Deterrence

Crime and Punishment: Critical Essays in Legal Philosophy
Series Editor: Thom Brooks

Titles in the Series:

Retribution
Thom Brooks

Deterrence
Thom Brooks

Shame Punishment
Thom Brooks

Juvenile Offending
Thom Brooks

Sentencing
Thom Brooks

Deterrence

Edited by

Thom Brooks

University of Durham, UK

ASHGATE

Published by
Ashgate Publishing Limited
Wey Court East
Union Road
Farnham
Surrey GU9 7PT
England

Ashgate Publishing Company
110 Cherry Street
Suite 3-1
Burlington, VT 05401-3818
USA

www.ashgate.com

British Library Cataloguing in Publication Data.
A catalogue record for this book is available from the British Library.

The Library of Congress has cataloged the printed edition as follows: 2013949702

ISBN 9781409451211

MIX
Paper from responsible sources
FSC® C013985

Printed in the United Kingdom by Henry Ling Limited,
at the Dorset Press, Dorchester, DT1 1HD

Contents

PART IV DETERRENCE AND CAPITAL PUNISHMENT

PART V DETERRENCE AND CORPORATE CRIME

PART VI CRITICS

Acknowledgements

Ashgate would like to thank the researchers and the contributing authors who provided copies, along with the following for their permission to reprint copyright material.

American Society for Criminology for the essay: Raymond V. Liedka, Anne Morrison Piehl and Bert Useem (2006), 'The Crime-Control Effect of Incarceration: Does Scale Matter?', *Criminology and Public Policy*, **5**, pp. 245–75. Copyright © 2006 American Society for Criminology.

Cengage for the essay: Thom Brooks (2012), 'Deterrence', in *Punishment*, New York: Routledge, pp. 35–50. Copyright © 2012 Thom Brooks.

Georgetown Law Journal for the essay: Paul H. Robinson and John M. Darley (2003), 'The Role of Deterrence in the Formulation of Criminal Law Rules: At Its Worst When Doing Its Best', *Georgetown Law Journal*, **91**, pp. 949–1002. Copyright © 2003 Georgetown Law Journal Association.

Harvard Law Review Association for the essays: Paul H. Robinson (2001), 'Punishing Dangerousness: Cloaking Preventive Detention as Criminal Justice', *Harvard Law Review*, **114**, pp. 1429–56. Copyright © 2001 the Harvard Law Review Association; Dan M. Kahan (1999), 'The Secret Ambition of Deterrence', *Harvard Law Review*, **113**, pp. 413–500.

Northwestern University School of Law for the essays: Raymond Paternoster (2010), 'How Much Do We Really Know about Criminal Deterrence?', *Journal of Criminal Law and Criminology*, **100**, pp. 765–823. Copyright © 2010 Northwestern University, School of Law; Matthew Haist (2009), 'Deterrence in a Sea of "Just Deserts": Are Utilitarian Goals Achievable in a World of "Limiting Retributivism"?', *Journal of Criminal Law and Criminology*, **99**, pp. 789–821. Copyright © 2009 Northwestern University, School of Law.

Ohio State University for the essay: Zachary Hoskins (2011), 'Deterrent Punishment and Respect for Persons', *Ohio State Journal of Criminal Law*, **8**, pp. 369–84. Copyright © 2011 Zachary Hoskins.

Oxford University Press for the essays: Victor Tadros (2011), 'Punishment and Duty', in *The Ends of Harm: The Moral Foundations of Criminal Law*, Oxford: Oxford University Press, pp. 265–92. Copyright © 2011 Victor Tadros; John Stuart Mill (1986), 'Speech in Favour of Capital Punishment', in Peter Singer (ed.), *Applied Ethics*, Oxford: Oxford University Press, pp. 97–104. Copyright © 1986 Oxford University Press; David A. Anderson (2002), 'The Deterrence Hypothesis and Picking Pockets at the Pickpocket's Hanging', *American Law and Economics Review*, **4**, pp. 295–313. Copyright © 2002 American Law and Economics Association.

School of Law, Stanford University for the essays: Cass R. Sunstein and Adrian Vermeule (2005), 'Is Capital Punishment Morally Required? Acts, Omissions, and Life–Life Tradeoffs', *Stanford Law Review*, **58**, pp. 703–50; Assaf Hamdani and Alon Klement (2008), 'Corporate Crime and Deterrence', *Stanford Law Review*, **61**, pp. 271–310.

John Wiley and Sons for the essays: Anthony Ellis (2003), 'A Deterrence Theory of Punishment', *Philosophical Quarterly*, **53**, pp. 337–51. Copyright © 2003 The Editors of the *Philosophical Quarterly*; Ernest van den Haag (1985), 'Refuting Reiman and Nathanson', *Philosophy and Public Affairs*, **14**, pp. 165–76. Reproduced with permission of Blackwell Publishing Ltd.

Every effort has been made to trace all the copyright holders, but if any have been inadvertently overlooked the publishers will be pleased to make the necessary arrangement at the first opportunity.

Publisher's Note

The material in this volume has been reproduced using the facsimile method. This means we can retain the original pagination to facilitate easy and correct citation of the original essays. It also explains the variety of typefaces, page layouts and numbering.

Series Preface

Crime and punishment grip the imagination and concerns of both the public and policymakers raising several serious challenges. Can punishment be justified? If so, then what purpose (or purposes) does it have? Which practices best cohere with this purpose(s)? These and many other questions are addressed with rigour and insight in this new book series.

Crime and Punishment: Critical Essays in Legal Philosophy comprises an authoritative and comprehensive set of five volumes reprinting the most influential essays by leading international figures engaged in this field. Each volume is organized thematically with a general introduction to provide an accessible launching pad to the latest research.

The first volume is on *Retribution*. This approach to punishment is widely held to be the oldest such view. Retributivists traditionally claim that punishment must be deserved and proportionate to what is deserved. This volume of essays covers several topics, including desert, proportionality, retributivist emotions, capital punishment and mercy. The second volume is a collection of essays about what is often regarded as the second oldest theory of punishment: *Deterrence*. This is the idea that punishment is justified by its effectiveness at deterring potential future offenders from committing crime. Topics covered include deterrence and crime reduction, incapacitation and the death penalty.

The next two volumes focus on particular issues. The third volume examines the latest research into *Shame Punishment*. Shame punishments are understood in multiple ways, such as an attempt to improve crime reduction through deterrence or as an effort at moral education. This volume covers topics such as shame and desert, shaming and dignity, shame and deterrence, and shame and restorative justice. The fourth volume is *Juvenile Offending* and it considers whether we should punish offenders differently because of their age as well as how this might be best achieved. Topics included are risk factors, the justification of punishing youth differently from adults and restorative justice for juvenile offenders.

The final fifth volume is about punishment as imprisonment: *Sentencing*. This volume examines sentencing in theory and practice, the Model Penal Code and use of sentencing guidelines, punitive restoration and the unified theory of punishment and alternatives to sentencing.

This *Crime and Punishment: Critical Essays in Legal Philosophy* book series covers exciting and innovative contemporary work by the leading international figures in the field today writing on retribution, deterrence, shame punishment, youth offending and sentencing. Each essay has been carefully selected for inclusion to ensure the seminal work available in English is brought together in one series for easy reference by students, practitioners, scholars and the general public.

THOM BROOKS
Series Editor
Reader in Law, Durham Law School, Durham University

Introduction

Introduction

Deterrence is one of the oldest and most powerful theories about punishment. Deterrence claims that punishment is justified through preventing future crimes. The argument that punishment ought to secure crime reduction occupies a central place in criminal justice policy: would the public support a system that made crime *more* likely? And this is the site for much debate: should the state deter offenders through the threat of punishment? What available evidence is there about the effectiveness of deterrence? Is deterrence even possible? This book brings together the leading work on deterrence from the dominant international figures in the field. Deterrence is examined from various critical perspectives, including its diversity, its relation with desert, the relation of deterrence with incapacitation and prevention, the role deterrence has played in debates over the death penalty, deterrence and corporate crime and illuminating insight by critics.

This introduction will consider each of these topics with primary reference to the important contributions to our thinking about deterrence carefully selected for inclusion in this collection. This survey of leading work will highlight the key debates and issues pertaining to contemporary research about deterrence.

Deterrence Theory

Deterrence is a simple idea understood in complex ways. The simple idea is that punishment is justified by its effects. The complexity is in how this simple idea is conceived more specifically as the effect on crime reduction through the threat of punishment. Deterrence is not merely about less criminal offending, but less future offending because of the fear of punishment. Deterrence is then a theory that addresses issues about psychology and human behaviour: how might the threat of punishment ensure potential offenders have a change of mind and choose to be law-abiding?

The first part includes essays by Paul H. Robinson and John M. Darley, Raymond Paternoster and Thom Brooks examining deterrence from broad and critical perspectives. Robinson and Darley (Chapter 1) argue that while deterrence has been a centrepiece for much sentencing policy, it offers a poor strategy for thinking about punishment. This is because the effectiveness of deterrence rests on an unstable foundation and that greater efforts to secure deterrence might generate crime in unexpected ways. A deterrence policy might be counterproductive. This critique is precise. Robinson and Darley accept that '[h]aving a punishment system does deter' (p. 5) and punishing offenders does produce a general effect on influencing the conduct of others. Deterrence has been used not only to justify particular punishments, but also in the decriminalization of offences where it has been argued punishment would lack a deterrent effect if used, such as in cases of suicide. However, they reject the view that we can deter crime 'through the manipulation of criminal law rules and penalties' (p. 5) in a forensic examination. Such reforms are often poorly communicated to the public and their effects largely assumed rather than evidence-based. Moreover, there can be problems where the pursuit of deterrence runs contrary to publicly shared views about penal justice. The punishment justified by deterrence may be different from what a majority might believe 'just'. This speaks to the difference between consequentialist concerns about future effects and non-consequentialist (and retributive) views about justice that are independent from any future effects. Where there is this gap, there may be a fear that deterrence could have unintended effects that undermine its effectiveness. Deterrence-based sentencing policy might produce more crime and not less.

Raymond Paternoster (Chapter 2) examines deterrence theory through a critical and historically informed perspective. Paternoster argues that while the idea that punishment deters has strong appeal it remains difficult to confirm precisely how strong an effect deterrence might create. There is a gap between what deterrence claims and what it does deliver. Deterrence aims to manipulate incentives: if threatened punishment is sufficiently likely and severe, then potential offenders should modify their behaviour and avoid crime. Paternoster claims there is evidence to confirm many offenders operate through a consideration of costs and benefits. The problem is not that offenders lack rationality, but rather the criminal justice system is not sufficiently well constructed to exploit it. If the system was better designed, we would be able to secure a greater deterrent effect. So the general problem is not that deterrence fails to work, but rather that the system we have is unsatisfactory for a deterrence-based sentencing policy.

Thom Brooks (Chapter 3) concludes this part with a wide-ranging exploration of deterrence. Brooks argues deterrence can be understood in different ways where each has consequences for how we design policy. For example, *macro-deterrence* (or 'general' deterrence) considers the possible deterrence effects on the general public. *Micro-deterrence* (or 'specific' deterrence) considers the possible deterrence effects on a particular individual. How we construct and implement a sentencing policy designed to secure deterrence may differ widely where we pursue macro-deterrence or micro-deterrence. Macro-deterrence requires reductions in crime on the whole, but which might not be best suited for combating offending for specific individual offenders.

Brooks highlights several other issues. One is the *geography of crime*: crime reduction is often focused exclusively on crimes affecting the general public, but this gets wrong the geography of crime. This is because crimes are not confined to public places: criminality is possible both within and outside prisons (p. 119). Another issue is *the problem of difference* for deterrence (p. 123). Different individuals or social groups may respond differently to particular deterrent threats. This is a problem for macro-deterrence: any such punishment is threatened to all, but the effects may differ by individuals and groups. A further issue is *the problem of time and changing effects* (pp. 123–24). Deterrent power changes over time. So a punishment may have very different effects in response to changing social conditions. While retribution might claim one particular punishment is always 'just' or 'deserved' for specific types of offenders, deterrence proponents cannot make such boasts and instead must constantly revise which punishment is justified based upon available evidence. One consequence is that the same types of offenders might be punished very differently depending on the likely effects given the broader circumstances.

A final issue raised by Brooks concerns deterrence and knowledge limits. Deterrence is not a view about ending crime (which might be an impossible ideal), but rather crime reduction.

This operates within a series of assumptions. In order to be deterrent, a potential offender must have knowledge about (a) all possible crimes that might be committed, (b) all possible sentences for these crimes, (c) the likelihood of arrest and charging for possible crimes, (d) the likelihood of conviction for possible crimes and (e) likely effect of conviction for possible crimes. The problem, of course, is that much, if not all, of this is unknown to even many academics working in this area. A bigger problem still: can we even *know* about any deterrence effect? How many murders or thefts of bicycles *would* have taken place in your neighbourhood if not for potential future murderers and bike thieves becoming *deterred* by the threat of punishment? We can measure crime reduction over time and draw some tentative conclusions from this, but can we ever have secure knowledge that *deterrence* (and not mere crime reduction) has taken place? Brooks offers serious doubts about the possibility of having any certain knowledge about deterrence.

Deterrence and Desert

The single biggest challenge to deterrence is a specific worry about desert. If punishment is justified by its deterrent effect, then the problem is that deterrent punishment might justify the punishment of innocent persons if this had a deterrent effect. The problem with desert is that deterrent punishment might not require a person deserve punishment to receive punishment. If only those who deserve selection for punishment should be punished, then deterrence appears to violate a fundamental principle governing sentencing distribution. Or does it?

Anthony Ellis (Chapter 4) offers a new theory about deterrence designed to overcome this problem. Ellis argues that the use of force against another can only be justified in self-defence. Punishment can be justified likewise as a form of self-defence. Punishment works as a system of threats: penal threats are addressed to each individual. If a person fails to heed such threats, then punishment is justified. Each person punished is deserving of such treatment because he or she has broken the law and, in so doing, failed to heed an official threat. So the problem of punishment of the innocent is avoided while defending a deterrent theory of punishment. However, this view addresses some questions while creating others. Which threats should the state sanction and should the modern state be in the business of threatening its citizens in this way? Why argue the justification of a system of threats also justifies specific sentences and how is the latter set?

Matthew Haist (Chapter 5) considers the idea of 'limiting retributivism' (also called 'negative retributivism') where desert is a necessary, but insufficient justification for punishment. We first ask whether a criminal possesses desert and, if so, consider how the punishment deserved could be tailored to produce beneficial consequences. Limiting retributivism is thought to 'limit' retributivism because this focus on the production of beneficial consequences makes more likely less severe punishments than would be permitted by retribution. This claim is doubtful: if greater severity is necessary for crime reduction, this view of punishment may well justify sanctions more severe than retribution. Nonetheless, the attractiveness of this model is that it brings together retribution and utilitarianism in a hybrid model.[1] Haist argues that such a model should be rejected because it is likely to lead to under-deterrence. If we are serious about improving punishment's ability to deter future offenders, then we might

1 Hybrid theories of punishment are explored in great depth in Brooks (2012), pp. 87–148.

have greater success by rejecting limiting retribution and opting for a more utilitarian-friendly model grounded in insights from behavioural psychology.

Zachary Hoskins (Chapter 6) defends deterrence against objections that it fails to respect persons. Retribution is often thought to fare better. Individuals are punished because they deserve punishment: the justificatory focus is on the individual offender and his punishment set in proportion to what he deserves. Retribution may then respect persons because it can account well for their individuality. Deterrence is believed to do much less well because it is often used as a general deterrent (in terms of macro-deterrence) to all. The punishment of this or that person might become incidental to the broader project of securing crime reduction through the macro-deterrence of all. Hoskins argues deterrence can respect offenders as moral persons. A system of deterrence bound by adequate safeguards need not treat offenders as a means to some end nor exclude offenders from the moral community (see Morris, 1986). Curiously, the defence of using deterrence is here largely dependent not on the merits or otherwise of deterrence, but the underlying foundational justice of non-deterrence factors that set the limits for the use of deterrence.

The final chapter in this part is an essay from *The Ends of Harm* by Victor Tadros (Chapter 7). The infliction of pain on citizens requires significant justification. Retribution claims that punishment can be justified because it can be intrinsically good where deserved. The alternative is to argue that punishment can be justified because of its consequences. The problem with alternatives is about their limits: if punishment is justified by its consequences, then limitations might be counterproductive to achieving certain ends. But if no limits are recognized, then punishment becomes deeply objectionable: should the state be justified in using *any* severity of punishment provided it helps achieve some ends? Does the end justify any means, such as punishing the innocent in some cases?

Tadros defends a new alternative where punishment is justified on the basis of its instrumental benefits and grounded by non-consequentialist principles governing harm to others. This is the duty view of punishment: criminal offenders have duties arising from their wrongdoing that make permissible their punishment as a means to the good of others. The duty view of punishment is part of a wider position on self-defence. Self-defence is about not harming others and offenders should provide their victims with protections against wrongdoing by other people. We may accept that there may be negative duties arising from an offender's crime that may place him or her in some obligation to rectify damage caused. However, it is unclear how negative duties arise in every such case of criminal wrongdoing. This is because not all crimes cause harm to others (see Brooks, 2013). If not all crimes are harms (or at least not other-regarding harms), then this view of punishment does not appear broad enough to capture all the kinds of crimes we would want to include in any theory of punishment. The cost of providing an alternative theory of deterrence that might meet several traditional objections might be a partial theory about punishment, or rather a theory of punishment that might address a partial set of crimes.

Deterrence, Incapacitation and Prevention

This part considers deterrence through incapacitation and prevention. One way offenders might be deterred, it is said, is by incarceration: no crimes can be committed when potential offenders are placed behind prison bars. One possible problem is that it is unclear whether incapacitation is acting as a deterrent, that is, as a threat to potential offenders. Crime reduction is certainly one aim of deterrence theories of punishment, but deterrence does not seek only to reduce crime, but to do so in particular ways, namely, by *deterring* through the use of threats. So the relation between deterrence and incapacitation is uncertain and perhaps even tenuous. A second way is through prevention and such an approach is more closely aligned with micro deterrence where deterrence efforts are addressed to specific individuals to deter him or her from future offending.

Paul Robinson (Chapter 8) considers the relation between dangerousness and punishment. Much criminal justice policy has been focused on addressing the challenge of dangerousness in various forms. These include so-called 'three strikes and you're out' legislation whereby offenders are seen as too dangerous upon a third eligible offence to remain outside prison. Or others might include anti-terrorism measures grounded in a climate of emergency, such as preventative detention. Still others might include increasing the severity of punishment for those convicted of child sex offences as persons too dangerous to be treated otherwise.

Robinson provides a compelling argument that we should have the criminal justice system serve as the primary mechanism for preventing future crimes as this may seriously damage other goals concerning institutional justice we want to achieve. Indeed, many measures established to help better address dangerous crimes may be likely to create more harm than do good and so prove counterproductive. One issue is the gap between policies designed to address dangerous crimes and a public conception of justice. There is a danger this gap is becoming too large and, if it is, this can have seriously damaging effects on criminal justice more widely in terms of the public losing confidence in the system as a whole. A second issue is that much of the current debate is insufficiently evidence-based. If it took the evidence more seriously, then sentencing policy might make a greater effort to account for 'empirical' desert: the informed view of justice we share publicly.

Raymond V. Liedka, Anne Morrison Piehl and Bert Useem (Chapter 9) consider empirical and theoretical work on the deterrence effect from incapacitation: does prison lead to greater deterrence? The research is mixed with some claiming such an effect can be found with other research casting doubt on these findings. Liedka and colleagues examine these competing literatures. They find that imprisonment does contribute to some effect on reducing crime rates. Their main finding is that this effect is not constant: an increasing prison population has beneficial effects only up to a certain point afterwards it leads to accelerating declining marginal returns that move more quickly than previously thought. Prison can work to some degree and only to a point. Policy-makers should have greater attentiveness to the empirical impact of exploding prison populations which may prove both costly and counterproductive.

Deterrence and Capital Punishment

Perhaps the most frequent question asked about the death penalty is: does it deter? This part considers three arguments in favour. The first is a famous speech given by John Stuart Mill in 1868 during his brief time as a Member of Parliament in the House of Commons. Mill (Chapter 10) argues that to deprive a criminal 'of the life of which he has proved himself to be unworthy' is the most 'appropriate' and 'impressive' mode of punishment that society can distribute (p. 298). So some offenders should be executed not because others may be deterred, but because it would be deserved. But Mill believes capital punishment can and does have a deterrent effect. For Mill, punishment 'acts principally through the imagination' and 'to be measured by the impression it makes on those who are still innocent' (p. 300). Capital punishment ought to remove the temptation 'we', the innocent public, have to perform capital offences. We execute deserving murderers to secure the deterrence of others. While some might argue that even if justified we should be concerned about ensuring proper safeguards, Mill claims that many rules are 'too favourable to the prisoner' (p. 303). Yet, while human judgement may be fallible, this is no reason against justifying capital punishment: instead, for Mill, this ensures that any such sentence will be undertaken with an extreme of care.

Ernest van den Haag (Chapter 11) takes up various challenges concerning the alleged intrinsic injustice of capital punishment. One argument is that murderers may deserve execution, but such a punishment is uncivilized. Van den Haag counters with the query of to whom is it uncivilized and which should we take sides with. If death is deserved, then the death penalty is just and any society claiming to be 'civilized' should not betray a commitment to justice. A civilized society is a just society: if capital punishment can be justified, then this should be honoured.

A second argument is about process. The distribution of death sentences is more likely to be given to some and not others. One explanation is racial discrimination in sentencing. If only some deserving murderers receive death sentences, then the concern is the system of distribution is institutionally unjust and so capital punishment is unjustified. Van den Haag notes again that poor distribution is not a reason to stop any distribution of just deserts. If some deserving persons are sentenced to death and no undeserving persons, then this is a reason to improve the system and not end it. Elsewhere, Brooks (2011) argues that the solution for defenders of capital punishment is to ensure more deserving persons are selected for execution. If only some of the deserving are selected, then the problem is we should select more. Ultimately, there are other problems for capital punishment pertaining to desert: can we ever be secure in the knowledge any person is innocent where recent innovations in forensic science can readily prove mistakes have been made in cases that have otherwise been conducted flawlessly, commanded unanimous verdicts by juries and after all appeals have been exhausted? Some would argue we cannot be and this is a compelling reason for retributivists and others to reject the death penalty (see Brooks, 2004, 2011).

Van den Haag considers the concern that deterrence is unknowable or at least unconfirmed. He argues that even if there is no *empirical* confirmation of deterrence from capital punishment, there is still *intuitive* evidence. So while the data may be inconclusive, we need only look into ourselves. It is implausible, he argues, to believe no one is deterred by the death penalty because it seems so intuitively obvious that it must have at least some effect. This reply is interesting, if not compelling as much recent research by behavioural economists has shown that many of the things we take to be intuitively obvious are factually untrue. Deterrence and capital punishment may be another casualty, too.

The final essay included here is by Cass R. Sunstein and Adrian Vermeule (Chapter 12). They argue that we should focus more specifically on what they call life–life tradeoffs. If we take persons seriously and if there is some deterrent effect from the use of capital punishment, then we may be morally obligated to sentence to death deserving persons. This is because it protects the lives of innocent persons. Government has a responsibility to protect its citizens. If it knew that failing to use capital punishment rendered more likely the murders of innocent persons *who would have lived if capital punishment were used*, then government can honour its obligation to its citizens by using the death penalty. This is not an argument grounded on what anyone deserves (although the focus is on persons, such as murderers, that are thought potentially to deserve execution), but rather on the justice of preventing future deaths through the use of penal threats. Much of this 'moral' argument rests on a claim about the current state of the empirical evidence. One issue is the reliability of this evidence and it has already been suggested there is much reason to question it. A second issue is the question of whether any such deterrent effect is confirmable and there is much reason to question this as well. A final issue is that any effect today may disappear tomorrow and return next week: deterrence evidence may be in flux if confirmable and known. There are many 'ifs' to consider, but this piece has helped illuminate a new (and controversial) argument in the longstanding debate about whether the death penalty is justified because of any deterrent effect.

Deterrence and Corporate Crime

Deterrence has informed policy-making across several areas and many of these have been discussed above. A more recent area concerns corporate criminal liability. Some critics believe that we ought not to bring the business world into the realm of the criminal law. This is because any criminal sanction may bring long-term negative consequences for a convicted offender that may become all the greater when it affects a corporation. But this is also a powerful argument in favour of deterrence: the mere threat of criminal sanction may be desirable because firms will have a powerful incentive to contain, if not avoid, any misconduct.

Assaf Hamdani and Alon Klement (Chapter 13) challenge this conventional thinking. They argue that severe penalties might, in fact, discourage the monitoring of misconduct and so prove counterproductive. Instead of making firms *more* responsible for fear of avoiding punishment and its negative effects, the consequences from severe penalties might make firms *less* robust in avoiding liability. Hamdani and Klement still maintain a deterrence model is attractive, but they argue it may work best where there is a greater reliance on purely financial penalties. Deterrence can work, but only where it is largely financial and more precisely targeted. This does not entail that penalties should *only* be financial to be effective. In essence, we might wish to endorse a more micro-deterrence-level approach to thinking about corporate crime than macro-deterrence.

Nevertheless, it remains unclear precisely how far deterrence might work. Perhaps deterrence may work in a way more intelligible because firms respond more clearly to costs and benefits in the pursuit of business and remaining solvent. We might more readily witness changes in corporate activities in response to regulation in a way we do not discern with private individuals where their motivations and decision-making are masked. However, the minds of individuals are not much more hidden from view than the inner workings of firms by the public. Deterrence may be one part of a wider regulatory strategy, but perhaps such a strategy will be grounded in some alternative principle or justification.

Critics

This book concludes with two essays by leading critics of deterrence theory. Dan M. Kahan (Chapter 14) offers a fascinating insight into the ambition of deterrence. So how important *is* deterrence in our debates about justice? Kahan argues that deterrence plays a relatively small role in shaping policy preferences. While many citizens may claim to support a policy because of deterrence, deterrence is not a major factor for their support. Kahan says that 'the real significance of deterrence theory lies not in what it says but in what it stops us from saying' (p. 412).

One example is capital punishment (see pp. 432–47). Persons supporting the use of capital punishment most often claim they support it because it deters potential murderers. Interestingly, persons stating the opposite and claiming to reject capital punishment most often claim they do so because it does not deter. But it gets even more interesting. Facts about deterrence change as conditions change. If deterrence were proven to have no effect on murder rates, persons supporting capital punishment because they believe it deters murderers *would still* support the use of capital punishment for the new reason that murderers deserve execution. If, however, deterrence were proven to deter murderers, persons who did not support capital punishment because they believe it did not deter murderers *would still* reject capital punishment for the new reason that the state should not execute its citizens. This is an example where people often claim deterrence plays a central role for why they accept a particular view; but, in fact, it plays little role if any. Attitudes about capital punishment are formed around views about value, such as whether someone does or does not deserve execution for murder. The hypothesis about why people falsely state deterrence plays an important role is that doing so might sound and appear more objective. It is as if to say: my judgement about this contentious issue is not a mere *subjective* statement about value (that might reveal something about me that might be controversial), but rather this is an *objective* conclusion about facts. Deterrence has the ambition of leading the discourse and how it is framed, but it is a mere chimera. The consequence is that debates about deterrence are much ado about nothing: what matters is what we value and not whether or not deterrence plays some role (see Carlsmith *et al.*, 2002). This conclusion is echoed in other work: Samuel R. Gross (1998) has argued that choosing whether to support a policy like capital punishment is like choosing which baseball team to support – it is a judgement based upon personal values and too often not evidence-based.

This book concludes with a powerful essay by David A. Anderson (Chapter 15). Deterrence assumes that active (and potentially active) criminals weigh costs and benefits before engaging in crime. Do criminals make rational decisions to engage in crime that can be influenced by deterrence? Anderson casts serious doubt on any such project. He argues that about 76 per cent of active criminals and 89 per cent of the most violent criminals either perceive no risk of arrest or no thought about their possible punishment. Drugs, mental health problems, fight-or-flight and other factors all inhibit deterrence from playing the role in practice that policy-makers intend in theory. It was said that pickpockets made their money pinching coins from the pockets of people in the crowd as all eyes looked up to see another pickpocket hanging for his crimes. Such punishments might have some effect on the public where many would never commit such crimes anyway – deterrent punishment might be a way of preaching to the converted and reaffirming views by the non-criminal public that such crimes should be punished severely. But they may not have the effect, or any effect, on intended parties. The failure of deterrence in practice was not recognized when hanging pickpockets was more common nor is it properly recognized now centuries later.

Conclusion

Deterrence is a powerful theory of punishment and a major factor for much sentencing policy. Its central idea that punishment is justified by its beneficial consequences through crime reduction has won many adherents. Deterrence is controversial and debates continue over how it is best conceived, how it is best practised, how it might be measured and even whether it is possible.

Deterrence is also a broad tent encompassing a wide range of theories and perspectives. This collection brings together the leading critical work on deterrence from contemporary exponents and most powerful opponents. These essays seek to deepen our collective understanding of this important view about punishment to shed greater light on future possibilities.

References

Brooks, Thom (2004), 'Retributivist Arguments against Capital Punishment', *Journal of Social Philosophy*, **35**, pp. 188–97.

Brooks, Thom (2011), 'Retribution and Capital Punishment', in Mark D. White (ed.), *Retributivism: Essays on Theory and Practice*, Oxford: Oxford University Press, pp. 232–45.

Brooks, Thom (2012), *Punishment*, New York: Routledge, pp. 87–148.

Brooks, Thom (2013), 'Criminal Harms', in *Law and Legal Theory*, Leiden: Brill, pp. 149–61.

Carlsmith, Kevin M., Darley, John M. and Robinson, Paul H. (2002), 'Why Do We Punish? Deterrence and Just Motives for Punishment', *Journal of Personality and Social Psychology*, **83**, pp. 284–99.

Gross, Samuel R. (1998), 'Update: American Public Opinion on the Death Penalty – It's Getting Personal', *Cornell Law Review*, **83**, pp. 1448–75.

Morris, J.M. (1986), 'The Structure of Criminal Law and Deterrence', *Criminal Law Review*, pp. 524–34.

Part I
Deterrence Theory

[1]

The Role of Deterrence in the Formulation of Criminal Law Rules: At Its Worst When Doing Its Best

PAUL H. ROBINSON* AND JOHN M. DARLEY**

TABLE OF CONTENTS

---

* Colin S. Diver Distinguished Professor of Law, University of Pennsylvania Law School.

** Warren Professor of Psychology, Princeton University. The authors wish to acknowledge the contributions of participants of faculty workshops at the law faculties of the University of Pennsylvania, Northwestern University, Cornell University, Rutgers University–Camden, Notre Dame University, the University of Minnesota, and at the Law and Public Affairs Program at Princeton University. Also appreciated are comments by Eric Posner, Ariel Porat, and Dan Kahan, and research assistance by Gabriel Posner, David Wang, Amanda Adrian, Kenworthey Bilz, and Danielle Estrada.

INTRODUCTION

For the past several decades, the deterrence of crime has been a centerpiece of criminal law reform. Lawmakers have sought to optimize the control of crime by devising a penalty-setting system that assigns criminal punishments of a magnitude sufficient to deter a thinking individual from committing a crime.

Although this seems initially an intuitively compelling strategy, we suggest it is a poor one; poor for two reasons. First, its effectiveness rests on a set of assumptions that on examination cannot be sustained. Second, deterrence strategies may have hidden crimogenic costs—that is, they may generate crime in unexpected ways.

Experience has taught us to be precise about exactly what we are saying about the effectiveness of a deterrence strategy. There seems little doubt that having a criminal justice system that punishes violators, as every organized society does, has the general effect of influencing the conduct of potential offenders. This we concede: Having a punishment system does deter. But there is growing evidence to suggest skepticism about the *criminal law's* deterrent effect—that is, skepticism about the ability to deter crime through the manipulation of criminal law rules and penalties. The general existence of the system may well deter prohibited conduct, but the formulation of criminal law rules within the system, according to a deterrence-optimizing analysis, may have a limited effect or even no effect beyond what the system's broad deterrent warning has already achieved. We suggest that, while it may be true that manipulation of criminal law rules *can* influence behavior, it does so only under conditions not typically found in the criminal justice systems of modern societies. In contrast, criminal lawmakers and adjudicators formulate and apply criminal law rules on the assumption that they *always* influence conduct. And it is this taken-for-granted assumption that we find so disturbing and so dangerous. In Part I we briefly summarize the social science literature that prompts our skepticism as to whether the criminal law deters, showing that potential offenders do not know the law, do not make rational choices, or do not perceive an expected cost for a violation that outweighs the expected gain.

In sharp contrast, the assumption that legal formulation decisions will have a direct deterrent effect on conduct, has been used in crafting nearly every aspect of criminal law, from defining the rules of conduct, to formulating principles of liability, to determining offense grades, to setting sentencing rules and practice.[1] On close inspection, we conclude that much of this is more a style of conversation—"deterrence speak"—than a true reliance upon deterrence analysis. But true reliance on deterrence is evident in a variety of rules that produce substantial deviations from what other principles for distributing liability and punishment, such as just deserts, would provide. We document these two phenomena in Part II.

1. Deterrence is not criminal law's only ex ante function. Deterrence speaks to discouraging prohibited conduct. But criminal law also *requires* that certain conduct be performed, a command carried in the law's creation of legal duties to act. Further, the criminal law *authorizes*, under special circumstances, conduct that otherwise is prohibited, the circumstances being set out in the criminal law's justification defenses. The same caution about legal rules influencing conduct applies to these ex ante commands as it does to deterrence. For the same reasons that we are skeptical of the influence of doctrinal formulations to deter conduct, we are skeptical of the criminal law's ability to induce conduct, at least in the way lawmakers assume when they create legal duties and justification defenses.

Even if one concludes that deterrence skepticism overstates its case, there remain reasons for serious concern. We argue that, even on the most cautious reading of the available studies, enough is known to urge an end to the past practice of formulating criminal law based on a deterrence-optimizing analysis. In Part III we offer four primary arguments. First, a disabling problem for deterrence as a principle for the distribution of liability and punishment is its need for information that is neither available nor likely to be available any time in the foreseeable future. Formulating criminal law rules according to a deterrence analysis can produce erroneous results if based upon missing or unreliable data. In fact, inadequately informed analyses could produce criminal law rules that reduce, rather than increase, the possibility of deterrence. In such an informational void, we argue, it makes sense to follow a distributive principle that at the very least can achieve its objectives.

Further, even if full and perfect information were available, we argue that the dynamics of deterrence are dramatically more complex than has been supposed. The deterrent process involves complex interactions, like substitution effects, that make deterrent predictions enormously difficult. And the deterrent process is a dynamic rather than a static one. The manipulation of a criminal law rule may well increase its deterrent effect as hoped, but that effect can itself change the existing conditions and require a new and different deterrence calculation. Part III.A examines deterrence's informational and complexity problems.

Second, once it is recognized that *any* distributive principle for criminal liability and punishment will produce some deterrent effect—if any is to be had—a deterrence-based distribution makes sense only if it can provide meaningfully greater deterrent effect than that already inherent in competing distributions that advance other valuable goals, such as doing justice.

Third, the important implication of our argument is that deterrence can do better than another distribution—such as a justice distribution[2]—only if and where the two distributive principles deviate. Thus, a deterrence-based distribution can deter better than a justice-based distribution only if and where it deviates from a just result. But it is just these instances of deviation from justice in which it is most difficult to achieve a deterrent effect. People assume the law is as they think it should be, according to their own collective notions of justice. Thus, the simple prerequisite of making the deterrence-based rule known becomes a serious task. Further, it is in these deviation-from-justice cases that the system's deterrence-based rules are least likely to be followed. Because people commonly think of criminal liability and punishment in terms of justice rather than deterrence, the exercise of police, prosecutorial, and judicial discretion, as well as jury nullification, commonly subvert application of deterrence-

2. By "justice distribution" we mean a distribution according to the shared intuitions of justice of the community bound by the law. For a detailed discussion of "justice distribution" and how it can be determined, see generally PAUL H. ROBINSON & JOHN M. DARLEY, JUSTICE, LIABILITY & BLAME: COMMUNITY VIEWS AND THE CRIMINAL LAW (1995), and in particular Chapter 7, at 201–15.

based deviation rules, thus subverting the deterrence program and confusing the deterrence message. Parts III.B and C detail these arguments.

Fourth, even if one assumes for the sake of argument that a deterrence-based distribution produces a greater deterrent effect than a justice-based distribution—despite the former's special deviation problems—there is reason to be concerned that the deterrence-based distribution simultaneously produces crime. Because it deviates from the community's shared intuitions of justice, the deterrence-based distribution can undercut the criminal law's moral credibility, lessening its own crime-control power as a moral authority—a dynamic that we suspect can have significant crimogenic effect. Thus, even if a deterrence-based distribution did successfully produce a greater deterrent effect than a justice-based distribution, that greater deterrent effect might be offset by its greater crimogenic effect in undercutting the moral authority of the criminal law. These are the potential costs, referred to above, that are incurred by a deterrence-based system. Part III.D details these arguments.

We believe that optimizing deterrence through doctrinal manipulation is possible, but only under narrow conditions not typical in American criminal justice. There are possibilities for reform that might broaden these conditions, but also serious limitations, due in large part to the sacrifices such reforms would demand: in greater financial cost, in infringing upon interests of privacy and freedom from governmental intrusion, in compromising basic notions of procedural fairness, and in doing injustice and failing to do justice. Our conclusion is that if one takes a realistic view of deterrence, even after plausible reforms are made, little increase in the deterrent effect of doctrinal manipulation would be produced, and not enough to justify its continued use as the standard mechanism of criminal lawmaking. Part IV offers a more realistic view of deterrence: the particular conditions under which it may work and the possibilities, and impossibilities, for improving its performance.

I. GROWING REASONS TO BE SKEPTICAL OF CRIMINAL LAW DETERRENCE

If a criminal law rule is to deter violators, three prerequisites must be satisfied: The potential offender must know of the rule; he must perceive the cost of violation as greater than the perceived benefit; and he must be able and willing to bring such knowledge to bear on his conduct decision at the time of the offense. But as we describe elsewhere,[3] one or more of these hurdles typically block any material deterrent effect of doctrinal manipulation. The social science literature suggests that potential offenders commonly do not know the law, do not perceive an expected cost for a violation that outweighs the expected gain, and do not make rational self-interest choices.

3. *See* Paul H. Robinson & John M. Darley, *Does the Criminal Law Deter? A Social Science Investigation*, 24 OXFORD J. LEGAL STUD. (forthcoming 2004).

A. KNOWLEDGE HURDLE

The available studies suggest that most people do not know the law, that even career criminals who have a special incentive to know it do not, and that even when people think they know the law they frequently are wrong. Potential offenders typically do not read law books and their ability to learn the law, even indirectly through hearing or reading of particular cases, is limited by the fact that the legal rule is just one of hundreds of variables that influence a case disposition. To divine the operative liability rule, hidden as it is under the effects of all the other variables, would require both a higher number of reported cases than those to which potential offenders are exposed and a mind for complex calculation beyond that which is reasonable to expect.[4]

B. PERCEIVED NET-COST HURDLE

The possibilities of deterrent effect are further weakened by difficulties in establishing a punishment rate that would be meaningful to potential offenders, avoiding the delay in imposition of punishment that seriously erodes its deterrent effect, and establishing and modulating the amount of punishment imposed. First, establishing some base expectation of a meaningful chance for punishment is a necessary condition to any deterrent effect. Yet, the perceived probability of punishment is low to the point where the threatened punishment commonly is not thought to be relevant to the potential offender.[5] Second, a delay between violation and punishment can dramatically reduce the perceived cost of the violation. Even if the punishment is certain, the more distant it is, the more its weight as a threat will be discounted. Further, the strength of the punishment memory—that is, its recalled punitive "bite" as a perceived threat for a future violation—is dramatically reduced as the length of delay increases. Unfortunately, in modern criminal justice such delay is substantial.[6]

Third, as to the amount of punishment, there is no question that any system that can impose punishment can produce a credible deterrent "bite." The challenge for a deterrence-based system is to modulate the threatened punishment bite as the program for optimum deterrence requires. Lawmakers assume they have the greatest control over this aspect of the cost-benefit calculus in that they can modulate the bite by simply altering the length of prison term. But, in reality, the studies suggest that this aspect of the cost-benefit balance is neither simple nor predictable. The forces at work in determining perceived amount of punishment are complex. For example, the "hedonic adaptation" and "subjective well-being" studies suggest that one's standard for judging perceived punitive effect changes over time and conditions. For example, both paraplegics and lottery winners return to their original state of well-being despite their dramatically changed circumstances. Thus, as a prison term continues, it can

4. *Id.* at § 1.A.
5. *Id.* at § 1.C(i) (Probability).
6. *Id.*

become increasingly less painful in effect, although its cost per unit time remains constant, making it increasingly less cost effective.[7]

In addition, it appears that it is the intensity of the punishment experience, rather than its duration, that is of significant effect. Indeed, because the remembered intensity is highly influenced by the end-point intensity, which we note above decreases over time, it is possible that the overall remembered bite of a prison term decreases as the length of the term increases! Therefore, while legislatures and judges believe they can reliably manipulate the amount of punishment threatened by simply manipulating the length of the prison term, such manipulation does not provide the punishment bite they assume.[8]

There is a failure of "special deterrence" when a person who serves a prison term does not experience the pain that conventional wisdom suggests he will. "Special deterrence" is the degree to which a punishment, once experienced, reduces the likelihood of the person who experienced the punishment risking a similar punishment by offending again in the future. The defender of the "general deterrence" approach to behavior control may point out that the difficulties we note do not pose similar difficulties with respect to modulating general deterrence among the population that has not experienced prison time, because that population would not have had the opportunity to discover that prison is not as painful as expected. For those who have not yet experienced prison, it is the imagined horribleness of a prison sentence that keeps them from committing crimes.

We do not think this distinction does much to rescue the deterrence approach to rule formulation. First, some of our other difficulties with the deterrence approach, such as the legal knowledge hurdle, apply to general deterrence as well as special deterrence. Second, given the generally known high rate of recidivism among criminals, the lack of special deterrence for future crimes among this group is a considerable failure. Third, those most at risk for committing their first crime are likely to have a good many ex-convicts among their acquaintances and in their neighborhoods, and will learn from them that "prison time isn't so bad." In other words, the diffusion of the prison experience information weakens general deterrence among the group at high risk of crime commission.

C. RATIONAL DECISIONMAKING HURDLE

Finally, there is a host of conditions that interfere with the rational calculation of self-interest by potential offenders: drug or alcohol use, personality types inclined toward impulsiveness and toward discounting consequences, and social influences such as the arousal effect of group action and the tendency of group members to calculate risk in terms of group rather than individual interests. Further, these conditions are disproportionately high among deterrence's pri-

7. *Id.*
8. *Id.*

mary target group: those persons for whom criminal conduct is not already ruled out by their own internalized norms or by those of their family or peers. This bodes ill for effective deterrence because it precludes, or at least diminishes, a rule's deterrent effect even if the rule is known and is backed by what is perceived as a meaningful threat of punishment. We can expect greater deterrent possibilities when dealing with more rational target audiences, such as white-collar offenders. Unfortunately, the more serious and more common offenses tend to be committed by persons less likely to exercise rationality.[9]

D. CUMULATIVE EFFECT

The most serious problems for deterrent effect stem from the combined effect of all three of these hurdles. A well-known rule carrying a credible threat of punishment that exceeds the benefit of the offense will be ineffective nonetheless in deterring a person caught up in rage, group arousal, and drug influence, as is the case with many gang-related offenses. A rational calculator who fears any form of punishment even if the likelihood of it is slight, nonetheless will not be deterred by a rule that he does not know, as where a homeowner shoots to protect his home, unaware that the law does not allow deadly force in protection of property alone. And a rule well-known by a rational calculator as carrying a meaningful penalty nonetheless will not deter if the chance of getting caught is seen as trivial, as illustrated by rampant tax cheating.[10]

II. THE TRADITIONAL ASSUMPTION THAT THE FORMULATION OF CRIMINAL LAW DOCTRINE WILL INFLUENCE CONDUCT

This view of a limited deterrent effect stands in stark contrast to the view of criminal lawmakers of the past four decades, who have relied heavily, if not primarily, on deterrence analysis in formulating criminal law rules on the assumption that deterrence is relevant to every aspect of criminal law doctrine. Deterrence is said by some commentators to be the criminal law's "primary purpose"[11] or its "core purpose."[12] The Model Penal Code drafters—for whom the Code's "dominant theme is . . . prevention" and its "major goal is to forbid and prevent" crime[13]—see incapacitation and desert as merely "subsidiary themes."[14] Most criminal law course books at their start introduce students to deterrence principles as part of the standard litany for analyzing criminal law

9. *Id.* at § 1.B.

10. *Id.* at §§ 1.D–E.

11. 1 WAYNE R. LAFAVE & AUSTIN W. SCOTT, JR., SUBSTANTIVE CRIMINAL LAW § 2.1, at 103 (2d. ed. 1986); *accord* GLANVILLE WILLIAMS, CRIMINAL LAW § 191, at 601 (2d ed. 1961).

12. Warren v. United States Parole Comm'n, 659 F.2d 183, 188 (D.C. Cir. 1981).

13. MODEL PENAL CODE § 1.02 explanatory note at 14 (1985).

14. "Subsidiary themes are to subject those who are disposed to commit crimes to public control [and] to prevent the condemnation of conduct that is without fault. . . ." *Id.*

doctrine.[15] As is illustrated below, criminal code commentaries, court opinions, legislative histories, and sentencing hearing transcripts are full of the language of deterrence in justifying every manner of criminal law rule and practice.

A. DOCTRINAL FORMULATIONS CALCULATED TO DETER, OR TO AVOID UNDERCUTTING DETERRENCE

1. Prohibitions

The most common use of deterrence rationales is in shaping the criminal law's prohibitions.[16] Explicit reliance on a deterrence rationale also is used to justify decisions *not* to criminalize certain conduct, often on the view that a sanction would be ineffective or unnecessary as a deterrent. Such a rationale is offered to explain, for example, the decriminalization of suicide,[17] attempted suicide,[18] failing to pay a valid debt,[19] self-abortion and the preparation of home-made abortifacients,[20] and limiting the "joyriding" offense to the person who actually operates or aids in the operation of the vehicle, thereby excluding

15. *See, e.g.*, SANFORD H. KADISH & STEPHEN J. SCHULHOFER, CRIMINAL LAW AND ITS PROCESSES: CASES AND MATERIALS 101–02 (7th ed. 2001); RICHARD G. SINGER & MARTIN K. GARDNER, CRIMES AND PUNISHMENT: CASES, MATERIALS, AND READINGS IN CRIMINAL LAW 87–94 (2d ed. 1996).

16. *See, e.g.*, *infra* text accompanying notes 110–17 (describing instances where deterrence is the explicit justification given for obvious harms). The deterrence rationale also is used to prohibit conduct not because that conduct is harmful in itself but because the prohibition will make some other conduct, which is harmful, more difficult. Thus, in criminalizing the receipt of stolen property, it is explained: From a practical standpoint, it is important to punish receivers *in order to discourage theft*. "The existence and functioning of the 'fence,' i.e., a dealer who provides a market for stolen property, is an assurance to thieves, and especially to professional thieves, of the ability to realize gain from their unlawful activity." MODEL PENAL CODE § 223.6 cmt. at 232 (1980).

17. GLANVILLE WILLIAMS, THE SANCTITY OF LIFE AND THE CRIMINAL LAW 305 (1957).

18. According to the Model Penal Code § 210.5 cmt. at 94 (1980):

> [A]ttempted suicide is . . . not criminal under the Model Code, for [suicide is not a crime and Section 5.01 attempt] is limited to situations where the actor engages in inchoate behavior that has as its object the completion of conduct that the law declares to be criminal. . . .
>
> . . . .
>
> The judgment underlying the Model Code position is that there is no form of criminal punishment that is acceptable for a completed suicide and that criminal punishment is singularly inefficacious to deter attempts to commit suicide. There is scant reason to believe that the threat of punishment will have deterrent impact upon one who sets out to take his own life. By definition, the person who commits what could be denominated a criminal attempt to commit suicide intends to succeed. It seems preposterous to argue that the visitation of criminal sanctions upon one who fails in the effort is likely to inhibit persons from undertaking a serious attempt to take their own lives.

19. *Id.* § 223.8 cmt. at 258–59 (reasoning that insolvencies cannot be deterred by threat of criminal sanction because they commonly result from factors out of the control of the debtor).

20. *Id.* § 230.3 cmt. at 438:

> It is apparent from the foregoing that criminal liability of the woman for an abortion committed on herself was not useful in suppressing self-abortion . . . [T]his section favors exemption from criminal liability, except in the late-pregnancy situation specially covered by Subsection (4). The prospect of prosecution is unlikely to deter the unhappy woman who is not restrained by morality, physical danger, expense, and ignominy.

See also id. § 230.3 cmt. at 439–40 (declining to criminalize home-made abortifacients).

willing passengers.[21]

Similarly, a deterrence rationale is used in formulating liability doctrines determining who should be held criminally liable. For example, the deterrence rationale is used both in support of[22] and in opposition to[23] the use of corporate-enterprise liability, in support of limiting the liability of corporate officials to the board of directors or high management,[24] and both in support of[25] and in opposition to[26] the use of vicarious liability.

Deterrence is also used as the guiding rationale in the formulation of inchoate liability rules. For example, it is used in support of the proximity test for attempt,[27] in support of limiting the renunciation defense to cases where the offender is successful in avoiding the offense,[28] and in opposition to an impossibility defense for inchoate liability.[29] For example, in justifying a renunciation defense to attempt, the Model Penal Code drafters explain:

> [The defense] provide[s] actors with a motive for desisting from their criminal designs, thereby diminishing the risk that the substantive crime will be committed. While under the proposed subsection such encouragement is held out at all stages of the criminal effort, its significance becomes greatest as the actor nears his criminal objective and the risk that the crime will be completed is correspondingly high. . . .
>
> . . . .
>
> . . .[B]ecause of the importance of encouraging desistance in the final stages of the attempt, the defense is allowed even when the last proximate act has occurred but the criminal result can be avoided, as for example when the

21. *See id.* § 223.9 cmt. at 273 (explaining that the threat of liability for the operator is enough to deter such offenses).

22. *See* Brent Fisse, *Reconstructing Corporate Criminal Law: Deterrence, Retribution, Fault, and Sanctions*, 56 S. CAL. L. REV. 1141, 1147–54 (1983) (arguing that the stigma of criminal conviction and punishment has a significant deterrent effect on corporations).

23. The argument is that corporate-enterprise liability makes a scapegoat of the corporation, allowing the corporate officials to escape liability and, therefore, undercuts deterrence. *See* LAFAVE & SCOTT, *supra* note 11, § 3.10, at 365; WILLIAMS, *supra* note 11, § 283, at 865.

24. *See* MODEL PENAL CODE § 2.07 cmt. at 336, 340 (1985) (reasoning that this is where the deterrent effect—through pressure by shareholders—is clear).

25. *See* Davis v. City of Peachtree City, 304 S.E.2d 701, 703 (Ga. 1983) (stating that deterrence is the objective of holding liquor store owners liable for employee alcohol sales to minors); *cf.* LAFAVE & SCOTT, *supra* note 11, § 3.9, at 352–57 (asserting that while vicarious liability is useful for deterrence purposes, it should not be used for moral condemnation and that fines, not imprisonment, should be imposed).

26. Some have opposed vicarious liability because if the actor himself has not done anything wrong, then there is no need for deterrence. *See, e.g.*, Commonwealth v. Koczwara, 155 A.2d 825, 828 n.1 (Pa. 1959).

27. *See* MODEL PENAL CODE § 5.01 cmt. at 323 (1985); LAFAVE & SCOTT, *supra* note 11, § 6.2, at 33; WILLIAMS, *supra* note 11, § 203, at 631–32.

28. *See* MODEL PENAL CODE § 5.01 cmt. at 360 (1985).

29. *See* Jerome B. Elkind, *Impossibility in Criminal Attempts: A Theorist's Headache*, 54 VA. L. REV. 20, 33–34 (1968) ("When a man makes a harmless attempt to commit a crime, he may well try again, perhaps more effectively. The voodoo witchdoctor may use a gun next time. Thus the purposes of special deterrence and neutralization can be served by punishing even the marginal cases.").

> fuse has been lit but can still be stamped out. If, however, the actor has put in motion forces that he is powerless to stop, then the attempt has been completed and cannot be abandoned.[30]

Similar kinds of behavioral control reasoning are found in justifying liability rules for solicitation[31] and conspiracy.[32]

2. Culpability Requirements, Mitigations, and Excuse Defenses

The belief of lawmakers that doctrinal manipulation can enhance or maintain deterrent effect appears as well in the formulation of culpability requirements, mitigations, and excuse defenses. For example, in *United States v. Park*,[33] the president of Acme Markets, Inc., a national retail food chain with approximately 36,000 employees, 874 retail outlets, twelve general warehouses, and four special warehouses, was held criminally liable for violations of the Federal Food, Drug, and Cosmetic Act when a company warehouse in Baltimore held food in a building that could be exposed to contamination by rodents, even though there was no indication that Park was negligent as to the violation.[34]

30. MODEL PENAL CODE § 5.01 cmt. at 359–60 (1985).

31. *See id.* § 5.02 cmt. at 365–66 (1980).

32. *See id.* § 5.03 cmt. at 458 (footnotes omitted):

> [T]he law [of conspiracy] should afford a significant incentive to persons to desist from pressing forward with their criminal designs.
>
> The [renunciation] test adopted . . . is consistent with those in the attempt and solicitation sections. First, the circumstances must manifest complete and voluntary renunciation of the actor's criminal purpose. Second, he must take action sufficient to prevent consummation of the criminal objective. The kind of action that will suffice varies for the three different inchoate crimes. Since attempt involves only an individual actor, abandonment will generally prevent completion of the crime, although in some cases the actor may have to put a stop to forces that he has set in motion and that would otherwise bring about the substantive crime independently of his will. The solicitor, on the other hand, has incited another person to commit the crime, unless the solicitation is uncommunicated or rejected; consequently, the Code requires that he either persuade the other person not to commit the crime or otherwise prevent its commission. Since conspiracy involves preparation for crime by a plurality of agents, the objective will generally be pursued despite renunciation by one conspirator, and the Code accordingly requires for a defense of renunciation that the actor thwart the success of the conspiracy.
>
> The means required to thwart the success of the conspiracy will of course vary in particular cases, and it would be impractical to endeavor to formulate a more specific rule. As a general matter, timely notification to law enforcement authorities will suffice, and this result accords with the similar means of exoneration allowed an accomplice who terminates his complicity prior to the commission of the substantive crime.

33. 421 U.S. 658 (1975).

34. *Id.* at 660. It could be argued that Park was blameworthy for his failure to take sufficient remedial steps after being informed of the violation because he ordered a cleanup but gave this order to the same people who had allowed the problem to occur. But, while one might argue that the government could have shown Park's negligence, the point is that the *Park* opinion allows statutes that do not require such a showing and thus allows criminal liability even if it is clear that no such showing can be made and that the defendant acted entirely reasonably. *See* Norman Abrams, *Criminal Liability of Corporate Officers for Strict Liability Offenses—A Comment on* Dotterweich *and* Park, 28 UCLA L. REV. 463, 476–77 (1981).

Such strict liability has been defended on the following deterrence grounds:

> [A] person engaged in a certain kind of activity would be more careful precisely because he knew that this kind of activity was governed by a strict liability statute. . . . [T]he knowledge that certain criminal sanctions will be imposed if certain consequences ensue might induce a person to engage in that activity with much greater caution than would be the case if some lesser standard prevailed.[35]

Another useful example is found in the well-known case, *Regina v. Dudley & Stephens*,[36] in which the defendants, adrift in an open boat at sea and soon to die from starvation, killed and drank the blood of a near-death cabin boy, an act that kept them alive long enough to be rescued.[37] They were convicted of murder and sentenced to death.[38] The court denied their claim of a necessity defense in large part because it feared that recognition of such a defense would undercut criminal law's prohibitions at a time when its deterrent threat must be at its strongest:

> It must not be supposed that in refusing to admit temptation to be an excuse for crime it is forgotten how terrible the temptation was; how awful the suffering; how hard in such trials to keep the judgment straight and the conduct pure. We are often compelled to set up standards we cannot reach ourselves, and to lay down rules which we could not ourselves satisfy. But a man has no right to declare temptation to be an excuse, though he might himself have yielded to it, nor allow compassion for the criminal to change or weaken in any manner the legal definition of the crime. It is therefore our duty to declare that the prisoners' act in this case was wilful murder, that the facts as stated in the verdict are no legal justification of the homicide; and to say that in our unanimous opinion the prisoners are upon this special verdict guilty of murder.[39]

The court then proceeded to pass sentence of death upon the prisoners.[40]

---

35. Richard A. Wasserstrom, *Strict Liability in the Criminal Law*, 12 STAN. L. REV. 731, 736 (1960). Wasserstrom also notes that people may be deterred from engaging in the strict liability activity altogether, out of concern that they might not be able to avoid the prohibited harm. "[T]he presence of strict liability offenses might have the added effect of keeping a relatively large class of persons from engaging in certain kinds of activity." *Id.* at 737.

36. 14 Q.B.D. 273 (1884). For more details on this case, see PAUL H. ROBINSON, CRIMINAL LAW CASE STUDIES 14–18 (2d ed. 2002); A.W. BRIAN SIMPSON, CANNIBALISM AND THE COMMON LAW: THE STORY OF THE TRAGIC LAST VOYAGE OF *THE MIGNONETTE* AND THE STRANGE LEGAL PROCEEDINGS TO WHICH IT GAVE RISE (1984).

37. *Dudley & Stephens*, 14 Q.B.D. at 273–75.

38. *Id.* at 288.

39. *Id.*

40. *Id.* The defendants' sentence was afterwards commuted by the Crown to six months imprisonment. *Id.*

The influence of a deterrence rationale is also apparent in the formulations of the test for negligence. Many jurisdictions continue to use a purely objective standard against which to judge a person's culpability for failing to be aware of a prohibited risk. They refuse to take account of the particular capacities of the person at hand—of whether the person had the capacity to have met the reasonable person standard—for fear that any individualization would undercut the force of the law's prohibitions.

Thus, in *State v. Williams*,[41] loving parents with little education and limited intelligence were held to have breached the reasonable person standard in failing to get needed medical care for their seventeen-month-old child, who died of complications from what began as a toothache.[42] The court ruled that it was sufficient negligence to support liability for manslaughter if "the conduct of a defendant, regardless of his ignorance, good intentions and good faith, fails to measure up to the conduct required of a man of reasonable prudence."[43] Reliance upon a purely objective, unindividualized negligence standard is justified in much the same way as the result in *Dudley & Stephens*[44]: it is necessary to maintain a clear standard of conduct. Holmes, for example, concludes that the reason for adopting it is the criminal law's "immediate object and task to establish a general standard . . . of conduct for the community, in the interest of the safety of all."[45]

To give just a few of many possible examples, deterrence arguments are used in the following areas: in opposition to[46] and in support of strict liability offenses;[47] in opposition to liability based upon negligence;[48] in support of liability for negligent homicide[49] and negligent assault with a deadly weapon;[50]

41. 484 P.2d 1167 (Wash. Ct. App. 1971).

42. Id. at 1169–70.

43. *Id.* at 1171. Similarly, in *Edgmon v. State*, 702 P.2d 643, 645 (Alaska Ct. App. 1985), the court held that the "peculiarities of a given individual—his or her intelligence, experience, and physical capabilities—are irrelevant in determining criminal negligence since the standard is one of a reasonably prudent person."

44. *See supra* text accompanying notes 36–40.

45. Commonwealth v. Pierce, 138 Mass. 165, 176 (1884); *see also* Richard Singer, *The Resurgence of Mens Rea: II—Honest but Unreasonable Mistake of Fact in Self Defense*, 28 B.C. L. REV. 459, 489 (1987) (describing the movement among legal scholars and courts to apply an objective and pragmatic standard to "achieve the greatest good: deterrence of negligent and more culpable actors").

46. This argument is made on the grounds that someone who lacks mens rea need not be deterred. *See* Herbert L. Packer, *Mens Rea and the Supreme Court*, 1962 SUP. CT. REV. 107, 109.

47. *See* Wasserstrom, *supra* note 35, at 736; Janet S. Harring, Note, *Liability Without Fault: Logic and Potential of a Developing Concept*, 1970 WIS. L. REV. 1201, 1207. Deterrence arguments also have been used in resolving related issues. *See* Steven S. Nemerson, Note, *Criminal Liability Without Fault: A Philosophical Perspective*, 75 COLUM. L. REV. 1517, 1550 (1975) (arguing that mens rea, even if burden of proof is shifted to defendant, is not a good alternative because it would result in significant loss of deterrence).

48. This argument is made on the grounds that such persons are not deterrable. *See* JEROME HALL, GENERAL PRINCIPLES OF CRIMINAL LAW 137 (2d ed. 1960); WILLIAMS, *supra* note 11, § 43, at 122.

49. "Criminal punishment of negligent homicide is not impotent to stimulate care that might otherwise not be taken." MODEL PENAL CODE § 210.4 cmt. at 86 (1980).

50. In order to induce "special care and restraint." *Id.* § 211.1 cmt. at 191.

in support of an objective unindividualized standard of recklessness;[51] in support of a purely objective, unindividualized standard for the provocation mitigation to murder;[52] in opposition to the individualized extreme emotional disturbance mitigation in murder cases;[53] in support of the partial responsibility mitigation in murder;[54] in support of recognizing an insanity defense,[55] an immaturity defense,[56] and a duress defense;[57] in support of a reasonableness requirement for a mistake as to a justification defense,[58] an involuntary act defense,[59] a statute of limitation,[60] and an entrapment defense;[61] and in opposi-

---

51. *See* ROYAL COMMISSION ON CAPITAL PUNISHMENT, 1949–1953, at 52–53 (1953) (in the context of involuntary manslaughter); *see also supra* text accompanying notes 41–43 (discussing *Williams* case).

52. *See* ROYAL COMMISSION, *supra* note 51, at 52–53.

53. As the Model Penal Code states:

> Unlike provocation, diminished responsibility is entirely subjective in character. It looks into the actor's mind to see whether he should be judged by a lesser standard than that applicable to ordinary men. It recognizes the defendant's own mental disorder or emotional instability as a basis for partially excusing his conduct. This position undoubtedly achieves a closer relation between criminal liability and moral guilt. Moral condemnation must be founded, at least in part, on some perception of the capacities and limitations of the individual actor. To the extent that the abnormal individual is judged as if he were normal, to the extent that the drunk man is judged as if he were sober, to the extent, in short, that the defective person is judged as if he were someone else, the moral judgment underlying criminal conviction is undermined. The doctrine of diminished responsibility resolves this conflict in favor of an individualistic and subjective determination of criminal liability. But this approach has its costs. By evaluating the abnormal individual on his own terms, it decreases the incentives for him to behave as if he were normal. It blurs the law's message that there are certain minimal standards of conduct to which every member of society must conform.

MODEL PENAL CODE § 210.3 cmt. at 71 (1980).

54. *See id.*

55. *See* ABRAHAM S. GOLDSTEIN, INSANITY DEFENSE 12–13 (1967).

56. *See* SIR EDWARD COKE, THE THIRD PART OF THE INSTITUTES OF THE LAWS OF ENGLAND 4 (R.H. Helmholz & Bernard D. Roams, Jr., eds., William S. Hein Co. 1986) (1797).

57. *See* MODEL PENAL CODE § 2.09 cmt. at 374–75 (1985); WILLIAMS, *supra* note 11, § 246, at 756.

58. As Herbert Wechsler and Jerome Michael stated:

> To concede a privilege to kill only in cases of actual necessity is to lay down a rule that must either be disregarded or else must operate to deny freedom of action even in cases where the necessity exists and not merely in those where is does not. On the other hand, no such onerous limitation on freedom of action is imposed by requiring that men exercise the degree of care to appraise the facts correctly which is appropriate to the situation. It is desirable to deter men from acting without exercising such care. . . .

Herbert Wechsler & Jerome Michael, *A Rationale of the Law of Homicide: I*, 37 COLUM. L. REV. 701, 736 (1937).

59. *See* LAFAVE & SCOTT, *supra* note 11, § 3.2, at 275–76.

60. *See* Yair Listokin, *Efficient Time Bars: A New Rationale for the Existence of Statutes of Limitations in Criminal Law*, 31 J. LEGAL STUD. 99, 99 (2002) ("Because potential criminals tend to discount the future at higher rates than society, punishing crimes long after they are committed will be inefficient. Punishments after a long lag have only a nominal deterrent effect, while they may cost society substantial sums.").

61. *See* MODEL PENAL CODE § 2.13 cmt. at 406–07, 412 (1985) (stating that the defense is an "attempt to deter wrongful conduct on the part of the government" and that "[t]he primary justification for the defense . . . is to discourage unsavory police tactics").

tion to recognizing a general reasonable mistake of law excuse[62] and a duress defense.[63] Deterrence arguments also have been used to support particular formulations of excuse defenses. For example, deterrence rationales have been used to support definitions of insanity that cover both cognitive impairment and control dysfunction[64] and to support definitions of insanity that exclude control dysfunction.[65]

3. Grading Judgments

An assumption that doctrinal formulations control deterrent effect also is reflected in the rationales offered for setting offense grades. An example is found in the popular felony-murder rule, which treats even a purely accidental killing as murder. The rule's traditional rationale assumes that a deterrent threat of severe sanctions if a death occurs will make felons more careful to avoid accidental injury:

> [I]f experience shows, or is deemed by the law-maker to show, that somehow or other deaths which the evidence makes accidental happen disproportionately often in connection with other felonies, or with resistance to officers, or if on any other ground of policy it is deemed desirable to make special efforts for the prevention of such deaths, the law-maker may consistently treat acts which, under the known circumstances, are felonious . . . as having a sufficiently dangerous tendency to be put under a special ban. The law may, therefore, throw on the actor the peril, not only of the consequences foreseen by him, but also of consequences which, although not predicted by common experience, the legislator apprehends.[66]

The rule is thought to have the useful collateral effect of providing an additional deterrent to felonies generally, especially to dangerous felonies.[67]

---

62. *See* LAFAVE & SCOTT, *supra* note 11, § 5.1, at 586–87. Dan Kahan argues against recognizing a reasonable mistake of law defense for fear that it will encourage persons to engage in conduct close to the line of criminality. Dan M. Kahan, *Ignorance of Law Is an Excuse—But Only for the Virtuous*, 96 MICH. L. REV. 127, 129 (1997).

63. 2 SIR JAMES FITZJAMES STEPHEN, A HISTORY OF THE CRIMINAL LAW OF ENGLAND 107 (William S. Hein & Co. 1980) (1883) ("[I]t is at the moment when temptation to crime is strongest that the law should speak most clearly and emphatically to the contrary.").

64. *See* People v. Hubert, 51 P. 329 (Cal. 1897); MODEL PENAL CODE § 4.01 cmt. at 156–60 (Tentative Draft No. 4, 1955); John Barker Waite, *Irresistible Impulse and Criminal Liability*, 23 MICH. L. REV. 443, 454 (1925); Herbert Wechsler, *The Criteria of Criminal Responsibility*, 22 U. CHI. L. REV. 367, 374 (1955).

65. *See* State v. Green, 6 P.2d 177 (Utah 1931); MODEL PENAL CODE § 4.01 cmt. at 173 n.24 (1985) (arguing for the ALI test—excusing one who "lacks substantial capacity to appreciate the criminality of his conduct or to conform his conduct to the requirements of law"—as the best formulation for excluding from liability only the undeterrables).

66. OLIVER W. HOLMES, THE COMMON LAW 59 (1881).

67. *See* Jenkins v. State, 230 A.2d 262, 268–69 (Del. 1967) ("[The] rational function of the felony-murder rule is to furnish added deterrent to the perpetration of felonies which, by their nature or by the attendant circumstances, create a foreseeable risk of death.").

Another example of adjusting grade to enhance deterrence is found in the "three strikes" and other habitual offender statutes. Part of their justification no doubt is the incapacitation of dangerous offenders by predicting future dangerousness from repeated past offenses. But such provisions also have been justified on deterrence grounds.[68] As the federal sentencing guidelines explain, "General deterrence of criminal conduct dictates that a clear message be sent to society that repeated criminal behavior will aggravate the need for punishment with each recurrence."[69] Indeed, it is in the context of habitual offender statutes that it has been argued that "deterrence is the surest ground for punishment."[70]

Rummel v. Estelle[71] illustrates such deterrence reliance. Thirty-year-old Rummel made his living through petty larceny and fraud. His pathetic check forgery was usually easy to discover, and he was caught and convicted several times. On a hot summer day, Rummel offered to fix a bar's broken air conditioner for $129.75, but actually had no intention of doing so. He was caught and convicted of theft, a felony under then-existing state law. After the state presented evidence of two prior felonies, a "three strikes" recidivist statute required that Rummel receive a sentence of life in prison without parole. The United States Supreme Court denied his appeal, concluding that the statute did not violate the

68. According to *Rummel v. Estelle*, for example:

> The purpose of a recidivist statute such as that involved here is not to simplify the task of prosecutors, judges, or juries. Its primary goals are to deter repeat offenders and, at some point in the life of one who repeatedly commits criminal offenses serious enough to be punished as felonies, to segregate that person from the rest of society for an extended period of time.

445 U.S. 263, 284 (1980); *see also* Dan Lungren, *Three Cheers for Three Strikes: California Enjoys a Record Drop in Crime*, POL'Y REV.: J. AM. CITIZENSHIP, Nov.–Dec. 1996, at 34, 36–37 (1996) (recognizing California's Three Strikes Law as having a large deterrent effect); William Clairborne, *"Three Strikes": Tough on Courts Too; California's Sentencing Law Leads to Criminal Justice Logjam*, WASH. POST, Nov. 7, 1995 at A1 (noting that "Three Strikes" supporters expect a deterrent effect over time); Walt Yost, *"Three Strikes" Law is Hardball That Works, Says Scully*, SACRAMENTO BEE, Apr. 21, 1996 at N7 (reporting the Sacramento County District Attorney's comments that the Three Strikes law deters criminals and has led to a dramatic decrease in the California crime rate).

69. U.S. SENTENCING GUIDELINES MANUAL § 4A, introductory cmt. at 317 (2002).

70. As Chief Judge Posner stated in *United States v. Jackson*:

> Indeed, deterrence is the surest ground for punishment since retributive norms are so unsettled and since incapacitation may, by removing one offender from the pool of offenders, simply make a career in crime more attractive to someone else, who is balanced on the razor's edge between criminal and legitimate activity and who now faces reduced competition in the crime 'market.'

5 F.2d 1195, 1199 (7th Cir. 1987) (Posner, C.J., concurring) (citing Isaac Ehrlich, *On the Usefulness of Controlling Individuals: An Economic Analysis of Rehabilitation, Incapacitation, and Deterrence*, 71 AM. ECON. REV. 307 (1981)).

71. For a more detailed account of the Rummel case, see Rummel v. Estelle, 498 F. Supp. 793 (W.D. Tex. 1980). *See also Appeals Court Upholds Life Sentence for San Antonian*, SAN ANTONIO EXPRESS-NEWS, Jan. 13, 1979; *Courts to Review Tough Texas Law: Billy Sol Bilks Companies Out of Millions; Rummel's Fraud Totals $229.11. Estes Serving 10 Years – Rummel Gets Life*, SAN ANTONIO EXPRESS-NEWS, Sept. 9, 1979, at 14A; Tom Nelson, *Rummel Ordered Released for Appeal*, SAN ANTONIO EXPRESS-NEWS, Oct. 4, 1980, at 11C; *S.A. Man Finally Free After 8-Year Ordeal*, SAN ANTONIO EXPRESS-NEWS, Nov. 15, 1980, at 2-A C; *S.A. Man Gets Life*, SAN ANTONIO NEWS, Apr. 13, 1973, at 20D.

Eighth Amendment's prohibition against cruel and unusual punishment.[72] Rummel's crime, a minor fraud, hardly seems to deserve life imprisonment without parole. Indeed, the cumulative impact of his entire criminal career—whether or not he had been formally sanctioned and punished for his earlier crimes—does not seem to merit such severe liability, at least on justice grounds. Yet "three strikes" laws are willing to tolerate this deviation from justice, partly in the name of general deterrence.

The use of grading determinations to optimize deterrent effect has been offered in support of a variety of offense grade aggravations, such as grading according to type of victim (old, young, or police officer)[73] or location (selling drugs near schools).[74] Similarly, deterrence arguments have been used in the following scenarios: in support of a separate offense of robbery (rather than relying upon the distinct offenses of theft and assault);[75] in support of grading a vehicular killing while intoxicated as manslaughter even without a showing of negligence or causation;[76] in opposition to application of the felony-murder rule to killings by non-felons during the felony;[77] in support of application of the felony-murder rule to killings by non-felons;[78] in support of the premeditation

72. *Rummel*, 445 U.S. at 284–85.

73. *See, e.g.*, 720 ILL. COMP. STAT. ANN. § 5/9-1 (West 2002) (elevating sentence for first degree murder: Defendant can get the death penalty if the victim was, inter alia, a police officer, a minor under 12 years of age, or an adult over 60 years old).

74. *See, e.g.*, 720 ILL. COMP. STAT. ANN. § 570/401(c)(2), 570/407 (West 2002) (elevating sentence for illegal drug sales near a school; for example, the sale of one 14-gram bag of cocaine normally is a Class 1 felony carrying a fine of not more than $250,000 but if the same quantity is sold on school grounds, it is a Class X felony with a fine not more than $500,000).

75. MODEL PENAL CODE § 222.1 cmt. at 98 (1980) (comparing the robber, who "menaces his victims with actual or threatened violence," and the "stealthy thief," who chooses not to confront his victim, and arguing that the penalty attached to theft is not enough to deter the robber).

76. *See, e.g.*, Baker v. State, 377 So.2d 17, 19 (Fla. 1979), stating:

> Is section 860.01(2) [Florida's DWI punishment law] a rational response to a real problem? We must respond that (i) the problem of drunken drivers operating motor vehicles on the highways of this state is pernicious and real, and (ii) the response embodied in section 860.01(2) can be justified on deterrence grounds. Both are supported by our recent decision in Ingram v. Pettit, 340 So.2d 922 (Fla. 1976), where, in the context of a civil action for punitive damages, the statistics regarding fatalities resulting from accidents where drinking was a contributing factor are recited, and the public policy of punishment of drunk drivers as a deterrent is recognized.

77. *See, e.g.*, Campbell v. State, 444 A.2d 1034, 1038 (Md. 1982) (declining to convict one co-felon of felony murder where the second co-felon was killed by a police officer during the course of an armed robbery, and noting that "the mere coincidence of homicide and felony is not enough to satisfy the requirements of the felony-murder doctrine." (citation omitted)).

78. *See* People v. Washington, 402 P.2d 130, 136–39 (Cal. 1965) (Burke, J. dissenting) ("If a victim . . . seizes an opportunity to shoot first when confronted with robbers with a deadly weapon . . . any 'gun battle' is initiated by the armed robbers. In such a situation, application of the felony-murder rule supports, if not compels, the conclusion that the surviving robber committed murder." (citations omitted)).

aggravation for first degree murder;[79] in rejecting a mere grade reduction for renunciation (preferring a complete defense);[80] in support of grading inchoate liability less than that for the substantive offense[81] and, where it is graded the same as the substantive offense, in support of making an exception to this rule for first degree felonies;[82] in support of grading theft of livestock more than other thefts of equal or greater value because the former are particularly easy to commit and difficult to detect;[83] in support of a lower grade for nonconsensual intercourse by mistake or trick rather than by force;[84] in support of grading theft by the amount stolen;[85] in support of reduced grading for "joyriding" (in comparison to theft);[86] in support of grading credit card fraud of even a nominal amount as at least a misdemeanor;[87] in support of grading incest no higher than a class three felony even if extreme moral indignation of the community would call for a higher grade;[88] in support of a relatively low

---

79. *Cf.* F. LINDMAN & D. MCINTYRE, THE MENTALLY DISABLED AND THE LAW 356 (1961) (discussing whether there should be decreased liability for unpremeditated killing because only those capable of thoughtful deliberation are likely to be deterred by threat of heavier sanction).

80. The Model Penal Code states:

> In considering the significance to be attached to abandonment of a criminal attempt, one solution that was rejected in drafting the Model Code was reduction of penalty in the event of abandonment. Insofar as encouragement of desistance is concerned, reductions in sanction would have to be very great to have a substantial impact on those already engrossed in a criminal attempt; indeed, it is unlikely that anything short of complete immunity would suffice.

MODEL PENAL CODE § 5.01 cmt. at 362 (1985) (footnote omitted).

81. *See id.* § 5.05 cmt. at 490 (1980).

82. *See id.*, stating:

> It is doubtful . . . that the threat of punishment for the inchoate crime can add significantly to the net deterrent efficacy of the sanction threatened for the substantive offense that is the actor's object, which he, by hypothesis, ignores. Hence, there is a basis for economizing in use of the heaviest and most afflictive sanctions by removing them from inchoate crimes.

83. *See* State v. Clark, 632 P.2d 841, 843 (Utah 1981).

84. "Subsection (2)(c) deals in effect with an aggravated instance of seduction by trick, a kind of activity that most women can prevent and that can be deterred by sanctions less severe than those applicable to sexual imposition on a physically helpless female." MODEL PENAL CODE § 213.1 cmt. at 331 (1980).

85. According to the Model Penal Code:

> Shorter sentences should be sufficient to deter those who have not as much to gain. On the other hand, longer sentences are called for in the case of offenders who realize greater sums. Escalation of penalty according to amount stolen decreases the incentive for crime that greater profits might induce.

Model Penal Code § 223.1 cmt. at 139 (1980).

86. "Temporary takings do not require more severe deterrents" than this. *Id.* § 223.9 cmt. at 276 (1985).

87. *See* MODEL PENAL CODE § 224.6 cmt. at 322 (1980) (reasoning that these methods of defrauding lend themselves to repeated violations by transients and, consequently, that grading can have an effect on real-world behavior).

88. According to the Model Penal Code:

> [Incest] is classified as a third-degree felony, carrying an ordinary-term maximum sentence of five years. This is based on the judgment that so heavy a threat will be enough to deter those

grading of perjury;[89] and in support of a grading reduction for a kidnapper who "voluntarily releases the victim alive and in a safe place prior to trial."[90]

4. Sentencing Decisions

Sentencing judges and sentencing guideline drafters share the assumption of code drafters and appellate judges that their decisions will influence the extent of the criminal law's deterrent effect. As an example, consider the case of DeSean McCarty, a young African-American from a crime-ridden, South Chicago neighborhood.[91] McCarty agreed to provide drugs to an acquaintance in return for the use of the latter's friend's car. The exchange was made, but McCarty did not return the car at the agreed time. A few days later, a police cruiser drove by McCarty sitting in the car. Not wanting to get caught in a stolen car with drugs, he sped off, then abandoned the car and fled on foot. A police vehicle, in giving chase, ran down and killed an officer pursuing McCarty on foot. McCarty was convicted for the death of the officer under the Illinois felony-murder rule, which characterizes any death caused in the course of a felony as first degree murder.[92] As has already been noted,[93] the felony-murder rule itself has strong deterrent backing. The sentencing judge in *McCarty* also thought to advance deterrence through the exercise of his sentencing

---

> people who are deterrable. Use of heavier penalties to reflect extreme moral indignation seems both unnecessary and unwise.

MODEL PENAL CODE § 230.2 cmt. at 422–23 (1980).

89. *See* MODEL PENAL CODE § 241.1 cmt. at 142 (explaining that "third degree felony sanctions are adequate to deter all deterrable perjury").

90. According to the Model Penal Code:

> If the most severe sanctions are available once some harm has come to the victim, there is no remaining incentive not to do further harm. Thus, while causing harm to the victim will aggravate the offense as explained above, the actor may still escape the extreme sanctions of a first-degree felony by preserving the life of the victim and voluntarily releasing him alive and in a safe place prior to trial.
>
> The effect of this scheme is to provide at every stage an incentive to release the victim and not to inflict any further harm.

MODEL PENAL CODE § 212.1 cmt. at 233–34 (1980).

91. For a more detailed account of the McCarty case, see Telephone Interview by C. Todd Inniss, Eve Brensike, and Colette Routel with Frank Rago, Public Defender, Markham Public Defender's Office (Feb. 1999) (notes on file with authors). *See* PAUL H. ROBINSON, CRIMINAL LAW CASE STUDIES 1–5 (2d ed. 2002); Sarah Karp, *Mother Copes with Cop's Death; Markham Officer Struck by Harvey Police Car*, DAILY SOUTHTOWN, Sept. 22, 1997, at 1; Karen Mellen, *Reckless Abandon; Families Want Driver Charged with Murder*, CHI. TRIB., Oct. 7, 1998, at A1; T. Shawn Taylor, *Cops Arrest Teen Linked to Officer's Fatal Chase; Police Want Subject Held Accountable*, CHI. TRIB., Sept. 23, 1997, at Metro Southwest 1; T. Shawn Taylor, *Markham Cop's Death Becomes Murder Case; Bond Hearing Set in Fatal Police Chase*, CHI. TRIB., Sept. 24, 1997, at Metro Southwest 1.

92. Illinois continues to read the felony-murder rule broadly where it applies, although the rule's application has been limited to "forcible" felonies. ILL. COMP. STAT. ANN. § 5/9-1(a)(3) (West 2002). *See, e.g.*, People v. Lowery, 687 N.E.2d 973, 979 (Ill. 1997) (upholding a felony-murder conviction where the victim shot at the fleeing robber with a gun that the robber had dropped, accidentally killing a bystander).

93. *See supra* notes 77–78.

discretion. While he could have mitigated the harshness of the rule, he instead imposed a sentence of forty years in prison, explaining that he hoped the sentence would deter others from leading the police on high-speed chases.[94]

This sort of deterrence rationale is common in the formulation of a wide range of sentencing rules and policies,[95] including the following: arguments in support of the death penalty;[96] empirical evidence for the efficacy of the death penalty;[97] arguments in support of automatic imposition of the death penalty for prisoners already sentenced to life imprisonment who kill;[98] arguments in support of jail time for drunk driving;[99] arguments in support of extending the statutory maximum for fines to double the pecuniary gain;[100] arguments in support of applying a mandatory penalty enhancement for a subsequent offense to a second offense on a simultaneous conviction;[101] arguments in support of higher fines for corporate offenders;[102] arguments in support of a judicially imposed minimum term of imprisonment;[103] arguments in support of fines for

94. *See* People v. McCarty, Circuit Court of Cook County, No. 97 CR 27339, Sentencing Transcript 00392:11–13 (Sept. 15, 1998).

95. *See* Gary Becker, *Crime and Punishment: An Economic Approach*, 76 J. POL. ECON. 169, 191–93 (1968) (assuming that the commission of an offense is a function of the size of the fine and the probability of conviction, and arguing that courts should set both the fine and probability at levels "that induce offenders to commit just Ô [optimal number of] offenses."); John R. Lott, *Do We Punish High Income Criminals Too Heavily?* 30 ECON. INQUIRY 583, 584, 605 (1992) (pointing out that the probability of conviction has a greater deterrent effect on the wealthy because they face additional lost income due to damage to their reputations); George J. Stigler, *The Optimum Enforcement of Laws*, 78 J. POL. ECON. 526, 530–31 (1970) (arguing that "rational law enforcement" must have "expected penalties increasing with expected gains so there is no marginal net gain from larger offenses" in order to achieve the optimal number of offenses).

96. *See, e.g.*, Gregg v. Georgia, 428 U.S. 153, 183 (1976) (discussing two social purposes of capital punishment: retribution and deterrence).

97. *See* Enmund v. Florida, 458 U.S. 782, 799 (1982) (plurality opinion) (arguing against the death penalty for felony murder because death is not caused often enough in the commission of a felony to make the death penalty an effective deterrent); *see also* authorities collected at WAYNE R. LAFAVE, MODERN CRIMINAL LAW 25 n.27 (3d ed. 2000); Hashem Dezhbakhsh, *Does Capital Punishment Have a Deterrent Effect? New Evidence from Postmoratorium Panel Data*, 5 AM. L. & ECON. REV. 344 (2003).

98. MODEL PENAL CODE § 210.6 cmt. at 132–33 (1980).

99. *See* Leon S. Robertson et al., *Jail Sentences for Driving While Intoxicated in Chicago: A Judicial Policy That Failed*, 8 LAW & SOC'Y REV. 55, 57 (1973) ("Chicago officials concluded that the fatalities involving alcohol resulted mainly from social drinking and that 7-day jail sentences for persons convicted of DWI would deter social drinkers from drinking an amount likely to involve them in fatal crashes.").

100. MODEL PENAL CODE § 6.03 cmt. at 61 (1985) (arguing that a fine equal to double the pecuniary gain "is thought to be of maximum deterrent utility. Pocketbook sanctions are likely to be most effective in the context of pocketbook offenses.").

101. *See* United States v. Bernier, 954 F.2d 818, 820 (2d Cir. 1992) (reasoning that a federal statute ordering enhanced sentence for the second of two simultaneous convictions for using a firearm during the commission of a violent crime reflects Congress's intent to deter multiple commissions of a crime with a gun: "an enhanced deterrent effect is felt (if at all) as soon as the first crime is committed, rather than later, when the first conviction is obtained . . . the lesson is to be learned, if necessary, all at once.").

102. MODEL PENAL CODE § 6.04 cmt. at 65 (1985).

103. *Id.* § 6.06 cmt. at 128.

offenses of pecuniary gain;[104] and guidelines for the exercise of judicial discretion in setting the length of a prison sentence[105] and the amount of a fine.[106]

B. DOCTRINAL FORMULATIONS CALCULATED TO REQUIRE OR AUTHORIZE CONDUCT

The assumption that the doctrinal manipulation of criminal law rules can optimize deterrence is one application of a larger assumption that criminal law formulations can influence conduct "on the street." The same assumption is equally suspect when criminal law rules are formulated that require conduct or authorize conduct that is normally prohibited.

1. Justification Defenses

When crafting justification defenses, lawmakers assume that their formulation of the defense will in fact guide the conduct of a person acting under the justifying conditions. Thus, in disallowing the use of force to resist an unlawful arrest, the drafters of the Model Penal Code explain: "[T]hose who are subjected to arrest or to search should be encouraged to submit rather than respond with force, and thus should not be entitled to rely upon . . . errors [by the officer] as a justifying basis for the resort to defensive force."[107] Indeed, many justification provisions have highly detailed rules about what a person may and may not do under a particular set of conditions. For example, a person may use force that is necessary for self-defense against unlawful aggression; however, that person may not use deadly force, unless deadly force or serious bodily injury is threatened. Furthermore, even if deadly force or serious bodily injury is threatened, a person may not use deadly force if that person can retreat in safety; yet that person need not retreat if he is in his own home or place of business, unless he was the initial aggressor or unless he is assailed at his place of work by a person who works at the same place.[108] Indeed, the Model Penal Code drafters prefer such detailed rules in part because they believe the law should and can give people specific guidance.[109]

---

104. *Id.* § 7.02 cmt. at 239–40.

105. *See, e.g.*, *id.* arts. 6–7 intro. at 2–3 (explaining that the code's directing courts to consider, inter alia, "whether a lesser sentence will depreciate the seriousness of the defendant's crime" reflects "the principle of general deterrence, though it puts to the court a more realistic inquiry than whether a particular penalty for a particular offender is necessary to deter others.").

106. *Id.* § 7.02 cmt. at 240–41 (reasoning that, because deterrent effect of a particular fine depends on wealth of defendant, a court must take that into account in sentencing).

107. *Id.* § 3.09 cmt. at 148.

108. *Id.* § 3.04(1), (2)(b).

109. *See id.* § 5.01 cmt. at 359, 362; § 5.03 cmt. at 458 (assuming that the Code's detailed rules will in fact influence conduct). According to the Model Penal Code:

> Any increase in precision does involve some sacrifice of flexibility in respect to unusual or unforeseen circumstances; but it was deemed important that people be able to understand on what occasions the use of force is allowable, and that jurors have the benefit of legislative judgments on that score. It was believed that the law on this subject could influence behavior and moral perspectives, encouraging members of the community not to employ force when immediate emotional reaction might support its use but enlightened morality would reject it.

This attempt of lawmakers to control situations of conflicting interests through the formulation of justification defenses is present in a wide variety of justification rules, including, for example, the following: rules barring the use of force to resist an unlawful arrest, in order to avoid an escalation of violence;[110] rules limiting the use of deadly force to defense against threats of death or serious bodily injury;[111] rules disallowing the use of deadly force if a person can retreat in safety;[112] rules barring the use of force to recapture movable property from a person acting under claim of right, in order to avoid an escalation of violence;[113] rules requiring a request to desist before using force;[114] rules barring citizens—but not officers—from using deadly force to arrest;[115] rules

---

> The alternative of a general standard of reasonableness would largely forfeit these advantages and would leave judgment to the uninstructed responses of particular juries.

Id. § 3.04 cmt. at 34–35. Subsequent legislative revisions have followed the Model Penal Code in adopting fairly detailed provisions on self-defense and other justifications for the use of force. *See* sources collected at Paul H. Robinson, *Criminal Law Defenses*, § 132 n.1.

110. According to the Model Penal Code:

> [T]here ought not to be a privilege to employ force against a public officer who, to the actor's knowledge, is attempting only to arrest him and subject him to the processes of law. It should be possible to provide adequate remedies against illegal arrest without permitting the arrested person to resort to force—a course of action highly likely to result in even greater injury to himself than the detention. . . . [I]t is believed to be entirely sound that the encouragement be in favor of judicial resolution of the legality of the arrest, rather than self-help.

Id. § 3.04 cmt. at 42–43 (1985) (footnotes omitted).

111. *Id.* § 3.04 cmt. at 48 ("[T]he discouragement of the infliction of death or serious bodily injury is so high on the scale of preferred societal values that such infliction cannot be justified by reference to the protection of an interest of any lesser pretensions, with the possible exception of dispossession from one's own dwelling.").

112. *Id.* § 3.04 cmt. at 54 ("[T]he protection of life has such a high place in a proper scheme of social values that the law should not permit conduct that places life in jeopardy, when the necessity for doing so can be avoided by the sacrifice of the much smaller value that inheres in standing up to an aggression.").

113. *Id.* § 3.06 cmt. at 74.

114. *Id.* § 3.06 cmt. at 90 ("[O]n many occasions such a request will end a potential confrontation, for example, when the aggressor is acting under a mistake of fact and the request clarifies some matter.").

115. According to the Model Penal Code:

> [T]he use of deadly force is restricted by Paragraph (ii) of Subsection (2)(b) to those who, under the law of the jurisdiction, are authorized to act as peace officers and to those who are assisting persons whom they believe are authorized to act as peace officers. Where the purpose to be served is the apprehension of persons to answer criminal charges, it has seemed important, in an age of firearms, to restrict the use of deadly force to situations where official personnel are involved, or at least are believed to be involved. This will mean, for the most part, that deadly force will be justified only at the instance or under the control of people who have been trained in the restraint that should be exhibited upon such occasions. It is thus an important limitation on the extent to which the private citizen can use force solely for the purpose of effecting arrest. By the same token, however, it does not penalize the private citizen who comes to the aid of a peace officer and either assists him under his direction or continues a course of conduct begun before the officer became disabled. It thus reflects what is believed to be an appropriate balance between the needs of effective law enforcement and the desirability of discouraging private resort to violence.

Id. § 3.07 cmt. at 116 (footnote omitted).

allowing a defense for mistake in the defense of others, for fear that failure to do so would deter people from helping others;[116] and rules limiting a mistake defense for citizens making an arrest, as a means "of discouraging private vigilante activity."[117]

2. Duties and Liability for Omissions

The same sort of assumption that the formulation of criminal law doctrine will influence conduct is found in the creation of a variety of legal duties, backed up by the threat of criminal liability for a failure. Examples include the duty to return or to report property lost or mislaid by another,[118] to take reasonable measures in some instances to prevent or to mitigate a catastrophe,[119] and to eject tenants engaging in prostitution.[120] In each instance, the lawmaker has created the legal duty under the belief that, by doing so, the duty will induce people to perform as the law commands.

C. "DETERRENCE SPEAK" VERSUS DEVIATIONS FROM JUSTICE

1. Deterrence Speak

Too much attention perhaps has been paid to the use of deterrence rationales; often, "deterrence" may be merely a common way that modern criminal law theorists have chosen to express themselves. Instead of saying "conduct X is harmful" and, therefore, should be criminalized, it is common to say "conduct X should be deterred." Instead of saying "the conduct was involuntary" and, therefore, should be exculpated, it is common to say, "the conduct is non-deterrable."

This deterrence speak is common in a variety of contexts in which the end result is to suggest a rule that makes sense under nearly any distributive principle, including that of doing justice. It is used, for example, as the explanation for criminalizing the following: intercourse with young children;[121] tampering with private records;[122] incest;[123] corruption in sporting

116. *Id.* § 3.05 cmt. at 65–66.

117. *Id.* § 3.07 cmt. at 129.

118. *See, e.g.*, *id.* § 223.5 (1980).

119. *See, e.g.*, *id.* § 220.2(3) (1985).

120. *See, e.g.*, *id.* § 251.2(2)(g).

121. *Id.* § 213.1(1)(d) cmt. at 329 ("[T]he central goal of subsection (1)(d) . . . is to deter intercourse with very young children.").

122. *Id.* § 224.4 cmt. at 312 ("In a highly organized society where accuracy of corporate and other records is nearly as important as accuracy of public records, the need for deterring those who would tamper with records for the purpose of deceiving or injuring anyone or to conceal wrongdoing seems reasonably clear.").

123. *Id.* § 230.2 cmt. at 406 ("The incest prohibition regulates erotic desire in two ways that contribute to preservation of the nuclear family. First, the prohibition controls sex rivalries and jealousies within the family unit . . . . Second, by ensuring suitable role models, the incest restriction prepares the individual for assumption of familial responsibility as an adult.").

events;[124] retaliation against participants in official proceedings;[125] witness tampering;[126] bail jumping;[127] obstruction of a public passageway;[128] and public indecency.[129] Deterrence speak also has been used to support greater punishment for armed robbery than for unarmed robbery.[130] These criminalization decisions are hardly startling. One could as easily say in each instance that such conduct ought to be criminalized because "it is harmful and condemnable conduct."[131] In other words, a deterrence explanation for the rule does not necessarily suggest that the writer has relied upon a deterrence cost-benefit analysis and has concluded that the deterrent benefits outweigh the deterrent costs. Rather, such deterrence language simply may reflect what has come to be the common mode of expression in modern criminal law analysis.

Indeed, some deterrence explanations are so frivolous as to strongly suggest that no actual deterrence analysis has been made, for any such analysis would surely suggest a different or at least a more nuanced conclusion. For example, as noted above, some writers offer a deterrence explanation for providing excuse defenses, such as insanity,[132] immatu-

124. *Id.* § 224.9 cmt. at 338 ("It seems clear that this type of activity should be deterred in order to prevent wholesale fraud in both legal and illegal betting and to maintain the integrity of the amateur and professional sport.").

125. *Id.* § 240.4 cmt. at 68 ("At the time the Model Code was drafted, there were some criminal statutes covering retaliation against jurors, court officials, and witnesses. The considerations that call for deterring retaliation against these persons would seem equally applicable to participants in other official proceedings and to public servants generally.") (footnote omitted).

126. *Id.* § 241.6 cmt. at 163 ("[T]he basic purpose . . . of the crime is to deter conduct that affects the integrity of the criminal justice system.").

127. *Id.* § 242.8 cmt. at 283 ("The purpose of Section 242.8 is to deter those who would obstruct justice by failure to appear for trial or service of sentence.").

128. *Id.* § 250.7 cmt. at 399–400 ("The purpose of this section is twofold: to prevent the danger and inconvenience that may result from unjustified obstruction of public passage; and, at the same time, to withdraw the threat of penal sanctions from lawful assembly.").

129. *Id.* § 251 intro. note at 447 ("The common goal of these provisions is to protect against the open flouting of community standards regarding sexual or related matters.").

130. LAFAVE & SCOTT, *supra* note 11, at § 8.11, at 456, n.108 ("[T]he greater punishment is awarded for armed robbery so as to deter the dangerous person who is actually capable of inflicting death or serious bodily harm.").

131. One could even say, in some cases, that the conduct suggests a dangerousness in the actor, thus calling for incapacitation.

132. *See* LAFAVE & SCOTT, *supra* note 11, § 4.1, at 431 (arguing that punishing offenders will discourage them from committing crimes in the future but such punishment "'can be effective only with men who can understand the signals directed at them by the [criminal] code, who can respond to warnings, and who can feel the significance of the sanctions imposed on violators.' Punishment, therefore, is not at all likely to deter the insane individual from future antisocial conduct.") (quoting ABRAHAM S. GOLDSTEIN, THE INSANITY DEFENSE 12–13 (1967)); *see also* MODEL PENAL CODE § 4.01, app. B, at 198–200 (1985) (detailing the correspondence between Dr. M. S. Guttmacher and H. Wechsler debating how to determine insanity in order to "define the nondeterrables" for purposes of drafting exculpatory provisions of Model Penal Code). A similar argument is made in support of a rule barring the death penalty for insane offenders. *See* LAFAVE & SCOTT, *supra* note 11, § 4.4, at 481 ("[T]he insane prisoner may be spared the death penalty without weakening the deterrent effect of that penalty. Taking

rity,[133] or duress.[134] They reason that a general deterrent purpose:

> . . . would not be served by conviction and punishment of the insane, for 'the examples are likely to deter only if the person who is *not* involved in the criminal process regards the lessons as applicable to him,' which he is likely to do 'only if he identifies with the offender and with the offending situation.' It is unlikely that the sane person . . . will identify with the insane defendant, and thus the insane cannot be effectively used as a deterrent example to others.[135]

One may speculate that the conclusion in favor of recognizing an insanity defense came first to the writer, and that the above analysis is simply a best effort at giving the obligatory deterrence argument to justify the desired conclusion. In fact, a true deterrence analysis would suggest the opposite conclusion, or at least would reveal conflicting deterrent interests. While the insane defendant at hand might not be deterrable and will be seen by third parties as different from themselves, there is every reason to think that if general deterrence works at all, it would be advanced by sanctioning the insane offender. Indeed, the insane offender provides a unique opportunity for the law to make clear just how serious it is about punishing a violation. "If the law sanctions even an insane offender," it might be understood as saying, "make no mistake that it will sanction you if you commit this offense." Indeed, punishing the insane offender may be the only means by which the law can dissuade those potential offenders who assume that, if caught, they can escape the threatened sanction by falsely claiming insanity as an excuse. Further, there is a deterrence argument for imposing greater liability in all cases of excuse in which either internal or external forces press an actor toward a violation. In arguing against a duress defense, for example, Stephen notes that "it is at the moment when temptation to crime is strongest that the law should speak most clearly and emphatically to the contrary."[136]

Thus, general deterrence arguments seem clearly to favor denying recogni-

---

the life of an insane person does not serve as an example to others, for a potential offender would not consider the possibility of escaping the death penalty by becoming insane after the conviction.").

133. *See* LAFAVE & SCOTT, *supra* note 11, § 4.11, at 567 ("'The early common law infancy defense was based upon an unwillingness to punish those thought to be incapable of forming criminal intent and not of an age where the threat of punishment could serve as a deterrent.'" (quoting COKE, *supra* note 56, at 4)).

134. *See id.* § 5.3, at 615 ("It has been suggested that [the duress defense] ought to apply, without regard to a balancing of harms done and avoided, where the unlawfully threatened harm is such that the threat of criminal punishment for doing the harmful conduct does not serve to deter the defendant. . . ."); WILLIAMS, *supra* note 11, § 246, at 756 ("Whether or not it was socially better that the *litera legis* should be violated, there are limits to the efficacy of the threat of punishment in controlling conduct. If the accused was in thrall to some power that could do him more harm than the legal sanction, the legal sanction must be ineffective and therefore should be removed.").

135. *See* LAFAVE & SCOTT, *supra* note 11, § 4.1, at 431–32 (quoting ABRAHAM S. GOLDSTEIN, THE INSANITY DEFENSE 13 (1967)).

136. *See* STEPHEN, *supra* note 63, at 107.

tion of excuse defenses. In opposition, the obvious reason to recognize excuse defenses—and likely the real reason driving even deterrence speak writers to such recognition—is that criminal law would be seen as grossly unjust if it denied excuses. The utilitarian must be concerned about this because it would tend to undermine the law's moral credibility with the community, which in turn would entail serious negative consequences.[137] But, if the analytic traditions of the day do not allow such justice-based objections to a doctrine, then some may feel compelled to fabricate whatever deterrence arguments are available to reach the desired result.

One may speculate about the reasons for such continuing reliance upon deterrence speak when it seems so awkward. Kahan argues the following:

> Deterrence theory helps to cool . . . expressive disputes. Its disembodied idiom of costs and benefits elides the points of moral contention that motivate public positions on . . . disputed issues. Citizens of diverse commitments converge on the deterrence idiom to satisfy social norms against contentious public moralizing. . . . Ultimately, the deterrence idiom takes the political charge out of contentious issues and deflects expressive contention away from the criminal law.[138]

Whatever the reasons for its use, the practice highlights just how pervasive is the deterrence orientation of modern criminal law. Deterrence has become not only the standard analytic form, but also the standard expressive form, determining how we are to think and talk about problems of criminal law theory. And this suggests a larger danger: If, as we argue here, doctrinal formulation can have limited deterrent effect, then the current deterrence speak may mislead users into questionable results in a wide range of doctrines.

2. Deterrence Rationales That Do Real Work: Deviations from Justice

As demonstrated above, the law often engages in "deterrence speak" by providing a fabricated deterrence justification for a legal formulation that is, in truth, based on other considerations. In contrast, some legal formulations are truly grounded upon deterrence analysis and are designed to produce punishment results with maximum deterrent effect. However, as illustrated by some of the examples discussed earlier in this Part, deterrence often comes at the expense of justice. It is worth revisiting these examples, because it is precisely these situations in which deterrence analysis is of greatest concern. Recall that the social science literature summarized in Part I suggests that it is rarely possible to optimize deterrence successfully through doctrinal manipulation. As a result, where deterrence-based formulations conflict with justice, deterrence

137. For a discussion of the tension between a deterrence-based system and contemporary notions of justice, see *infra* Part III.c.

138. Dan M. Kahan, *The Secret Ambition of Deterrence*, 113 HARV. L. REV. 413, 416–17 (1999).

analysis produces real injustice for little or no benefit. In contrast, where deterrence analysis nevertheless reliably does justice, little is lost.

Consider again these instances of deterrence-based doctrines that conflict with justice. The felony-murder rule applied in the *McCarty* case, authorized—and a deterrence-focused sentencing judge imposed—a forty-year sentence for fleeing from police.[139] In *Dudley & Stephens*, the need to keep clear the deterrent threat against killing and cannibalism demanded the death penalty, even though the court essentially conceded that it was imposing a standard of conduct that it might not have been able itself to meet.[140] In *Park*, the president of Acme Markets, Inc., a national retail food chain with approximately 36,000 employees, 874 retail outlets, twelve general warehouses, and four special warehouses, was held criminally liable for a health violation in one of the company warehouses, even though Park was not negligent as to the violation.[141] In *Rummel*, the defendant was given a life sentence for a $129.75 air conditioner repair fraud because of his prior felony convictions of a similar nature.[142] In *Williams*, loving parents of limited intelligence and education were convicted of criminally negligent homicide when their failure to get medical care for their baby led to his death, despite their likely inability to meet the purely objective standard of care the court insisted upon.[143] In each case, the lawmakers and courts used deterrence explanations to help justify both the liability rules and the exercise of discretion that produced case dispositions in conflict with justice.

How do these five cases fare in light of the deterrence-skeptical conclusions summarized in Part I? One or more of the deterrence prerequisite hurdles is likely to prevent a deterrent effect for many, if not most of these deterrence optimizing cases. For example, McCarty, who was convicted of felony-murder and received a forty-year sentence for fleeing from police, probably knew nothing of the felony-murder rule or its application to him when he chose to flee. Nor will others like him be likely to apply the intended lesson in their drug-addled brains when the next police car appears. For Dudley, and others like him, for whom a painful death looms, little, if anything, will deter; and the price paid in *Dudley & Stephens* to reinforce the prohibition on killing hardly seems worth the cost in injustice, especially given how well-known the no-killing rule already is. In contrast, people like Rummel might not commit air conditioning and similar types of fraud if they knew it would result in life imprisonment, but few are likely to perceive a meaningful chance of suffering such a sentence for this sort of fraud. They would be right: they have a greater chance of being struck by lightning. Most of such potential offenders probably do not even know that a life imprisonment rule is applicable to them. (Do you know the terms of your state's habitual offender statute, or even if it has one?)

139. *See supra* text accompanying notes 91–94.
140. *See supra* text accompanying notes 36–40.
141. *See supra* text accompanying notes 33–34.
142. *See supra* text accompanying notes 71–72.
143. *See supra* text accompanying notes 41–43.

Similarly Park, as the executive of a large and respectable corporation, would undoubtedly be appalled at the thought of a criminal conviction, but he also is not likely to know about the rodent droppings in Baltimore. Even assuming that he knew of the droppings and that counsel kept him well informed on relevant statutes, someone in Park's situation would likely see criminal liability in the absence of even negligence as so remote on the facts as to be irrelevant. (If executives did think the chance of such strict criminal liability was meaningful, we would have few volunteers for Park's vacant position.) The Williamses, and other parents like them, will know little of the criminal law's liability rules or the nuances of the alternative negligence standards and in any case, will have no reason to think such rules are applicable to them because their baby only has a toothache.[144] Yet these dubious contributions to the law's deterrent threat are purchased at some considerable expense, in both the injustices they do and the reputational damage they cause to a criminal justice system that is seen as indifferent to doing justice.

III. THE CASE AGAINST USING DETERRENCE AS A DISTRIBUTIVE PRINCIPLE

There are a number of reasons why one might decide against constructing a justice system based entirely on the logic of deterrence. The most obvious reason not to use deterrence to formulate criminal law rules comes from our prior conclusion that such doctrinal manipulation to optimize deterrence will rarely achieve its desired effect. While deterrence may be a good reason for having a criminal justice system that punishes violators, it is at best ineffective as a guide for distributing liability and punishment within that system. In Hart's terminology,[145] deterrence is a sound justificatory purpose but a poor distributive principle.

We concede that some doctrinal manipulation can have a deterrent effect. A recent event in Afghanistan makes this point starkly. The new leaders in Aliabad introduced a practice that worked to reduce what they regarded as lawlessness: The bullet-ridden bodies of robbers were hung from a tank barrel outside the village for two days.[146] This practice is likely to have a deterrent effect. Less draconian practices can work too. In specific situations, publicly-known rules can deter, if those rules (1) target actors who are dispositionally rational in circumstances that allow for rationality; (2) provide for a high rate of violation detection; and (3) provide a reasonable certainty of punishment following the detected violation. But even in such optimal situations, problems remain with formulating criminal law rules based upon deterrence analysis.

144. *See id.*

145. *See* H. L. A. HART, PUNISHMENT AND RESPONSIBILITY 1–28 (1968).

146. C.J. Chivers, *New Leaders Send a Signal By Hanging Bandit's Body*, N.Y. TIMES, Dec. 3, 2001, at B4.

A. THE DIFFICULTIES OF DETERRENCE: THE INFORMATION AND COMPLEXITY PROBLEM

We have argued that, contrary to the expectations of scholars and lawmakers, the ability of doctrinal manipulation to produce an alteration of deterrent effect is highly limited, both in the instances in which it is at all plausible and in the extent of influence on deterrent effect that is possible. From this we conclude that scholars and lawmakers are rarely warranted in using deterrence arguments to justify doctrinal rules. Even where the prerequisites for deterrence exist, we think the use of deterrence analysis in the formulation of criminal law is dangerous. In this section, we argue that, when examined at the level of detail necessary to build a deterrence-based liability system, the causal connection between doctrine and effect is so complex and based upon so many factors about which we know little, that reliance upon deterrence arguments can easily lead to doctrinal formulations that reduce rather than increase deterrence. Without better information and without a better grasp of the complexities of the doctrine-effect dynamic, we cannot know which result will be produced.

Consider the wide range of factors that are relevant to a deterrence calculation. We would need to know, for example, what the potential offender perceives about the following: the chance of getting caught, convicted, and punished; the amount of punishment associated with each of the possible conviction outcomes; the degree of painfulness associated with each possible punishment outcome (for example, how painful the potential offender considers, say, a $10,000 fine, two weeks in jail, a three year prison sentence, or solitary confinement for life?); the likely delay in any anticipated punishment; and the anticipated benefit of the contemplated offense.

Further, we need a sense of the equation that assigns the appropriate weights for each of these factors. For example, we noted previously that if the probability of punishment were high—that is, if a potential offender is highly likely to get caught for drunken driving or running a red light—even moderate punishments seem sufficient to deter the conduct. As the likelihood of punishment declines the deterrent effect soon becomes greatly reduced or even negligible.[147] This suggests that the probability of punishment should be more heavily weighted in the deterrence equation than should the intensity of the punishment.[148] A deterrence calculation would need to sort out just how much more weight should be given to probability of punishment than to the other factors in the equation.

Consider as well the difficulty of translating the parameters of the prison sentence that can be controlled by the authorities into the degree of deterrent effect produced by the contemplation of the pain of serving that sentence at some time in the future. Two translations are needed. The first is what is called the "psychophysical" translation. In general, a doubling of the intensity of a stimulus in terms of the physical system units in which that intensity is

147. *See supra* text accompanying notes 5–6.
148. For an illustration of this principle, see *supra* text accompanying note 146.

measured is not generally experienced by the person perceiving that stimulus change as a doubling of its intensity.[149] But annoyingly for predictive purposes, depending on the exact physical stimulus in question, it is sometimes perceived as more than a doubling in psychological intensity, and sometimes as less, and it also depends on the initial intensity of the stimulus from which the physical doubling takes place.

The calculations for this psychophysical translation are quite daunting to contemplate making, but it is probably the case that the need for the second translation introduces even more complexity. What the person who is contemplating a crime must do to make the calculation of whether a prison sentence is of enough magnitude to deter him from the contemplated crime, is not to estimate the level of discomfort, pain or dread that the sentence causes him to feel *now*, but to estimate the negative magnitude he *would* feel, if he experienced that sentence some time in the future. Without going into great detail about the rapidly growing psychological literature on this topic, it seems fair to say that people are often confident in their ability to forecast how they will feel if a major positive or negative life event happens to them in the future. If the major event does happen, it turns out that their predictions about their post-event feelings are quite poor. People are poor "affective forecasters."[150]

Still further, one cannot underestimate the ability of erroneous data concerning one factor to distort the calculation. Deterrence calculations are not intuitive: Their results will depend upon the numbers, not a general principle that itself may make good sense. For example, one aspect of deterrence analysis would want to impose a greater punishment on a more serious offense, if for no other reason than to deter a person who has committed the lesser offense from proceeding to commit the greater one. Thus, murder receives a more severe punishment than does assault or burglary to keep the burglar who is discovered by the home owner from killing the home owner to avoid being identified.

However, imagine a situation where the punishment rate was high for the more serious offense and low for a less serious offense. In fact, the punishment

149. The relationship between the measured intensity of a stimulus and the psychological intensity of the stimulus perceived by the observer is described by the following function: $S = kI^b$, where S is the perceived intensity, I is the intensity of the stimulus in physical units, the exponent b varies depending on the physical properties of the stimulus, and k is simply a constant depending on the units of measurement being used. Light has a $b = 0.33$, which means that, as a very dim light doubles in brightness, it more than doubles in perceived brightness, but after it reaches a brightness of a certain intensity, a doubling in the physical brightness is perceived as much less than a doubling of perceived brightness. On the other hand, if the stimulus is an electric shock, b = about 3.5. This means that at low intensities of electric shock, as the shock doubles in intensity it does not feel twice as painful. However, at moderate levels of shock, a doubling of physical intensity is more than twice as painful. *See* JOHN DARLEY, SAM GLUCKSBERG & RONALD KINCHLA, INTRODUCTORY PSYCHOLOGY 73–74 (1991) for a more complete discussion of these findings.

150. *See generally* Daniel Gilbert & Jane Ebert, *Decisions and Revisions: The Affective Forecasting of Changeable Outcomes*, 82 J. PERSONALITY & SOC. PSYCHOL. 503 (2002).

rate for murder is approximately thirty times greater than for burglary.[151] One wants the total punishment cost to be high enough to deter the potential offense and, as we have already established, the probability of punishment is an important determinant of the total punishment cost. This creates the necessity, within a deterrence analysis, to increase the punishment on a low capture-rate offense.[152] Therefore, depending on exactly how the punishment weight calculations come out, a deterrence optimizing theorist might conclude that one should have a greater penalty for the less serious offense! The point is not a hypothetical one. Recall, for example, the drug laws passed in various states in the belief that drug possession and use was highly dangerous to society and highly contagious. Legislators, driven by the logic of deterrence, set prison terms for possession of relatively small amounts of cocaine—and in some states for possession of marijuana—considerably higher than those for various crimes of violence.[153]

Even if one had good information on the basic conditions that may influence deterrent effect, the calculations are all the more complex because of the potential feedback effects that one's proposed rule might itself trigger. That is, one rule might make sense given the conditions that presently exist, but the introduction of that rule might quickly change the conditions. For example, Neal Katyal points out that substitution effects are important to consider because an increased penalty for a lesser offense may encourage the commission of a greater one.[154] One might be inclined to increase the threatened punishment in order to deter an offense of moderate harm, but before doing so one must consider whether the potential offender will substitute an offense of more serious harm. There are drug addicts who steal to obtain money for their addictive habits. If we increase the punishment for thefts from empty buildings, will we cause addicts to turn to assaulting citizens to gain the money to support their habits? A deterrence perspective generates these types of complex and dynamic considerations.

Consider another example. Oren Bar-Gill and Alon Harel suggest that while we normally think of the crime rate as a product of the factors that affect deterrence, such as the probability and amount of the expected sanction, in fact the reverse can also be true: The crime rate can be a determinant of probability

151. *See* Robinson & Darley, *Does Criminal Law Deter?*, app. at Table 1, col.(d), *available at* http://www.law.upenn.edu/fac/phrobins/OxfordDeterrenceAppendix.pdf (unpublished appendix to Robinson & Darley, *supra* note 3).

152. In contrast, the fact that a high punishment-rate offense, is rarely committed, signals that deterrence is being achieved with the existing punishment. Therefore, there is not only no need to increase the punishment amount, but also a possibility of decreasing it because it may be inefficiently high.

153. A number of these intuition-defying comparisons are cited in Paul H. Robinson, *Dissent from the United States Sentencing Commission's Proposed Guidelines*, 77 J. CRIM. L. & CRIMINOLOGY 1112 (1986).

154. *See generally* Neal Kumar Katyal, *Deterrence's Difficulty*, 95 MICH. L. REV. 2385 (1997).

and amount of the expected sanction.[155] For example, a higher crime rate makes fewer resources available per crime and reduces the probability of detection; a lower crime rate may have a reverse effect. An increased rate of crime also might delay the imposition of punishments—due to congested courts, for example. Such delays cause the future punishment discount to be incrementally higher, reducing the perceived punishment cost. A decrease in crime rate might have the reverse effect.[156]

Thus, one might set rules based on present conditions but then, as soon as one's rules began to take effect, they might cause those conditions to change. In other words, not only does reliable deterrence analysis require information that is not now available and an understanding of the interrelation among the relevant factors that we do not now have, but it also requires a constant updating of the analysis because the relevant factors themselves are constantly in motion. These are not circumstances under which it makes much sense to set criminal law doctrine according to attempts at deterrence analysis.

B. A COMPARISON OF DETERRENT EFFECTS

We assume that most people would see value in having a criminal justice system that, broadly speaking, does justice either for instrumentalist or retributivist reasons.[157] Advocates for a deterrence-based distribution argue not that doing justice has no value but that crime reduction through precisely adjusted deterrent punishments has a greater value. But deterrent system advocates certainly would concede that a deterrence-based distribution of punishment is not the only distribution that will have a deterrent effect. Indeed, any one of a number of different kinds of distributive principles for assigning punishment will provide some deterrent effect. Thus, a deterrence-based distributive principle cannot be justified simply by showing that it generates a deterrent effect. To prefer a deterrence-based distribution to the just-deserts-based system that we advocate, it must be shown that the deterrence-based distribution provides greater deterrence than the justice-based distribution.

This last point is not often recognized for a number of reasons. People tend to believe that the threat of punishment is all that deters those who are "criminally

155. Bar-Gill and Harel wrote:

> The expected sanction is determined by the size of the sanction and by the probability of apprehension and conviction (hereafter "the probability of punishment"). Both components of the expected sanction are influenced by the rate of crime. A higher crime rate may either increase or decrease the probability of punishment, depending on the law enforcement technology and the internal organization or modus operandi of the criminal community. Similarly, a higher crime rate may either increase or decrease the magnitude of the sanction, through its influence on the social sanction, which is a component of the overall sanction.

Oren Bar-Gill & Alon Harel, *Crime Rates and Expected Sanctions: The Economics of Deterrence Revisited*, 30 J. LEGAL STUD. 485, 485–86 (2001).

156. *See id.*

157. *See generally* PAUL H. ROBINSON & MICHAEL T. CAHILL, LAW WITHOUT JUSTICE: HOW AND WHY CRIMINAL LAW DELIBERATELY SACRIFICES JUSTICE (forthcoming 2004).

inclined."[158] If one believes that crime reduction is achieved only by the potential criminal's awareness of the punishments that would follow the commission of the crime, then there can be no alternative to a justice system that relies on making precise adjustments in criminal punishments to achieve deterrent effects. But if one takes a broader view of the forces that keep individuals from committing crimes another conclusion becomes possible: Evidence suggests that there is considerable crime-reducing potential in a distribution of punishment that tracks the principles of justice shared by the community—what we have called a "justice based" system for the distribution of punishment. This crime-reducing potential is achieved in at least two complex ways: the first involves application of social pressures to those who might commit crime; the second involves fostering internal norms—moral prohibitions—against committing crime among those who might otherwise do so.

Evidence suggests that both social influence[159] and internalized norms[160] are powerful forces governing individual conduct,[161] even more powerful than the threat of official conviction and punishment by the criminal justice system.[162] One might argue that the social influence forces are also triggered by criminal conviction, thus adding to the deterrent effect of official sanction, but the available studies suggest that the effect of social influence and internalized norms are independent, without significant interactive effect.[163] The social influence forces generated by the mobilization of community stigmatization against the criminally convicted can be quite powerful, and can include the loss of any prospects of being hired into decent jobs or having friends or marriage

158. *See* Catherine A. Sanderson & John M. Darley, *I Am Moral But You are Deterred: Differential Attributions About Why People Obey the Law*, 32 J. APPLIED SOC. PSYCHOL. 375, 375–88 (2002).

159. *See* Paul H. Robinson & John M. Darley, *The Utility of Desert*, 91 NW. U. L. REV. 453, 469 (1997) ("The normative pressures from other people, generally experienced as an external force by the actor, function like the more formal deterrence mechanisms were thought to function. People obey the social norms of their groups because those groups have rewards to give for doing so and sanctions for failing to do so.").

160. *See generally* Marc G. Gertz & Leroy C. Gould, *Fear of Punishment and the Willingness to Engage in Criminal Behavior: A Research Note*, 23 J. CRIM. JUST. 377 (1995) (finding that study participants' tendency toward criminal behavior was dependent on their prior actions and internal notions of whether the action was wrong).

161. *See* Kahan, *supra* note 62 at 127–30 (arguing in support of the "ignorance is no excuse" maxim with the understanding that the laws reflect social morals not held by all members of society, but which are required for the effect they will have on the conduct of potential offenders); *see generally* Dan M. Kahan, *Social Influence, Social Meaning, and Deterrence*, 83 VA. L. REV. 349 (1997) (describing the effects of social influences on individual behavior, and arguing that laws that suppress public criminality have a preventative effect by suppressing such social and peer influences).

162. *See* TOM R. TYLER, WHY PEOPLE OBEY THE LAW 64 (1990) ("The most important normative influence on compliance with the law is the person's assessment that following the law accords with his or her sense of right and wrong; a second factor is the person's feeling of obligation to obey the law and allegiance to legal authorities."); Scott Decker et al., *Perceptual Deterrence Among Active Residential Burglars: A Research Note*, 31 CRIMINOLOGY 135, 145 (1993) ("Penalty only had an influence on offender decision making in combination with anticipated gain or perceived risk.").

163. *See* Daniel S. Nagin & Raymond Paternoster, *Enduring Individual Differences and Rational Choice Theories of Crime*, 27 LAW & SOC'Y REV. 467 *passim* (1993).

partners from among the respectable segments of the community.[164] However, these informal sanctions will occur only if the criminal law has moral authority with the community. If it has moral authority, the threat of stigmatization provides a highly cost-efficient means of crime reduction because it requires no government expenditures, as compared to the $20,000 cost of imprisonment per inmate per year.[165]

The effect of informal sanctions goes further. A criminal law with moral authority can produce stigmatization of the offender by those in the community who become aware of his offense even without arrest and criminal conviction by the legal authorities. If the criminal law has such moral credibility that it has the force of social norms, then a violation of the criminal law may trigger moral condemnation by those who know of the offender's violation, even if the law enforcement authorities do not, thus greatly increasing the criminal law's reach in preventing crime.[166]

Finally, a number of studies suggest that a legal code that is perceived as having moral credibility can provide a clear set of guidelines around which childhood and adolescent socialization can coalesce.[167] Those so socialized obey the law not because they fear the penalties for not doing so, but because they regard the laws as specifying the right conduct, and thus there is a moral imperative to "do as the law says you should do." People report that this, rather than the threat of arrest, is generally why they obey the laws that they consider to have moral credibility.[168]

In summary, before a deterrence-based distribution is to be preferred, it must

164. *See* Harold G. Grasmick & Robert J. Bursik, Jr., *Conscience, Significant Others, and Rational Choice: Extending the Deterrence Model*, 24 LAW & SOC'Y REV. 837, 837 (1990) ("We propose that significant others and conscience function as agents of social control in a manner similar to the state."); Daniel S. Nagin, *Deterrence and Incapacitation*, *in* THE HANDBOOK OF CRIME & PUNISHMENT 345, 351–53 (Michael Tonry ed., 1998); Kirk R. Williams & Richard Hawkins, *Perceptual Research on General Deterrence: A Critical Review*, 20 LAW & SOC'Y REV. 545, 564–66 (1986) (discussing the "attachment costs" of an arrest: "negative consequences for relationships with close friends and relatives").

165. JAMES J. STEPHAN, U.S. DEP'T OF JUSTICE, STATE PRISON EXPENDITURES, 1996, iv (1999).

166. *See* ROBINSON & DARLEY, *supra* note 2, at 201–03 ("recent empirical evidence suggests that the law's most powerful mechanism for gaining compliance lies not with the negative force of the deterrent threat but rather with the positive force of the law as an arbiter of proper conduct. Most people obey the law not because they fear punishment but because they see themselves as persons who want to do the right thing."); Paul H. Robinson, *Why Does the Criminal Law Care What the Lay Person Thinks Is Just? Coercive Versus Normative Crime Control*, 86 VA. L. REV. 1839, 1840 (2000) ("The crime control power of criminal law's moral credibility works in a different way [than the coercive effect of a deterrent threat]. . . .[I]t works through unofficial avenues to bring the potential offender to see the prohibited conduct as unattractive because it is inconsistent with the norms of family or friends and, even better, with the person's own internalized sense of what is acceptable."); Robinson & Darley, *supra* note 159, at 456 ("[A] distributive theory that tracks the community's perceived principles of justice has a greater power to gain compliance with society's rules of lawful conduct."); *see also id.* at 457, 468–71 (discussing the powerful effect of moral and social forces on deterring crime).

167. *See* LAW, JUSTICE, AND THE INDIVIDUAL IN SOCIETY: PSYCHOLOGICAL AND LEGAL ISSUES 29–84 (June Tapp & Felice J. Levine eds., 1977).

168. *See* Sanderson & Darley, *supra* note 158; *supra* note 166.

be shown that its deterrent effect exceeds that of a just deserts distribution, which may be difficult to do. Evidence suggests that the gains of the just deserts system may be quite substantial, although they tend to be hidden if one takes the perspective that crime control is achieved only through the direct deterrence of the threat of criminal punishment.

C. WHERE DETERRENCE DEVIATES FROM JUSTICE, IT CONFRONTS SPECIAL DIFFICULTIES

As we have argued, a deterrence-based system for punishment can do better than a just-deserts-based system only when its rules deviate from the justice-based system. But for a number of reasons, it is just these instances of deviation in which it is most difficult to get a deterrent effect. First, citizens are quite unlikely to know the content of the law at exactly the point that the law deviates from their own notions of justice. People instead assume the law is as they think it should be, according to their own collective notions of justice. Several studies have demonstrated this. For example, a survey of New Jersey citizens found that they perceived that the morally appropriate penalty for attempts at crimes was an increasing prison sentence the nearer the perpetrator came to committing the crime. But even an attempt that came in "dangerous proximity" to the completed crime was penalized less than the completed crime. The respondents also reported that the New Jersey state laws essentially matched their moral intuitions. But they were wrong. As a state that follows the Model Penal Code, New Jersey penalizes any attempt at a crime that goes past a substantial step toward its completion as heavily as it penalizes the completion of the crime.[169]

Another study tested the knowledge of criminal law rules that are applicable to the general population: for example, rules governing whether it is a crime to fail to turn in lost property, or whether it is lawful to use deadly force if necessary to protect property. Subjects were drawn from five states, each with fairly similar criminal codes. Each state followed the most common American formulation—the "majority" rule—with respect to most offenses, but each state also followed a divergent "minority" approach on one or more offenses. The testing revealed that citizens in all of the states had generally the same view of the existing legal rule, thus, were generally ignorant of their state's position on the law—though they did not always think the rule was that held by the majority. Again, their perceptions of what the laws held were better predicted by their attitudes about what the laws should be than by the actual content of the laws.[170]

As the above studies make painfully clear, just making the justice-deviation rule known to those whose behavior it is designed to control becomes a special task for those who seek to manipulate behavior by deterrence-driven changes in

169. John M. Darley et al., *Community Standards for Defining Attempt: Inconsistencies with the Model Penal Code*, 39 AM. BEHAV. SCIENTIST 405, 414 (1996).

170. John M. Darley et al., *The Ex Ante Function of the Criminal Law*, 35 LAW & SOC'Y REV. 165, 168–79 (2001).

the laws. People assume the law is as they think it should be, according to their perceptions of shared intuitions of justice. Thus, it is in the deviation cases that criminal law has its greatest difficulty conveying its rule because it is in those cases that the legal system must affirmatively change the community's initial contrary assumption about what the law provides. We see no evidence of attempts to bring changes in the law into the community's collective consciousness; a scan of the newspapers in the capitals of the studied states showed no particular publicity about the deviant laws the legislatures were enacting.[171]

Furthermore, rules that deviate from shared notions of justice are less likely to be followed during criminal justice adjudications because those who take the various discretionary roles within the criminal justice system are likely to have the same moral intuitions as the other members of the community and are likely to allow those intuitions to influence their decisions. The exercise of police, prosecutorial, and judicial discretion, as well as jury nullification, will commonly be subversive of deviation rules, thereby confounding the deterrent program and certainly confusing the deterrent message. A jury may refuse to convict a person, even if the legal rules seem to call for it, if the jurors believe it would be unjust to do so.[172] Prosecutors may similarly exercise discretion in subversion of rules that produce what they see as unjust results. Judges, by exercising sentencing discretion or approving lenient plea bargains, also may subvert the deterrence-based stance of the system, moving it in the direction of justice considerations. So if it is these adjudication decisions that the deterrence theorist is counting on to perform the needed re-education task, the hope seems a vain one. Decisionmakers are often likely to follow their own intuitions of justice and ignore the law's contrary rule, or at least look for ways to minimize the rule's effect. And this kind of distortion in application means that case dispositions often obfuscate, rather than clarify, the legal rule sought to be conveyed.

Given that we think that the justice system should be explicitly formed around justice considerations, it might be thought that we should applaud all of these processes that move the system in that direction. However, the problem is that this sort of subversion of deterrence-based rules is likely to be uneven. We earlier cited the *McCarty* case in which a judge acted specifically to deter others from criminal involvement, giving a strikingly high sentence under a broad felony murder rule for the accidental death of an officer resulting from McCarty's flight.[173] But certainly there are cases in which other judges have treated similarly-situated defendants more leniently based on justice intuitions.

To generalize, juries, prosecutors, and judges may deal more leniently with

171. *Id.* at 185.

172. *See* Irwin A. Horowitz, *The Effect of Jury Nullification Instructions on Verdicts and Jury Functioning in Criminal Trials*, 9 LAW & HUM. BEHAV. 25 *passim* (1985).

173. *See supra* text accompanying notes 91–94.

offenders who are physically attractive,[174] racially matched to the jurors,[175] more capable of mustering legal resources to defend themselves, or who are otherwise advantaged in public opinion. And, on the other side of the coin, it is also possible for the justice system to accuse and convict those who are regarded as deviants within the community based on "crimes" for which others would not be prosecuted. So one problem with "under the table" intrusions of justice into a deterrence-based legal system is the unevenness with which they may occur, an unevenness that is likely to be discriminatory, rather than random.

A further problem with this intrusion is that its workings often need to be disguised. If the judge is applying justice considerations in cases in which the deterrence-based legal rules dictate another outcome, then case dispositions, and the texts that promulgate them, are likely to be exercises in obfuscation rather than clarity. This, too, is likely to generate contempt for legal rulings.

D. CREATING CRIMINALS: THE PROBLEM OF OFFSETTING CRIMOGENIC EFFECT

Finally, certain consequences of a solely deterrence-based system for defining crimes and assigning punishments can lead to increases in criminal activity because citizens realize, with some shock and dismay, that the legal code does not embody their own sense of justice. Assume that a deterrence-based distribution has managed to clear the hurdle of showing a deterrent effect greater than that inherent in a justice-based distribution. Its next problem is that it also is likely to generate certain quite substantial costs associated with its deviation from community standards of justice. Of particular concern here is the injury that a deterrence-based distribution will cause to the criminal law's potential for influencing conduct through social pressures, internalized norms, and stigmatization.

Recent research suggests that when citizens assign penalties that they think are appropriate for a particular crime, they do so from a justice rather than a deterrence perspective.[176] As this suggests, a deterrence-based system will generate conflict with the community's shared intuitions of justice. Laypersons do not distribute punishment according to the criterion of optimizing deterrence but rather according to their shared notions of justice.[177] And often the factors that maximize deterrence will conflict with the community sense of justice.[178] Part II gives many illustrations of the point. We highlighted several: McCarty's

---

174. *See* John Clark, *The Social Psychology of Jury Nullification*, 24 LAW & PSYCHOL. REV. 39, 48 (2000) ("[T]he way a defendant is physically perceived has a direct bearing on one's degree of responsibility.").

175. Erick L. Hill & Jeffrey E. Pfeifer, *Nullification Instructions and Juror Guilt Ratings: An Examination of Modern Racism*, 16 CONTEMP. SOC. PSYCHOL. 6 *passim* (1992).

176. *See* Kevin Carlsmith, John Darley & Paul H. Robinson, *Why Do We Punish? Deterrence and Just Deserts as Motives for Punishment*, 83 J. PERSONALITY & SOC. PSYCHOL. 1 *passim* (2002).

177. *See id.*

178. As Robinson notes:

felony-murder liability and forty-year sentence for fleeing from police; Dudley's murder liability for killing the sick cabin boy to stay alive; Park's criminal liability for the rodent droppings in Baltimore of which he had no culpability; the Williamses manslaughter liability for failing to recognize that their child needed medical care; and Rummel's life imprisonment for committing a $129 air conditioning fraud under a "three strikes" statute.[179]

Deterrence's conflict with the community's shared intuitions of justice will generate costs that are not immediately apparent if one takes only a deterrence perspective on the forces producing law-abiding behavior. This conflict may result first in the community's sense that specific laws are unjust, which in turn may spread to a generalized contempt for the criminal justice system. Legal codes then no longer serve as a guide to just and moral behavior; they no longer become the core of a set of normative rules that citizens use to regulate their behavior. Further, each citizen will realize that the community no longer regards the criminal law as providing this guidance. This means that the citizen does not think that he or she will lose standing in or be condemned by the community if he or she transgresses some legal rule generated from a deterrence-based rather than a justice-based perspective. If the community comes to view the law as being irrelevant to justice—or worse, as violating justice—then a lawbreaker will not be stigmatized by the community. He or she may even be regarded as a Robin Hood, working to produce what the community considers to be justice, in defiance of the unjust legal system and its enforcers. According to this analysis, distributing punishment in a way that conflicts with shared lay intuitions of justice undercuts the criminal law's moral authority and thereby reduces its crime reduction effect.

Many analyses of the effects of Prohibition in the 1920s suggest that this undercutting process does in fact occur.[180] Recently, two sets of experimental studies demonstrate empirically the beginnings of this process. In both sets of studies, the respondents discover that the legislature has or is in the process of passing laws that the respondents can be predicted to find to be in conflict with their own moral intuitions. In the first set of studies, respondents read what they took to be newspaper stories in which a person was sentenced to a prison term

---

> Deterrence frequently conflicts with desert . . . where some abnormal condition external to the actor, such as duress, coercion, or nonjustified necessity, contributes to the actor's criminal conduct. Because the conditions rather than the actor are judged responsible for the conduct, the actor is held blameless . . . and thus is acquitted or receives a reduced sentence. On the other hand, the same coercive conditions can create the need for a greater rather than lesser deterrent threat. Greater sanctions would provide a needed additional deterrent in the face of unusual pressure to commit the offense.

Paul H. Robinson, *Hybrid Principles for the Distribution of Criminal Sanctions*, 82 NW. U.L. REV. 19, 27 (1987).

179. *See supra* text accompanying notes 33–43, 71–73, 91–94. For a full discussion of how wide-ranging are the criminal law's doctrines of deviation from desert, see ROBINSON & CAHILL, *supra* note 157.

180. *See, e.g.*, SEAN DENNIS CASHMAN, PROHIBITION: THE LIE OF THE LAND (1981).

for behavior that most of the respondents did not consider criminal.[181] For those who did not consider the conduct criminal, their reported willingness to defer to the law in other instances decreased. Specifically, "they were more inclined to oppose incumbent legislators and prosecutors and to take actions aimed at effective legal reforms—including the possibility of violating other laws in the course of trying to get the offending law changed."[182] The first set of studies also reported that respondents were more willing to take actions that violated the law, less likely to call on or cooperate with the police, and more likely to engage in vigilante action against suspected wrongdoers.[183] Particularly germane to our argument, they rated themselves less likely to use the law to guide their behavior in situations in which they themselves were unsure about the right thing to do.[184] In the second set of studies, one group of respondents read about a legislature seriously considering adopting laws that the respondents perceived as unjust.[185] Another group read about a legislature considering laws that the respondents considered just. Those who read about the unjust laws "were more willing, as a general matter, to flout unrelated laws . . . . This willingness to disobey extended far beyond the unjust law in question, resulting in participants expressing plans to flout unrelated laws in their everyday lives."[186] The author concludes that what she calls the "flouting thesis"—the idea that the perceived justice of one law can influence the intention to comply with unrelated laws, is empirically supported.[187]

To summarize, at the level of social and moral influence, the criminal law can harness these forces only by building up its own moral credibility with the community.[188] Its task, in psychological terms, is to convince the community of both the moral validity of the lines it draws between conduct that is acceptable and unacceptable, and the justice of the degree of liability and punishment it imposes for unacceptable conduct. If the criminal law manages to persuade the community on both scores, then in a specific case in which members of the community do not have an independent opinion about the rightness or wrongness of certain conduct,[189] they will follow the legal code's guidance and obey

181. *See* Erich Greene, Effects of Disagreements Between Legal Codes and Lay Intuitions on Respect for the Law, abstract, iv–v (unpublished Ph.D dissertation, Princeton University 2003) (on file with authors).

182. *Id.* at 43.

183. *Id.* at 43–44.

184. *Id.* at 36.

185. Janice Nadler, Flouting the Law: Does Perceived Injustice Provoke General Non-Compliance? (unpublished manuscript, Northwestern University School of Law: Law & Economics Research Paper Series, Research Paper No. 02-9) (Apr. 1, 2002), *available at* http://ssrn.com/abstract_id=353745 (last visited Oct. 25, 2003).

186. *Id.* at 1.

187. *Id.*

188. *See generally* ROBINSON & DARLEY, *supra* note 2, at 5–7, 201–03; Robinson & Darley, *supra* note 159, at 456–57, 468–71.

189. For example, notice that the criminal code drafters attempted this sort of persuasion when they criminalized the complex of actions and knowledge that defines "insider trading."

the law.

Continuing the analogy with credibility and persuasion further provides greater understanding of some of the costs risked by a criminal justice system that deviates from justice. A broadly accepted general finding in the psychology of persuasion is that a communicator who has credibility can achieve greater persuasion than one with less credibility.[190] One way of gaining credibility is by having the recipient of the communication see the source as having similar values to the recipient. Research shows that communications coming from communicators whose values are close to the recipient's are more persuasive than those coming from communicators who are seen as having dissimilar values.[191] The import of this for our purposes is this: If the criminal justice system is seen as making a number of decisions that are based on a deterrence stance, rather than the justice perspective that the community holds, the community will realize that the justice system does not share the community's underlying values of justice. The justice system will, therefore, lose the power to persuade the community to follow its guidance in spheres of behavior in which the community does not have well-formed opinions about what conduct is right and wrong. Much of what we have been arguing can be summed up by saying "reputation matters," and the reputation that matters for the criminal justice system is that it functions to impose just punishment on wrongdoers.

To summarize, if the criminal justice system is driven solely by deterrence considerations, it potentially forfeits the gains achieved when the system is regarded by the community as based on justice considerations. This could amount to a considerable loss, albeit a loss that is extraordinarily difficult or impossible to calculate. And, as we argue, there is a second cost, which is the potential crimogenic effect stemming from citizens' perceptions of injustice arising from the system's contradiction of justice concerns. Even if one assumed for the sake of argument that there would be some greater deterrent effect of a deterrence-based distribution of punishment over a justice-based distribution of punishment, one would still question whether this marginal benefit exceeds the losses that a deterrence-based system would incur.

Combined with the problems of unavailable information and complexity discussed in Part III.A, our conclusion is this: By generating punishment rules driven by deterrence analysis, one could suffer the crimogenic costs of deviating from justice and get nothing for it. Indeed, it might even be the case that a justice distribution would have greater inherent deterrent effect than the deterrence-based rule. In general, if we cannot make reliable deterrence calculations—if we don't know whether we are really increasing deterrence or in fact decreasing it—we suggest that we are better off following a distributive prin-

190. *See* RICHARD E. PETTY & JOHN T. CACIOPPO, ATTITUDES AND PERSUASION: CLASSIC AND CONTEMPORARY APPROACHES 61–62 (1981).

191. *See* George R. Goethals & R. Eric Nelson, *Similarity in the Influence Process: The Belief-Value Distinction*, 25 J. PERSONALITY & SOC. PSYCHOL. 117, 121 (1973).

ciple that will at least achieve its stated goal, such as doing justice under the community's shared intuition of justice. That is likely to achieve considerable deterrent force in the process.

IV. THE POSSIBILITIES AND IMPOSSIBILITIES OF IMPROVING DETERRENT EFFECT

We have argued thus far that under existing conditions in modern criminal justice systems, the formulation of criminal law rules cannot normally materially increase deterrence. But perhaps existing conditions could be changed so that doctrinal manipulation could enhance deterrence. In this Part we discuss how a deterrent effect might be enhanced, if at all, and describe situations in which doctrinal manipulation might actually have a deterrent effect. Our goal is to give a more realistic view of deterrence as a distributive principle, a view that criminal lawmakers can use as a touchstone before relying upon deterrence analysis. To telegraph our conclusion, it is this: Avenues of reform to enhance deterrent effect are available, but most are unconstitutional or are unattractive because of the sacrifices they require. Within the realm of plausible reforms, one could work to foster conditions that favor the success of doctrinal manipulations designed to have deterrent effect, but such conditions would remain the exception rather than the rule.

A. ENSURING THAT THE TARGET AUDIENCE KNOWS, DIRECTLY OR INDIRECTLY, OF THE RULE DESIGNED TO INFLUENCE THEIR CONDUCT

As Part I notes, most people do not know the law; even career criminals who have a special incentive to know it do not; and even when people think they know the law they frequently are wrong. Potential offenders typically do not read law books and their ability to learn the law, even indirectly through hearing or reading about particular cases, is limited by the fact that the legal rule—and often there are many rules interacting to produce the case result—is just one of dozens of variables at play in a case disposition. It is not reasonable to expect that potential offenders would either know of prior cases or have the capacity for the complex calculations that would be necessary to grasp the operative liability rule hidden under the effects of numerous other variables.

But there are some situations in which the criminal law rule can and will be known, and there are ways in which knowledge of it can be increased. First, a bare prohibition itself is the easiest rule to convey, in part because its effects can be dramatic. Either the police can arrest for such conduct or they can not, and the police decisions will become known within the target population. The more noteworthy the prohibition, or repeal of a prohibition, the more widely it will be known. For example, if the legislature decriminalizes robbing convenience stores on weekends, the fact would be quickly reported and would likely quickly increase robberies.

However, the rule often is not known, even for rules as simple as those defining the law's prohibitions. Is it criminal to fail to help a stranger in serious danger if one can do so without endangering oneself? Is it criminal for a private person to keep a dead body without burial or cremation? Is it criminal to fail to try to find the owner when you come upon a valuable mislaid item? Most people can only guess—often incorrectly—about these criminal law commands. The answer in each case is: It depends upon which jurisdiction one is in.

There are some situations in which the knowledge necessary for deterrence can be conveyed to the potential offender at the time and place of the potential offense, such as where the witness on the stand is reminded of the penalty for perjury,[192] where life term inmates are informed of their special eligibility for the death penalty for certain crimes while in prison,[193] where an offender is told after an arrest for seduction that there is a "marriage defense" to the crime,[194] where road signs inform felons of a special duty to register in the jurisdiction,[195] or where a kidnapper is told that he will receive a lesser sentence if he releases the victim alive.[196] But such opportunities for special education are not typically available, and the government often does not take advantage of them when they are.

One could imagine requiring high school seniors to pass a knowledge-of-the-law examination to graduate, much as we give rules-of-the-road examinations before issuing a driver's license. It would be useful for graduates to know the serious penalties associated with domestic violence, the conduct that constitutes criminal harassment, and whether it is a crime to tape-record one's own phone conversation without permission of the other party. But government tends to rely instead on the maxim "ignorance or mistake of law is no excuse,"[197] pushing the full burden of education, unrealistically, on each individual.

One also could imagine criminal codes written using "plain language draft-

192. MODEL PENAL CODE § 241.1 cmt. at 94 (1980).

193. *See, e.g.*, CAL. PENAL CODE § 4500 (West 2002); 720 ILL. COMP. STAT. ANN. § 5/9-1(b)(10) (West 2002); N.Y. CRIM. PROC. LAWS § 400.27 (McKinney 2002); N.Y. PENAL LAWS § 125.27 (McKinney 2002); TEX. PENAL CODE ANN. § 19.03 (Vernon 2001). All statutes listed provide life imprisonment status as special aggravating factor for death penalty.

194. Modern codes often reject this once common defense. See MODEL PENAL CODE § 213.3 cmt. at 396.

195. *See, e.g.*, CAL. HEALTH & SAFETY CODE § 11590 (West 2002) (requiring registration of controlled substance offenders); CAL. PENAL CODE § 290 (West 2002) (requiring registration of sex offenders); 730 ILL. COMP. STAT. ANN. § 150/3 (West 2002) (requiring registration of sex offenders); N.Y. CORRECT. LAW § 168-e (McKinney 2002) (requiring that, upon release, sex offender must be informed of duty to register); Lambert v. California, 355 U.S. 225, 229 (1957) (holding that Los Angeles felon registration ordinance violated due process because the defendant had no knowledge of his duty to register).

196. MODEL PENAL CODE § 212.1 cmt. at 232–33 (1980).

197. *See, e.g.*, Commonwealth v. Mash, 48 Mass. (7 Met.) 472, 473 (1844) (finding a woman liable for polygamy, despite the fact that her first husband left home one morning saying that he would return immediately but was not heard from again for over three years, leading her to believe him dead); People v. Marrero, 422 N.Y.S.2d 384, 387–88 (App. Div. 1979) (finding prison guard liable for criminal possession of a weapon even though he reasonably believed that he was a "peace officer" and therefore not required to have a gun permit); City of West Allis v. Megna, 133 N.W.2d 252, 254 (Wis. 1965) (holding tavern-keeper liable for permitting a minor to loiter in the tavern, even though he had relied in good faith on the minor's identification card, which was later determined to be false).

ing" techniques,[198] but in reality such laws contain mountains of technical legalese that even lawyers must work to understand.[199] Similarly, one could increase the chances that the legal rule could be known and followed by keeping rules simple. Being able to reduce a rule to a slogan that can be widely advertised, such as "Use a gun, go to jail," might help. By contrast, the standard modern criminal code's complex self-defense rules cited above appear rather silly.[200] It would be unrealistic to think that a person could know—and in the pressure of an attack, follow—those complex rules. But one could distill the rules to highlight the basic principles that guided their formulation. The defensive force rule might read simply: "In order to defend yourself against an unlawful attack, you can use only the force that is necessary and that is not disproportionate to the harm threatened."[201]

One might be able to increase the complexity of a rule if it applied primarily to a group of persons who could be specially trained, such as police officers or public officials. Thus, a code might provide detailed rules governing the use of force by officers during an arrest;[202] or rules governing entrapment; or detailed rules limiting a public official's ability to sell political influence;[203] or even detailed rules for doctors performing abortions.[204] More complex rules could also be applied to target groups that have the ability and are on notice of their need to specially educate themselves, such as rules governing the conduct of corporate officials, who can look to corporate counsel.

One final observation concerns criminal law rules of general application. As noted in Part I, while people rarely know "the law," they generally assume that the criminal law is as they would expect it to be. That is, they use their own intuitions of justice and their own assessments of what is harmful or wrongful as the basis for assumptions of what the criminal law must provide. This

---

198. *See generally* Gregory J. Odorizzi, *Plain Language—Incentives and Recent Developments in the Federal Government*, 79 MICH. BAR J. 1210 (2000) (describing the efforts in federal agencies and the Clinton Administration to use "plain language" in their documents); Tom Goldstein, *The Law; Drive for Plain English Gains Among Lawyers*, N.Y. TIMES, Feb. 19, 1988 at B7.

199. *See, e.g.*, Paul H. Robinson, *Why a New Criminal Code?*, *in* 1 FINAL REPORT OF THE ILLINOIS CRIMINAL CODE REWRITE AND REFORM COMM'N xvi (Paul H. Robinson, Rep., State of Illinois Jan. 2003), *available at* http://www.idoc.state.il.us/ccrc/files/frv1_introductory_materials.pdf (last visited Oct. 26, 2003).

200. *See supra* notes 108–09 and accompanying text.

201. *See, e.g.*, 2 FINAL REPORT OF THE ILLINOIS CRIMINAL CODE REWRITE AND REFORM COMM'N, § 416, at 74 (Paul H. Robinson, Rep., State of Illinois Jan. 2003). The Final Report discusses the following Rule:

> Section 416. Defense of Person
>
> (1) The use of force against an aggressor is justified when and to the extent such conduct is immediately necessary to defend oneself or another person against the aggressor's use of unjustified force.
>
> (2) Definition. "Unjustified" conduct is conduct that satisfies the objective elements of an offense and is not justified by this Article.

202. MODEL PENAL CODE § 3.07 cmt. at 122 (1985).

203. *Id.* § 240.7 cmt. at 85 (1980).

204. *Id.* § 230.3 cmt. at 429.

suggests that the criminal law can ensure greater knowledge of its commands, with little or no need for special education efforts, if its rules track shared community views. Conversely, it would be difficult to get compliance with rules that appear to conflict with lay expectations, such as a rule barring force necessary to recapture property from a thief if the thief acts under a mistaken claim of right,[205] barring resistance to an unlawful arrest,[206] or barring use of deadly force necessary for self-defense if one can retreat.[207] Where the law's rule conflicts with lay intuition, a special education drive will be needed.

But this is more bad news for the use of deterrent analysis in formulating criminal law doctrine. Using deterrence as a distributive principle has effect—that is, it can be argued that deterrence is preferable to a "perceived justice" (shared community intuitions) distribution—only when it produces results *that deviate from* such a justice distribution. Yet it is just these instances of deviation in which ignorance and mistake by the target audience is at its greatest. And it is just these instances of deviation in which the law must not only educate but must overcome the mistaken notion of the rules that people otherwise will have.

B. ENSURING THAT THE TARGET AUDIENCE PERCEIVES A MEANINGFUL NET COST TO A VIOLATION

Part I noted the many difficulties in establishing a punishment rate that would be meaningful to potential offenders, both in avoiding the delay in imposition of punishment that seriously erodes its deterrent effect, and in establishing and modulating the amount of punishment imposed, as an effective deterrence distribution of punishment must do. This Section discusses several reforms that could improve the system's ability to make and modulate the threat of punishment, but concludes that the potential for improvement is, at best, modest.

1. Probability

The empirical studies seem to agree that increasing the probability of punishment provides a better chance of strengthening deterrence than increasing the severity of punishment.[208] Establishing some base expectation of a meaningful chance of punishment is a necessary condition to any deterrent effect. Yet, we have previously noted just how low is the perceived probability of punishment[209]—a perception that results from the very low actual rates of punishment,

205. *See id.* § 3.06 cmt. at 74 (1985); *see also* ROBINSON & DARLEY, *supra* note 2, at 68–69 (discussing an empirical study that suggests a difference between the legal rule and lay intuition concerning the use of force in protection of property).

206. *See* MODEL PENAL CODE § 3.04 cmt. at 42–43 (1985); *id.* § 3.09 cmt. at 148.

207. *See id.* § 3.04 cmt. at 54; *see also* ROBINSON & DARLEY, *supra* note 2, at 56–57, 64 (citing an empirical study suggesting a difference between the legal rule and lay intuition concerning the use of deadly force in self-defense).

208. *See* Jeffrey Grogger, *Certainty v. Severity of Punishment*, 24 ECON. INQUIRY 297 (1991); Ann Dryden Witte, *Estimating the Economic Model of Crime with Individual Data*, 94 Q. J. ECON. 57 (1980).

209. *See supra* note 5.

and is further exacerbated by the human tendency to heavily discount a future event. Sentencing discretion contributes to the uncertainty of punishment, as does the discretion of the many other participants in the criminal justice system, from police officers, to prosecutors, to jurors, whose exercise of discretion regularly allow offenders to escape punishment or get less than they might. Such uncertainty can nurture in all cases a hope of avoiding punishment.

There appears little that can be done to improve the perceived probability of punishment. Increasing punishment certainty would require improving clearance rates—the rates at which offenders are arrested for given offenses—and conviction rates. The more important factor to address may be clearance rates, for they account for the greatest "leakage" of offenders escaping punishment.[210] Yet such increases would require one or all of the following: a significant increase in the amount we spend on law enforcement and criminal justice; an increase in the intrusiveness we suffer from law enforcement; and a reduction in the procedural safeguards we provide in criminal adjudications. The reality is that most people think they already pay too much in taxes,[211] and limitations on investigative intrusiveness and on adjudication procedures typically are constitutionally based, and thus, unchangeable by legislative action. No doubt progress could be made around the edges, assuming people were willing to suffer the tradeoffs—higher taxes, more governmental intrusion, and fewer procedural safeguards—but the kind of dramatic changes that would be required to alter our current abysmal clearance rates significantly seem unlikely.

An additional complication in making such reforms—even if people were willing to make the tradeoffs required for them—is their effect on the criminal justice system's reputation for procedural fairness, which, like its reputation for moral credibility, has crime-control implications. A system perceived as procedurally unfair will not earn the legitimacy required for the acquiescence and support, by defendants, witnesses, jurors, and officials—by extension by citizens in general—that the system needs to operate effectively. For example, we might obtain a higher conviction rate by lowering the standard of proof from the demanding "beyond a reasonable doubt." But would criminal convictions retain even their current level of credibility if we did?

Tom Tyler and Yuen Huo, surveying a large sample of Chicago residents, found that the degree to which respondents felt that they had received fair treatment at the hands of the police predicted those respondents' general confi-

210. *See* ROBINSON & DARLEY, *supra* note 2, at tbl.1, col.(c) (noting that only 8.1% of all burglaries, 14.4% of all rapes, and 7.8% of all assaults result in an arrest).

211. Some studies suggest a greater willingness to pay for crime control measures than had been previously reported. *See* Mark A. Cohen et al., Willingness-to-Pay for Crime Control Programs (Nov. 2001) (unpublished manuscript), *available at* http://www.ssrn.com/abstract=293153 (last visited Oct. 26, 2003). Of course, these expressions of willingness show a willingness to pay if the expenditures would in fact reduce a particular kind of crime. There is little reason to think that such additional funds could actually produce the crime reduction demanded, in which case the willingness to pay would evaporate.

dence in legal authorities and, importantly, the degree to which they felt obliged to obey the law.[212] Tyler and Huo, reporting on the National Center for State Courts survey, showed that responses to such statements as "the courts are concerned with people's rights" predict respondents' evaluations of the court system and their willingness to obey the laws. To summarize, people "were strongly influenced by whether they believed that the police and the courts treated people with respect, dignity, and fairness, and did not harass them or subject them to rude or inappropriate treatment."[213] The point here is that the reputation of the criminal justice system for fair and respectful treatment of people is central to its ability to enlist voluntary compliance from citizens with the law, and the "procedural byproducts" of a criminal justice system that organizes itself to increase arrest rates may bring about highly consequential losses in citizens' perceptions of procedural legitimacy.

2. Delay

We have noted that the delay between violation and punishment can dramatically reduce deterrent effect.[214] The more distant punishment is, the more its weight as a threat will be discounted, even if the punishment is certain. Further, when punishment is imposed, the strength of the punishment memory—that is, its recalled punitive "bite" as a perceived threat for a future violation—is dramatically reduced as the length of delay increases.[215] But, as with reforms to increase probability, decreasing the delay in punishment—perhaps by forcing defendants to trial more quickly or by giving law enforcement greater authority to intrude into personal affairs to find offenders more quickly—would require increases in resources or changes in procedural rules that could be held unconstitutional, or if not, would require unpopular trade-offs and could injure the criminal justice system's reputation for fairness and, thereby, its legitimacy.

3. Amount

Part I noted that the greatest difficulties relevant to "amount" of punishment lie not in establishing a punitive bite but rather in manipulating it reliably so as to optimize deterrence. The aspect of perceived net cost over which lawmakers assume they have the greatest control is the amount of the threatened punishment, or its total punitive bite. Legislatures and judges believe they can manipulate the amount of punishment threatened by simply adjusting the length of the prison term. But such manipulation of sentence length does not provide the degree of change in punishment amount that lawmakers and judges expect, and indeed may have the opposite effect. The forces at work in determining the

212. TOM R. TYLER & YUEN J. HUO, TRUST IN THE LAW: ENCOURAGING PUBLIC COOPERATION WITH THE POLICE AND COURTS 179 (2002).

213. *Id.* at 191.

214. *See supra* note 6.

215. *See id.*

perceived amount of punishment are considerably more complex than has been assumed.[216] The effect of this dynamic for punishment is that each additional unit of imprisonment adds increasingly less to the total punishment amount. Yet the cost of each unit remains essentially constant. Thus, as duration increases, each unit becomes increasingly less cost-effective, which is not a promising state of affairs when one wishes to use increases in duration as the primary means of increasing punishment amount. But as we saw, even this may be a wildly optimistic picture of the effectiveness of using duration to modulate punishment bite. The "duration neglect" studies suggest that total punishment bite has little to do with duration, and more to do with maximum peak intensity and end point intensity.[217] Given the predictable drop in intensity over time, the end point intensity decreases with increased duration. Thus, a longer sentence may have less remembered punishment bite than a shorter one. If this theory is empirically confirmed, both of its implications are devastating for deterrence's ability to increase total bite by increasing duration. First, as noted, increasing duration may have the reverse effect on total bite. Second, "duration neglect" means that the only effective means of increasing total punishment bite is to increase the intensity of the punishment experience.

But the criminal justice system in the United States, and probably in any liberal democracy, has little ability to increase punishment intensity beyond its current level. Earlier times saw attempts to do so, in the invention of increasingly excruciating tortures and humiliations, such as having an offender's bones broken and body ripped apart while still alive ("drawing" and "quartering"[218]), or in repeated near-drownings ("dunkings"[219]), which apparently produced a horrible suffocation sensation. But there would be neither the political will to provide nor the public acceptance of such torture today, nor of nearly anything much more unpleasant than the current prison experience. Imprisonment at "hard labor" might be tolerated by some, but would have its details scrutinized for unconstitutional "cruel and unusual punishment."[220] For example, in one

216. Recall the hedonic adaptation and "subjective well-being" studies, which suggest that both paraplegics and lottery winners return to their original state of well-being despite their dramatically changed circumstances. *See supra* note 7 and accompanying text.

217. *See supra* text accompanying notes 7–8. "Duration neglect" refers to the following phenomenon: any experience, whether of pleasure or pain, has a duration of a certain length. The total experience of pleasure or pain, therefore, is the moment by moment pleasure or pain, times the duration of the experience. But now suppose that the experience is in the past, and the question is about the person's *remembered* experience of pleasure or pain. A startling empirical finding has emerged: If we are talking about the experience of pain, as we would when talking about a prison sentence, the remembered experience of pain is a function of the worst moment of pain, and the experience of pain at the end of the period. The experienced duration of pain has almost no effect on the remembered summary of the painfulness of the experience. *Id.*

218. 2 SIR FREDRICK POLLOCK & FREDRICK W. MAITLAND, THE HISTORY OF ENGLISH LAW 500–01 (Cambridge University Press 2d ed. 1968).

219. A. EARLE, CURIOUS PUNISHMENTS OF BYGONE DAYS 11, 17 (1896) (discussing the use of the "dunking stool" to punish women who spoke too much).

220. *See generally* LAFAVE & SCOTT, *supra* note 11, § 2.14, at 248–49 (reviewing constitutional limitations on modes of punishment); *cf.* Weems v. United States, 217 U.S. 349, 405–06 (1910)

recently reported case, a judge's attempt to bar the use of television, as part of a sentence of home detention, was challenged by defense attorneys, who persuaded the Second Circuit to temporarily stay the television ban.[221]

Even if more intense punishments were not held unconstitutional, they might well be counterproductive. As we discussed in Part III.C, a criminal justice system that is seen as barbaric or as dispensing disproportionate punishment would likely lose moral authority within the community and, with it, the crime-control power that such moral authority can bring. One practical example is stigmatization, which can be highly effective in influencing conduct and has none of the financial costs of imprisonment, but is dependent upon the criminal justice system having earned a reputation for reliability in making criminal liability judgments that accord with the community's shared intuitions of justice. A system would quickly lose its moral credibility if it distributed cruel or disproportionate punishment, or liability based upon any number of the factors that deterrence analysis would make central to liability and punishment, but which are unrelated to moral blameworthiness.[222]

The best option may be to explore ways of increasing the punishment bite—consistent with human dignity, as the community's moral sense demands—through minor adjustments to prison conditions. This could be achieved either through more dignified, shorter, but more unpleasant terms, or through non-incarcerative alternatives, which have the advantage of being less expensive. For example, if it is the unpredictability of prison life that makes its aversiveness fresh, then it might be possible to increase that uncertainty and shorten the prison term over which it is experienced. For less serious crimes there are a number of alternatives to prison sentences that people would perceive as having a punitive "bite" comparable to that of a short prison term.[223] This means that it is possible to create a sentence of the appropriate severity that would be a mix of these experiences, such as home confinement, labor-intensive community service, weekends in jail, and fines. Again, it might be possible to rotate offenders through a variety of these punishment options, which might keep the aversiveness of the experiences fresh. There is a moral tightrope to be walked

(scrutinizing a Philippine statute that imposed a hard-labor sentence for falsifying public documents, and finding the sentence so disproportionate as to violate the Eighth Amendment).

221. Benjamin Weiser, *A Sentence of No TV? Unusual, Yes, but Cruel?*, N.Y. TIMES, March 7, 2002, at A1. Whether or not the defendant ultimately prevails, it says something about the extent of scrutiny of "different" punishments that the Second Circuit would grant the stay.

222. A deterrence-based system might look to, for instance, the difficulty of detecting a crime, reasoning that if the system can catch only one out of the hundred people who commit some easily-hidden crime, it is necessary to punish the one with dreadful severity to keep the "punishment weight" constant and to deter others. Or, to accomplish general deterrence of the population, one might give an exemplarily severe sentence to a case that one knew was generating a great deal of public interest so the sentence would be widely publicized.

223. *See generally* George Gescheider et al., *Psychophysical Measurement of the Judged Seriousness of Crimes and Severity of Punishments*, 19 BULL. PSYCHONOMIC SOC'Y 275–78 (1982); Robert Harlow et al., *The Severity of Intermediate Penal Sanctions: Psychophysical Scaling Approach for Obtaining Community Perceptions*, 11 J. QUANTITATIVE CRIMINOLOGY 71–95 (1995).

here. One is attempting not to increase the objective negativity of the punishments, but to increase the perceived negativity.

One last point on deterrent limitations of sentences, especially imprisonment: Most of what we have said so far focuses on legislative action in setting offense grades and their sentencing consequences. Even if a legislature found the most deterrent-efficient set of punishment rules and enshrined them in the criminal code, such rules would not necessarily produce the intended modulation of punishment amount required by a deterrence-based system. Judges, not legislators, impose sentences, and given the wide sentencing discretion that American judges traditionally have had and continue to have in the vast majority of states, judicial discretion not legislative policy will determine deterrent effectiveness.

For this reason, mandatory minimum sentences have become popular in many states.[224] But such legislative sentencing creates the danger—increasingly recognized in public discourse—of increased community perceptions of injustice, which, as before, can undercut the criminal law's moral authority. On the other hand, judicial discretion left unchecked produces unjustified disparity in the sentencing of similar cases, which also can produce perceived injustice.[225] The community expectation is that punishment should depend upon what the offender has done, not on the sentencing judge to whom he happens to be assigned.

Judicial discretion is also troublesome because it can produce not only inconsistency among different judges but inconsistency among a single judge's different cases. For example, when a judge picks out one case or another with which to "make an example"—a practice typically justified on deterrence grounds[226]—the sentence is likely to be inconsistent with other cases of similar

224. *See, e.g.*, Gary T. Lowenthal, *Mandatory Sentencing Laws: Undermining the Effectiveness of Determinate Sentencing Reform*, 81 CAL. L. REV. 61, 61–63 (1993).

225. One survey of federal judges revealed that:

> While one-fourth of the judges thought rehabilitation was an extremely important goal of sentencing, 19 percent thought it was no more than 'slightly' important; conversely, about 25 percent thought 'just deserts' was a very important or extremely important purpose of sentencing, while 45 percent thought it was only slightly important or not important at all.

S. REP. No. 98-225, at 41 n.18 (1983) (citing INSLAW, Inc. et al., *Federal Sentencing: Toward a More Explicit Policy of Criminal Sanctions* III-4 (1981)). Research also confirms that these differences in philosophy do indeed translate into different sentences. One study done by the judiciary gave 50 judges the same 20 cases to sentence. The differences in sentences were staggering. In one extortion case, for example, sentences ranged from twenty years' imprisonment and a $65,000 fine to three years' imprisonment and no fine. *Id.* at 42–44. This same disparity in sentencing is reflected in the sentences given in real cases every day. One study compared the sentences imposed in the different federal circuits. For forgery, as an example, the average sentence ranged from 30 months in the Third Circuit to 82 months in the District of Columbia. *Id.* at 41 n.21 (citing Whitney North Seymour, *1972 Sentencing Study for the Southern District of New York*, 45 N.Y.S.B.J. 163, 167 (1973)). For interstate transportation of stolen motor vehicles, the extremes in average sentences were 22 months in the First Circuit and 42 months in the Tenth Circuit. *Id.* at 41 n.21. *See generally* MARVIN E. FRANKEL, CRIMINAL SENTENCES: LAW WITHOUT ORDER (1973).

226. *See, e.g.*, McCarty Sentencing Transcript, *supra* note 94, at 00392:11–13 ("a sentence does need to be imposed that would deter others from committing such crime, a high speed chase with the police").

seriousness. The point of "making an example" of an offender is to give a higher sentence than what one ordinarily would give in such a case in order to boost the deterrent message. But this suggests that each instance of "making an example" risks the criminal justice system's reputation for fairness and uniformity in application.

Further, "making an example" of an offender can backfire. The open acknowledgment that offenders may not ordinarily be given such a punishment may tell listeners that the publicized punishment is not the regular punishment, and thus not the punishment they should expect if they commit the offense, especially given that they will be sentenced at a later time and by a different judge. The more newsworthy the "example," and the more widely it is reported—normally desirable in a deterrence paradigm—the more unusual and atypical the sentence may be perceived as being. A more effective deterrent approach would be to advertise the consistency with which sentences are given. That is difficult to do with today's high degree of judicial sentencing discretion.

A common means of compensating for the inconsistency among sentencing judges has been to have the real determination of sentence length made after the public sentencing, by a centralized authority such as a state-wide parole commission. But this solution creates its own problems, the most important of which is the (accurate) perception that the sentence publicly announced after trial does not in fact represent the real punishment. The real sentence in such a system comes to be understood, especially by those familiar with the operation of the system, as much less than the official sentence announced. The extent to which the announced sentence is discounted can be substantial. In some jurisdictions, including the federal system until recent reforms, a sentence of many years imprisonment can mean that the offender is in fact eligible for immediate release.[227] When this truth becomes known, as it generally does in an open society, it is no surprise to find that the credibility of the system's punishment threat has been damaged. Further, once burned, the public may wonder, "If the system is misleading us on this issue, on what other issues is it similarly misleading?" This is not a good condition for projecting a credible punishment threat, but rather offers the worst of both worlds: It undercuts the deterrent threat meant to be carried by the publicly announced sentences, and simultaneously ensures the inconsistency and injustice that will undermine the system's moral credibility.

Perhaps the best that one can do to improve the credibility of the punishment

227. In the federal system before the Sentencing Reform Act of 1984, any offender was eligible for immediate release unless the sentencing judge explicitly imposed a term of parole ineligibility, which, even if imposed, could never exceed one-third of the publicly announced sentence. 18 U.S.C. § 4205 (1982). *See also* S. REP. NO. 98-225, at 48 (1983) ("[A] court-imposed term of imprisonment in excess of one year frequently has little to do with the amount of time that an offender will spend in prison. The announced term represents only the maximum length of time the offender may spend in prison if he earns no good time credits and if the Parole Commission does not set a release date that falls before the date of expiration of the sentence.").

threat is to institute reforms such as sentencing guidelines that regularize sentences[228] and "truth in sentencing" reforms that require offenders to serve all or most of the sentence imposed.[229]

C. ENSURING THAT THE TARGET AUDIENCE IS CAPABLE OF AND WILLING TO BRING A PERCEIVED THREAT OF PUNISHMENT TO BEAR ON THEIR CONDUCT DECISIONS

Part I noted that there are a host of conditions that interfere with rational calculation of self-interest in potential offenders, such as drug or alcohol use, personality types inclined toward impulsiveness and toward discounting consequences, and social influences such as the arousal effect of group action and the tendency of group members to identity with group rather than individual interests. Furthermore, these conditions are disproportionately high among deterrence's target group—those persons for whom criminal conduct is not already ruled out by their own internalized norms or by those of their family or peers.[230] This bodes ill for effective deterrence because it precludes, or at least diminishes, a rule's deterrent effect, even if the rule is known and is backed up by what is perceived as a meaningful threat of punishment.

Can the rational calculation of self-interest among potential offenders be improved? Our present perspective may suggest an interesting twist on the modern skepticism about the effectiveness of treatment and rehabilitation programs. While it may not be realistic to think that criminals can be "rehabilitated" into good citizens, it is somewhat more realistic to think that the behavioral sciences could find a way to make potential offenders more able to exercise rational self-interest in response to a perceived threat of punishment. While current treatment techniques may not be able to make potential offenders good people, perhaps they could increase their susceptibility to being deterred!

There are various practical, procedural, and conceptual problems with creating effective regimes for increasing deterrent effects. Many would involve special monitoring programs that were enforced as conditions of parole. Mark Kleiman has suggested one such set of impositions under which a monitoring program is likely to reduce drug or alcohol consumption.[231] The essence of the program is a high frequency of testing for consumption of the banned substance,

---

228. [S]entencing in the Federal courts is characterized by unwarranted disparity and by uncertainty about the length of time offenders will serve in prison.

> The lack of reasonable consistency in the sentences handed down by the courts is due in large part to the lack of a comprehensive Federal sentencing law. . . . This disparity is fair neither to the offenders nor to the public.

S. REP. NO. 98-225, at 49 (1983).

229. The federal system, for example, now requires that an offender serve 85% of the sentence imposed. That is, only a 15% reduction is allowed as credit for good behavior in prison. 18 U.S.C. § 3624 (2002) (providing that prisoners may qualify for good behavior credit of up to 54 days for each year served).

230. *See supra* note 9 and accompanying text.

231. Mark A.R. Kleiman, *Coerced Abstinence: A Neopaternalist Drug Policy Initiative*, *in* THE NEW PATERNALISM: SUPERVISORY APPROACHES TO POVERTY 182–219 (Lawrence Mead ed., 1997).

with graduated and at least initially non-draconian punishments for violation that increase in a step-wise fashion. To be sure, such programs are not always possible to design, are somewhat costly to administer, and do not produce perfect success in preventing people from pursuing crime. However, the shift in focus that we propose here could better capture the potential that does exist in these programs. While such programs may not prevent crime directly, carefully selecting the programs to use and the offenders for which they are used might lead a potential criminal to engage in the rational, self-interest calculation that will, in turn, permit traditional criminal law deterrence to accomplish its task.

One suggestion for increasing the effectiveness of treatment programs consists of increasing the level of surveillance until detection of lapses is nearly certain. Daily breath-analyzer tests for those who drink and drive or daily urine tests for those who use drugs will at least sort out those who have the "will power" to restrain themselves from lapsing when the penalties for lapsing are nearly certain. Those who continue to lapse under these detection conditions may require more incarcerative treatments to keep them from committing crimes while under the influence of alcohol or drugs. One can imagine that these sorts of high-frequency surveillance programs can be costly. But those costs need to be compared to the costs expended to keep the offenders in prison. Further, costs can be reduced by utilizing recent developments in computational power and electronic surveillance. There are now breath-analyzers that can be coupled to car ignitions to keep people from driving if they have consumed alcohol. It is now possible to have drug abusers randomly beeped to, for instance, give a blood sample that could be remotely tested for illicit drugs. Should these methods fail, electronically enforced daily periods of "house arrest" could allow an offender to continue employment while being restricted from other activities. These procedures are remarkably intrusive, even Orwellian, but they perhaps violate the person's autonomy and dignity less than the alternative, which is generally prison.

One final point on clearing the rational-choice hurdle: The absence of rational decisionmaking seems greater for offenses that do not require sustained planning efforts. This is true both because persons who can so plan are also likely to be able to calculate self-interest, and because the longer the planning stage the greater the opportunity for self-interest to intervene and override impulsiveness or the other forces toward irrationality. This suggests that, if rehabilitation programs are to be revised to enhance a potential offender's self-interest calculation, the primary target for such treatment is not the white-collar criminal who may have been the primary client of rehabilitation programs in the past, but rather the more dysfunctional, perhaps impulsive offender.[232]

232. It may be that the movement toward "crime prevention through environmental design" seeks to do this, to cause the perceived physical barriers to successful crime completion to be greater and more time and energy consuming, so that the potential criminal's good sense intervenes, and he decides not to attempt the crime. Much of the literature on reduction of crime via environmental design is reviewed

It is also true that we can expect more rational calculations of self-interest if the potential offender fully understands the governing criminal law rules, as stated in our previous discussion regarding clear and straightforward statutes.[233] The reforms discussed there for improving the comprehensibility of the law increase the likelihood that a potential offender can at least understand the rule enough to include its implications in his calculations of self-interest. An obvious suggestion would be to simplify the rules—for example, about what conduct is legitimate in self-defense or what is or is not a case of date rape.

V. SUMMARY AND CONCLUSION

We do not dispute that having a criminal justice system that imposes punishment can and does deter violations. The system's generalized threat of punishment provides a clear disincentive to crime. It does not follow, however, that the manipulation of rules for determining liability and punishment within that system—traditionally governed by deterrence analysis—can send the more nuanced messages that are needed to influence the conduct of potential offenders in a more precise way. It could happen. But the conditions under which it could happen are the exception rather than the rule: a potential offender who is at least indirectly aware of the rule intended to influence his conduct; a perception that the immediate benefit of the crime is less than the delayed and doubtful possibility of a distant punishment; a sufficiently rational actor who is sufficiently free of decision-distorting influences to be able and willing to respond to the manipulation of rules by altering his conduct; and a resulting deterrent effect not so incrementally dissipated as to be trivial. We suggest that the infrequency of being able to achieve a meaningful deterrent effect through doctrinal manipulation reveals that the deterrent-analysis tradition of modern criminal law scholars, judges, and lawmakers is seriously out of touch with the reality of its limitations.

Indeed, while there may be situations in which doctrinal manipulation can have the desired deterrent effect, such an effect is most difficult and most unlikely in those situations where a deterrence distribution actually does some real work. That is because a deterrence-optimizing distributive principle only has effect—it only provides an advantage over a justice-based distributive principle—where it deviates from justice. But it is in just these deviation cases that achieving a deterrent effect is most difficult and most doubtful.

This is so because people assume the law is as they think it should be, according to their perceptions of shared intuitions of justice. It is in the deviation cases that criminal law has its greatest difficulty conveying its rule, for it is here that the legal system must affirmatively change the community's

and critiqued in C. Ray Jeffery & Diane Zahm, *Crime Prevention Through Environmental Design, Opportunity Theory, and Rational Choice Models*, *in* 5 ADVANCES IN CRIMINOLOGICAL THEORY 323 (Ronald V. Clarke & Marcus Felson eds., 1993).

233. *See supra* text accompanying notes 197–207.

initial incorrect assumption about what the law provides. Further, it is the deviation cases in which the system will find it most difficult to educate by example, through case dispositions, because it is in these cases that prosecutors and juries are most likely to follow their own intuitions of justice and ignore the law's contrary rule—or at least look for ways to minimize the rule's effect. This kind of distortion means that case dispositions often obfuscate rather than clarify the legal rule sought to be conveyed. Further, and most importantly, the tendency of system participants to undercut the deviation rules—be it through the exercise of prosecutorial or enforcement discretion, sentencing discretion, jury nullification, or other methods—means, obviously, that the planned deterrence program will be frustrated.

But even if a deterrence-based doctrinal manipulation did result in some marginal deterrence effect, there would be good reason to reject it in favor of a justice distribution that tracks the community's shared intuitive principles. Such a just-deserts distribution provides some deterrent effect. Thus, as we pointed out above, a deterrence distribution can provide an advantage only to the extent that it deviates from justice and, by such deviation, provides a greater deterrent effect. But such a deterrence-based distributional system incurs costs that are often not recognized by its advocates. This is so because the deterrence-based system would provide added deterrent effect only if the community members were aware that the legal codes deviated from their sense of what was morally right, either by being draconian in criminalizing actions that the community regarded as not immoral, or failing to criminalize actions that the community does think are immoral.

But it is just these rules that deviate from the community's sense of justice that most undercut the criminal law's moral credibility with the community and thereby reduce the law's long-term crime control power. In the community governed by a criminal justice system that punishes what the community regards as morally appropriate actions, the laws are obeyed only under threat of apprehension by what comes to be seen as an oppressive police force and judicial system. Thus, even if a deterrence distribution has a net immediate crime-control benefit over a justice distribution, over time that benefit may be outweighed by the slowly building crimogenic effect that results when citizens come to hold their criminal justice system in contempt. Lawmakers' constant emphasis on tweaking a doctrine's deterrent effect, even at the expense of justice, may not only be a waste of time, energy, and resources—it may actually have the counterproductive effect of increasing, rather than decreasing, crime.

[2]

HOW MUCH DO WE REALLY KNOW ABOUT CRIMINAL DETERRENCE?

RAYMOND PATERNOSTER*

This Article discusses the deterrence of crime through sanctions. It begins with a brief intellectual history of deterrence theory in the work of Cesare Beccaria and Jeremy Bentham, two Enlightenment philosophers who created the conceptual foundation for later deterrence and rational choice theory. Although a prominent intellectual current by the end of the 1700s, interest in deterrence and rational choice based theories of criminal offending was later eclipsed by more biologically and psychologically based explanations. Interest in deterrence theory and the deterrent effect of legal sanctions was not rekindled until the mid-1960s. This Article discusses the particular and important role of the Journal of Criminal Law and Criminology *in publishing the works of both those who were highly critical of deterrence theory and those who wished to keep it alive, though vividly aware of the lack of any empirical support for it. This Article discusses the theoretical connections that are presumed by the deterrence process and briefly reviews some important empirical studies pertaining to each of those presumed causal connections. The empirical evidence leads to the conclusion that there is a marginal deterrent effect for legal sanctions, but this conclusion must be swallowed with a hefty dose of caution and skepticism; it is very difficult to state with any precision how strong a deterrent effect the criminal justice system provides. At the very least, there is a great asymmetry between what is expected of the legal system through deterrence and what the system delivers. There is greater confidence that non-legal factors are more effective in securing compliance than legal threats. It is argued that the empirical evidence does support the belief that criminal offenders are rational actors, in that they are responsive to the incentives and disincentives associated with their actions, but that the criminal justice system, because of its delayed imposition of punishment, is not well constructed to exploit this rationality.*

---

* Department of Criminology, Maryland Population Research Center, University of Maryland. The author would like to thank Shawn Bushway for reading and commenting on a previous draft of this manuscript, and for being a constant source of insight and a good argument.

I. INTRODUCTION

The concept of deterrence is quite simple—it is the omission of a criminal act because of the fear of sanctions or punishment. While not the entire premise, deterrence is certainly an important foundation of the criminal justice system. Law enforcement exists both to apprehend wrongdoers and to convince would-be wrongdoers that there is a risk of apprehension and punishment if they commit a crime. Laws that provide a host of different sanctions for the commission of criminal offenses (fines, probation, imprisonment) serve notice that criminal statutes contain a credible threat that—it is hoped—will inhibit those who have been punished from committing additional crimes (specific deterrence) and those who have not yet offended from committing crimes at all (general deterrence). Particular criminal justice policies such as police "crackdowns," enhanced enforcement in and surveillance of high crime areas or "hot spots," mandatory minimum sentences, sentencing enhancements for firearm possession, "three-strike" laws, and others are all enacted with the expectation that they will successfully engineer the crime rate down through deterring offenders and would-be offenders. It is reasonable to argue that a belief or expectation that sanction threats can deter crime is at the very heart of the criminal justice system.

In spite of its central importance, and the very high expectation we have that legal punishment and criminal justice policies can inhibit crime, we do not have very solid and credible empirical evidence that deterrence through the imposition of criminal sanctions works very well. While we have an abundance of research about specific police, judicial, and correctional policies, as well as more general theoretical work about deterrence mechanisms, the evidence to date, while suggesting that there is a deterrence return to all that we do about crime, is more than a little flimsy. In essence, while we can say that there likely is a deterrent effect to the workings of the criminal justice system,[1] it is difficult to determine how strong an effect it is and why that effect is not stronger than we might think it should be. This Article explores at least two very important reasons why the empirical evidence in support of criminal deterrence is so weak: (1) it is

[1] It is easy enough to see that criminal deterrence frequently and effectively influences our actions. We all "throw out the anchor" on the highway when we spot a patrol car. We generally do not park in handicapped-only parking spots. We do not light up a joint at the movies. Burglars like to break into unoccupied homes. Drug deals are typically made in the shadows and not out in the open where police can see. But while we know that deterrence works in the absence of doing nothing about crime, we are decidedly less certain about relative or marginal deterrent effects. For example, does increasing the number of police officers reduce crime? Does adding three years to a prison sentence for the use of a gun deter firearm-related felonies? Does an increased use of incarceration deter crime better compared with previous levels of incarceration?

very difficult to isolate and measure a deterrent effect precisely because a great many things must happen before deterrence can occur; (2) it just may be very difficult to generate strong deterrent effects through the legal system because the system is unable to exploit human rationality effectively. This Article examines selective features of the empirical deterrence terrain (more comprehensive reviews of the literature are both abundant and recent) with the intention of providing a glimpse of what we know about criminal deterrence and how our knowledge is very imprecise, how difficult it is to come by that knowledge, and what features of the legal system and its delivery of sanctions, and of people may contribute to our lack of precise knowledge about deterrence.

The Article begins with a brief intellectual history of deterrence and the role of the *Journal of Criminal Law and Criminology* in that history. The following section discusses the causal mechanisms that define how the process of deterrence works. This causal process links the workings of the criminal justice system (the objective properties of punishment) to the perceptual properties of punishment held by individuals to crime and, in turn, both of these properties of punishment to crime. A causal effect of deterrence requires that each of the three links in this chain be present. Subsequent sections briefly review selected empirical studies about each one of the necessary causal connections in deterrence. The Article concludes with a more speculative discussion about what it is about the criminal justice system and about human beings that contributes to the generally weak, generally imprecise empirical support for criminal deterrence through legal sanctions.

II. A Brief Intellectual History of Deterrence Theory in Criminology

A. Intellectual Roots

There are two standard, but nonetheless productive, sources to consult for an understanding of the intellectual history of deterrence theory. The first is an essay, *On Crimes and Punishments* (*On Crimes*), written in 1764 by the Enlightenment philosopher Cesare Beccaria,[2] and the second is Jeremy Bentham's *An Introduction to the Principles of Morals and Legislation* (*Introduction to the Principles*), published in 1789.[3] Although Beccaria is often cited as the founder of the classical school of criminology,

[2] Cesare Beccaria, On Crimes and Punishments (Henry Paolucci trans., Macmillan 1986) (1764).

[3] Jeremy Bentham, The Principles of Morals and Legislation (Prometheus Books 1988) (1789).

On Crimes does not really contain a fully developed theory of crime as much as Bentham's does. Beccaria's *On Crimes* is best thought of as a collection of principles that an enlightened ruler might use to make the administration of his legal system more systematically rational and therefore, Beccaria would argue, efficient.[4] Nevertheless, the essay does contain discussions about the characteristics of punishment that form the foundation of deterrence theory.[5] Bentham's *Introduction to the Principles* contains a more fully articulated theory of crime that provides a better foundation for a rational choice theory of crime.[6]

On Crimes begins by clearly describing Beccaria's purpose—not to question authority, but to make the exercise of authority more rational:

> Whoever might wish to honor me with his criticism should therefore begin by understanding clearly the design of this work, a design which, far from diminishing legitimate authority, must serve to increase it, if reasoning rather than force can prevail among men, and if benevolence and humanity justify it in the eyes of all.[7]

Becarria was an Enlightenment thinker who was repulsed by the cruelty and barbarism of the legal codes under the *anciens regimes* throughout Europe.[8] These codes allowed such practices as secret accusations, torture, convictions without trial, and a host of not only cruel but disparate punishments.[9] These practices were offensive to Beccaria because their irrationality made them ineffective for crime control.[10] What Beccaria proposed in their place was a corpus of principles for authorities to follow that would make their rule more rational and, therefore, more effective.[11] He proposed a system of legal reforms that included clearly written laws, a restrained judiciary, the abolishment of torture and secret accusations, and a proportionality between the harm produced by the crime and the amount of punishment visited upon the offender.[12]

Becarria argued that the motivation to commit crime was found in ubiquitous self-interest, which he referred to as "the despotic spirit[] *which is in every man*,"[13] and that the "tangible motives"[14] to commit crime had to be countered by punishments. But the power of the sovereign is not

[4] *See* BECCARIA, *supra* note 2.

[5] *Id.* at 10-13.

[6] BENTHAM, *supra* note 3.

[7] BECCARIA, *supra* note 2, at 4.

[8] *Id.* at 3-4.

[9] *See id.* at 17-20, 25-28.

[10] *Id.* at 8-9.

[11] *Id.* at 17-19.

[12] *Id.* at 93-99.

[13] *Id.* at 12 (emphasis added).

[14] *Id.*

limitless; instead, the authority of the sovereign is premised on the consent of the governed—the social contract in Enlightenment terms—wherein each person surrenders only a limited part of his or her freedom in exchange for protection against others who would harm him or her.[15] In Chapter 23 of *On Crimes*, Beccaria argued that punishment must be proportionate to the crime: crimes that cause the greatest damage to society should be punished the most severely, and the least serious crimes should result in the least painful punishments.[16]

Even before this, however, Beccaria presented (in Chapter 20) a proposition that has been axiomatic in deterrence theory ever since. Certain punishment is a much more effective deterrent than severe punishment:

> One of the greatest curbs on crimes is not the cruelty of punishments, but their infallibility .... The certainty of a punishment, even if it be moderate, will always make a stronger impression than the fear of another which is more terrible but combined with the hope of impunity; even the least evils, when they are certain, always terrify men's minds ....[17]

He argued that punishments that are certain, severe enough to sufficiently offset the anticipated gains of crime, and arrive immediately after the crime would make for a more effective legal system than the system that existed at the time, which combined great cruelty and the seemingly random exercise of mercy.[18] Very much the original deterrence theorist, Beccaria's position was that the self-interest to commit crime has to be thwarted by legal punishment that is certain, proportional, and swift.[19]

In the penultimate chapter of *On Crimes*, Beccaria made an interesting observation that is returned to at the end of this Article. Chapter 41 is entitled "How to Prevent Crimes," and Beccaria began this chapter with the observation that "[i]t is better to prevent crimes that to punish them."[20] Of course, the reader could not be blamed for thinking that after forty chapters he had already fully explained how crimes can be prevented—crime can be deterred by the threats provided by a rational and efficient legal system of punishment, the structure of which makes up the first forty chapters of *On Crimes*. While Beccaria believed, without a doubt, that clearly defined laws that enjoy a great deal of consensus, are enforced equally, and are associated with certain and measured punishment could secure compliance, he also seemed keenly aware of the limitations of the legal system in the

[15] *Id.* at 12-13.

[16] *Id.* at 62-64.

[17] *Id.* at 58.

[18] *Id.* at 58-59.

[19] *Id.* at 46-47, 55-57, 62-64.

[20] *Id.* at 93.

prevention of most crime.[21] He argued that "the surest but most difficult way to prevent crimes is by perfecting education," by which he meant moral education or self-restraint—education on virtue.[22] Education allows individuals to avoid evil by enabling them to make better choices rather than securing their compliance through punishment, "which obtains only simulated and momentary obedience."[23] In terms of creating the conditions for maximum freedom and minimum evil (by both crime and punishment), Beccaria, in the end, seemed to appeal more to Rousseau's *Emile*[24] than to Bentham's *Panopticon*.[25]

While *On Crimes* provides the enlightened authority with practical policies to make legal systems more rational and efficient, it is thin with respect to any developed theory of crime or criminal conduct. Beccaria provided no real theory of behavior other than that crime is driven by self-interest, which resides in everyone. Bentham, however, offered a more developed intellectual source for deterrence theory's model of human conduct. It is in Bentham where one finds the notion of utility as the weighted balance between two opposing considerations—pleasure (benefits) and pain (costs)—that is the guide to conduct.[26] In the very first paragraph of *Introduction to the Principles*, Bentham argued that human behavior is directed by the twin goals of the attainment of pleasure and the avoidance of pain: "Nature has placed mankind under the governance of two sovereign masters, *pain* and *pleasure*. It is for them alone to point out what we ought to do, as well as to determine what we shall do."[27] The "masters" of pleasure and pain operate through the principle of utility—actions that bring pleasure provide utility, and those that bring pain provide disutility. The happiness of the individual is maximized when the sum total of their actions brings them more utility than disutility, and the self-interested individual is presumed to behave in such a way as to maximize his individual utility.[28] In talking about the general inclination to action in later chapters of *Introduction to the Principles*, Bentham stated in Chapter 3:

> Sum up all the values of all the pleasures on the one side, and those of all the pains on the other. The balance, if it be on the side of pleasure, will give the good tendency of

[21] *Id.* at 93-99.

[22] *Id.* at 98.

[23] *Id.* at 99.

[24] JEAN JACQUES ROUSSEAU, EMILE: OR ON EDUCATION (Dartmouth Coll. Press 2010) (1762).

[25] JEREMY BENTHAM, PANOPTICON (1787).

[26] BENTHAM, *supra* note 3, at 1.

[27] *Id.*

[28] *Id.* at 31.

> the act upon the whole, with respect to the interests of that individual person; if on the side of pain, the bad tendency of it upon the whole.[29]

In Chapter 7, he explained that "[t]he general tendency of an act is more or less pernicious, according to the sum total of its consequences: that is, according to the difference between the sum of such as are good, and the sum of such as are evil."[30] Utility for individuals, then, is the net difference between the benefits and costs of actions; among alternative courses of action, the individual will choose that which has the greater sum of benefits over costs.

In subsequent chapters, Bentham discussed the characteristics of pleasure and pain and, in the process, developed a theory much broader in scope than a strict version of deterrence theory[31]—a theory that resembles what a century later would be called rational choice theory in criminology.[32] He stated in Chapter 3 that there are four general sources of pleasure and pain: (1) physical, (2) political, (3) moral or popular, and (4) religious.[33] With respect to crime, an example of physical pleasure would be the feeling of exhilaration or "high" one gets from using drugs; an example of physical pain would be getting shot by a homeowner when trying to break into her house at night. Political pain would include the stock of legal sanctions used by authorities. Examples of the moral or popular pleasure and pain of criminal conduct include, respectively, the sense of prestige and reputation that one might get from some as a result of being involved in crime and the blast of censure and approbation received from more conventional others. Religious pleasure consists of the sense of a rewarded afterlife for good conduct, and the pain consists of the anticipation of damnation.

As one can see, in discussing this very diverse variety of pleasures and pains that ultimately determine the utility of one's actions, Bentham developed a substantially more general theory of behavior in *Introduction to the Principles* than Beccaria did in *On Crimes*. In addition to the pains presented by legal punishments, Bentham's theory includes a host of informal sanctions, imposed by the self and social others, in addition to a wide consideration of the specific pleasures that can be experienced by criminal behavior not under the direct control of legal authorities.[34] In addition to the different types or sources of pain and pleasure, Bentham

[29] *Id.* (emphasis omitted).

[30] *Id.* at 70.

[31] *See generally id.* at 97-130.

[32] *See generally* THE REASONING CRIMINAL: RATIONAL CHOICE PERSPECTIVES ON OFFENDING (Derek B. Cornish & Ronald V. Clarke eds., 1986).

[33] BENTHAM, *supra* note 3, at 25.

[34] *See id.* at 24-42.

argued that there is an important variation in several characteristics—or their elements or dimensions—including intensity, duration, certainty, propinquity, fecundity, and purity.[35] Later, in Chapter 5 of *Introduction to the Principles*, Bentham provided a comprehensive list of the specific kinds of pleasures (the pleasures of the senses, a good reputation, wealth) and pains (physical pains, being poor, having an ill reputation).[36] At the end of Chapter 5, Bentham remarked, with respect to crime specifically, that the inclination to offend consists of a desire to attain the above pleasures and avoid the pains and that the punishment of the offender is inflicted, and is justified in being inflicted, by imposing one or more of the pains.[37] Finally, while it is clear that he had no well-developed understanding of psychology, in Chapter 6 Bentham implied that the pleasures and pains that are the important determinants of utility, and therefore behavior, are those that are seen by the individual and not necessarily those that objectively exist: "[p]ain and pleasure *are produced in men's minds* by the action of certain causes. But the quantity of pleasure and pain runs not uniformly in proportion to the cause; in other words, to the quantity of force exerted by such cause."[38]

In spite of what (for the times) was a fairly well-developed theory that explained the cause of crime, what the reaction or response to crime should be, and how those reactions or responses should be apportioned, when the profession of criminology initially developed, it did not build its foundation upon the works of either Beccaria or Bentham, but on the biological/psychological model of psychiatrists like Pinel, Pritchard, and Rush, who all believed that criminal behavior was more likely to be the result of a pathological mind than anything else and that such a pathology affected only a minority of persons.[39] From an early emphasis on criminality due to individual conditions, such as moral insanity, it was but a short-step to criminal anthropologists' concepts of atavism, degeneration, and feeble-mindedness.[40] This movement of the study of crime from the more philosophical works of Beccaria and Bentham to biological positivism was due to several sources including the growing influence of natural science (Darwin's *On the Origin of Species* was published in 1859[41]), the prestige of the medical profession, and the political advantages of a view of

---

[35] *Id.* at 29-32.

[36] *Id.* at 33-42.

[37] *Id.* at 41.

[38] *Id.* at 43 (emphasis added).

[39] NICOLE RAFTER, THE CRIMINAL BRAIN: UNDERSTANDING BIOLOGICAL THEORIES OF CRIME 19-21 (2008).

[40] *Id.* at 65-70.

[41] CHARLES DARWIN, ON THE ORIGIN OF SPECIES (Penguin 2003) (1859).

crime that attributed its causes to individual pathology rather than some defect of the political or social system.[42] Whatever the appeal of the biological positivists, criminology would turn its back for nearly two centuries on deterrence theory, as well as the more general idea that the motivation to commit crime was something that everyone possessed and that crime, like any other human activity, was rational and motivated by considerations of utility.

B. RESURRECTION OF DETERRENCE THEORY

Over the years, the *Journal of Criminal Law and Criminology* (*Journal*) has played a prominent role in both helping to bury deterrence theory and later reviving it. The general ill-repute in which deterrence theory was held in the field of criminology before the mid-twentieth century was nicely captured in an article by Hans von Hentig that appeared in the *Journal* in 1938.[43] Von Hentig, a former associate editor of the *Journal*, argued that there are large groups of persons who are simply immune to the deterrence-like threats of the law including those motivated by love or maternal instincts, the young and women who tend to be impetuous, those motivated by ideology, the "have-nots," and the feeble-minded.[44] According to von Hentig, Bentham's belief that persons are moved by the consequences of their actions, the pursuit of pleasure and avoidance of pain, "appear[s] to be unreal and simple-minded, when we think of the enormous multiformity and complication of life."[45] To von Hentig, as to most criminologists at the time and even later, something so complicated and serious as crime requires an equally complicated and serious answer.[46] These criminologists believed that, in order to deal with crime on the policy level, one must first take a comprehensive study of the individual offender to discover what factors or forces are operating to produce him. Only through the scientific study of the individual offender can we develop a sense of the complex causal factors in crime, which is necessary before we can begin to deal with them. In making a more general criticism of deterrence theory, von Hentig made a very insightful point that is returned to in the conclusion of this Article. According to von Hentig, deterrence is doomed to fail because the pleasure of committing a criminal act is a "near object" while the cost provided by the legal system is a "long-distance

[42] IAN TAYLOR, PAUL WALTON & JOCK YOUNG, THE NEW CRIMINOLOGY: FOR A SOCIAL THEORY OF DEVIANCE 38-40 (1973).

[43] Hans von Hentig, *The Limits of Deterrence*, 29 J. AM. INST. CRIM. L. & CRIMINOLOGY 555 (1938).

[44] *Id.* at 557-60.

[45] *Id.* at 560.

[46] *Id.* at 561.

danger," very much in the remote future and therefore unable to offset the more immediate advantages of crime.[47]

Two other articles in the *Journal* made arguments conceptually similar to von Hentig's that were in opposition to the use of punishment to deter wrongdoing and secure compliance with rules. In his article entitled "Is Punishment Necessary?," Jackson Toby took a position that was characteristic of many criminologists and sociologists of his time.[48] According to Toby, the use of punishment to create conformity through deterrence is not necessary because "[t]he socialization process prevents most deviant behavior... [and] [o]nly the unsocialized (and therefore amoral) individual fits the model of classical criminology and is deterred from expressing deviant impulses by a nice calculation of pleasures and punishments."[49] While punishment in the Durkheimian sense of strengthening the moral convictions of citizens is necessary, punishment in order to deter cannot hold much promise.[50] Much the same position was taken from a psychological perspective just one year later by James B. Appel and Neil J. Peterson.[51] They argued that psychological learning principles are inconsistent with the idea that punishment could inhibit behavior under normal circumstances.[52] To be effective, they argued, deterrence requires either extreme (and likely cruel) forms of punishment or repeated applications of punishment.[53] In the full spirit of the reigning rehabilitative model of the time, Appel and Peterson concluded that punishment is "essentially an ineffective way to control or to eliminate the behavior of the punished person."[54]

Although adherents were certainly in the minority, not all scholars were dismissive of deterrence theory. In fact, three articles published in the *Journal* were instrumental in keeping the deterrence doctrine intellectually alive until it could be fully revived in the late 1960s. The first of these was by Johannes Andenaes. The *Journal* published his ultimately influential article in 1952, almost two decades after von Hentig's and in the midst of the popularity of the medical model of deviance and the rehabilitation

---

47 *Id.* at 559 (emphasis omitted).

48 Jackson Toby, *Is Punishment Necessary?*, 55 J. CRIM. L., CRIMINOLOGY & POLICE SCI. 332 (1964).

49 *Id.* at 333 (citing ÉMILE DURKHEIM, THE DIVISION OF LABOR IN SOCIETY 89 (1947)).

50 *Id.* at 333-34.

51 James B. Appel & Neil J. Peterson, *What's Wrong with Punishment?*, 56 J. CRIM. L., CRIMINOLOGY & POLICE SCI. 450 (1965).

52 *Id.* at 452-53.

53 *Id.*

54 *Id.* at 453.

model of corrections.[55] In his article, Andenaes argued for what he called the "general preventive effect of punishment."[56] The general preventive effect of punishment includes general deterrence but is much broader than that, also including the moralizing effect that punishment may have and its effect in creating a habit of conformity.[57] Andenaes's perspective was distinctive, however, in its stance against the prevailing popular and scientific winds as embodied in the assertion that punishment could play an important role in securing compliance.[58] He acknowledged that the consideration of the general preventive effects of punishment had, over the years, taken a back seat to the individual preventive effects.[59] The individual preventive effects of punishment include rehabilitation or reformation of the offender as well as incapacitation and specific deterrence.[60] Andenaes also asserted that at least one of the reasons why punishment for general preventive effects was not more popular within the scientific and policy communities was because there was not a sound empirical basis for the proposition that punishment had general deterrent, moralizing, or habituating effects:

> These views on the relationship between general prevention and the magnitude of punishment are built upon abstract reasoning . . . . It must be admitted at once that only very little support for the proposition is to be educed from experience—in the first place because the general-preventive effect is always hard to ascertain, and second because there has never been a systematic gathering of material which could illuminate the question.[61]

At the conclusion of his article, Andenaes simply noted that "the empirical data are still lacking . . . [and] we shall not have firm ground to stand on before a systematic investigation is made into the effect of penal law and its enforcement on the citizen's behavior."[62]

To get a sense of the resistance to Andenaes's efforts to bring forward a discussion of the role of punishment in deterrence in the existing intellectual current of the time, the *American Catholic Sociological Review* published a review of his article wherein the reviewer noted that Andenaes's "approach, which talks of eliminating crime by means of more effective law enforcement and heavier penalties, is at first repugnant to the

---

[55] Johs Andenaes, *General Prevention—Illusion or Reality?*, 43 J. CRIM. L., CRIMINOLOGY & POLICE SCI. 176 (1952).

[56] *Id.* at 177.

[57] *Id.* at 179.

[58] *Id.* at 179-180.

[59] *Id.* at 175.

[60] *Id.* at 180.

[61] *Id.* at 193.

[62] *Id.* at 197.

democratic citizen and smacks of the police state."[63] The reviewer acknowledged that Andenaes may have had a point about the moralizing effects of punishment, but that "the empirical data on crime prevention are still lacking."[64]

The review of Andenaes's article was followed just two years later by an article by John Ball in the *Journal* entitled "The Deterrence Concept in Criminology and Law."[65] Ball too was clearly aware of the fact that most criminologists thought that punishment is archaic and barbaric, that crime is really due to some underlying individual pathology, and that the only way to reduce it is through the rehabilitation of individual offenders.[66] As a result of this concern with reformation, most scholars either ignored deterrence theory or "incorrectly and prematurely dismissed [it] as invalid."[67] Ball's point, much like Andenaes's, was that rather than dismiss deterrence on ideological grounds, there needed to be empirical research conducted so that a scientific evaluation of the theory could be undertaken.[68] Ball went much farther than simply lamenting the absence of an existing empirical foundation for deterrence theory; he articulated a comprehensive research agenda. Two very critical points in that agenda were that it is very likely that any empirical deterrent effect for punishment (1) depends upon the certainty of punishment, and (2) requires an understanding of would-be offenders' perceptions of punishment rather than the objective properties of punishment.[69] As Ball wrote, "A law can have no deterrent influence upon a potential criminal if he is unaware of its existence."[70] These two points would play an important role in the subsequent development of deterrence theory.

In 1965, the *Journal* published the third important article pertaining to deterrence theory; C. Ray Jeffery, who was at the time the Editor of the *Journal*'s Book Review section, penned the article.[71] Entitled "Criminal

---

[63] Joseph G. Green, Jr., Periodical Review, 14 AM. CATHOLIC SOC. REV. 57, 57 (1953). (reviewing Andenaes, *supra* note 55).

[64] *Id.*

[65] John C. Ball, *The Deterrence Concept in Criminology and Law*, 46 J. CRIM. L., CRIMINOLOGY & POLICE SCI. 347 (1955).

[66] *Id.* at 347-48.

[67] *Id.* at 348.

[68] *See* Andenaes, *supra* note 55.

[69] Ball, *supra* note 65, at 351.

[70] *Id.*

[71] C. R. Jeffery, *Criminal Behavior and Learning Theory*, 56 J. CRIM. L., CRIMINOLOGY & POLICE SCI. 294, 294 (1965). A paper by Schmideberg published in the *Journal* five years before Jeffery's also presented a staunch defense for the use of punishment for deterrent purposes. Melitta Schmideberg, *The Offender's Attitude Toward Punishment*, 51 J. CRIM. L., CRIMINOLOGY & POLICE SCI. 328 (1960).

Behavior and Learning Theory," the article's primary focus was the author's interest in crafting a learning theory of criminal behavior that drew upon the work of Edwin Sutherland and B. F. Skinner.[72] Since punishment is an integral part of operant learning theory, Jeffery spent some time discussing its role in criminal behavior.[73] He argued that the experimental evidence that was accumulating in psychology supported the position that punishment (or at least its certainty) can play a constructive role in deterring criminal behavior.[74] There are, however, three features about legal punishment that prevent it from being an even more effective deterrent: (1) legal punishments are generally very uncertain, (2) they are only imposed long after the crime has been committed and so have low celerity, and (3) the pleasures of crime are immediate and so carry greater weight than the delayed costs of crime in the would-be offender's calculus.[75] In a point that is returned to at the end of this Article, Jeffery noted that an unfortunate feature of punishment and criminal behavior is that "[t]here are no aversive stimuli in the environment *at that moment*."[76]

C. MODERN REVIVAL OF DETERRENCE THEORY

Although the classical school's advocacy of deterrence theory had come dangerously close to being scientifically discredited and the best that one could say of it was that it was politely ignored by both academics and penal reformers, it continued to have its group of supporters. Influential articles published in the *Journal* and a few other social scientific journals and law reviews kept the belief in the deterrent effect of punishment alive, if only on life-support.[77] Rejection of the deterrence doctrine seemed to be based more upon ideological than empirical grounds as both friend and foe of deterrence noted that the empirical base was exceedingly thin.[78]

In spite of the neglect and criticism heaped upon deterrence theory by generations of criminologists and other scholars interested in crime, two articles appeared in 1968 that revived interest in deterrence theory—one by

---

72 Jeffery, *supra* note 71, at 294.

73 *Id.* at 294-295.

74 *Id.* at 299.

75 *Id.*

76 *Id.* (emphasis added).

77 *See generally* Daniel S. Nagin, *Criminal Deterrence Research at the Outset of the Twenty-First Century*, *in* 23 CRIME & JUSTICE: A REVIEW OF RESEARCH 1 (Michael Tonry ed., 1998); Raymond Paternoster, *The Deterrent Effect of the Perceived Certainty and Severity of Punishment: A Review of the Evidence and Issues*, 4 JUST. Q. 173 (1987).

78 There was, however, excellent empirical research on the deterrent effect of capital punishment on homicide rates. *See* THORSTEN SELLIN, THE DEATH PENALTY (1959). Even those who argued that capital punishment was not an effective deterrent acknowledged that this does not necessarily mean that other types of punishment are not capable of deterring.

an economist and one by a sociologist. The article by economist Gary Becker was premised on an understanding of crime that was similar to Bentham's,[79] while sociologist Jack P. Gibbs's article drew more from Beccaria.[80] Both articles ignited great interest in empirically testing some of the hypotheses of deterrence theory. After Gibbs's and Becker's articles, there were scores of empirical studies of the effect of sanctions and sanction threats, and that scholarly effort continues to the present day.[81] At long last, the battle between deterrence and other possible state responses to crime was waged, at least in part, on empirical grounds.

Becker made an explicit point of rejecting existing theories of crime that presumed that offenders possess some sort of extraordinary motivation based upon strain or psychological abnormalities and, instead, argued that crime was due to rational self-interest and could be understood like any other kind of economic activity: "[A] useful theory of criminal behavior can dispense with special theories of anomie, psychological inadequacies, or inheritance of special traits and simply extend the economist's usual analysis of choice."[82] The economist's "usual analysis of choice" was a rational choice model of criminal behavior that

> assumes that a person commits an offense if the expected utility to them exceeds the utility he could get by using his time and other resources at other activities . . . . Some persons become "criminals," therefore, not because their basic motivation differs from that of other persons, but because their benefits and costs differ.[83]

Becker argued that, in the expected utility model, the decision to offend is made up of the costs and benefits of both crime and non-crime.[84] The costs include the formal legal punishments available for a crime, and Becker noted that the certainty of legal penalties are more important than their severity.[85] Though obviously less sophisticated than Becker, Bentham's theory of crime contained many of the same principles: criminal behavior requires no special motivation; behavior is a product of the utility of actions; the utility of an action is the net difference between the benefits and

---

[79] Gary S. Becker, *Crime and Punishment: An Economic Approach*, 76 J. POL. ECON. 169, 170 (1968).

[80] Jack P. Gibbs, *Crime, Punishment, and Deterrence*, 48 SOUTHWESTERN SOC. SCI. Q. 515, 515-16 (1968).

[81] *See generally* JACK P. GIBBS, CRIME, PUNISHMENT, AND DETERRENCE (1975); FRANKLIN E. ZIMRING & GORDON J. HAWKINS, DETERRENCE: THE LEGAL THREAT IN CRIME CONTROL (1973); Nagin, *supra* note 77; Paternoster, *supra* note 77.

[82] Becker, *supra* note 79, at 170.

[83] *Id.* at 176.

[84] *Id.* at 177-78.

[85] *Id.* at 178.

costs of that action; other things being equal, the action with the greatest utility will be selected among alternatives.[86]

Gibbs's article that same year was much more Beccarian in that it focused exclusively on the role of punishment in criminal behavior and adopted a specific theory of criminal deterrence by legal sanctions rather than the more general expected utility theories of Bentham and Becker.[87] Gibbs was less interested in discussing notions of utility and the diverse benefits and costs of crime than he was in the more specific question of whether or not actual punishment, implemented by authorities, was effective in reducing crime. Gibbs also initiated an agenda of empirical research on the subject—something that had been missing throughout the previous two centuries—that examined the relationship between the certainty and severity of punishment in individual states and their crime rates.[88] The importance of Gibbs's article is that it provided an empirical example of how deterrence research could be done, and his finding of an inverse relationship between the certainty of punishment in a state and the homicide rate provided some support for those who believed that there was something to the deterrence argument. Gibbs created convincing operational definitions of the certainty and severity of punishment for homicide across the several states and argued that if the deterrence doctrine was valid, then states where the certainty and severity of punishment were higher would have lower homicide rates.[89] This is precisely what he found, providing empirical evidence that perhaps punishment is effective in generating compliance with the laws.[90] Gibbs's confirmation of general deterrence initiated a veritable cottage industry of deterrence research among sociologists and criminologists.[91] Subsequent research examined the deterrence of crimes other than homicide, entertained new measures of the certainty and severity of punishment, and pursued nagging methodological issues such as possible feedback effects between crime and punishment.[92] By the early to mid-1970s, empirical and theoretical work in deterrence was a vibrant field, and the publication of two important books, Zimring and Hawkins's *Deterrence: The Legal Threat in Crime Control*

---

[86] *See generally* BENTHAM, *supra* note 3.

[87] Gibbs, *supra* note 80.

[88] *Id.* at 523-25.

[89] *Id.* at 519-20.

[90] *Id.* at 524-25.

[91] For descriptions of this research, see GIBBS, *supra* note 81; ZIMRING & HAWKINS, *supra* note 81; Nagin, *supra* note 77.

[92] Paternoster, *supra* note 77. *See generally* Nagin, *supra* note 77.

and Gibbs's *Crime, Punishment, and Deterrence,* greatly helped to solidify interest in deterrence.[93]

Two important theoretical developments in deterrence work occurred later in the mid-1980s. One development was that scholars began to understand deterrence theory as a theory about the *perception* of sanction threats and the relationship between those perceptions and self-reported behavior.[94] This stood in contrast to research and theorizing from the mid-1960s to the late 1970s, which mainly dealt with the objective properties of punishment.[95] The charge began when Geerken and Gove developed a perceptual theory of deterrence,[96] after which scholars began to understand deterrence as a social psychological theory of threat communication and to realize that if the objective properties of punishment are important, it is only because they affect crime through individual perceptions.[97] The restatement of deterrence as a perceptual theory, and therefore a theory at the individual or micro-level, led to another outpouring of deterrence research that began in the mid-1970s and continues to the present day.[98]

In addition to a conception of deterrence that emphasized a perceptual dimension, a second important theoretical development in deterrence theory occurred in the mid-1980s. Traditionally, deterrence theory had been restricted to the proposition that the imposition or the threat of the imposition of *formal legal sanctions* was related to crime.[99] The definition of deterrence provided by Gibbs is a perfect example of this: "Deterrence can be thought of as the omission of an act as a response to the perceived risk and fear of punishment for *contrary* behavior. Since the deterrence

---

[93] *See* GIBBS, *supra* note 81; ZIMRING & HAWKINS, *supra* note 81.

[94] GIBBS, *supra* note 81, at 115.

[95] *See, e.g.*, Gibbs, *supra* note 80; Charles H. Logan, *General Deterrent Effects of Imprisonment*, 51 SOC. FORCES 64 (1972); Charles R. Tittle, *Crime Rates and Legal Sanctions*, 16 SOC. PROBS. 409 (1969).

[96] Michael R. Geerken & Walter R. Gove, *Deterrence: Some Theoretical Considerations*, 9 LAW & SOC'Y REV. 497 (1975); *see also* Gordon P. Waldo & Theodore G. Chiricos, *Perceived Penal Sanction and Self-Reported Criminality: A Neglected Approach to Deterrence Research*, 19 SOC. PROBS. 522 (1972).

[97] GIBBS, *supra* note 81, at 15-16.

[98] *See, e.g.*, Waldo & Chiricos, *supra* note 96; Linda Saltzman et al., *Deterrent and Experiential Effects: The Problem of Causal Order in Perceptual Deterrence Research*, 28 J. RES. CRIME & DELINQ. 172 (1982); Maynard L. Erickson, Jack P. Gibbs & Gary F. Jensen, *The Deterrence Doctrine and the Perceived Certainty of Legal Punishments*, 42 AM. SOC. REV. 305 (1977); Thomas Loughran et al., *Reassessing the Certainty Effect in Deterrence Theory: Insights From Prospect Theory* (Jan. 25, 2010) (unpublished manuscript, on file with author).

[99] *See* GIBBS, *supra* note 81, at 2.

doctrine focuses on crime, the acts in question are violations of criminal laws and the punishments are 'legal.'"[100]

Later, the conceptual boundaries of deterrence theory were gradually expanded. In 1986, Williams and Hawkins argued that any inhibition of crime that was brought about directly or indirectly by the threat of legal sanctions should be considered part of the deterrence process.[101] They drew a distinction between punishment that is based upon the criminal act itself and punishment that is based upon any legal reaction to the criminal act.[102] For example, if I refrain from drinking and driving because I fear that my spouse will think less of me if she finds out that I have been drinking and driving, my inhibition is not due to deterrence but to an extralegal process (social censure or embarrassment). However, if I refrain from drinking and driving because I fear that if I am *arrested* my spouse will think less of me because of the arrest, then since her disapproval is triggered by the arrest and not the act itself, my avoidance of drinking and driving is to be considered an instance of deterrence. Williams and Hawkins essentially added a new cluster of right-hand-side variables to the deterrence equation so that it included inhibition due to the threat of legal punishment, and inhibition due to the threat of social censure, commitment costs (fear of losing my job if arrested), and any self-imposed costs (guilt if I were arrested).

Around the same time, rational choice models of crime were being developed in criminology,[103] and these models were decidedly inspired by both Bentham and Becker in that they included the full range of anticipated benefits and costs of crime.[104] In content they were very much what Bentham described, and they were called subjective expected utility models because they were predicated on the perceived or subjectively understood costs and benefits of criminal offending,[105] something that Ball argued for three decades earlier in the *Journal*.[106] At this point, a pure deterrence model was blended into a more general rational choice model of crime in which anticipated legal costs are simply one of several factors considered by rational and reasoning would-be offenders.

---

[100] *Id.* at 2.

[101] Kirk R. Williams & Richard Hawkins, *Perceptual Research on General Deterrence: A Critical Review*, 20 LAW & SOC'Y REV 545, 561-66 (1986).

[102] *Id.* at 558-61.

[103] *See* CORNISH & CLARKE, *supra* note 32.

[104] Pamela Lattimore & Ann Witte, *Models of Decision Making Under Uncertainty: The Criminal Choice*, *in* THE REASONING CRIMINAL 129, *supra* note 32, at 131-34.

[105] *Id.*

[106] Ball, *supra* note 65, at 351.

With this basic history of deterrence theory completed, the next section provides a summary of the major hypotheses and research questions posed by the theory. This is followed by a brief examination of the existing empirical support for each of the hypotheses.

III. BASIC PRINCIPLES OF DETERRENCE THEORY

Deterrence theory is a theory of crime that presumes that human beings are rational enough to consider the consequences of their actions and to be influenced by those consequences.[107] Generally, as self-interested and relatively free agents, human beings are influenced by the benefits and costs of their actions. Virtually any human activity can be understood as resulting in both benefits and costs, and persons are presumed to be rational enough to weigh the costs and benefits of any action and any reasonable alternative courses of action. The behavior with the greatest advantage of benefits over costs (the one resulting in greater utility) is presumed to be the behavior with the highest probability of being acted upon. Deterrence theorists presume, therefore, that human beings are self-interested, rational, and reasoning creatures.[108] An implication of this view is that an innate propensity to commit crime is not possessed by some people but not by others (the Positive School's notion of "differentiation" between criminals and non-criminals)[109] but instead resides in everyone.[110] Since we are all motivated by self-interest, we all have the capacity to commit crime when the benefits of crime exceed the costs. Similarly, we are all motivated to go to college or get married if the benefits of post-secondary education and marriage are thought to be greater than the costs. In other words, crime is no different than other behavior and criminals are no different than non-criminals—what differs across people are their assessments of the costs and benefits of different lines of action.[111]

As a human activity, crime comes with its own stock of benefits and costs. As suggested above, the decision to commit crime is no different than the decision to go to college or to get married—it is made by reasonable, rational agents who are self-interested and select behaviors that provide more rewards than costs. This means that crime does not have to be explained by any extraordinary motivation—or any motivation at all—

[107] DAVID M. KENNEDY, DETERRENCE AS CRIME PREVENTION: RECONSIDERING THE PROSPECT OF SANCTION 15-23 (2008); ZIMRING & HAWKINS, *supra* note 81, at 106-08.

[108] *See generally* BENTHAM, *supra* note 3; GIBBS, *supra* note 81; ZIMRING & HAWKINS, *supra* note 81.

[109] *See* TAYLOR ET AL., *supra* note 42, at 24-26.

[110] *Id.*

[111] Lattimore & Witte, *supra* note 104.

other than self-interest.[112] Most of the time, people are not compelled to commit criminal acts[113] but do so when the expected benefits outweigh the expected gains. A key term in deterrence theory, therefore, is the notion of *utility*, which simply refers to the total satisfaction that is derived from a course of action or consumption.[114] A very simple equation to express the basic premise of deterrence theory is that an individual will decide to offend if:

$$\text{U(Crime)} = p_1 \text{ (Benefits of Crime)} + p_2 \text{ (Costs of Crime)} + p_3 \text{ (Benefits of Non-Crime)} + p_4 \text{ (Costs of Non-Crime)} \qquad (1.1)$$

This equation states that the utility of crime is equal to the sum of the benefits of crime (easy money, the "high" of drug use, prestige, or "rep"), the costs of crime (getting arrested, getting convicted, going to jail, loss of family respect, not seeing one's children while in jail or prison), the benefits of non-crime (a steady and safe income from a job, physical security from not being shot or falling ill from ingesting bad drugs), and the costs of non-crime (low wages, feeling like a failure from a low-prestige job). The p's reflect the probability of each event occurring. The utility of crime, then, is determined not only by the outcomes, but by the probability of those outcomes.

One of the costs of crime is the possible legal punishment, including being arrested for committing the act, getting convicted of the crime, and being subjected to some kind of punishment as a result of conviction (jail, probation, prison, or, in some jurisdictions for some crimes, death). Deterrence theorists presume that punishment by the legal system will increase the cost of—and therefore inhibit—crime.[115] There are three properties of legal punishment that are related to its cost, the (1) certainty, (2) severity, and (3) celerity (or swiftness) of punishment. Other things being equal, a legal punishment is more costly when it is more certain (more likely than not to be a consequence of crime), severe (greater in magnitude), and swift (the punishment arrives sooner rather than later after the offense). This leads to the three key hypotheses that can be deduced

[112] BENTHAM, *supra* note 3, at 1-2.

[113] The fact that most crime can be explained as rational and self-interested behavior does not mean that all crime has to be so explained in order for the theory to be valid. Some crimes are committed by people who are under the influence of strong compulsions or emotional forces that co-opt or minimize rational thinking. *See* Daniel Ariely & George Loewenstein, *The Heat of the Moment: The Effect of Sexual Arousal on Sexual Decision Making*, 19 J. BEHAV. DECISION MAKING 87 (2006) (showing the effect of emotions on decision making); George Loewenstein, *Out of Control: Visceral Influences on Behavior*, 65 ORGANIZATIONAL BEHAV. & HUM. DECISION PROCESSES 272 (1996) (same).

[114] BENTHAM, *supra* note 3, at 2-3.

[115] GIBBS, *supra* note 81, at 5, ZIMRING & HAWKINS, *supra* note 81, at 1-9.

from deterrence theory, which have served to guide empirical research over the past fifty years:[116]

H_1: The greater the certainty of legal punishment, the lower the crime rate.

H_2: The greater the severity of legal punishment, the lower the crime rate.

H_3: The greater the celerity of legal punishment, the lower the crime rate.

The important deterrence variables are, then, certainty, severity, and celerity. There are two levels of these punishment properties, an objective level and a subjective (or perceptual) level. In general, the criminal justice system is premised in part on the expectation that having rigorously enforced laws and appropriate penalties that are applied with reasonable swiftness will lower crime by deterring punished persons from offending again and deterring would-be offenders from committing new crimes. How certainly, severely, and swiftly a jurisdiction *actually responds* to crime constitutes the objective properties of punishment.[117] For example, if ten of every one hundred armed robbers are arrested in City X, then the objective certainty of arrest for armed robbery is 0.10. If the average prison term imposed by judges for those convicted of armed robbery is seven years, then one indicator of the objective severity of punishment is seven years in prison.

A legal jurisdiction can hope to reduce crime by increasing the number of law enforcement officers on the street, thereby increasing the certainty with which an offender would be caught for misdeeds.[118] This was the intention of President Clinton's effort in 1994 to add 100,000 new police officers by the year 2000.[119] Increasing the number of police officers on the street was an attempt to increase the *objective* certainty of punishment. A jurisdiction can also attempt to reduce crime by increasing the penalty or punishment for an act even without affecting its certainty. For example, many states have passed felony firearm laws that enhance the severity of punishment for a felony offense if the offender uses or threatens to use a firearm.[120] The purpose of such laws is to increase the cost of the crime and deter would-be offenders from using guns when committing crimes.

Of course, even Bentham was aware that the objective properties of punishment work to inhibit crimes by increasing how the certainty, severity,

---

116 GIBBS, *supra* note 81, at 5.

117 *Id.* at 8.

118 *See generally id.*; KENNEDY, *supra* note 107; MARK A.R. KLEIMAN, WHEN BRUTE FORCE FAILS: HOW TO HAVE LESS CRIME AND LESS PUNISHMENT (2009).

119 William N. Evans & Emily G. Owens, *COPS and Crime*, 91 J. PUB. ECON. 181, 182 (2007).

120 KENNEDY, *supra* note 107, at 10, 13.

and celerity of punishments are perceived by would-be offenders.[121] In other words, legislators establish and modify the objective properties of punishment with the expectation that the *perceptual properties of punishment* will be affected. The perceptual properties of punishment are those properties that are *thought to exist* in a jurisdiction by its population of offenders and would-be offenders.[122] For example, in the hypothetical jurisdiction above in which ten out of one hundred armed robbers were arrested, the objective certainty of arrest for armed robbery was 0.10. It may be, however, that would-be armed robbers think that the probability of being caught and arrested if they commit armed robbery is much higher (0.25) or much lower (0.05) than what it actually is. Similarly, a state may pass a felony firearm law, enhancing the penalty for felonies committed with a gun, hoping to reduce the proportion of such crimes. The state would pass such a law with the expectation that the increased punishment that could be inflicted under the law will be recognized by the public, including would-be felons.

Deterrence theorists presume that there is a strong positive correlation between the objective and subjective (perceptual) properties of punishment. The relationship between these two properties of punishment cannot, however, be taken for granted. This relationship is first of all empirical, and the relationship between the two likely falls far short of unity. Moreover, the subjective properties of punishment are likely affected by things other than the objective properties of punishment. Since the objective properties of punishment matter for deterrence theory only to the extent that the perceptual properties are affected, the magnitude and nature of the relationship between the objective and perceptual properties of punishment is an important consideration for deterrence theory and public policy.[123] At its core, therefore, deterrence theory is a social psychological theory of threat communication in which the causal chain runs from the objective properties of punishment through the perceptual properties of punishment to crime.

The causal process of deterrence is illustrated in Figure 1. The dashed line connecting the objective properties of punishment to crime indicates that crime control policies are frequently manipulated to reduce crime and operate under the assumption that the perceptual properties of punishment will change as well, without explicit empirical proof that they have changed. The important conclusion to be drawn from Figure 1 is that in

[121] BENTHAM, *supra* note 3, at 43.

[122] GIBBS, *supra* note 81, at 7.

[123] *Id.* at 115.

Figure 1

Causal Process of Deterrence

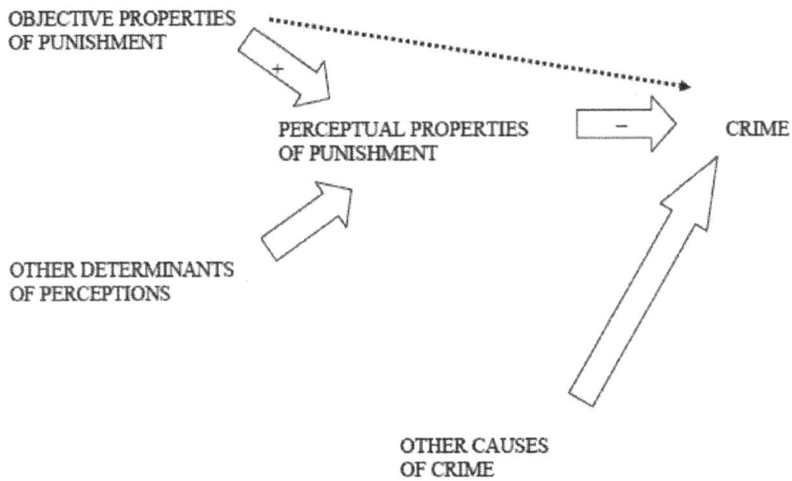

order for deterrence to occur, a lot must happen. For an increase in the number of police officers to affect the crime rate, for example, there must be a perception among the class of would-be offenders that the certainty of punishment has increased, and this increase must be connected to their refraining from crime. Similarly, whether or not the certainty of enforcement or punishment increases with the use of incarceration, it cannot have a deterrent effect unless it affects the perceptions of those who are contemplating offending and those intentions to offend are altered by the increased risk of sanctions.

From the causal schema in Figure 1, one can deduce some more precise deterrence hypotheses that can be subject to empirical tests:

> H_1: Other things being equal, there should be an inverse relationship between the objective properties of punishment (certainty, severity, celerity) and the crime rate.
>
> H_2: Other things being equal, there should be a positive relationship between the objective properties of punishment (certainty, severity, celerity) and the perceptual properties.
>
> H_3: Other things being equal, there should be an inverse relationship between the perceptual properties of punishment (certainty, severity, celerity) and measures of criminal offending.

Figure 1 illustrates the causal process assumed by deterrence theory at the most general level. I use this model as the basic framework for discussing the empirical literature pertaining to deterrence theory

The causal process of deterrence is made up of three distinct links. The first link is that between the objective properties of punishment and crime rates. It is presumed that the law enforcement and punishment policies of legal jurisdictions are inversely related to crime levels in those jurisdictions.[124] If this relationship can be demonstrated empirically, it can be attributed to a deterrent effect only if: (a) there is a link between criminal justice practices and perceptions of those practices on the part of offenders and would-be offenders and (b) the reduction in crime is not due to some other mechanism (such as the incapacitation of high-rate offenders). Research on the link between the objective properties of punishment and crime rates assumes, but does not demonstrate, that the second link—that between the objective and perceptual properties of punishment—exists.[125] The third link in the process is that between the perceived properties of punishment and some measure of self-reported offending.

There is a substantial volume of existing research about the possible deterrent value of various criminal justice policies (policing practices, sentencing, and prison) and aggregate levels of crime, and between perceptions of sanction threats and offending at the individual level.[126] There is much less research, however, on the relationship between the objective and perceptual properties of punishment.[127]

IV. THE RELATIONSHIP BETWEEN OBJECTIVE SANCTIONS AND CRIME RATES

The first hypothesis states that there should be an inverse relationship between the objective properties of legal sanctions and crime rates. More specifically, increasing the certainty, severity, and celerity of legal sanctions should result in lower levels of crime. A very good point to begin this analysis of deterrence is long-term crime trends in the United States. Figure 2 shows the rate of property and violent index crimes for the United States over the period from 1962 to 2008. It reveals that, from the early 1960s until the 1980s, there was a steady increase in both property and violent index crimes. From the late 1970s until about the mid-1980s, both rates of crime slightly declined. There followed several years of increases in crime, particularly for violent index offenses, with both rates reaching

---

124 *Id.* at 5.

125 *See* Nagin, *supra* note 77, at 26

126 KENNEDY, *supra* note 118, at 9-14

127 Nagin, *supra* note 77, at 5-6.

peaks in 1991. After 1991, however, there was a consistent and substantial decline in the rate of both property and violent crime up to the year 2000—what has become known as "the great crime drop."[128] Both property and violent crime rates continued to decline in the years leading up to 2008, but at a much slower rate. The decline in crime over the period from 1990 to 2008 was very gradual and consistent, but also remarkable in its cumulative magnitude. By 2008, the rate of violent crime was down about 66% from its level in 1992, while the property crime rate had declined by about 53%. This decline in crime occurred across all regions of the country, in both urban and rural areas, and for all index crime categories.[129] Quite literally, the bottom fell out of crime. In trying to account for this dramatic and long-term decline in crime, it is imperative to examine the criminal justice system and determine whether changes in deterrence-related policies might have had a hand creating the decline. A couple of suspects come readily to mind—the police and the use of imprisonment.

Figure 2

Property and Violent Crime Rate in the United States, 1962-2008

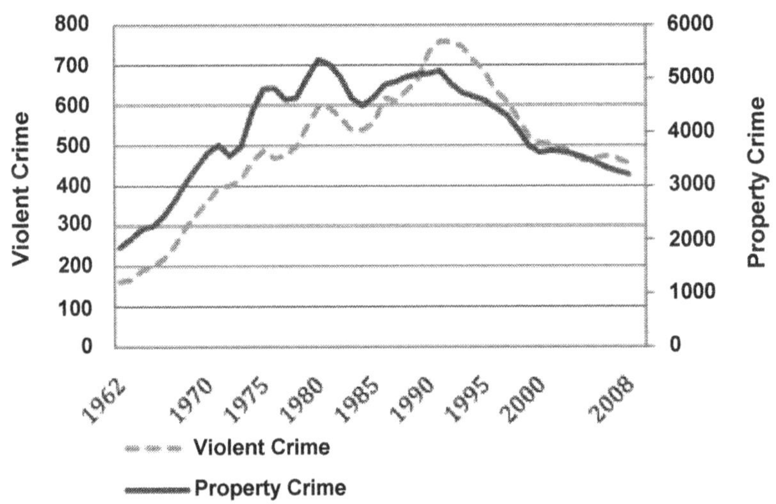

Source: Uniform Crime Reports.

[128] ALFRED BLUMSTEIN & JOEL WALLMAN, THE CRIME DROP IN AMERICA 1-12 (2000).

[129] UNIFORM CRIME REPORTING PROGRAM, DEP'T OF JUSTICE, CRIME IN THE UNITED STATES—2001: SECTION 2: CRIME INDEX OFFENSES REPORTED 64 tbl.1 (2002), *available at* http://www.fbi.gov/ucr/cius_01/01crime2.pdf. *See generally* FRANKLIN E. ZIMRING, THE GREAT AMERICAN CRIME DECLINE (2007).

A. THE ROLE OF THE POLICE IN DETERRENCE

In 1994, President Clinton signed the Violent Crime Control and Law Enforcement Act, which initiated many policies aimed at increasing the deterrent bite of the law, including new firearms restrictions, tougher sentencing laws, and a plan to put 100,000 new police officers on the street.[130] There is evidence that, as a result of federal funding, there was a noticeable increase in the number and per capita rate of police officers in the United States beginning in the early 1990s.[131] Although it is difficult to say for sure, one estimate indicated that there was an increase of approximately 50,000 to 60,000 police officers in the United States (a per capita expansion of about 14%).[132] The intended effect of putting more police officers on the streets was to increase the objective probability or certainty of arrest, with a subsequent deterrent effect on the crime rate. In addition to a sheer increase in numbers, however, police began experimenting with more targeted strategies of enforcement in the 1990s. They started using technology to identify geographic areas of high crime or "hot spots," and they engaged in "crackdowns" that targeted particular kinds of crime, such as drug dealing and weapons offenses, with enhanced enforcement.[133] It is possible that the rather dramatic decrease in crime observed in the United States since the 1990s was due to the combination of more police and better policing.

With respect to the role of the police, many scholars have concluded—although there is some dispute about this—that at least some of the decline in crime rates can be attributed to an increase in the number of police and the increased certainty of punishment associated with that increase.[134] That an increase in police presence would have the effect of producing some reduction in crime can be anticipated by previous research that showed a connection between the two. James Q. Wilson and Barbara Boland conducted one of the first comprehensive studies of the general effect of police behavior on crime rates.[135] They examined the effect of aggressive

[130] Pub. L. No. 103-322, 108 Stat. 1796 (1994).

[131] BRIAN A. REAVES & MATTHEW J. HICKMAN, BUREAU OF JUSTICE STATISTICS, U.S. DEP'T OF JUSTICE, POLICE DEPARTMENTS IN LARGE CITIES, 1990-2000 (2002).

[132] Steven D. Levitt, *Understanding Why Crime Fell in the 1990s: Four Factors That Explain the Decline and Six That Do Not*, 18 J. ECON. PERSPS. 163, 177 (2004).

[133] Christopher S. Koper & Evan Mayo-Wilson, *Police Crackdowns on Illegal Gun Carrying: A Systematic Review of Their Impact on Gun Crime*, 2 J. EXPERIMENTAL CRIMINOLOGY 227, 228-51 (2006); Leavitt, *supra* note 132, at 172.

[134] *See* JOHN ECK & EDWARD R. MAGUIRE, *Have Changes in Policing Reduced Violent Crime?: An Assessment of the Evidence*, *in* THE CRIME DROP IN AMERICA 207 (Alfred Blumstein & Joel Wallman eds., 2000).

[135] James Q. Wilson & Barbara Boland, *The Effect of the Police on Crime*, 12 LAW & SOC'Y REV. 367 (1978).

police patrolling practices (having patrol units on the street stopping cars and issuing moving citations) on robbery rates in thirty-five American cities.[136] Consistent with the expected deterrent effect of increased police activity, they found that robbery rates across cities were inversely related to the arrest ratios for robberies—in cities in which a higher proportion of robberies resulted in an arrest, the robbery rate was lower.[137] In addition, they found that the arrest ratio for robbery was higher in those cities that employed more aggressive police patrolling practices.[138] The authors concluded that more police cars out on the street "doing something," such as issuing citations, increased their visibility, creating a higher certainty and severity of punishment (as evidenced by higher arrest ratios), which in turn is related to lower crime rates.[139]

Robert J. Sampson and Jacqueline Cohen replicated Wilson and Boland's work in a study of all 171 U.S. cities with populations greater than 100,000 in 1980.[140] Sampson and Cohen examined the relationship between aggressive policing (defined as the number of arrests per police officer for disorderly conduct and driving under the influence) and robbery and burglary rates. Similar to Wilson and Boland, they found that police aggressiveness was associated with increased levels of arrest certainty for both robbery and burglary.[141] These two sets of findings suggest that what the police do can affect the objective certainty of punishment.

Thomas B. Marvell and Carlisle E. Moody and Steven D. Levitt conducted two additional studies about the deterrent effect of sheer police presence. In both studies, the researchers examined the relationship between the number of police officers per capita (in forty-nine U.S. states and fifty-six large cities during the period from 1973 to 1992 for Marvell and Moody, and in fifty-nine U.S. cities from 1970 to 1992 for Levitt) and measures of serious felony crime rates.[142] Consistent with deterrence theory, Marvell and Moody found a significant inverse relationship between the number of police officers and state-level homicide, robbery, and burglary rates.[143] At the city level, a deterrent effect was found for total

---

[136] *Id.* at 372-74.

[137] *Id.* at 375-76.

[138] *Id.* at 378.

[139] *Id.*

[140] Robert J. Sampson & Jacqueline Cohen, *Deterrent Effects of the Police on Crime: A Replication and Theoretical Extension*, 22 LAW & SOC'Y REV. 163, 169 (1988).

[141] *Id.* at 175-83.

[142] Thomas B. Marvell & Carlisle E. Moody, *Specification Problems, Police Levels, and Crime Rates*, 34 CRIMINOLOGY 609, 623 (1996); Steven D. Levitt, *Using Electoral Cycles in Police Hiring to Estimate the Effect of Police on Crime*, 87 AM. ECON. REV. 270, 271 (1997).

[143] Marvell & Moody, *supra* note 142, at 630.

crimes, homicide, robbery, burglary, larceny, and auto theft. Moreover, the magnitude of the effects were non-trivial; they estimated that each additional police officer resulted in a reduction of about four crimes at the state level and twenty-four crimes at the city level.[144] Similarly, Levitt found that an increase in the number of police reduced crime by an average of approximately 5% to 8% across different crime types—with a greater effect for violent than property crimes.[145] With a different identification strategy than that used in his earlier paper, Levitt found, in a city-level data set which included 122 cities and covered the years from 1975 to 1995, that the number of police officers reduced both the violent and property crime rate by approximately 5%.[146]

There are, then, empirical grounds for the belief that at least some of the crime drop since the 1990s was due to the increase in the number of police officers. New York City experienced the largest drop in crime for any major U.S. city over this time period, with declines that were about twice the national average; it also experienced a uniquely dramatic increase in the number of police officers.[147] Zimring noted that in the ten-year period from 1990 to 2000, New York City had a 23% increase in the number of police per 100,000 population, compared with only a 2.6% increase in police per capita in nine of the other largest U.S. cities.[148] The New York Police Department (NYPD) also modified its style of policing during that decade, introducing the COMPSTAT management/organization system, which promised a more rationally targeted allocation of police resources. There were other changes to the way the NYPD did its police work during this period including a "zero tolerance" policy with respect to minor offending.[149] It was believed that more certain and severe enforcement of public drunkenness, littering, panhandling, and other public order laws would have a broader deterrent effect by serving notice that the police were vigilant about all crime. Given the "stew" of many changes in policing undergone by the NYPD during that time period, it is exceedingly difficult to separate any unique sources of deterrence.[150] Nevertheless, there is some evidence that police size and strategy had some deterrent

[144] *Id.* at 632.

[145] Steven D. Levitt, *supra* note 142, at 280-83 tbl.5 (1997).

[146] Steven D. Levitt, Reply, *Using Electoral Cycles in Police Hiring to Estimate the Effect of Police on Crime: Reply*, 92 AM. ECON. REV.1244, 1245, 1248-49 tbls.3 & 4 (2002).

[147] *See* ZIMRING, *supra* note 129, at 137 fig.6.1, 145 fig.6.5, 149 fig.6.7.

[148] *See id.* at 149 fig.6.7.

[149] *Id.* at 149-52.

[150] *Id.* at 156-58.

impact on crime, although the magnitude of that impact is very difficult to gauge.[151]

In one study, Hope Corman and H. Naci Mocan examined serious felony crime rates (murder, robbery, burglary, motor vehicle theft) in New York City during the period from 1970 to 1996 and how changes in those rates reflected changes in the monthly number of arrests and the number of police officers in the NYPD.[152] Consistent with a deterrent effect, they found that murders, robberies, burglaries, and thefts of motor vehicles significantly declined in response to increases in the arrest rate for each crime, and that robberies and burglaries declined with increases in the number of police officers.[153] Rosenfeld and his colleagues examined whether COMPSTAT had an impact on New York City homicide rates over the 1992-2001 period.[154] They concluded that the decline in both general homicides and gun-related homicides in New York City did not deviate from the average decline experienced in other cities, indicating that those decreases were not likely due to the introduction of COMPSTAT.[155] However, they did not analyze whether the general decline in crime in New York City since 2001 was due to COMPSTAT.[156]

A few studies have looked specifically at whether and how much of the crime decline in the 1990s in the United States could be attributed to more police officers. These additional hires were due to federal funding from the 1994 Crime Control Act through the COPS program.[157] Evans and Owens examined both the hiring of new police officers and the effect of those newly hired officers on city-level crime rates.[158] Using annual data from 1990 to 2001 from 2,074 cities (each with a population over 10,000), they found that the more officers that were added to city police departments, the lower the rates for all seven index offenses.[159] The reduction in crime was statistically significant for auto thefts, burglaries, robberies, and aggravated assaults and was marginally significant for murder.[160] Levitt estimated that the COPS program increased the number

---

[151] *Id.* at 168.

[152] Hope Corman & H. Naci Mocan, *A Time-Series Analysis of Crime, Deterrence, and Drug Abuse in New York City*, 90 AM. ECON. REV. 584, 586-87 (2000).

[153] *Id.* at 595-601.

[154] Richard Rosenfeld et al., *Did* Ceasefire, Compstat, *and* Exile *Reduce Homicide?*, 4 CRIMINOLOGY & PUB. POL'Y 419, 428 (2005).

[155] *Id.* at 431, 432 fig.1.

[156] *See id.* at 431-33.

[157] Evans & Owens, *supra* note 119, at 181.

[158] *Id.*

[159] *Id.* at 195-99 tbls.5 & 6.

[160] *Id.* at 195.

of police officers per capita by 14% during the 1990s.[161] He further estimated that the increase in the number of police during this time period was responsible for a 5% to 6% reduction in crime, accounting for between one-fifth and one-tenth of the overall drop in crime.[162]

To be fair, not all scholars agree with Levitt's assessment. John Eck and Edward Maguire published an extensive review of the existing research on the relationship between the number of police officers and crime rates and whether police force size was related to the downturn in crime.[163] Two interesting things came out of their review. First, they were struck with the general lack of quality in a great deal of this research. Out of forty-one studies that they identified as helpful in dealing with the issue, they found only nine that dealt rigorously enough with methodological problems to come to a confident conclusion.[164] Second, based upon their review of these nine studies, they concluded that the police had no real effect on the drop in crime over the 1990s: "[T]he research suggests that hiring more police officers did not play an independent or consistent role in reducing violent crime in the United States."[165]

In addition to this research on police presence, a substantial body of literature examines the deterrent effect of particular police practices on the crime rate, such as "police crackdowns" on certain kinds of crime or intensive law enforcement in high-crime areas known as "hot spots."[166] The idea behind police crackdowns and hot-spot policing is to increase the certainty of arrest and punishment for particular crimes or particular

[161] Levitt, *supra* note 132, at 177.

[162] *Id.* at 177.

[163] ECK & MAGUIRE, *supra* note 134.

[164] *Id.* at 217.

[165] *Id.*

[166] *See generally* DAVID M. KENNEDY, DETERRENCE AND CRIME PREVENTION: RECONSIDERING THE PROSPECT OF SANCTION (2009); Mark A.R. Kleiman, *The Effect of Intensive Enforcement on Retail Heroin Dealing, in* STREET-LEVEL DRUG ENFORCEMENT: EXAMINING THE ISSUES 3 (Marcia R. Chaiken ed., 1988); Lawrence W. Sherman, *Police Crackdowns: Initial and Residual Deterrence, in* 12 CRIME AND JUSTICE: A REVIEW OF RESEARCH 1 (Michael Tonry & Norval Morris eds., 1990); Lawrence W. Sherman, *Policing for Crime Prevention, in* EVIDENCE-BASED CRIME PREVENTION 295 (Lawrence W. Sherman et al. eds., 2002); Anthony A. Braga, *Hot Spots Policing and Crime Prevention: A Systematic Review of Randomized Controlled Trials*, 1 J. EXPERIMENTAL CRIMINOLOGY 317 (2005); Christopher S. Koper & Evan Mayo-Wilson, *Police Crackdowns on Illegal Gun Carrying: A Systematic Review of Their Impact on Gun Crime*, 2 J. EXPERIMENTAL CRIMINOLOGY 227 (2006); David Weisburd, *Hot Spots Policing Experiments and Criminal Justice Research: Lessons from the Field*, 599 ANNALS AM. ACAD. POL. & SOC. SCI. 220 (2005); Mark A. R. Kleiman, *Bringing Back Street-Level Heroin Enforcement* (John F. Kennedy Sch. of Gov't, Program in Criminal Justice Policy and Mgmt., Working Paper No. 80-01-08, 1986).

geographic areas with greatly intensified police activity.[167] For example, if there is a two-block area in a given city in which the crime rate is particularly high (prostitution, drug sales, robberies), extra police could be assigned, traffic flow restricted, an on-site booking facility set up, and a cleaning up of vacant areas and abandoned buildings, all in a concerted effort to bring additional law enforcement muscle to the area. One would expect the increased police presence and law enforcement activity to increase the perception among would-be offenders that the certainty and severity of sanctions has increased and that, as a result of these changed perceptions, crime will be deterred.[168] Reviews of this literature are more optimistic than definitive. Many studies are simply too poorly conducted to draw precise or even realistic assessments about whether the particular police effort deterred crime. Many studies, in fact, show that even with massive police effort the return in reduced crime is marginal.[169] At least some of these studies show that crime is reduced in a given area while the crack-down or enhanced police presence exists, but that crime quickly returns to its pre-intervention level soon after the program ends.

Interestingly, these studies frequently show that there is evidence of crime displacement, whereby crime increases in areas geographically proximate to the targeted area.[170] What program evaluators must do, therefore, is balance the deterrent effects achieved in one area with the crime displacement effects that occur in other areas. Although troubling from a policy perspective, that criminals simply "move around the corner" in response to increased police presence to commit crime in another area is perfectly compatible with (and indeed expected by) deterrence theory and the belief in a rational offender.[171] A reasoning offender would respond to the increased probability of legal sanctions in one area by relocating to an area with a lower certainty of apprehension. The rational offender would then return to his normal "haunts" once the extra police activity brought on by the crackdown in the original area is removed.[172] Those committing

---

[167] KENNEDY, *supra* note 166, at 10-11.

[168] *Id.*

[169] *See generally id.*; Richard A. Berk, Reaction Essay, *Knowing When to Fold 'Em: An Essay on Evaluating the Impact of* Ceasefire, Compstat, *and* Exile, 4 CRIMINOLOGY & PUB. POL'Y 451 (2005); Rosenfeld et al., *supra* note 154. For an example, see the evaluations of the Boston youth violence crackdown known as "Operation Ceasefire." *See* KENNEDY, *supra* note 166, at 8; Berk, *supra* note 169, at 455-59; Rosenfeld et al., *supra* note 154, at 434-35.

[170] David Weisburd & John E. Eck, *What Can Police Do to Reduce Crime, Disorder, and Fear?*, 593 ANNALS AM. ACAD. POL. & SOC. SCI. 42, 52 (2004).

[171] David Weisburd et al., *Does Crime Just Move around the Corner?: A Controlled Study of Spatial Displacement of Crime Control Benefits*, 44 CRIMINOLOGY 549 (2006).

[172] Nagin, *supra* note 77, at 9-11.

crimes in the targeted area may rationally reduce their level of offending until they notice that the risk is either not as great as they thought or police enforcement has slackened or withdrawn.[173]

What can we say about this very copious body of research on both the number of police and policing styles intended to deter crime? Unfortunately, nothing precise. It is undoubtedly true that increasing the number of police officers who patrol an area does lower the amount of crime in that area, targeted police work with enhanced activity likely lowers crime, and at least some part of the "great crime drop" can be attributed to an increase in the number of police officers added to the force as a result of federal funding. But even these very minimal conclusions must be taken with a healthy dose of skepticism, and we can say with even less confidence *how much* deterrent effect extra police officers and targeted policing have had.

We should conclude that it is only *probably* true that added police contributed to the crime drop for several reasons. First, from 1990 to 2000, in addition to an increase in the number of police officers in many U.S. cities, there was also great experimentation with different policing strategies. It is difficult to disentangle the impact of more police from the impact of what those police were doing.[174] Second, while it is true that crime rates dropped while cities were adding more police officers to their force—including the greatest decline in New York City, which also had the greatest increase in number of police officers—the relationship between more police and a reduction in crime is not always clear.[175] Figure 3 shows the percent change in the number of police per 100,000 residents and the percent change in the rate of violent index crime for a selection of U.S. cities over the years 1990-2000. While many cities saw an increase in the number of police and a corresponding reduction in violent crime, this was not always the case. For example, San Diego experienced approximately a 45% decline in violent crime with only a 1% increase in its police force.[176] Dallas saw more than a 40% reduction in violent crime along with an 8% *reduction* in the size of its police force.[177] Seattle saw a sizable reduction in crime (about 44%) with a 9% reduction in its police force. Philadelphia had a 10% increase in its police per capita but an equally sized increase in crime.[178] Baltimore had a 20% increase in its police with no discernable

[173] *Id.*

[174] ZIMRING, *supra* note 129, at 149-52.

[175] *See* REAVES & HICKMAN, *supra* note 131.

[176] *Id.* app. A at 10, app. D at 13.

[177] *Id.*

[178] *Id.*

effect on crime.[179] Clearly, while the number of police can influence the amount of crime a city experiences, we do not know how much it matters, and other things seem to matter a great deal as well.

Figure 3

Percent Change 1990-2000 in the Number of Sworn Police and the Violent Crime Rate (per 100,000)

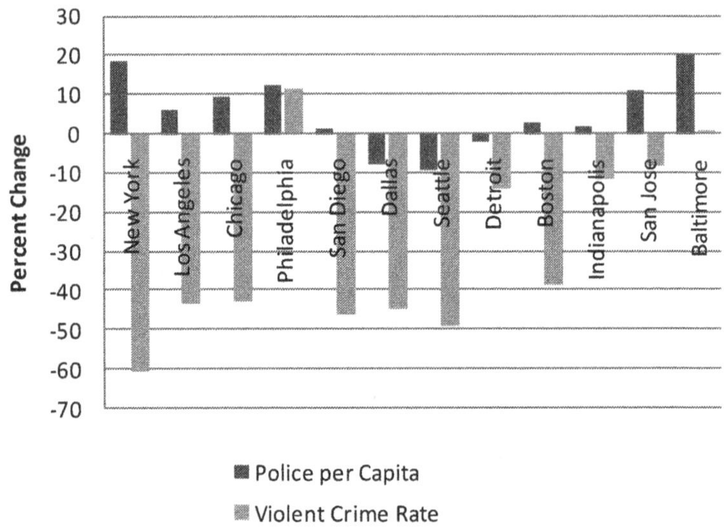

Source: Bureau of Justice Statistics Special Report. Police Departments in Large Cities, 1990-2000. May 2002. Washington, D.C.: U.S. Department of Justice.

New York City did observe the most dramatic decline in it crime rate of any U.S. city from 1990 to 2000, and it did so while increasing the size of its police force more than any other city. It also introduced new police strategies such as COMPSTAT and "zero tolerance" policies. However, questions have been raised about the veracity of the NYPD's crime statistics program under COMPSTAT.[180] A survey given to a group of more than one hundred retired NYPD captains and higher ranking officers indicated that they were aware of consistent and non-trivial efforts to produce lower crime statistics by "down-grading" citizen reports. Down-grading can entail either deliberately not recording certain crimes or putting

[179] *Id.*

[180] William K. Rashbaum, *Retired Officers Raise Questions on Crime Data*, N.Y. TIMES, Feb. 7, 2010, at A1.

pressure on citizens to withdraw their reports.[181] Part of COMPSTAT's program was to make individual police precinct commanders responsible for reductions of crime in their area to the point that people perceived that careers were at stake if crime did not go down. Many who responded to the survey complained that city officials put great pressure on individual precinct commanders to reduce crime by any way possible.[182] In the past, eleven police officials including four precinct commanders were disciplined by the department for attempting to tamper with crime statistics.[183] In fairness, it must be mentioned that the COMPSTAT system had been independently reviewed by the state comptroller and a New York University professor who both concluded that the NYPD crime data were accurate and reliable.[184] In addition, even conceding that police meddling with citizen complaints may have occurred, in order to have substantially contributed to a large share of the crime drop, the "fudging" of police statistics would have to have been done in virtually every major and mid-sized U.S. city since the crime drop occurred everywhere.[185]

There is one other general point to be made here about how much one can attribute the crime drop in the United States to policies of the criminal justice system including enhanced police presence. Following Zimring's advice that comparisons of U.S. and Canadian crime statistics are instructive, Figure 4 shows the rate of violent and property crime for Canada over the years 1962-2008, and Figure 5 shows the homicide rate for Canada and the United States.[186] Much like the United States, Canada experienced a rise in crime that peaked in the early 1990s. From 1990 to 2000, Canadian crime rates fell as did those in the United States, though not by as much for violent crimes. From 1990 to 2000, the Canadian violent crime rate fell by 10% while its property crime rate fell by 45%. It is perhaps more instructive to compare particular crime categories for the United States and Canada (Table 1). With the exception of auto theft, the general crime drop experienced by Canada is comparable to that found in the United States. From 1990 to 2000, the homicide rate declined by 39% in the United States and by 34% in Canada, and the rape rate declined by 22% in both countries. Robberies decreased more in the United States than

[181] *Id.*

[182] *Id.* Complaints about police officials lowering crime by "cooking the books" have been made about other city police departments such as Atlanta, Baltimore, Dallas, New Orleans, and Washington. *Id.*

[183] Rashbaum, *supra* note 180, at A1.

[184] *Id.*

[185] *Id.*

[186] SARA BEATTIE & AMY MOLE, CANADIAN CTR. FOR JUSTICE STATISTICS, POLICE RESOURCES IN CANADA, 2007 15 (2007); *see also* ZIMRING, *supra* note 129, at 107-34.

Figure 4
Rate of Violent and Property Crime in Canada, 1962-2008

Source: Canadian Center for Justice Statistics

Figure 5
Homicide Rate in the United States and Canada, 1962-2008

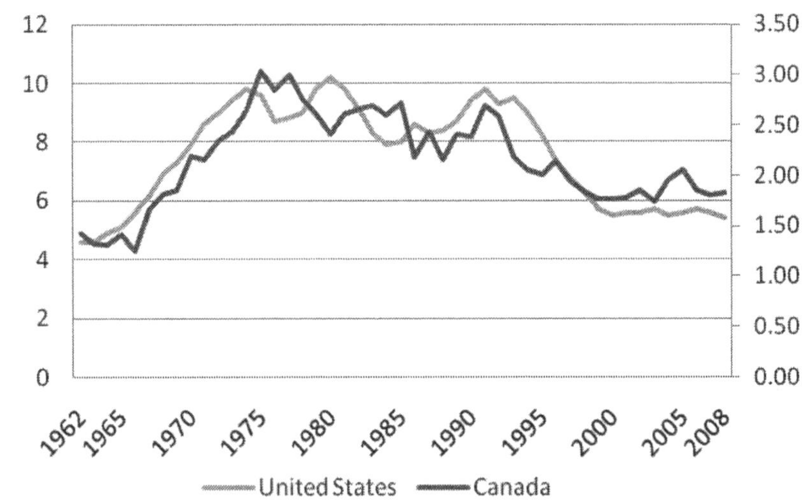

Source: Uniform Crime Reports and Canadian Centre for Justice Statistics.

Table 1

Changes in Crime in United States and Canada, 1990-2000[187]

	United States	Canada
Homicide	-39%	-34%
Rape	-22%	-22%
Aggravated Assault	-24%	-62%
Robbery	-44%	-13%
Burglary	-41%	-30%
Auto Theft	-37%	26%
Larceny	-23%	-39%

Canada (-44% compared to -13%), as did burglaries (-41% compared to -30%), but for both aggravated assault (-24% for the United States and -62% for Canada) and larcenies (-23% for the United States and -39% for Canada), the crime drop was greater in Canada.[188]

The interesting thing about Figures 4 and 5 and Table 1 is that Canadian property and violent crime rates fell at about the same time and level of magnitude and with the same duration as the rates in the United States, but Canada experienced a 10% *decline* in the number of police officers per 100,000 residents from 1990 to 2000.[189] Compare the 1980-2000 property and violent crime rates for Canada in Figure 4 and the homicide rate in Figure 5 with the trend in police per 100,000 residents reported in Figure 6. Crime was declining in Canada at a time when the number of police officers per capita was also *declining*, unlike the case for the United States. It is not likely that an increase in the presence of the police in the United States had a spill-over effect on Canadian crime rates. Other more general but not yet identified or understood factors must have been operating.[190] These data undermine any bold assertion that the great crime decline in the United States was unequivocally due to the deterrence provided by more police. While it is *likely* true that crime came down in the United States due to more police, it really is not clear at all the extent of police's role in deterrence. What we are left with, then, is that clearly police presence deters crime, but it is probably very difficult to say with any degree of precision how much it deters. Let us take Levitt's estimate as a reasonable guess that increasing the size of the police force by 10% will reduce crime by about 4% or 5%.[191]

---

[187] Zimring, *supra* note 129, at 16 tbl 1.3.

[188] BEATTIE & MOLE, *supra* note 186, at 108 fig.5.1.

[189] *Id.* at 15.

[190] ZIMRING, *supra* note 129, at 131-32.

[191] Levitt, *supra* note 132, at 177.

Figure 6

Police per 100,000 population in Canada, 1980-2000

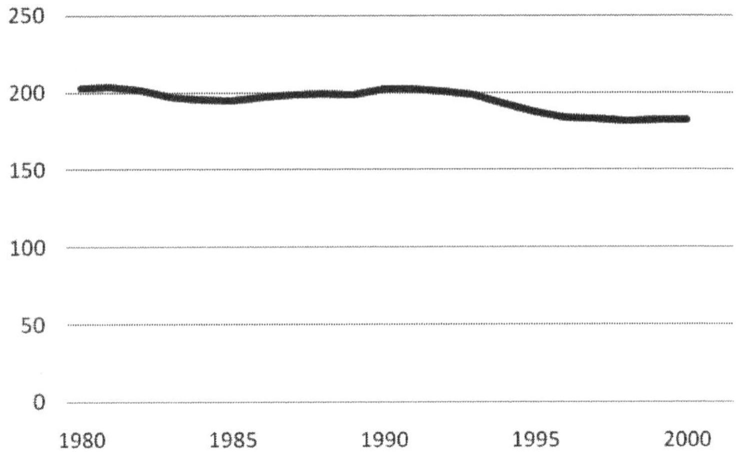

Source: Beattie and Mole, 2007.

B. THE ROLE OF IMPRISONMENT IN DETERRENCE

One of the most substantial punishments that the criminal justice system has in its arsenal of sanctions is imprisonment. Going to prison is a costly and painful possible outcome of committing crime. If the deterrence doctrine is true, there should be an inverse relationship between the use of imprisonment and crime. For example, the economist Steven Levitt conducted a very clever and convincing study of the relationship between imprisonment and crime rates.[192] He was fully aware of the problem of simultaneity between imprisonment and crime rates (they can mutually affect each other) and so used prison overcrowding legislation in a state (court orders to reduce overcrowding) to act as an instrumental variable for changes in the probability of imprisonment. Court orders to reduce overcrowding in some state prison systems led to a substantial reduction in the number of inmates and thus a decline in the probability of a convicted offender going to prison.[193] Using data that covered the years 1971-1993, Levitt concluded that likelihood of imprisonment had a non-trivial crime reduction effect. He estimated that each additional man-year of

[192] Steven D. Levitt, *The Effect of Prison Population Size on Crime Rates: Evidence from Prison Overcrowding Litigation*, 111 Q. J. ECON. 319 (1996).

[193] *Id.* at 330-44, 348.

imprisonment resulted in the reduction of fifteen index crimes.[194] It is not entirely clear from Levitt's analysis, however, how much of the crime avoided was due to deterrence and how much to incapacitation—the fact that high-rate offenders get locked up and cannot commit crimes. Other estimates of the effect of prison on crime come from Spelman, who argued that the "elasticity" of crime with respect to incarceration is between -0.2 and -0.4.[195] "Elasticity" is a statistical way of expressing the effect of a change in one factor on the change in another. An elasticity of -0.2 indicates that a 10% increase in incarceration would result in a 2% decline in crime.[196]

We can also study the relationship between changes in the rate of incarceration and crime rates over time to give us some sense as to whether imprisonment acts as a deterrent to crime. Recall that from the early 1990s until the present day the crime rate in the United States dramatically declined. The rate of imprisonment during this same period also increased rather dramatically, by some 52%. Figure 7 shows the index violent crime and homicide rates in the United States from 1980 to 2008 along with the rate of incarceration. It shows that the decline in serious crime and the most serious crime (homicide) came during a period when the incarceration rate was doubling.[197] One can look at this figure and be led easily to think that perhaps some part of the great crime drop was due to the increase in incarceration.

A great deal of scholarly interest has been directed at trying to understand the relationship between the great crime drop and the increased use of imprisonment. There are excellent summaries of this literature available,[198] and I am again selective here. There is a general consensus that the decline in crime is, at least in part, due to more and longer prison sentences, with most of the controversy being over how much of an effect imprisonment had. After an extensive empirical analysis, Spelman concluded that between 4% and 21% of the crime drop could be attributed to the expansion of incarceration.[199] Levitt concluded that the increase in

---

[194] *Id.* at 345-46.

[195] William Spelman, *What Recent Studies Do (and Don't) Tell Us About Imprisonment and Crime*, 27 CRIME & JUST. 419, 485 (2000).

[196] *Id.*

[197] BUREAU OF JUSTICE STATISTICS, U.S. DEP'T OF JUSTICE, REPORTED CRIME IN UNITED STATES-TOTAL, http://bjsdata.ojp.usdoj.gov/dataonline/Search/Crime/State/statebystaterun.cfm?stateid=52 (last visited July 9, 2010) (crime data); BUREAU OF JUSTICE STATISTICS, U.S. DEP'T OF JUSTICE, TOTAL CORRECTIONAL POPULATION, http://bjs.ojp.usdoj.gov/index.cfm?ty=tp&tid=11 (last visited July 9, 2010) (incarceration data).

[198] *See generally* BLUMSTEIN & WALLMAN, *supra* note 128.

[199] Spelman, *supra* note 195, at 109.

Figure 7

Rate of Incarceration, Violent Crime, and Homicide in the United States 1980-2008

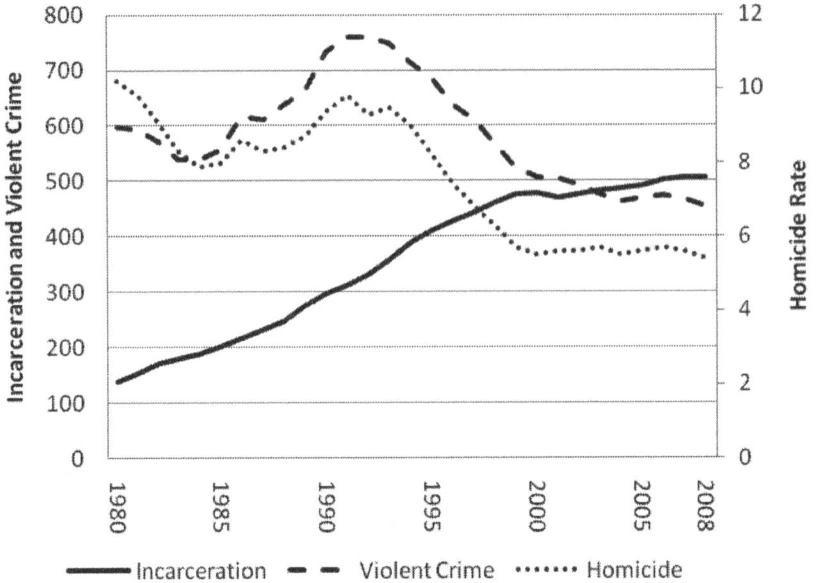

Source: Uniform Crime Reports, 2008. Bureau of Justice Statistics, 2010.

the use of imprisonment from 1990 to 2000 was responsible for about one-third of the declining crime rate.[200]

In other words, both authors would agree that some part of the decline in crime since the 1990s was due to the increased use of incarceration in the United States, and that we can attribute anywhere from 20% to 30% of the crime drop to imprisonment. As was the case with the role of police presence in reducing crime, however, I would suggest some caution and humility in accepting these conclusions. First, it is probably very safe to say that the threat of imprisonment does indeed act as a general deterrent and *probably* is responsible for *some share* of the recent crime drop. I say *probably* and *some share* because, as with the role of more police, it is really difficult to make any more definitive conclusions about the deterrent effect of imprisonment for four reasons.

First, the evidence to date is consistent with the fact that putting more people in prison can, to some degree, lower the crime rate, but it is not clear

[200] Levitt, *supra* note 132, at 178-79.

how this crime reduction occurs. Putting more people behind bars can reduce crime by deterring them but also by incapacitating high-rate offenders. While it may be true that increased imprisonment does lower crime, it is far more difficult to say with any authority how much of that crime reduction is due to deterrence and how much to incapacitation. For policy purposes, I readily admit that it probably does not make much difference why crime goes down in response to greater incarceration, but if one is trying to determine the causal mechanisms behind the decline it certainly does. Further, one could argue that since both the probability of imprisonment and the length of imprisonment increased since the 1990s, both deterrence and incapacitation are equally compelling explanations.[201]

Second, any explanation that the crime drop of the 1990s should be attributed to the increased use of incarceration certainly would have to explain how that is compatible with the earlier time trend for incarceration and crime shown in Figure 6. In the decade from the early 1980s to the early 1990s, the rate of violent crime was *rising* while the incarceration rate was doubling. If a greater reliance on incarceration reduces crime by deterrence (or even incapacitation), why did it take so long to have any effect on the crime rate?

Third, one also needs to explain why if imprisonment was responsible for lowering the crime rate in the United States from 1990 to 2000, Canada had an almost equally impressive decline in crime without a huge expansion of incarceration like that in the United States? The rate of incarceration in Canada *declined* by about 10% from 1993 to 2001, at about the same time that U.S. rates were doubling, and both countries experienced a substantial reduction in crime.[202]

Fourth, before one can unambiguously conclude that the policies of the criminal justice system, such as increased incarceration (and increased police presence), lowered the crime rate through deterrence, one has to be confident that another link in the deterrence process exists—that between the objective and perceptual properties of punishment. For something like increased incarceration or increased law enforcement to have a general deterrent effect, would-be offenders would have to be aware of the heightened risk. In the absence of a relationship between the objective and perceptual properties of punishment, confidence in general deterrence as the

---

[201] Marc Mauer, *The Hidden Problem of Time Served in Prison*, 74 SOC. RES. 701, 701-02 (2007); *see also* Steven D. Levitt, *Why Do Increased Arrest Rates Appear to Reduce Crime: Deterrence, Incapacitation, or Measurement Error?*, 36 ECON. INQUIRY 353 (1998).

[202] SARA JOHNSON, CANADIAN CTR. FOR JUSTICE STATISTICS, ADULT CORRECTIONAL SERVICES IN CANADA (2004), *available at* http://dsp-psd.communication.gc.ca/Pilot/Statcan/85-002-XIE/0100485-002-XIE.pdf.

main causal mechanism responsible for driving down the crime rate would be shaken. It is to this connection that I turn next.

V. The Link Between the Objective and Perceptual Properties of Punishment

If criminal justice practices, such as enhanced police activity in particular areas or the increased use of incarceration, have a general deterrent effect on criminal activity, it must be because there is a causal link between the objective and perceptual properties of punishment. As Ball wrote in his paper that appeared in the *Journal*, the "deterrent effect of a law obviously depends upon the individual's knowledge of the law and the punishment prescribed."[203] An important component of the deterrence doctrine, and the criminal justice system itself, is that persons are aware of actual punishment practices and are aware of changes in those practices when they occur. This does not mean that the correlation must be unity, but certainly one should expect to see at least a robust correlation between the objective and perceptual properties of punishment. Phillip Cook similarly argued that although the public's perceptions of sanction threats "are not accurate, [they] do tend to be systematically related to criminal justice system activities."[204] Interestingly, if the correlation is moderate to large, then aggregate-level studies that relate the objective properties of punishment to crime rates do provide valid insight into the deterrence process, but perceptual studies about deterrence were initiated in part because of skepticism about this causal link. One would also expect that one's perceptions of punishment are not immutable but change in response to changes in objective conditions and changes in that person's experiences. In other words, while a person's current perceptions are certainly related to some prior set of perceptions, they are nonetheless updated in response to new information if persons behave rationally.

The expected robust correlation between the objective and perceptual properties of punishment, and the updating of perceptions in response to new information about risks and magnitudes of punishments, would seem to be core assertions at the heart of deterrence theory. There is evidence that would-be offenders are not completely unmindful of the objective risks and costs they run if they commit crimes, but the correlations are rather meager and must be disappointing to believers in deterrence. In fact, one of the "dirty little secrets" of deterrence is that there really is not much evidence in

[203] Ball, *supra* note 65, at 351.

[204] Phillip Cook, *Research in Criminal Deterrence: Laying the Groundwork for the Second Decade*, *in* 2 Crime & Justice: An Annual Review of Research 211, 222 (Norval Morris & Michael Tonry eds., 1980).

support of a strong correlation between the objective and subjective properties of punishment. Perhaps the more unfortunate fact is that although this may be one of the most crucial links in the deterrence process, it is the one that we know the least about.

What evidence do we have about how would-be offenders perceive legal sanctions? Two early studies conducted in California lead to the conclusion that the public does not know very much about the maximum and minimum punishments provided by law for different offenses, nor is the public very aware of any changes to those punishments, and inmates of California prisons were only slightly more informed.[205] Anderson also found that convicted felons who had been imprisoned were unmindful of the possible consequences: 18% reported that they no idea what the penalty would be for their criminal act, and another 35% stated that they didn't even consider the possible penalty before committing the crime that got them into prison.[206] Many ethnographic accounts of offenders also suggest that in deciding whether or not to commit a crime, the probability of getting caught and the severity of punishment are not well known.[207]

Another thing researchers have discovered is that offenders do not see increments in punishment in the same way that they are intended to see them. Because people have what economists call subjective discount rates (a point that is returned to at the conclusion of this Article), they reduce in their minds the cost of things that are more distant in time (much like we do when we reduce the "pain" of buying something by using a credit card rather than cash). To demonstrate this, Kent A. McClelland and Geoffrey P. Alpert asked a sample of 152 recently arrested persons to provide estimates for several different types and levels of legal punishments.[208] Consistent with subjective discounting, they found that a five-year prison sentence was rated to be only twice as severe as a one year sentence, and a twenty-year sentence was judged to be just a little more than one-half times

[205] *See* CAL. ASSEMBLY COMM. ON CRIMINAL PROCEDURE, DETERRENT EFFECTS OF CRIMINAL SANCTIONS (1968); Zimring & Hawkins, *supra* note 81, at 143.

[206] David A. Anderson, *The Deterrence Hypothesis and Picking Pockets at the Pickpocket's Hanging*, 4 AM L. & ECON. REV 295, 305 (2002).

[207] *See* NEAL SHOVER, GREAT PRETENDERS: PURSUITS AND CAREERS OF PERSISTENT THIEVES 151-74 (1996); KENNETH D. TUNNELL, CHOOSING CRIME: THE CRIMINAL CALCULUS OF PROPERTY OFFENDERS 60-85 (1992); RICHARD T. WRIGHT & SCOTT H. DECKER, BURGLARS ON THE JOB: STREETLIFE AND RESIDENTIAL BREAK-INS 127-33 (1994); RICHARD T. WRIGHT & SCOTT H. DECKER, ARMED ROBBERS IN ACTION: STICKUPS AND STREET CULTURE 59-60 (1997).

[208] Kent A. McClelland & Geoffrey P. Alpert, *Factor Analysis Applied to Magnitude Estimates of Punishment Seriousness: Patterns of Individual Differences*, 1 J. QUANTITATIVE CRIMINOLOGY 307, 309-10 (1985).

more severe than a ten-year sentence.[209] In a later study, Eleni Apospori and Alpert reported that a sample of arrested offenders perceived a ten-year prison sentence as only four times more severe than a one-year sentence, a twenty-year sentence only six times more severe, and a twenty-year sentence was judged to be less than one and one-half times more severe than a ten-year sentence.[210]

There is other evidence to suggest that would-be offenders' perceptions of the certainty and severity of punishment are not strongly related to the objective properties of punishment and are, therefore, not likely to be very accurate nor responsive to policy changes. Irving Piliavin and colleagues found that a measure of the perceived risk of formal punishment was unrelated to a respondent's prior arrests and convictions.[211] Julie Horney and Ineke Haen Marshall found that the total number of arrests an individual had accumulated and whether a person had been arrested for every criminal offense he or she had committed were unrelated to perceptions of the certainty of arrest.[212]

Most damaging of all to deterrence theory is a study by Gary Kleck and colleagues.[213] They interviewed 1,500 adult residents of fifty-four large urban counties and asked them about their perceptions of the certainty, severity, and celerity of punishment in their county.[214] An example of a question about the perceived certainty of punishment measure was: "In the past 10 years in your county, out of every 100 robberies known to the police, about how many do you think resulted in the arrest of the robber?"[215] One measure of perceived severity was: "Out of every 100 persons convicted of robbery in your county, about how many do you think are given a jail or prison sentence?"[216] For the celerity of punishment: "For persons convicted of robbery, what do you think is the average amount of time that passes between the day the offender is arrested and the day they were sentenced in court?"[217] Comparable county-level measures of the

---

[209] *Id.* at 311-14.

[210] *See* Eleni Apospori & Geoffrey Alpert, Research Note, *The Role of Differential Experience with the Criminal Justice System for Changes in Perceptions of Severity of Legal Sanctions over Time*, 39 CRIME & DELINQ. 184, 189 (1993).

[211] Irving Piliavin et al., *Crime, Deterrence, and Rational Choice*, 51 AM. SOC. REV. 101, 114 (1986).

[212] Julie Horney & Ineke Haen Marshall, *Risk Perceptions Among Serious Offenders: The Role of Crime and Punishment*, 30 CRIMINOLOGY 575, 586 (1992).

[213] Gary Kleck et al., *The Missing Link in General Deterrence Research*, 43 CRIMINOLOGY 623 (2005).

[214] *Id.* at 635-36.

[215] *Id.* at 634.

[216] *Id.*

[217] *Id.* at 635.

objective levels of the certainty, severity, and celerity of punishment in the county were obtained from the Bureau of Justice Statistics and Uniform Crime Reports.[218] The important question that Kleck and colleagues asked was whether persons had higher perceptions of the certainty, severity, and celerity of punishment in counties where the actual levels were higher. They did not. The correlations between perceived and actual punishment levels were consistently weak, averaging a Pearson's correlation of 0.02, and none was larger than 0.13.[219] At the bivariate level, less than 2% of the variance in perceived sanction threats was explained by actual levels of sanctions.[220] This null finding was true when the full sample of respondents was stratified into those who had at least one prior arrest (the "experienced") and those with no prior arrests.[221] In multivariate analysis, county-level measures of punishment characteristics were unrelated to individual perceptions of sanction threats.[222] This was true for each different measure of certainty, severity, and celerity of punishment and for each of four different offenses (homicide, robbery, assault, burglary) studied. The variance explained in these multivariate models were all very small, with the largest being 0.08.[223]

Lance Lochner argued that a person's perceptions about the certainty of arrest should depend upon "an individual's own (past) criminal behavior and arrest outcomes, the criminal and arrest outcomes of others around him, and more general signals that may come from local arrest rates or neighborhood conditions."[224] He examined this deterrence hypothesis with two different data sets—the National Youth Survey (NYS) and the National Longitudinal Survey of Youth (NLSY97).[225] Estimating an ordinary least squares regression model with the perceived probability of arrest for auto theft in the NLSY97 as the dependent variable, Lochner found that the objective certainty of punishment as measured by the country-level arrest rate for auto theft was *unrelated to the perceived level of certainty.*[226] Even more disturbing for deterrence theory is the fact that Lochner was only able to explain 3% of the variance in the perceived certainty of arrest.[227] There

---

[218] *Id.* at 633-34

[219] *Id.* at 642.

[220] *Id.*

[221] *Id.* at 643 tbl.2.

[222] *Id.* at 645-51 tbls.3, 4, 5, 6, 7, 8 & 9.

[223] *Id.* at 647 tbl.5.

[224] Lance Lochner, *Individual Perceptions of the Criminal Justice System*, 97 AM. ECON. REV. 444, 445 (2007).

[225] *Id.* at 444.

[226] *Id.* at 450.

[227] *Id.* at 449 tbl.2.

was no measure of the local objective arrest rate in the NYS, but Lochner found that the perceived probability of arrest was unrelated to the perception that crime or disorder was a problem within one's neighborhood. Like the analysis of the NLSY97 data, the amount of explained variance in perceptions was very small, from 4% to less than 1%.[228]

Horney and Marshall's, Piliavin et al.'s, Kleck et al.'s, and Lochner's studies not only show that there is not a strong relationship between objective sanctions and perceived sanctions; in none of these were the researchers able to explain much of the variance in perceived sanction threats. Piliavin and colleagues explained only 7% of the variance in their measure of formal sanction risk.[229] In Horney and Marshall's study, the explained variance of the perceived risk measures varied by offense but only ranged from 0.05 to 0.13.[230] Kleck et al.'s study also varied by offence and only ranged between 4% and 8%.[231] Lochner explained only 3% of the variance in his model of perceived punishment.[232]

This inability to explain much of the variance in perceptions of sanction threats is another dirty little secret in deterrence research. What makes this more remarkable is that in each of the studies mentioned above, the models are fairly well-specified with appropriate right-hand-side variables that theoretically should matter. In addition, it is not as if predictions of future states are difficult to explain, as scholars have been able to better explain other kinds of perceptions, such as perceptions of college attendance, fertility, smoking, and mortality.[233] We really do not know very much about how perceptions of punishment are formed, and we are no better informed than we were when Daniel S. Nagin concluded ten years ago that "[t]he literature on the formation of sanction risk perception is small and narrow in scope."[234] However, it is not only an important theoretical question about deterrence, but it has critical policy significance. If perceptions of sanction threats are not directly tied to objective practices

228 *Id.* at 452 tbl.4

229 Piliavin, *supra* note 211, at 111 tbl.4.

230 Horney & Marshall, *supra* note 212, at 584 tbl.2.

231 Kleck et al., *supra* note 213, at 647 tbl.5.

232 Lochner, *supra* note 224, at 227. The models of Matsueda et al. are also consistent with Horney & Marshall's, Lochner's, and Kleck's in that the amount of explained variance of perceptions of punishment were low (ranging between 0.03 and 0.26), even with lagged values of the dependent variable in the model. Ross Matsueda et al., *Deterring Delinquents: A Rational Choice Model of Theft and Violence*, 71 AM. SOC. REV. 95, 108-09 tbl.2 (2006).

233 Wandi Bruine de Bruin et al., *Can Adolescents Predict Significant Life Events?*, 41 J. ADOLESCENT HEALTH 208 (2007); Baruch Fischhoff et al., *Teen Expectations for Significant Life Events*, 64 PUB. OPINION Q. 189 (2000); Michael Schoenbaum, *The Accuracy of Teens' Expectations of Future Smoking*, 28 AM. J. PREVENTIVE MED. 274 (2005).

234 Nagin, *supra* note 77, at 17.

in the criminal justice system, then they will not be responsive to or easily manipulated by criminal justice policy.

We do not know very much about how perceptions are formed, but, in a bit of good news for deterrence theory, we do know that once formed perceptions are modified by experiences, both one's own experiences and the experiences of others. This is good news for deterrence theory because people have shown themselves to be capable Bayesians. Prior perceptions of the risk of punishment are generally modified downward when people commit crimes and get away with it—this has been called the "experiential effect" in the literature.[235] People also generally increase their perceptions of the risk of punishment when they do get caught.[236] Lochner also found that, in both the NYS and NLSY97 datasets, there was evidence of updating of perceptions in response to one's own behavior—those who committed crimes and were not arrested had lower perceptions of the certainty of punishment.[237] What was interesting, however, is that while there was a significant relationship between arrests for a serious crime and perceived certainty, it was insignificant when arrest for *any* offense was used. This implies that attempts by authorities to crack down on minor crimes in "zero tolerance" campaigns are not likely to spill over to affect beliefs about the probability of arrest for more serious crimes.[238]

Finally, Shamena Anwar and Thomas A. Loughran estimated a Bayesian model of perceptual updating on the basis of one's experience.[239] An important characteristic of their research is that it was conducted with a high-risk sample of offenders—youth who have been convicted, either in juvenile or adult court, of a serious felony offense.[240] They too found that the experience of an arrest increased one's risk perceptions, although the magnitude of the effect was rather modest. An individual who committed a crime and was arrested for it increased his or her perceptions of the

[235] Saltzman et al., *supra* note 98, at 180-84.

[236] *See* Horney & Marshall, *supra* note 212, at 584 tbl.2; Lochner, *supra* note 224, at 454 tbl.5; Matsueda et al., *supra* note 232, at 111.

[237] Contrary evidence was found by Pogarsky and colleagues who reported that those who had experienced an arrest had lower perceptions of the risk of punishment compared with those not arrested. They analogized this to the "gambler's fallacy" whereby once arrested, offenders think that they are due a streak of good luck before the next arrest. Greg Pogarsky & Alex R. Piquero, *Can Punishment Encourage Offending? Investigating the 'Resetting' Effect*, 40 J. RES. CRIME & DELINQ. 92 (2003); Greg Pogarsky et al., *Modeling Change in Perceptions about Sanction Threats: The Neglected Linkage in Deterrence Theory*, 20 J. QUANTITATIVE CRIMINOLOGY 343 (2004).

[238] Lochner, *supra* note 224, at 456 tbl.6 (presenting results for male offenders).

[239] Shamena Anwar & Thomas A. Loughran, *Testing a Bayseian Learning Theory of Deterrence among Serious Juvenile Offenders* (Apr. 1 2010) (unpublished, on file with author).

[240] *Id.* at 23.

certainty of punishment by only 5%, compared with those who had not been arrested.[241] This increase in perceived risk was greater for less experienced offenders (for whom the information of an arrest would be more novel) than for the more experienced.[242] Unfortunately for both a more general deterrent effect and for the deterrent effectiveness of "zero-tolerance" policing of minor offenses, the effect of an arrest was crime specific. Getting arrested for a violent crime did not affect one's perceptions of the risk for committing a property offense.[243]

To summarize, contrary to the deterrence doctrine, subjective probabilities of punishment held by individuals do not appear to vary systematically with the actual or objective probabilities. Levitt observed over ten years ago that "there are a number of obstacles to effective deterrence. First, criminals may be poorly informed about the likelihood of detection."[244] The research to date, though sparse, does suggest that would-be offenders are not well-informed about the actual risks of sanctions. Nor do we know very much about how perceptions are formed. However, consistent with a rational actor assumption, research has shown that individuals' assessments of the risk of being legally sanctioned are affected by their and others' experiences with committing crimes with impunity and with getting arrested. Those individuals who commit crimes and get away with them, and who know of others who have had the same experiences, are more likely to lower their estimate of the risk of crime. Individuals who get arrested do update their perceptions of risk, usually by increasing the estimate they have about the risk of another arrest (although whether a gambler's fallacy exists, and there is a resetting of one's risk following an arrest, is yet to be determined). What is troubling is that perceptions of sanction threats are generally not well explained at all. We know very little about exactly how perceptions of punishment certainty, severity, and celerity are formed and this is one of the most glaring holes in the deterrence literature. Further, while perceptions of sanction threats do increase in response to an arrest, consistent with the deterrence process, Anwar and Loughran's research suggests that this effect is very modest.[245] The fact that perceptions of sanction threats are not strongly related to the actual levels of punishment does not speak well of the ability of the criminal justice system to regulate criminal conduct through polices aimed at making punishment more certain, severe, or swift.

---

[241] *Id.* at 28.

[242] *Id.* at 30.

[243] *Id.* at 30-32.

[244] Levitt, *supra* note 201, at 353.

[245] Anwar & Loughran, *supra* note 239, at 28.

VI. THE LINK BETWEEN PERCEIVED SANCTION THREATS AND CRIME

The link between perceptions of the certainty, severity, and celerity of punishment and self-reported involvement in crime has been extremely well researched, with a line of empirical studies that dates back to the early 1970s.[246] The question that this line of research attempts to address is, "Whatever the source of individual perceptions of sanction threats, is there an inverse relationship between perceptions of the certainty, severity, and celerity of punishment and involvement in crime?"[247] The research in this area has gone through a number of methodological developments. In the first stage, respondents were asked about their current perceptions of the certainty and severity of punishment for certain acts and their previous self-reported involvement in those acts. This line of cross-sectional survey data consistently revealed that those who perceived the certainty of punishment to be higher were less likely to report involvement in crime (the results were not as consistent for perceived severity).[248] While these findings were initially taken as evidence of a deterrent effect for perceived sanction threats, it became clear that since the self-reported behaviors were lagged (usually by one year) before the perception measures, the inverse correlation captured not deterrence but an "experiential effect."[249] This experiential effect reflects the fact that those who committed crimes usually got away with it, and they adjusted their perceptions downward in response to that new information.[250]

---

[246] *See* Waldo & Chiricos, *supra* note 96, at 522-28. There is virtually no research on the role of the swiftness or celerity of punishment on self-reported crime. *See* Daniel S. Nagin & Greg Pogarsky, *Integrating Celerity, Impulsivity, and Extralegal Sanction Threats into a Model of General Deterrence: Theory and Evidence*, 39 CRIMINOLOGY 865 (2001) (providing a recent exception). This is another one of the gaping holes in deterrence research. This may be due to the fact that it is not entirely clear which direction the deterrence hypothesis would predict. Early deterrence theorists like Beccaria clearly argued that punishment must be swift in order to be effective

> because when the length of time that passes between punishment and the misdeed is less, so much the stronger and more lasting in the human mind is the association of these two ideas, crime and punishment; they then come insensibly to be considered, one as the cause, the other as the necessary inevitable effect.

BECCARIA, *supra* note 2, at 56 (emphasis omitted). Empirical work by Loewenstein however, questions this. George Loewenstein, *Anticipation and the Valuation of Delayed Consumption*, 97 ECON. J. 666 (1987). Findings from some of his experiments suggest that, given the choice, people would like to get their punishment over as quickly as possible and that punishment delayed is seen as more costly than if given immediately. *Id.* at 667-69.

[247] *See* Waldo & Chicoros, *supra* note 96, at 525-27.

[248] For a review, see Paternoster, *supra* note 77.

[249] Saltzman et. al., *supra* note 233, at 180-84

[250] *Id.*

The second stage adopted a similar survey methodology but utilized panel data so that perceived sanction threats were measured before the incidence of offending—now perceptions were generally lagged by one year. These studies too showed inverse relationships between perceptions of certainty and crime (but not generally severity), but they were much reduced in magnitude from those found in cross-sectional research.[251] Moreover, multivariate models consistently indicated that informal sanctions were more responsible for inhibiting criminal conduct than the fear of formal sanctions. Nevertheless, panel survey data did provide some support for the deterrence doctrine at least with respect to the perceived certainty of punishment.[252]

Three recent examples of the use of survey data to study deterrent effects on behavior by Ross Matsueda et al., Lochner, and Loughran et al. are especially informative. Matsueda and colleagues examined the relationship between the perceived certainty of arrest and subsequent delinquency using panel data from the Denver Youth Study.[253] Consistent with deterrence theory, they found that net of other known explanatory factors, those youth who believed they would be arrested for committing crime were less likely to report doing it in the subsequent year.[254] This deterrent effect held for both self-reported violent crimes and theft.[255] Consistent with a more general model, they also found that the perceived benefits of criminal offending comprised an important factor, and the estimated effect for the perceived costs and benefits of offending were of roughly the same magnitude.[256] Although they found evidence of deterrent effects, Matsueda and colleagues were careful in noting that the deterrence factors *were not* the most important determinants of crime and that the modest effects on crime reduction would suggest caution in using the criminal justice system as the primary tool for compliance:

> [G]iven that the United States has one of the highest arrest and imprisonment rates among Western nations, increasing the perceived probability of arrest by 0.1 would likely involve draconian steps by the criminal justice system. This implies that policies for increasing the objective probability of punishment, *by themselves*, may be of limited value for reducing the crime rate substantially . . . . Indeed, the modest explained variance in your models of theft (seven percent) and violence (nine percent)

---

[251] For reviews, see Nagin, *supra* note 234, at 12-16; Paternoster, *supra* note 248, at 185 tbl.3; Travis Pratt et al., *The Empirical Status of Deterrence Theory: A Meta-Analysis*, *in* TAKING STOCK: THE STATUS OF CRIMINOLOGICAL THEORY 367, 383 (Francis T. Cullen et al. eds., 2006).

[252] *See* Paternoster, *supra* note 77, at 191-94

[253] Matsueda et al., *supra* note 232, at 103.

[254] *Id.* at 114-15 tbl.3.

[255] *Id.*

[256] *Id.*

suggests that other processes, such as socialization and embeddedness in institutions, may dwarf the effects of punishment and suggest more efficient policy interventions.[257]

Lochner examined deterrent effects in two different data sets, the National Longitudinal Survey of Youth (NLSY97) and the National Youth Survey (NYS), both nationally representative panel data sets.[258] Using an estimate of the perceived probability of arrest for auto theft in the NLSY97, Lochner found that it was inversely and significantly related to self-reported subsequent involvement in auto theft and theft of something worth more than $50.[259] The effect was not large; a 10% increase in the perceived probability of arrest was estimated to reduce auto theft by 7% and serious theft by only 4%.[260] Matsueda cautions that it might take draconian criminal justice policies to increase the perceived probability of punishment appreciably. This and the fact that Lochner found that the arrest rate in the area was unrelated to the individual's perceptions of the probability of arrest further limit the public policy implications of these findings. In addition, recall that in Lochner's research one measure of the objective certainty of punishment, the county-level arrest rate, had no deterrent effect on self-reported auto theft or serious property theft.[261] In the analysis of NYS data, Lochner estimated the relationship between crime-specific perceptions about the probability of arrest for two types of theft, breaking and entering, and attacking someone, on one hand, and self-reported subsequent involvement in those acts, on the other.[262] All coefficients were negative, as predicted by deterrence theory, and Lochner estimated that an increase of ten percentage points in the perceived probability of punishment reduced involvement in serious thefts by about 3% and auto theft by about 8%.[263]

Loughran and colleagues investigated the functional form of the deterrence model using data from a sample of juvenile offenders who were convicted of a serious felony in either juvenile or adult court.[264] Respondents were asked how likely is it that they would be caught and arrested for the following crimes: fighting, robbery with gun, stabbing someone, breaking into a store or home, stealing clothes from a store,

---

257 *Id.* at 117.

258 Lochner, *supra* note 224, at 444.

259 *Id.* at 457.

260 *Id.* at 458.

261 *Id.* at 454 tbl.5.

262 *Id.* at 457-58.

263 *Id.* at 458.

264 Loughran et al., *supra* note 98.

vandalism, and auto theft.[265] They were also asked to self-report the frequency of their involvement in seventeen different delinquent/criminal offenses that reflected the offenses in the perceptions questions.[266] Summary scales were created both for the perceived risk of arrest and for self-reported offending. They found evidence of a non-linear, inverse relationship between the risk of arrest and offending.[267] Perceptions about the risk of arrest had no effect on self-reported offending when the estimated risk was below some tipping point (an estimated probability of arrest of 0.30).[268] In addition, there was a point of diminishing deterrence returns at the upper end of the perceived risk of arrest distribution. When the perceived probability of arrest was within the range from 0.30 to 0.70, a 10% increase of perceived risk was associated with a statistically significant decrease of more than one half of an offense on average.[269] However, when the perceived probability of arrest was over 0.70, a 10% increase of perceived risk was associated with a much smaller decrease of only about 0.159 of an offense on average.[270] Taken together, these results suggest that the marginal deterrent effect of a change in certainty is substantially greater—that is, nearly 3.5 times larger—for individuals in the mid-range of the continuum, as compared to those in the upper ranges.[271] Two important implications of this are that the observed deterrent effects are very modest in magnitude, and while sanction threat certainty must be above a certain threshold to be credible, beyond a certain point it returns a much diminished deterrent benefit.

In the third stage of perceptual deterrence research, researchers recognized that perceptions of sanction threats should optimally be measured at the time that would-be offenders are contemplating committing a crime.[272] This recognition led to the development of so-called scenario studies. In this type of research, respondents are provided with a description of the commission of a crime that is as realistic as possible. For example, the respondent may be asked to imagine himself in a bar and to believe that he has had enough alcohol to put himself above the legal limit. He is told that he could either drive home himself (and thus drive while

---

[265] *Id.* at 13.

[266] *Id.* at 14.

[267] *Id.* at 16-18.

[268] *Id.* at 18.

[269] *Id.* at 20.

[270] *Id.* at 21.

[271] *Id.*

[272] In addition, if perceptions are not stable over time, then the longer the lag between the measurement of perceptions and behavior the greater the possibility of measurement error which would bias any observed relationship to zero.

drunk) or get a ride with someone but then be forced to get back to the bar the next morning the get their car. The respondent typically would then be asked to estimate the risk of being caught for drunk driving if he was to drive himself home, estimate the severity of the punishment he would receive if he was caught, and then estimate the probability that he would drive home in the described situation. The findings from these scenario studies consistently show support for deterrence theory, at least with respect to the perceived certainty of punishment. Those who think they are likely to get caught are less likely to evade paying their taxes, drive while drunk, steal things, cheat in school, act in a sexually aggressive manner, act violently, or engage in various acts of corporate crime.[273]

A study by Nagin and Pogarsky is deserving of special scrutiny because it presents one of the most theoretically sophisticated deterrence models in the literature and it combines the elements of perceived certainty, severity, and celerity.[274] Nagin and Pogarsky argue that crime will be committed when the expected benefits outweigh the expected costs:[275]

$$\text{U(Benefits)} > p\ \text{U(Legal Costs + Extralegal Costs)} \qquad (2.1)$$

Here, the extralegal costs include such things as social censure and self-inflicted guilt, and p is the perceived risk of being sanctioned. This is the traditional deterrence model in which crime is expected to be reduced when either the probability of punishment, p, or the perceived severity of legal punishment (arrest) increases, modified by the inclusion of a parameter that captures the conceptual spirit of the celerity of punishment. For example, it is not clear that netting $500 immediately from a theft is exactly offset by the probability of a $500 fine at sometime in the future. Traditional theory holds that only if the cost is expected to arrive quickly after the act—theoretically as quickly as the benefit—is there an offset. Delay makes the severity of the punishment diminish because it is not immediate and not as severe. If would-be offenders would prefer to delay their punishment, we should expect to see a celerity effect.[276]

273 See Nagin, *supra* note 77, for a review.

274 Nagin & Pogarsky, *supra* note 246.

275 *Id.* at 872.

276 There is no theoretical reason why this has to be true, and Loewenstein has empirically found evidence for the counter position that persons would prefer to get their punishment over quickly rather than have it delayed. Loewenstein, *supra* note 246, at 667-68. The idea that punishment which is to be delivered later is actually perceived to be more painful is consistent with the concept of "dread." *Id.* at 667. The notion of dread makes things conceptually messy for deterrence theory because while there is an empirical basis for thinking that gains are discounted in the future, we have no knowledge as to whether or not this is symmetric with respect to losses.

In response to this, Nagin and Pogarsky add another parameter to equation 2 above, δ, which is a discount factor that assigns a weight to future costs.[277] The model becomes:

$$\text{U(Benefits)} > \delta_t\, p\, \text{U(Legal Costs + Extralegal Costs)} \qquad (2.2)$$

Here, the expected legal and extralegal costs of offending are scaled by δ_t and by r, where $\delta_t = 1/(1 + r)$. The extent to which costs are scaled depends upon how many time periods the legal and extralegal sanctions are delayed, which is the celerity of punishment, and r, which is the individual's discount rate. The discount rate is the extent to which the person reduces the value of future objects; those with a high discount rate are more impulsive and less patient (Cook has argued that individual discount rates may make deterrence through the legal system problematic).[278] Notice what happens to the costs of crime when the discount rate increases from 0.10 to 0.20 (and the delay is equal to one time period). When r=0.10, the discount factor is equal to 0.91. As Nagin and Pogarsky illustrate, when the present value of a fine is $1,000, the value delayed by one time period falls to $909 with a discount fact of 0.91.[279] When the discount rate is increased from 0.10 to 0.20, the discount factor becomes 0.83 and the value of a $1,000 fine for a more impulsive individual is $833. They also show how the discount factor provides an operational understanding of the celerity of punishment. At a fixed level of impulsivity (r), the longer the expected delay in punishment (or, as t increases) the discount factor also increases. So if r=0.10 and the delay in punishment is over two periods, then the discount factor is 0.83 and the present value of a $1,000 fine is $833.

According to this deterrence model, the utility of crime decreases as legal and extralegal costs increase. The utility of crime also decreases as the probability of punishment, captured by p, increases. The magnitude by which punishment produces a disutility is also a function of the value of the discount factor δ_t for each individual—as it decreases the person places less weight on the cost of future punishment. As can be seen, the value of δ_t declines as t, the time between the act (or celerity), increases.

Although Nagin and Pogarsky did not directly confront this issue, notice that if George Loewenstein is correct, persons do not view delayed punishment more favorably but want to get their punishment over as quickly as possible.[280] If true, then celerity would have an inverse weight, such that delayed punishment is perceived to be more costly than more immediate punishment. Whether or not celerity is a positive or negative

[277] Nagin & Pogarsky, *supra* note 246, at 872.

[278] Cook, *supra* note 204, at 232-33.

[279] Nagin & Pogarsky, *supra* note 246, at 872.

[280] Loewenstein, *supra* note 246, at 667-68.

weight is one of the interesting issues deterrence researchers need to address in the future.

Nagin and Pogarsky collected data using a hypothetical drunk driving scenario and a sample of college students to test their deterrence model.[281] They found that the perceived certainty and severity of legal punishment had a significant effect on expressed intentions to drive while drunk, but the perceived celerity of punishment did not. As in virtually every deterrence study to date, the perceived certainty of punishment was more important than the perceived severity. The perceived extralegal costs of punishment (the cost of hiring a lawyer) was at least as good at explaining intentions to drive drunk as the anticipated fines. The effect of the perceived severity was far less for those who were more present-oriented than those who were more future-oriented. Nagin and Pogarsky's work is important, not only for putting celerity back on the table for deterrence scholars to debate and examine, but for getting deterrence theorists to think about the role of stable individual characteristics, such as one's discount rate or time orientation, in the deterrence process.

As well as being one of the most interesting and informative perceptual deterrence studies, Nagin and Pogarsky's findings summarize this entire body of perceptual deterrence literature.[282] As seen across a diverse variety of offenses and with different methodologies (panel survey and scenarios), the evidence seems to suggest that there is a modest deterrent effect for the perceived certainty of legal punishment on behavior, no consistent effect for the perceived severity or celerity of punishment (though the latter needs additional research), an even stronger effect for the certainty of non-legal or informal sanctions, and finally, a modest to strong effect for the perceived benefits or gains from offending. The conclusion that Nagin came to in his earlier review of the deterrence literature seems equally accurate today: "[A] consensus has emerged among perceptual deterrence researchers that the negative association between sanction risk perceptions and offending behavior or intentions [to offend] is measuring deterrence."[283] The dispute may occur over how large the effect is. Other reviewers of the perceptual deterrence and rational choice literature, for example, have noted that the magnitude of these observed deterrent effects have not been particularly large relative to other explanatory factors. Travis Pratt and colleagues conducted a meta-analysis of the perceptual deterrence literature and concluded that "the mean effect sizes of the relationships between crime/deviance and variables specified by deterrence theory are

[281] Nagin & Pogarsky, *supra* note 246, at 874-75.

[282] *Id.* at 872-84.

[283] Nagin, *supra* note 77, at 15.

modest to negligible."[284] The safest conclusion from the literature thus far would be that the perception of certain legal and extralegal sanctions does seem to act as a modest deterrent factor, but that the perceived severity and celerity of punishment do not appear to be effective deterrents to crime, and we know virtually nothing about celerity. The remaining question to be addressed in the conclusion is why we do not find more dramatic and impressive deterrent effects. Is it because people are not rational as deterrence theory requires, or is it that the criminal justice system is not set up to best exploit that rationality?

VII. CONCLUSION

The remark offered at the beginning of this Article still seems relevant at the end—the literature seems to suggest that there is a marginal deterrent effect to some changes in criminal justice policy. It is reasonable to believe that increasing the number of police officers on the street does deter some amount of crime, and increasing the risk of incarceration does as well. The literature on the specific deterrent effect of imprisonment (whether those who are punished do not return to crime when released) was not reviewed here, but it has been reviewed elsewhere very recently, and the evidence does not suggest that either imprisonment itself or the length of imprisonment is effective in deterring crime for those who experience it.[285] There is very little evidence to support the notion that there is a robust relationship between the objective and perceived properties of punishment, though offenders do rationally update their risk estimates in response to their own and others' experiences. Finally, while there may be disagreement about the magnitude, there does seem to be a modest inverse relationship between the perceived certainty of punishment and crime, but no real evidence of a deterrent effect for severity, and no real knowledge base about the celerity of punishment.[286]

---

[284] Pratt et al., *supra* note 251, at 383.

[285] *See* Anthony N. Doob & Cheryl Marie Webster, *Sentence Severity and Crime: Accepting the Null Hypothesis*, *in* 30 CRIME AND JUSTICE: A REVIEW OF RESEARCH 143 (Michael Tonry ed., 2003); Daniel S. Nagin et al., *Imprisonment and Reoffending*, *in* 38 CRIME AND JUSTICE: A REVIEW OF RESEARCH 115 (Michael Tonry ed., 2009).

[286] In addition to the work on the specific deterrent effect of imprisonment, space prevented the review of other literatures that speak to the possibility of a deterrent effect. For example, one important but unaddressed issue is whether or not there is a marginal deterrent effect as one transitions from the juvenile justice system to the adult system. There is evidence in favor of deterrence from studies that show a sharp drop in crime when youth reach the age of adulthood and move from the very much more lenient juvenile justice system to the more punitive adult justice system. Steven D. Levitt, *Juvenile Crime and Punishment*, 106 J. POL. ECON. 1156 (1998). However, while Hjalmarsson found that the perceived risk of arrest and punishment increases at the age of majority, there was no consistent relationship between this increased perception of risk and self-reported

A puzzling question is why deterrent effects reported in the literature are not stronger. Does it mean that people are not rational and do not behave rationally? Or does it mean that the criminal justice system might not be the best place to see deterrent effects given how it the system works? In other words, perhaps offenders are rational, or at least rational enough to be effectively deterred by sanction threats, but the criminal justice system is not capable of exploiting that rationality.[287]

The evidence to date with respect to deterrence does speak clearly about the role of rational choice in criminal offending. It says that while offenders and would-be offenders may not be perfect Bayesians or perfectly rational, they certainly are rational in the sense that they respond to incentives and disincentives. For example, research at the individual-level shows that people are affected by their perceptions about the risk of getting caught for misconduct and that these perceptions are sensitive to the outcomes of behavior. Perceptions of the risks of crime are pushed downward when people commit crimes and get away with them and are pushed upward when they get arrested. Policy studies about the policing of "hot spots" and police "crackdowns" do generally show that there is at least an initial general deterrent effect in response to the enhanced presence of the police and police actions, and that offenders rationally readjust their perceptions of the risk of sanctions and reduce their offending. Or rationally noticing that enforcement in one area has increased, they "move around the corner" and commit crimes elsewhere until the "heat is off." Evidence of crime displacement, then, while troublesome for policy evaluations is perfectly consistent, and even expected, under the assumptions of deterrence and rational choice theory.

---

involvement in criminal behavior. Randi Hjalmarsson, *Crime and Expected Punishment: Changes in Perception at the Age of Criminal Majority*, 11 AM. L. & ECON. REV. 209, 240-44 (2009). There is also evidence counter to deterrence theory which fails to show that permissible concealed gun laws have a negative impact on crime. Jens Ludwig, *Gun Self-Defense and Deterrence*, *in* 27 CRIME AND JUSTICE: A REVIEW OF RESEARCH 363 (Michael Tonry ed., 2000). Finally, there is an abundant literature on whether or not the death penalty is an effective deterrent to homicide with strong statements by some that it is a very effective deterrent, while others offer compelling grounds to think that it really has no effect. *See generally* Ethan Cohen-Cole et al., *Model Uncertainty and the Deterrent Effect of Capital Punishment*, 11 AM. L. & ECON. REV. 335 (2009); John J. Donahue & Justin Wolfers, *Estimating the Impact of the Death Penalty on Murder*, 11 AM. L. & ECON. REV. 249 (2009); John J. Donahue & Justin Wolfers, *Uses and Abuses of Empirical Evidence in the Death Penalty Debate*, 58 STAN. L. REV. 791 (2005); Cass R. Sunstein & Adrian Vermeule, *Is Capital Punishment Morally Required? Acts, Omissions, and Life-Life Tradeoffs*, 58 STAN. L. REV. 703 (2005).

[287] Special thanks to Shawn Bushway for hammering this point into my head as only he can.

Even the finding that prison sentences or longer prison sentences do not deter—and may actually slightly increase the risk of recidivism—is consistent with a rational choice view of offending.[288] While prison, and more rather than less prison, may send a deterrent message to would-be offenders that punishment is credible and severe, it may, in the longer-term, make it much more difficult for those who have been imprisoned to desist when they leave the penitentiary. There is an abundant literature that vividly describes the many and onerous obstacles to employment, housing, and full civic participation that ex-offenders face upon release from prison.[289] These obstacles have the effect of decreasing the utility of non-offending. Confronted by the fact that employment is substantially impaired because of their criminal record, public housing is restricted, and other penalties to citizenship exist, crime subsequent to imprisonment may be the more rational alternative for some past offenders. Much of the deterrence literature, then, is perfectly consistent with a rational choice understanding of criminal behavior. But if offenders and would-be offenders are indeed rational, why are deterrent effects for legal sanctions so meager in the literature?

The answer to this question must remain speculative at the moment but it was hinted at very early on in the intellectual history of deterrence theory and the intellectual history of the *Journal of Criminal Law and Criminology*.[290] Both Bentham and Beccaria argued that in order to be effective in offsetting the perceived benefits of crime, punishment must come soon after the offense. Beccaria said it most directly: "The more promptly and the more closely punishment follows upon the commission of a crime, the more just and useful it will be."[291] The reason prompt punishment is more "useful" is because it is important "that the crime and the punishment be intimately linked to together, if it be desirable that, in crude vulgar minds, the seductive picture of a particularly advantageous crime *should immediately call up the associated idea of punishment*."[292]

Although both Beccaria and Bentham have been accused of having had a primitive idea of human learning, they actually had a quite sophisticated

---

288 *Cf.* Doob & Webster, *supra* note 285.

289 *See generally* DEVAH PAGER, MARKED: RACE, CRIME, AND FINDING WORK IN AN ERA OF MASS INCARCERATION (2007); Shawn D. Bushway, *The Impact of Arrest on the Job Stability of Young White American Men*, 35 J. RES. CRIME & DELINQ. 454 (1998); Shawn D. Bushway, *Labor Market Effect of Permitting Employers Access to Criminal History Records*, 20 J. CONTEMP. CRIM. JUST. 276 (2004); Christopher Uggen et al., *Citizenship and Reintegration: The Socioeconomic, Familial, and Civic Lives of Criminal Offenders*, 605 ANNALS AM. ACAD. POL. & SOC. SCI. 281 (2006).

290 *See, e.g.*, von Hentig, *supra* note 43.

291 BECCARIA, *supra* note 2, at 55.

292 *Id.* at 57.

understanding of the limits of criminal deterrence. Beccaria clearly argued that for a deterrence system to be most effective, the crime should immediately trigger in the would-be offender's mind the anticipated punishment. The benefit of the crime, the "seductive picture" of it, is immediate and must in turn be countered in the person's mind by the comparably immediate anticipation of punishment. Beccaria was fully aware of the pull of immediate pleasure and that most of us are more attracted by the immediate benefits of action than we are by the long-term costs: "[T]he more vulgar [people] are, the more apt they are to act merely on immediate and familiar associations, ignoring the more remote and complex ones."[293] For deterrence to work well, the would-be offender, tempted by the immediate gains of committing the crime, must be able to quickly conjure up in her mind the anticipated pain of punishment. To assist them in that conjuring up of the punishment in their mind, the criminal justice system must make punishment swift. However, in the criminal justice system, not only are punishments uncertain, they are far in the future compared with the benefits of offending. The criminal justice system, because it has other imperatives (justice must be served and justice frequently takes time), is not culturally positioned to exploit the rationality of offenders.

Criminal deterrence may have its limits precisely because the legal costs are far removed in time and people find it difficult to feel the pain of the longer-term consequences of their actions. The critic of deterrence von Hentig referred to the pains of the criminal law as a "long-distance danger" and noted that "the criminal seems to be in part a human specimen, whose appetites and desires are irresistibly attracted by a near object."[294] The problem of being seduced by "near objects" is perhaps more general than von Hentig thought. Think for a moment of the predicament of the dieter tempted by a delicious slice of chocolate cake. The pleasures are powerful and immediate, and the pain of added pounds is down the road, removed in time. The cake would be eaten unless this dieter can imagine in their mind an immediate cost—say the feeling of defeat at breaking her diet or shame at succumbing to the seduction. In order to offset the immediate pleasure of eating the chocolate cake, the tempted dieter would have to be able to perceive an immediate pain of breaking the diet. In a series of absolutely fascinating research papers, a group of behavioral economists and psychologists referred to this immediate discomfort or pain as the "pain of paying."[295] They specifically ask why people purchase things they clearly

[293] *Id.* at 56.

[294] Von Hentig, *supra* note 43, at 559 (emphasis omitted).

[295] Brian Kuntson et al., *Neural Predictors of Purchases*, 53 NEURON 147, 147 (2007); Scott Rick et al., *Tightwads and Spendthrifts*, 34 J. CONSUMER RES. 767, 768 (2007).

cannot afford, sometimes becoming spendthrifts; the answer, they argue, is that many of us find it difficult to feel the "pain of paying," we defer payment with credit cards or don't *really* pay for it by using debit cards.[296] Unable to feel the immediate pain of paying, we buy what we don't need to buy, we eat and drink what we shouldn't eat and drink, and we gamble when we should save. The "limit[] of deterrence" is that formal legal sanctions may be too far removed in time to provide that immediate pain of paying.[297] This was precisely the point made by Jeffery in his *Journal* article when he noted that a most unfortunate feature about legal punishment and criminal behavior, and the reason why criminal sanctions cannot be relied upon to generate conformity, is that "[t]here are no aversive stimuli in the environment *at that moment*."[298]

Without suggesting at all that legal sanctions should be abandoned because Andenaes was absolutely correct when he asserted that legal sanctions serve to reinforce our notion of morality, and because there is evidence of modest marginal deterrent effects of the law, we might take Beccaria's advice in the next to the last chapter of *On Crimes* to heart and consider that our best effort at securing compliance with rules may come much earlier in life through education and prevention.[299] Maybe Beccaria had it right and the answer to America's crime problem is to be found in the *Emile* and not the *Panopticon*.

Finally, it is also very likely that the distal punishment of the criminal justice system not only fails to constructively exploit rationality, it does, to its detriment, effectively exploit a common feature of decision making under uncertainty—time discounting. As Cook brought up three decades ago, people have a tendency to "discount" future events.[300] This discounting would account for the fact that even those who have experienced punishment, on average, rate a ten-year prison sentence as much less than twice as severe as a five-year sentence.[301] When we think we are greatly enhancing deterrent effects by doubling the length of sentences, then, we likely have a far lessened impact on the offending calculus of offenders. Time discounting applies to the entire panoply of sanctions available in the arsenal of the legal system, punishments occur in the future, and their certainty and severity may be greatly discounted in making a decision as to whether to commit a crime or not. Whatever sanctions the criminal justice system may have available for offenders or

[296] Knutson et al., *supra* note 295, at 151-52; Rick et al., *supra* note 295, at 767-69.

[297] Von Hentig, *supra* note 43, at 559.

[298] Jeffery, *supra* note 71, at 299 (emphasis added).

[299] BECCARIA, *supra* note 2, at 93-98.

[300] Cook, *supra* note 204, at 232-33.

[301] McClelland & Alpert, *supra* note 208, 311 tbl.1.

would-be offenders, their effectiveness in deterring crime is naturally diminished by their lack of temporal proximity to the offending decision. This lends further humility in expecting that the law and legal institutions can play the most important role in securing compliance to important social norms.

[3]

Deterrence

Thom Brooks

Introduction

Deterrence has traditionally been understood as the primary alternative to retributivism. Both have been at loggerheads for literally centuries. It is easy to see why. Retributivists give special attention to a criminal's desert for a past injustice: it is primarily a backward-looking theory of punishment. Deterrence is primarily a forward-looking theory of punishment: deterrence proponents give special attention to deterring future criminality. Therefore, deterrence offers us a very different focus and understanding of the purpose of punishment. This chapter will clarify the leading theories of deterrence to determine their promise and potential problems.

What is deterrence?

Deterrence theories of punishment claim that the general justification of punishment is deterrence. Deterrence proponents argue that a key feature of punishment should be its ability to make crime less frequent, if not end. Punishment that merely harmed criminals and lacked any clear beneficial effects may even be seen as cruel. Instead, punishment may be justified on account of the good consequences that it makes possible. These may include deterrence of criminality.

Deterrence proponents have traditionally argued that people are deterred by the threat of punishment. Many classic defenders of deterrence have been utilitarians. Generally speaking, utilitarians argue that we seek pleasure and avoid pain. The threat of punishment is a pain to be avoided. Punishment deters because we want to avoid the pains of punishment. For example, David Hume argues:

> 'Tis indeed certain, that as all human laws are founded on rewards and punishments, 'tis suppos'd as a fundamental principle, that these motives have an influence on the mind, and both produce the good and prevent the evil actions.[1]

Utilitarians often assume that individuals are naturally selfish. We are influenced by external influences, not least social influences including the threat of punishment. The idea is that punishment may have a deterrent effect upon us because we are naturally selfish and we would normally choose to avoid the pain of punishment. We choose to be law abiding after making a rational choice calculus: the burdens of potential punishment outweigh the benefits from crime.

Deterrent punishment helps realize an important good. The political community has enacted a criminal law. If the criminal law is just, then it is right that we encourage others to act in accordance with it and avoid criminality. Punishment can play a positive role in protecting the security of us all in deterring potential criminals.[2] This idea has its roots in Plato's writings:

> It is appropriate for everyone who is subject to punishment rightly inflicted by another either to become better and profit from it, or else be made an example to others, so that when they see him suffering whatever it is he suffers, they may be afraid and become better.[3]

This defence of deterrence is shared by a great many today. For example, Ted Honderich argues that punishment may be acceptable simply because it deters'.[4] Acceptance of deterrence may lie in the beneficial consequences it might produce.

Deterrent punishments can take several forms, such as general or specific deterrence. General deterrence is often understood as the public threat of punishment and specific deterrence as the individual's experience of punishment. An alternative view of this distinction is between *macrodeterrence* (general deterrence) and *microdeterrence* (specific deterrence).[5] Macrodeterrence concerns society in general. It asks how we might best construct deterrent punishments for society at large. This analysis focuses on the crime and steps that could be taken to deter persons from crime. Macrodeterrence judges success on the basis of how well punishment acts as a general deterrence.

Microdeterrence focuses on the criminal. It asks how we might deter an individual from crime. This view finds expression in a brief essay by John Stuart Mill: 'You do not punish one person in order that another may be deterred. The other is deterred, not by the punishment of the first, but by the expectation of being punished himself'.[6] Microdeterrence judges success on the basis of how well punishment acts as a specific deterrent for particular individuals.

Macrodeterrence and microdeterrence offer different perspectives on how we might approach the construction of deterrent punishments. However, these different perspectives need not translate into conflicting viewpoints. Instead, the two should be understood as working together in approaching the same project from different angles. Furthermore, they may overlap so that general and specific deterrence may be achieved together.

The way we construct deterrent punishments may take several forms, such as fear, incapacitation, and reform. The first form is the traditional understanding of deterrence. Deterrent punishments are public threats: individuals are deterred from criminality by the fear of threatened punishment if they engage in criminality. This fear of threatened pain is what motivates individuals to remain law abiding. If the public is sufficiently afraid of threatened punishment, then the public will not offend.

The second form of constructing deterrent punishments is *incapacitation*. This view, first argued for by William Paley, has a long history as well.[7] The incapacitation approach argues that the criminal can be said to be deterred from criminality by virtue of his becoming imprisoned. For example, the idea is that all potential criminals have something in common: they are not imprisoned. Whatever prison's deterrent effects upon the general public, prison has an undeniable deterrent effect on imprisoned criminals: they cannot commit crimes while imprisoned. The incapacitation approach does suffer from at least two serious problems. The first is that it may compel us to imprison everyone. If our desired goal is to deter as much crime as we can and no imprisoned person can commit crime, then we can deter more crime by imprisoning more people. Moreover, we can deter all crime when we imprison (virtually) everyone.[8]

This position is highly objectionable because incapacitation is not reducible to punishment, nor vice versa.[9] Recall that we should understand punishment as a response to crime: punishment must be of a person for breaking the law. The first problem for incapacitation is that it might justify the imprisonment of innocent persons in order to prevent future crime. The second problem is that criminality does not stop at the prison gate: criminals can and do (and perhaps always have) committed crimes within prisons. Such crimes include assaults and abuse of controlled substances. Not only might incapacitation insufficiently guard against objectionable implications, but it rests on a mistake about *the geography of crime*, namely, that crimes are not confined to public places or private homes, but they may take place in prisons as well. Criminality is possible both within and outside prisons. A deterrent theory of punishment must recognize this fact about the geography of crime, a feature too often overlooked and unnoticed.[10]

A final form that deterrence might take is reform. Future criminality might be deterred because criminals have become reformed. I will highlight this further understanding of deterrence as reform in the next chapter.

Deterrence and crime reduction

Deterrence is about crime reduction, but not all crime reduction is evidence of deterrence. This is because deterrence is one approach amongst many to reduce crime. One method of crime reduction may be the rehabilitation of offenders. Rehabilitated offenders are reformed and refrain from future criminality, which assists crime reduction efforts. But this is not deterrence. Deterrence theories aim to reduce crime by deterring potential criminal offenders. They are deterred where they choose against crime because they desire to avoid punishment. Crime reduction may be a result of deterrence, but deterrence is not the only method for achieving crime reduction. It is important to recognize that deterrence is one of many penal strategies for achieving crime reduction because it highlights that there may be significant differences in how we approach crime reduction. So if there was evidence that crime has been reduced over a period of time, then this is not necessarily evidence that crime reduction was a result of deterrence. Deterrence may always aim at crime reduction, but not all crime reduction is a result of deterrence.

Deterrence and desert

The problem most commonly associated with deterrence is the problem of punishing the innocent: deterrence should be rejected because it could justify the punishment of innocent persons. This problem is frequently used by retributivists to argue that retribution should be preferred over deterrence because only retribution takes criminal desert seriously. Let me explain this debate further.

Retributivists argue – in what we might call *the standard view* – that punishment should be distributed only where it is deserved. Retribution is a deontological theory in that punishment is not justified by its effects, but desert. Deterrence is instead a consequentialist theory whereby punishment is justified where it has specific consequences, such as a deterrent effect. This difference gives rise to a disagreement about how we justify the punishment of criminals. One criticism of deterrence is that, as Hegel argues, 'to justify punishment in this way is like raising one's stick at a dog; it means treating a human being like a dog instead of respecting his honour and freedom'.[11] For critics like Hegel, deterrence fails to honour people in failing to offer them reasons for good citizenship and avoidance of criminality.

We might respond that this criticism misses its target. Deterrence does offer reasons to citizens to refrain from criminality: if citizens engage in crime, the state threatens to impose punishment. Nor need this be problematic where citizens believe. Deterrence proponents might also claim that retributivists are no better. Both declare that criminals will be punished in advance. One important difference is that deterrence proponents believe that the threat of punishment may have a deterrent effect. We should expect potential criminals to reconsider participating in criminal activity to avoid the possibility of punishment. Retributivists may accept a similar analysis. While retributivists might argue that the severity of punishment is not set with a view of any future deterrent effect, retributivists may still claim that the *wrongness* of a crime should weigh on the conscience of potential criminals and contribute to their reconsidering any criminal activity. Deterrence proponents are mistaken to believe that the only deterrent effect to be found is in the threat of punishment and not the gravity of a crime's wrongfulness.

Deterrence proponents might reply that its aim is to reduce criminal activity by rendering it sufficiently unattractive. One relevant factor will be the threat of punishment, but a second factor will be the criminal act itself. Citizens may find criminal activity unattractive because they wish to avoid the possibility of punishment, but also because they agree with the laws governing their relations. Cesare Beccaria says:

> What are the true and most effective laws? They are those pacts and conventions that everyone would observe and propose while the voice of private interest, which one always hears, is silent or in agreement with the voice of the public interest.[12]

The result is that perhaps deterrence does aim to manipulate the incentive structure for citizens in order to reduce crime. No plausible theory of punishment claims that criminal activity is desirable or good. If punishment could be used to reduce crime by winning the agreement of citizens and deterring potential criminals, then these should be compelling arguments in its favour.

This raises a deeper concern often raised by retributivists against deterrence. Let us accept that the reduction of crime is desirable or even good. The traditional argument against deterrence is that it might permit the punishment, or even execution, of the innocent. The objection is as follows. Deterrence proponents believe that punishment is justified, at least in part, by its deterrent effects. If these effects were obtained by punishing the innocent, then punishment would be justified because it would have a deterrent effect. If deterring potential criminals is what matters, then this does not rule out our only punishing criminals. The objection is that we should never punish the innocent for crimes they did not commit. Deterrence is an objectionable penal aim because it might justify punishing innocent people.

This concern is not lost on leading proponents of deterrence. In fact, it is difficult to find any major figure who accepts the possibility of punishing the innocent under any circumstances: the worry that deterrence approaches would lead to the punishment of the innocent is largely a criticism about deterrence approaches and not a policy that deterrence proponents espouse. All place clear limits on how deterrence should be pursued. Examples abound. Plato argues that the criminal should receive 'due punishment for the wrongdoing he commits'.[13] Fichte similarly claims that 'in a well-governed state, no innocent person should ever be punished'.[14] Bentham likewise rejects the punishment of the innocent.[15] Beccaria is a possible exception. He argues it is necessary to execute an innocent person if his death was 'the *only* real way of restraining others from committing crimes'.[16] However, this is not much of a concession to critics of deterrence approaches if we believed that such cases might be so rare as to be virtually non-existent.

We might then argue that deterrence theories are at best impure. Each would appear to accept some retributivist core that punishment must first be deserved before it can be punished and never imposed on the innocent. The difference would then appear to be that deterrence theories link the severity of punishment with expected future effects rather than the gravity of a crime's wrongfulness. If true, then these deterrent theories might be understood as *negative retributivist* theories of punishment. Negative retributivists argue that desert is necessary, but not sufficient for punishment. Punishment is distributed where other non-desert factors obtain.[17]

Deterrence proponents need not accept that their 'deterrence' theories are in fact a species of retributivism. Another compelling perspective is the following.[18] The state issues threats: if citizens perform a crime, then they will be punished for it. The state then punishes those persons who have failed to heed such threats.[19] So the state only punishes those persons who have failed to obey its threats and, thus, the state aims to deter without punishing the innocent. The state punishes to make good on its original threat to punish crimes: these threats would lack substance if the state failed to make good on its promise. Only those who break the law are subject to punishment: 'The threat is addressed to each individually, and each is punished because he, individually, chose to ignore the threat; the others, and their potential behaviour, are irrelevant'.[20] This understanding of deterrence punishes only the guilty, but not on grounds of desert. Deterrence theories can avoid justifying the punishment of innocent people.

One final consideration is criminals who resist deterrence: *the problem of the undeterrable*. Retributivists, on the standard view, would punish the undeterrable because punishment is deserved. Future consequences are irrelevant. This is untrue for deterrence, where future consequences take centre stage. The undeterrable are not a major problem for theories of macrodeterrence: while some may not be deterred, punishment may be justified where it leads to reductions in crime for the general population. The situation is different with the microdeterrence of an individual offender. If a person is genuinely resistant to changing his behaviour in response to any deterrent efforts, then specific deterrence would fail in like cases. The problem of undeterrable criminals raises an important difficulty for microdeterrence accounts. If certain persons cannot be deterred, then punishment is not justified because it will not have any deterrent effect on them. Punishment might only be justified on grounds of macrodeterrence were it possible to have a deterrent effect on others, or the deterrable.

Deterrence and difference

Deterrence theories of punishment aim to deter potential criminals from criminality. Our focus is on constructing a suitable deterrent for members of a political community. This is a consequentialist approach: the deterrent proponent aspires to secure a particular consequence, namely, reduced criminality. The target is the political community and this raises several potential problems concerning *the problem of difference.*

The first potential problem is that we cannot hope to find any *single* punishment that might have the same deterrent effect for everyone everywhere. A penal threat may have a greater effect upon you than me. There are several reasons why this is the case. One reason is that deterrence is specific to local social conditions: what works as a deterrent in one political community may lack a similar effect in other communities. So a punishment may have a different deterrent effect or none at all in different political communities. Furthermore, this problem may not merely exist between political communities, but it may also exist within political communities. Call this *the problem of domestic difference.* Some social groups within the same political community may respond differently to the same deterrent threats. A second reason why deterrent punishments may differ between communities is that deterrence is linked with particular crimes and these crimes may differ from one community to the next. Therefore, deterrent punishments for crimes may not hold universally where there is disagreement between different political communities on what is included within the criminal law. This is only a problem for a global theory of deterrent punishment: deterrence may only be a genuine possibility within a political community.

The second potential problem is that what may deter today may not deter tomorrow. This is *the problem of time and changing effects.* Whatever knowledge we have of deterrent effects is always knowledge of the past: the owl of Minerva takes flight at dusk.[21] The fact that some were deterred last year or even yesterday may be no guarantee that we can expect a similar number to be deterred today or next month. The deterrent power of punishment constantly changes over time in response to social conditions. Therefore, the deterrent potential of any punishment is always in flux and subject to constant change. One problem is that this potential may only be known after the fact; the deterrent potential of present punishments is always a matter of guesswork to some degree. We can never say that any one punishment is always best to maximize the deterrence of potential criminals for any crime. This is because we can only guess at likely future effects and these effects are subject to constant revision.

The use of the same punishment may have different deterrent effects in different communities and be subject to constant change over time. These issues highlight the deep complexity associated with deterrence and the challenges for presenting global theories of deterrence. These concerns do not entail that we cannot know whether there are deterrent effects from the threat of punishment, but rather that such knowledge is complex and difficult to acquire.

The data on deterrence

Deterrence proponents offer a theory of punishment linked to empirical claims. They argue not only *that* punishment should be designed to bring about deterrence, but that punishment *has* a deterrent effect. Deterrence is an evidence-based approach to criminal justice. So what do the data reveal?

The big problem for deterrence theories is that punishment does not appear to have much, if any, confirmed deterrent effect.[22] There is much disagreement about the best measures of deterrence and indications of success or failure, but several conclusions have become established in recent years concerning criminals who have been imprisoned. Many reoffend upon release. For example, most criminals who are imprisoned receive sentences of 12 months or less. Approximately 60 per cent will reoffend and often within weeks of release.[23] One study of American prisoners released since 1994 found that two-thirds were arrested for a serious misdemeanour or felony within three years, and half of these were reconvicted for new crimes. The study concluded that 'no evidence was found that spending more time in prison raises the recidivism rate'.[24]

These results have been confirmed in several international studies which have also cast doubt on whether there is any link between time served and reoffending.[25] For example, the British Prime Minister's Strategy Unit has concluded that 'there is no convincing evidence that further increases in the use of custody would significantly reduce crime'.[26] Increasing prison sentences may be popular with the public, but the evidence is that such policies place greater pressures on taxpayers for no substantive improvements upon recidivism rates. The public may often support 'tough on crime' policies whereby penal tariffs rise ever higher, but such support lacks sufficient evidence that it works. The main consequence is much higher costs without improvements in crime reduction.[27]

Perhaps surprisingly, even threats of severe punishment have not been conclusively shown to possess a deterrent effect, and decreased offending has not been strongly linked with increasing the severity of punishments.[28] One example is California's so-called 'Three Strikes and You're Out' law. This motto refers to baseball where a batter is 'out' after receiving three strikes. Anyone convicted of a third strike-eligible crime faces a minimum 25 year imprisonment. This is irrespective of the seriousness of the crimes committed. It might be expected that – even if an unreasonable policy – such a high penal tariff would have some clear deterrent effect, but the findings are surprising. The deterrent effect appears small and is estimated at about 2 per cent or less.[29] The policy has led to an explosion in the prison population and contributed to the further problem of prison overcrowding.[30] Thus, even fairly severe threats of punishment have not conclusively demonstrated a clear deterrent effect, but these penal experiments have contributed to ever higher costs for little, if any, public benefit.

A common criticism is that imprisoning criminals makes them better criminals. For example, criminals may be thought to become transformed into *criminal labourers* through imprisonment: the 'professional' thief, for example. Some claim that imprisonment may even be *criminogenic* because it may contribute to more crime and not less.[31] The contributing problems are that imprisonment often leads to offenders 'losing their jobs, their homes and their families'.[32] While we would expect those with the longest prison sentences to be most likely to reoffend, this is not supported by most evidence. Most released prisoners will reoffend, but these persons often serve sentences of less than one year. Recidivism rates drop for all criminals serving more than one year in prison: the longer a criminal is imprisoned, the less likely he is to reoffend upon release. This may have more to do with the crimes associated with longer sentences and the greater professional support these inmates can expect to receive, as well as the age of offenders upon release. It is worth noting that criminals given suspended sentences and community sentences reoffend less often than criminals imprisoned for under a year.[33] If our aim is to reduce crime rates, then the use of prison may be counterproductive. This may be counterintuitive: we might expect the burdens of imprisonment to deter better than community service, but deterrence proponents must support policies that best meet their preferred penal goals. If alternatives to prison work best, then these alternatives should be endorsed.

None of this need deny that crime rates have ever fallen. Instead, the issue is that where we find lower crime rates there are often non-deterrence factors to account for such changes.[34] For example, there is evidence that crime rates may be linked to the number of males aged between 15 and 24 years: the greater the number of males, the higher the expected crime rates.[35] There is also evidence that increased economic insecurity leads to both rising crime rates and a greater public fear of crime. It has been claimed that 'individuals who are worried about their economic stability may be more likely to fear criminals, who could further threaten their increasingly tenuous economic positions'.[36] Furthermore, Steven Levitt and Stephen Dubner argue:

> It is true that a stronger job market may make certain crimes relatively less attractive. But that is only the case for crimes with a direct financial motivation—burglary, robbery, and auto theft—as opposed to violent crimes like homicide, assault, and rape. Moreover, studies have shown that an unemployment decline of 1 percentage point accounts for a 1 percent drop in nonviolent crime.[37]

One clear result is that a strong job creation strategy ensuring low unemployment rates is not only good economics, but a good criminal justice policy leading to lower crime rates and lower public fear of crime.

Not all studies have failed to find substantive deterrent effects. However, these studies often conclude that these effects are modest at best. For example, the results often reveal that the effects of deterrence upon crime rates is at most between about a 2 to 5 per cent decrease in crime following a 10 per cent increase in the prison population.[38] If this is true, then prison may have an identifiable deterrent effect. However, the effects do not appear large and come at a significant cost to taxpayers.

Judging success

Discussions about the data on deterrence inevitably raise important questions about what constitutes 'success' for any deterrence theory of punishment. We have at least three options:

(1) Deterrent theories of punishment aim for any deterrent effect.
(2) Deterrent theories of punishment aim for any substantial effect.
(3) Deterrent theories of punishment aim for a complete effect.

The first option is too weak and the third is too strong. The first option claims that the aims of deterrent punishment are satisfied where *any* deterrent effect may be identified. This is too weak. Suppose we have two different punishments. The difference between them is that one punishment is known to deter a small handful and the other punishment lacks any known effect. The deterrence proponent would seem compelled to prefer a punishment with *any* deterrent effect over an alternative that *lacked* any effect. But would this remain true if a very small effect were only made possible by way of inflicting great pain? The deterrence proponent is not a retributivist: she does not link a punishment's severity with what is deserved, but rather what has a deterrent effect. But this is not quite right. Deterrence proponents argue that deterrence is a central justification of punishment. Therefore, deterrence should not have a mere negligible presence, but it should play a clearer role in punishing. If deterrence is the justification of punishment, then it must also play some clear – and not merely tangential – role. Deterrence is *reductivist*: its goal is the reduction of crime. A deterrent approach that can promise no more than little, if any, reduction in crime is not much worth its name.

The third option is too strong. While we may hope that a great many will be deterred from criminality, we cannot expect our hope will be realized. There is a little appreciated fact about crime that I call *the fact of crime in society*. It is a fact that any society will have crime if it has a criminal law. This fact is not always recognized by proponents of deterrence. For example, Johann Gottlieb Fichte argues:

> Punishment is not an absolute end ... Punishment is a means for achieving the state's end, which is public security; and its only purpose is to prevent offenses by threatening to punish them. The end of penal law is to render itself unnecessary. The threat of punishment aims to ... never be necessary.[39]

However noble its aim of seeing punishment wither on the vine one day, it is pure fantasy to believe that crime will ever disappear so long as we are governed by the rule of law.[40] Laws are not made to be broken, but are broken inevitably nonetheless by carelessness as well as design. There is little point in creating *a utopia of crimelessness*, but much promise in aspiring to restrict the fact of crime in society as best as is possible. Penal theorists may disagree on the ultimate justification of punishment, but they should all prefer less crime and lower recidivism.

The fact that crime is ever present does not mean we should accept crime however it is found. Deterrence proponents should not be satisfied with punishments with negligible deterrent effects nor aspire to full or 'perfect' deterrence. Instead, deterrence proponents defend deterrence as a substantial consequence of justified punishment. This leads us to endorse the second option. A successful deterrence theory is one that can demonstrate a substantial deterrent effect. So what would such an effect look like? It is difficult to pinpoint any specific figure, but surely 2–5 per cent falls far below any plausible indication of a 'substantial deterrent effect'. Nevertheless, our knowledge about the deterrence effects, if any, for any crime is 'exceedingly thin'.[41]

Deterrence, intuitions, and knowledge limits

Many deterrence proponents naturally assume that punishment has a deterrent effect notwithstanding contrary findings by existing studies. For example, James Q. Wilson says:

> People are governed in their daily lives by rewards and penalties of every sort ... To assert that 'deterrence doesn't work' is tantamount to either denying the plainest facts of everyday life or claiming that would-be criminals are utterly different from the rest of us.[42]

It is assumed that we, the community, know the laws that govern us. Ignorance of the law is no defence from future punishment.[43] It is also assumed that the burdens of punishment should outweigh expected benefits from possible criminal activity. Where this obtains, individuals engaged in a cost-benefit analysis will rationally choose to avoid crime. It would be irrational to commit a crime where the costs outweigh expected benefits. The deterrent effect of punishment is intuitively true. Evidence to the contrary is opposed to our most basic intuitions about criminal justice. Or so deterrence proponents may argue.

There are many reasons why this intuitive justification of deterrence is problematic. First, there is little evidence to suggest that criminals weigh costs and benefits in the way many deterrence models assume.[44] Criminals appear to rely on little more than guesswork about their possible likelihood of arrest and conviction.[45] But this is not all. In short, deterrence may assume too much. Michael Davis says: '"Deterrent" does not have any relation to actual or probable crime without assumptions about the rationality of criminals, the efficiency of police, the likelihood that the penalty will not itself make the crime glamorous, and so on'.[46] How many people would have stolen a car last week, if the laws had been different? How many people were deterred from any crime because of any specific legislation? If punishment deters criminals, then it might be possible to have some idea about how to answer these questions. Yet, such answers remain elusive.[47]

For example, deterrence presupposes knowledge about crimes, possible sanctions, the likelihood of arrest and conviction. There are many reasons to believe these articles of faith do not cohere with reality. First, only a few citizens will have knowledge about even a majority of crimes and perhaps no one knows them all. If citizens are to conduct a rational choice assessment weighing the costs and burdens of criminal activity, then they must have satisfactory knowledge about what counts as criminal activity. Most lack this knowledge. Punishment fails to serve its deterrent function where citizens do not know what is criminalized. Perhaps punishment might have a more limited deterrent function on a crime-by-crime basis. For example, many may be unaware about the full range of property crimes, but many will know that murder is criminalized. Punishment may only have a deterrent function for those crimes that citizens have sufficiently satisfactory knowledge about. The problem is that citizens lack such knowledge about most crimes.[48] Citizens cannot be deterred from crimes that they are unaware of.

Second, citizens lack knowledge about most crimes *and* they lack knowledge about possible sanctions for most crimes. This is perhaps a more serious problem than the first. While citizens may not know all crimes, they might still identify a plentiful core acknowledging arson, burglary, murder, and theft amongst others. However, their knowledge of what possible sanctions would relate from a conviction for any of these crimes is even worse. I have lectured on criminal law and punishment in several countries and before many distinguished audiences: not once has anyone been able to correctly identify the tariff for arson for any jurisdiction.[49] Can you? This is despite the fact that all recognize arson as a serious crime. If academics, lawyers, and policymakers are unsure about how arson might be punished, then there is reason to believe the lay public would perform no better. The problem is that punishment cannot have a deterrent effect where citizens do not know how their crimes might be punished.

Third, suppose we possess satisfactory knowledge about crimes and their possible punishments. We would still require satisfactory knowledge *in addition to this* about the likelihood of our arrest and conviction. The facts are startling: the majority of crimes are unsolved. Murders have the highest detection rates, but these are often no better than about 80 per cent. Do you know the likelihood of your being arrested or convicted for benefit fraud or illegal trading? Or for any crime? Punishment cannot have a deterrent effect where citizens do not know crimes, how their crimes might be punished, the likelihood of arrest for crimes, nor the likelihood of punishment.

There is a further issue concerning imprisonment. Many prisoners remain imprisoned beyond their official release date. There are an estimated 2,500 prisoners in the UK alone in this position. The justification is that they remain imprisoned because they have been found to remain a threat to the general public.[50] It is unclear whether or not this improves future deterrence for crimes that may involve imprisonment. On the one hand, this may be relatively unknown by persons potentially affected and so not enter into risk calculations about engaging in crime. On the other hand, the possibility that a prison sentence represents a minimal term and may be for life could have a potential deterrent effect if it is communicated effectively to persons potentially affected. It is perhaps shocking how little effort governments expend on informing the public about possible criminal sanctions. Whatever the reality of deterrence, there is a clear need for improved communication between governments and their citizens to better educate them about criminal punishment.

Many deterrence proponents claim that it is at least intuitively true that punishment has a deterrent effect. We have seen that few studies have shown any substantial deterrent effect. Furthermore, there is little reason to believe that citizens could be deterred by punishment for most crimes. This is because citizens lack sufficient relevant knowledge necessary for deterrence to obtain. Citizens do not know most crimes, know less about possible punishments for crimes, and know little, if anything, about the likelihood for arrest and conviction. It is clear that there is a need for greater communication about such matters with the general public to improve their knowledge in these areas. The intuitive evidence for deterrence seems limited to persons with perfect information about crimes, punishments, and other factors that no one has in fact. The conclusion to be drawn is not that deterrence is impossible, but rather that it is substantially more difficult to determine and perceive than we may initially recognize. Nevertheless, there remains something attractive about a society where crime reduction works, all things considered. But whether crime reduction should be achieved through deterrence or an alternative approach is another consideration.

Should government deter?

Consider the proper role of government. Should government deter? This concern may take many forms, such as whether governments should endorse some alternative justification of punishment. I do not want to address such matters here, but instead focus on a very specific concern that is often overlooked in discussions about deterrence. Surprisingly, this concern arises within the writings of John Stuart Mill, an advocate of deterrence. He offers the following worry: 'the preventive function of government, however, is far more liable to be abused'.[51] Perhaps governments should deter. The problem is this power is most likely to become abused.

Let me address this worry in the following way. It may be argued that a central task of any government is enforcing its laws. The government will have a clear interest in addressing criminality. Deterrence is one way of addressing criminality: governments should address criminality by deterring it, leading to crime reduction. One classic objection to deterrence is that governments fail to treat their citizens with the dignity that they deserve. Deterrence measures may lead governments to treating their citizens as a means to some goal rather than an end in their own right.

We might reply that we use people as a means all the time.[52] For instance, we use taxi drivers to take us to our destinations or we use waitresses to serve us our meals and so on. The question is not whether we use others, but rather whether we use others in a justifiable way.[53] There is a difference between paying another for a consensual service and demanding someone is imprisoned. Nevertheless, this difference does not reflect a problem with the respect of dignity for the imprisoned. Respect can be secured in our ensuring a person is only imprisoned for criminality: no person need be treated merely as a means by deterrence theories of punishment. Thus, deterrence can address people as moral agents and deterrence need not be understood as little better than addressing people like animals.[54]

Mill's worry is not that deterrence denies dignity to others, but that deterrence is more liable to abuse by governments than alternative theories of punishment. Recall that there is a link between the justification of law and the justification of punishment: *there can be no justified punishment for an unjustified law*.[55] If laws are justified, then it becomes possible to justify punishment for criminality. One problem is that governments may use greater threats to deter persons from violating unjustified laws. This might make a bad situation much worse.

Let me explain this point further. Suppose, following Cesare Beccaria, that deterrent punishments should aim to 'make the strongest and most lasting impression on the minds of men, and inflict the least torment on the body of the criminal'.[56] If our aim is to make the biggest impression with the least damage to the criminal, then perhaps our use of punishment should aspire to mislead the public into believing punishments are much worse than they are. This brings us to a famous illustration by Jeremy Bentham: 'If hanging a man *in effigy* would produce the same salutary impression of terror upon the minds of people, it would be a folly or cruelty ever to hang a man *in person*'.[57] The *effect* from punishment is of crucial significance for deterrence proponents. If this effect might be gained without harming anyone through punishment, then such an alternative may prove tempting. Deterrence does not aim to be cruel, but to reduce crime, and such an alternative might fulfil this ambition.

Beccaria argues that 'it is better to prevent crimes than to punish them'.[58] If this is true, then the state may be tempted to broadcast mock punishment in attempts to mislead the public. But this need not be the only result. Instead, governments might attempt to reduce crime without resorting to misleading the public. One reason would be concerns about the likely impact of the public gaining knowledge about any deceit. Mock executions may prove effective where the public are deceived, but backfire catastrophically where the public learn the truth about such matters. Many governments have moved to a greater emphasis on strict liability with the easier convictions this approach brings, albeit for often relatively minor punishments. While governments have many reasons to reduce crime, most do not appear to run afoul of Mill's warning about the likelihood of the abuse of power in the pursuit of prevention strategies. This does not conclusively prove that government should deter, but instead offers some evidence to believe that Mill's warning is not a deciding objection against deterrence.

Conclusion

This chapter has considered the problems and prospects of deterrence approaches. The problems are considerable. First, there is little evidence that deterrence works in any substantive sense. Most studies show limited, if negligible, effects for even severe threats of punishment. Second, there is little evidence that intuitive judgements about deterrence hold much water. These judgements rest upon various assumptions about the knowledge people have about criminal justice that they do not possess. Where we find reduced crime rates, there are often other factors that seem best to explain these changes.

There is also a curious paradox. The public strongly support a 'tough on crime' approach despite a lack of evidence that this approach has any significant beneficial effects. In fact, voters are more likely to vote for candidates who claim a 'tough on crime' policy even where those voters might otherwise favour alternative approaches, such as rehabilitation. Deterrence theories of punishment claim justification because they lead to crime reduction. The problem is that the evidence is inconclusive at best and perhaps even counterintuitive.

There are also clear prospects. The fact that conclusive evidence is lacking does not entail that no evidence can be found, but only that the jury is still out. People may have limited knowledge about criminal justice, but so then we might rely on a more modest understanding of how deterrence might apply. The threat of punishment is clearly one possible factor for potential criminals to desist from engaging in crime. Moreover, crime reduction is desirable: we would prefer a society with less crime to others, all things considered.

The project of deterrence may prove more challenging to offer than its defenders have claimed, but it remains an approach to punishment of real importance.

Notes

1 David Hume, *A Treatise of Human Nature*, 2nd ed., ed. L. A. Selby-Bigge (Oxford: Oxford University Press, 1978): 410.

2 See Mill, *On Liberty*, 10.

3 Plato, 'Gorgias', in *Complete Works*, 525b-c.

4 Ted Honderich, *Punishment: The Supposed Justifications* (Harmondsworth: Penguin, 1969): 59.

5 This important distinction could be further understood as a macro-level approach to deterrence (macrodeterrence) and a micro-level approach to deterrence (microdeterrence). I believe that our understanding of deterrence and deterrent strategies is aided when considering this subject through this distinction.

6 J. S. Mill, 'On Punishment' in *Collected Works of John Stuart Mill*, vol. 21, ed. John M. Robson (Toronto: University of Toronto Press, [1834] 1984): 78.

7 The classic exposition of the incapacitation theory of punishment is William Paley's *Principles of Penal Law* in 1771.

8 The objection includes the qualification of 'virtually' (as in 'virtually everyone') as there would be a need for some persons to administer prisons housing everyone else. Imprisoning everyone is impossible even in a hypothetical case, but this counterexample remains an important argument against incapacitation.

9 Punishment is not always incapacitation. This is because we understand punishment to take more potential forms than imprisonment, but include community sentences, fines, and other possibilities. This is a break from some academic discussions of 'punishment' that have understood 'punishment' as 'imprisonment', especially since Feinberg's distinction between fines and punishment as noted in chapter 1. However, our more inclusive understanding of punishment as a response to crime (and not only responses involving imprisonment) is much closer to how punishment is understood in debates over criminal justice policy by policymakers.

10 This fact about the geography of crime may further problematize the possibility of deterrence. We should not only look to reductions in crime rates amongst the public (e.g. the standard scenario), but also to effects within prison walls. If deterrence is about crime reduction and crime takes place in public and prison, then we must adopt a wider perspective of approaches to crime reduction than often held.

11 Hegel, *Elements of the Philosophy of Right*, §99 Addition.

12 Beccaria, *Of Crimes and Punishments*, 51. Similarly, Green argues that 'will, not force' explains just political obligation although he ultimately rejects deterrence theories. See T. H. Green, *Lectures on the Principles of Political Obligation* (London: Longmans, 1941): sect. 113–36.

13 Plato, 'Gorgias', in *Complete Works*, 472e.

14 J. G. Fichte, *Foundations of Natural Right*, ed. Frederick Neuhouser (Cambridge: Cambridge University Press, 2000): 232.

15 See Bentham, *An Introduction to the Principles of Morals and Legislation*, 93–4.

16 Beccaria, *Of Crimes and Punishments*, 46 (emphasis added).

Notes

17 We will examine negative retributivism in further detail in chapter 5.
18 The argument here summarizes Anthony Ellis, 'A Deterrence Theory of Punishment', *Philosophical Quarterly* 53 (2003): 338–51.
19 See Zachary Hoskins, 'Deterrent Punishment and Respect for Persons', *Ohio State Journal of Criminal Law* 8 (2011): 373–4.
20 Ellis, 'A Deterrence Theory of Punishment', 345.
21 See Hegel, *Elements of the Philosophy of Right*, preface.
22 See Anthony Doob and Cheryl Webster, 'Sentence Severity and Crime: Accepting the Null Hypothesis' in Michael Tonry (ed.), *Crime and Justice: A Review of Research*, vol. 30 (Chicago: University of Chicago Press, 2003): 143–95. Some have claimed there is a deterrence effect via incapacitation (or 'incapacitation effect') whereby crime rates have risen in specific cases closely following criminals leaving prison. However, they have not argued that the solution to this problem is to give all criminals life sentences to reduce crime; instead, the argument is that imprisoning most criminally minded persons will reduce crime rates. See Durlauf and Nagin, 'Imprisonment and Crime', 30 and Steven D. Levitt and Stephen J. Dubner, *Freakonomics: A Rogue Economist Explores the Hidden Side of Everything* (New York: Harper Perennial, 2009): 119–29.
23 See Ministry of Justice data at http://open.justice.gov.uk/home/.
24 Patrick A. Langan and David J. Levin, *Recidivism of Prisoners Released in 1994* (Washington, DC: Bureau of Justice Statistics, 2002): 2.
25 For example, see G. Matthew Snodgrass, Arjan A. J. Blokland, Amelia Haviland, Paul Nieubeerta, and Daniel S. Nagin, 'Does the Time Cause the Crime? An Examination of the Relationship between Time Served and Reoffending in the Netherlands', *Criminology* 49 (2011): 1149–94.
26 Patrick Carter, *Managing Offenders, Reducing Crime: A New Approach* (London: Prime Minister's Strategy Unit, 2003): 15.
27 Carter, *Managing Offenders, Reducing Crime*, 10. The situation is no less true in the United States. See ibid. 15 and Editorial, 'The Crime of Punishment', *New York Times* (6 December 2010): A26.
28 See Easton and Piper, *Sentencing and Punishment*, 113.
29 See Durlauf and Nagin, 'Imprisonment and Crime', 28.
30 See *Brown* v. *Plata*, 563 U.S. (2011).
31 See Durlauf and Nagin, 'Imprisonment and Crime', 14, 21–3 and Michael Tonry, 'Less Imprisonment is No Doubt a Good Thing: More Policing is Not', *Criminology & Public Policy* 10 (2011): 138, 140–1.
32 Tonry, 'Less Imprisonment is No Doubt a Good Thing', 143 (quoting Kenneth Clarke).
33 See Ministry of Justice, *2011 Compendium of Re-Offending Statistics and Analysis* (London: Her Majesty's Stationery Office, 2011): 3–4. Reoffending rates do not generally differ between men and women. See Ministry of Justice, *Adult Re-Convictions: Results from the 2009 Cohort (England and Wales)* (London: Her Majesty's Stationery Office, 2011): 14.
34 For example, Levitt and Dubner argue that the US murder rate fell largely as a result of the legalization of abortion: 'the pool of potential criminals had dramatically shrunk'. See Levitt and Dubner, *Freakonomics*, 4. For other factors, see David Lazar (ed.), *DNA and the Criminal Justice System: The Technology of Justice* (Cambridge: MIT Press, 2004) and Barry Sheck, Peter Neufeld, and Jim Dwyer, *Actual Innocence: When Justice Goes Wrong and How to Make It Right* (New York: American Library, 2003).
35 See Cassia C. Spohn, *How Do Judges Decide? The Search for Fairness and Justice in Punishment* (Thousand Oaks: Sage, 2002): 285.

Notes

36 Sarah Britto, '"Diffuse Anxiety": The Role of Economic Insecurity in Predicting Fear of Crime', *Journal of Crime and Justice* (2011) (DOI:10.1080/0735648X.2011.631399).
37 Levitt and Dubner, *Freakonomics*, 109.
38 See R. Liedka, A. Piehl, and B. Useem, 'The Crime-Control Effect of Incarceration: Does Scale Matter?', *Criminology and Public Policy* 5 (2006): 245–75 and T. Marvell and C. Moody, 'Prison Population and Crime Reduction', *Journal of Quantitative Criminology* 10 (1994): 109–39.
39 J. G. Fichte, *Foundations of Natural Right*, 228.
40 I am grateful to Brian O'Connor for suggesting this idea to me.
41 Richard L. Lippke, *Rethinking Imprisonment* (Oxford: Oxford University Press, 2007): 41.
42 James Q. Wilson, *Thinking About Crime,* 2nd ed. (New York: Vintage Books, 1985): 121.
43 See Ashworth, 'Ignorance of the Criminal Law', 1–26.
44 For example, see Mandeep K. Dhami and David R. Mandel, 'Crime as Risk Taking', *Psychology, Crime and Law* (2011): 1–15. Thaler and Sunstein argue that only 'Econs', a fictional understanding of people as *homo economicus* and not people like you or me, make such rational choice calculations. Behavioural models must rely upon new models for predicting policy effects. See Richard Thaler and Cass Sunstein, *Nudge: Improving Decisions about Health, Wealth, and Happiness* (London: Penguin, 2008).
45 See Thomas A. Loughran, Raymond Paternoster, Alex R. Piquero, and Greg Pogarsky, 'On Ambiguity in Perception of Risk: Implications for Criminal Decision Making and Deterrence', *Criminology* 49 (2011): 1029–61.
46 Davis, 'How to Make the Punishment Fit the Crime', 735.
47 There is also 'the fallacy of the warden's survey research': the warden observes the many undeterred criminals at his prison and concludes that deterrence does not work. This is a fallacy because the warden reaches this conclusion without any consideration of the possible supermajority outside his prison that were deterred. See Albert Dzur and Alan Wertheimer, 'Forgiveness and Public Deliberation: The Practice of Restorative Justice', *Criminal Justice Ethics* 21 (2002): 15. The problem is not that we cannot know how many people have been deterred, but only how crime rates have changed over time.
48 This is not surprising, in part, because there can be much confusion. Take capital punishment for murder in the United States. The crime of murder is not unitary, but differs: the crime of murder where the victim is a private citizen is separate from the crime of murder where the victim is the US President. Each is criminalized by different jurisdictions and may have different tariffs. For example, murder is normally part of state statutes. While most states have legalized capital punishment, a significant minority have not. Whether or not the murder of another private citizen may warrant the possibility of execution will differ from state to state. Furthermore, the crime of murder of the US President does not fall under any state law, but under federal law and federal law permits the possibility of execution. A person found guilty of the murder of the US President in a state that did not accept capital punishment for murder might still be executed for his crime in that state. This is because he would be guilty of a federal crime even though the act took place in an abolitionist state. This illustration highlights that even the punishment of murder is not straightforwardly clear given the complex relationship between state and federal laws in the United States.

Notes

49 The punishment for arson differs across states. For one example, see http://firemarshal.state.md.us/crimes.htm. The punishment of arson in the UK is found in the Criminal Damage Act (1971). I leave it to the reader to discover the sanction for arson in his or her jurisdiction. This exercise further underscores the difficulty of penal threats having any clear deterrent effect where knowledge about possible sanctions is confusing or difficult to obtain for even the most serious crimes.

50 See Alan Travis, 'Governors Urge Fast Release of 2,500 Prisoners', *The Guardian* (12 October 2010): 8.

51 Mill, *On Liberty*, 95.

52 See Hoskins, 'Deterrent Punishment and Respect for Persons', 374–5.

53 For example, see Martha C. Nussbaum, '"Whether from Reason or Prejudice": Taking Money for Bodily Services', *Journal of Legal Studies* 27 (1998): 693–724.

54 Theorists who argue that deterrence does not address people as moral agents cite a passage from Hegel as supporting evidence. Hegel says (of Paul Johann Anselm Ritter von Feuerbach's theory of deterrence) that '[t]o justify punishment in this way is like raising one's stick at a dog; it means treating a human being like a dog instead of respecting his honour and freedom'. While Hegel did reject deterrence as a primary ground of punishment, he does not oppose deterrence within a unified theory of punishment. See Hegel, *Elements of the Philosophy of Right*, §99 Addition and Thom Brooks, 'Hegel and the Unified Theory of Punishment' in *Hegel's Philosophy of Right* (Oxford: Blackwell, 2012): 103–23.

55 The claim that 'there can be no justified punishment for an unjustified law' does not run afoul of the naturalistic fallacy. This is because what is central is the establishment of justification rather than the establishment of (moral) justice.

56 Beccaria, *Of Crimes and Punishments*, 42.

57 Jeremy Bentham, *The Works of Jeremy Bentham*, vol. 1: *Principles of Penal Law* (New York: Russell & Russell, 1961): 398.

58 Beccaria, *Of Crimes and Punishments*, 74.

Part II
Deterrence and Desert

[4]

A DETERRENCE THEORY OF PUNISHMENT

By Anthony Ellis

I start from the presupposition that the use of force against another is justified only in self-defence or in defence of others against aggression. If so, the main work of justifying punishment must rely on its deterrent effect, since most punishments have no other significant self-defensive effect. It has often been objected to the deterrent justification of punishment that it commits us to using offenders unacceptably, and that it is unable to deliver acceptable limits on punishment. I describe a sort of deterrent theory which can avoid both of these objections.

I

If punishment is to be justified, it must be predominantly by reference to deterrence. I hold this for two reasons, neither of which I can argue for here.

First, each of the so-called retributive theories is either internally incoherent or has implausible moral implications.

Secondly, even if there were an otherwise acceptable retributive theory of punishment, we should have to reject it, for I believe that violence is justified only in self-defence against aggression, that is to say, against behaviour violating a constraint which one has a right to uphold in self-interest (as is usual, I include in this the defence of others' self-interest). This claim, of course, does not itself restrict us to a deterrent theory, for it is consistent with other possible justificatory aims: direct prevention, for instance, or reform. But most punishments have no significant preventative effect, and are not intended to have any; and their beneficial reformative effect is scarcely more pronounced.

The simplest version of the deterrence theory of punishment, that we may punish offenders to deter other potential offenders, has usually been rejected, for two reasons.

First, the theory commits us to accepting that in punishing one person in order to deter others we are unacceptably *using* him. There have been many ways of trying to avoid this. For now, I shall simply register my agreement with Tony Honoré that none of them will work.[1] Broadly, attempts to avoid the problem hold that punishing offenders to deter others does not unacceptably use them (because, for instance, they have implicitly assented in advance to this treatment, or because they deserve their punishment), or that they have forfeited the right not to be used. But I think that the objection is correct, and the only response a proponent of the theory could make would be to accept this, and simply tough it out.

Secondly, the theory lays down no acceptable limits on punishment. Presumably if we are concerned simply with deterring offenders, then the appropriate level of punishment should be whatever is necessary to deter. And this might be, in particular cases, either too lenient or too severe. Of course, we can solve the problem by laying down independent moral constraints upon the acceptable levels of punishment.[2] But this may seem *ad hoc*; one might have hoped for a more unified theory, one in which the point of the institution itself generates the constraints.[3]

In this paper I shall sketch a deterrent theory which avoids these objections.

II

The theory understands punishment as a form of self-defence. I shall assume that we have the right to use force in legitimate self-defence. I shall also assume that groups may use force in self-defence, and that a society or a nation may do so. Do we, in addition, have the right to threaten retaliation against potential aggressors in order to deter them? It seems plausible to think that at least sometimes we do; all else being equal, it must surely be better to try to prevent aggression rather than to have to deal with it forcefully when it occurs. Of course, all else may not be equal. Greater force may have to be used to deter aggression than would be required to deflect it once it has started. Or the methods used to deter could be intrinsically unacceptable. Or the threat may have little chance of succeeding, or may even constitute a perverse incentive to potential aggressors. But in the absence of such factors, threats of retaliation are surely acceptable. However, this raises a familiar question: if it is indeed permissible to *threaten* some level of retaliation to deter aggression, is it also permissible to *carry out* that retaliation if the threat fails to work? The justification for threatening is that it will prevent aggression (and any harm involved in a self-defensive

[1] Tony Honoré, *Responsibility and Fault* (London: Hart, 1999), p. 19.

[2] This is the position of H.L.A. Hart (or one of his positions): see *Punishment and Responsibility* (Oxford: Clarendon Press, 1968), ch. 1.

[3] Cf. P. Montague, *Punishment as Societal-Defense* (Lanham: Rowman & Littlefield, 1995), p. 91.

response). If the threat does not work, however, that justification will not carry over into a justification for carrying out the threat, for carrying out the threat will, by hypothesis, do nothing to prevent these harms. Retaliation, then, seems unjustified (at least by the principles of self-defence).

But what if in addition to merely issuing the threat I somehow *bound myself* to carry it out?[4] I mean by this not just that I pledged myself to carry it out, but that I somehow made it the case that if the threat were ignored, retaliation would be inevitable. We could suppose, for instance, that I constructed a booby-trap surrounding my domain which, once it was constructed, I could not dismantle, and whose operation was automatic as soon as anyone crossed my border; I might then, with the intention of deterring anyone from crossing the border, announce that I had done this. If the threat of retaliation failed, the actual retaliation would be automatic.

When retaliation against an offender is carried out by such an automatic system (I shall just say 'punished' from now on), can he complain that he is being used? Initially, at least, it hardly seems so. That charge was based on the claim that offenders were being made to suffer in order to modify the behaviour of others, and that seems no longer true. After all, it may be known that the offender's punishment will have no such effect; how then can it be said that he is being punished in order to deter others? His punishment is simply a direct response to his own action, carrying no thought of how it may affect others.

However, the core of the worry may remain. Any particular offender's punishment may be known to have no deterrent effect, but the fact that punishments are actually administered must play some role, otherwise it would not be justifiable to go beyond a system in which the threat is merely a bluff. The obvious role is making the threat credible to others. It may then seem that the actual offender is punished because the system requires that offenders in general must be punished in order to maintain the general effectiveness of the system. And this may seem essentially no different from a system in which we pick a number of people and punish them as a deterrent demonstration to others, knowing that, for whatever reason, some of these punishments would not in fact serve that purpose: here each offender could correctly say that he was being used to deter others, even though, in some cases, the particular punishment would not have that effect.

[4] Warren Quinn also used this idea in a discussion of punishment: see 'The Right to Threaten and the Right to Punish', *Philosophy and Public Affairs*, 14 (1985), pp. 327–73. Daniel Farrell has shown that Quinn's argument rests upon a premise which is false: see 'On Threats and Punishments', *Social Theory and Practice*, 15 (1989), pp. 125–54. The idea that punishment can be justified as a form of self-defence has also been defended by Montague (see *Punishment as Societal-Defense*), and by Farrell: see, for instance, 'Deterrence and the Just Distribution of Harm', *Social Philosophy and Policy*, 12 (1995), pp. 220–40, and 'On Threats and Punishments'.

But maintaining the credibility of the threat is not the only reason we could have for making it a genuine one. We could imagine that, for various reasons, a bluff might actually work – sufficiently so at least to maintain the system's effectiveness. In such circumstances, there might still be reasons to make the threat a real one. It may simply be more convenient. Or again, a system of bluffs would require dishonesty, and we might object to that. There is, of course, an indefinite number of further possible reasons, having nothing to do with the deterrent effectiveness of the system. So long as one of these is our reason, no one is punished because the system requires that offenders must be punished in order to maintain the deterrent effectiveness of the system. This should remove the last vestige of the worry that offenders are being used. It would in no sense be true that they are being punished in an attempt to modify the behaviour of others. The threat is addressed to each individually, and each is punished because he, individually, chose to ignore the threat; the others, and their potential behaviour, are irrelevant.

There are, of course, other possible problems with such retaliatory systems. One is that such systems may seem to involve the intention to cause harm at a point in time when this harm may be known to have no beneficial effects. But that is a tendentious description. Less tendentiously, the system requires that at time t_1, with the intention of preventing an evil, we set in motion an irreversible process, which, if our intention is not realized, will cause harm at t_2. Now it is certainly impermissible to intend, *tout court*, to cause pointless harm; but it does not follow from this that it is impermissible to intend to prevent harm by setting in motion a train of events which will, if one's intention is not realized, cause harm. That will depend upon the totality of the circumstances, and in particular whether the agent has observed certain conditions which I shall outline later.[5]

A different sort of problem we may call the problem of scatter: unless the system's method of detection were infallible, the threat would be triggered even by innocent people whom the system mistakenly took to be aggressors. (Who is 'innocent' is a problem to which I shall return.) But this does not by itself make such systems impermissible, for there are clearly circumstances in which it is permissible knowingly to put innocent people at risk as long as this is not our aim. Indeed, we do this constantly in our criminal justice systems, requiring only that benefits and risks be appropriately balanced. And so long as there is the appropriate balance, there is, as yet, no objection to such deterrent threats.

[5] There is, of course, an immense and ancient literature to which I cannot here do justice on the logic of the intentions embedded in threats. For a relevant discussion, see Farrell, 'A New Paradox of Deterrence', in J.L. Coleman and C.W. Morris (eds), *Rational Commitment and Social Justice: Essays for Gregory Kavka* (Cambridge UP, 1998), pp. 22–46.

One way of making it easier to achieve that balance would be by making the system slightly less automatic, allowing it to be stopped when there is reason to think that an apparent aggressor is in fact innocent. I might do this by dividing the operation into different functions and placing each in the hands of a different person. So one agent might be authorized to apprehend suspected aggressors, another might be authorized to decide whether they really were aggressors, and another might be authorized to administer punishment if appropriate. But no one would have authority to deactivate his part of the system except in special circumstances. From my point of view, this system would be substantially similar to the simpler model I sketched a moment ago. Once I have issued my threat, I have nothing further to do in order for an aggressor to be punished: from my point of view it is now automatic. It can now properly be said that the aim of the system is deterrence, but that no one is punished in order to deter others.

III

It may seem that this model is too remote from reality to tell us anything about punishment in the real world. However, I shall suggest that it is a useful model of criminal justice systems in the USA and UK.

A criminal statute, we may say, lays down a threat, which we can think of as a threat of retaliation against anyone in violation of its prohibition. And it is, in the important sense, like the threat in the model I have suggested: once someone has transgressed, the procedure goes forward fairly automatically. Legal systems differ, of course. In some, such as the German and Austrian systems, prosecution of all offences is, in principle, mandatory where there is adequate evidence to sustain a conviction. In others, such as the UK and US systems, there is broad discretion at most levels. It is enough, of course, for my present purposes that we can imagine a realistic system in which the normal course, though not necessarily mandatory, is prosecution. And, I shall suggest, this is the best understanding of the US and UK systems.

The procedure is automatic in the sense in which the system just imagined is automatic – a system which, of course, was meant to reflect the separation of powers that characterizes modern democracies. The legislature issues threats, but it has no authority to decide whether those threats are acted on in particular cases. Prosecutors and police have that authority; but they in turn have no authority to decide whether a convicted person is punished. Actually, in some jurisdictions the police can deal with fines for minor traffic offences. And in some systems prosecutors are empowered to dismiss cases if the accused is prepared to pay some compensation to the victim, or even make a payment to a charity nominated by the prosecutor. Judges (and jurors) decide upon sentences, but only in accordance with previous law. Punishment is then in the hands of the executive, which, in general, has no authority not to administer due punishment. It could be said that we, through the legislature, issue a threat; 'we', however, cannot revoke it. From 'our' point of view, punishment is automatic.

This may seem to ignore the discretion exercised by each branch of the penal system. The police are granted some authority not to pursue a complaint, or merely to issue a warning to an offender; a prosecutor may choose not to prosecute a case; a judge typically has some discretion in sentencing. There are also exceptions to the general picture I have sketched, such as the power of executive clemency. And in so far as this discretion extended to permit the authority to take account of the deterrent effects of particular punishments it would, of course, reintroduce the original worry.

That discretion does so extend in our own legal systems seems clear. But we are not bound to this. Though there is much discretion in the operation of the law, none of it is arbitrary. When an offender has been apprehended, the default presumption is that he will be prosecuted and punished, and at every level, if the law is not to take its normal course, this should be because allowing it to take its normal course would be against 'the public interest'. I need not now give a full account of what is meant by that phrase, but it need not be, and is not, construed in a narrowly utilitarian way: it already encompasses notions of what is just or fair, for instance. It would not, then, be an unrealistically radical step to embody in this notion the value of individuals, which lays a moral constraint upon merely using them. So we can plausibly say that if, at any stage in a particular case, the question is raised of whether the law should take its normal course, that question should not be answered by reference to whether the normal course will deter others. (The UK Criminal Justice Act 1991 signalled a clear move away from deterrent considerations in sentencing: individual sentences were to be based primarily upon the 'seriousness' of the offence, with the possibility of incapacitative sentences for some offenders who posed a great risk to the community.)

We have, then, a system in which the legislature issues a threat whose execution is, from its point of view, automatic: it need, and can, do nothing further to ensure that it is carried out. Of course those who are involved in carrying it out are granted some discretion in this. But so long as that discretion does not extend to deciding individual cases on the basis of deterrent effectiveness, it can correctly be said that the point of the penal system is to deter, but that the offender is not punished in order to deter others.

IV

I turn now to the limits on punishment. If deterrent threats are made in self-defence, then they are subject to the principles of self-defence, a central one of which is that it is permissible to use in self-defence only such force as is 'reasonably necessary'. What does that mean?

Imagine that I have only three possible responses to an act of aggression already under way: doing nothing, rational persuasion, and counter-force. What I may permissibly do will be a matter of the likely costs and benefits, broadly construed.

For each course of action, the primary benefit aimed at will be that the threatened harm is avoided or minimized. So we need to know both how great the threatened harm is, and how likely it is to occur given each course of action. If the threatened harm is slight and merely speculative, then normally the correct course of action will be to do nothing, though in such circumstances there will usually be alternatives besides the three just mentioned. At the other extreme, a high probability of serious harm if I do not use force will often justify it. But not always: in particular, if it has in any case no chance of warding off the threat, then it will be pointless violence, and cannot be justified under the principles of self-defence.

As to what count as costs, there will be some dispute. Some will consider the harm to the aggressor a cost, but others will not. Most would think that the degree of the aggressor's responsibility would need to be taken account of, but not necessarily as limiting the victim's rights; it may be unkind to use force against an 'innocent threat', but it is not necessarily unjust. Some may consider it a (moral) cost to oneself to indulge in violence, even if it is justifiable to do so, whereas others will not. But there are some costs that are clear: a forceful response to aggression may simply trigger a forceful counter-response on the part of my aggressor, for instance; or it may cause harm to innocent third parties. And on any plausible view, forceful action will in general be more costly than non-forceful action.

These considerations, which I shall refer to as 'the restraining considerations', determine when it is reasonable to use force, and how much force it is reasonable to use. Dispute about their precise content can be settled only by appeal to their source. About that too, of course, there will be dispute, and I can do little more here than state baldly what I believe it is. It stems, I believe, from the general social necessity to minimize the use of violence. It is clear that we need disincentives to violence, and recognizing the right to self-defence is one of the most important of them. But forceful self-defence itself needs restrictions, for it too poses dangers: it may spill over into, or be confused with, vengeance, with all of the attendant dangers; it may be used as a cloak for violence desired for other ends; it may provoke further violence from the aggressor, either in self-defence or in revenge; and it poses dangers to those who are uninvolved. On the other hand, an absolute prohibition on the use of force would obviously not be desirable, for this would remove a major disincentive to aggression. And it would not be generally adhered to; most would think that, in its encouragement of aggression, the prohibition made no sense, and they would not respect it. In any case, self-interest would ensure that people would not routinely forego the use of force when this entailed a significant sacrifice to themselves.

So a compromise has to be found between an absolute prohibition and no restriction at all. It is impossible to say with precision just where it will be located. But the guiding principle will be that the use of force should be confined to limits we can sensibly expect people to abide by, and force which is reasonably necessary is simply force within those limits. There will, obviously, be some disagreement about what those limits should be; but there is also considerable agreement. Virtually everyone agrees, for instance, that the victim of aggression should be required to forego self-defensive force when there is a significant disparity between the harm threatened and the amount of force required to thwart it: this is a restriction that normal people will see the point of, and will generally abide by. And when it is reasonably necessary to use force, the restriction on the amount of force that may be used has of course the same point. Its effect is to reduce forceful countermeasures to the level that we can sensibly demand. We require, then, that victims should sometimes be prepared to sustain some loss when responding forcefully to an aggressor by choosing a less forceful measure than they might prefer. There is, of course, no way in practice of saying precisely how great a loss it is reasonable in general to require; it is no surprise, therefore, that judgements vary over this matter.

To turn now to *deterrent threats*, again imagine that I have three possible responses to a threat of aggression: I may do nothing, I may try to persuade potential aggressors not to aggress, or I may threaten them with retaliation in order to deter them.

The restraining considerations operate much as before: we need to know the scale and likelihood of the threatened harm, the likelihood of success of each course of action, and the costs of each course. But different factors will now become salient. (They, or counterparts, are of course present in the case of direct self-defence too.) For instance, since we are dealing with merely potential aggression, we shall need to think of how tempting is the aggression to potential aggressors: the more tempting it is, the greater the harm it will be justified to threaten (other things being equal). There is also the possibility that the threat may act as a perverse incentive, or that retaliation will lead some to seek revenge. And if we are talking of semi-automatic systems of retaliation, the possible harm to innocent third parties will loom much larger.

It may seem natural to think that it would be permissible to threaten in deterrence all and only that which it would be permissible to do in direct self-defence. But this is not, of course, correct. The restraining considerations mentioned above generate crucial divergences. First, we may take account of the probability that the threat itself may work, and the retaliation thus may not be triggered. This will often relax the limits. Indeed, other things being equal, there would perhaps be no limit at all on what might be threatened if we could be absolutely sure that the threat would be effective.

On the other side, there is the crucial question of immediacy. Potential aggressors can often be deterred by the threat of much less force than would be required to prevent their aggression once it has started. (It may be necessary for you to kill someone who is trying to kill you; but he might have been deterred if you had let it be known that if someone kills you, your friends will administer him a beating.) More generally, all sorts of resources that might have been available in advance will not be available in the heat of the moment.

The issue of immediacy also raises the question of scatter. If I booby-trap my house, and post a notice to this effect, the trap may still be triggered by innocent intruders who have not seen the notice. This problem is not confined to self-defensive threats, of course: it applies also to direct self-defence. But it is presumably a more serious problem in the case of automatic and semi-automatic systems of threatened retaliation than in most cases of direct self-defence, and requires a greater stringency in the restrictions governing their use.

Further complications arise when we move from *individual* self-defensive deterrence to *collective* self-defensive deterrence on the part of society against those who aggress against its members; there will then be special empirical facts, and, arguably, special normative considerations to take account of. But the goal of reducing violence will still be appropriate. A threat of retaliation may be a successful disincentive against aggression. But even, or perhaps especially, when wielded by the government, it must be hedged about with restrictions. For one thing, we are rightly reluctant to give government more coercive power than is necessary, for its agents are ordinary people, as likely to misuse power as others. And we are reluctant to allow government to resort to force too easily, for this is a lapse from the ideal relationship between government and citizens. And even when serious punishment is completely justified, it is likely to foster alienation from the government on the part of at least some citizens (the family and friends of the offender, for instance). There is also the question of likely harm to innocents. As well as the wrongly convicted, there are others, such as the innocent families of properly convicted offenders. And the more serious the punishment we threaten, the greater the costs we shall feel constrained to pay in the attempt to avoid miscarriages of justice. The government is required, then, not to use the threat of punishment to prevent crime if there is a reasonable, less violent alternative; and it may threaten no more than is reasonably required for deterrence.

So though the principles are the same, what it is permissible for an individual to do in direct self-defence will often diverge from what it is permissible for society to threaten in self-defensive deterrence. Overlooking this may make it seem that punishment and self-defence are morally separate phenomena:

> Proportionality in punishment ... is more rigorous than proportionality in self-defence. Using the death penalty for rape, for example, violates the principle of proportional punishment.... Yet if a woman is threatened by rape, she may legally resist by killing the aggressor. Even legal systems that have abolished the death penalty permit the use of deadly force in the defence of vital interests. While proportionality in punishment requires that the sentence fit the crime, clearly more is permitted in self-defence.[6]

Fletcher speaks here of a distinction between what is permissible in self-defence and what is permissible in punishment. But we could equally well think of it as a distinction between what is permissible in direct, individual self-defence and what is permissible in collective, self-defensive deterrence. A woman faced with imminent rape faces an immediate, serious threat, which there may be no way of repelling, short of killing her attacker. A legislature deciding upon the sentence for rape faces a different problem. Its problem is to deter potential rapists, and a threat of death is not reasonably necessary for this end; for the most part, the threat of lesser punishment achieves it. So an individual woman may kill in order to resist rape, whereas the state may not punish rapists by killing them.

But if the threat of imprisonment works only 'for the most part', why should we not say that a threat of death, which may have greater deterrent force, is reasonably necessary?

First, threats of death would be unlikely to achieve the desired result. Most of those who are not deterred by the threat of relatively heavy prison

[6] George P. Fletcher, *A Crime of Self-Defense: Bernhard Goetz and the Law on Trial* (New York: Free Press, 1988), p. 29.

sentences would not be significantly more effectively deterred by the threat of capital punishment. In addition, juries would generally be unwilling to send rapists to their deaths, and this would decrease its deterrent value. This problem might be alleviated by restricting capital punishment to only a few types of rape; but this would increase the uncertainty attaching to the consequences of the offence and would correspondingly reduce its deterrent value again. Secondly, even if it did decrease the number of rapes, we should have to set against that the likely costs. They include the destruction of human life. Many people would think this justifiable to prevent an otherwise certain rape, but not justified as part of a somewhat speculative process designed to deter possible rapes. The likelihood of wrongful convictions would also strike most people as an unacceptable cost.[7] The point is illustrated in most legal systems. A woman immediately threatened with rape may kill to protect herself. But in most civilized jurisdictions she may not, in order to deter potential rapists (or even potential murderers), display a deadly weapon with intent to use it; and even those jurisdictions which allow the open carrying of firearms would baulk at a woman booby-trapping her body with a bomb which would explode if she were attacked; these measures would pose an unreasonable threat to innocent people. The government, in adopting measures to deter rapists, is in the same position.

In order to explain the phenomenon remarked by Fletcher, then, we do not need principles of punishment intrinsically more restrictive than the principles of self-defence. On the other hand, if we derive the principles of punishment from the principles of self-defence, then anything that is permissible in direct self-defence will indeed be permissible, in some imaginable circumstances, in deterrent threats. Imagine, for instance, a desert island inhabited by two people, one of whom is a determined rapist who can be deterred only by the genuine threat of death. Would it in those circumstances be permissible to set up a deterrent threat of automatic deadly retaliation? In these unlikely circumstances, it might be. It would depend in part upon the amount of violence that this threat, and its realization, might themselves trigger, and in part upon the relative evaluation of sexual autonomy and human life. About that latter consideration the protective-deterrent theory has itself, like other theories of punishment, nothing to say. All that can be said is that *if* it is permissible to kill to avoid an otherwise certain rape, *then* there will be some conceivable circumstance in which it would be permissible to mount a credible threat of death to deter a potential rapist. But the legal system in the real world never finds itself in circumstances like these.

[7] Since 1973 'At least 96 people have been exonerated and freed from death rows in 22 states' (*The New York Times*, August 24th, 2001).

V

What would a legal system look like that followed these principles?

The range of offences that could be punished would be those alone which could plausibly be brought under the umbrella of self-defence. It would be impermissible to punish behaviour merely on the ground that it was immoral. And it would be impermissible to punish behaviour which harmed only the agent. The most obviously punishable behaviour would be paradigm acts of aggression, such as rape and murder. But regulatory offences, such as traffic offences, would also be covered, since the relevant regulations, if legitimate, are constraints that we are justified in protecting in self-interest.

It would have a robust and plausible requirement that the punishment should fit the crime: it would restrict punishment to what it is reasonable to threaten in order to deter the offence. Deterrent considerations, however, would play no further part in the treatment of particular cases.

A particular aspect of the idea that the punishment should fit the crime is the idea that the innocent should not be punished, and the deterrence theory can explain this. Punishment is retaliation against those who have ignored a warning. The system is set up so as to be triggered by those who ignore that warning, not by others; and no acceptable self-defensive intention would be achieved by setting it up in any other way. 'Punishing' those who are innocent, then, will have no justification, for they have not failed to comply with the warning. Unless we were, unacceptably, using them in a deterrent display, there would thus be no way of bringing their punishment under the umbrella of self-defence.

We could, of course, set up the system so that innocents might suffer the 'retaliation'. We could issue threats to punish the innocent relatives of potential lawbreakers, for instance. Or we could threaten to harm entire groups when only certain members of the group transgress. But it is clear that punishment in these circumstances would be *using* people. Those who are punished would, either directly or indirectly, be made to suffer as part of an attempt to modify the behaviour of others; the deterrence theory can quite consistently object to that.

Questions of guilt and innocence, of course, refer to more than whether the defendant committed the prohibited act. First, punishment is hedged around with the requirements of *mens rea*, or responsibility. One is not punished at all unless one acted in an appropriate state of mind. And the severity of one's punishment may depend upon one's state of mind when one committed the offence, whether one did it deliberately or negligently, for instance. Secondly, the law recognizes a number of excuses, such as necessity or duress, which can lead to an acquittal or mitigation of sentence. All of this may seem to reflect nothing of self-defence, for our right of self-defence against one who threatens us does not turn upon his level of responsibility, or whether he is coerced into harming us. Why, then, are such questions so important in the law?

Taking responsibility first, a requirement of responsibility enters into the limits of self-defence as soon as we move from direct self-defence to deterrent threats. The reason is simple: there is no point in issuing threats to those who cannot heed them, and any violence occasioned by such threats would therefore be without justification. Anyone who suffered such violence would have been done an injustice. The law, then, may not justifiably threaten with punishment, for instance, the severely mentally ill, and so may not punish them. (It may, of course, detain them for the safety of themselves and others.) The threat of punishment is not addressed to them.

But some of the mentally ill, kleptomaniacs, for example, are capable to some degree of being deterred, and threats, though they may eventually be ignored, are not without effect. Is it then permissible to punish such people? If it would not be pointless to threaten them with punishment, then punishment, within the restraining considerations, would not be unjust. So they may be punished without injustice. It is a misfortune for them that they suffer this obsession; but others are not required to bear the burden of their misfortune, and may use whatever force is reasonably necessary to protect themselves against its consequences. Whether carrying out punishment in such circumstances would be stupid, or callous, are, of course, different questions.

To turn now to negligence, we seem to have the same right of self-defence against a negligent threat as against a deliberate one. But, typically, the law treats deliberate misconduct more severely than negligent misconduct. How can that be, if punishment is a form of self-defence?

We do indeed have the same rights of self-defence against negligent and deliberate threats, but when we think about self-defensive deterrence, as opposed to direct self-defence, we should be more concerned about the prospect of deliberate misconduct than the prospect of negligent misconduct. Deliberate misconduct is in general more likely to cause harm than negligent misconduct: we have more reason to be concerned about someone who intends to kill than about someone who simply drives his car recklessly, for, in general, the former will pose a much more serious threat. Additionally, deliberate misconduct threatens the fabric of the social order in a way negligence does not. Further, it is generally easier to deter negligent behaviour, which requires only more care, than deliberate misconduct, which requires abandoning a positively desired course of action. All of this, other things being equal, justifies a correspondingly less forceful measure.

To turn now to excuses, such as coercion, the actions of one who is severely coerced are guided by reasons, and so this is not like the case of the mentally ill. On the other hand, we can be quite sure that those who are severely coerced will not respond to threats of punishment (those who coerce them will usually find it easy to ensure this); so threats would again be pointless, and any violence they involved would be unjustified. So legal threats are not addressed to those who are severely coerced; coercion is an excuse. (Typically, only severe coercion is an excuse. It does not usually excuse in murder cases. But if threats of punishment are no more likely to deter potential murderers than others, coercion should be an excuse here too, as some legal theorists have argued.)

Does this mean that it is unjustifiable to issue threats of punishment whenever we are sure that this will not deter? And does that in turn mean that it is unjustifiable to threaten punishment to hard-core, recidivist criminals? The answer to the first question is 'Yes'; to the second question 'No'. 'Hard-core recidivist criminals' may offend whatever we do, but they would commit far more offences if they had *carte blanche* to do so. Deterrent effectiveness is always a matter of degree, and one who eventually offends may none the less have been deterred *to some degree*, in the sense that the range of circumstances in which he would offend is restricted. The threat is thus not pointless, and the violence it involves may be justifiable.

I shall deal with one last issue, the law of attempts. An unsuccessful attempt to commit a crime may itself be a separate crime: one who tries to murder but fails may be convicted of attempted murder. This may seem odd from the point of view of the deterrence theory:

> those who set about crime intend to succeed and the law's threat has all the deterrent force it can have if it is attached to the crime; no additional effect is given to it if unsuccessful attempts are also punished.[8]

But the deterrence theory can explain why we have separate offences of attempt. If we were setting up a system of semi-automatic retaliation, we should not set it up so that the retaliation would be triggered only by the completed offence. Our first thought might be that we should set it up, if possible, so that it would be triggered *before* the offence was complete, indeed as soon as the offender had fully committed himself to his course of action. But the issue is more complicated. Given the goal of reducing violence, a rational strategy would not only be to give potential aggressors an incentive

[8] Hart, *Punishment and Responsibility*, p. 128. (Hart thinks that this is a 'fallacy'.)

not to aggress in the first place; we should also want to give actual aggressors an incentive to desist from their actions even when they had embarked on them, and to give them such an incentive for as long as reasonably possible. However, if we set the trigger point very late, we might encourage potential offenders to embark on offences, and to continue with them at inconvenience to others, knowing that they could later withdraw if it seemed prudent. If, on the other hand, we set the trigger point very early – as soon as they had started planning the act, for instance – then this would deprive offenders of what might have been an effective incentive to desist once the act was under way; in addition, enforcing this would require enormous resources, and considerable general deprivation of liberty. The challenge, then, is to find the point at which one's self-defensive strategy would be optimized within the restraining considerations mentioned earlier.[9]

This goal in turn makes intelligible why unsuccessful attempts are usually punished less severely than completed attempts. The emphasis on moral desert that characterizes many theories of punishment makes this puzzling.[10] But from the point of view of the protective-deterrence theory, moral desert will of course not be the issue. All that will be relevant are the considerations mentioned earlier: roughly, what will be the likely costs and benefits of threatening various levels of retaliation against, say, unsuccessful attempts? We have reason to want offenders to desist from their offences even when they have already embarked upon them; given this, it would be perverse to threaten them with the full punishment as soon as they embark on the offence, for then they would have no incentive to desist as soon as the likelihood of apprehension is as great as when the offence is accomplished. A natural thought would be a sliding scale of retaliation: roughly, and other things being equal, the further along the course of his action the offender had progressed, the greater would be the retaliation. This would not, of course, be practical in the criminal law. Our best approximation is to fix a point at which an attempt really has been made, as opposed to mere preparations, and a point at which the attempt has been completed; between those two points we punish, but less severely than for the completed attempt.

Virginia Commonwealth University

[9] And we find in jurisprudential thought just what we should expect, given this aim. But for a different approach, see Duff, *Criminal Attempts* (Oxford: Clarendon Press, 1996).

[10] Duff has tried to explain the puzzle in *Criminal Attempts*. I have criticized Duff's argument in my 'Criminal Attempts', *Journal of Applied Philosophy*, 15 (1998), pp. 207–12.

[5]

DETERRENCE IN A SEA OF "JUST DESERTS": ARE UTILITARIAN GOALS ACHIEVABLE IN A WORLD OF "LIMITING RETRIBUTIVISM"?

MATTHEW HAIST*

Recent scholarship on theories of criminal punishment has increasingly focused on retributivist justifications for punishment. While within this retributivist camp opinions differ as to the particulars of such policies, there is general agreement that criminals getting what they deserve, that is, their "just deserts," should be the underlying goal and rationale of the criminal justice system. From this point, these scholars argue that a criminal should receive punishment according to what the criminal deserves. Some forms of retributivism, however, have attempted to draw support from other theories of criminal punishment. By borrowing elements of other theories, specifically utilitarian theories, scholars have attempted to bolster support for retributivist policies. A particularly well received form of retributivism and the focus of this Comment, "limiting retributivism," argues that a range of punishments will fall within the criminal's just deserts, and that utilitarian concepts can alter the punishment within the aforementioned range. This Comment scrutinizes limiting retributivism's appeal to utilitarian theories of punishment to determine if such a system of punishment can achieve many of the outcomes sought by utilitarian theories, specifically deterrence.

This Comment argues that the answer to this question, while complex, is ultimately no. *I begin my inquiry by expounding on the history of retributive and utilitarian theories of punishment, and the specific concepts of limiting retributivism and what "factors" exist in determining a criminal's just deserts. Then, I shift focus and analyze the practical effects of these factors in light of recent behavioral psychology and behavioral law and economics research on cognitive biases. Subsequently, I describe why these insights into human psychology and the effects of cognitive biases, as*

* J.D., Northwestern University School of Law, 2009; A.B., Davidson College, 2003. I would like to thank the editorial staff of the *Journal of Criminal Law and Criminology* for their comments and corrections, and as always, my parents, David and Louise.

applied to the retributive factors in determining just deserts, will actually lead to under-deterrence of criminal activity. I develop this point by acknowledging that while this research also questions utilitarianism's proposal for deterrence through ex ante *incentives, the under-deterrence effect of limiting retributivism is far higher than that of utilitarianism. I also highlight why such under-deterrence is fundamentally contrary to utilitarian goals of punishment. I end by arguing that, given the insights of behavioral psychology, utilitarian goals of punishment are not sufficiently accomplished under limiting retributivism. A more pure form of utilitarianism is required to achieve utilitarian goals with hard and fast criminal rules with no appeal to or use of other theories of punishment. I also propose that utilitarians, in collaboration with behavioral law and economics scholars, can further understanding of how the criminal law may incorporate behavioral psychology insights to create more effective* ex ante *incentives.*

I. INTRODUCTION

The question of why we should punish criminals is age-old, and elicits many more answers than the lay person would imagine. Punishing what society deems wrong or unwise seems to be an integral part of any civilization.[1] Specific guidelines for punishment date back to Hammurabi's Code,[2] while theoretical and philosophical justifications for punishment can be seen as early as Aristotle.[3] Simply put, criminal justice is, and has always been, at the center of public concern, so much so that modern societies often view and compare themselves to one another through the lens of what we now call criminal justice.[4] Given the importance of criminal justice to obtaining a safe and prosperous society, recent developments in the field must constantly be monitored to ensure that we operate under a theory of criminal punishment that either is optimally in

[1] I have not found any evidence or instance of a society that does not have a form of punishment.

[2] HAMMURABI'S CODE OF LAWS (c. 1780 B.C.E.) (L.W. King trans.), *available at* http://www.fordham.edu/halsall/ancient/hamcode.html (last visited May 1, 2009).

[3] ARISTOTLE, NICOMACHEAN ETHICS 200-01 (Roger Crisp trans., Cambridge Univ. Press 2000).

[4] One only needs to look toward the Europeans' general view of the death penalty and their detestation of continued U.S. support for such punishment to see evidence of this comparison. Justice Scalia's concurring opinion in *Kansas v. Marsh* highlights this point. 126 S. Ct. 2516, 2532 (2006) (Scalia, J., concurring) ("There exists in some parts of the world sanctimonious criticism of America's death penalty.").

line with our concepts of morality or best serves to provide the needed security.[5]

Fortunately, scholars have spent much time and effort increasingly so within the past twenty to thirty years—debating this issue.[6] These debates affect our view of which system of criminal punishment is ideal, and demonstrate that the discussion is never-ending.[7] Criminal justice has evolved over the millennia and will continue to do so over the next. Under Hammurabi's Code, the punishment for almost any crime was death.[8] Under the Qur'an, crimes were given specific punishments, yet required a particular level of proof to be established to find guilt.[9] English common law guaranteed a criminal defendant a right to trial by his or her peers.[10] And our founding fathers added the right against self-incrimination and the prohibition of cruel and unusual punishment, while preserving the English common law right to trial by jury.[11]

---

[5] If one gives credence to social contract theory, security and safety is the principal reason individuals enter society in the first place. Therefore, preservation of individuals' interests, be they bodily integrity, property interests, or general liberties, should be the main priority and obligation of government. *See* THOMAS HOBBES, LEVIATHAN 121 (Richard Tuck ed., rev. student ed., Cambridge Univ. Press 1996) (1651) ("A *Common-wealth* is said to be *Instituted* . . . [so] that Man, or Assembly of men . . . live peacefully amongst themselves, and be protected against other men."); JOHN LOCKE, TWO TREATISES ON GOVERNMENT 269-78 (Peter Laslett ed., Cambridge Univ. Press 2002) (1698); JEAN-JACQUES ROUSSEAU, *THE SOCIAL CONTRACT* AND *THE FIRST AND SECOND DISCOURSES* 163-64 (Susan Dunn trans., Yale Univ. Press 2002).

[6] *See, e.g.*, Albert W. Alschuler, *The Changing Purposes of Criminal Punishment: A Retrospective on the Past Century and Some Thoughts About the Next*, 70 U. CHI. L. REV. 1 (2003); Russell L. Christopher, *Deterring Retributivism: The Injustice of "Just" Punishment*, 96 NW. U. L. REV. 843 (2002); Richard S. Frase, *Punishment Purposes*, 58 STAN. L. REV. 67 (2005); Norval Morris, *Desert as a Limiting Principle*, *in* PRINCIPLED SENTENCING 201 (Andrew von Hirsch & Andrew Ashworth eds., 1992); Alice Ristroph, *Desert, Democracy, and Sentencing Reform*, 96 J. CRIM. L. & CRIMINOLOGY 1293 (2006); Paul H. Robinson & John M. Darley, *The Utility of Desert*, 91 NW. U. L. REV. 453 (1997).

[7] *See supra* note 6.

[8] HAMMURABI'S CODE OF LAWS, *supra* note 2 (stating, for example, in Code number six that "[i]f any one steal the property of a temple or of the court, he shall be put to death, and also the one who receives the stolen thing from him shall be put to death," and in Code number fourteen that "[i]f any one steal the minor son of another, he shall be put to death").

[9] AN INTERPRETATION OF THE QUR'AN [THE KORAN], *Al-mā'idah* 5:38, at 113 (Majid Fakhry trans., bilingual ed., N.Y. Univ. Press 2002) ("As for the thieves, whether male or female, cut off their hands in punishment for what they did . . . .").

[10] *See* 3 WILLIAM BLACKSTONE, COMMENTARIES ON THE LAWS OF ENGLAND 349 (Dawsons of Pall Mall 1966) (1768); *see also* A.E. DICK HOWARD, MAGNA CARTA: TEXT AND COMMENTARY § 39 (Univ. Press of Virginia 1964) (1215) ("No free man shall be taken, imprisoned, disseised, oulawed, banished, or in any way destroyed, nor will We proceed against or prosecute him, except by the lawful judgment of his peers and by the law of the land.").

[11] U.S. CONST. amend. V, VII-VIII.

This evolution of criminal procedures and customs has been accompanied by rigorous academic debate over the goals and rationales of criminal punishment.[12] The progression can be seen from its beginning under Aristotle,[13] to the nineteenth century works of Immanuel Kant[14] and Jeremy Bentham,[15] and into the twentieth and now twenty-first centuries.[16] Today, the debate largely involves three theories of criminal punishment: utilitarianism, retributivism, and denunciation—although denunciation tends to take a back seat to the first two frameworks.[17]

Some modern scholars have attempted to form theories of punishment by mixing the three concepts into a single theory of punishment, or have argued in favor of one theory through appeals to another.[18] A common argument is to support a retributivist system of punishment, but with attempts to appeal to certain utilitarian concerns.[19] The most widely accepted form of this theory is Norval Morris's "limiting retributivism."[20] This Comment attempts to further the debate over theories of criminal punishment by investigating whether such retributivist appeals to utilitarianism are valid and can achieve utilitarian goals. Specifically, this Comment seeks to determine whether Morris's limiting retributivism theory, and its appeal to utilitarian concepts, can achieve utilitarian goals.

I undertake to answer this question in five parts. Part II presents a brief historical overview of theories of criminal punishment in order to provide the reader with sufficient background and context to understand the recent movements in this debate. Part III then describes the current movement of scholarship towards the retributivist camp, the several factors that potentially determine the severity of a criminal's punishment under a retributive theory of punishment, and, finally, this camp's attempted appeal to utilitarianism. Part IV describes the concept of limiting retributivism in

---

[12] *See supra* note 6.

[13] ARISTOTLE, *supra* note 3, at 200-01.

[14] IMMANUEL KANT, THE PHILOSOPHY OF LAW: AN EXPOSITION OF THE FUNDAMENTAL PRINCIPLES OF JURISPRUDENCE AS THE SCIENCE OF RIGHT 194-204 (W. Hastie trans., Edinburgh, I.&T. Clark 1887) (1796).

[15] JEREMY BENTHAM, AN INTRODUCTION TO THE PRINCIPLES OF MORALS AND LEGISLATION (1781), *reprinted in* 1 THE WORKS OF JEREMY BENTHAM 1, 83-96 (John Bowring ed., Thoemmes Press 1995) [hereinafter MORALS AND LEGISLATION]; JEREMY BENTHAM, PRINCIPLES OF PENAL LAW (1843), *reprinted in* 1 THE WORKS OF JEREMY BENTHAM, *supra*, 365, 396-97.

[16] *See supra* note 6.

[17] JOSHUA DRESSLER, UNDERSTANDING CRIMINAL LAW 14-19 (4th ed. 2006).

[18] *Id.* at 11-24.

[19] *See* Norval Morris, *Punishment, Desert and Rehabilitation*, *in* SENTENCING 257 (Hyman Gross & Andrew von Hirsch eds., 1981).

[20] *See* Ristroph, *supra* note 6, at 1301-02.

greater detail. Part V describes why limiting retributivism's appeal to utilitarianism cannot succeed. In doing so, it utilizes recent behavioral psychology research to demonstrate how the structure of retributivist punishment leads to under-deterrence of crime. Specifically, it highlights how the factors involved in determining punishment under retributivism are affected by cognitive biases. Part VI then acknowledges that the same behavioral psychology research challenges utilitarianism's attempt to create sufficient and optimal *ex ante* incentives. However, while utilitarianism without any adjustment for cognitive biases leads to a one-time under-deterrent effect, limiting retributivism essentially creates a "double" under-deterrent effect. Because of this double effect, limiting retributivism's appeal to utilitarianism fails. Thus, based on this behavioral psychology research, utilitarian goals of punishment, and deterrence in particular, are best served through a purely utilitarian theory of punishment. Finally, this Part provides insights into how utilitarian punishment may be improved through the use of behavioral psychology research.

II. BACKGROUND

Retributive and utilitarian theories of criminal punishment are the two predominant theories of punishment discussed today.[21] The two theories are often thought of as the two opposing concepts of what criminal punishment should be.[22] The debate between the two camps is by no means a recent phenomenon. It has evolved over hundreds of years and will probably continue to advance over the next hundred years.[23] But before we address the history and development of this debate, it is necessary here to give a quick synopsis of each theory.

A. RETRIBUTIVISM

Retributivism posits that punishment is necessary because society must engage in some form of retribution against those who violate its laws.[24] Its central tenet defines *punishment* as society's response to a criminal action that has occurred in the past.[25] The value of the punishment of the crime is

---

[21] DRESSLER, *supra* note 17, at 19.

[22] *See id.*

[23] *See, e.g.*, Alschuler, *supra* note 6.

[24] *See* GEORG WILHELM FRIEDRICH HEGEL, HEGEL'S PHILOSOPHY OF RIGHT §§ 90-104 (T.M. Knox trans., Oxford Univ. Press 1978) (1821); *see also* KANT, *supra* note 14, at 196 (describing retaliation as the only principle capable of determining "the quality and quantity of a just penalty").

[25] *See* R.A. DUFF, TRIALS AND PUNISHMENTS 4 (1986) (noting that retributivism "find[s] the sense and justification of punishment in its relation to a past offence").

in the punishment itself;[26] when someone has committed a crime, they simply deserve to be punished.[27] "Punishment that gives an offender what he or she deserves for a past crime is a valuable end in itself and needs no further justification."[28] Furthermore, society is morally obligated to punish wrongdoers.[29]

B. UTILITARIANISM

Utilitarian theories of criminal punishment stem from general utilitarian concepts. Joshua Dressler suggests that "[t]he purpose of all laws is to maximize the net happiness of society."[30] Therefore, punishment should only be administered if it results in an overall benefit to society.[31] Only when punishment leads to more aggregate pleasure than aggregate pain is punishment justified.[32] As John Robinson and John Darley argue, "Punishment for a past offense is [only] justified by the future benefits it provides."[33] In this manner, utilitarian theories are sometimes referred to as "consequentialist" because they are concerned solely with how punishment will affect future actions and with society's future aggregate happiness.[34] Punishment can do this in two main ways. First, it can deter future criminals from committing crimes; second, it can either incapacitate criminals or rehabilitate them so that they cannot or will not engage in future crimes.[35]

C. HISTORY

The history of these two theories of punishment is extensive. Each has enjoyed the support of legal scholars and intellectual giants, and each has had its periods of dominance.[36] While the specifics of the theories may have changed over the years, their foundations have remained constant. Retributivism has always been concerned with punishing criminals as

---

[26] *See* Stanley I. Benn, *Punishment*, *in* 7 THE ENCYCLOPEDIA OF PHILOSOPHY 29, 30 (Paul Edwards ed., 1967) ("[T]he punishment of crime is right in itself . . . .").

[27] *See id.*

[28] Robinson & Darley, *supra* note 6, at 454.

[29] *See* John Rawls, *Two Concepts of Rules*, 64 PHIL. REV. 3, 5 (1955).

[30] DRESSLER, *supra* note 17, at 14.

[31] *See* BENTHAM, MORALS AND LEGISLATION, *supra* note 15, at 83-84.

[32] *See id.*

[33] Robinson & Darley, *supra* note 6, at 454.

[34] *See* Christopher, *supra* note 6, at 848 ("Consequentialist theories justify punishment . . . on the actual, good consequences that are attained, for example, deterrence of a crime . . . .").

[35] Robinson & Darley, *supra* note 6, at 453.

[36] *See, e.g.*, Alschuler, *supra* note 6.

simple punishment for their crimes,[37] while utilitarianism has valued the punishment of criminals because of the benefit society may reap as a result of such punishment.[38]

Retributivism can trace its origins far into the past.[39] From the time of antiquity through the middle-ages, many criminal justice systems were based largely on the concept of retributivism—the criminal getting what he or she deserved.[40] Indeed, retributivism can be seen in biblical and Talmudic forms of justice.[41] The existence of early forms of retributivism is not surprising when one considers the emotional aspects of this theory—punishment based in large part on a feeling that the perpetrator deserves the punishment.[42]

But retributivism was not solely a legal or emotional justification for punishment. It was also justified on moral and philosophical grounds.[43] Arguing in support of these justifications for punishment, Immanuel Kant wrote that "[p]unishment can never be administered merely as a means for promoting another Good . . . ."[44] On the contrary, "Punishment ought to be pronounced over all criminals proportionate to their internal wickedness."[45] In this sense retributive punishment could be thought of as a moral or ideological and philosophical need to condemn wrongdoers. Hegel provided an even more comprehensive justification of retributivism.[46] He concluded that crimes needed to be negated in order to re-establish equivalence in society, and that negation could only be achieved through punishment.[47] Retribution was the link between the crime and the punishment.[48]

---

37 *See infra* text accompanying notes 39-48.

38 *See* BENTHAM, MORALS AND LEGISLATION, *supra* note 15, at 83.

39 *See* IGOR PRIMORATZ, JUSTIFYING LEGAL PUNISHMENT 12 (1989).

40 *See id.*

41 *Id.* at 13 ("The history of the retributive view of punishment begins with the biblical and [T]almudic ethical and legal ideas.").

42 *Cf.* PRIMORATZ, *supra* note 39, at 13 (describing the moral aspect of retributive punishment, which this Comment posits will often equate to an emotional aspect of retributive punishment).

43 *See id.*

44 KANT, *supra* note 14, at 195.

45 IMMANUEL KANT, THE SCIENCE OF RIGHT (1790), *reprinted in* 42 GREAT BOOKS OF THE WESTERN WORLD: KANT 447 (Robert Maynard Hutchins ed., 1989).

46 *See* Markus Dirk Dubber, *Rediscovering Hegel's Theory of Crime and Punishment*, 92 MICH. L. REV. 1577, 1577-78 (1994).

47 *Id.* at 1581-82.

48 HEGEL, *supra* note 24, at § 101.

Utilitarian theories of punishment, while perhaps not as old as retributivism, may also date back several millennia.[49] While early retributivism may have called for a thief to have his or her hand cut off (also potentially a utilitarian response), it is possible that a decision to imprison the thief instead of, or in addition to, cutting off his or her hand reflected utilitarian values. After all, the utilitarian principle of incapacitation asserts that while in prison, the thief is no threat. Seen in this light, utilitarian concepts may date back almost to the beginnings of civilization. Indeed, utilitarian justifications for punishment can be seen as early as in the work of Plato. In *Protagoras*, Plato argued that punishment for punishment's sake was "taking blind vengeance like a beast."[50] He continued, "No, punishment is not inflicted by a rational man for the sake of the crime that has been committed—after all one cannot undo what is past . . . ."[51]

The medieval and early modern eras witnessed the continued development of utilitarian thought. St. Thomas Aquinas argued that the purpose of punishment required that some good emerge from the punishment.[52] Later in the millennium, Thomas Hobbes indicated support for utilitarian forms and rationales of punishment. He argued that society should be "forbidden to inflict punishment with any other design[], than for the correction of the offender, or direction of others."[53] The utilitarian rationale in this statement appears undeniable.

Yet it was not until the writings of Jeremy Bentham in the eighteenth and nineteenth centuries that utilitarianism was most clearly articulated.[54] Although it was John Stewart Mill who actually coined the term *utilitarianism* to describe the doctrine,[55] it was Jeremy Bentham who first proposed his theory that society's goal should be to maximize utility, that is, to maximize the amount of aggregate pleasure and minimize the amount

---

[49] A more recent example can be seen in the work of John Locke. LOCKE, *supra* note 5, at 273 (noting that a crime may be punished for future restraint).

[50] PLATO, PROTAGORAS, *reprinted in* THE COLLECTED DIALOGUES OF PLATO 308, 321 (Edith Hamilton & Huntington Cairns eds., 1982) (stating that punishment is permissible if "the [punisher's] intention be directed chiefly to some good, to be obtained by means of the punishment of the person who has sinned").

[51] *Id.*

[52] II ST. THOMAS AQUINAS, SUMMA THEOLOGICA, *in* 20 GREAT BOOKS OF THE WESTERN WORLD, second part, part I, question 92, art. 2, at 215 (Robert Maynard Hutchins ed., founders ed. 1952) ("And it is the fear of punishment that law makes use of in order to ensure obedience . . . .").

[53] HOBBES, *supra* note 5, at 106.

[54] *See* BENTHAM, MORALS AND LEGISLATION, *supra* note 15, at 83-86.

[55] JOHN STUART MILL, UTILITARIANISM (Oskar Piest ed., Bobbs-Merrill Co. 1957) (1861).

of aggregate pain in society.[56] Criminal punishment, therefore, was only acceptable if it increased future pleasure or decreased future pain. Using his theory of utility, Bentham was the first to clearly argue that prevention of future crimes should be the primary goal of punishment. "General prevention ought to be the chief end of punishment, as it is its real justification."[57] Because criminal acts decrease aggregate happiness in society, prevention of such acts increases aggregate happiness.

The influence of Bentham's and others' works on utilitarianism and their influences on the criminal justice system cannot be overstated. Bentham, in particular, accurately touched on all the issues mentioned by previous academics and philosophers, and weaved those concerns into a comprehensive and conclusive theory that could be applied to life in general.[58]

Following Bentham, we see the emergence of applications of utilitarian principles of punishment by prominent legal scholars.[59] Several famous American scholars and judges adopted and further developed utilitarian theories of punishment. Oliver Wendall Holmes, Jr., for example, wrote in 1881 that "prevention would . . . seem to be the chief and only universal purpose of punishment."[60] He openly supported deterrence as a chief principle of punishment:

> If I were having a philosophical talk with a man I was going to have hanged . . . . I should say, I don't doubt that your act was inevitable for you but to make it more avoidable by others we propose to sacrifice you to the common good. You may regard yourself as a soldier dying for your country if you like. But the law must keep its promises.[61]

John H. Wigmore described deterrence as "the kingpin of the criminal law."[62]

As the twentieth century progressed, the movement towards utilitarian theories of punishment grew in its influence.[63] Even the Supreme Court

---

[56] *See* BENTHAM, MORALS AND LEGISLATION, *supra* note 15, at 1-13.

[57] BENTHAM, PRINCIPLES OF PENAL LAW, *supra* note 15, at 396.

[58] *See* PRIMORATZ, *supra* note 39, at 13.

[59] *See infra* text accompanying notes 60-62.

[60] OLIVER WENDELL HOLMES, JR., THE COMMON LAW 46 (Little, Brown & Co. 1945) (1881).

[61] Letter from Oliver Wendell Holmes, Jr., to Harold J. Laski (Dec 17, 1925), *in* 1 HOLMES-LASKI LETTERS: THE CORRESPONDENCE OF MR. JUSTICE HOLMES AND HAROLD J. LASKI, 1916-1925, at 806 (Mark DeWolfe Howe ed., 1953).

[62] Harry Olson, Homer Cummings & John H. Wigmore, *A Symposium of Comments from the Legal Profession: The Loeb-Leopold Case (Concluded)*, 15 J. AM. INST. CRIM. L. & CRIMINOLOGY 395, 401 (1924).

[63] However, this period can be differentiated between adoptions of rehabilitation and deterrence as governing theories. *See* Alschuler, *supra* note 6, at 6-14.

appeared to have found the virtues of the philosophy. In 1949, the Court held that "[r]etribution is no longer the dominant objective of the criminal law."[64] Three years later the Court spoke of the "tardy and unfinished substitution of deterrence and reformation in place of retaliation and vengeance as the motivation of public prosecution."[65]

The latter half of the twentieth century saw a continued development of utilitarian principles that nicely dovetailed into the philosophy of the emerging law and economics movement.[66] This movement sought to craft legal rules that created *ex ante* incentives that would lead to efficient outcomes in a variety of situations.[67] The utilitarian concepts of using criminal punishments to decrease the amount of future crime through deterrence played right into the law and economics movement and its use of *ex ante* incentives to create optimal care and activity levels.[68] By creating a bright-line rule of harsh punishments, potential criminals are incentivized not to commit a crime.[69]

As discussed above, during this period incapacitation and deterrence became important goals of the criminal justice system.[70] Professor Albert Alschuler highlights the use of law-and-economics-based deterrence policies during the period with the example of federal income tax evasion penalties.[71] Even though physically stealing $100,000, for example, from the government would appear to most of us as worse than avoiding paying $100,000 worth of income tax, income tax evasion was punished much more severely than outright theft.[72] The justification was that tax evaders were caught less often than thieves; therefore, harsher penalties were necessary to create a sufficient deterrent effect.[73]

As the twentieth century wore on, utilitarian justifications for punishment seemed to be gaining a foothold in American criminal jurisprudence.[74] Yet this blossoming of acceptance of utilitarian concepts

---

[64] Williams v. New York, 337 U.S. 241, 248 (1949).

[65] Morissette v. United States, 342 U.S. 246, 251 (1952).

[66] *Cf.* Alschuler, *supra* note 6, at 11 (noting economists' views on criminal punishment).

[67] *See, e.g.*, Steven Shavell, *Criminal Law and the Optimal Use of Nonmonetary Sanctions as a Deterrent*, 85 COLUM. L. REV. 1232 (1985).

[68] *See id.*

[69] *See id.*

[70] *See* Alschuler, *supra* note 6, at 11.

[71] *Id.*

[72] *Id.*

[73] *Id.* at 11 n.61 ("Especially in light of the limited number of criminal tax prosecutions relative to the estimated incidence of such violations . . . deterring others from violating the tax laws is the primary consideration underlying these guidelines." (citing U.S. SENTENCING GUIDELINES AND POLICY STATEMENTS § 2T4.1 (April 1987))).

[74] *Id.* at 9-12.

of punishment was not to last. A "renaissance" of retributivist thought was soon to challenge utilitarian theory.[75] This recent movement towards retributivism as the predominant school of American criminal jurisprudence is discussed in the next Part.

III. MODERN RETRIBUTIVISM

As recently as the middle to late twentieth century, many scholars and judges were still under the assumption that retributive theories of punishment had either been thoroughly defeated or served little to no purpose in the criminal justice system.[76] In 1972, Justice Thurgood Marshall declared that "no one has ever seriously advanced retribution as a legitimate goal of our society."[77] A criminal law scholar in the 1950s claimed that "[p]unishment as retribution belongs to a penal philosophy that is archaic and discredited by history."[78] Even the drafters of the Model Penal Code seemed to virtually ignore the role of retributivism in criminal punishment.[79] The 1962 draft included retribution as a limiting principle while seemingly including every other plausible justification as a legitimate and primary rationale and purpose for punishment.[80] In such a hostile atmosphere, a reemergence of retributivism seemed highly unlikely; yet, exactly such a reemergence has occurred, and with great strength and influence.[81]

Over the last quarter of the twentieth century and into the early part of the twenty-first century, retributivism has reestablished itself as the dominant theory behind criminal justice.[82] That this revolution in thought about criminal punishment has occurred is disputed by few scholars[83] and can be seen in a plethora of examples.[84] One scholar noted that "[t]here has been a steady rise in the popularity of retributivism over the last decade,

---

[75] *See* Martin R. Gardner, *The Renaissance of Retribution—An Examination of Doing Justice*, 1976 WIS. L. REV. 781, 781.

[76] *See supra* text accompanying notes 63-75; *infra* text accompanying notes 77-80.

[77] Furman v. Georgia, 408 U.S. 238, 363 (1972) (Marshall, J., concurring).

[78] Austin MacCormick, *The Prison's Role in Crime Prevention*, 41 J. CRIM. L. & CRIMINOLOGY 36, 40 (1951).

[79] *See* MODEL PENAL CODE § 1.02 (Proposed Official Draft 1962).

[80] *Id.*

[81] *See* Christopher, *supra* note 6, at 845-47.

[82] *Id.*

[83] *But see* Gerald Leonard, *Towards a Legal History of American Criminal Theory: Culture and Doctrine from Blackstone to the Model Penal Code*, 6 BUFF. CRIM. L. REV. 691, 692 n.6 (2003) (arguing that there has not been a revolution of retributivist thinking).

[84] *See* Christopher, *supra* note 6, at 845; Gardener, *supra* note 75, at 784; Ristroph, *supra* note 6, at 1293.

which is surprising given its near death in the 1950s and 1960s."[85] Such sentiments are seen through the works of several other criminal law scholars.[86]

These scholarly insights about the reemergence of retributivism were based on strong examples in a number of contexts. In *Spaziano v. Florida*, the United States Supreme Court acknowledged the role of retribution in criminal justice.[87] The Court stated that retribution "is an element of all punishments society imposes."[88] State courts, too, adopted a more retributivist slant when interpreting criminal punishment statutes.[89] Additionally, several states adopted retributivist principles of punishment into their penal codes.[90] Pennsylvania's penal code went so far as openly advocating retribution as the primary purpose of criminal punishment: "The sentencing guidelines provide sanctions proportionate to the severity of the crime [that] . . . establishes a sentencing system with a primary focus on retribution . . . ."[91]

While the specific event that triggered the reemergence of retributivism is highly debated, the reasons for its reemergence are more agreed upon.[92] Although several reasons existed for the growth, three are predominant. First, retributivism altered its rhetoric away from talk of retribution and towards criminals getting their just deserts.[93] In other words, retributivism no longer spoke of victims or society taking vengeance on the criminal, but instead spoke of the criminal getting what he or she deserved for committing the crime. Second, retributivism received a facelift in the form of much scholarly development of its concepts and philosophical arguments and justifications.[94] This development helped modernize retributivist thought and moved retributivism away from its

---

[85] Jean Hampton, *Correcting Harms Versus Righting Wrongs: The Goal of Retribution*, 39 UCLA L. Rev. 1659, 1659 (1992).

[86] *See, e.g.*, Richard S. Frase, *Limiting Retributivism*, *in* THE FUTURE OF IMPRISONMENT 83, 90-104 (Michael Tonry ed., 2004); Gardener, *supra* note 75, at 784; Kyron Huigens, *The Dead End of Deterrence, and Beyond*, 41 WM. & MARY L. REV. 943, 980 n.152 (2000); Sanford H. Kadish, *Fifty Years of Criminal Law: An Opinionated Review*, 87 CAL. L. REV. 943, 978 (1999).

[87] 468 U.S. 447, 462 (1984).

[88] *Id.*

[89] *See* Michelle Cotton, *Back with a Vengeance: The Resilience of Retribution as an Articulated Purpose of Criminal Punishment*, 37 AM. CRIM. L. REV. 1313, 1326-27 (2000) (citing examples of state courts adopting retributivist rationales for criminal punishment).

[90] *See, e.g.*, Act Operative July 1, 1977, ch. 4.5, 1976 Cal. Stat. 5140 (codified as amended at CAL. PENAL CODE § 1170(a)(1) (West 2004 & Supp. 2009)).

[91] 204 PA. CODE § 303.11 (2008).

[92] Christopher, *supra* note 6, at 846 n.6.

[93] *See* Ristroph, *supra* note 6, at 1299-1301.

[94] *See id.* at 1299-1300.

archaic image of an "eye for an eye" punishment.[95] Lastly, many retributivists developed and adopted new systems of retributivism that attempted to appeal to other theories of punishment.[96] For purposes of this Comment, I focus on limiting retributivism's appeal to utilitarianism, and will now discuss the three developments in great detail.

The rhetoric of retributivism had always been one of its weakest points.[97] A system that speaks of the basis of punishment in terms of vengeance is bound to evoke bad connotations similar to reactions towards vigilante justice.[98] This rhetoric leads to retributivism being "portray[ed] . . . as glorified vengeance, [a] celebrat[ed] and codif[ied] . . . brutal and inhumane impulse to harm those who harm us."[99] In response to these negative images associated with the term retribution, retributivism scholars have adopted less severe and more egalitarian-sounding rhetoric.[100] The newly chosen motto was "just deserts." When a person commits a crime, his or her actions deserve punishment in accordance with the severity of the crime and his or her moral culpability.[101]

This change in rhetoric has largely achieved its goals.[102] "The emphasis on desert seems to have helped disassociate retribution from revenge, for it allows punishment theorists to draw on a concept that has more neutral philosophical status."[103] Thus, instead of being punished because of revenge or hatred, the criminal receives his or her just deserts as punishment.[104]

This change in rhetoric accompanied a change in retributivism's underlying philosophy as well.[105] While opinions differ within the philosophy of modern retributivism, there is consistency in the emergence of the use of egalitarian principles within those theories.[106]

---

95 *See id.* at 1299-1306.

96 *See id.*

97 *See id.*

98 *See id.* at 1298-99.

99 *Id.* at 1299.

100 *Id.*

101 *See* Frase, *supra* note 6, at 73 (citing ANDREW VON HIRSCH, CENSURE AND SANCTIONS 29-33 (1993); Richard S. Frase, *Excessive Prison Sentences, Punishment Goals, and the Eighth Amendment: "Proportionality" Relative to What?*, 89 MINN. L. REV. 571, 590 (2005)).

102 *See supra* text accompanying notes 81-86.

103 Ristroph, *supra* note 6, at 1300.

104 *See id.*

105 *See* Herbert Morris, *Persons and Punishment*, *in* SENTENCING, *supra* note 19, at 93.

106 *See* Ristroph, *supra* note 6, at 1300 ("These egalitarian arguments have won much support.").

Herbert Morris was one of the pioneering supporters of the new theoretical basis for retributivism.[107] Morris argued that the law should create equal rights and responsibilities for all members of society.[108] When an individual commits a crime, the perpetrator violates this equal distribution.[109] The criminal receives the benefit of others not committing crimes, but violates his responsibility not to commit crimes against others.[110] Punishment, therefore, is simply society restoring the balances of benefits and burdens of the law.[111]

Other retributivists consider a criminal act to consist of the criminal declaring he is more important than the victim.[112] By delivering just deserts as punishment, society signals that the criminal is not, in fact, more valuable than the victim, demonstrating the victim's equality through the punishment of the criminal.[113]

Lastly, retributivists attempted to reconcile retributivism with utilitarianism to gain adherents among traditional supporters of utilitarian theories of punishment.[114] While, historically, retributivism and utilitarianism were viewed as diametrically opposed and mutually exclusive theories of punishment, late twentieth century scholars were able to create a system that bridged the gap.[115]

The most influential of these scholars was Norval Morris, not to be confused with Herbert Morris.[116] Morris established the limiting retributivism model of criminal punishment.[117] Limiting retributivism did not follow the typical retributivist concept that punishment should be based and predicated on a criminal getting his or her just deserts.[118] Instead, desert and moral blameworthiness served as a limiting principle, "a principle that, though it would rarely tell us the exact sanction to be

---

[107] *See* Morris, *supra* note 105, at 93-95.

[108] *Id.*

[109] *Id.*

[110] *Id.* at 95 ("[I]t is just to punish those who have violated the rules and caused the unfair distribution of benefits and burdens. A person who violates the rules has something others have—the benefits of the system—but by renouncing what others have assumed, the burdens of self-restraint, he has acquired an unfair advantage.").

[111] *See* WOJCIECH SADURSKI, GIVING DESERT ITS DUE: SOCIAL JUSTICE AND LEGAL THEORY 229 (1985).

[112] *See, e.g.*, Jean Hampton, *An Expressive Theory of Retribution*, *in* RETRIBUTIVISM AND ITS CRITICS 1, 5-6 (Wesley Cragg ed., 1992).

[113] *Id.* at 6-11.

[114] *See, e.g.*, Morris, *supra* note 19, at 257-59.

[115] *See* DRESSLER, *supra* note 17, at 19.

[116] *See* Morris, *supra* note 19, at 257-59.

[117] *Id.*

[118] *Id.*

imposed . . . would nevertheless give us the outer limits of leniency and severity which should not be excluded."[119] Despite the fact that Morris used retributivism as a limiting principle, his theory can still be seen as located squarely within the retributivist camp of theories of punishment.

Morris acknowledged the fundamental difficulties in determining with precision a prisoner's just deserts. Instead, retributivism would often lead to a range of possible penalties.[120] While we can be sure that some penalty is either too little or too much, we cannot always know exactly what the correct retributivist penalty should be.[121] This leads to Morris's use of retributivism as a limiting principle instead of a guiding principle, as mentioned above.[122]

Within the range of penalties dictated by retributivism's limiting principles, other theories of criminal punishment are utilized to increase or decrease the sentence to achieve those theories' goals.[123] One such theory, supported strongly by Morris himself, was "parsimony," which essentially held that a criminal's punishment should be no more severe than needed.[124] This served as a further limiting principle that had to be addressed before any other considerations could result in an increase or decrease in punishment within the acceptable range. For this Comment, however, the most important theory to which Morris's limited retributivism attempted to appeal was utilitarianism.

Limiting retributivism appealed to utilitarian concerns in two main ways. First, and of lesser concern, it created increased uniformity in sentences, which was believed to be of utilitarian value.[125] More uniform sentences would create a clear indication of the level of punishment that a criminal would receive and thus was thought to have a deterrent effect.[126] Second, and more importantly, within sentence parameters a judge could factor in utilitarian concerns such as incapacitation or deterrence to increase or decrease the severity of the sentence.[127] Thus, "desert permits the reasonable pursuit of utilitarian aims even as it forestalls the dangers of

---

[119] *Id.* at 259.

[120] *Id.*

[121] *See* Ristroph, *supra* note 6, at 1301-02 (noting that "[t]he 'limiting retributivism' model attributed to Norval Morris begins with the recognition that our intuitions about how much punishment a given offender deserves are often imprecise").

[122] *See, e.g.*, HERBERT L. PACKER, THE LIMITS OF THE CRIMINAL SANCTION 66 (1968) ("I see an important limiting principle in the criminal law's traditional emphasis on blameworthiness . . . . But it is a *limiting* principle, not a justification for action.").

[123] *See* Morris, *supra* note 19, at 264.

[124] *See* NORVAL MORRIS, THE FUTURE OF IMPRISONMENT 60-62 (1974).

[125] *See* Frase, *supra* note 6, at 74-75.

[126] *Id.*

[127] *Id.* at 76-77.

excessive utilitarianism."[128] In light of these developments, Norval Morris's theory of limiting retributivism seemed to succeed at bridging the gap between retributivism and utilitarianism.

As a result of its ability to appeal to both retributivism and utilitarianism, limiting retributivism became a widely accepted theory of criminal punishment.[129] Some sentencing guidelines, where theories of criminal punishment are put to practice, are evidence of such acceptance. Some of the guidelines, Minnesota's for example, seem to be adopting limiting retributivism as their guiding principles.[130]

IV. LIMITING RETRIBUTIVISM

Because of its extreme success,[131] limiting retributivism is the model of retributivism I will focus on in the remaining portions of this Comment. Here, a more detailed description of limiting retributivism is necessary to highlight how it functions in practice, how it specifically appeals to utilitarianism, and what factors are involved in determining the upper and lower bounds of acceptable levels of punishment.

As previously mentioned, limiting retributivism seeks to create a system of criminal punishment in which retributivist principles determine upper and lower limits of a criminal's potential range of punishment.[132] The criminal's culpability and moral blameworthiness are the relevant factors in assessing the upper and lower limits of punishment.[133] While determining an appropriate, specific punishment may create difficulties for scholars and practitioners, creating a range of possible punishments is easier, although not without its own difficulties.

Professor Martin Redish claims that when interpreting constitutional text, you may not always know when your interpretation is the correct one, but you do know when it is the wrong one.[134] The text provides a range of

---

[128] Ristroph, *supra* note 6, at 1302.

[129] One scholar noted that limiting retributivism has become a "widely endorsed and adopted model." Frase, *supra* note 6, at 76. Another stated that it is "[o]ne of the most widely followed reconciliations of desert with utilitarian aims." Ristroph, *supra* note 6, at 1301.

[130] Minnesota's sentencing guidelines seem to have adopted limiting retributivism to some degree. *See* Richard S. Frase, *Sentencing Guidelines in Minnesota: 1978–2003*, 31 CRIME & JUST. 131, 149 (2005) ("Thus, for most defendants, the guidelines essentially retain the traditional indeterminate sentencing system and its utilitarian values, subject only to retributive 'caps' set by the presumptive duration of stayed prison terms.").

[131] *See* Frase, *supra* note 6, at 76; Ristroph, *supra* note 6, at 1301.

[132] *See supra* text accompanying notes 116-24.

[133] ANDREW VON HIRSCH, DOING JUSTICE: THE CHOICE OF PUNISHMENTS 69 (1976).

[134] *See* Martin H. Redish & Karen L. Drizin, *Constitutional Federalism and Judicial Review: The Role of Textual Analysis*, 62 N.Y.U. L. REV. 1, 22 (1987) (citing Frederick

possible interpretations, and it should be quite clear when you have exceeded that range.[135] This same idea can apply to creating an acceptable range of punishments for a criminal. You cannot always know if a certain punishment is correct, but you can know if it is either too severe or too lenient. If a criminal steals a car, we intuitively know that a one-day prison sentence is far too low, while a fifty-year sentence is far too high. Yet we may not know if a ten-year or a fifteen-year sentence is more appropriate.[136]

While upper and lower limits can be very roughly determined through intuitive retributivist beliefs given a specific crime, how do we determine different ranges of punishments from one type of crime to another? In other words, how do limiting retributivists determine that an appropriate range of punishments for theft is one to five years, for example, while an appropriate range for rape is ten to twenty? The answer is much the same as how limiting retributivists determine the appropriate range for a single crime: there are intuitive sensibilities about punishments. There is a general belief that some crimes are more morally reprehensible than others.[137] People tend to agree that rape is a far more reprehensible crime than mere theft. These general beliefs about the varying degrees of reprehensibility of crimes are supported by empirical evidence.[138] Almost all people, across all groups, when asked to rank crimes from least-worst to worst, rank them in similar manners.[139] This evidence bolsters limiting retributivism's appeal to intuition to create upper and lower limits by demonstrating that such intuition is inherent in human nature and, therefore, in some sense, not arbitrary. Although the fact that differing crimes receive different levels of punishment seems obvious, it is still important to note that the range of punishment from crime *A* to crime *B* is justified in a similar manner as that of ranges of potential punishments within a single type of crime. Both differences are based on moral culpability. This fact can be seen in the Model Penal Code, which ranks crimes and states of required knowledge, implying differing levels of moral culpability for each mens rea.[140]

Once we have accepted that limiting retributivism can successfully create a range of acceptable punishments, we are faced with how utilitarian

---

Schauer, *An Essay on Constitutional Language*, 29 UCLA L. REV. 797, 828 (1982)).

[135] *See id.*

[136] This example is taken from Ristroph, *supra* note 6, at 1302.

[137] *Cf.* VON HIRSCH, *supra* note 133, at 66-71 (arguing that the existence of differing punishments for different crimes implies that certain crimes are worse than others).

[138] Joseph E. Jacoby & Francis T. Cullen, *The Structure of Punishment Norms: Applying the Rossi-Berk Model*, 89 J. CRIM. L. & CRIMINOLOGY 245 (1998).

[139] *Id.*

[140] *See* Kevin R. Reitz, *Reporter's Introduction* to MODEL PENAL CODE: SENTENCING 1, 3-4 (Discussion Draft 2006).

principles may be met and goals achieved within those ranges. Here, utilitarian concepts such as incapacitation or deterrence are utilized.[141] The judge or sentencing guidelines determine the range of punishments available for certain crimes, given the type of crime and the criminal's culpability and moral blameworthiness, and then utilitarian concerns are used to determine the adequate punishment within that range.[142]

According to supporters of limiting retributivism, these adoptions of utilitarian principles can have demonstrable effects and thus serve utilitarian purposes.[143] Limiting retributivism's use of utilitarian principles can serve utilitarianism's twin goals of incapacitation and deterrence; examples of each follow.

Suppose a person has robbed a grocery store. The upper and lower bounds for this theft are one to ten years. The trial judge discovers that this individual has been previously convicted of theft, assault, and attempted robbery, and received jail terms of one year, six months, and one year, respectively. Given this individual's demonstrated propensity to commit crime, utilitarians consider this criminal a threat to society—that is to say, the criminal's demonstrated propensity to commit crimes indicates he is likely to commit future crimes and thus is bound to cause pain to others. Therefore, society will be better off if this individual is put in jail for a long time where he cannot hurt others. Thus, with these considerations in mind, a judge may sentence this individual to ten years in prison, the maximum allowed. This same logic is behind the "three strikes and you're out" rule of many state penal codes.[144] This example is a clear demonstration of an appeal to incapacitation principles of utilitarianism.

Now let us consider another hypothetical. An individual is convicted of attempted rape. The range of acceptable punishments for attempted rape is two to twenty years. Let us also assume that this crime was committed in a state or county where it was known that a very low percentage of rape or attempted rape victims took actions against their perpetrators and pursued criminal charges. In this regard, a very low percentage of people committing rape or attempted rape end up being charged with the crime, and an even lower percentage will be found guilty and sentenced to a term of imprisonment. In light of this low rate, a very high level of punishment may be required to create sufficiently strong incentives that will convince potential rapists that they should not commit the crime. Simple economic calculations support this statement. If there is a 10% chance of being found

---

[141] *See* MORRIS, *supra* note 124, at 60-62.

[142] *See id.*; *see also* Frase, *supra* note 6, at 76-77 (explaining the concept of limiting retributivism and Morris's role in its development).

[143] *See* MORRIS, *supra* note 124, at 60-62.

[144] *See, e.g.*, CAL. PENAL. CODE § 667(e)(2) (West 1999).

guilty and an expected jail time of five years, then the expected harm to the rapist is a six-month jail sentence. On the other hand, if the expected jail time is twenty years, the expected harm is a two-year sentence. According to simple law and economic principles, the higher expected harm will create greater incentives not to commit the crime.[145] Given this information, the judge decides to award twenty years in an attempt to demonstrate to the community that one found guilty of attempted rape will face twenty years imprisonment.[146] This decision to sentence one found guilty of rape or attempted rape to the highest possible prison term, according to the law and economics theory previously mentioned, creates stronger incentives not to commit rapes, and therefore serves as a deterrent, the other main goal of utilitarianism.[147] This example demonstrates limiting retributivism's appeal to deterrence.

But this leaves us with our last, and, as we will see, most important question. Retributivists claim that the level of culpability and moral blameworthiness of the offender determines the upper and lower bounds of permissible punishment.[148] This seems simple enough, yet how are culpability and moral blameworthiness quantified? I cannot imagine a retributivist would ever claim that a man with Down syndrome was as culpable or morally abject for committing assault as a full-grown man with average intellect. Neither, I imagine, would a retributivist say the permissible range of punishments should be the same for a young child who commits theft as for an adult. The question is then: what factors are utilized when determining the upper and lower bounds of permissible punishment, given the fact that people committing the same crime may have varying degrees of culpability and moral blameworthiness?

Scholars and judges have dealt with this problem by viewing desert on a case-specific basis.[149] By looking at the specifics of each case, the judge can determine the most appropriate range of punishment in line with the defendant's culpability and moral blameworthiness, and the severity of the crime.[150] "Desert is typically understood to be a highly individual matter, in the sense that to be deserving or not is dependent on particular traits of the individual."[151] One scholar goes as far as describing desert as based "as

---

145 *See* Shavell, *supra* note 67, at 1235.

146 This example is similar to the federal income tax evasion example mentioned *supra*, in the text accompanying notes 70-73.

147 *See* Shavell, *supra* note 67, at 1235.

148 *See generally* Ristroph, *supra* note 6.

149 *Id.* at 1321.

150 *Id.*

151 *Id.*

much or more on circumstances and personal characteristics as on physical actions and harm."[152]

Several commentators have acknowledged that each individual's desert may differ greatly.[153] Various conditions or situations exist that may increase or decrease a criminal's culpability and moral blameworthiness, and hence alter his or her desert.[154] Such factors range from mental ability to age.[155] I refer to these issues of personal characteristics and circumstances as "aggravating" and "mitigating" factors. An aggravating factor is any factor that increases a criminal's desert, while a mitigating factor is any factor that decreases a criminal's desert. While the academic discussion of the list of possible aggravating and mitigating factors is nowhere near complete, I posit that based on the underlying structure of retributivism and its dependency on moral blameworthiness, that list will be lengthy.

Aggravating and mitigating factors play a large role in determining a criminal's just desert. For example, how blameworthy is a poor baker stealing bread from his employer to feed his family? What about a situation in which a man thinks his actions are saving the lives of many, yet actually result in several deaths? Or a ten-year-old child who accidentally shoots and kills his sister? Most would not argue that these three people are just as morally culpable and blameworthy as those who stole or murdered in cold blood, for fun or revenge. I believe these three situations illustrate how many factors could be used to alter the range of potential punishments under a limiting retributivism theory of punishment.[156]

In conclusion, limiting retributivism, in its current form, consists of determining a range of potential punishments by utilizing all the various aggravating and mitigating factors that affect the defendant's moral culpability, and then altering the punishment within those parameters to serve utilitarian purposes. As we will see in the following Part, this system

---

[152] Alschuler, *supra* note 6, at 19.

[153] *See, e.g.*, JOEL FEINBERG, *Justice and Personal Desert*, *in* DOING AND DESERVING: ESSAYS IN THE THEORY OF RESPONSIBILITY 55, 61 (1970).

[154] *See, e.g.*, Kadish, *supra* note 86.

[155] *See* Ristroph, *supra* note 6, at 1314-27.

[156] Although I have not seen any scholarly writings that have argued this point, I believe it is a natural and logical progression of the concept of retributivism in general. Given that moral blameworthiness and culpability are what defines an individual's desert, I cannot see how the examples I illustrated would not affect one's level of desert. In order to preclude such factors from entering the debate of what the individual's just deserts are, retributivists will need to create a different rationale or measuring stick for desert. A possibility could be having some sort of free will requirement, in other words, describing moral blameworthiness as being able to understand the import of your decision, its likely outcome, yet nonetheless going forward with the action.

is questionable because the existence of so many aggravating and mitigating factors itself will lead to severe under-deterrence, due to the effects of cognitive biases. Regardless of the resulting adjustments for utilitarian concerns within the acceptable range of punishments, the overall deterrent effect of this system is inadequate. The following Part describes why utilitarian concerns about deterrence and *ex ante* incentives are not adequately addressed by limiting retributivism.

V. LIMITING RETRIBUTIVISM, UTILITARIANISM, AND COGNITIVE BIASES

Over the past several decades, behavioral psychologists have made numerous discoveries that have questioned previous assumptions about human behavior.[157] These discoveries have questioned the neo-classical image of human beings as rational beings capable of making well-informed, reasoned decisions.[158] In contrast to the optimal rational behavior humans were imagined to possess, they "exhibit bounded rationality, bounded self-interest, and bounded willpower."[159] In other words, human psychology and behavior prevent people from acting or behaving as entirely rational beings, as they have often been thought to be. With these new insights into the true nature of human psychology, several old theories, specifically theories of criminal punishment, must be adjusted to accommodate this new information.

In essence, behavioral psychologists have discovered over the past several decades what many already thought to be true: human beings simply are not rational.[160] Yet research has shown that the extent to which human beings are irrational, and the impact of this irrational behavior, is far greater than previously predicted.[161] Errors in human judgment are not simply the effect of emotion creeping into the decision-making process and temporarily overriding the individual's rationality; rather, they are the effect

[157] Ironically, the decision to engage in such research was, in large part, a reaction to the law and economics movement's description of human beings as rational decision-makers. *See* William M. Goldstein & Robin M. Hogarth, *Judgment and Decision Research: Some Historical Context*, *in* RESEARCH ON JUDGMENT AND DECISION MAKING 3, 5 (William M. Goldstein & Robin M. Hogarth eds., 1997); Robin M. Hogarth & Melvin W. Reder, *Introduction* to RATIONAL CHOICE: THE CONTRAST BETWEEN ECONOMICS AND PSYCHOLOGY 1, 5 (Robin M. Hogarth & Melvin W. Reder eds., 1987).

[158] *See supra* note 157.

[159] Christine Jolls, Cass R. Sunstein & Richard Thaler, *A Behavioral Approach to Law and Economics*, 50 STAN. L. REV. 1471, 1471 (1998).

[160] *Id.* at 1473.

[161] Jon D. Hanson & Douglas A. Kysar, *Taking Behavioralism Seriously: The Problem of Market Manipulation*, 74 N.Y.U. L. REV. 630, 633 (1999).

of systematic cognitive biases that affect all of human nature.[162] Studies have demonstrated that human beings are, in many ways, fundamentally irrational. By demonstrating the existence of such cognitive biases as the hindsight bias,[163] the entity effect,[164] and the representative heuristic effect, behavioral psychologists have demonstrated just how irrational we are.[165]

Hindsight bias refers to the phenomenon in which human beings, once knowledgeable of the outcome of some situation, develop a sincere belief that they would have predicted the actual outcome.[166] This may seem like common sense—hindsight is 20/20—yet the extent of this bias is remarkable. Suppose a patient comes into a hospital with a set of symptoms. Doctors know that given these symptoms, there is a 33% chance the patient has disease *A*, a 33% chance that the patient has disease *B*, and a 33% chance that the patient has disease *C*. Before actual diagnosis, several doctors, knowledgeable about all three diseases and their symptoms, are asked the probability that a patient with this set of symptoms has each of the three diseases. Virtually every doctor will say there is a 33% chance that the patient has each disease. The doctors are then presented with a description of a patient with the exact same symptoms, but told the patient had disease *B*. They are then asked, if they had seen this patient before he was diagnosed, what would be the predicted probability of the patient having each of the three diseases. In one study of the hindsight bias, the doctors claimed they would have predicted disease *B* was more than 50% likely to be the cause of the patient's symptoms. Clearly, the responses in both situations should be the same—33% for each disease—yet the results were not so.[167] The doctors all exhibited hindsight biases. The practical effect of this bias on the legal world is huge. How should we view an expert doctor's testimony at a medical malpractice suit with the effect of hindsight bias in mind?[168]

---

[162] J. St B.T. Evans, *Bias and Rationality*, *in* RATIONALITY: PSYCHOLOGICAL AND PHILOSOPHICAL PERSPECTIVES 6, 6 (K.I. Manktelow & D.E. Over eds., 1993) (noting that humans exhibit "a whole range of systematic errors and biases").

[163] *See, e.g.*, Hal R. Arkes et al., *Eliminating the Hindsight Bias*, 73 J. APPLIED PSYCHOL. 302, 305 (1988).

[164] *See, e.g.*, Lee Ross et al., *Perseverance in Self-Perception and Social Perception: Biased Attributional Processes in the Debriefing Paradigm*, 32 J. PERSONALITY & SOC. PSYCHOL. 880, 882-83 (1975) (referring to the "entity effect" as the perseverance phenomenon).

[165] *See, e.g.*, SUSAN T. FISKE & SHELLEY E. TAYLOR, SOCIAL COGNITION 142-79, 245-94 (2d ed. 1991) (1984).

[166] *See* Arkes et al., *supra* note 163, at 305.

[167] *See id.* at 305, 306 tbl.1.

[168] *See, e.g.*, Susan J. LaBine & Gary LaBine, *Determinations of Negligence and the Hindsight Bias*, 20 LAW & HUM. BEHAV. 501, 510-11 (1996).

The entity effect is another example of a cognitive bias that affects human decision-making.[169] Research in this field demonstrates that if humans are presented with a hypothetical situation and a set of related facts, they will continue to maintain their belief in a conclusion drawn based on the facts even after they have learned that those facts are false. Thus, if given a set of facts and then asked to create a hypothesis based on those facts, even if those facts are later proved to be entirely false, people still hold on to their initial hypotheses and fundamentally believe it is correct. This tendency is called the entity effect.[170]

Another example of a cognitive bias that affects decision-making is the availability bias. This refers to the phenomena in which individuals, faced with a decision, give far too much credence to anecdotal evidence that is particularly salient to them, instead of depending on relevant, known statistical evidence.[171] For example, suppose that a person lives in city *X*. Recently, two of the person's friends have had their cars stolen. The person is asked by another friend whether car theft is a big problem in city *X*. Previously the person was provided with statistical evidence demonstrating that, compared to other cities, city *X* has a very low rate of car thefts. Nonetheless, the person will probably still say, and genuinely believe, that car thefts are a big problem in city *X*, despite the evidence to the contrary.

With these examples of cognitive biases in mind, we move to those biases that affect our issue specifically. That is, we will examine which cognitive biases will be triggered by the adoption of limiting retributivism with its aggravating and mitigating factors and what the effects of those biases will be. The biases are motivated reasoning,[172] optimistic bias,[173] cognitive dissonance,[174] and control illusion.[175]

A. MOTIVATED REASONING

Motivated reasoning is a combination of several cognitive biases and describes the tendency in humans to reach desired conclusions in an

---

[169] *See* Ross et al., *supra* note 164, at 882-83.

[170] *Id.* at 883-84.

[171] *See* Matthew Rabin, *Psychology and Economics*, 36 J. ECON. LITERATURE 11, 30 (1998).

[172] *See, e.g.*, Ziva Kunda, *The Case for Motivated Reasoning*, 108 PSYCHOL. BULL. 480 (1990).

[173] *See, e.g.*, Neil D. Weinstein, *Unrealistic Optimism About Future Life Events*, 39 J. PERSONALITY & SOC. PSYCHOL. 806, 806 (1980).

[174] *See, e.g.*, Neil D. Weinstein & William M. Klein, *Resistance of Personal Risk Perceptions to Debiasing Interventions*, 14 HEALTH PSYCHOL. 132, 138-39 (1995).

[175] *See, e.g.*, Ellen J. Langer, *The Illusion of Control*, 32 J. PERSONALITY & SOC. PSYCHOL. 311, 311-13 (1975).

apparently unbiased manner.[176] Specifically, given a set of facts, humans are more likely to reach the conclusion that they want, without actually being aware of this predisposition. When making decisions, "one [naturally] accesses only a biased subset of the relevant beliefs and rules."[177] Thus people "perceive and interpret evidence in a manner designed to confirm initial hypotheses, but [they] construct[] the initial hypotheses themselves through biased cognitive processes designed to 'reason' toward a desired conclusion."[178] This bias has significant, real-world importance. For example, people may often convince themselves they have not had too much to drink, and that even if they are above the legal limit, they can still handle a car. These individuals honestly believe in such a statement despite the fact that the majority of people in this situation cannot, in fact, drive safely.[179] Unfortunately, "the practice of motivated reasoning appears to be a universal and, perhaps, immutable characteristic of human nature."[180]

B. OPTIMISM BIAS

Optimism bias describes how human beings are simply overly optimistic about factors affecting their lives.[181] Despite the fact that many people purport to believe that they are unlucky or that bad things always happen to them, deep-down people are extremely optimistic.[182] Regardless of how aware of statistics or actuarial calculations people are, they still often believe bad things will not happen to them while good things will. For example, people are twice as likely to think their children will be gifted than is statistically probable,[183] while they are six times more likely to think they will own a home than statistics suggest.[184] "One particular manifestation of this bias is the tendency of people to underestimate their own chance of suffering some adverse outcome even when they accurately state or even overstate everyone else's chance of suffering the same outcome."[185]

---

[176] *See* Kunda, *supra* note 172, at 480.

[177] *Id.* at 493.

[178] Hanson & Kysar, *supra* note 161, at 654.

[179] *Cf.* Kunda, *supra* note 172, at 495-96 (discussing examples of the motivated reasoning bias; the example given here, while not explicitly supported by Kunda's article, is a logical progression).

[180] Hanson & Kysar, *supra* note 161, at 654.

[181] *See* Weinstein, *supra* note 173, at 806.

[182] *See* Neil D. Weinstein, *Optimistic Biases About Personal Risks*, 246 SCI. 1232, 1232 (1989).

[183] *See* Weinstein, *supra* note 173, at 810.

[184] *Id.*

[185] Hanson & Kysar, *supra* note 161, at 656.

Optimism bias stems from several sources, chief among them the belief that risk is avoidable through individual action. In other words, the individual believes that while something bad may happen to others, he or she knows how to handle the situation and, as a result, will not suffer the same outcome.[186] Optimism bias is one of the most prevalent biases and, unfortunately, also one of the most "indiscriminate and indefatigable" ones.[187]

C. COGNITIVE DISSONANCE

Cognitive dissonance is somewhat of a subset of both optimism bias and motivated reasoning.[188] It describes the general tendency of people to ignore or undervalue information that contradicts more positive information about oneself.[189] Behavioral psychologists believe cognitive dissonance stems from individuals seriously believing themselves to be "smart, nice people."[190] Anything that contradicts this self-image is ignored or downplayed.[191] The effect of this cognitive feature is that "[i]n the face of a known risk . . . individuals come readily to the opinion that they themselves—unlike the average person—are relatively immune, and they hold onto these optimistic assessments tenaciously."[192] Thus, "[p]eople prefer to believe that they are intelligent and are not subjecting themselves to a substantial risk."[193] The impact of this type of bias should be clear: people think more highly of themselves and their abilities than they should.

D. CONTROL ILLUSION

The illusion of control is one which leads individuals to attribute random events to their own actions; in effect, they believe they can control, to some extent, random events.[194] Several studies have demonstrated this bias's effects in a variety of situations.[195] The important point here is that

---

[186] *See, e.g.*, Laurie J. Bauman & Karolynn Siegel, *Misperception Among Gay Men of the Risk for AIDS Associated with Their Sexual Behavior*, 17 J. APPLIED SOC. PSYCHOL. 329, 344-45 (1987).

[187] Hanson & Kysar, *supra* note 161, at 657.

[188] *Cf.* Weinstein & Klein, *supra* note 174, at 138-39.

[189] *Id.*

[190] George A. Akerlof & William T. Dickens, *The Economic Consequences of Cognitive Dissonance*, 72 AM. ECON. REV. 307, 308-09 (1982).

[191] *Id.*

[192] Hanson & Kysar, *supra* note 161, at 658 (footnotes omitted).

[193] *Id.*

[194] *See* Langer, *supra* note 175, at 311-13.

[195] *See, e.g.*, Ellen J. Langer & Jane Roth, *Heads I Win, Tails It's Chance: The Illusion of Control as a Function of the Sequence of Outcomes in a Purely Chance Task*, 32 J.

people believe that their control of a situation is merited by the actual situation.

E. LIMITING RETRIBUTIVISM

With these biases in mind, we now look to limiting retributivism doctrines and their use of aggravating and mitigating factors to determine the appropriate range of punishment. The salient issue here is the theory's open and public support of the use of these aggravating and mitigating factors. The entire concept of a defendant's moral culpability rests on determining how immoral or blameworthy the defendant and his or her actions are. Unfortunately, when this theory openly advocates the use of these aggravating and mitigating factors, it links directly into cognitive biases, where it becomes problematic.

If the potential criminal is aware of the use of aggravating and mitigating factors in determining sentencing ranges, his or her decision-making will be affected by the interaction of his or her cognitive biases and his or her knowledge of the factors in the present situation that may be considered in sentencing. Before a person's decision to commit or not to commit a crime, all four of the aforementioned biases will play their respective roles in his or her judgment process. Although these biases will be present whether or not there are aggravating and mitigating factors, the fact that these factors may play a role in any punishment received will be shown to exacerbate the effects of these biases. How will these cognitive biases affect a criminal's decision-making process, given that the criminal knows that aggravating and mitigating factors may play a role in sentencing?

Because of cognitive biases, a person debating whether or not to commit a crime may be comforted by several facts that the criminal believes to be true. First, the criminal probably does not believe that he or she will be caught in the first place. Second, if he or she is caught, he or she will believe that he will receive a sentence or punishment on the lower end of the range of permissible punishments. As a result of his or her cognitive biases, the criminal is likely to genuinely believe that the jury or the judge will find, given the particular facts of the case, that he or she does not have a high degree of moral culpability. For example, if the person has a history of abuse as a child, or has a poor family that needs to be fed, or if the crime contemplated is non-violent in nature, a person may believe that these or other factors will lead the jury or the judge to find that the

---

PERSONALITY & SOC. PSYCHOL. 951 (1975); Amos Tversky & Daniel Kahneman, *Judgment Under Uncertainty: Heuristics and Biases*, 185 SCI. 1124, 1129 (1974).

defendant's just desert is on the low end of the range of permissible punishments.

Given the existence of motivated reasoning, we can see that all of the above statements contribute to the hypothesis about potential punishment for the crime contemplated that a person would likely create, given the set of facts as he or she believes them to be, when engaging in the decision-making process of whether to commit a crime. The truth is that the criminal's hypotheses or predictions about any aggravating or mitigating factors that will affect his or her punishment are probably not accurate, but instead are highly influenced by cognitive biases. In other words, because of inherent cognitive biases, a person will conclude that, if caught and found guilty, he or she will not receive a harsh sentence even though a more balanced and rational interpretation of the facts would actually lead to a different conclusion. As mentioned above, the potential criminal's thought process is an example of motivated reasoning. The jury or judge will likely have a more balanced and rational interpretation of the facts and circumstances surrounding the crime.

The same person will also exhibit the optimism bias. If his or her cognitive processes are being filtered through the optimism bias, a person will believe that the judge will not be harsh on him because he or she honestly thinks he or she, and his or her situation, is different. The person will think the judge will be far more likely to find mitigating factors and far less likely to find aggravating factors. As a result, the individual will believe that the judge will determine that the appropriate punishment is on the very low end of the scale.

In addition, the person may suffer from cognitive dissonance in the decision-making process. This person may anticipate a lenient judge, for example, because he or she believes that he or she is a nice person. The judge will see that he or she is a good person who may have simply fallen on some bad luck, as he himself believes. Alternatively, he or she may think he or she is smart enough to outwit the system or the judge. In the mind of the would-be criminal, all of the potential aggravating factors will not be important to the judge, who will see through all of the district attorney's ploys to cast the defendant in a bad light and see him or her for who he or she really is—a good person who made a mistake and had lots of forces out of his or her control pushing him or her towards committing the crime. The criminal believes that he or she is either not very morally culpable, or can convince the judge that he or she is not morally culpable. Therefore, the criminal believes that the judge will grant him or her a range of sentences on the lower end of the spectrum. Of course, the criminal's confidence in his or her good nature or ability is likely unfounded.

Lastly, the would-be criminal may believe that he or she has a way to convince the jury or the judge to be lenient on him. He or she may believe that he or she has a secret method to put the judge or the jury in a good mood or to make them sympathetic to his or her pleas. While there is a chance the defendant may actually have a method to achieve these goals, it is more likely he or she is simply demonstrating control illusion and, in fact, will be unable to control the judge or jury.

While the examples given above are not examples of purely one type of cognitive bias or another, they combine to demonstrate the collective effects of these biases on a criminal's psychology and, thus, how the criminal's decision-making process may be affected. Together, these illustrations demonstrate how a person may anticipate a sentence far lower than he or she rationally should. The open use of aggravating and mitigating factors in determining sentences plays strongly into the effects of these cognitive biases. By openly admitting that they are used in determining sentences, limiting retributivism is, in essence, advertising directly to these biases. Reliance on them in determining sentencing simply adds more factors into which cognitive biases can play, with the effect of altering the criminal's expectations.

This may have a disastrous effect if one abides by a utilitarian theory of punishment. Under limiting retributivism, the use of these aggravating and mitigating factors in determining punishment will lead to would-be criminals anticipating punishments extremely below those which they may actually receive. Here, another law and economics example is useful. Suppose the existence of aggravating and mitigating factors leads criminals to believe that the average sentence will be one year, while the average sentence is in fact five years. The deterrence effect of the punishment, then, is five times lower than it should be. In essence, the very existence of these factors in determining punishment may lead to a person's anticipation of less prison time and hence under-deterrence.

Utilitarianism cannot be reconciled with a system that leads to such under-deterrence. Regardless of whether within the permissible punishment ranges utilitarian principles are utilized, the primary basis on which the range of punishment is decided is contrary to the goals of utilitarianism. Such a retributivist appeal to utilitarianism is similar to a store attempting to appeal to penny-wise shoppers by increasing the price of their goods by five dollars and then giving two-dollar coupons. When the system of determining punishment leads to under-deterrence, the subsequent use of utilitarian concerns is of lesser to no value.

VI. ACHIEVING UTILITARIAN GOALS

Limiting retributivism's use of aggravating and mitigating factors in determining punishment will likely result in strong under-deterrence of crime. Insights into human behavioral psychology demonstrate this fact.[196] Therefore, limiting retributivism proponents' attempts to appeal to supporters of utilitarian theories of criminal punishment should be rebuffed as contrary to utilitarian aims. However, establishing that limiting retributivism does not sufficiently serve utilitarian goals does not end the debate. A careful reader will notice that the cognitive biases identified by behavioral psychologists, and used here to suggest the failure of limiting a retributivist system of punishment to achieve utilitarian goals, may also be used to challenge utilitarian systems of punishment as well. After all, the same cognitive biases that lead criminals to irrationally believe they will either not be caught or will be found innocent may also affect deterrent levels in a purely utilitarian system. In this section, I defend the argument that utilitarians should reject limiting retributivism appeals to utilitarian goals because cognitive biases create a double under-deterrent effect under a limiting retributivism system while they create only a single under-deterrent effect under a utilitarian system. Furthermore, I highlight possible methods to adjust utilitarian policies to accommodate previously mentioned research in behavioral psychology and to better achieve utilitarian goals.

Given the research in behavioral psychology, utilitarians face a difficult task in arguing in further support for utilitarian theories of punishment, specifically deterrence-based punishment. Because behavioral psychologists have shown that people do not rationally react or respond to facts, it could be argued that all of the deterrence efforts of utilitarianism will ultimately fail. Critics of utilitarianism will argue that this research proves that utilitarian goals of deterrence are unreachable and therefore utilitarianism is an unworkable system of punishment. Yet, these arguments that utilitarianism is an unworkable system fail under scrutiny.

The evidence that people do not act as rational individuals, the basis of much of utilitarianism and of law and economics, weakens the allure of utilitarianism; yet it does not destroy the theory altogether. Optimism bias, the illusion of control, motivated reasoning, and cognitive dissonance all serve to decrease the overall deterrent effect of criminal punishment; however, they do not destroy all deterrent effect. Whether because criminals think they have less of a chance of getting caught or judges will be lenient with them if caught, the overall expected harm that a criminal will anticipate will be lower than it should be. The reason behind this sub-optimal deterrent level is the effect of cognitive biases.

---

[196] *See supra* Part IV.

But does this mean that punishment has no deterrent effect? The answer is *no*. While the deterrent effect is not optimal, it still exists, albeit in a weaker form. At this point, one may wonder, is this not the same argument used to discredit retributivism's appeal to utilitarianism? Was not the fact that retributivism led to under-deterrence the very reason it was held to be contrary to utilitarian goals? The answer is *yes*, but only to a degree. The real question then becomes which system creates a stronger deterrent effect?

To answer this question, one needs to determine which system is more affected by these cognitive biases: limiting retributivism or utilitarianism. In a limiting retributivism system, two factors exist that will lead to under-deterrence. First, the use of basic utilitarian principles to alter a sentence within the acceptable range will not have as much deterrent effect as one would hope. Second, the open use of mitigating and aggravating factors in determining punishment will create further under-deterrence.[197] Both steps in the determination of punishment under limiting retributivism, creating the range of permissible punishment and altering the specific punishment within that range, deter at a sub-optimal level. Utilitarianism does not face this double under-deterrence effect. Under a utilitarian system, the general deterrent effect of the punishment will be less than ideal, but no other factors will further reduce the deterrent effect. In other words, there is likely only one point where cognitive biases create sub-optimal deterrence levels.

An example will demonstrate this difference appropriately. The crime at issue is auto theft. Suppose it is an ideal world, where people act according to the classic economic view of human beings as rational and the optimal level of deterrence is created by a punishment of twenty years. In other words, this punishment provides the ideal deterrent effect. In a utilitarian system, one found guilty of this crime will face a twenty-year sentence if caught and convicted. Now, let us assume that human nature, as defined by behavioral psychology, will result in a 20% decrease in the deterrent effect, either because criminals expect not to get caught, or because they expect leniency in sentencing, or for whatever other reason. Whereas under the previous scenario of completely rational human behavior, a stated punishment of twenty years in jail has an expected punishment of twenty years, now there is an expected punishment of sixteen years. Thus, with cognitive biases in mind, a twenty-year sentence no longer creates the optimal deterrence level because criminals will expect a sixteen-year sentence. The utilitarian system has two options: (1) increase the punishment by 25% to twenty-five years, so the aggregate effect is

[197] *See supra* Part III.

twenty years of expected punishment, resulting in the optimal deterrence level or (2) accept less-than-ideal deterrent levels—an 80% effective deterrent effect.

Now analyze this situation under a limiting retributivism system of punishment. Under a limiting retributivism system, assume that the range of punishment for someone convicted of stealing a car is fifteen to twenty-five years. Because of the open use of aggravating and mitigating factors in determining sentencing, the potential car thief will expect a 20% decrease in the applied range. Now, he or she expects a range of twelve to twenty years instead of fifteen to twenty-five. The anticipation of a decreased range of punishment, which as mentioned above stems from cognitive biases, is the first way in which limiting retributivism under-deters.

Next, the criminal will further expect his or her sentence to be 20% less than is probable within the range. This occurs because the criminal will anticipate this second level of decision-making by the judge—he or she will know that the judge has discretion to sentence within a given range. At this point, cognitive biases may lead the criminal to expect or anticipate a specific level of punishment within the range that is less than what is actually likely, given the facts of the case. This is where the second level of under-deterrence occurs in limiting retributivism. Within the eight-year range, the facts of the case may indicate four years of added punishment, yet the criminal's prediction of this number is affected by his or her biases, and as a result he or she will predict 3.2 years of added punishment. Thus the criminal's expected punishment will be 15.2 years (12 years plus 3.2 years).

Thus, the aggregate deterrence level will be closer to the optimal level under a utilitarian system. Under utilitarianism the potential criminal will expect a 16 year sentence, while under limiting retributivism he or she will expect a 15.2 year sentence. Because deterrence levels are higher under a utilitarian system of punishment than under a limiting retributivism system, adherents of utilitarian theory must reject limiting retributivism. Using a utilitarian system will lead to greater deterrence and decrease the likelihood of future crimes. Accordingly, utilitarianism provides the greatest level of deterrent effects. Thus, for those who hope the law can have a deterrent effect by creating *ex ante* incentives for individuals not to commit crimes, utilitarianism is the only system and theory of punishment that is acceptable. If one is steadfast in the belief of the value of using *ex ante* incentives, the only system permissible is that which comes closest to creating optimal levels, which is utilitarianism.

Yet this does not mean that utilitarians have won and should pack up and go home happy. As has been demonstrated, utilitarian systems of punishment may still not result in optimal levels of deterrence. Human psychology undoubtedly decreases the deterrent effect of criminal laws. Anyone who believes the law can and should create ideal levels of incentives to create optimal outcomes, including most proponents of utilitarian theories of punishment, has much more work to do.

As the recent developments in the fields of behavioral law and economics indicate, the goal of optimal outcomes may still be reached if we tailor laws in recognition of cognitive biases or create laws—or, more specifically, systems of punishment—that minimize the effects of these biases.[198] In fact, unbeknownst to lawyers at the time of the rules' creation, several legal rules can be seen as methods to overcome cognitive biases.[199] An excellent example of such a law is the "business judgment rule" in corporate law. This rule essentially states that when challenging a business decision of a company executive, all that is required to defend the decision—absent any evidence of self-dealing—is that it was in some way rational, even if not the best decision.[200] In essence, this rule can be seen as compensating for the existence of hindsight bias by declaring that the outcome is not important at all, and saying that if there was any reasonable rationale for making the decision that was ultimately made, then the decision is legitimate.[201]

While the example of the business judgment rule demonstrates how behavioral psychology insights can help craft better laws, or justify previously existing ones, these laws are examples of *ex post* reasoning. What concerns utilitarians are *ex ante* incentives. The cognitive biases that affect *ex ante* incentives are very different than those that affect *ex post* decisions. In other words, the hindsight effect, highlighted by the business judgment rule example, focuses more on a person's view of a situation after that situation has occurred, and thus is unlikely to have effects on *ex ante* decision-making and hence *ex ante* incentives. Unfortunately, biases that affect such decision-making, for example, optimism bias and motivated reasoning, have been demonstrated to be extremely difficult to adjust for or to alter.[202]

Utilitarians face a tough challenge, but one that may not be insurmountable. Utilitarianism has been demonstrated to have at least some effect on deterring criminals. Further investigations may prove that cognitive biases are, in fact, correctable. If not, other, more correctable biases may be further investigated and applied. Insight into such biases

---

[198] *See* Jolls, Sunstein & Thaler, *supra* note 159, at 1522-41.

[199] *Id.*

[200] Smith v. Van Gorkom, 488 A.2d 858, 872 (Del. 1985).

[201] Jolls, Sunstein & Thaler, *supra* note 159.

[202] Hanson & Kysar, *supra* note 161, at 657.

may not lead to a system of perfect deterrence, but it may assist utilitarians in crafting laws that are better able to deter criminals. Through the research, use, and adoption of laws tailored to accommodate for, or to alter, cognitive biases, deterrence levels may be increased.

VII. CONCLUSION

Recent developments in retributivist theory have resulted in the creation of a limiting retributivism system of criminal punishment. Such a system attempts to appeal to utilitarian concerns in an effort to garner support from those who desire the criminal law to serve utilitarian purposes. Utilitarians must reject this appeal, however, because it leads to lesser deterrent levels compared to those expected under a properly utilitarian system of punishment.

Recent developments in behavioral psychology suggest reasons why the limited retributivist system of punishment may lead to sub-optimal deterrence levels. Limiting retributivist systems of punishment are affected by cognitive biases on two separate occasions, leading to a double under-deterrence effect, while utilitarian systems of punishment only face a single under-deterrence effect. Simply put, cognitive biases suggest that limiting retributivism systems of punishment will lead to higher levels of under-deterrence than will utilitarian systems of punishment. In light of these inferences, utilitarians must resist the appeals of proponents of limiting retributivism and insist on a more rigid utilitarian system of punishment.

Utilitarians must engage in further research in an effort to mitigate the effects of cognitive biases on deterrence levels. The *ex ante* incentives that utilitarians wish to create through the law may be improved if laws are drafted to account for—and overcome—demonstrated cognitive biases.

[6]

Deterrent Punishment and Respect for Persons

Zachary Hoskins*

This article defends deterrence as an aim of punishment. Specifically, I contend that a system of punishment aimed at deterrence (with constraints to prohibit punishing the innocent or excessively punishing the guilty) is consistent with the liberal principle of respect for offenders as autonomous moral persons. I consider three versions of the objection that deterrent punishment fails to respect offenders. The first version, raised by Jeffrie Murphy and others, charges that deterrent punishment uses offenders as mere means to securing the social good of crime reduction. The second and third are developed by R.A. Duff. The second holds that deterrent punishment inappropriately excludes offenders from the moral community. The third charges that deterrent punishment offers community members the wrong sorts of reasons to comply with the law. I conclude that each of these objections fails. A system of punishment aimed at deterrence (suitably constrained) is consistent with respect for offenders as moral persons.

I. Introduction

Deterrence-based accounts of punishment have been criticized frequently because they are unable to rule out occasionally punishing innocent citizens, or disproportionately punishing guilty ones, if doing so would yield net deterrent benefits.[1] In response to these sorts of objections, some theorists have argued that although considerations of deterrence cannot ground a complete justification of punishment, they may nevertheless shoulder some of the justificatory burden. Perhaps most notably, H.L.A. Hart contended that consequentialist considerations such as crime prevention represent the central aim of punishment, but that particular impositions of punishment should be constrained by the familiar principles that only the criminally guilty should be punished, and only in

---

* Ph.D., 2011, Washington University in St. Louis. I am grateful to Richard Dagger, Larry May, Christopher Heath Wellman, and David Wood for their helpful comments on earlier drafts of this paper.

1 *See, e.g.*, David Boonin, The Problem of Punishment 41–52 (2008); John Braithwaite & Philip Pettit, Not Just Deserts: A Republican Theory of Criminal Justice 46 (1990); Deirdre Golash, The Case Against Punishment: Retribution, Crime Prevention, and the Law 43–44 (2005); W.D. Ross, The Right and the Good 56–57 (1930); H.J. McCloskey, *An Examination of Restricted Utilitarianism*, 66 Phil. Rev. 466, 468–69 (1957); H.J. McCloskey, *Utilitarian and Retributive Punishment*, 64 J. Phil. 91, 93–102 (1967).

proportion with the seriousness of their crimes.[2] Constrained by principles such as these, deterrence as an aim of punishment looks significantly more appealing.

Even with these constraints, however, deterrence as an aim of punishment has been subject to a further line of criticism. Here, the objection is not that in some cases considerations of deterrence might permit the punishment of law abiders, but rather that punishment aimed at deterrence fails to respect offenders as autonomous moral agents—or in Kantian terms, as ends in themselves.[3] This challenge is particularly powerful. It does not merely charge that deterrent punishment might allow, in certain cases, the disrespectful treatment of offenders; if this were the charge, then perhaps constraints could be articulated, similar to the constraints against punishing the innocent, to rule out such treatment. The objection here, however, is that punishment aimed at deterrence *by its nature* fails to treat offenders with respect.[4] If the charge is valid, then additional constraints will not help.[5]

This paper defends deterrence as an aim (in my view, the central aim) of punishment against this objection that deterrent punishment fails to respect offenders as moral persons. I examine three prominent ways in which this charge has been fleshed out. First, some theorists, such as Jeffrie Murphy, have objected that punishing with the aim of deterrence uses the offender as a mere means to secure some social benefit, namely, crime reduction.[6] The second and third versions of the objection have been developed thoroughly by R.A. Duff. A system of criminal law and punishment aimed at deterrence, Duff claims, offers reasons for compliance that are inappropriate to autonomous moral agents, and it implicitly excludes criminals from membership in the political community.[7] Duff offers these as aspects of the same line of critique,[8] but I argue below that they are in fact separate charges and thus merit distinct consideration. I contend that none of these objections ultimately succeeds. That is, none of them establishes that punishment aimed at deterring crime fails to demonstrate appropriate respect for persons. Specifically, a deterrent system of punishment—bounded by appropriate constraints on who may be punished and how severely—does not treat offenders as mere means to securing certain social goods, it does not offer inappropriate reasons

---

2 H.L.A. HART, *Prolegomenon to the Principles of Punishment*, *in* PUNISHMENT AND RESPONSIBILITY: ESSAYS IN THE PHILOSOPHY OF LAW 1, 8–13 (2d ed. 2008). *See also* Don E. Scheid, *Constructing a Theory of Punishment, Desert, and the Distribution of Punishments*, 10 CANADIAN J.L. & JURISPRUDENCE 441, 449–50 (1997) (imposing punishments "only on offenders for their offenses and only in appropriate amounts"). For a somewhat different sort of disaggregation of the relevant questions, see ROSS, *supra* note 1, at 61–64.

3 Jeffrie G. Murphy, *Marxism and Retribution*, 2 PHIL. & PUB. AFF. 217, 218–19 (1973).

4 *Id.*

5 *Id.* at 219.

6 *See id.*

7 R.A. DUFF, PUNISHMENT, COMMUNICATION, AND COMMUNITY 13–14 (2001).

8 *See id.* at 13.

for compliance with the law, and it does not implicitly exclude criminals from membership in the political community.

In Part II, I examine and refute the objection that deterrent punishment uses offenders as mere means to securing the social goal of crime reduction. In Part III, I take a closer look at Duff's account and contend that he actually offers two distinguishable versions of the respect-based objection. In Parts IV and V, I examine each of these objections in turn, and I conclude that neither succeeds. Ultimately, deterrence is a permissible aim for a system of criminal punishment; that is, punishment aimed at deterring crime can be consistent with respect for moral persons.

II. Does Deterrence Use Offenders as Mere Means?

One way to interpret the charge that deterrent punishment fails to respect offenders as persons is that such punishment appears to use offenders as mere means to deterring crime. Jeffrie Murphy, for instance, has written of deterrence that "a guilty man is, on this theory, being punished because of the instrumental value the action of punishment will have in the future. He is being used as a means to some future good—e.g., the deterrence of others."[9] Such punishment thus appears inconsistent with maintaining proper respect for offenders as autonomous moral agents.

Murphy's characterization of the good being sought as "the deterrence of others" points to a sense in which we might think one form of deterrence can be especially problematic.[10] That is, it might seem bad enough that punishment subjects offenders to hard treatment with the aim of promoting the social good of crime reduction. A critic might further point out, however, that one type of deterrence, general deterrence, seeks to achieve this social good by treating offenders in certain ways in order to affect others' behaviors, to persuade others to comply with the law. Special deterrence may also seem troubling insofar as it subjects an offender to hard treatment to bring about the social good of crime reduction, but at least it treats the offender in this manner with the aim of affecting her own future behavior, of persuading her to comply with the law in the future, rather than treating her in this way to affect others' behavior. Thus, insofar as this objection is valid, it strikes particularly hard at general deterrence.

We might respond to this line of critique by pointing out that political communities also harm law abiders for the sake of promoting some greater good. Construction of a new highway may be beneficial to the community generally, but it may harm those who live nearby (perhaps by generating noise pollution or diminishing property values). Similarly, those with a communicable disease may be forced to endure certain restrictions of their liberties in the interest of protecting

---

9 Murphy, *supra* note 3, at 219. *See also* BOONIN, *supra* note 1, at 60–61; DUFF, *supra* note 7, at 13–14.

10 Murphy, *supra* note 3, at 219.

public health. If harming some for the greater benefit of others is permissible in cases such as these and numerous others, then perhaps harming offenders to benefit the public by deterring crime is similarly permissible.

David Boonin rejects this line of response, however, because he believes it overlooks the distinction between intending harm and foreseeing harm.[11] Boonin points out that cases such as those described above—the highway construction, or quarantining those with a communicable disease—"do not involve intentionally harming some people in order to benefit others. Rather, they involve intentionally doing acts that foreseeably cause some harm to some people and provide greater benefits to many others."[12] He continues:

> [T]he fact is that punishment stands alone as the one instance in which the state not only does an act that predictably harms some of its citizens, but in which it acts with the explicit aim of causing harm. Punishment is utterly anomalous in this respect. This is precisely what makes punishment distinctively difficult to justify in the first place.[13]

Thus, for Boonin, a deterrent system of punishment is objectionable because it intentionally harms some to benefit others. The harm is the means by which the good is achieved, not merely a foreseeable consequence.

Given that the ultimate aim of a system of deterrent punishment is to reduce crime, however, I suggest that actual inflictions of punishment are not the means by which the system seeks to achieve this aim. Rather, the *threat* of punishment is intended to do the deterrent work.[14] A deterrent system of punishment communicates a threat to everyone in the community: if you do these acts, you will be subject to punishment. Consider that if the threat of deterrent punishment were perfectly effective, no one would violate the community's laws, and thus, no one would be punished. Actual instances of punishment, then, are best seen as cases where the deterrent threat failed.[15] The inflictions of harm that constitute punishment are not the means by which the good of crime reduction is achieved; rather, the means by which deterrent systems of punishment aim to reduce crime is by issuance of a threat. Obviously, in the real world, deterrent systems of punishment are not perfectly effective. Individuals continue to commit crimes

---

[11] BOONIN, *supra* note 1, at 61–62.

[12] *Id.* at 62.

[13] *Id. See also* Nathan Hanna, *Say What? A Critique of Expressive Retributivism*, 27 LAW & PHIL. 123, 124–28 (2008) (discussing hard treatment and suffering as part of the definition and essential characteristics of punishment).

[14] One might worry that the threat of punishment is itself a sort of coercive sanction, in that its aim is to change incentives so that, in effect, it restricts citizens' viable options. I consider this point more below.

[15] S.I. Benn noted this point. S.I. Benn, *An Approach to the Problems of Punishment*, 33 PHIL. 325, 330 (1958).

despite the existence of the deterrent threat. In these cases, such individuals are harmed in the ways characteristic of punishment. But such individuals are foreseeably rather than intentionally harmed. Again, this is because the intention of a deterrent system of punishment is that everyone should take the threat seriously and avoid criminal behavior (and, in turn, punishment).

Boonin insists, however, that the intended-harm element is essential to our conception not only of deterrent punishment, but of punishment in general.[16] He writes:

> When the state punishes someone, . . . it inflicts various harmful treatments on him *in order* to harm him. It is not merely that in sentencing a prisoner to hard labor, for example, we foresee that he will suffer. Rather, a prisoner who is sentenced to hard labor is sentenced to hard labor *so that* he will suffer, and if a given form of labor turned out to be too pleasant and enjoyable, he would be sentenced to some other form of labor for precisely that reason.[17]

Boonin may be correct with respect to punishment whose central aim is retribution, or perhaps even special deterrence (although even on these accounts there would presumably be plausible considerations cautioning against lengthening or altering sentences once they had been issued). His point is mistaken, however, with respect to general deterrence. In a system of punishment aimed at general deterrence, sentences are not imposed to inflict suffering on the offender, but rather to maintain a credible threat to the public generally. Typically, of course, the more severe the sentence, the more the offender will suffer *and* the more credible the threat will be. But the concern, from the perspective of general deterrence, is not how much an offender suffers, but rather how effectively the general public is deterred from committing the given offense. In fact, if the credible threat could be maintained without harming any offenders, then this would be entirely acceptable based solely on considerations of general deterrence.[18] Punishment aimed at

---

[16] BOONIN, *supra* note 1, at 12.

[17] *Id.* at 13.

[18] This point, in fact, grounds a distinct objection commonly leveled against deterrent punishments generally: insofar as the deterrent threat is what is crucial, the legal authority might be justified in some cases of merely pretending to punish offenders. This prospect is particularly troubling to those with the retributivist intuition that the guilty deserve to suffer. Advocates of deterrence as an aim of punishment might respond to this objection in various ways: they might contend that the public's likely discovery of the pretend punishment cases could undermine the general deterrent effect of the threat, or that whereas general deterrence constitutes one aim of punishment, there are others (retribution, reform, etc.) that rule out the possibility of pretending to punish. Whether these or other responses would be persuasive need not worry us here, because the question of whether general deterrence would permit pretend-punishing is a distinct one from the question of whether punishments aimed at general deterrence treat offenders as mere means. For present purposes, the relevance of the pretend-punishing objection is that it underscores that

general deterrence, then, is best characterized not as intentionally harming some to benefit others, but rather as intentionally threatening everyone, and then foreseeably harming those who nevertheless commit crimes.

Suppose, however, that I am wrong about this. Suppose that punishment aimed at deterrence is in fact best understood as intentionally harming some to benefit others. This is still not enough to establish that such punishment would violate the Kantian principle of respect for persons. It is widely recognized that this principle does not forbid treating others as means, but as *mere* means. We frequently treat others as means to our own or other people's ends, and we typically consider such treatment permissible. I ask a taxi driver to take me to my destination, our country sends soldiers to fight in a war to protect our interests, or I ask a friend to lend me money. The taxi driver, the soldiers, and my friend are all treated as means to others' ends (mine, or in the case of the soldiers, the country's), but we do not find these cases objectionable as long as they are not treated *merely* as means. The relevant question for this version of the respect-based objection, then, is whether deterrent punishment treats offenders merely as means to the social good of crime reduction.

There are good reasons to doubt that punishing for deterrence uses offenders merely as means to the end of crime reduction. First, note that insofar as the institution of punishment yields a deterrent effect, those who commit crimes typically will have reaped benefits from the existence of this institution just as law abiders have done. Perpetrators of crime are also, like other community members, potential victims of crime. Thus, insofar as the institution of punishment helps to deter crime, it protects the safety and security of everyone.

One might respond that an offender may still be treated merely as a means when she is harmed in the interest of securing this social good, even if the social good is also a good for the offender herself. If our legal system sanctioned the occasional punishment of innocent people for the purpose of achieving the beneficial deterrent effect, for instance, then these individuals would be used as mere means even if they themselves had benefited from the deterrent effects of the institution generally. Thus, even if both offenders and law abiders enjoy the general benefits of deterrent punishment, this fact by itself appears insufficient to assure that such punishment avoids using offenders as mere means.

Deterrent punishment with prohibitions on punishing the guilty is relevantly different, however, from a system of deterrent punishment (even an overall beneficial one) that allows the punishment of the innocent. To punish law abiders would be to treat them in ways that were not responsive to choices they had actually made, and thus it would fail to respect them as autonomous moral agents. Respectful treatment requires, at least, that we treat others according to what they have actually done (or failed to do); punishing those who have violated no criminal laws fails to meet this minimal standard of respect. Notice, though, that a deterrent

---

punishment-as-general-deterrence aims to reduce crime not by harming offenders but rather by issuing a threat.

system of punishment does not only offer to each community member the benefits that come from reduced crime. Deterrent punishment constrained by the retributivist principle against punishing the innocent also allows each individual to choose whether she will risk suffering the harms associated with punishment. Such a system offers everyone a choice: comply with the law, or be subject to punishment. Thus, unlike the innocent person who is punished to achieve the deterrent effect, the offender's punishment is a response to the choice she made to violate the law. Given that her punishment is a response to her own free choice, the fact that the aim of punishing her is to deter others from committing similar crimes (or her from committing similar crimes in the future) does not imply that she is treated *merely* as a means to this end. Hart expresses this essential idea, as he describes the institution of punishment as "*offering* individuals including the criminal the protection of the laws on terms which are fair, because they not only consist of a framework of reciprocal rights and duties, but because within this framework each individual is given a *fair* opportunity to choose" between complying with the law or facing punishment.[19]

Still, even if an institution of deterrent punishment offers benefits to everyone, and even if it offers each community member equally a choice about whether to endure the threatened sanction, one might still object that this choice itself is coercive, that it employs the threat of harm to restrict citizens' viable options. Richard Burgh objects to Hart's account by offering what he considers an analogous case, in which terrorists take a group of people hostage and tell each that "if he attempts to escape, he will be beaten."[20] The terrorists treat all of the hostages equally, and they stay true to their pledge to beat only those hostages who try to escape.[21] "Simply because a hostage is given a fair opportunity to avoid being beaten," Burgh concludes, "it does not follow that his beating is just."[22] Even if the terrorists "were to inform the hostages that if they do as they are told they will receive positive benefits," beating those who tried to escape would be unjust.[23] Burgh concludes that, analogously, deterrent punishment cannot be justified on grounds that it provides a choice either to comply with the law and reap benefits from others' compliance or to break the law and suffer punishment.[24]

Contrary to Burgh's charge, however, there is a fairly straightforward difference between the choice offered by the institution of deterrent punishment and the choice offered by the terrorists. Given that the terrorists violate each hostage's liberty rights, the hostages' choice is either not to do that which they have a moral right to do (namely, leave) or to be beaten. So the terrorists use the

---

19 HART, *supra* note 2, at 22–23.

20 Richard W. Burgh, *Do the Guilty Deserve Punishment?*, 79 J. PHILOSOPHY 193, 199 (1982).

21 *Id.*

22 *Id.*

23 *Id.* at 200.

24 *Id.*

prospect of force to persuade the hostages not to do what they have a right to do. A system of deterrent punishment, however, employs the prospect of force to persuade community members not to do the sort of acts that they have a moral obligation not to do.[25] Thus, the relevant question is whether a system of punishment that provides significant benefits to community members generally, and that offers a choice *either* not to commit acts that one has moral obligations not to commit *or* to be harmed, is coercive in a way that renders it inconsistent with respect for moral persons. Given that such a system offers each community member benefits, treats each according to her own choices, and seeks to persuade citizens not to do that which they have a moral obligation not to do anyway, I suggest that such a system is consistent with respecting individuals, even those punished, as autonomous moral agents.

Kant himself provides support for the view that punishment, properly constrained by the retributivist principle, may aim at deterrence while nevertheless respecting the offender.[26] A criminal, he writes, "must previously have been found *punishable* before any thought can be given to drawing from his punishment something of use for himself or his fellow citizens."[27] Although Kant's full view of punishment continues to be the subject of substantial debate,[28] in this passage he suggests that deterrence is a permissible aim, which for him means that it does not use the individual as a mere means, as long as punishments are limited to those who are guilty of crimes.[29]

I conclude that punishment aimed at deterrence does not use offenders as mere means, and thus this version of the respect-based objection fails. Still, Kant's respect principle instructs us not only not to use others as mere means, but also to respect them as ends in themselves.[30] Respecting people as ends may require more than merely not using them as mere means. Perhaps, then, there is a sense in which punishment aimed at deterrence nevertheless violates the respect principle. In the following three parts, I consider what I take to be the most thorough and compelling development of this sort of objection, by R.A. Duff.

---

[25] This is the case, at least, when the laws backed by deterrent punishment are justified. By contrast, unjust laws (e.g., laws allowing, or requiring, what is morally prohibited) backed by deterrent punishment would be analogous to Burgh's terrorist example. As such, a system of deterrent punishment backing such laws would fail to respect those punished as moral persons.

[26] *See* IMMANUEL KANT, THE METAPHYSICS OF MORALS (1797), *reprinted in* IMMANUEL KANT: PRACTICAL PHILOSOPHY 353, § 6:331, at 473 (Mary J. Gregor ed. & trans., 1996).

[27] *Id.*

[28] *See, e.g.*, Thom Brooks, *Kant's Theory of Punishment*, 15 UTILITAS 206, 208–15 (2003); Thomas E. Hill, Jr., *Kant on Wrongdoing, Desert, and Punishment*, 18 LAW & PHIL. 407, 408–09 (1999); David Sussman, *Shame and Punishment in Kant's* Doctrine of Right, 58 PHIL. Q. 299, 302–09 (2008).

[29] *See* KANT, *supra* note 26, at 473.

[30] *See id.*

III. DUFF'S CRITIQUE OF DETERRENCE

R.A. Duff conceives of the criminal law as fundamentally a communicative enterprise.[31] He argues that a system of punishment that aims to deter potential offenders is inappropriate for a liberal political community committed to respecting its members *as* members of the community.[32] Essentially, this is because deterrent punishment communicates in prudential rather than moral terms:

> The law of [a liberal political] community, as its common law, must address its members in terms of the values it embodies—values to which they should, as members of the community, already be committed. It portrays criminal conduct as wrongful in terms of those values; and the reasons that citizens have to refrain from such conduct, the reasons to which the law refers and on which it depends, are precisely the moral reasons that make such conduct wrong. A purely deterrent law, however, addresses those whom it seeks to deter, not in terms of the communal values that it aims to protect, but simply in the brute language of self-interest. It thus addresses them, not as members of the normative community of citizens, but as threatening outsiders against whom the community must protect itself. It implicitly excludes them from membership of the citizen community by no longer addressing them in terms of that community's values.[33]

Duff is concerned, commendably, that offenders should be treated as moral persons, and in fact as continuing members of the community, rather than merely as the "['they'] against whom 'we,' the law-abiding, must protect ourselves."[34] His concern is well founded; it is all too easy, and too common, to assume that the criminal act necessarily demonstrates a criminal, perhaps even irredeemably criminal, character. Duff urges us, however, always to regard the person guilty of a criminal offense as nevertheless one of us, a member of our community who may come to share (or recommit to) the moral values that the community endorses.[35] Despite the significant virtues of Duff's account, however, I contend that his objection to punishments aimed at deterrence misses its mark. There is a real sense in which a system of punishment aimed at deterring crime (with appropriate constraints) can nevertheless demonstrate appropriate respect for criminal offenders, and thus avoid being objectionably exclusionary.

Note that Duff actually offers two critiques of systems of punishment aimed at deterrence—two ways in which such systems of punishment fail to treat

---

[31] DUFF, *supra* note 7, at 79.

[32] *Id.* at 78.

[33] *Id.* at 78–79.

[34] *Id.* at 78.

[35] *Id.*

individuals with appropriate respect as autonomous moral agents. First, deterrent punishment offers individuals the wrong sort of reasons to comply with the law. It offers merely prudential reasons to comply—i.e., to avoid incarceration, community service, etc.—rather than the appropriate moral reasons—i.e., that the prohibited acts are morally condemned by the community. Second, by offering merely prudential reasons, rather than making the sort of moral appeal that is appropriate to members of a liberal political community, a deterrent system of punishment implicitly excludes those it addresses from membership in the community. It fails to respect them as fellow community members who, as members, share (or should share, and can come to share) the community's moral values. Punishing to deter is thus exclusionary, Duff believes, in that it reinforces the distinction between "us," the law-abiding citizens, and "them," the criminals, rather than treating offenders as continuing to be fellow members of our community.

Duff implies that the second critique follows from the first. That is, he indicates that a system of punishment aimed at deterrence excludes certain individuals from the political community *because* it offers them the wrong sort of reasons (i.e., prudential reasons) to comply with the law.[36] In fact, however, these are distinct critiques. The charge that deterrent punishment is exclusionary rests on the notion that it treats offenders differently from law abiders. It perpetuates the distinction between "us" (the law abiders) and "them" (the criminals) and implicitly excludes "them" from the community in which "we," as law abiders, are still included as members. By contrast, the objection that punishment aimed at deterrence provides the wrong sort of reasons to comply with the law does not depend on its offering *different* reasons to offenders and to law abiders. Rather, a system of punishment might offer the same inappropriate reasons for compliance to everyone. As such, it would not treat one group (offenders) as less a part of the political community than another group (law abiders). It would not perpetuate the objectionable "we" and "they" distinction, because such a system would communicate the same message, and offer the same reasons, to everyone.[37] Thus, whereas one objection contends that deterrent punishment offers the wrong sort of reasons, the other contends that such punishment inappropriately offers different reasons to different members of the community.

I suggest, then, that these two critiques warrant distinct consideration. We should ask, first, if punishment aimed at deterrence communicates a different message to (or provides different reasons to, or in some other way excludes)

---

[36] *Id.* at 78–79.

[37] One might respond that such a system of punishment would then be exclusionary of everyone. But if everyone is excluded, then we must ask, excluded from what? Duff's point is that deterrent punishments exclude offenders from their communities, but if all community members (law abider and offender alike) were excluded, then it is not clear what community would remain for those excluded to be excluded *from*. Thus, central to the charge that deterrent punishment excludes certain community members is the claim that it treats some (the excluded) differently from others (the included).

criminals from the political community generally; and second, if the reasons such a system of punishment offers for complying with the law are themselves the wrong sort of reasons to offer fellow members of the political community. I consider each of these critiques in turn and contend that, ultimately, each fails. A system of punishment aimed at deterrence communicates the same message to everyone in the political community. Thus it does not implicitly exclude anyone. Furthermore, a deterrent system of punishment is compatible with demonstrating appropriate respect to all members of the community as members who share (or should share, and can come to share) the community's fundamental moral values.

IV. IS DETERRENT PUNISHMENT EXCLUSIONARY?

The first objection evident in Duff's account is that a system of punishment aimed solely at deterrence implicitly excludes offenders from their community. It treats offenders as the "they" against whom "we," the law-abiding members of the community, must protect ourselves. Thus it fails to treat offenders with appropriate respect. Given Duff's conception of the criminal law as a fundamentally communicative enterprise,[38] the worry with deterrent punishment is that, insofar as it offers the offender only prudential reasons why she should not have committed, say, theft or tax evasion, it fails to communicate with her as (still) a member of the community. A more appropriate message to a community member would appeal to the moral reasons that her act was wrong, namely, that such acts violate important moral values that the community shares (and thus that she, as a member of the community, should also share).

The thrust of the "exclusion" objection to deterrent punishment, then, is that once a member of the community commits a crime, the criminal law stops talking to her as it talks to law abiders, to whom it offers appropriate, moral reasons not to violate the law. Instead, it begins to talk with her in the language of mere prudence, as though this is the only language she is capable of understanding. As such, it inappropriately excludes her from membership in her community.

One might understandably be tempted to respond here that the offender, in committing her crime, essentially excludes *herself* from membership in the community—or at least, that she demonstrates that she does not share the community's moral values. If so, then it may seem appropriate for a system of punishment to communicate to her solely in the language of prudence rather than in the language of the community's moral values. Duff rejects this argument, however, for several reasons, the most persuasive of which is that it is empirically dubious.[39] Often, criminal acts are not evidence that offenders have no regard for the community's moral values, but rather

[38] DUFF, *supra* note 7, at 79.

[39] *Id.* at 84.

> [T]hat their regard is not wholehearted, or consistent, or always sufficient to overcome the temptations of self-interest. They—or rather *we*, since these comments surely apply to many of us—are not wholly deaf to the law's moral appeal, though we do not attend to it consistently or carefully enough.[40]

Duff is right to caution against assuming that an individual's criminal act is evidence of a complete rejection, or lack of regard, for the community's values.

There is a more fundamental problem, however, with the claim that deterrent punishment somehow communicates to offenders differently from law abiders, and thus excludes offenders from the political community. The message communicated by a system of punishment aimed at deterrence essentially takes the form of a threat: if you commit some criminal act, then you will be liable to having some form of suffering inflicted on you. It is important to consider, however, to whom this message is communicated. For deterrent punishment to be exclusionary, to create the sort of "we-they" dichotomy that concerns Duff, it would have to be the case that a system of deterrent punishment communicates one (prudential) message only to criminal offenders, and that law abiders, by contrast, receive another (moral) appeal that is appropriate to members of the political community.

But this is doubly wrong. First, a system of deterrent punishment communicates its prudential message, its threat, to everyone. For those who have not committed a crime, the prospect of punishment offers reasons not to do so (i.e., it acts as a general deterrent). For those who do commit crimes, their punishments—or more specifically, the unpleasant prospect of another term of punishment in the future—provide reasons not to recidivate (i.e., they act as a special deterrent). From the perspective of deterrent punishment, then, everyone is a potential offender (or reoffender), and such a system of punishment communicates the same prudential message to everyone. Therefore, and secondly, if law abiders receive the moral appeal that Duff believes is appropriate to members of the political community, the source of this appeal is not the system of deterrent punishment. Rather, the moral appeal must come from somewhere else, such as, perhaps, the criminal laws themselves. But if it is the criminal laws that communicate the moral message, that declare certain actions to be morally condemned by the community, the intended audience of this communication is everyone, law abider and offender alike. Thus, it is not the case that, in receiving the prudential message of a deterrent system of punishment, offenders are treated differently from others in the community, who are exclusive recipients of the moral message. It appears that deterrent punishment is not essentially exclusionary in the way Duff indicates.

There are other ways, of course, in which existing penal practices tend to exclude offenders from the community. Imprisonment, by its nature, removes

---

40 *Id.*

offenders physically from the larger community. Beyond this, prisoners are typically excluded from participation in the political process, most obviously by being denied the vote.[41] Also, offenders are excluded from access to basic financial services (bank accounts, credit, insurance), not only during their incarceration but often, in practice, even after their release.[42] These and other forms of exclusion should be troubling to members of a liberal political community who are concerned to treat individuals, even offenders, with respect as autonomous moral agents. But notice that such forms of exclusion are not distinctively characteristic of systems of punishment aimed at deterrence (and constrained in the ways suggested earlier). Because punishment involves the restriction of offenders' liberties in ways that law abiders' liberties are not restricted, issues of exclusion will always arise. But such issues are not distinctive of systems of punishment aimed at deterrence. Rather than communicating differently to offenders and law abiders, and thus perpetuating the "we-they" distinction that concerns Duff, systems of punishment aimed at deterrence regard everyone equally as potential offenders. They communicate the same message, namely, if you commit a crime, then you will be liable to being harmed. I conclude, then, that punishment aimed at deterrence is not exclusionary as Duff charges.

V. Does Deterrent Punishment Offer the Wrong Sort of Reasons for Compliance?

Given that deterrent punishment communicates the same reasons to everyone, the question then becomes whether these reasons are appropriate. Duff contends that they are not. He writes, "The criminal law of a liberal polity, and the criminal process of trial and conviction to which offenders are subjected, are communicative enterprises that address the citizens, as rational moral agents, in the normative language of the community's values."[43] Additionally, the institution of punishment, a constitutive element of the institution of criminal law generally, must similarly communicate in moral rather than prudential terms. A system of punishment aimed at deterring criminals, however, aims to secure general compliance with the law by means of a threat, rather than by moral appeal. Thus, Hegel famously objected: "To base a justification of punishment on threat is to

41 In the United States, only Maine and Vermont allow incarcerated felons to vote. *The Sentencing Project Interactive Map*, THE SENTENCING PROJECT, http://www.sentencingproject.org/map/map.cfm (last visited Nov. 19, 2010). A number of states go further than this, imposing a lifetime voting ban on anyone with a felony conviction, even those who have served their sentences. *See id.*

42 Gaynor Pengelly, *Give Prisoners Bank Accounts*, THIS IS MONEY (Oct. 25, 2010), http://www.thisismoney.co.uk/savings-and-banking/article.html?in_article_id=517136&in_page_id=7&position=moretopstories. For a fuller discussion of types of exclusion, see DUFF, *supra* note 7, at 75–77.

43 DUFF, *supra* note 7, at 80.

liken it to the act of a man who lifts his stick to a dog. It is to treat a man like a dog instead of with the freedom and respect due to him as a man."[44] Like Hegel, Duff worries that the prudential terms in which deterrent punishment communicates with community members, the prudential reasons it gives them to comply with the community's laws, are not the sort of reasons that are appropriate to offer to autonomous members of a liberal political community, who endorse (or could come to endorse) the community's moral values.[45]

I offer a couple of responses to this worry. First, punishment may communicate a prudential message to community members without communicating a *solely* prudential message. In my view, the good of punishment, the reason we should want such an institution, is that it plays a key role in ensuring the well-being of community members. Thus, the proper aim of punishment is to prevent or reduce crime by offering potential wrongdoers reasons not to offend. Punishment may serve this aim by supplying potential offenders with prudential reasons not to offend (reasons such as the desire to avoid the harms characteristic of incarceration, etc.), but it may also provide moral reasons. As is commonly recognized, punishment involves not only what Joel Feinberg called a "hard treatment" aspect but also an expressive aspect in that punishment expresses the community's condemnation of the offender for her criminal act.[46] Even before the commission of a crime, however, the threat of punishment also expresses the community's condemnation not of a particular offender but rather of the offense itself. If a potential offender receives and accepts this message of condemnation, it may play a role in persuading her not to do what she otherwise would have done. If so, then even if the fear of punitive suffering also played a role in dissuading her, I suggest that she is treated with the respect due to her as a moral person. Thus, even if a system of punishment's central aim is to provide prudential reasons for compliance, this does not preclude its also providing moral reasons.

Second, even if a system of punishment did provide *solely* prudential reasons to comply with the law, this does not show that the criminal legal system more generally fails to communicate with community members as moral persons. I agree with Duff that the criminal law should appeal to citizens as moral agents who share (or should share, and can come to share) the community's values. But punishment is only one aspect of the criminal legal system. Suppose we grant, then, that a community through its criminal statutes declares certain acts to be wrong and makes a moral appeal to community members to comply, whereas trials and convictions communicate a message of deserved moral censure to the wrongdoer and urge the wrongdoer "to understand and accept the censure as justified."[47] Why, then, must punishment also make a moral appeal? Why is it

[44] GEORG WILHELM FRIEDRICH HEGEL, HEGEL'S PHILOSOPHY OF RIGHT 246 (T.M. Knox trans., 1942).

[45] DUFF, *supra* note 7, at 80.

[46] JOEL FEINBERG, *The Expressive Function of Punishment*, 49 MONIST 397, 397–423 (1965).

[47] DUFF, *supra* note 7, at 80.

inappropriate for the institution of punishment to communicate a solely prudential message?

First, one might argue that the criminal legal system must be univocal in the message it communicates to community members, and that this message must be a moral rather than a prudential one. Thus, the institution of punishment, as one element of the criminal law generally, must communicate a moral message. It is not clear why this should be so, however. We can grant, with Duff, that the criminal legal institution should communicate a moral message to community members while still: (a) recognizing that distinct elements of the institution can communicate different messages; (b) maintaining that the criminal statutes themselves, and perhaps the process of trial and conviction, sufficiently communicate the moral message; and thus, (c) denying that punishment must communicate this same message. Notice, too, that if the entire criminal legal system must be univocal in its moral message, much more than deterrent punishment would be prohibited. The practice of plea bargaining, for one, would appear unjustifiable if prudential appeals were inappropriate in criminal law. More reasonable, I suggest, is to claim that the criminal law should address community members in moral terms, and in fact that the moral message should be central, but that as long as this moral message is present, prudential appeals also have an appropriate role.

A second possible response is that whereas the criminal law need not, in principle, communicate only a moral message, the prudential message of deterrent punishment is inappropriate in practice because it tends to drown out the moral message. That is, perhaps the threat of punishment is so powerful that it tends to focus community members' attention on the prudential reasons not to commit crimes and causes them to lose sight of the moral appeal. Andrew von Hirsch, who conceives of punishment as offering prudential reasons to supplement the (sometimes insufficiently motivating) moral reasons supplied by the criminal law, advocates a "decremental strategy" according to which prescribed sentences would be reduced gradually to levels at which the prudential reasons they offered would not drown out the moral reasons for compliance with the laws.[48] Duff is skeptical of such a strategy, however, as he believes that sentences mild enough so as not to overwhelm the moral message with the prudential threat would be too mild to achieve much deterrent effect at all.[49] By contrast, sentences sufficiently severe to provide any genuine deterrent effect would replace, rather than merely supplement, the moral appeal.[50]

I suggest that this worry, that the prudential appeal of deterrent punishment may drown out the moral message of the criminal law generally, inaccurately depicts the relationship of the moral and prudential appeals. Rather than accepting that a stronger prudential message will tend to weaken the moral message

---

48 ANDREW VON HIRSCH, CENSURE AND SANCTIONS 36–46 (1993).

49 DUFF, *supra* note 7, at 88.

50 *Id.*

comparatively, why not acknowledge that the prudential threat actually can reinforce the moral appeal? Granted, an institution of punishment aimed at deterrence provides prudential reasons to comply with the community's laws. But the existence of such an institution also invites us to consider, or remind ourselves, why our community believes that these laws, and the interests they protect, are of sufficient moral weight that we are willing to invoke the threat of hard treatment to help ensure that they are not violated. Rather than drowning out the moral message of the criminal law, as Duff fears—the message that certain acts are prohibited because society regards them as significant moral violations—deterrent punishment can reinforce this message, as it underscores that protecting community members from such violations is sufficiently important to warrant the infliction of harm as a response.

The prudential message of deterrent punishment, therefore, is compatible with the criminal law's communication of a moral appeal to community members, and thus with respecting them as autonomous moral agents. On one hand, a system of punishment aimed at deterrence may nevertheless provide moral as well as prudential reasons for compliance. On the other hand, even if punishment itself provides only prudential reasons, the criminal legal system need not be univocal. As long as the moral message is communicated prominently (by the laws themselves and the process of trial and conviction), respect for persons does not require that the institution of punishment communicate in moral terms. I conclude, then, that this third articulation of the respect-based objection fails.

VI. CONCLUSION

In closing, it is worth emphasizing again the scope of the defense of deterrence that I have offered here. Specifically, I have not aimed to defend deterrence as sufficient to ground a complete justification of punishment. Rather, my focus has been on deterrence as the aim of punishment, constrained by certain considerations such as the retributivist principles against punishing the innocent or excessively punishing the guilty. Critics of deterrence, such as Murphy and Duff, claim that even as one element of this sort of hybrid account of punishment, deterrence is objectionable because it fails to treat individuals with appropriate respect as autonomous moral agents. I have contended, however, that on what I take to be the three most plausible articulations of this critique, it nonetheless fails. Constrained in certain ways, then, I conclude that deterrence is a permissible aim of punishment.

[7]

Punishment and Duty

Victor Tadros

Introduction

Punishment typically involves intentionally inflicting harm on an offender in response to the crime that she has committed. It is difficult to justify punishment. One reason is that punishment involves the intentional infliction of harm. And, many people believe, it is much more difficult to justify inflicting harm intentionally than inflicting harm as a side effect of a good action.

One way to justify punishment, which is endorsed by retributivists, is to show that the suffering that is imposed by punishment is intrinsically good. If this were true, it might then be argued that it is permissible intentionally to harm offenders either for its own sake, or for the good of others, because it is permissible to do a good thing, the imposition of suffering on those who deserve it, for its own sake or for the good of others. The imposition of deserved suffering would not be the kind of harm that engages the principle that we cannot intend to harm a person for the sake of a greater good.

As we saw in Part I, there are many reasons to be sceptical about this view. It is difficult to believe that suffering can be intrinsically good, and it is difficult to believe that the imposition of suffering on offenders using costly state institutions is warranted even if it is. So this way of meeting the objection raised to state punishment—that it involves the intentional infliction of harm—is at best very controversial.

An alternative approach is to defend punishment in the light of consequentialism. But this approach is often criticized convincingly. Consequentialist theories of punishment find it difficult to defend plausible restrictions on punishment. On a consequentialist view, it seems permissible to punish an innocent person, or to punish a guilty person disproportionately, if these things will do more good than harm. These problems arise due to the fact that consequentialism is a radically revisionist moral theory. Most people endorse some constraints on the pursuit of the good. One of the most important constraints, that I explored in Part II, is the *means principle*. Punishing the innocent seems wrong, even if this will prevent greater harms, because it would harm the innocent person as a means to the greater good.

Here I explore an alternative approach. On this approach punishment is to be justified on the basis of its instrumental benefits. But this is done in the light of the non-consequentialist principles governing harm to others that I outlined in Parts II and III. The idea is to show that although it is generally wrong to harm a person as a means to the good of others, explaining why punishment of the innocent is wrong, it may be permissible to harm offenders as a means to the good of others. The view that I defend is based on the duties that offenders incur as a result of their wrongdoing. We can call it the *duty view* of punishment.

A natural way to begin is to explore similarities between punishing offenders and self-defence. This approach is attractive for two reasons. First, self-defence, like punishment, involves intentionally inflicting harm on others. Self-defence is justified by non-consequentialists as an exception to the general principle that it is wrong intentionally to harm others in pursuit of a greater good. We may even defend ourselves against attacks, most people believe, in pursuit of a *lesser* good if the person we harm is morally responsible for attacking us. And yet, secondly, desert, as a basic moral idea, does not play an important role in most work on self-defence. It is recognized that the harm that is done to attackers is bad, but it is permissible to do that bad thing to them to prevent them from completing their attacks.[1]

Defensive theories of punishment are becoming increasingly popular and sophisticated but they also face unresolved difficulties. My purpose here is to develop a more satisfactory justification of punishment that draws part of its moral force from consideration of self-defence cases. Punishment is not *quite* like self-defence in its justification, I will suggest. Although it has defensive aims, punishment is justified in virtue of obligations that offenders owe, primarily to their victims, and derivatively to other people in virtue of having violated their primary duty not to wrongfully harm others. That is in contrast to self-defence, which is concerned with enforcing the primary duty that people have not to harm others rather than the secondary duties that are incurred through wrongdoing. The obligation to respond to one's wrongdoing, I will suggest, requires offenders to provide their victims with protection against wrongdoing by other people. The implication of this view is controversial amongst self-defensive theories of punishment. As it permits harming wrongdoers to deter others, it justifies what we call general deterrence.

Before beginning with the argument itself, I should note that my purpose in this chapter is almost completely limited to the moral question of whether it is permissible to harm wrongdoers for reasons of general deterrence. There are important and difficult questions about state punishment: whether the state has the right to punish, whether it has a duty to punish, and whether it has the exclusive right and duty to punish. I take up these questions in the next chapter.

I. Elimination and Manipulation

Consider the following:

Self-Defence. Arnold wrongfully attacks Debbie. The only way for Debbie to prevent herself from being killed is to kill Arnold.

[1] See, further, the discussion of desert in self-defence in chapter 8.

Everyone except the most committed pacifist will agree that Debbie is permitted to harm Arnold in self-defence. Now consider:

Punishment. Oswald attacks Doris and Doris is killed. Oswald is made to suffer in order to deter others from killing.

Is this wrong? Many people think so. I think not. What differences between *Self-Defence* and *Punishment* might lead people to conclude that the former is justified whereas the latter is not?

Here's one difference. Although harm is inflicted intentionally in both cases, in *Self-Defence* killing Arnold itself eliminates a threat whereas in *Punishment* Oswald is harmed as a means to avert an independent threat. The concern that general deterrence harms offenders as a means is one of the main reasons why it has been rejected by non-consequentialists.[2] Some people think that it may be permitted intentionally to harm another if harming that person eliminates a threat that they pose (eliminative harming) but that it is wrong intentionally to harm another person as a means to avert a threat that they do not pose (manipulative harming).

We explored this distinction in the previous chapter. The difference between eliminative harming and manipulative harming is roughly this. A person's presence in a particular place at a particular time, in particular circumstances, or doing particular actions, might constitute the problem that we face. We wish to move the person from that place, or alter their circumstances, so that they don't pose the problem. This is true in *Self-Defence*. In *Punishment*, in contrast, Oswald does not necessarily constitute a threat any longer. And the permission to punish offenders does not plausibly depend on the idea that they continue to pose threats to us. We face threats, but they may not come from Oswald. To avert the threats that we face, we can manipulate Oswald. But, it might be argued, doing so is wrong.

As I noted in the previous chapter, the distinction between eliminative and manipulative harming is morally important. The restrictions on the former are more stringent than the restrictions on the latter. But manipulative harming is at least sometimes permitted. Recall this case from chapter 8:

Hit Man. I hire a hit man to kill you, a complete innocent. The only way for you to avert the threat is to pull me in front of you, using me as a shield.

It is not wrong for you to use me as a shield. That is so even though my presence no longer poses a threat. This is so even if I could not call the hit man off if I wanted to. If I were obliterated from the face of the earth the threat would still be there. And yet you may harm me manipulatively to avert it.

Of course, it would be wrong for you to use an innocent bystander as a shield in these circumstances. Manipulative harming of an innocent bystander is wrong

[2] See, for example, R A Duff *Punishment, Communication, and Community* (Oxford: OUP, 2001) 16–19.

unless the harm that he will suffer is very much less serious than the harm to be averted. This suggests that culpable responsibility for a threat makes a significant difference to the permissibility of manipulative harm.

Why is this so? Here's a brief summary of the argument from chapter 8. When I, through my wrongful action, create a threat to you, I must bear significant costs to prevent that threat from being realized. For it is only by doing this that I will abide by my stringent obligation not to harm you. If I fail to fulfil that obligation, it is permissible for you manipulatively to harm me for that purpose. Unlike the innocent bystander, I have an enforceable duty to help you, and hence I may permissibly be harmed as a means for the sake of the end that I have a duty to serve. Why is the duty that I incur, in consequence of my wrongful action, enforceable? This is for the reason that were I not to do my duty you would be very seriously harmed and compensation for that harm is both unlikely to be made and likely to be inadequate. In other words, as it is urgent that I do my duty and that I do it now, you may force me to do it.

II. Responsibility and Harm

Here's a second difference between *Self-Defence* and *Punishment*. Killing Arnold harms him to avert a threat that he is (culpably) responsible for creating. But in *Punishment* Oswald is harmed to avert threats that he bears no responsibility for creating. He may not even causally contribute to those threats. Some will think that it is permissible manipulatively to harm a person to avert threats that she has (culpably) created but that it is wrong manipulatively to harm a person to avert a threat that she is not (culpably) responsible for creating. The claim that it is wrong to harm even a culpable attacker to avert a threat that she is not responsible for creating is familiar in the philosophy of self-defence, and is commonly endorsed. As I noted in chapter 8, we should reject this view, at least in this stark form. Here, I will extend that argument to show how it applies to the case of punishment. Before coming to that, let us consider two responses that have been developed to meet this problem within the context of defensive theories of punishment.

i) Deriving the Right to Punish from the Right to Threaten

One response, the most familiar version of which is defended by Warren Quinn,[3] seeks to derive the justification of punishment from our right to threaten. Making a threat involves expressing a conditional intention to harm. If you do x, I say, I will do y. In standard cases, x involves wrongdoing and y involves a harm that you will

[3] 'The Right to Threaten and the Right to Punish' in *Morality and Action* (Cambridge: CUP, 1993).

suffer. A threat is sincere when the person making the threat *forms* the conditional intention that he expresses. The criminal law threatens punishment, and in punishing offenders we carry out the threat. If we are justified in threatening people we are justified in carrying out the threats, or so it is argued.

This view aims to justify punishment not in virtue of the future goods that will be secured through punishment. Rather, punishment is to be justified in order to secure the value of the threat that the criminal law makes. As punishment is necessary to secure that value, punishment is justified. This view has the apparent virtue that we justify harming wrongdoers with reference to them alone and not to others whose behaviour we might affect by punishing them. It may also seem attractive in that each act of punishment is justified in a purely backwards-looking way. It refers only to the threats that have already been made and not to future harms that will be prevented.

An important feature of this view is the idea that the right to threaten is independent of, and prior to, the right to punish. Focusing on the fact that we are sometimes permitted to make insincere threats helps to demonstrate the plausibility of this idea. Suppose that you are about to kill my child. I cannot prevent you from doing this if you try. But I can credibly threaten you that if you kill my child I will kill two of yours. If I do so you will refrain from killing my child. Although it is permissible for me to make this threat it would obviously be wrong for me to kill your children if you were to ignore it. The fact that I have the right to make the threat indicates that it is not wrong to attempt to persuade you that I have immoral intentions. That is justified in virtue of the fact that making the threat does not harm your children and may avert a very serious threat to my child. One must be very committed to the obligation not to lie to regard lying as wrong in this case. This case demonstrates that the right to threaten does not depend on the right to carry out the threat, and may be completely independent of it.

The more difficult question is whether it can ever be permissible to make *sincere* threats in the absence of a forward-looking reason in favour of carrying out the threat if the threat is ignored. The difficulty stems from this familiar problem. I may have a good reason to make a sincere threat. But what if the threat is ignored? What reason do I have to carry the threat out? And what could motivate me to carry it out?

To see the difficulty, consider the following example. Suppose that you are wrongfully about to destroy my car. I threaten you that if you do I'll break your leg. You destroy my car. What reason do I now have to break your leg? The car is gone. Breaking your leg would be all harm with no good to outweigh it. If I reject the retributivist claim that we are permitted to harm others to ensure that they get the suffering that they deserve, and I cannot appeal to forward-looking considerations, carrying out the threat would seem to be not only wrong, but also difficult to motivate.[4] From this we might conclude that unless we can point to

[4] I could sincerely threaten you, believing that I will carry out the threat out of revenge. Assuming that acting out of revenge is wrong, this idea would involve creating a threat,

forward-looking considerations to motivate us in carrying out our threats it is only ever permissible to make insincere threats. Insincere threats might sometimes be effective. Some people might be good liars. Sincere threats might also permissibly be made, but only if we can find a forward-looking reason to carry out the threat once the condition in the threat is satisfied.

One obvious forward-looking reason is to protect our ability to make credible threats in the future.[5] But if we appeal to this reason the apparently distinctive virtue of a threat-based theory is undermined. For, on the theory as it stands, it would no longer be possible to avoid the challenge that wrongdoers are harmed as a means to avert future threats by others. We would carry out our threats to maintain our capacity effectively to threaten in the future. But that capacity is important to us only to protect ourselves against future threats.[6]

One response to this concern claims that the sincerity of a threat contributes to its effectiveness. We are justified in improving our prospects by threatening sincerely. But that improvement in our prospects depends on our ability to bind ourselves to execute our threats. If it is permissible to make a sincere threat, it might be argued, it is permissible to bind ourselves to execute our threats, and hence execute them if they are ignored. Suppose, for a moment, that the formation of a conditional intention to do something guarantees doing it if the condition is fulfilled. Now return to the case where I threaten you that if you destroy my car I'll break your leg. If I am a poor liar, my threat might be more convincing if it is sincere. So the best way for me to avert the threat to my car is to form the intention to break your leg if you destroy my car. And I would be justified in forming such an intention, we might think.

Why might that be so? First, you have already wronged me by threatening me with the destruction of my car, so you are liable to be threatened. Secondly, making the threat helps to protect me, albeit imperfectly, from having my car destroyed. And thirdly, drawing on our discussion in chapter 8, you are protected against being harmed by me. You can avoid being harmed simply by refraining from destroying my car, something that you are already required to do.

So if I form the conditional intention to carry out the threat, my prospects are significantly improved and yours are not significantly eroded. My prospects are improved in that my car is less likely to be destroyed. Yours are not significantly eroded in that you can avoid suffering the harm at no significant cost to yourself. You might find it frustrating that you cannot destroy my car, but as destroying the

believing that one will act wrongly in carrying it out. This may be true, but it will not help to rescue the view under consideration. I consider the related possibility of encouraging or accepting the corrupt motives of punishers to secure the value of making threats below.

[5] Daniel Farrell defends this view. I discuss it below.

[6] See also J McMahan 'Paradoxes of Abortion and Prenatal Injury' (2006) 116 *Ethics* 625, 645.

car would be wrongful, your frustration is not a reason against permitting me to make the threat. Making the threat, in that case, is justified in the same way as it would be justified, under certain conditions, to develop an automatic machine to break the legs of people who destroy cars.[7]

The difficulty with this argument is that human agency is not mechanical. If I form a conditional intention that I will break your leg if you destroy my car, once you destroy my car I retain a choice whether to break your leg. Furthermore, at least if I am being rational, the reason that I had for making the threat cannot provide a reason to carry it out. All of the value that making the threat may have had—i.e. the protection that it gave to my car—has now gone. In fact, I should conclude that any value that I thought existed in making the threat has been shown not to exist. For the threat was ineffective. Once you have destroyed my car how can I be motivated by the fact that I mistakenly thought that threatening you was valuable? And what reason for action could that mistaken belief give me?

If I lack any reason or motivation to carry out an ineffective threat my ability to form the conditional intention to break your leg is undermined. When I threaten you with a broken leg I will realize that if the condition in the threat obtains I will have no reason to carry out the threat. And I will recognize that I won't be motivated to carry out the threat. I cannot be said to *have* a conditional intention to *v* if I believe that I will not *v* if the condition obtains. And I have every reason to form that belief.[8]

It might be argued that we could avoid this problem by making our punishment practices more mechanical. We could do this by constraining the discretion of criminal justice officials. Criminal justice officials would be given the task of identifying and punishing the guilty. They would be required automatically to punish those found guilty.[9] But this idea does little to avoid the problem. For it would be difficult to see why criminal justice officials should accept their role of punishing guilty people on this basis. Officials would object to carrying out punishment on the grounds that it could not possibly deter an offence that has already been committed. In accepting their role as criminal justice officials, they would form the conditional intention to punish offenders. But why would they form such conditional intentions if they could find no rationale for executing them?

[7] Automatic machines have played a significant role in self-defensive theories of punishment. See, further, L Alexander 'The Doomsday Machine: Proportionality, Punishment and Prevention' (1980) 63 *The Monist* 199 and W Quinn, 'The Right to Threaten and the Right to Punish'.

[8] For related discussion, see G Kavka 'Some Paradoxes of Deterrence' (1978) 75 *Journal of Philosophy* 291 and D Farrell 'On Threats and Punishments' (1989) 15 *Social Theory and Practice* 125. Quinn ('The Right to Threaten and the Right to Punish') tries to rebut this objection at 97–9, but not, I think, successfully.

[9] See A Ellis 'A Deterrence Theory of Punishment' (2003) 53 *Philosophical Quarterly* 337.

Perhaps we could persuade criminal justice officials to be retributivists, or refrain from dissuading them from being retributivists, knowing that their view is false. We could do that to inculcate in them the false belief that they have good reason to carry out the threats that we make. We should be glad (all things considered) that such morally evil people exist.[10] But, for one thing, we should at least hope that our system of criminal justice does not require us to corrupt criminal justice officials to serve our purposes. For that would involve corrupting them as a means to secure the good, which would itself be a form of manipulative harm. And even were it permissible to corrupt officials for this reason, we would be provided only with very unstable support for our deterrence aims. As John Rawls noted in his rule-utilitarian account of punishment,[11] in the long term, when attempting to render our institutions stable, we ought not to rely on our ability to lie convincingly.

ii) Responsibility and Security

Another response to the concern that it is wrong manipulatively to harm offenders to avert threats for which they are not responsible aims to show that offenders *are* responsible for future threats. If we could show that criminal wrongdoing causes our future security to be eroded we could justify manipulatively harming offenders to avert the enhanced threats that we face through such wrongdoing.

Why might criminal wrongdoers be responsible for future threats? As Daniel Farrell argues, through their wrongdoing wrongdoers might encourage other people to think that we are vulnerable, leading them to attack us.[12] Return to the case involving my car. I threaten you that if you destroy my car I will break your leg. You destroy my car. If I were not to execute my threat other people would see that my threats are insincere. They will know that once the condition in my threat is fulfilled I will not be motivated to execute my expressed intention. In order to avert these threats that will otherwise come about I may execute my intention. You would be harmed as a means, in this case, but only as a means to avert threats that you wrongfully create.

It is true that it is wrong for you to undermine my credibility by wronging me. This can be demonstrated by focusing again on permissible but insincere threats. Return to the case where I make an insincere threat to you that I will kill two of your children if you kill my child. It would be wrong for someone else to undermine my threat by explaining to you that I am a good person who would

[10] David Lewis endorses this view in the context of nuclear deterrence. See 'Devil's Bargains and the Real World' in *Papers in Ethics and Social Philosophy* (Cambridge: CUP, 2000) 205–8. It is more plausible in that context because the harm to be averted is so great.

[11] 'Two Concepts of Rules' in *Collected Papers* (Cambridge, Mass.: Harvard UP, 1999).

[12] See, especially, D M Farrell 'Deterrence and the Just Distribution of Harm' (1995) *Social Philosophy and Policy* 220, 233–5. This idea is also implicit in M Otsuka *Libertarianism Without Inequality* (Oxford: OUP, 2003) ch.3.

not dream of executing the threat. That person would wrongfully undermine my ability to lie to protect my children. It follows that it is also wrong for you to undermine my ability to make future threats by killing my child. It is more difficult to see this because we are focused primarily on the homicide itself. But whilst nothing can now be done to prevent the homicide occurring, something can be done to restore my eroded security. You may be harmed as a means to that end.

Where the threat that I make is proportionate, this at least sometimes provides a reason to execute my threats. If you destroy my car in the previous example I have a choice. Either I refrain from breaking your leg, in which case other people will think that I am vulnerable to future attacks, or I break your leg. If it is proportionate to do so, I am permitted to break your leg to avert future threats that your wrongdoing causes. They are threats that you are responsible for creating. This provides a limited justification of general deterrence. We may manipulatively harm wrongdoers, but only to avert threats that they are responsible for creating, hence avoiding the objection to punishment under consideration.

This argument is convincing but its implications for punishment are implausibly modest. The limit on the magnitude of punishment would be based not on the gravity of the wrong itself, but on its effects on our security. We can illuminate the problem by demonstrating that wrongful conduct does not always erode security. Whether it does will depend on the visibility of the wrongdoing. Suppose that you destroy my car in circumstances where no one else will find out about it. The view under consideration would provide me with no reason to carry out my threat against you. For my ability to threaten others would be untouched.[13]

Perhaps it might be argued that failing to execute my threat erodes my security with respect to you. But that will depend on whether you continue to pose a threat to me. You may be a reformed character, or you may have already achieved what you wanted, and so pose no threat to me at all. The amount of punishment that I would be permitted to impose on you would, in consequence, be modest at best. It is difficult to believe that it is wrong to punish a serious offender if that person neither poses any future threat nor is responsible for eroding our security.

III. Responsibility and the Duty to Protect

So far, we have seen that although a satisfactory argument from self-defence for the justification of punishment has been provided, its implications are implausibly modest. If we accept the principle that it is permissible manipulatively to harm a person only in order to avert a threat that the person is responsible for creating, we must accept that we have no right to punish those who pose no future threat to us

[13] Conversation with Jeff McMahan helped me to clarify my views here.

and who are not responsible for the threats created by anyone else. Criminal offending would then go unpunished if it was a one-off and it was secretive enough.

If we want to justify punishing such offenders on defensive grounds, we must reject the restriction on harming offenders only to avert threats for which they are responsible. That is controversial. Many people who write about self-defence endorse that restriction and so we will have to proceed carefully. But we have already seen good reason to reject a strict version of that restriction in chapter 8. Let me summarize the argument briefly here.

The responsibility restriction is one very strict way of understanding the relationship between responsibility and liability. A person's liability to be harmed as a means to avert a threat depends on the person being responsible for the threat. We might understand the responsibility restriction as a restriction on the scope of a person's duties to prevent or compensate for the harms that she causes. This idea draws on the discussion of *Hit Man* above. The person hiring the hit man was liable manipulatively to be harmed to avert the threat only because he is required to fulfil his duty to prevent, or to compensate for, the harm that he has created through his wrongful action.

But the responsibility restriction is too strict. Recall our discussion of the following case in chapter 8:

Double Hit Man 2. Evelyn hires a hit man to kill Wayne. Fred has also hired a hit man to kill Wayne. Both hit men arrive at the same time. Because of where they are standing, Wayne can only use Fred as a shield against Evelyn's hit man and Evelyn as a shield against Fred's hit man. He manages to do that, resulting in the deaths of Evelyn and Fred.

It seems obviously wrong that Wayne is required to sacrifice his life in this case rather than using Evelyn and Fred as shields. The justification for the conclusion that he is permitted to use Evelyn and Fred in this way is as follows. If Evelyn could give up her life in order to avert the threat that she has faced she ought to do that, and the same goes for Fred. Consequently each of them ought to authorize Wayne to use them as a shield to avert the threat for which they are individually responsible. It just so happens that it would not help to do this. They are in the wrong places to be used successfully.

If Evelyn cannot fulfil her duty on her own, though, she has a duty to get someone else to help her. What she could try to do is to get Fred to take her place. Fred has the same duty as Evelyn. And Fred, were he properly motivated, would want Evelyn to take his place and protect Wayne to avert the threat for which *he* is responsible. In that case, Fred and Evelyn ought to form and execute an agreement to protect Wayne by fulfilling each other's duties to avert the threat that they are responsible for creating. In that way Evelyn and Fred could avoid harming Wayne.

If they cannot form and execute such an agreement, however, or they refuse to do so, Wayne can permissibly use them as a shield to avert the threats that he faces.

For were he to do so he would merely force them to fulfil their duty: to make themselves available, together, to avert the threats to Wayne. In that way they would only be made to bear the cost that they are required to bear in order to fulfil their obligation to avert the threats that they have created. This idea is bolstered by the argument in chapter 6 which demonstrated that there is no important difference between harming someone as a means to an end and forcing a person to do her duty to secure that end.

I abstracted the following argument for this proposal. Suppose that A has an enforceable duty to do *x* and B has an enforceable duty to do *y*. The duties are important and are reasonably similar in stringency and kind, and there is no particular reason why A must perform his own duty and B must perform his own duty. Only A can *y* and only B can *x*. If these things are true, A and B have an enforceable duty to form and execute an agreement to perform each other's duties. If A and B fail to do that, or are unable to do so, it is permissible manipulatively to harm A and B to ensure that they do not breach their duties. A and B can be harmed only to some magnitude less than the degree that they would have been required to suffer in performance of their own duty.

A duty will be enforceable if doing the duty is necessary to avert a great harm and compensation will be inadequate, or will be unlikely to be forthcoming, if the duty is breached. That is so in *Double Hit Man 2*. This argument implies that we must relax the idea that a person may be harmed only to avert a threat that she is responsible for creating. This conclusion should be accepted by those who think that responsibility is important in grounding our duties—for that is the very idea to which we have appealed in explaining why we must depart from the responsibility-based view.

IV. Punishment as Remedy for Breach

The argument that I have just considered rests on the duty that people have to ensure that they do not wrongfully harm others. But whilst this argument provides us with good reason to doubt the responsibility constraint on manipulative harming it does not on its own justify general deterrence. We can see this by focusing on another significant difference between *Self-Defence* and *Punishment*. In *Self-Defence* we are concerned with preventing Arnold breaching his duty not to harm Debbie. In *Punishment*, in contrast, Oswald's duty not to harm Doris has already been breached. Our focus must shift from preventing harm to responding to harm already done.

i) Future Protection as a Remedy

One puzzling feature of Farrell's view that I identified above is that in determining the scope of a person's liability to manipulative harm he focuses only on the offender's responsibility for future threats. Punishment is not owed in virtue of the harm that he has caused but in virtue of the threats of harm that he has wrongfully created. That has the odd implication, which we have already discussed, that the person whose crime *has* no future effects of this kind cannot be punished for this crime. It is also in tension with the idea that punishment should be *for the crime*, and not only *for the future effects of crime*. The best understanding of the idea that punishment should be for the crime is not just that committing a crime is a necessary condition of punishment, or that punishment would be a good thing in virtue of the crime having been committed, but rather that a person who has wrongfully harmed another owes duties to the person whom she has harmed—duties to respond appropriately to the harm that she has caused. We vaguely allude to this idea when we say that the wrongdoer must 'pay a debt to society' for his crime.

This idea helps to explain something else that drives people to retributivism: the idea that something is amiss when a serious wrongdoer is not punished. As I argued in Part I of this book, this is best explained not by the fact that the suffering of wrongdoers is good in itself, but rather that offenders who are not punished have a duty that is unfulfilled. We feel an impulse to ensure that the very important duties that offenders owe in virtue of their wrongdoing are fulfilled, and that leads to our sense that something is seriously wrong when the person continues to live in society without suffering any burden.

The duties that a person owes in virtue of having wrongfully harmed others flow naturally from the duties that the person breached in the first place. If a person breaches her duty, the duty is not obliterated. It remains to be fulfilled as well as the person can. For example, if a person breaches a promise, his duty to fulfil the promise as well as he can still remains. If I promise you to do some work on Tuesday and I don't turn up, I ought to get someone else to do the work just as well as I would have on Tuesday. If I can't do that, I ought to do the work on Wednesday. To put things in more general terms, we can say that if a person has a duty to v and he breaches that duty, he retains a duty to do the next best thing.[14]

Of course, in the law, damages rather than specific performance provide the standard remedy for breach of contract. But this fact about the law can be explained. Requiring specific performance would be difficult to enforce and would often be undesirable to both parties. After all, the performance often cannot *really be* very specific in that by the time the court has determined that rectificatory obligations are owed the time at which the contract ought to have been performed has long passed. Furthermore, imposing specific performance on the defendant may be very burdensome. If the difference to the plaintiff is not great, damages are the appropriate remedy.[15]

[14] See, especially, J Raz 'Personal Practical Conflicts' in P Baumann and M Betzler *Practical Conflicts* (Cambridge: CUP, 2004). This idea is carefully explored in the context of tort law in J Gardner 'What is Tort Law For? Part 1: The Place of Corrective Justice' (2011) 30 *Law and Philosophy* 1.

[15] See also D Kimel *From Promise to Contract: Towards a Liberal Theory of Contract* (Oxford: Hart, 2005) 100–9.

Now let us consider a standard criminal wrong, say assault. If William has assaulted David he has breached his duty to David. He must now do the next best thing to fulfilling his duty not to assault David. What might that be? Perhaps he could provide David with monetary compensation for harming him. But if the assault is quite serious, damages will be inadequate as a response. And it will be very difficult to get William to provide David with compensation of this kind, especially if William is not very well off.

In some circumstances, though, perhaps he could do something that is closer to specific performance than providing David with compensation. Suppose that, just after William's assault, Wanda attacks David. William could prevent Wanda from harming David. We might conclude that he ought to do this. He cannot undo *his* assault. But he can put David in a position that is almost as good as he would have been in had William not assaulted him, by preventing the other person's assault on him.

Furthermore, just as I had to incur a cost to prevent the hit man I hired from harming you in *Hit Man*, so William would have been expected to bear a cost to prevent David being harmed by his assault had he been able to. As he can't prevent his own assault from occurring by bearing that cost, he can be expected to bear some cost, perhaps a less grave cost, to prevent Wanda from assaulting David. And if he is unwilling to do his duty it is permissible for David manipulatively to harm him for that purpose. For in doing so he will only make William bear a cost that he already has a duty to bear.

It might be objected to this that it is odd to require William to fulfil his rectificatory duty by requiring him to avert the threat that Wanda poses to David. We wouldn't normally think it an appropriate remedy for breach of a promise to require the promissor to prevent another person breaching their promise. If I breach my promise to work for you on Tuesday it would be odd to require me to compel someone else, let's call him Harry, to fulfil *his* promise to work for you as a remedy. Why not draw the same conclusion in the case of assault?

There are two related differences between assault and breach of promise that explain why we should not draw conclusions about the former case from the latter. The first is that a person who has breached a promise is normally capable adequately of rectifying the breach in other ways. Return to the case where I have breached a promise to do some work for you on Tuesday. I could either do the work on Wednesday, or I could prevent another person from breaching a promise to do some work for you on Tuesday. It will often be preferable for me to do the work on Wednesday. And if the other person breaches his promise to work for you on Tuesday, there may be adequate things that *he* can do, and be compelled to do, in response to the breach. Requiring those who breach promises to compel other people to fulfil their promises is unlikely to be the preferred option, even for the victim of the breach.

This is not the case with respect to assault. It is likely that William cannot adequately compensate David for assault. And if Wanda assaults David, it is likely that she will not be able adequately to compensate David for assault either. If William is not required to prevent Wanda from assaulting David, David will suffer a double loss. He will fail adequately to be compensated for either assault.

If William assaults David and then prevents Wanda from assaulting David, David is the victim of one assault—by William. Had William not assaulted David and then failed to prevent Wanda from assaulting David, David would also have been the victim of one assault—by Wanda. Thus, if William assaults David and then prevents Wanda from assaulting David, David would be in a position that is reasonably similar to the one that he would have been in had William done nothing at all.

Of course, he is still the victim of one assault, an assault that has gone uncompensated. This suggests that David is also owed compensation for the harm that he has suffered. The burden of compensation might appropriately be divided between Wanda and William. As we will see in a moment, William may be harmed to render David *better off* than he would have been had William not harmed him.

Wanda owes some contribution to compensating David, for she has benefited through William's action, in that she has been prevented from acting in a way that would have rendered her liable to be harmed. As I will suggest in a moment, there is a sense in which general deterrence benefits many people—it helps to ensure that they do not offend. Many of us, for this reason, can be expected to bear some cost to help compensate victims of crime.

Secondly, and this point is related, it is permissible for William to compel Wanda not to assault David independently of whether he has a duty to do this. We are permitted to use force to defend others against wrongful attacks. William may coerce her into doing what duty requires of her. But it is not normally permissible to coerce a person to fulfil their promises. Wanda has no complaint about being coerced by William. Harry, in contrast, has a complaint about being coerced by me into fulfilling his promise. Why might that be so? Again it is for the reason that compensation is typically adequate to rectify breach of promise when compared with assault.

That provides part of the explanation why breach of contract, which to some extent legalizes breach of promise, is part of the civil law whereas assault is criminalized.[16] The law, like morality, prohibits both assault and breach of contract. But it uses the threat of punishment, as well as a police force, to protect people only against assault and not against breach of contract. The reason for this is that we ought not to use force or the threat of force to compel a person to fulfil all of their obligations. Whether we are permitted to use force or the threat of force depends in part on whether compensation for breach of the obligation might be adequate in typical cases.

[16] See, further, V Tadros 'Criminalization and Regulation' in A Duff, L Farmer, S Marshall, M Renzo, and V Tadros *The Boundaries of the Criminal Law* (Oxford: OUP, 2010).

It might be argued that the adequacy of compensation is not all that matters in determining whether a wrong ought to be prohibited by the criminal or by the civil law. After all, it does not seem wrong to criminalize theft even though compensation might typically be adequate in response to theft. But there are other important considerations in criminalization decisions. For example, we must consider not only the adequacy of compensation were it to be provided but also the likelihood that we will be able to secure compensation in fact. It is no use claiming that a civil remedy is adequate if that remedy will, in very many cases, not be provided either because the wrongdoer cannot be found or because he cannot pay. These considerations help to motivate the criminalization of theft in contrast with breach of contract.

Of course, some will hope for a more principled basis upon which we can distinguish between criminal and civil wrongs. For example, some claim that criminal wrongdoing is public, in the sense that the public can call wrongdoers to answer for their wrongs, whereas civil wrongdoing is private, in the sense that the dispute is solely between the parties.[17]

I doubt very much that it is possible to find a principled distinction between civil and criminal wrongs of this kind that has plausible implications. The main reason not to criminalize breach of contract is that we tend not to need the kind of protection that punishment offers for breach of contract. We do not need it because we can normally identify the person who has breached the contract and they will often be in a position adequately to compensate us for our losses. There would be an argument in favour of criminalization were these things to be false. The distinction between the civil and criminal law turns in part on empirical considerations, which should not be surprising. Even many retributivists acknowledge that whether we should resort to criminalization of some conduct, and hence to sanction that conduct with punishment, depends on the effectiveness of other available options to regulate the conduct in question, including the use of the civil law.[18]

ii) The Transfer of the Right to Protection

I still haven't provided a complete justification of punishment. I have demonstrated only that the offender is liable to manipulative harm to prevent the victim from suffering further attacks. That provides us with a justification of general deterrence. But general deterrence would permissibly be used only to protect the victims against further threats. Would we be justified in punishing offenders in order to protect *other people* from criminal offending?

[17] For an argument for criminal wrongdoing as public wrongdoing, see S E Marshall and R A Duff 'Criminalization and Sharing Wrongs' (1998) 11 *Canadian Journal of Law and Jurisprudence* 7; R A Duff *Answering for Crime* (Oxford: Hart, 2007); and D N Husak *Overcriminalization: The Limits of the Criminal Law* (Oxford: OUP, 2007) 135–7.

[18] See, for example, D Husak 'The Criminal Law as Last Resort' (2004) 24 *Oxford Journal of Legal Studies* 207.

One way of answering this question draws on the earlier discussion of *Double Hit Man 2*. There we saw that a person who is culpably responsible for the creation of a threat can incur a duty to prevent the victim from being harmed by someone else on the basis of the following argument. Suppose that A has an enforceable duty to do *x* and B has an enforceable duty to do *y*. The duties are important and are reasonably similar in stringency and kind, and there is no particular reason why A must perform his own duty and B must perform his own duty. Only A can *y* and only B can *x*. If these things are true, A and B have an enforceable duty to form and execute an agreement to perform each other's duties. If A and B fail to do that, or are unable to do so, it is permissible manipulatively to harm A and B to ensure that they do not breach their duties. A and B can be harmed only to the degree that they would have been permitted to be harmed to fulfil their own duty were they able to do so, and perhaps less than that. A duty will be enforceable if doing the duty is necessary to avert a great harm and compensation will be inadequate, or will be unlikely to be forthcoming, if the duty is breached.

This argument has implications for the justification of punishment as well as self-defence. If punishing each wrongdoer can protect *other* victims of crime from future offending each wrongdoer ought to accept that he must be punished. Each wrongdoer ought to accept this because he ought to form an agreement with other wrongdoers to ensure that all victims of crime are protected. As part of the agreement to accept that he must be punished, each wrongdoer will do his best to ensure that his duty to protect his victim is fulfilled *by someone*.

Let us clarify this with an example. Suppose that Linda assaults Vera and Simon assaults Trevor. Linda has an obligation to prevent other people from assaulting Vera and Simon has an obligation to prevent other people from assaulting Trevor. If each of them can fulfil their obligation to do this only by forming and executing an agreement with the other, that is what they must do. And that gives rise to a permission manipulatively to harm each offender for the protection of each victim.

But this argument, whilst valid, cannot explain the full scope of the right to punish in a plausible way. So far we have justified punishment of offenders only to protect people who are already victims of crime from being victimized again. But when we punish people we *also* aim to protect people who have not yet been offended against. Suppose that after Linda assaults Vera there is no possibility that Vera can be assaulted again. What does Linda owe to Vera?

One answer might be as follows. Whilst Vera is safe, there are people who she cares about. *They* could be protected from being harmed by Linda. Suppose that Vera wishes her daughter, Veronica, to be protected from harm. Can Vera pass on her entitlement to protection to Veronica? This is perhaps more controversial. If we allow Vera to pass on her right to protection to Veronica, we extend the scope of the right that the victim has to manipulate the offender. But in cases where the offender has breached a very serious duty, and it is impossible adequately to compensate the victim for breach, we might think that this is the least that the offender owes to the victim.

The most obvious example of this is where the attacker has killed his victim. In *Punishment* Oswald has killed Doris. He obviously cannot benefit her. But he does have a duty to Doris's family. And that is because the closest that Oswald can now come to fulfilling his duty to Doris is to benefit Doris's family.[19] The same thing might be true in the case of Vera and Veronica. There is nothing that Linda can do to assist Vera that would be at all close to fulfilling her duty to Vera. The closest that Linda can come to doing her duty to Vera is to assist Veronica. And that is what she ought to do.

If this is right, the duty that wrongdoers owe to protect others from harm is quite extensive. But it is still not extensive enough. We can see this if we consider cases where the person harmed does not care about anyone else. Is it then permissible to punish the wrongdoer in order to protect other people from being harmed? The obvious question to ask is whether wrongdoers can be punished in order to protect all citizens of the state and whether this can be done even if the direct victim of the wrongdoing does not wish it to be done. That will require us to consider the role that the state has in protecting its citizens. Whether the state has such a role will depend on the permissions and obligations that citizens have to transfer their right to protection to other citizens. That is something that I will consider in the next chapter.

iii) Imminence and Deterrence

It might be argued that whereas in the examples I am considering the threat is imminent, when we use general deterrence, we prevent threats that are not imminent. We even prevent threats coming into existence at all. In fact, if deterrence works in the way that we hope that it will, we might think that it *should* prevent threats coming into existence. The existence of deterrent systems of punishment can help to create a culture in which intentions to commit wrongs are formed less regularly. Responding to deterrence, a person begins to see that wrongdoing is not an option simply for prudential reasons. This can help the idea that offending is not an option to become embedded in the person's psychology, so that she never considers wrongdoing.

I believe that deterrence has powerful effects of this kind in most modern democratic societies, and other societies as well. It plays a significant role in ensuring that people do not develop *inclinations* to offend. The personalities and judgements of citizens in these societies are shaped in a context where wrongdoing is already ruled out for reasons of prudence, both in their own minds and in the minds of those, such as parents, teachers, and carers, who shape their moral psychology. I also believe that this is one of the most attractive features of deterrence. Those who

[19] For a similar idea in a different context, see M Ridge 'Giving the Dead Their Due' (2003) 114 *Ethics* 38.

doubt the deterrent effects of the criminal law tend to focus on its ability to motivate people who have the inclination to commit crime. But this fails to acknowledge the much more profound effect that criminal justice institutions can have. We see the effects of criminal justice much more clearly by comparing societies where the criminal justice system is reasonably effective in discovering and punishing criminals with societies where it is not. In the latter case, I suspect, we will find many more people with the inclination to commit criminal wrongs for the reasons to which I have alluded. Whilst I cannot demonstrate this to be the case, let us work on the assumption that I am right about this speculative claim.

The question we must address, in the light of this, is whether it is permissible to harm a person to prevent others forming intentions to commit wrongs, some of which would lead to threats that we face. It might be argued that this does not follow from the permissibility of harming a person as a means to avert an imminent threat. A comparison might be drawn here with self-defence. Many people believe that it is permissible to defend oneself even against a culpable attacker only if the threat faced is imminent. It would be wrong to use force against a person who has an intention to attack unless the threat is now *posed* by the attacker.

This comparison is not apt, however. For in this case, the person harmed has *already completed* her attack. One of the main reasons in favour of an imminence requirement—that we should not harm a person until we are sure that she is a threat to us—is not engaged in this case. Furthermore, it is surely much better to harm a person to prevent wrongful intentions being formed than it is to avert threats that are posed to us. Imagine that, given your wrongdoing, I could harm you to degree x to avert a threat of magnitude y. There are two different ways I could do this. Either I could harm you now, preventing another person from forming the intention to commit a wrong of magnitude y, or I could harm you later, averting the threat of magnitude y that the person posed. There is no special reason why I should wait to harm you. You have already committed your wrong, so you are already liable to be harmed. And there are good reasons for you to prefer being harmed now for reasons of deterrence rather than used as a means to avert a threat posed. If you were used as a shield later, for example, we will have much less control over the degree to which you are harmed. Punishing you now can be done in a controlled way, perhaps even in a way that can benefit you.

There is an even more important reason why we should prefer harming you for reasons of deterrence rather than allowing you to be used as a means in other ways. Harming you now for reasons of deterrence *does* provide a significant benefit to others. Inculcating a culture in which people do not form intentions to do wrong is a significant social benefit. One reason why this is so is that it helps to ensure that these people are less likely to be morally corrupt. Forming wrongful intentions and trying to act on them makes a person morally corrupt, and it is worse for people that they are corrupt in this way.

As I argued in chapter 5, this reason is often less powerful than the reason to prevent others from being harmed, but it is nevertheless significant. To it we can add the fact that a person who does form the intention to harm others and in consequence poses a threat to them becomes liable to be harmed to avert the threat. Preventing people from forming the intention to harm others by creating a culture of compliance prevents people from becoming liable to be harmed in this way. The state should aim to prevent wrongdoing partly in order to protect victims against wrongdoing. But it should also do so in order to prevent people being liable to be harmed for preventive, compensatory, or punitive reasons. Educating people not to offend aims to benefit both the person educated and the person who might be a victim of his crimes. The criminal justice system has a role in supporting this positive outcome.

Deterrence, then, has twin benefits to those who would otherwise try to commit offences—it helps to ensure that they are better people and it helps to ensure that they are protected from harm. We have very strong reasons to prefer using wrongdoers as a means to deter others than we have to use them as a means to avert imminent threats. We can predict that were it not for the deterrence effects of the criminal law, there would be very many wrongdoers, and *their* lives, as well as the lives of those they harm, would go significantly worse as a result. This is one of the great attractions of deterrence.

V. Beyond Rectification

I have grounded my justification of general deterrence in the duty that offenders have to rectify the wrongs that they have perpetrated. It might be argued that even if this argument is sound, it does not capture in an adequate way what is special about criminal punishment. There are two versions of this objection to consider. One version focuses on the demand that offenders focus on their own wrongdoing. Wrongdoing is *personal*. I cannot rectify a wrong that I have perpetrated by preventing the wrongs of others. A second version of the objection focuses on the fact that a person may be able to prevent serious wrongdoing of others at modest cost to himself. If so, he would seem to have fulfilled his rectificatory duties. And yet it seems that the punishment imposed on him would, intuitively, be too modest.

i) Rectification, Recognition, and Reconciliation

Here is the first version of the objection. The account I have offered is focused only on the wrongdoing of others. It does not demand the appropriate kind of response from the offender. Preventing the wrongdoing of others does not focus appropriately on the offender's wrong itself. It is strangely impersonal in that it aims to nullify the offender's wrong by nullifying wrongs committed by others.

To see this concern more clearly, return to the case of David, William, and Wanda. It might be argued that if William protects David against Wanda's assault, William will not have responded to his wrongdoing in a *completely* appropriate way. Surely there is still something lacking, some remaining reason that can justify us in punishing William even after he has protected David. He may have prevented David from Wanda, but that does not amount to an adequate response to *his own* wrongdoing.

In responding to this objection, the first thing to note is that I *can* compensate you for a lesser harm by preventing you from suffering a greater harm. Here's a case that helps to demonstrate this. Suppose that you are unconscious and a villain is about to cut off your right arm. He agrees to refrain from doing that if I cut off your left arm. You are right-handed and I know that you would prefer to lose your left arm. I am permitted to cut off your left arm, or so I believe. Protecting you against having your right arm cut off is more than sufficient compensation for the loss of your left arm.

Things are different in David's case, of course. One difference is that David has already suffered harm for some time, and we must take that into consideration in determining the scope of William's duty to protect David. The appropriate comparison, then, is with a case in which I harm you now to avert a greater future harm. This implies that William's obligation to protect David will have been fulfilled only if he averts a threat to David that is of a significantly greater magnitude than the harm that he has caused him.

A similar response is appropriate when we are asked to consider a further distinguishing feature of David's case. Not only has David been harmed, he has been harmed unjustly. Whilst I can fully compensate you for a harm that I have caused by protecting you against other harms, it will be argued, I cannot fully compensate you for any injustice I have perpetrated against you by doing this. If I act in order to save your right arm, I do nothing wrong in cutting off your left arm. And so there is no injustice to compensate you for. But William owes David compensation not only for harming him but also for the injustice of his action.

It might be argued that in preventing Wanda's attack William has prevented David from being harmed unjustly by Wanda. So he has compensated David not only for the harm that he has suffered but also for the injustice that has been done to him. Preventing the injustice of others, we might think, is an inadequate response to one's own injustice. In the case of harm, we have seen that we can compensate for one's harmful act by preventing a greater harm perpetrated by another person. But this doesn't seem to be the right conclusion in the case of injustice. I can respond adequately to the injustice that I have perpetrated only by full recognition and apology. I cannot respond to my own wrongdoing simply by preventing the wrongdoing of another. This idea lies at the heart of communicative theories of punishment.[20] As I noted in chapter 5, I am to a degree sympathetic to this idea, even if I doubt that it is very significant in justifying state institutions of punishment.

[20] See, especially, R A Duff *Punishment, Communication, and Community*. Duff has criticized my account of punishment for failing to acknowledge this idea. See 'In Response' in R Cruft, M Kramer, and M Reiff *Crime, Punishment, and Responsibility: The Jurisprudence of Antony Duff* (Oxford: OUP, forthcoming). In his criticism Duff wrongly attributes to me the

But this idea only shows that the duties of offenders are more extensive than those that ground the permission to harm them for reasons of general deterrence. It does not show that it is wrong to harm offenders for reasons of general deterrence. Indeed one thing that seems mistaken about Antony Duff's version of the communicative theory of punishment is that it is almost exclusively focused on repairing the relationship between the offender and the victim and pays relatively little attention to how the harm caused may be repaired.[21]

On the view that I defend, offenders may be harmed because that would provide at least part of the appropriate response to the wrong that they have perpetrated. We need not establish that general deterrence provides an *exclusive* justification of punishment. If we are required to punish offenders to satisfy the victim's demand for recognition, we have a further reason to impose punishment on offenders.

The justification of general deterrence is, I believe, crucial to justifying state punishment. It is crucial in that it is the only thing that could plausibly justify using significant state resources to develop and maintain the kind of criminal justice institutions that are necessary for the maintenance of civil society.[22] Once we have sufficient justification for setting up these institutions, though, we may use them to pursue other aims. Recognition by the offender, in that case, becomes a legitimate aim of our criminal justice system.

This fact may also have implications for institutional design. Our demand that the offender recognizes that what he has done is wrong can help to structure the way in which we harm the offender. We can harm him in a way that is likely to protect victims and others from harm and that at the same time can help to persuade him to recognize that what he has done is wrong. He takes on the burdens of protection, and does so in a way that can achieve the further goal of reconciling the offender with the victim and with the broader community.

As I noted in chapter 5, we should not be too confident about the ability of our institutions to achieve recognition and reconciliation. Criminal justice has typically fared very poorly in that regard. But achieving recognition and reconciliation is a legitimate aim of the criminal justice system. If punishing offenders in a way that can promote recognition and reconciliation does not undermine the aim of protection, we have good reason to punish offenders in that way.

To conclude, punishing offenders for reasons of general deterrence would ensure that they fulfil a significant part of the duty that they owe to their victims. General deterrence may not provide an *exclusive* justification of punishment. If we are

view that preventing wrongdoing by another person could amount to a *complete* response to a person's wrongdoing. I do not believe this, and there is no reason for me to rely on the idea.

[21] The idea that compensation may be impossible and the idea that it may be insufficient are somewhat run together in Duff's account. See *Punishment, Communication, and Community* 94.

[22] See, further, chapter 5.

required to punish offenders to satisfy the victim's demand for recognition, we have a further reason to impose punishment on offenders.

ii) Easy Compensation

That brings us to the second version of the objection under consideration. We might think that a justification of punishment that is based on rectificatory duties is inadequately modest in cases where rectification is easy to provide, or could be provided by others. It is true that punishment aims at more than rectification. We can justify this, I will suggest, on the basis that the duties that a person incurs as a result of having wronged another are more extensive than the duty of compensation. It is permissible to harm an offender to a greater degree than is necessary fully to compensate the victim for having been wronged. The offender may be harmed to make the victim *better off* than he would have been had he not been wronged by the offender.

Suppose that William protects David against Wanda's attack. Being much stronger than Wanda, he does this without bearing any significant burden himself. Do we retain any right to punish him? As I have already noted, it may be that William owes David more than protection against Wanda's attack. Other justifications of punishment might make it permissible to punish William to some degree. It would nevertheless seem unsatisfactory that a significant part of William's duty to David has been fulfilled at such a modest cost.

One immediate response is as follows. If William has protected David from harm at little cost to himself he has done nothing to fulfil the duty that he owes to David in consequence of his wrongdoing. The reason for this is that William would owe a duty to protect David in this case *even if he hadn't wronged him.* We have a duty to rescue each other from harm if we can do so at relatively little cost to ourselves. If he does not bear any significant cost in protecting David from Wanda's attack, William cannot claim that he has fulfilled his rectificatory duty to David. For he would only have done what he would have had a duty to do independently of his wrongdoing. The obligation that William owes to protect David is an obligation that is owed *over and above* obligations of protection that he already has. Until he incurs a cost that he would not have had a duty to incur were it not for his wrongdoing, his duty to protect David will remain. And he can be punished in order to ensure that he incurs that cost. The magnitude of punishment that it is permissible to impose on wrongdoers may vary with the costs that they must incur in order to fulfil their protective duties. But that is hardly an objection: it is familiar that we vary the magnitude of punishment depending on its deterrence effects, and many retributivists accept this idea.[23]

[23] See, for example, A von Hirsch *Censure and Sanctions* (Oxford: OUP, 1993) and J Tasioulas 'Punishment and Repentance' (2006) 81 *Philosophy* 279.

Imagine that William could prevent Wanda's attack on David being completed at some cost to himself. William has come to recognize that what he did was wrong, and wishes to do his duty in protecting David. Suppose that the ordinary duty to rescue would require William to rescue David at a cost of his finger, but not at a cost of his foot. If William rescues David at a cost of his finger, David may still punish William for his original attack. For William has done only what duty already required of him regardless of his earlier assault. If William loses his foot in rescuing David, in contrast, it might be argued that David may not punish William. For William has rectified the situation in preventing David from suffering a harm similar to the one he caused, and has done so in response to a duty that he incurred as a result of his original wrongdoing.

Whilst plausible, this response is also inadequate. It does seem that full rectification, even if the offender is acting beyond the duties that he would otherwise have to rescue the victim, does not provide a constraint on punishment. There may be ways in which one person can protect another from a further harm at little cost to himself or herself, and yet the one person lacks a duty to protect the other. For example, suppose that a wealthy person in a just state could pay for extra security for the person harmed by paying more than her fair share of taxes. If all that wrongdoers owe is compensation, the wealthy person could discharge her duty without much cost to herself.

A related objection concerns multiple attackers. In the civil law, when a person is harmed through a wrongful act we divide up the compensatory burden between the number of people who caused the harm. If four people are liable to pay compensation to the victim, each person pays a quarter of the compensation owed. The more people there are who are liable for causing a certain magnitude of harm, the less the compensation that is owed by each person. But we do not think in the same way in the criminal law. Where there are multiple offenders who cause the harm, the magnitude of punishment to be suffered by each does not depend on the number of offenders.

If we ground punishment in rectificatory obligations that are incurred as a result of harming the victim, we might be led to counter-intuitive conclusions in such cases. Each offender will owe the victim only a proportion of the total security that she is owed, and so, where there are multiple offenders who cause harm, the punishment will be reduced to reflect the fact that the total amount of security that is owed to the victim is to be divided between the offenders.

There are responses that we can make to this problem even within the limits of a rectificatory model of punishment. The first thing to note is that in many cases involving multiple offenders the magnitude of the harm increases with an increase in the number of offenders. Being attacked by a mob, or being gang raped, is normally more harmful than being attacked or raped by a single person. So the magnitude of security that is owed to the victim will often be different in cases involving multiple offenders when compared with single offenders.

Secondly, as we will see in chapter 14, the liability of offenders is not only grounded in the harm that they cause to their immediate victim. It is also grounded in the fact that when a person commits a wrong we have good reason to make ourselves secure from that person. If we divert security resources to one person we make ourselves less secure from others. We have reason to believe that those who have threatened us once will threaten us in the future. That helps to explain why it is permissible to punish offenders for the inchoate crimes they commit—were we not to do so attempters would be responsible for us being harmed by others. They would be responsible because we would, through their actions, have fewer resources to meet threats that others pose. Similarly, we might argue that those who offend in groups pose greater security risks to us than those who offend individually, and so they have greater liability to be harmed to avert future threats that we face. Furthermore, each member of a group of offenders may be punished for reasons of special deterrence, to avert threats that they will otherwise pose in the future. They may also be punished to help secure recognition for the crimes that they commit.

But again, whilst these responses are plausible, they do not go to the heart of the problem. There seems to be a fundamental difference between compensation and punishment of this kind. Compensation only aims to neutralize the effects of the harm that the perpetrator has cased. Punishment, in contrast, is not limited by this aim. It appears permissible to punish offenders even if doing so does more than merely rectifying the harm caused by the wrongful conduct.

This idea can be recast in the language of duties, and it helps to vindicate the duty view of punishment that I defend. Seen in this way, the heart of the problem posed by easy compensation and by groups of offenders is that our compensatory duties are fulfilled when we have done what is required to rectify the harm that we have caused. The duties that underpin punishment, in contrast, are not. They remain even once the harm has been adequately rectified. This suggests that we must move beyond rectification in setting the duties that offenders incur as a result of their wrongdoing.

We have justified general deterrence on the grounds that offenders owe compensatory duties to victims as a result of their wrongdoing. This can be defended on quite modest assumptions. A more ambitious theory of punishment along these lines aims to show that the duties that are incurred as a result of serious wrongdoing are set not only by the benefit that is provided to the victim of crime, but also by the extent of the burden that is suffered by the wrongdoer. Punishment may be meted out to an offender, rendering him worse off, even if this renders the victim and others better off than they would have been had the original wrongdoing not been perpetrated.

Let us consider an example to examine this idea more closely. Suppose that Jake assaults Sally. Jake could prevent Sally from being assaulted again. He is now a reformed character and he prevents Sally from being assaulted again. He does so at some cost to himself that he would not be required to bear for her sake. For example, he paid Mike to protect her when he would not otherwise have been required to do so. Although it seems as though Sally has been compensated for her loss by having the future assault prevented, it seems right that Jake retains a duty towards Sally. Jake is required to do more, not because Sally has not been fully compensated but because Jake is not rendered sufficiently *badly* off. If Jake manages to benefit Sally at little cost to himself, we will have a sense that he has 'got away' with his crime. It seems right that Jake does retain a duty in this case. He can be expected to continue to benefit Sally at a cost to himself even if this renders her much better off than she would have been had she not been assaulted by him in the first place.

Of course, we may think that this result is true for the kinds of reasons that Farrell pointed to in his argument about punishment that I considered earlier: were we not to punish Jake more severely, our threats to other wealthy people would be rendered ineffective, for they would believe that they could offend and compensate later at little cost to themselves. Were we not to punish Jake more severely, in this case, we would all be rendered more insecure than we ought to be as a result of his actions. But there seems more to the case than this. Jake's duty would remain even were his act impossible to discover.

Some may think that this points to the significance of desert in grounding punishment: we can justify punishing Jake, in this case, because it is good that he is worse off. But that is not the right conclusion to draw from the case. The relevant point is not that it is good that Jake suffers, but rather that he may be made to suffer for Sally's sake at a cost to himself even if, as a consequence, she benefits overall from having been assaulted by him. The case is still concerned with the duties that Jake owes to Sally—his suffering is not to be endorsed in a way that is independent of these duties. And it is justified not for its intrinsic value but for its instrumental effects.

Consider the following:

Three Threats. Three boulders have wrongfully been rolled down a hill towards Jane. Bob is responsible for Boulder 1, which, when it hits her, will harm Jane to magnitude x. Other people, acting independently, are responsible for the two other boulders. Boulder 2, if it hits Jane, will harm her to magnitude x. Boulder 3, if it hits Jane, will harm her to magnitude $2x$. The threat created by Bob cannot be averted. Had it been possible to do so, it would have been permissible for Jane to harm Bob to magnitude y to protect her from Boulder 1. She could use Bob as a means to divert either Boulder 2 or Boulder 3. If she uses Bob to divert Boulder 2 Bob will suffer very minimal injuries. If she uses Bob to divert Boulder 3 Bob will be harmed to a greater degree, but less than y.

For the sake of simplicity let us assume that the degree to which a person is harmed overall is cumulative in a simple scalar fashion. Being harmed to magnitude $2x$ is twice as bad as being harmed to magnitude x. Being harmed to magnitude $3x$ is three times as bad as being harmed to magnitude x and so on.

Suppose that Jane is permitted to harm Bob as a means to avert Boulder 2 but not Boulder 3. If that is true, Jane suffers no greater harm than she would have suffered were Bob not to have rolled Boulder 1 at her. To see this, imagine that Bob had not rolled his boulder at her. She would not then be permitted to harm him as a means to avert the threat posed by either of the other boulders rolling towards her. She would then be harmed to magnitude $3x$. And that is exactly the magnitude of harm that she suffers if she harms Bob to avert Boulder 2. Bob, though, suffers only minimal harm if she does that.

Nevertheless, it seems intuitive that Jane may harm Bob to avert Boulder 3 rather than Boulder 2 even though that would render her better off than she would have been had Bob not rolled his boulder. Bob would then suffer to a greater degree than he would were he to be harmed to protect Jane from Boulder 2. But he is liable to suffer to an even greater degree to avert his own boulder. And although Jane would be rendered better off than she would have been had Bob not rolled a boulder at her, she is still worse off than she ought to be *all things considered*—she will still wrongfully be harmed to magnitude $2x$.

We can see that desert is not playing a very significant role in our judgements about this case from the fact that the permissibility of Jane harming Bob depends on the instrumental benefits that she enjoys by harming him. To see this, imagine that Boulder 3 would not harm Jane at all. If she uses Bob as a means to protect herself from Boulder 2 she will be prevented from being further harmed. If she pushes Bob in front of Boulder 3, he will suffer to the same degree that he would have suffered to avert the threat that he posed, but Jane would not be protected from further harm. Suppose that there is no way of harming Bob any further after this sequence of events. If he is used to prevent Jane being harmed by Boulder 2, he will only have suffered minor injuries.

I believe that Jane has a decisive reason to harm him to block Boulder 2 even though the harm that he suffers is minimal. This suggests at least that her right to use Bob as a means to protect herself is much more important than reasons of desert. But I think that it is further true that there is *no reason* to push Bob in front of Boulder 3. Were desert a significant factor in explaining our judgements about this case, it would seem that there is a conflict in this variation between ensuring that Jane is protected from Boulder 2 and ensuring that Bob gets what he deserves. But it is difficult to feel the force of any such conflict. We might think it a shame that Bob cannot be used as a means further to protect Jane. If we are not able to use him, though, there is little reason to harm him.

Why should we regard it as permissible for Jane to harm Bob in a way that renders her better off than she would have been had he not rolled his boulder? Our decision is between the following options: 1) permit Jane to reduce the extent to which she is wrongfully harmed by using Bob in a way that significantly harms him; or 2) minimize the harm that Bob will suffer by restricting Jane's permission to use him to ensure only that the effects of his wrongdoing are neutralized.

Here is one reason to conclude that we should endorse a permission for Jane to use Bob to render herself better off than she would have been had he not harmed her. Bob could have avoided being harmed to this degree simply by refraining from threatening Jane. He has already rendered himself liable to be harmed to magnitude y by wrongfully posing a threat to Jane. It is just that we cannot harm him to this magnitude to prevent the threat that he poses being realized. The grounds that we have to object to a principle permitting him to be harmed to magnitude y are, in consequence, significantly diminished.

Improving Jane's security from wrongdoing, in contrast, is something that we are strongly motivated to do. If we don't permit her to harm Bob to avert Boulder 3, she will be much worse off than she ought to be. Although she will not be significantly worse off than she would have been had Bob not attacked her, she will be significantly worse off than she would be in a just world—a world where everyone abides by their moral obligations. We will wish to save her from this fate. If this is right, we ought to permit Jane to harm Bob to avert Boulder 3 even though Bob prevents a threat that is greater than the threat that he posed to Jane.

Now return to the case of Jake and Sally that I discussed earlier. By paying Mike, Jake has ensured that Sally is harmed to no greater degree than she would have been harmed had he not assaulted her. But he is liable to be harmed to a greater degree to avert threats that she faces. His duties of protection are set by the extent to which it would have been permissible for him to avert the original threat that he posed to Sally. Hence, in paying Mike to protect Sally, he has not fulfilled his duty towards her. It would be permissible to harm him to a much greater degree in order to benefit Sally further by protecting her against a broader range of threats that she might face. Hence, even though he has already ensured that Sally has not been disadvantaged by his wrongdoing, he may nevertheless be punished.

This idea, I should say, is more controversial than the idea that punishment is justified simply on a compensatory basis. It rests on the idea that the duties that a person incurs as a result of wrongdoing are not limited to ensuring that the person harmed is as well off as she would have been had this person not committed the wrong that he committed. Because I could have been harmed as a means to avert a threat that I posed as a result of my wrongdoing, I may now be harmed as a means to an equivalent degree to avert other threats, even threats of a greater magnitude than the harm that I caused. We do not need this idea to defend general deterrence as the foundation of a theory of punishment. But we do need it to ensure that our theory of punishment is not implausibly modest.

Conclusions

My aim in this chapter was to show that general deterrence provides a central part of the justification of punishment in moral theory. The main objection to the use of punishment for reasons of general deterrence is that this would involve harming offenders as a means to the good of others. This objection, I have shown, is unfounded. It is true that offenders would be harmed as a means to the good of others. But doing this is consistent with the best understanding of the *means principle* and its limits. Harming offenders as a means is justified as it involves enforcing the duties that offenders have to protect their victims and others from future harms. This, of course, only provides a moral theory of punishment. What we wish to justify is *state* punishment. That involves consideration of a further range of questions, to which I turn in the next chapter.

Part III
Deterrence, Incapacitation and Prevention

[8]

PUNISHING DANGEROUSNESS: CLOAKING PREVENTIVE DETENTION AS CRIMINAL JUSTICE

*Paul H. Robinson**

Laypersons have traditionally thought of the criminal justice system as being in the business of doing justice: punishing offenders for the crimes they commit.[1] Yet during the past several decades, the justice system's focus has shifted from punishing past crimes to preventing future violations through the incarceration and control of dangerous offenders. Habitual-offender statutes, such as "three strikes" laws, authorize life sentences for repeat offenders.[2] Jurisdictional reforms

---

* Edna and Ednyfed Williams Professor of Law, Northwestern University.

[1] Modern academics have become comfortable with using nondesert crime-control principles, such as deterrence and the incapacitation of dangerous people, to govern the distribution of criminal punishment. Laypersons, however, generally do not share this perspective. *See, e.g.*, John M. Darley, Kevin M. Carlsmith & Paul H. Robinson, *Incapacitation and Just Deserts as Motives for Punishment*, 24 LAW & HUM. BEHAV. 659, 659 (2000) (noting that empirical studies suggest that laypersons do not take account of correlates of future criminality in setting punishment, especially if protective mechanisms other than the criminal justice system are available, but that they instead look to blameworthiness); Cass R. Sunstein, David Schkade & Daniel Kahneman, *Do People Want Optimal Deterrence?*, 29 J. LEGAL STUD. 237 (2000) (discussing two experiments that suggest that people do not spontaneously think in terms of optimal deterrence, and that people would have objections to policies based on the goal of optimal deterrence); Kevin M. Carlsmith, John M. Darley & Paul H. Robinson, Why Do We Punish? Deterrence and Just Deserts as Motives for Punishment 24 (Nov. 15, 2000) (unpublished manuscript, on file with the Harvard Law School Library) (noting empirical studies that imply that laypersons do not consider publicity or difficulty of detection in setting punishment).

[2] *See, e.g.*, 18 U.S.C. § 3559 (1994) (requiring life imprisonment on a third serious violent felony conviction); MONT. CODE ANN. § 46-18-219 (1999) (requiring life imprisonment without the possibility of release after a second or third felony conviction, depending on the felonies committed); *see generally* JOHN CLARK, JAMES AUSTIN & D. ALAN HENRY, "THREE STRIKES AND YOU'RE OUT": A REVIEW OF STATE LEGISLATION 9–10 (Nat'l Inst. of Justice: Research in Brief, NJC 165369, 1997) (noting that many states have expanded pre-existing repeat-offender statutes); NAT'L CONFERENCE OF STATE LEGISLATORS, "THREE STRIKES" SENTENCING LAWS 24 (1999) (noting that between 1993 and 1999, twenty-four states and the federal government enacted "three strikes" laws and that nearly all states have some type of sentence enhancement applicable to habitual offenders).

have decreased the age at which juveniles may be tried as adults.[3] Gang membership and recruitment are now punished.[4] "Megan's

The protective rationale for these laws is evident in the legislative history of the federal three strikes statute. After citing the "problem [of] a significant percentage of crimes . . . committed by people who previously have committed crimes" and concluding that, to date, "the response of the criminal justice system to both violent crime and recidivism has been inadequate," the Report of the House of Representatives states that the purpose of the legislation is "to take the Nation's most dangerous recidivist criminals off the streets and imprison them for life." H.R. REP. NO. 103-463, *reprinted in* H.R. 3981, 103d Cong., at 3–4 (codified at 18 U.S.C. § 3559 (1994)). Senate Majority Leader Trent Lott explained the need for the federal legislation by noting that "[t]here is no doubt that a small hardened group of criminals commit most of the violent crimes in this country" and that "[m]any of the people involved in these crimes are released again and again because of the 'revolving door' of the prison system." 139 CONG. REC. 27,822–23 (1993).

[3] Between 1992 and 1995, forty-one states passed laws making it easier to try juveniles as adults. MELISSA SICKMUND, HOWARD N. SNYDER & EILEEN POE-YAMAGATA, NAT'L CTR. FOR JUVENILE JUSTICE, JUVENILE OFFENDERS AND VICTIMS: 1997 UPDATE ON VIOLENCE 30 (1997). Twenty-nine states now allow the prosecution of ten-year-olds for at least one offense. *See* HOWARD N. SNYDER & MELISSA SICKMUND, NAT'L CTR. FOR JUVENILE JUSTICE, JUVENILE OFFENDERS AND VICTIMS: A NATIONAL REPORT 88 (1995). Some of these states require juvenile court judges to agree to the transfer of juveniles to adult court, others leave the decision to transfer to prosecutorial discretion, and still others require the transfer for certain offenses. *See id.* at 85–89; *see generally* Eric K. Klein, *Dennis the Menace or Billy the Kid: An Analysis of the Role of Transfer to Criminal Court in Juvenile Justice*, 35 AM. CRIM. L. REV. 371, 401–09 (1998) (discussing the problems that result when children are tried as adults). According to a recent Justice Department report, "every state now has at least one provision to transfer juveniles to adult courts." KEVIN J. STROM, PROFILE OF STATE PRISONERS UNDER AGE 18, 1985–97, at 1 (Bureau of Justice: Special Report, NCJ 176989, 2000). As of 1997, twenty-eight states had statutes that automatically excluded certain types of offenders from juvenile court jurisdiction, fifteen states permitted prosecutors to file some juvenile cases in adult criminal courts directly, and forty-six states allowed juvenile court judges to send cases to adult courts at their discretion. *Id.* at 2. As a result of such changes, the number of young people sent to prison rose from 18 per 1000 violent crime arrestees under age eighteen in 1985 to 33 per 1000 arrestees in 1997. *Id.* at 5 tbl.4.

Legislative histories provide further evidence of the protective rationale underlying these reforms. The report for the 1994 California legislation, for example, explains the need for lowering the age of criminal prosecution from sixteen to fourteen by noting that "the public is legitimately concerned that crimes of violence committed by juveniles are increasing in number and in terms of the level of violence," and concluding that the legislation "is a rational response to the legitimate public desire to address what is a serious problem." A.B. 560, 1993–1994 Leg., Reg. Sess. (Cal. 1994) (enacted). The Congressional Research Service similarly summarizes the rationale for such state legislation: "locking up dangerous kids so that they will not commit further crimes." CONG. RESEARCH SERV., PUB. NO. 95-1152 GOV, JUVENILES IN THE ADULT CRIMINAL JUSTICE SYSTEM: AN OVERVIEW 5 (1995). Federal legislation that the House passed and that is pending in the Senate would reduce the age of presumptive adult prosecution to fourteen and would allow prosecution at thirteen for violent offenses and drug offenses. The "Background and Need for the Legislation" section of the bill indicates that "[i]n America today no population poses a larger threat to public safety than juvenile criminals." H.R. REP. NO. 105-86, at 14 (1997).

[4] *See, e.g.*, NEV. REV. STAT. 193.168 (1999) (enhancing criminal penalties for felonies committed to promote criminal gang activities); OKLA. STAT. ANN. tit. 21, §§ 856(D)–(F) (West Supp. 2000) (creating a crime encompassing gang recruitment activities); CAL. PENAL CODE § 186.22(a) (West Supp. 2001) (providing special penalties for facilitating gang crime); *see generally* Bart H. Rubin, Note, *Hail, Hail, The Gangs Are All Here: Why New York Should Adopt a Comprehensive Anti-Gang Statute*, 66 FORDHAM L. REV. 2033 (1998) (discussing the attributes of anti-gang statutes). The California statute is part of the state's Street Terrorism and Enforcement Prevention Act, which was a response to "a state of crisis which has been caused by violent street gangs whose

Law" statutes require community notification of convicted sex offenders.[5] "Sexual predator" statutes provide for the civil detention of sexual offenders who remain dangerous at the conclusion of their criminal commitment.[6] New sentencing guidelines increase the sentence of offenders with criminal histories because these offenders are seen as the most likely to commit future crimes.[7] These reforms boast as their common denominator greater official control over dangerous persons, a rationale readily apparent from each reform's legislative history.[8]

members threaten, terrorize, and commit a multitude of crimes against the peaceful citizens of their neighborhoods." CAL. PENAL CODE § 186.21 (West Supp. 1998).

This list of recent reforms focusing on dangerousness is not exhaustive. Many death penalty provisions also use dangerousness explicitly as a ground for imposing the death penalty rather than life imprisonment. *See, e.g.*, VA. CODE ANN. § 19.2-264.2 (Michie 2000); WASH. REV. CODE ANN. § 10.95.070(8) (West Supp. 1999); WYO. STAT. ANN. § 6-2-102(h)(xi) (Michie 1999). Sometimes lack of dangerousness is a mitigating factor in death penalty cases. *See, e.g.*, MD. CODE ANN., Crimes and Punishments § 413(g)(7) (1996). Occasionally criminal history is considered in sentencing instead of dangerousness. *See, e.g.*, ARK. CODE ANN. § 5-4-604(31) (Michie 1997); OKLA. STAT. tit. 21, § 701.12(1) (1991); CAL. PENAL CODE § 190.3(c) (West 1999); *see also* People v. Hawkins, 897 P.2d 574, 597 (1995) (finding that it was not error for a prosecutor to argue that the future dangerousness of the defendant was a factor weighing in favor of the death penalty). Correctional officers are sometimes required to exclude allegedly dangerous offenders from certain release programs. N.Y. LEGIS. EXEC. ORDER 5.1 (1996). Some shaming penalties are designed to "prevent future dangerous acts, rather than punish past action." Art Hubacher, *Every Picture Tells a Story: Is Kansas City's "John TV" Constitutional?*, 46 U. KAN. L. REV. 551, 587 (1998) (internal quotation marks omitted).

[5] Federal legislation creates financial incentives for states to enact such sexual offender registration statutes. 42 U.S.C. §§ 14071(g), (i). Most states have done so. *See, e.g.*, NAT'L INST. OF JUSTICE, SEX OFFENDER COMMUNITY NOTIFICATION 1 (Feb. 1997).

[6] Washington was the first state to pass such a law. *See* WASH. REV. CODE § 71.09 (1992). Other states have since enacted similar laws. *E.g.*, IOWA CODE § 901A.1 *et seq.*; KAN. STAT. ANN. § 59-29a01 (1994); MINN. STAT. §§ 253B.18, .185 (1994); WIS. STAT. ANN. § 980 (West 1998). The constitutionality of the Kansas statute was challenged in December, 1996. *See* Kansas v. Hendricks, 521 U.S. 346, 350 (1997) (sustaining the act). At that time, six states had such statutes — the other five being Arizona, California, Minnesota, Washington, and Wisconsin — and thirty-eight states, including New Jersey and New York, filed amicus briefs successfully urging the Justices to uphold the law. *Id.* at 371.

The promulgation of the Kansas statute was based on a finding that "sexually violent predators generally have anti-social personality features which are unamenable to existing mental illness treatment modalities[,] and those features render them likely to engage in sexually violent behavior[,] and that sexually violent predators' likelihood of engaging in repeat acts of predatory sexual violence is high." KAN. STAT. ANN. § 59-29a01 (1994).

[7] *See, e.g.*, U.S. SENTENCING GUIDELINES MANUAL ch. 4, pt. A (1998–99); *id.* at ch. 5, pt. A (providing guideline sentences as a function of "Offense Level" and "Criminal History Category"); ARIZ. REV. STAT. § 16-90-801(b)(1) (1995); DEL. CODE ANN. tit. 11, § 6580(c)(1) (1995); WASH. REV. CODE ANN. § 9.94A.010(1) (West 1985).

The rationale for heavy reliance upon criminal history in sentencing guidelines is its effectiveness in incapacitating dangerous offenders. As the *Guidelines Manual* of the United States Sentencing Commission explains, "the specific factors included in [the calculation of the Criminal History Category] are consistent with the extant empirical research assessing correlates of recidivism and patterns of career criminal behavior." U.S. SENTENCING GUIDELINES MANUAL 289 (1999).

[8] *See supra* notes 2–7.

Although the individual legislative histories make clear that a preventive rationale has motivated each of these reforms, the system's general shift from punishment toward prevention has not been accompanied by a corresponding shift in how the system presents itself. While increasingly designed to prevent dangerous persons from committing future crimes, the system still alleges that it is doing criminal "justice" and imposing "punishment." Yet it is impossible to "punish dangerousness." To "punish" is "to cause (a person) to undergo pain, loss, or suffering *for a crime or wrongdoing*"[9] — therefore, punishment can only exist in relation to a past wrong. "Dangerous" means "likely to cause injury, pain, etc."[10] — that is, dangerousness describes a threat of future harm. One can "restrain," "detain," or "incapacitate" a dangerous person, but one cannot logically "punish" dangerousness.

Why the shift to preventive detention? Why the wish to keep the old criminal "punishment" facade? These are the starting points of inquiry in this Commentary. It concludes that the trend of the last decade — the shifting of the criminal justice system toward the detention of dangerous offenders — is a move in the wrong direction. The difficulty lies not in the laudable attempt to prevent future crime but rather in the use of the criminal justice system as the vehicle to achieve that goal. The approach perverts the justice process and undercuts the criminal justice system's long-term effectiveness in controlling crime. At the same time, the basic features of the criminal justice system make it a costly yet ineffective preventive detention system.

Segregation of the punishment and prevention functions offers a superior alternative. Punishment and prevention are fundamentally different; they rely on different criteria and call for different procedures.[11] Punishment, especially through imprisonment, happily produces a beneficial collateral effect of incapacitation. If preventive detention is needed beyond the prison term of deserved punishment, it ought to be provided by a system that is open about its preventive purpose and is specifically designed to perform that function.

I. How Strong Is the Need for Increased Prevention?

It is difficult to deny that a society ought to be able to defend itself against persons who will cause serious harm. The goal of providing such protection underlies traditional civil commitment systems that detain persons who are dangerously mentally ill or who have contagious

---

[9] WEBSTER'S NEW WORLD COLLEGE DICTIONARY 1180 (2d ed. 1959) (emphasis added).

[10] *Id.* at 372.

[11] *See infra* pp. 1437–41.

diseases or drug dependencies.[12] In any case, political forces inevitably will press for protective measures if a perception of public vulnerability exists.

Given the history of crime rates, the recent enthusiasm for protective reforms is predictable. Despite recent declines, the violent crime rate remains more than three times higher than it was during the decade following World War II, when the baby-boomers, now the civic and political leaders, were growing up.[13] Today's aggravated assault rate is nearly four times what it was almost forty years ago.[14] News reports commonly celebrate that crime rates are back to the levels of the late 1970s, but fail to note that by that time the long unbroken string of annual crime increases had already tripled the rates of the 1950s.[15] Given the widening epidemic of juvenile crime, the unknown future effects of a wave of crack babies, and a host of other both predictable and unpredictable changes, the current decline in crime rates may not continue. Even if it did, the declining crime rate of the last eight years would have to continue unbroken for another three decades before crime levels returned to those enjoyed by baby-boomers as children.[16]

Even a return to the low crime rates of the 1950s would leave Americans with reason to be dissatisfied. As a result of the past decades of crime increases, people have seriously altered their lifestyles. We no longer let our children walk home from school. We dead bolt our doors, use "The Club" in our cars, and live in security-staffed apartment buildings and gated communities.[17] Current crime rates are high despite these precautions and would be even higher without them. Recapturing the security of life we enjoyed a half century ago would necessitate not only a return to the crime rates of the 1950s but

---

12 *See* Paul H. Robinson, *Foreword: The Criminal-Civil Distinction and Dangerous Blameless Offenders*, 83 J. CRIM. L. & CRIMINOLOGY 693, 711–14 & nn.57–68 (1993) (listing related authorities).

13 BUREAU OF JUSTICE STATISTICS, U.S. DEP'T OF JUSTICE, SOURCEBOOK OF CRIMINAL JUSTICE STATISTICS—1998, at 260 tbl.3.114 (Kathleen Maguire & Ann L. Pastore eds., 1999) [hereinafter SOURCEBOOK].

14 *Id.*

15 *Id.*

16 This takes into account a 7% decrease announced in preliminary data for 1999, FBI, U.S. DEP'T OF JUSTICE, PRELIMINARY ANNUAL UNIFORM CRIME REPORT — 1999, at 1 (1999), producing a total eight-year decline of 30.1%. *See also* Gary LaFree, *Social Institutions and the Crime "Bust" of the 1990s*, 88 J. CRIM. L. & CRIMINOLOGY 1325, 1340–43, fig.3 (1998) (showing that although the rates of rape, robbery, and aggravated assault are decreasing, further significant declines are needed to reach the 1950s' crime level).

17 A 1998 study reveals that 49% of the residents of the largest American cities avoided going out at night and 18% installed security systems. Steven K. Smith, Greg W. Steadman, Todd D. Minton & Meg Townsend, Criminal Victimization and Perceptions of Community Safety in 12 Cities, 1998, at 20–21 tbls.24 & 25 (NJJ 173940 1999), *available at* http://www.ojp.usdoj.gov/bjs/; *see also* SOURCEBOOK, *supra* note 13, at 121 tbls.2.41 & 2.42.

also the freedom of action enjoyed during that period. The seeming impossibility of such a return highlights how much we have lost to crime since the 1950s.

II. THE JUSTICE PROBLEMS

From this perspective, it is understandable that today's citizens are demanding greater protection and that legislators are seeking new ways to provide it.[18] But the use of the criminal justice system as the primary mechanism for preventing future crimes seriously perverts the goals of our institutions of justice.

Lowering the age for adult prosecution, with its longer terms of imprisonment, is likely to increase societal protection. Juveniles are committing an increasing number of serious crimes.[19] But decreasing the age at which a juvenile can be prosecuted as an adult increases the number of cases in which a young offender lacking the capacity for moral choice is nonetheless held criminally liable.

There is little dispute that many young offenders, especially those below the age of fifteen, lack the cognitive and control capacities of normal adults. Some may not appreciate the enormity of the consequences of their acts and others may lack normal behavior control mechanisms.[20] If an adult offender is similarly dysfunctional, due to insanity or involuntary intoxication for example, an excuse defense is generally available.[21] Yet a young offender impaired in a similar way

---

[18] Public opinion survey results rank crime as the second most serious problem facing the country, after "ethics, moral, family decline." SOURCEBOOK, *supra* note 13, at 96 tbl.2.1. A July 1999 survey found that 52% of the respondents believed that crime had risen in the previous year. *Id.* at 116 tbl.2.33. Public concern about crime rates continues in many communities, even after the crime drop. *See* Yvette Caig, *Crime Down 10 Percent in Fort Worth in 1997*, FORT WORTH STAR TELEGRAM, Jan. 13, 1998, at 1 (Metro) ("Although the release of the year-end crime statistics is cause for applause, the news comes amid heightened concern about a string of homicides since the new year began."); Bob von Sternberg, *Clearly, Life Is Good in Minnesota*, STAR TRIB. (Minneapolis-St. Paul), Jan. 27, 2000, at 1A ("The single national issue that concerns the largest number of Minnesotans is crime, cited by 13 percent of those polled — at a time when the rates of violent crime are plummeting.").

[19] Juveniles as a group are more dangerous persons today than a decade ago. For example, in 1976, juveniles between the ages of fourteen and seventeen accounted for 10.6 offenders per 100,000 in terms of murders and non-negligent homicides; by 1995, the figure had more than doubled to 23.0 offenders per 100,000. SOURCEBOOK, *supra* note 13, at 340 tbl.3.132.

[20] *See, e.g.*, ARTHUR T. JERSILD, CHARLES W. TELFORD & JANE M. SAWREY, CHILD PSYCHOLOGY 157 (7th ed. 1975); GLANVILLE WILLIAMS, CRIMINAL LAW: THE GENERAL PART 818 (2d ed. 1961) ("[I]t is only in a special sense that the child member of a delinquent gang can be said to know shoplifting or receiving stolen goods to be 'wrong.' He knows that such conduct is frowned upon by the police, and perhaps by his parents; but he does not himself feel it to be wrong.").

[21] Insanity, involuntary intoxication, and duress excuse a violator who has caused the harm or evil prohibited by an offense but who lacks the capacity to appreciate the wrongfulness of her conduct or to conform her conduct to the requirements of law. *See, e.g.*, MODEL PENAL CODE §§ 2.08(4), 2.09(1), 4.01(1) (1962). Because a person's lack of maturity can cause these same excus-

by immaturity has no defense or mitigation, because adult courts traditionally have not recognized an immaturity excuse.[22] Courts have had no need to make such an excuse available in the past for the obvious reason that juvenile courts dealt with the cases involving youthful offenders. The recent trend toward trying youths in adult courts has created the need for such an excuse defense, but none has been developed, perhaps because the defense would interfere with the goal of gaining control over dangerous offenders without regard to their blamelessness.

A more common and more damaging distortion of justice derives from the use of "three strikes" and other habitual-offender statutes, and the use of prevention-oriented sentencing guidelines that dramatically increase sentences for offenders with prior criminal records. These reforms affect nearly every case in which an offender has a prior criminal record.

Shocking cases of long-term imprisonment for minor offenses are well known. In *Rummel v. Estelle*,[23] for example, the defendant took $129.75 from a bar owner to fix the bar's air conditioner with no intention of actually doing so. His conviction for fraud was his third, qualifying him for a term of life imprisonment without the possibility of parole under an early "three strikes" statute.[24]

But problems are inherent not only in the shocking cases but in every case in which a habitual-offender statute or prior-record-based sentencing guideline applies. In these cases, the sentence imposed exceeds the deserved punishment, albeit to a less dramatic extent than life imprisonment for minor check fraud. The imposition of that excess punishment is, of course, the motivating goal of such statutes: they significantly increase the sentence beyond the level deserved for the crime because a prior record may predict future offenses. But the effect of such a policy is that the criminal justice system *regularly* imposes sentences that exceed the punishment deserved. Sentencing guidelines that give great weight to prior criminal records and "three strikes" and related habitual-offender provisions commonly double, triple, or quadruple the punishment imposed on repeat offenders.[25] An

---

ing conditions, an immaturity defense logically should be part of the criminal law's system of excuses. For a general discussion of the conceptual analogy among excuses, see PAUL H. ROBINSON, CRIMINAL LAW 477–94 (1997).

[22] Instead, states provide for the transfer of jurisdiction to juvenile court for all defendants below a given age. *See generally* 2 PAUL H. ROBINSON, CRIMINAL LAW DEFENSES § 175 (1984 & Supp. 1998).

[23] 445 U.S. 263 (1980). The three prior fraud convictions that qualified Rummel for a life term involved a total of $229.11. *Id.* at 265–66.

[24] *Id.* at 284–85.

[25] Under three strikes statutes, for example, the criminal history often quadruples the sentence that would be imposed for the identical offense by the identical offender with no criminal history.

initial portion of the sentence may well be deserved, but what follows is a purely preventive detention portion that cannot be justified as deserved punishment.

One can construct a theory that makes a prior criminal record relevant to deserved punishment, as Andrew von Hirsch has done.[26] By committing an offense after a previous conviction, an offender might be seen as "thumbing his nose" at the justice system. Such disregard may justify some incremental increase in punishment over that deserved by a first-time offender, but it seems difficult to justify the doubling, tripling, or quadrupling of punishment because of nose-thumbing.[27] The recidivist nature of a second robbery is only one of

A twenty-five year old offender committing a felony that normally carries a ten-year sentence, for which less than ten years ordinarily would be served, can get mandatory life imprisonment without the possibility of parole, which may mean a sentence of forty-five years or more. *See* CLARK, AUSTIN & HENRY, *supra* note 2, at 7–9, exhibit 9; *see also, e.g.*, DEL. CODE ANN. tit. 11, § 4214 (1995) (stating that a third felony conviction carries a life sentence for violations including kidnapping and aggravated robbery); 720 ILL. COMP. STAT. ANN. 5/33B-1 (West Supp. 1998) (stating that a third felony conviction carries a life sentence for violations including Class X felonies and criminal sexual assault).

Even the less drastic habitual-offender statutes, which have been in use for some time, can have a substantial effect on the amount of punishment inflicted on an offender. For example, the *Model Penal Code* provision, which is the structural model for many habitual-offender statutes, allows an "extended term of imprisonment" that essentially doubles the maximum authorized sentence for a repeat offender: the maximum sentence is increased from five years to ten years for a third-degree felony, from ten years to twenty years for a second-degree felony, and from twenty years to life imprisonment for a first-degree felony. MODEL PENAL CODE §§ 6.07, 7.03(3)–(4) (1962).

Even in the absence of either three strikes or habitual-offender statutes, sentencing guidelines that tie a sentence in part to an offender's criminal history provide for a similar increase in punishment for dangerousness. Under the *Guidelines Manual*, for example, an individual who commits a level 10 offense receives a sentence of 6 to 12 months if he has no criminal record but receives a sentence of 24 to 30 months if he has a significant record; an individual who commits a level 19 offense receives a sentence of 30 to 37 months if he has no criminal record but receives a sentence of 63 to 78 months if he has a significant record; and an individual who commits a level 37 offense receives a sentence of 210 to 262 months if he has no criminal record but receives a sentence of 360 to life imprisonment if he has a significant record. *See* U.S. SENTENCING GUIDELINES MANUAL ch. 5, pt. A, sentencing tbl. (1997).

[26] ANDREW VON HIRSCH, DOING JUSTICE: THE CHOICE OF PUNISHMENTS 85 (1976). But von Hirsch later withdrew much of his support for such a theory and relied instead on a different theory suggesting that a discount in punishment may be appropriate for first-time offenders. *See* ANDREW VON HIRSCH, PAST OR FUTURE CRIMES: DESERVEDNESS AND DANGEROUSNESS IN THE SENTENCING OF CRIMINALS 78–85 (1985) [hereinafter VON HIRSCH, PAST OR FUTURE CRIMES].

[27] If a nose-thumbing theory does not work, one might argue that additional punishment can serve as a sort of lingering suspended sentence from the past offenses. But that argument is inconsistent with the facts. None of the reforms that look to past criminal history consider whether the sentences for past offenses were carried out in full or suspended. In fact, none of the reforms consider prior sentences at all. Two offenders with identical criminal histories who commit identical present offenses will receive identical treatment under recent reforms even if one offender has served many long prison terms and the other has served none. Clearly, it is future dangerousness that is the concern; under the theory of the reforms, identical criminal history suggests identical dangerousness.

many characteristics that determine blameworthiness.[28] Lay intuitions may see the nose-thumbing as making the second robbery more condemnable than the first but not more condemnable than the second robbery itself, and certainly not twice as condemnable as the second robbery. But note that, although nose-thumbing may justify a minor portion of the dramatic increases imposed for a prior record, the theory allows proponents of preventive detention to implement their program unobtrusively within a system of criminal punishment.

Further, if such disrespect for law provided the impetus for these statutes, the aggravation of blameworthiness and increased punishment would apply to all offenses. That is, if nose-thumbing is itself condemnable, then it ought to be condemnable in every context, not just in selected contexts. Nose-thumbing through a second violent offense might be more condemnable than nose-thumbing through a second theft offense, but nose-thumbing through a second theft would hardly be irrelevant. Yet the three strikes provisions typically apply only to a limited class of offenses — commonly violent offenses[29] — and typically account for only certain kinds of criminal history — again, commonly a history of violent offenses.[30] It seems difficult to construct a desert theory of nose-thumbing disrespect that allows for such selective increases in punishment. But note that applying habitual-offender schemes only to violent offenses does make sense under a prevention rationale, however, because these offenses most demand prevention.

The criminal justice system's focus on dangerousness also causes, albeit less frequently, distortions of the reverse sort: failures of justice in which a person fails to receive the punishment he or she deserves. This kind of error can occur both in the assignment of liability and in the assessment of the proper amount of punishment. For example, the Model Penal Code provides a defense to inchoate liability if a person "presents [no] public danger" and the person's attempt was "inherently unlikely" to succeed.[31] Such a defense may make sense for a system designed to incapacitate the dangerous person because incarcerating the nondangerous attempter is a waste of preventive resources. But if the person believes his conduct will cause a criminal harm, the person deserves punishment whether or not the chosen method is likely to succeed. For example, the HIV-positive son who attempts to kill his

---

28 Von Hirsch agrees with this conclusion. *See* VON HIRSCH, PAST OR FUTURE CRIMES, *supra* note 26, at 131–36 (1985).

29 *See* CLARK, AUSTIN & HENRY, *supra* note 2, at 7–9, exhibit 9 (providing a table that lists the various offenses that states include in habitual-offender sentencing schemes).

30 *See, e.g.*, WASH. REV. CODE §§ 9.94A.030(23), 9.94A.030(27), 9.94.120(4) (1985); MD. ANN. CODE art. 27, § 643B (1996).

31 MODEL PENAL CODE § 5.05(2) (1962).

long-hated father by spitting on him[32] can escape liability if the killing method is impossible and he is not otherwise dangerous.[33] But if the son's intention to kill his father unjustifiably is real and he has shown a willingness to carry out the intention fully, his blameworthiness is clear.

Such failures of justice are more common in sentencing, at least in the discretionary systems that abounded two decades ago and that still exist in many jurisdictions. The judge who focuses on prevention instead of desert[34] will give a minor sentence for a serious offense if the offender is no longer dangerous. Thus, the recently discovered, elderly former Nazi concentration camp official can escape the punishment he deserves.[35]

These conflicts between pursuing justice and incapacitating dangerous persons should come as no surprise. Dangerousness and desert are distinct criteria that commonly diverge. Desert arises from a past wrong, whereas dangerousness arises from the prediction of a future wrong. A person may be dangerous but not blameworthy, or vice versa. Consider, for example, a mentally ill offender. A desert distributive principle acquits the dysfunctional person of all criminal liability because the person is not to blame for the offense; he deserves no punishment. But an incapacitation principle would impose liability and require incapacitation because the offender is dangerous.[36]

In a reverse set of cases, an incapacitation principle does not call for punishment of an offender even though the desert principle calls for conviction, as with the elderly Nazi official and the HIV-positive

---

32 For examples of such HIV-mistaken-effect attacks, see *State v. Smith*, 621 A.2d 493 (N.J. Super. Ct. App. Div. 1993).

33 Assume, for example, that the despised father subsequently dies from natural causes and the son is therefore no longer dangerous. Alternatively, consider the son who poisons a hated mother with watermelon juice, falsely believing that such juice can cause a fatal allergic reaction. The son is as blameworthy as an attempted murderer. Even if watermelon allergies do not exist, and even if the despised mother has since died of natural causes so that the son is admittedly no longer a danger to anyone, allowing a defense in this hypothetical is a failure of justice that the Model Penal Code provision promotes.

34 In a 1981 study, forty-five percent of judges did not think that "just deserts" was important. *See* S. REP. NO. 98-225, at 41 n.18 (1983) (citing INSLAW/Yankelovich, Skelly & White, Inc., Federal Sentencing III-4 (1981)); *see also* ANTHONY PARTRIDGE & WILLIAM B. ELDRIDGE, FEDERAL JUDICIAL CENTER, THE SECOND CIRCUIT SENTENCING STUDY: A REPORT TO THE JUDGES OF THE SECOND CIRCUIT (1974).

35 The Nazi official may now be a productive member of society, presenting no need for incapacitation or rehabilitation. Yet even if the circumstances of the Third Reich will never arise again, the offender is blameworthy, and the desert principle insists he receive punishment for his past offense.

36 Other utilitarian distributive principles also might impose liability. Punishing such an offender reinforces the general prohibition against such offenses; that is, it serves a general deterrent purpose. Moreover, such an offender may need rehabilitation.

spitter.[37] Because the person's conduct is harmless and the person is not otherwise dangerous, an incapacitation principle suggests that imposing criminal sanctions is a waste of resources.[38] The desert principle, in contrast, takes the person's attempt to kill as evidence of blameworthiness deserving punishment.

III. THE INEVITABLE CONFLICT BETWEEN DESERT AND DANGEROUSNESS AS DISTRIBUTIVE CRITERIA

The inherent conflict between incapacitation and desert has practical implications, as in the difference in the kinds of factors taken into account in assessing liability and determining sentences. If incapacitation of the dangerous alone determined the distribution of criminal sanctions, prison terms would be set according to those factors that best predicted future crime. The higher the likelihood of recidivism, the stronger the case for imprisonment and, often, the longer the sentence. One of the best predictors of future criminality is employment history.[39] Thus, unemployment for the two years preceding the crime could aggravate the grade of an offense or increase the imposed sentence. An offender's age and family situation are also good predictors of future criminality,[40] and thus could also determine the offender's liability and sentence: younger offenders and offenders without fathers in the home would receive longer prison terms. Indeed, if incapacitation of the dangerous were the only distributive principle, there would be little reason to wait until an offense were committed to impose criminal liability and sanctions; it would be more effective to screen

---

[37] Consider also the practitioner of "voodoo" who tries to kill by placing a spell or by sticking needles into a doll.

[38] It is this utilitarian reasoning that leads the Model Penal Code to provide a defense for an "inherently unlikely" attempt. *See supra* p. 1437.

[39] *See, e.g.*, DON M. GOTTFREDSON, LESLIE T. WILKINS & PETER B. HOFFMAN, GUIDELINES FOR PAROLE AND SENTENCING 41–67 (1978) (including employment history in a list of nine factors best predicting future criminality); PETER W. GREENWOOD WITH ALLAN ABRAHAMSE, SELECTIVE INCAPACITATION 105–06 (1982) (noting that employment history "is somewhat associated with . . . offense rates").

[40] Researchers have found age to be an effective predictor of future violence. *See, e.g.*, Joseph J. Cocozza & Henry J. Steadman, *Some Refinements in the Measurement and Prediction of Dangerous Behavior*, 131 AM. J. PSYCHIATRY 1012 (1974). Various aspects of an offender's family situation are also of predictive value. *See, e.g.*, Alfred Blumstein, David P. Farrington & Soumyo Moitra, *Delinquency Careers: Innocents, Desisters, and Persisters*, *in* 6 CRIME AND JUSTICE: AN ANNUAL REVIEW OF RESEARCH 187, 198 (Michael Tonry & Norval Morris eds., 1985). Greenwood identifies several other factors of predictive value: prior convictions of the instant offense type; incarceration for more than half of the preceding two years; conviction before the age of sixteen; time served in a state juvenile facility; drug use during the preceding two years; and employment during less than half of the preceding two years. GREENWOOD WITH ABRAHAMSE, *supra* note 39, at 50.

the general population and "convict" those found dangerous and in need of incapacitation.[41]

Yet openly relying on the factors relevant to an incapacitative principle would be offensive to a system of just punishment. A person does not deserve more punishment for an offense because he has a poor employment history, is young, or has no father in his household.[42] And certainly, no person deserves punishment before committing an offense.

The incapacitative principle not only focuses on different criteria than the desert principle, but also wholly neglects factors central to the desert principle. Even the nature of the crime committed may be of little relevance if the goal is prevention. Consider, for example, the Model Sentencing Act, which was drafted in the early 1960s and con-

---

[41] One study suggests that rapists may be distinguished from nonrapists based on their penile erection response to certain stimuli. Gene G. Abel, David H. Barlow, Edward B. Blanchard & Donald Guild, *The Components of Rapists' Sexual Arousal*, 34 ARCHIVES GEN. PSYCHIATRY 895, 895 (1977). If the predictive technique were sufficiently refined, a pure incapacitation distributive principle might find it an appropriate basis for distributing criminal liability. *See generally* Sanford H. Kadish, *The Decline of Innocence*, 26 CAMBRIDGE L.J. 273 (1968).

A similar analysis applies to the utilitarian crime-control principles of deterrence and rehabilitation. If deterrence were the sole distributive principle for liability and punishment, potential offenders' perceptions of the probability of apprehension would be highly relevant in determining the sanction needed to deter effectively. Offenses with a perceived low probability of apprehension would require more severe punishment to compensate for that perception.

Potential offenders' perceptions of the likelihood of conviction also can prove powerful. Thus, it may be useful to drop those requirements of liability that prosecutors find difficult to prove, such as culpability requirements (for example, intention and recklessness), because such reforms would increase the perceived likelihood of conviction.

A pure deterrence principle also would base liability on how widely the sanction is known. Just as an advertising executive willingly pays more for an advertisement that will reach more people, the cost of a higher criminal sanction is a good investment if its deterrent message will reach more people. Thus, greater news coverage of a case would aggravate the grade of the offense, lengthening the imposed prison term.

If rehabilitation governed the distribution of punishment, a person's amenability to treatment would act as the primary variable. Recall that fully indeterminate sentences were recently imposed in furtherance of the rehabilitative purpose. The length of the sentence was determined by the length of time necessary for rehabilitation of the offender — a factor eluding predetermination. The offender's term of imprisonment continued indefinitely until the offender was rehabilitated. Thus, a minor offense might call for long-term incarceration and a serious offense might call for no incarceration, if long-term treatment were required to avoid recidivism in the first case and no treatment were required in the second.

Indeed, with a pure rehabilitation principle, as with incapacitation, there is little reason to wait for an offense to occur. Screening of the population would determine those people likely to commit future offenses absent rehabilitative treatment, followed by the imposition of liability and sanctions to compel the required treatment and thereby to avoid the anticipated crime.

[42] Nor does a person deserve more punishment because his offense is one with a perceived low apprehension or conviction rate or because of aggressive news coverage — factors that increase the length of incarceration under a deterrence principle. Similarly, a person does not deserve more punishment because the kind of rehabilitation program that might help him takes longer than other programs — a factor that increases the length of incarceration under a rehabilitative principle.

siders only the purposes of rehabilitation and incapacitation of the dangerous. The Report of Model Act proudly points out:

> The [Act] diminishes [differences in] sentencing according to the particular offense. Under [the Act] the dangerous offender may be committed to a lengthy term; the non dangerous defendant may not. It makes available, for the first time, a plan that allows the sentence to be determined by the defendant's make-up, his potential threat in the future, and other similar factors, with a minimum of variation according to the offense.[43]

The point is that the traditional principles of incapacitation and desert conflict; they inevitably distribute liability and punishment differently. To advance one, the system must sacrifice the other. The irreconcilable differences reflect the fact that prevention and desert seek to achieve different goals. Incapacitation concerns itself with the future — avoiding future crimes. Desert concerns itself with the past — allocating punishment for past offenses.

IV. DENYING THE CONFLICT

One of the most troublesome aspects of the conflict between incapacitation and desert is the denial that it exists. People commonly believe that incapacitation and desert somehow can combine or reconcile in a way that allows both to achieve their objectives. The Model Penal Code of the American Law Institute, for example, lists all of the traditional purposes of sentencing, including incapacitation and desert, and then directs judges to fashion sentences that most effectively further all of the purposes.[44] The Code's commentary explains that if the purposes conflict in a particular case they should be "justly harmonized."[45] Other writers have suggested that these competing interests

---

[43] Council of Judges of the National Council on Crime and Delinquency, *Model Sentencing Act: Second Edition*, 18 CRIME AND DELINQUENCY 335, 341 (1972). There is disagreement as to whether a deterrence principle generates liability proportional to the seriousness of the offense. *Compare, e.g.*, Ernest van den Haag, *Punishment as a Device for Controlling the Crime Rate*, 33 RUTGERS L. REV. 706, 713 (1981) (suggesting that deterrence calls for proportionality), *with* Alan H. Goldman, *Beyond the Deterrence Theory: Comments on van den Haag's "Punishment as a Device for Controlling the Crime Rate"*, 33 RUTGERS L. REV. 721 (1981) (criticizing van den Haag's theory for its asymmetry and for its failure to allow punishment for all who deserve it).

[44] MODEL PENAL CODE § 1.02(2) (1962).

[45] The Commentary explains the Code's rationale:

> The section is drafted in the view that sentencing and treatment policy should serve the end of crime prevention. It does not undertake, however, to state a fixed priority among the means to such prevention, i.e., the deterrence of potential criminals and the incapacitation and correction of the individual offender. These are all proper goals to be pursued in social action with respect to the offender, one or another of which may call for the larger emphasis in a particular context or situation. What the Code seeks is the just harmonizing of these subordinate objectives, rather than the concentration on some single target of this kind. It is also recognized that not even crime prevention can be said to be the only end involved. The correction and rehabilitation of offenders is a social value in itself, as well as a preventive instrument. Basic considerations of justice demand,

are to be "balance[d],"[46] or "blended,"[47] or "accommodate[d]."[48]

But how can this be done? When incapacitation and desert conflict, the principles suggest different sentences, and a judge or sentencing commission must choose between purposes. Furthering one aim necessitates sacrificing the other. Or, if a judge averages the sentences advocated by the two conflicting purposes, the resulting sentence may serve neither function effectively.[49]

Norval Morris and others offer another argument to deny the existence of the conflict — a system may set sentences according to dangerousness without violating desert principles simply by avoiding any extreme disparity between levels of punishment and blameworthiness.[50] This view conceives of desert as having only vague requirements, which operate at the extremes of disproportionality. Under this view, desert requires no particular sentence; it merely sets the outer limits of a range of just punishments.

But to those who study the demands of desert, its requirements are not so vague or flexible. Von Hirsch, for example, notes that the principle of desert necessitates an ordinal ranking of cases[51] — justice requires that offenders of lesser blameworthiness receive less punishment than offenders of greater blameworthiness. Given the finite range over which the amount of punishment can vary and the large number of distinctions commonly recognized between degrees of blameworthiness, the punishment deserved in a particular case falls into a narrow range. The range is determined not by some special connection between that degree of blameworthiness and that amount of punishment, but by the need to distinguish a given case from the large number of other cases of distinguishable blameworthiness. Empirical research

---

> moreover, that penal law safeguard offenders against excessive, disproportionate or arbitrary punishment, that it afford fair warning of the nature of the sentences that may be imposed upon conviction and that differences among offenders be reflected in the just individualization of their treatment.

MODEL PENAL CODE § 1.02 cmt. at 2 (Tentative Draft No. 2, 1954).

[46] Stanley A. Cohen, *An Introduction to the Theory, Justifications and Modern Manifestations of Criminal Punishment*, 27 MCGILL L.J. 73, 81 (1981).

[47] REPORT OF THE CANADIAN COMMITTEE ON CORRECTIONS — TOWARD UNITY: CRIMINAL JUSTICE AND CORRECTIONS 188 (1969) (commonly referred to as the Ouimet Report).

[48] Cohen, *supra* note 46, at 73.

[49] *See generally* Paul H. Robinson, *Hybrid Principles for the Distribution of Criminal Sanctions*, 82 NW. U. L. REV. 19 (1987); Paul H. Robinson, *Why Does the Criminal Law Care What the Lay Person Thinks Is Just? Coercive Versus Normative Crime Control*, 86 VA. L. REV. 1939 (2000).

[50] *See* NORVAL MORRIS, THE FUTURE OF IMPRISONMENT 73–76 (1974); Norval Morris & Marc Miller, *Predictions of Dangerousness*, *in* 6 CRIME AND JUSTICE: AN ANNUAL REVIEW OF RESEARCH 1, 35 (1985).

[51] *See* VON HIRSCH, PAST OR FUTURE CRIMES, *supra* note 26, at 40.

supports this view.[52] Small differences in facts often create a significant shift in shared lay perceptions of the punishment deserved. (Note that it is the amount of punishment, not the means of punishment, that is constrained by desert. Thus, preventive concerns may properly guide the selection of a sentencing method without offending desert.[53])

V. THE UTILITY OF DESERT

The justice problems resulting from the conflict between incapacitation and desert are significant not only because doing justice is an important value in its own right — the nonconsequentialist, retributivist view — but also because doing justice can have important crime-prevention effects — the consequentialist, utilitarian argument. As I have argued elsewhere,[54] the moral credibility of the criminal law, built on community perceptions that the criminal justice system distributes liability and punishment justly, gives the criminal law crime-control power. If the criminal law has moral authority, it can stigmatize offenders and, for some, the fear of stigma will deter prohibited conduct. More importantly, moral authority gives the criminal law persuasive power to label as morally condemnable conduct that was not previously seen as such. That is, a criminal law with moral credibility can facilitate the internalization of norms that counsel against prohibited conduct. It is this internalization of norms by individuals and their family and acquaintances that has the greatest effect in controlling conduct, more than threats of official liability and punishment. Finally, a criminal law with moral authority can influence conduct by helping to shape community norms. Norms relating to drunk driving and domestic violence, for example, have evolved in part because more severe criminal penalties and related reforms painted such conduct as more morally condemnable than previously thought.

---

52 *See, e.g.*, PAUL H. ROBINSON & JOHN M. DARLEY, JUSTICE, LIABILITY, AND BLAME: COMMUNITY VIEWS AND THE CRIMINAL LAW 229–71, 273 (1995) (reporting empirical studies of lay intuitions on a broad range of substantive criminal law issues, the results of which indicate substantial agreement among subjects). Presented with a dozen scenarios describing similar but different cases, subjects in the studies generally agreed on the rank and even relative relation of the cases as to the amount of punishment deserved. Some of the subjects imposed generally longer sentences, some generally shorter sentences, but both harsh and lenient sentencers typically agreed on the *pattern* of relative blameworthiness among the cases, even in instances in which the factual differences among the cases were slight. Further, the agreement among subjects extended across gender, education, income, political affiliation, and most other significant demographic variables. *See id.* at 223, 226.

53 Paul H. Robinson, *Desert, Crime Control, Disparity, and Units of Punishment*, *in* PENAL THEORY AND PRACTICE: TRADITION AND INNOVATION IN CRIMINAL JUSTICE 93–105 (Antony Duff, Sandra Marshall, Rebecca Emerson Dobash & Russell P. Dobash eds., 1994).

54 *See generally* Paul H. Robinson & John M. Darley, *The Utility of Desert*, 91 NW. U. L. REV. 453 (1997).

The strength of these crime-control powers of criminal law is a function of the criminal law's moral credibility. A criminal justice system in the business of preventive detention, rather than administration of justice, can expect no more moral authority than that afforded doctors who determine whether a mentally ill person is sufficiently dangerous to be civilly committed. Requiring the criminal justice system to distribute punishment according to predictions of future dangerousness rather than blameworthiness for past crimes can only undercut the system's moral credibility. Citizens initially pleased by the added protection that preventive detention reforms provide, nonetheless may accurately perceive that the system is no longer in the business of doing justice. As criminal liability is increasingly disconnected from moral blameworthiness, the criminal law can exercise less moral authority to change norms or to cause the internalization of norms. In the long run, then, using the criminal justice system as a mechanism for preventive detention may undercut the very crime prevention goal that is offered to justify such use.

VI. CLOAKING PREVENTIVE DETENTION AS CRIMINAL JUSTICE

It is ironic that the perversions of justice suffered in the name of prevention actually produce a seriously flawed prevention system. These prevention difficulties arise primarily because of the perceived need to cloak preventive measures as doctrines of criminal punishment to make them appear consistent with a criminal *justice* system that imposes *punishment*.

Why should this be so? If reformers want to detain dangerous offenders, why not adopt a system that is open about its preventive detention nature and its intention to fill any preventive need remaining after criminal justice incarceration? Most jurisdictions allow civil commitment of persons who are dangerous because of mental illness, drug dependency, or contagious disease.[55] Why is there reluctance to detain preventively offenders who remain dangerous at the conclusion of their deserved criminal terms of imprisonment?

The intense controversy surrounding the preventive detention legislation of the 1960s may help to explain this reluctance.[56] Critics de-

---

[55] *See* Robinson, *supra* note 12, at 711–14 & nn.57–68.

[56] For a chronological list of preventive detention enactments, see Barbara Gottlieb, *The Pretrial Processing of "Dangerous" Defendants: A Comparative Analysis of State Laws* (Nat'l Inst. of Justice Study, 1984), *reprinted in* Report on Bail Reform Act of 1984, H.R. REP. NO. 98-121, app. A, at 90. The first statutes appeared in Alaska and Delaware in 1967, Maryland and South Carolina in 1969, Vermont in 1967 and 1969, and the District of Columbia in 1970. Despite the constitutional approval of pretrial preventive detention, United States v. Edwards, 430 A.2d 1321, 1343 (D.C. 1981), *cert. denied*, 455 U.S. 1022 (1982), many jurisdictions have refused to enact such a system. The twenty-four states authorizing pretrial detention are listed in Gottlieb, *supra*, at 76.

nounced the legislation as "Clockwork Orange"[57] and "'Alice in Wonderland' justice" in which the punishment precedes the offense[58] and as introducing a "police state"[59] and "fostering tyranny."[60] Opponents described it as "intellectually dishonest,"[61] characterized it as "one of the most tragic mistakes we as a society could make,"[62] and feared that it "would change the complexion of American justice."[63] Preventive detention was "simply not the American way."[64]

A large part of the perceived problem with the 1960s preventive detention legislation was that it provided *pretrial* preventive detention. In contrast, most current reforms provide preventive detention only after trial and conviction, an important difference.[65]

---

57 Glen Elsasser, *U.S. Defends Pretrial Jailings of Suspects Seen as Dangerous*, CHI. TRIB., Jan. 22, 1987, § 1, at 16 (quoting critics).

58 Elder Witt, *Preventive-Detention Statute Is Upheld as Constitutional*, CONG. Q. WKLY. REP., May 30, 1987, at 1141 (quoting Professor Alan Dershowitz).

59 *E.g.*, Ethan Bronner, *Court Upholds Pretrial Jailing*, BOSTON GLOBE, May 27, 1987, at 1 (quoting Justice Marshall); *Gotti Being Held Under Tough Bail Reform Act*, LAS VEGAS REV. J., Dec. 17, 1990, at A7; Caryle Murphy, *Law Allowing Denial of Bail Provokes Debate on Rights*, WASH. POST, Aug. 1, 1986, at A1 (quoting Judge Jon O. Newman); Herb Robinson, *Judge's Dilemma Delicate Balance in Bail Rulings*, SEATTLE TIMES, May 21, 1986, at A14.

60 James J. Kilpatrick, *A Cautious "Yes" on Preventive Detention*, SEATTLE TIMES, June 3, 1987, at A12 (citing Justice Marshall).

61 Edwin M. Yoder Jr., *A Gross Judicial Assault on Personal Liberties*, HOUSTON CHRON., May 31, 1987, at 2.

62 *Say 'No' to No Bail*, RECORD, N. N.J., Nov. 19, 1986, at A22 (quoting New Jersey Senate President John Russo, a former prosecutor).

63 Richard Lacayo, *First the Sentence, Then the Trial*, TIME, June 8, 1987, at 69.

64 Alan Dershowitz, *'Wonderland' Court Trashes Our Safeguards*, CHI. SUN-TIMES, June 7, 1987, at 11.

65 Not all of the dangerousness reforms can claim this distinction. If dangerousness rationales set the minimum conduct requirements for criminal liability — as in expanding the scope of attempt and conspiracy to include persons thought to be dangerous — the system encompasses people who would not otherwise have been judged sufficiently blameworthy to merit criminal conviction, but who now will be criminally convicted and detained. It is true that detention requires proof of certain past conduct, not just the prediction of future conduct, but if the past conduct is not itself condemnable but is taken as a predictor of future criminality, the distinction between pretrial preventive detention and the new "criminal conduct" is less clear.

Indeed, in some respects, one can argue that pretrial preventive detention is less objectionable than prevention-based expansions of criminal liability and punishment. The data suggest that after pretrial preventive detention, the detainee is almost always convicted of an offense. One would expect as much because the strength of the prosecution's case is one of the factors the judge must consider in determining whether to permit pretrial preventive detention. For example, under the federal pretrial preventive detention scheme, the judge must consider not only the offense charged and the defendant's dangerousness, but also "the weight of the evidence against the person." 18 U.S.C. § 3142(g)(2) (1984). At sentencing, the convicted offender receives credit toward the sentence for the time served during pretrial detention. In the end, then, a convicted offender is not materially harmed by the pretrial detention (although there may still be a risk of injustice and a breach of traditional due process). At least theoretically, an offender serves only the time deserved. The person caught in the prevention-based expansion of liability and punishment, in contrast, is subject to post-trial detention based solely on his predicted dangerousness.

Yet the primary criticism of pretrial preventive detention — that the sentence precedes the trial — can also be applied to the postconviction preventive detention reforms. Detention for longer than the deserved term of imprisonment is justified as preventing predicted *future* crimes. Such detention not only punishes an offense for which the detainee has not yet been convicted, but also punishes an offense that he has not yet committed.

But the ability to punish the uncommitted crime, and thereby prevent it, is the genius of the current system's cloaking of preventive detention as criminal justice. By obscuring the preventive nature of the liability and sentence, by making it appear not so entirely different from a criminal justice system of deserved punishment, the preventive detention controversy can be avoided entirely.

VII. THE PRACTICAL VALUE OF CREATING DESERT-DANGEROUSNESS AMBIGUITY

The practical advantage of cloaking preventive detention as criminal justice lies in the opportunity it provides to bypass the logical restrictions on preventive detention. First, if the justification for detention is dangerousness, then logically the government ought to be required periodically to prove the detainee's continuing dangerousness. If the dangerousness disappears, so does the justification for detention. However, if the detention is characterized as deserved punishment for a past offense, there is little reason to revisit the justification for the detention. The factors relevant to determining deserved punishment may be weighed at the time of sentencing: the offender's conduct, state of mind, and capacities at the time of the offense and the resulting harm or evil. Thus, characterizing preventive detention as deserved punishment obscures the need for periodic review.

Second, if a person is detained for society's benefit rather than as deserved punishment, the conditions of detention should not be punitive. The preventive detainee is not being punished but rather is suffering an intrusion of liberty for the benefit of society. The mentally ill, drug-dependent, or contagious disease detainee logically ought to and often does enjoy better conditions than the person suffering punishment.[66] In contrast, if confinement serves to impose deserved punishment, the offender has little justification for complaining about punitive conditions. One of the points of imprisonment is, within the bounds of human dignity, to induce suffering. By cloaking preventive

[66] *See, e.g.*, GLANVILLE WILLIAMS, CRIMINAL LAW: THE GENERAL PART 829–36 (2d ed. 1961) (discussing the practice and rationale for nonpunitive conditions of detention for civilly committed juvenile delinquents).

detention as deserved punishment, the system avoids having to justify its failure to provide nonpunitive conditions of preventive detention.

Third, prevention-justified restraint should logically be limited to the minimum required to ensure the community's safety. If house arrest, an ankle bracelet, drug therapy, or other alternatives to incarceration provide adequate protection, then greater levels of restraint cannot be justified.[67] No such minimum-restraint principle applies to deserved punishment. Indeed, Dan Kahan and others argue that imprisonment is a preferred form of punishment because of its expressive power of condemnation.[68] Cloaking preventive detention as criminal justice, then, permits authorities to avoid demonstrating that detention is the least intrusive restraint adequate for protection.

Finally, consistent with the preventive detention principle of minimum restraint, a detainee should be entitled to treatment if it can reduce the length or intrusiveness of the restraint. No similar claim to treatment is available if the justification for incarceration is retributive. The person incarcerated as deserved punishment has no greater claim to government-provided treatment than any other citizen.

Thus, reformers benefit from all of these practical implications by cloaking preventive detention as criminal justice. By continuing to present itself as "doing justice" — by obscuring the preventive nature of reforms with ambiguity as to their purpose — the system can provide preventive detention without the constraints that logically would attend an explicit preventive detention system.

VIII. SURREPTITIOUSLY DISCOUNTING THE SIGNIFICANCE OF RESULTING HARM

Diverting the criminal justice system from upholding justice to advancing preventive detention is not an entirely new phenomenon. The seeds of this shift from desert to dangerousness were planted at least as early as the 1950s with the rehabilitation movement. For example, the Model Penal Code, promulgated in 1962, generally grades inchoate of-

[67] *See generally* NORVAL MORRIS & MICHAEL TONRY, BETWEEN PRISON AND PROBATION: INTERMEDIATE PUNISHMENTS IN A RATIONAL SENTENCING SYSTEM 3, 176–220 (1990) (discussing a full range of sanctions between imprisonment and probation).

[68] *See, e.g.*, Dan M. Kahan, *Social Influence, Social Meaning, and Deterrence*, 83 VA. L. REV. 349, 362–63, 384 (1997) (suggesting that the form of punishment conveys a social meaning: "Imprisonment is an extraordinarily potent gesture of moral disapproval; because of the symbolic importance of individual liberty in American culture, there is never a doubt that society means to condemn someone when it takes that person's freedom away."); Dan M. Kahan, *What Do Alternative Sanctions Mean?*, 63 U. CHI. L. REV. 591, 594–605 (1996) (discussing the "expressive dimension" of punishment and the significance of imprisonment for moral condemnation). Of course, the more incarceration is used for preventive detention rather than deserved punishment for a past offense, the less clearly imprisonment will convey condemnation of a past wrong.

fenses the same as substantive ones.[69] Attempted rape has the same grade as rape, attempted arson the same as arson. The judgment implicit in such grading clearly conflicts with the strongly held lay belief that resulting harm aggravates an offender's blameworthiness and calls for greater punishment.[70] But the Code's grading approach makes sense if the goal is to maximize societal control over dangerous people. The offender who fails to cause harm because police are able to interrupt him may be as dangerous as the offender who completes the offense. The two are thus equal candidates for rehabilitation or, failing that, incapacitation.[71] This approach is consistent with the

[69] MODEL PENAL CODE § 5.05(1) (1962). The drafters explain:

> The theory of this grading system may be stated simply. To the extent that sentencing depends upon the antisocial disposition of the actor and the demonstrated need for a corrective sanction, there is likely to be little difference in the gravity of the required measures depending on the consummation or the failure of the plan.

MODEL PENAL CODE § 5.05(1) cmt. at 490 (1985). The drafters exempt inchoate offenses to commit a first-degree felony because of the overriding deterrent purpose. *Id.* at 489–90.

[70] *See* ROBINSON & DARLEY, *supra* note 52, at 14–28, 33–42 (1995).

[71] As the drafters explain, "[t]he primary purpose of punishing attempts is to neutralize dangerous individuals." MODEL PENAL CODE § 5.01 cmt. at 323 (1985); *see also id.* at 298 (stating that "the proper focus of attention is the actor's disposition"); *id.* at 331 (advocating the broadening of liability to permit the earlier apprehension of dangerous persons).

For another example of the Model Penal Code's concern with dangerousness, consider § 1.02 of the Code, which includes as one of "[t]he general purposes of the provisions governing the definition of offenses: . . . [t]o subject to public control persons whose conduct indicates that they are disposed to commit crimes." MODEL PENAL CODE § 1.02(1)(b) (1962).

In their definitions of offenses, the drafters reveal a shift in focus from desert to dangerousness. For example, the Model Penal Code alters the common law definition of attempt from requiring that a person come within some proximity of completing an offense — the so-called "proximity" test, of which the common law had several variations — to requiring only that a person have taken a "substantial step" toward the offense. It no longer matters whether the actor actually came close to committing a specific offense. All that is relevant is that the actor at some point externalized his intention to commit an offense, thereby revealing his dangerousness. The proximity tests were rejected because they focused on the nature of the actor's conduct rather than on "the proper focus of attention . . . the actor's disposition [to commit a crime]." *Id.* § 5.01 cmt. at 298.

Similar substantive criminal law reformulations abound in the Code. The Code's definition of conspiracy was altered so that it no longer requires that the actor in fact agree with another that one of them will commit an offense, but requires only that the actor thought he had agreed with another. *Compare, e.g.*, Archbold v. State, 397 N.E.2d 1071, 1073 (Ind. Ct. App. 1979) (requiring actual agreement), *with* People v. Schwimmer, 411 N.Y.S.2d 922, 928 (1978) (holding that a defendant can be found guilty of conspiracy even though the coconspirators did not have the requisite mens rea). *See generally* PAUL H. ROBINSON, CRIMINAL LAW 648 (1997) (discussing the bilateral agreement required at common law for conspiracy and the unilateral requirement of modern codes). This change logically follows from the drafters' view that conspiracy's purpose is "as a basis . . . for the corrective treatment of persons who reveal that they are disposed to criminality." MODEL PENAL CODE § 5.03 cmt. at 97 (Tentative Draft No. 10, 1960). There may be no real danger of an offense being committed if an actor only mistakenly believes he has conspired with another (an undercover officer, for example), but his agreement shows that he is the type of person who would be willing to join in such an agreement. Similarly, the Code drops the common law's unconvictable perpetrator defense to complicity; it is no longer relevant that the perpetrator had no intention of committing the crime. The accomplice is equally dangerous whether the perpetrator

Model Sentencing Act, which minimizes the significance of offense seriousness.[72]

This approach — discounting the significance of resulting harm and offense seriousness in assessing punishment — became somewhat less attractive in the mid-1970s, when the limited ability of social and medical science to rehabilitate offenders became clear.[73] Crime and the consequent need for criminal justice would not disappear through the power of clinical advances, as had been hoped.[74] But an important step had been taken: the disconnect between criminal punishment and desert had been formally legitimized.

Reformers soon realized that even if rehabilitation was unrealistic, at the very least incapacitation would prevent future crimes. Hence, the modern ideas for reform developed — three strikes, lowering the age of eligibility for prosecution as an adult, and others. If desert does not constrain the criminal justice system, then liability and punishment can be distributed in any way that the current crime-control utilitarian calculus suggests may reduce crime.

Rather than openly recharacterize the system to reveal its nature as preventive detention, the reformers, then as now, appeared anxious to maintain the false image of a system of criminal punishment. If the drafters believed that resulting harm should be irrelevant to grading, they could have simply eliminated all result elements from the Model Penal Code's offense definitions and defined all offenses in terms of conduct and accompanying mental state: "Engaging in conduct by which one intends to . . ." burn a building, falsify an official document, or injure another. Why retain the result elements, implying that the Code considers resulting harm, only to negate the effect of the result elements by grading inchoate conduct the same as the completed offense? One might speculate that the drafters saw value in maintaining the appearance, although not the spirit, of a criminal punishment system.

---

actually intended to commit the crime or not. Still another example is the Code's reformulation of the objective requirements of complicity that allows liability for the full substantive offense on proof that a person tried but failed to assist. MODEL PENAL CODE § 2.06(3)(a)(ii) (1962) (assigning liability when an individual "aids or agrees or attempts to aid"). That the failed assister in fact contributed nothing to the offense does not reduce his display of dangerousness in trying to assist.

72 *See supra* p. 1441.

73 By 1974 Robert Martinson concluded in his survey article: "I am bound to say that these data, involving over two hundred studies and hundreds of thousands of individuals as they do, are the best available and give us very little reason to hope that we have in fact found a sure way of reducing recidivism through rehabilitation." Robert Martinson, *What Works? — Questions and Answers About Prison Reform*, 35 PUB. INT. 22, 49 (1974).

74 *See, e.g.*, COUNCIL OF JUDGES, NAT'L COUNCIL ON CRIME & DELINQUENCY, MODEL SENTENCING ACT (2d ed. 1972) art. 1, § 1, *reprinted in* 18 CRIME AND DELINQUENCY, 335, 344 (1972) ("The purpose of penal codes and sentencing is public protection. Sentences should not be based upon revenge and retribution.").

IX. THE PREVENTIVE DETENTION PROBLEMS

It is evident, then, that there are various ways in which the current criminal justice system surreptitiously provides preventive detention at the expense of just punishment. Ironically, such cloaked preventive detention also seriously impedes the system's preventive effectiveness. For example, instead of examining each offender to determine the person's actual present dangerousness, the current system uses prior criminal record as a proxy for dangerousness. Prior record has some correlation with dangerousness and, with the assertion of the "nose-thumbing" theory, has plausible deniability as to its perverting justice.[75] But prior record is only a rough approximation of actual dangerousness, and its use in preventive detention guarantees errors of both inclusion and exclusion.

A scientist's ability to predict future criminality using all available data is poor;[76] using just the proxy of prior criminal history, a scientist's prediction is even less accurate. It is often true that a person who has committed an offense will do so again. But it is also frequently false — many offenders do not commit another offense.[77] An explicit assessment of dangerousness would reveal that many second-time offenders are no longer dangerous, yet these offenders receive long preventive terms under three strikes statutes and criminal-history-based guidelines. At the same time, an explicit assessment of dangerousness would reveal that many first-time offenders are dangerous; yet these offenders are not preventively detained under three strikes statutes and criminal-history-based guidelines.[78]

---

75 *See supra* pp. 1435–36.

76 For a review of the available studies, see Stephen J. Morse, *Blame and Danger: An Essay on Preventive Detention*, 76 B.U. L. REV. 113, 126 n.39 (1996). Morse concludes that "the ability of mental health professionals to predict future violence among mental patients may be better than chance, but it is still highly inaccurate, especially if these professionals are attempting to use clinical methods to predict serious violence." *Id.* at 126.

77 *See* Office of the Legislative Auditor, State of Minnesota, *Recidivism of Adult Felons*, *at* http://www.auditor.leg.state.mn.us/ped/1997/pe9701.htm (reporting that 55% of all felony offenders in the study were not convicted of a subsequent offense during three years following their initial arrest and finding that homicide offenders had one of the lowest recidivism rates); *see also* Bureau of Justice Statistics Special Report, Recidivism of Prisoners Released in 1983 (1989).

78 The chronic spouse abuser who turns to obsessive violence when the battered spouse leaves may have no criminal history — battering spouses are often able to persuade their victims not to press criminal charges — yet the abuser may present a clear and immediate danger. Similarly, a stalking and threat offense, depending on its circumstances, may suggest a high risk of serious danger. *See, e.g.*, JOHN DOUGLAS & MARK OLSHAKER, OBSESSION 266 (1998). Yet most such offenses would not trigger the dangerousness add-on provisions that are components of recent reforms. That is, even if the circumstances and nature of the offense suggest a life-threatening level of violence, a system that looks to criminal history rather than to dangerousness will have no grounds to detain the perpetrator.

Indeed, this particular cloaking device stands good prevention on its head. Evidence suggests that criminality is highly age-related.[79] Whether due to changes in testosterone levels or something else, the offending rate drops off steadily for individuals beyond their twenties. The prior-record cloak leads us to ignore younger offenders' future crimes when they are running wild, and to begin long-term imprisonment, often life imprisonment under "three strikes," just when the natural forces of aging would often rein in the offenders. Offenders with their criminal careers before them are not detained because they have not yet compiled their criminal resumes, whereas offenders with their criminal careers behind them are detained because they have the requisite criminal records. Such a scheme produces a costly prevention system of prisons full of geriatric life-termers. Simultaneously, the scheme leads to ineffective prevention, because the system does little during the period in a criminal's life when the need for preventive detention is greatest. A rational and cost-effective preventive detention system would more readily detain young offenders during their crime-prone years and release them for their crime-free older years. Yet the need to cloak preventive detention with deserved punishment prompts the use of prior record as a substitute for actual dangerousness.

An equally counterproductive aspect of the cloaked system is its mandating of fixed ("determinate") sentences immediately following a guilty verdict. In determining the length of a deserved sentence, all of the relevant information is known at the time of sentencing — the nature of the offense and the personal culpability and capacities of the offender. Thus, sentencing judges determining deserved punishment have little reason to impose any sentence other than a fully determinate one (that is, one that sets the actual release date) immediately after trial. A system that instead allows a subsequent reduction of sentence, as by a parole board, undercuts deserved punishment. Citizens become cynical that a just sentence will be undermined by early re-

[79] For example, only 15% of those arrested for crime in 1994 were in their forties or older, although that age group made up 40% of the U.S. population. BUREAU OF JUSTICE STATISTICS, SOURCEBOOK OF CRIMINAL JUSTICE STATISTICS — 1995, at 397 tbl.4.4 (1996). In contrast, persons in their thirties made up 25.3% of arrests but accounted for only 16.9% of the population. *Id.* Persons between the ages nineteen and twenty-nine made up 37.1% of arrests but only 15.9% of the population. *Id.* Homicide arrest rates suggest an even greater drop-off in criminality with age in 1993: 11.9 of 100,000 males in the thirty-five to forty-four age bracket were arrested for homicide. *Id.* at 423 tbl.4.18. Of those aged twenty-five to twenty-nine, the rate was more than two and a half times higher, 30.0 per 100,000. *Id.* For those between twenty-one and twenty-four, the rate was almost five times higher, 56.8. *Id.* Of those between eighteen and twenty, the rate was almost eight times higher, 91.3. The trend of the last several decades has been toward even less criminality by middle-aged persons. In 1970, the homicide arrest rate for males between thirty-five and forty-four was two-thirds higher than it was in 1993 — 19.5 per 100,000 versus 11.9 per 100,000. *Id.* Yet the current reforms will detain a greater number of middle-aged offenders for a longer period of time.

lease.[80] It is this cynicism that gives rise to demands for "truth in sentencing" and to the legislative response of establishing determinate terms and abolishing early release on parole.[81]

Therefore, to maintain its justice cloak, the preventive system must follow this practice of imposing determinate sentences soon after trial. But this practice is highly inappropriate for effective prevention. It is difficult enough to determine a person's present dangerousness — whether he would commit an offense if released today. It is much more difficult to predict an offender's future dangerousness — whether he would commit an offense if released at the end of the deserved punishment term in the future. It is still more difficult, if not impossible, to predict today precisely how long the future preventive detention will need to last. Yet that is what determinate sentencing demands: the imposition now of a fixed term that predicts preventive needs far in the future.

A sentencing judge or guideline drafter is left to the grossest sort of speculation, inevitably doomed to setting either a term too long — thus unfairly detaining a nondangerous offender and wasting preventive resources — or a term too short — thus failing to provide adequate prevention. In deciding between these two bad choices, decisionmakers commonly opt for errors of the first sort rather than the second, resulting in the recent increases in the terms of imprisonment.

A rational preventive detention system would do what current civil commitment systems do: make a determination of present dangerousness in setting detention for a limited period, commonly six

---

80 The public probably infers that early release is common from the plethora of well-publicized anecdotes in which predictably dangerous criminals are released earlier than their sentences dictate, only to quickly return to their criminal ways. *See, e.g.*, James Wootton, *Truth in Sentencing — Why States Should Make Violent Criminals Do Their Time*, 20 U. DAYTON L. REV. 779, 779–80 (1995) (citing the case of a nun murdered in 1993 by a convicted killer who had been sentenced to eighteen to twenty years in 1979, subsequently escaped and after his eventual recapture was released on parole in 1991); Editorial, *Honesty at Prison Gate*, GRAND RAPIDS PRESS, July 12, 1998, at D2; Richard P. Jones, *Thompson Signs Bill Ending Parole: State Lawmaker Calls for 3,000 New Prison Beds To Handle Inmate Increase*, MILWAUKEE J. SENTINEL, June 16, 1998 (reporting that when the parole bill was signed, 58% of all new prisoners received sentences of four years or less; with parole, they were released in two years or less); *Time To Face the Truth on Prisons*, CHI. TRIB., Aug. 28, 1995, § 1, at 14 (describing the public as "continually outraged by stories of violent offenders who serve half their time and commit other heinous acts when released").

81 One of the prime motivations for the federal Sentencing Reform Act of 1984, which among other things abolished the United States Parole Commission, was an attempt to reestablish credibility with an emphasis on "truth in sentencing" that determinate sentences bring. *See, e.g.*, U.S. SENTENCING COMM'N, SENTENCING GUIDELINES AND POLICY STATEMENTS 1.2 (1987) (stating that "Congress first sought *honesty* in sentencing . . . to avoid the confusion and implicit deception" arising out of the then-extant indeterminate sentencing system).

months, and then periodically revisit the decision to determine whether the need for detention continues.[82]

Other inefficiencies resulting from the use of the cloak are found in the method of restraint. A rational preventive detention system would follow a principle of minimum intrusion: a detainee would be held at the minimum level of restraint necessary for community safety. If house arrest or regular medication would provide the same level of community safety as imprisonment, then the former choices would be preferred as less intrusive to the offender and less costly to society. Implementing deserved punishment, in contrast, may often require a prison term to reaffirm the community's strong condemnation of the offense. House arrest or regular medication may be unacceptable substitutes if they are perceived as trivializing the offense. If preventive detention must operate under the cloak of criminal justice, it too often must follow the punishment preference for imprisonment even in situations in which prevention would be satisfied with less intrusive restraint.

The preventive detention system hidden behind the cloak of criminal justice not only fails to protect the community efficiently but also fails to deal fairly with those being preventively detained. As noted above, the inaccuracies created by the use of prior record as a substitute for actual dangerousness result in the unnecessary detention of a greater number of nondangerous offenders. The inaccuracies created by the use of determinate sentences can have the same effect. In cases in which a nonincarcerative sentence would provide adequate protection, the use of a prison term provides one more example of needless restraint.

But the unfairness generated by the cloak of criminal justice extends to other aspects of the preventive detention system, such as the conditions of detention. Punitive conditions are entirely consistent with a punishment rationale for the incarceration. But if an offender has served the portion of his sentence justified by deserved punishment and continues to be detained for entirely preventive reasons, punitive conditions become inappropriate.

Similarly, an offender being preventively detained should logically have a right to treatment, especially if such treatment can reduce the length or intrusiveness of the preventive detention — this constitutes a

[82] *See, e.g.*, IDAHO CODE § 66-337(a) (Michie 2000) (requiring department directors to examine a patient's need for commitment at the end of the first ninety days and every one hundred twenty days thereafter); R.I. GEN. LAWS § 40.1-5.3-4(f) (1997) (permitting courts to commit dangerous persons, but requiring courts to review such orders every six months); S.D. CODIFIED LAWS ANN. § 27A-10-14 (Michie 2000) (requiring a board to review a patient who has been committed for mental illness at least once every six months for the first year and at least once every twelve months thereafter).

specialized application of the principle of minimum restraint. If treatment can reduce the necessary individual sacrifice,[83] the offender ought to receive it.

X. SEGREGATING JUSTICE AND PROTECTION

Real world problems commonly present us with conflicting interests that cannot be reconciled but can only be compromised. The natural conflict between fair trials and a free press, for example, cannot be resolved; these competing interests must be balanced. Each must be sacrificed to some extent to accommodate the other. Society's interest in effective investigation of crime competes with individuals' interest in privacy, and Fourth Amendment analysis, the standard mechanism for resolving this competition, strikes a complex balance between the two.

Fortunately, however, there is no need to compromise either justice or prevention to advance the other, for the conflict between justice and prevention can be avoided by simply segregating the two functions into two systems. The first would be a criminal justice system that focused exclusively on imposing the punishment deserved for the past offense, and the second would be a post-sentence civil commitment system that considered only the protection of society from future offenses by a dangerous offender.

The sticking point in this proposal is not in having a criminal justice system that is guided only by justice. Most lay persons assume that the criminal justice system has always sought this goal. The difficulty comes, instead, with the open acknowledgment of a system of preventive detention.

There is some precedent for preventive detention. As noted, all states currently have some form of civil commitment operating to protect society.[84] Additional direct precedent exists in that many states currently have post-criminal-incarceration civil commitment of some criminal offenders, typically "sexual predators."[85] Under these civil commitment systems, the government can attempt to detain an offender at the conclusion of his criminal term if the government can show continuing dangerousness.[86]

---

83 For example, a number of encouraging studies have recently suggested that comprehensive treatment of pedophilia has a ninety percent or better success rate. *See* Robert E. Freeman-Longo, *Reducing Sexual Abuse in America: Legislating Tougher Laws or Public Education and Prevention*, 23 NEW ENG. J. ON CRIM. & CIV. CONFINEMENT 303, 323 (1997).

84 *See supra* p. 1444.

85 *See supra* p. 1431.

86 Unlike the proposal made here, there is no indication that the current "sexual predator" legislation excludes reliance on dangerousness in setting the criminal commitment. It is less a segregated system than a cloaked system followed by a preventive detention system.

Despite the precedent, there are understandable concerns about creating a broader system of explicit preventive detention:[87] the *Gulag Archipelago* potential for governmental abuse is real. But if the alternative is the present system of cloaked preventive detention, the risk is worth taking. An explicit system of post-criminal commitment would better serve both the community and potential detainees.

To summarize the arguments above, under a segregated system, the community would be better off because such a system offers both more justice and increased protection from dangerous offenders. Giving the criminal justice system a better chance of doing justice is valuable for its own sake. It also creates greater moral credibility for the system, and thus greater long-term crime-control power. An explicit preventive detention system offers better protection, because it can directly consider a person's present dangerousness and more accurately predict who is dangerous. Such a system also enhances accuracy by allowing for periodic re-evaluations, in comparison with the present system's need to make a single prediction of dangerousness years in advance. Greater accuracy leads to more detention of the dangerous, better protection, and less detention of the nondangerous, thus saving resources.

A segregated system also benefits the potential detainees for many of the same reasons. Better accuracy in prediction means less detention of nondangerous offenders. Periodic re-evaluation leads to detention limited to periods of actual dangerousness. Acknowledging the preventive nature of the detention also logically suggests a right to treatment, a right to nonpunitive conditions, and the application of the principle of minimum restraint, meaning greater freedom among those who are detained.

Beyond the new limitations imposed on it, an open system of preventive detention ought to be preferred precisely because it is open rather than cloaked. No one can guarantee that a legislature or court will not attempt to abuse its power. But an open system makes it harder to abuse the system. The openly preventive nature of the system makes it susceptible to closer scrutiny, which the present cloaked system escapes. Instead of the current debates — which typically reduce to disagreements about, for example, whether "three strikes" sentences are "too long" — the debate would shift to the many aspects of preventive detention that cry out for debate: What is the reliability of

[87] The post-sentence civil commitment proposal might be held unconstitutional. Although the permissible scope of civil commitment has recently been expanded slightly, it still appears to require not only a finding of dangerousness, but also some additional factor, such as mental abnormality. Kansas v. Hendricks, 521 U.S. 346, 358 (1997) (citing *Heller v. Doe*, 509 U.S. 312, 314–15 (1993); and *Allen v. Illinois*, 478 U.S. 364, 366 (1986)). But this would be an odd result: barring the civil commitment with periodic review of dangerousness of a dangerous murderer, but permitting, as the Court did in *Rummel*, the life imprisonment without parole of a petty fraud offender.

the predictions of dangerousness? Is the threatened danger sufficient to justify the extent of intrusion on personal liberty? Are there less expensive or less intrusive measures that would as effectively protect the community? Under the current cloaked system, these issues escape examination and debate.

Imagine a legislature considering an explicit preventive detention statute that would provide life preventive detention on a third conviction for a minor fraud offense, the disposition provided by the statute in *Rummel*. Such legislation would be difficult to defend and would be unlikely to find support in any political quarter. Indeed, imagine the Supreme Court's review of *Rummel* if Rummel were being preventively detained. Life terms without the possibility of parole may be common and acceptable in a criminal justice system, in which horrible crimes deserve severe punishment. But life commitment with no further dangerousness review for a property offense would be preposterous on its face in a civil preventive detention system.

Some people will argue that it is simply not politically feasible in the United States today to create an explicit system of preventive detention, even one limited to dangerous felons about to be released from prison. Less feasible, however, is political inaction in the face of recurring serious offenses that are preventable. The inevitable pressure for protection will express itself in one form or another. If the only choices are an open preventive detention system and a cloaked one, both the community and potential detainees ought to prefer the open system. If there is a danger of governmental abuse of preventive detention, that danger is greatest when preventive detention is cloaked as criminal justice.

[9]

THE CRIME-CONTROL EFFECT OF INCARCERATION: DOES SCALE MATTER?*

RAYMOND V. LIEDKA
Oakland University

ANNE MORRISON PIEHL
Rutgers University

BERT USEEM
Purdue University

Research Summary:
Several prominent empirical studies estimate models of a constant proportional effect of prison on crime, finding that effect is substantial and negative. A separate literature argues against the crime-reducing effect of prison but mainly on theoretical grounds. This second literature suggests that the elasticity of the prison/crime relationship is not constant. We provide a model that nests these two literatures. Using data from the United States over 30 years, we find strong evidence that the negative relationship between prison and crime becomes less strongly negative as the scale of imprisonment increases. This revisionist model indicates that (1) at low levels of incarceration, a constant elasticity model underestimates the negative relationship between incarceration and crime, and (2) at higher levels of incarceration, the constant elasticity model overstates the negative effect.

Policy Implications:
These results go beyond the claim of declining marginal returns, instead finding accelerating declining marginal returns. As the prison population continues to increase, albeit at a slower rate, after three decades of phenomenal growth, these findings provide an important caution that for many jurisdictions, the point of accelerating declining

* Author names are ordered arbitrarily to reflect equal contribution. The authors thank Carlisle Moody and David Card for making data available and John M. Roberts, Jr. for helpful comments. Funding was provided by grants from the National Institute of Justice, National Science Foundation, and the Guggenheim Foundation. Points of view in the document are those of the authors and do not necessarily represent the views of either agency. Direct correspondence to Raymond V. Liedka, Department of Sociology and Anthropology, 518 Varner Hall, Oakland University, Rochester MI 48309 (rliedka@insightbb.com).

marginal returns may have set in. Any policy discussion of the appropriate scale of punishment should be concerned with the empirical impact of this expensive and intrusive government intervention.

KEYWORDS: Crime Rates, Prison Population, Mass Incarceration, Prison Buildup

Over the last 25 years, the population behind bars has grown at an astounding rate. From 200,000 inmates in 1973, the federal and state inmate population surpassed the one million mark in 1994, with more recent growth bringing the total to 1.4 million. Through much of this buildup period, researchers have disagreed over the effectiveness of the buildup in reducing the crime rate.

The terms of the debate are now familiar. One side argues that increasing prison will reduce the crime rate through deterrence and incapacitation. Deterrence refers to the mechanism that legal sanctions lower the crime rate by altering the incentives for behavior (Becker, 1968; Grasmick and Bryjak, 1980; Wilson, 1983). If society raises the cost of crime by imposing higher rates of imprisonment, then the incidence of criminal behavior will decline. Incapacitation refers to the mechanism that physical restraint will have a negative impact on the crime rate (Nagin, 1998; Spelman, 1994). An offender behind bars cannot commit new crimes against society, unless or until he or she returns to the streets. Therefore, absent full replacement (new criminals filling the niche left by those incarcerated), incapacitation will reduce crime over what it would otherwise have been.

Yet other researchers have not been convinced by the crime-reduction argument. During the middle stages of the buildup, some criminologists dismissed the prison expansion as a failure because rates of imprisonment were rising, but crime rates were steady. If prison works, why no reduction in crime?[1] William Chambliss (1999:130) observed: "Virtually everyone who studies or works in the criminal justice system agrees that putting people in prison is costly and ineffective." The National Criminal Justice Commission (Donziger, 1996:42), a panel of leading criminologists and civic leaders, sums up the research literature as showing "little or no correlation between rates of crime and the number of people in prison." One strand of this literature holds that a larger prison population even generates crime by negatively impacting individuals and communities (Rose and Clear, 1998).

1. This question was asked by Jerome Skolnick (1995:8) in his 1994 presidential address to the American Society of Criminology. Even recently, Marc Mauer (1999:192) argued that the prison buildup has had "relatively little" impact on the crime rate.

The landscape of the debate gained additional contours by the publication of several studies using econometric modeling to estimate the effect of prison and crime. These studies took advantage of the experience of the prison buildup to estimate the prison/crime elasticity, or the percentage reduction in crime that would result from a percentage increase in the imprisonment rate. Rigorous studies were conduced by Marvell and Moody (1994), Levitt (1996), and Witt and Witte (2000). All three found that increases in prison population had significantly reduced the U.S. crime rate. Even in the face of such evidence, however, some researchers continued to view the prison buildup with an exceedingly critical eye. These critics, however, did not rebut or otherwise assimilate the econometric studies, but they seemed to have dismissed their relevance. For example, David Garland (2001) published a broad ranging discussion of the role of punishment in modern society, critical of the heavy U.S .reliance on prison. Although Garland's discussion is highly erudite, drawing on many sources, it does not make reference to the econometric findings.

The end product was two strongly argued positions, making assertions about the same phenomenon, but not fully engaged with each other. The buildup critics pointed to the many possible side effects of the buildup. Yet as a research priority, the effect of prison on crime—prison's formal mission—should be central to any analysis of mass incarceration in U.S. society.

People accept institutions because society has certain problems to solve, and institutions may provide answers to those problems (Stinchcombe, 1997). One such problem is crime control.

This research synthesizes these two positions and arrives at a novel solution. We begin by considering in greater detail the extant research literature.

EMPIRICAL RESEARCH ON PRISON GROWTH

Formal data analyses that seek to estimate the effects of prison on crime rates fall into two branches of literature. One branch relies on data collected from surveys of inmates, in which inmates are asked about crimes they committed before their incarceration. Researchers then address policy issues concerning the number of "crimes averted" through possible changes in the level of imprisonment. The original survey work was performed at the Rand Corporation (Chaiken and Chaiken, 1982). Important analyses using these data include those by Peter Greenwood (1982) and Edwin Zedlewski (1987). Other researchers have developed the approach (Spelman, 1994), some using new data (Piehl and DiIulio, 1995; Piehl et al., 1999). Still others have challenged the approach (Meyer and Hopkins,

1991; Zimring and Hawkins, 1988). Certainly surveys are useful for profiling "who" is in prison at a particular time. The survey approach is superior to relying on official records, because the latter does not include crimes committed that went undetected. From the profiles, researchers estimate the kinds of crimes current inmates would commit if on the streets. The approach seems to capture the effects of prison incapacitation on crime.

A second branch takes a regression approach, in which the researcher examines whether changes in prison population covary with crime, net other factors. The advantages to a regression approach are two-fold. First, a regression approach deals with actual changes in the world, whereas the survey approach relies on a mental experiment ("what would be the result of not incarcerating those currently imprisoned?"). Second, a regression approach captures the full impact of prison on crime, whether through deterrence, incapacitation, or other potential mechanisms. As noted, the three "best" regression studies (Levitt, 1996; Marvell and Moody, 1994; and Witt and Witte, 2000) yield similar estimates. All three estimate that the elasticity of crime with regard to the prison rate is between –0.159 and –0.55.[2] That is, a 10% increase in the prison rate will result in a 1.6% to 5.5% drop in the crime rate.

We find it difficult to challenge the validity of the regression studies demonstrating that declining crime rates are due to increases in the prison population, particularly so when the replication below shows similar effects. Yet we are also persuaded to consider the proposal that the high levels of incarceration may increase crime because of the damage done to communities and the social network of young men and women. The crucial issue is not whether such effects occur; they most certainly do (Lynch and Sabol, 2004). Rather it is whether those effects overwhelm the crime-reducing mechanisms of prison—deterrence and incapacitation—which also most certainly occur.

Without modeling the details of the entire process, the "collateral damage" concept (Hagan and Dinovitzer, 1999) suggests two hypotheses. The first hypothesis is that the diminishing marginal returns to the crime-control effect of imprisonment will accelerate with ever greater increases in imprisonment. That is, the percentage reduction in crime rates caused by a percentage increase in imprisonment is smaller when incarceration rates are already high. This result would be indicated by a prison elasticity of crime that declines with the level of incarceration. We call this the less–less hypothesis: the higher the level of imprisonment, the weaker the effect of

2. Specifically, Marvell and Moody find an elasticity of –0.159, Levitt an elasticity of –0.379 for violent crime and –0.261 for property crime, and Witt and Witte an overall elasticity of –0.55.

incarceration to lessen crime. That is, as the prison rate exceeds a threshold, additional increases in the prison rate are less effective in causing less crime.

The second hypothesis is that, beyond a certain level, additional increases in imprisonment will lead to higher levels of crime, not lower ones. This "crime-augmentation" hypothesis is the logical extension of arguments that increased use of incarceration increases the potential pool of criminal offenders. The social damage of high rates of imprisonment outweighs their crime reduction effects. This hypothesis would be observed as a prison elasticity of crime shifting from negative to positive beyond some threshold level of incarceration.

SPELMAN'S ANALYSIS

We are not the first consider the possibility that the causal impact of prison on crime may depend on the scale of imprisonment. Spelman (2000) argued that the sharp downturn in crime rates during the 1990s observed at the national level, and likewise in a great many localities, cannot be attributed fully to the continued prison buildup—the crime drop would have occurred regardless. Using estimates from the literature of the prison-crime relationship, Spelman concluded that the prison buildup reduced the violent crime rate between 20% and 50%, with the rest of the decline from other factors. To explain the "excess" drop in crime, Spelman proposes that prison became a more effective force in reducing crime—that is, the elasticity increased over time. He attributes this increase to scale effects and increased efficiency in law enforcement.

More specifically, Spelman used a range of viable estimates for the crime elasticity of prison to derive estimates of what the trend in crime rates would have been in the absence of a prison buildup. These estimates were calculated by subtracting the estimated crime-reduction effect of prison expansion from the actual crime rate. He compared the trend in these estimates to the trend that did occur and observed that in both time series, there is a downturn in crime through the 1990s, beginning at the same point. This result forms the basis for his conclusion that the drop in crime during the 1990s would have occurred even without the prison buildup, although it would not have been as great. Unfortunately, Spelman's conclusion is an artifact of his method.

Spelman's calculations treat the observed prison population growth, the observed crime rates, and the crime elasticity of prison as independent of each other. They are not. Spelman draws the range of viable elasticities he considers from his own work estimating the effects of prison on crime from self-report data and the regression analyses of Levitt (1996) and Marvell and Moody (1994). But these estimates of the elasticity—certainly in the regression analyses—are determined from the empirical relation between crime and imprisonment. The elasticities are not independent of observed crime and imprisonment data trends; rather, the elasticity is a numerical statement of the relationship between the two.

This lack of independence means the relationship between the estimated elasticity and the prison buildup imposes limits on the calculation of the counterfactual (non-prison-buildup crime rates). Spelman's curve of the estimated non-buildup crime rate simply must mirror the observed path of the crime rate for any reasonable value of the elasticity. Given the elasticity, the counterfactual crime rate is pulled along, following the path of observed crime rates.[3] Spelman's conclusion—that the dip in crime rates in the 1990s would have occurred without the prison buildup—may or may not hold. His analysis, however, cannot adjudicate whether his conclusion holds. By construction, the historical time series of crime rates and Spelman's estimated time series must resemble each other.

If Spelman's work is empirically flawed, it does identify the problem: the need to consider whether prison's effectiveness changes with the scale of imprisonment rather than to presume that it would not vary over a period during which changes were dramatic. To test this idea directly, Spelman then estimated a regression model in which the crime elasticity of prison varies with the size of the prison population. He found that the effect of imprisonment became stronger as the size of the prison population grew larger (p. 122). In this part of the analysis, Spelman, however, improperly specified scale effects by including only the quadratic form of imprisonment in his model,[4] which meant that he was constrained to find one of only two possibilities—either the effect of prison is to increase crime and it gets stronger (increases crime even more) with larger prison

3. To demonstrate this, we only need to reconstruct the equation that produces Spelman's estimate of the non-buildup crime rate. This equation can be written as

$$\textit{Non-buildup crime rate increase}_t = \frac{\dfrac{\textit{violent crime rate}_t}{\textit{violent crime rate}_{t-1}}}{1+\varepsilon\left[\dfrac{\textit{prison populatiaon}_t}{\textit{prison population}_{t-1}}-1\right]}.$$

The numerator on the right-hand side is the observed increase in the violent crime rate, whereas the denominator is a function of the elasticity, ε, and it contains the observed increase in the prison population. Given that the values of elasticity that Spelman considers range from –0.30 to –0.50, the denominator will always be positive, falling between 0.9445 and 0.9979. This result forces the counterfactual crime rate increase to be a simple multiple of the observed crime rate, and the non-buildup crime trend to mirror the observed crime trend.

4. This must be the case for Spelman to get the expression for the elasticity reported on p. 122.

populations, or the effect of prison is to reduce crime and it gets stronger (decreases crime even more) with larger prison populations. (Of course, he also could have found no relationship between prison and crime.)

A proper specification of the scale effects model should include a linear term as well as the quadratic. A fair test of whether the prison-crime elasticity is constant should allow for a full set of alternative, perhaps complex, relationships. For example, the elasticity could start out negative, become weaker (less negative), and with continued growth in imprisonment, become positive. It is the goal of this study to conduct such a fully developed analysis.

DATA AND METHODS

The state-level panel data provided here on prison populations and crime rates covers the years 1972 through 2000, for all 50 states and the District of Columbia. The dependent variable is the state crime rate per 100,000 population, using the FBI's Uniform Crime Reports (UCR) Index.[5] The key independent variable is the prison inmate population (under state jurisdiction) per 1,000 state population. The state prison population for year *t* (SPP_t) is calculated as the average of the year-end population for year *t* and year *t - 1*.[6]

Table 1 presents summary statistics for all variables used in the model estimations to follow. The first column reports the mean of each variable, across all states and all years. The second column gives the standard deviation of each variable, calculated across all states and all years. The third column gives the standard deviation of state means, whereas the final column gives the standard deviation of yearly means. The last two columns show the relative variability across states and across years.[7]

The mean value of the crime index is 4947.74 per 100,000 population, or about 1 in 20. There is a lot of variation in index crime rates, most of which is across states. The across-state variation is nearly three times larger than the variation over three decades of time. The mean number of prison inmates is 2.42 per 1,000 population, or 1 in 446. Although there is substantial variation in this variable, it is approximately evenly divided across states and over time.

To control for differing age distributions of state populations, we use

5. This index includes crimes known to police in the following categories: homicide, forcible rape, robbery, aggravated assault, burglary, larceny/theft, and motor-vehicle theft.

6. The results are not sensitive to this particular timing convention. Results using other definitions are available from the authors.

7. For virtually all variables, the state and year mean standard deviations are both smaller than the overall standard deviation; this result occurs because in calculating a mean for each state or each year, some variability is lost.

TABLE 1. SUMMARY STATISTICS

	Mean	Standard Deviation (Overall)	Standard Deviation of State Averages	Standard Deviation of Year Averages
Index Crimes per 100,000 pop	4947.74	1442.25	1322.02	406.17
Prison Inmates per 1000 pop	2.42	1.97	1.45	1.18
% Population 16–19 (x100)	6.49	0.98	0.38	0.92
% Population 20–24 (x100)	8.14	1.27	0.48	1.10
% Population 25–34 (x100)	16.01	1.87	1.13	1.46
Unemployment Rate (%)	6.18	2.13	1.24	1.40
% Black Population	10.71	11.90	12.18	7.17
% Metro Population	65.85	22.16	22.27	4.35
Mean Wage	–0.01	0.10	0.09	0.01

NOTES: There are 51 states (including Washington, D.C.) and 29 years (1972–2000) for a total of 1479 observations. The data for 1972 are only used to create lagged values for 1973. Because of missing data for some states or some years on several of the variables, the data are reported for the 1308 cases on which complete data are available. These 1308 cases are the same ones employed in model estimation.

variable definitions similar to those of Marvell and Moody (1994). Specifically, these variables are the percentage of a state's population in the age groups of 16 to 19 years, 20 to 24 years, and 25 to 34 years.[8] For the proportion of the state population in the two younger age groups, there is about twice as much variation over time as there is across states.

We use a more extensive set of control variables than did Marvell and Moody. The first is the state unemployment rate. It is commonly argued that when unemployment increases, those without jobs will turn to criminal activity, either to sustain themselves or because their daily lives are less regulated. A second economic control variable is a measure of prevailing mean wages and salaries for males with a high-school education or less, corrected for inflation.[9] Gould et al. (Gould et al., 2002) have argued that, in predicting crime rates, wages are a more important measure of labor

8. Marvell and Moody (1994) used age groups 15–17 years, 18–24 years, and 25–34 years. The difference with the age groups here is negligible. The population variables in this study were constructed from U.S. Census data on the distribution by single year of age for each state. For example, the total number of persons in each state for each year of age between 16 and 19 is totaled and divided by the total state population to create the "percentage age 16-19" variable.

9. This variable is constructed in a manner following Gould et al. (2002). The yearly March CPS data from 1969 to 1998 were used to determine prevailing mean wages and salaries. Only males above the age of 18 years in the data with a high-school diploma or less were included. First, the income data were adjusted for inflation by using the national level Consumer Price Index (CPI-U) to 1998 dollars. Then, weighting by CPS weights, inflation-adjusted wage and salary income were regressed on dummy variables for race (white vs. nonwhite) and marital status (single vs other, married vs. other), and variables for age, education in years, and a proxy for labor force experience $((\text{age-educ})-6)^2$. These regressions were performed for each year separately. The

market conditions than the unemployment rate. They suggest this alternative as a better measure of the opportunity cost of crime, because the prevailing wage for unskilled workers is the true alternative to illicit gain. We find this argument sufficiently compelling to include a measure of wages in addition to the more commonly used unemployment rate. Variation in the unemployment rate is split evenly between the "across states" component and the "within states" component, but variation in wages occurs primarily across states. This finding suggests these two variables pick up somewhat different phenomena.

Two additional control variables are the percentages of the state population who are African-American and who reside in metropolitan areas. African-Americans are overrepresented among both perpetrators and victims of crime. Urban areas have higher levels of crime, possibly because of the concentration of viable crime targets or less guardianship over those targets. Virtually all variation in black and urban population is across states; the change over time is negligible.

EMPIRICAL MODEL

The baseline model presented here of the relationship between crime rates and incarceration rates can be written as

$$\ln(\textit{crime rate}_{it}) = b_0 + b_1 (\ln SPP_{i(t-1)}) + \sum b_k X_{kit} + \delta_i + \lambda_t + \varepsilon_{it}$$

where ln ($\textit{crime rate}_{it}$) is the natural logarithm of the UCR crime index for the i-th state in the t-th year, $\ln SPP_{i(t-1)}$ is the one-year lagged value of the natural logarithm of prison inmate population, X_{kit} represents the control variables, and δ_i and λ_t are fixed state and year effects. The log–log specification is chosen so the coefficients can be interpreted as elasticities. The fixed effects control for omitted variables that vary by state or year. The error term is modeled as a first-order autoregressive "AR(1)" process with $\varepsilon_{it} = \rho\varepsilon_{i(t-1)} + \upsilon_{it}$ where υ_{it} is the usual independent normally distributed error. This process is referred to as the Lag Model, because prison inmate population is entered in its lagged form. Estimation proceeds via maximum likelihood, weighted by state population. Robust standard errors are employed, known as the "sandwich" estimator or as White standard errors.[10]

weighted state means of the residuals from this procedure are then the measure of the prevailing wage and salary in each state.

10. Although the natural logarithm of crime rates is employed—a variance stabilizing transformation—there is slight evidence of heteroskedasticity from White's test. Results that employed non-weighted regressions and ordinary standard errors were similar. Indeed, these results indicate an even greater nonlinearity than the results presented here.

A model specification that incorporates an hypothesized non-constant elasticity is formulated as

$$\ln(crime\ rate_{it}) = b_0 + b_1(\ln SPP_{i(t-1)}) + b_2(\ln SPP_{i(t-1)})^2 + \sum b_k X_{kit} + \delta_i + \lambda_t + \varepsilon_{it}$$

This specification is the same one as in model (1), save for the addition of the quadratic term on the effect of SPP. This model is referred to as as the Quadratic Model because of its key characteristic. For this model, the elasticity is no longer constant, but equal to $b_1 + 2b_2(\ln SPP_{i(t-1)})$. The elasticity—the proportional effect of changes in prison population—now depends on the scale of the prison population. Depending on the values of the parameter estimates b_1 and b_2, the elasticity may be positive, negative, or even zero.

Note that if the coefficient on the quadratic term is not significantly different from zero, then the estimated elasticity is constant. This result would be evidence against the non-constant elasticity hypothesis, including the special case of the crime-augmenting effect of imprisonment hypothesis. This specification is also extended to a polynomial specification employing additional powers, the cubic and quartic of the logarithm of prison population.

The final specification is one wherein the logarithm of prison population is entered as a spline function, using the deciles of SPP to define the spline segments. This model can be written as

$$\ln(crime\ rate_{it}) = b_0 + b_1(\ln SPP_{1i(t-1)}) + \ldots + b_{10}(\ln SPP_{10i(t-1)}) + \sum b_k X_{kit} + \delta_i + \lambda_t + \varepsilon_{it}$$

where there is a different coefficient on the logarithm of state prison population at each decile of state prison population, which means that the elasticity of prison population can vary in a semiparametric way with the scale of punishment, and it does not impose the parametric shape of a quadratic or polynomial. Because it flexibly allows for a broad range of possible patterns for a non-constant elasticity (including constancy), it is theoretically the strongest specification.

SIMULTANEITY

An unavoidable issue in regressions of crime rates on incarceration rates is that of simultaneity bias. To interpret the estimates of a model as causal, one must view incarceration rates as exogenous to crime rates. However, it is plausible (even likely) that the process also operates in the opposite direction. Holding other variables constant, increases in crime rates eventually lead to a growth in the incarceration rate. When simultaneity occurs, the regression estimate of the effect of incarceration on crime will be a mixture of the effect one hopes to isolate (the crime-control effect of incarceration) and the effect of the opposite causal sequence (effect of crime rates on incarceration rates). But because these effects are in opposite directions, the estimated overall effect of incarceration will tend to be biased toward zero. Simultaneity bias should, therefore, result only in an underestimate, but not an overestimate, of the crime-control effects of incarceration.

Levitt (1996) employed an instrumental variable approach to resolve the simultaneity problem. The instrumental variable approach is to identify a variable that directly affects the rate of imprisonment, but it is otherwise unrelated to crime rates. Levitt used prison overcrowding litigation as an instrument to break the simultaneity. When crowding litigation occurs, prisons decrease their incarceration rate independently of the crime rate. One can then look to see whether this "artificial" lowering of the prison rate had an effect on the crime rate. Levitt found that it did.

Yet it is difficult to see how, if rising crime rates cause increases in prison populations, they do not also play a role in determining overcrowding litigation because the rising crime rate leads to the overcrowding. The instrument is correlated with the dependent variable through a simple causal sequence: more crime—more prison inmates—prison litigation. To that extent, the litigation instrument would not solve the simultaneity problem. Additionally, only 12 states experienced system-wide litigation during the period Levitt studied. A lot is riding, then, on whether the experience of the 12 states at a particular time can be generalized to the other 38 states, or even the same states at a different time. Yet, 7 of the 12 states are Southern states, whereas the remaining 5 are small states. One can view court intervention in Southern corrections as something akin to a revolution from above—that is, an effort by federal courts to modernize Southern corrections and bring them into the mainstream.[11] This issue greatly confounds the analysis, as it is not clear what the instrument is picking up in addition to slowed prison growth.

Moreover, federal judges implementing crowding caps cannot directly affect the number of offenders sent to prison. They can urge changed legislation, but short of this, the imprisonment decision remains largely with local prosecutors, judges, and juries. Remedies issued from the federal bench are primarily limited to early release or other "back end" solutions (Feeley and Rubin, 1998:387). Assuming Levitt's results are otherwise correct, this insight adds a degree of specificity to the findings: Early release programs cause the crime rate to rise. Yet, it is unclear whether front-end

11. On this point, see the pioneering study by Blake McKelvey (1977) and more recent contributions by Paul Finkelman (1985) and Malcolm Feeley and Edward Rubin (1998:150–158).

solutions have the same effect.[12]

Finally, the authors are concerned about technical issues with Levitt's choice of instrument. Weak instruments can exhibit finite-sample bias on the same order as the non-instrumental variable regression, even in large samples (Bound et al., 1995). An approximate estimate of the finite-sample bias is $1/F$, where F is the value of the F-test on the instruments in the first stage of the instrumental variables estimation (Bound et al., 1995:446). Levitt does not report the F-test on the instruments in his Table IV, but the replication here of his analysis produced an $F = 1.94$, which indicates a finite-sample bias approximately 50% of the bias of the non-instrumental variables regression.[13]

Even if Levitt's litigation instrument is problematic, is it still not better to use an imperfect instrument than none at all? Perhaps, but the instrument is not available for the most recent years of the prison buildup. The Prison Litigation Reform Act (PLRA), passed by Congress in 1996, changed the rules on judicial consent decrees (Schlanger, 2003). PLRA made it easier for state prison systems to terminate judicial arrangements meant to alleviate overcrowding. The legislation also made it more difficult for inmates to bring any new overcrowding litigation. Although Levitt might have identified a useful instrument for the period he considered, no comparable measure is available for more recent experience.

Marvell and Moody (1994) employed the Granger causality test to resolve the problem of simultaneity bias. Granger (1969) developed a statistical test to determine the direction of causality between two variables that may be affecting one another. This direction is found by testing for temporal precedence. Do changes in variable X precede changes in variable Y, or do changes in variable Y precede changes in variable X? This result is accomplished in practice by testing whether lagged values of an independent variable significantly predicts the outcome in the presence of lagged values of the outcome variable. One then reverses the procedure to

12. It is easy to imagine that the effect on the crime rate of releasing one inmate early differs from that of contracting the scope of incarceration to exclude one new admission. For one thing, the early release may well be of an inmate with a more serious offending history. On the other hand, that inmate may no longer be criminally active (either because he has been affected by the prison experience or because he has "aged out" of offending), whereas the "new" inmate is likely to have offended in the recent past.

13. This replication is not perfect, because there are about 100 fewer cases than Levitt reports using. The discrepancy is primarily from missing police data on all states for 1993. Levitt does report a p-value for a test of the instruments, and working backward from that p-value and the reported sample size and number of variables, it can be concluded that an $F = 2.90$ would be the minimum that Levitt obtained. This result would still indicate a finite-sample bias of approximately 33% of the bias from a non-instrumental variables estimation.

determine whether lagged values of the outcome variable predict the independent variable in the presence of lagged values of the independent variable.

The authors conducted Granger tests for all models. In every case, the result of the Granger test suggested that imprisonment is a causal factor for crime rates, but crime rates are not a causal factor for imprisonment rates. This result is similar to that reported by Marvell and Moody (1994). The uniformity and strength of the results of the Granger causality test give no indication that these model estimates suffer any ill effects of simultaneity.

STATIONARITY

The first step in the analysis is to conduct a panel unit-root test on the crime and prison-population variables to determine whether they are stationary. If they are non-stationary, this may produce spurious estimated regression effects and a misinterpretation of underlying relationships (Greenberg, 2001).

The Fisher λ-test proposed by Maddala and Wu (1999) is used, because it has the advantage of heterogeneity across cross-sections, does not require a balanced panel data set, and can incorporate different lag structures in each panel.[14] For the crime-rate data, assuming a lag length of four leads to a rejection of the unit root null hypothesis ($P_\lambda = 417.809$, df = 102, $p < 0.001$ for the Z statistic; $P_\lambda = 406.127$, df = 102, $p < 0.001$ for the T statistic) for a process with a non-zero mean. For the prison population series, assuming a lag-length of four leads to the rejection of the unit-root null hypothesis for one test statistic, but not the other ($P_\lambda = 411.810$, df = 102, $p < 0.001$ for the Z statistic; $P_\lambda = 80.831$, df = 102, $p < 0.939$ for the T statistic) for a process that is trend-stationary.

These results indicate that the crime and prison population series are probably not cointegrated. This finding is the same one that Greenberg (2001) found. Although rejection of a unit root does not guarantee that the series is I(0), the inclusion of year dummies effectively detrends the series, and they need not be overly concerned about potential spurious estimated effects. With this result, the authors proceed with a detailed analysis of this empirical model. However, because of the ambiguities of

14. ADF tests were conducted separately for each state, and the panel ADF test was constructed by combining the p-values for the ADF test from each state, p_i, following a procedure first presented by Fisher for combining independent hypothesis tests (the so-called Fisher λ-test; Fisher, 1932). As discussed in Maddala and Wu (1999), the test statistic is constructed as $P_\lambda = -2 \sum \ln p^i$ and is distributed as a chi-square statistic with df = 2N, where N is the number of states. Such a test construction can be followed for either the test statistic $Z = T(\hat{\rho}-1)$ or for the test statistic $T = {}^{(\hat{\rho}-1)}/_{\sigma_{\hat{\rho}}}$.

panel unit-root tests, the authors will consider a model appropriate for cointegrated series, such as would result if both the crime data and the prison population data contained unit roots, in their examination of robustness of the results.

RESULTS

The authors begin with a baseline model, updating the results from Marvell and Moody covering the more recent years of the prison expansion. They then turn to the quadratic model, their main interest, and then a series of extensions and robustness checks.

BASELINE MODELS

The results of estimating model (1) are reported in Table 2. The first model is a lagged model corresponding to the model specification of Marvell and Moody (1994), but covers a longer time period, 1973 to 2000.[15] It is estimated that a 10% increase in the prison population is associated with reductions in the crime rate of 0.63%, but the effect is not statistically significant.

The second column in Table 2 adds an extended set of control variables beyond the demographic age groups employed by Marvell and Moody. These additions include unemployment rates, a measure of prevailing wages for non-college-educated males, proportion of population that is African-American, and proportion of population living in metropolitan areas. The inclusion of these control variables provides a more complete specification for a crime equation.

The negative estimated SPP elasticity holds up in the extended model; indeed there is very little difference in the estimates. The estimated elasticity for Model 2 is –0.072, which indicates that a 10% increase in prison population would result in a reduction in the crime rate of 0.72%. This estimate is lower than those reported by Levitt or Marvell and Moody. There are several likely reasons for this difference, such as the inclusion of additional years of data, different sets of control variables, using weighted regressions and robust standard errors, and somewhat different model specifications.

The bottom line from this analysis is that smaller, although roughly similar crime-control effects of prison population are found as the extent literature has reported. These effects are not statistically significant, but they do attain significance when unweighted regressions are used. Although the

15. This replication of Marvell and Moody is not a precise replication, because the lagged specification of equation (1) discussed above is employed. However, in a later section of the paper, the Marvell and Moody analysis is more closely replicated with estimates from an error-correction model.

TABLE 2. ML REGRESSIONS OF Ln(CRIME RATES/100,000)

	Model 1 Lag Model	Model 2 Lag Model
Intercept	8.306***	8.129***
	(0.354)	(0.171)
lag [Ln (SPP/1000)]	–0.063	–0.072
	(0.046)	(0.044)
% Population 16–19	–0.177	1.106
	(4.323)	(3.973)
% Population 20–24	0.412	0.512
	(1.167)	(1.260)
% Population 25–34	–0.918	–0.715
	(1.002)	(0.901)
Unemployment Rate		0.820***
		(0.230)
% Black Population		1.377
		(0.889)
% Metro Population		0.147
		(0.228)
Mean Wage		0.045
		(0.027)
–2 log likelihood	–3457.0	–3490.7
BIC	–3126.7	–3144.7
df (parameters estimated)	84.0	88
N	1308.0	1308

*p < 0.05; **p <0.01; ***p < 0.001.
NOTES: For all models, an AR(1) error structure has been modeled.

magnitude of these effects differ from those reported in Marvell and Moody (1994), it is concluded that the addition of another decade's worth of data has not drastically changed the conclusions drawn in the empirical literature of the mid-1990s.

NON-CONSTANT STATE PRISON POPULATION ELASTICITY

Turn now to the estimation of the quadratic SPP effect model [Equation (2)]. Recall that we are interested in estimating a model that encompasses a non-constant SPP elasticity because it is plausible that the effect of incarceration might depend on the scale of incarceration.

We emphasize that our model goes beyond the more typical claim of declining marginal returns. Rather, it asserts *accelerating* declining marginal returns, that is, a percent reduction in crime that gets smaller with ever larger prison populations. To develop the contrast, a non-linear relationship between SPP and crime rates is already incorporated into the basic model through the elasticity specification. In those specifications, the elasticity is constant: The proportional rate of change in crime rates from proportional changes in incarceration rates is constant regardless of the actual level of imprisonment. The distinguishing characteristic of the current quadratic model is that the elasticity can vary: The proportional rate of change in crime rates from proportional changes in incarceration rates depends on the actual level of imprisonment. With this novel specification, models may reveal a pattern in which the declining marginal returns accelerate with the level of imprisonment. In particular, we explore whether a continual increasing of the incarcerated population will reduce the magnitude of prison's negative impact on crime rates.

To sum up, this "less–less" hypothesis—the negative effect of incarceration becomes less as levels of imprisonment increase—implies elasticities that decrease with the size of the incarcerated population, which means that the percentage decline in crime rates from a 10% increase in incarceration gets smaller with higher levels of imprisonment. Elasticities that become positive with the increasing size of the incarcerated population are implied by the crime-augmenting hypothesis.

The estimates of the Quadratic Model are reported as Model 1 in the first column of Table 3.[16] The coefficient of the linear term is –0.118, and the coefficient of the quadratic term is 0.050. Both effects are statistically significant; which is confirmed with a standard *F*-test of the joint hypothesis that both coefficients are simultaneously equal to zero ($p < 0.001$). A likelihood-ratio test comparing this Quadratic Model with the Lag Model (Model 2 in Table 2) demonstrates that the Quadratic Model better fits the data ($G^2 = 30.6$, df = 1, $p < 0.001$), which supports the non-constant elasticity hypothesis.

These estimates imply that the non-constant elasticity relating SPP and crime rates is statistically significant, with negative elasticities at low rates of imprisonment that become less strongly negative as the incarceration

16. An alternative approach to using lagged prison population as the key independent variable is to instrument for contemporaneous prison population using lagged values. This approach is somewhat difficult to implement in these nonlinear models, as it requires at least one instrument for each endogenous variable and the preferred models contain several variables to capture the nonlinearity in the endogenous variable. Although a full IV model was not implemented, we did investigate the sensitivity of the results to using this approach. OLS without an AR(1) closely approximates baseline results, and two-stage least squares was performed using the quadratic model presented here, with the third lag of prison population as the instrument. The results from this IV model are qualitatively and quantitatively similar to the results presented in the article: The point estimate increases somewhat on the level effect (becomes 1/3 more negative), and the standard errors increase modestly. Therefore, inference is not affected by this change in specification.

TABLE 3. ML REGRESSIONS OF Ln(CRIME RATES/100,000): NON-CONSTANT ELASTICITY SPECIFICATIONS

	Model 1 Quadratic Lag Model	Model 2 Polynomial Lag Model	Model 3 Spline Lag Model
Intercept	8.000***	7.922***	7.957***
	(0.248)	(0.228)	(0.249)
lag [Ln (SPP/1000)]	–0.118**	–0.138***	–0.103**
	(0.046)	(0.044)	(0.042)
lag $[\text{Ln (SPP/1000)}]^2$	0.050*	0.009	
	(0.022)	(0.025)	
lag $[\text{Ln (SPP/1000)}]^3$		0.022	
		(0.012)	
lag $[\text{Ln (SPP/1000)}]^4$		0.000	
		(0.004)	
Second Decile Increment			(0.042)
of lag [Ln (SPP/1000)]			(0.042)
Third Decile Increment			0.064
of lag [Ln (SPP/1000)]			(0.063)
Fourth Decile Increment			0.087
of lag [Ln (SPP/1000)]			(0.052)
Fifth Decile Increment			–0.012
of lag [Ln (SPP/1000)]			(0.044)
Sixth Decile Increment			–0.005
of lag [Ln (SPP/1000)]			(0.070)
Seventh Decile Increment			0.055
of lag [Ln (SPP/1000)]			(0.074)
Eighth Decile Increment			0.001
of lag [Ln (SPP/1000)]			(0.035)
Ninth Decile Increment			0.017
of lag [Ln (SPP/1000)]			(0.059)
Tenth Decile Increment			0.313***
of lag [Ln (SPP/1000)]			(0.072)
% Population 16–19	2.115	2.862	2.380
	(3.374)	(3.203)	(3.337)
% Population 20–24	0.624	0.945	0.909
	(1.282)	(1.338)	(1.297)
% Population 25–34	–0.444	–0.304	–0.274
	(0.830)	(0.795)	(0.791)
Unemployment Rate	0.835***	0.866***	0.857***
	(0.246)	(0.242)	(0.247)
% Black Population	1.462	1.841	1.730
	(1.111)	(1.461)	(1.319)
% Metro Population	0.170	0.218	0.210
	(0.219)	(0.217)	(0.223)
Mean Wage	0.043	0.040	0.039
	(0.027)	(0.026)	(0.026)
–2 log likelihood	–3521.4	–3539.6	–3533.3
BIC	–3171.5	–3181.8	–3151.9
df (parameters estimated)	89	91	97
N	1308	1308	1308

$*p < 0.05$; $**p < 0.01$; $***p < 0.001$.

NOTES: For all models, fixed state and year effects are included, along with an AR(1) error structure.

rates get bigger, eventually reaching an inflection point where the elasticity turns positive. This inflection point occurs when a state's incarceration rate is 3.25 persons per 1000 population. This value might seem very low, but it actually corresponds to the 78th percentile of the observed state imprisonment rates.

At the median value of SPP, the estimated elasticity under the Quadratic Lag Model is –1.014, which indicates that a 10% increase in SPP would lower crime rates by 1.01%. But at the 25th-percentile of SPP, that same 10% increase would reduce crime rates by 1.35%, and at the 75th-percentile, the reduction would only be 0.36%. This pattern is clearly consistent with the "less–less" hypothesis of diminishing proportional returns to the use of incarceration.

As indicated, a useful extension of the Quadratic Model is to consider a polynomial specification of imprisonment rates; this model has the advantage of greater generality of the parametric form over the imposed quadratic of the previous model. We consider a fourth-order polynomial of SPP for this extension. The extra powers included in the polynomial specification allow for more complex non-constant patterns in the SPP elasticity. Estimates of this Polynomial Model are reported in the second column of Table 3. What is found is that the only statistically significant term of the polynomial is the linear ($p < 0.01$) term, but the positive cubic effect does approach conventional levels of significance ($p < 0.0611$). The more powerful likelihood-ratio test finds the Polynomial Model better fitting ($G^2 = 18.2$, $df = 2$, $p < 0.02$) than the Quadratic Model, which indicates that the additional cubic and quartic terms do contribute to the explanation of crime rates provided here. The results of the Polynomial Model substantially parallel the general conclusion from the Quadratic Model.

At the median value of SPP, the estimated elasticity under the Polynomial Lag Model is –0.093, which indicates that a 10% increase in SPP would lower crime rates by about 0.93%. But at the 25th-percentile of SPP, that same 10% increase would reduce crime rates by 1.31%, and at the 75th-percentile, the decline would be only 0.31%. Again, the pattern is consistent with the less–less hypothesis.

Turning to the final empirical specification, it is found that spline estimates replicate the essential pattern observed in the Quadratic Lag and Polynomial Lag models. Note that the two statistically significant spline effects are the –0.103 coefficient for the first decile of the spline and the +0.313 coefficient for the tenth decile, which means that when SPP reaches the higher levels of the tenth decile, the elasticity becomes positive 0.210 (= –0.103 + 0.313). At levels of SPP below 4.292 inmates per 1000 population (the 90th percentile), a 10% increase in SPP decreases crime rates. Above this level, a 10% increase in SPP increases crime rates. The spline model can be viewed as a roughly hewn non-parametric approximation to the Quadratic Lag Model, and perhaps more strongly convincing because it does not impose a parametric form on the relationship.

The results from all three non-constant elasticity models are strongly consistent. The Quadratic Lag Model finds that at low-to-moderate levels of SPP, the estimated elasticity is negative, which indicates a crime-control effect of imprisonment. At higher levels of SPP, the quadratic term takes over, and the negative elasticity gets weaker, sliding closer to zero, until it reaches a level of SPP whereupon the elasticity actually becomes positive, which indicates a crime-augmentation effect of SPP. The Polynomial Lag Model parallels the Quadratic Model, because the two most significant effects are the linear and quadratic terms in the polynomial specification of SPP. Finally, the Spline model parallels the Quadratic Model in that the estimated elasticity is negative over much of the range of SPP, turning significantly positive when SPP exceeds 4.292 prisoners per 1000 population (demarcation of the tenth decile)—not so very different from the inflection point of 3.25 prisoners per 1000 population calculated from the parameter estimates of the Quadratic Model. Given the range and flexibility of these models, the general findings are strongly supported.[17]The evidence of these three non-constant elasticity models is compelling. All three are clearly better fits to the data than the constant elasticity model. All three roughly parallel each other in the pattern of the estimated effect of incarceration. They all indicate that the crime-control effect of imprisonment does lessen with greater increases in incarceration. They support the "less–less" hypothesis.

ROBUSTNESS

Because of the strong relationship between prison populations and time, one needs to be concerned that prison populations and time are both properly specified. If not, the non-constant elasticities estimated here may pick up the effects of unmeasured variables, which change over time. To examine the robustness of these regression results, the three specifications of the previous section—Quadratic Lag Model, Polynomial Lag Model,

17. These models can be compared with the more orthodox constant elasticity baseline model (Table 2, Model 2). The Quadratic Lag Model ($G^2 = 30.7$, df = 1, $p < 0.001$) and the Polynomial Lag Model ($G^2 = 48.9$, df = 3, $p < 0.001$) both fit better using a likelihood-ratio test. So does the Spline Model ($G^2 = 48.6$, df = 9, $p < 0.001$). The Spline Model cannot be directly compared with either the Quadratic or the Polynomial Model because they are not nested, but the Bayesian Information Criterion (BIC) statistic (Raftery, 1995) can be used to choose among them. The BIC is a penalized version of the likelihood, where parsimony is valued. The smaller the value of BIC, the better the model. Employing BIC, both the Quadratic (BIC = –3171.5) and the Polynomial Lag (BIC = –3181.8) models are preferred over the Spline Lag model (BIC = –3151.9). The Polynomial Lag model is only slightly preferred over the Quadratic Lag model.

and Spline Lag Model—were reestimated with state-specific linear and quadratic time trends, as reported in Table 4. Quadratic time trends are important to consider. Because crime rates over the past 25 years follow a roughly quadratic pattern, it is possible that the result of fitting quadratic SPP models is an artifact of the crime rate trend. State-specific quadratic time trends proxy any unmeasured effects at the state level, which might better account for the observed crime rate trend.

The addition of state-specific linear time trends eliminates the non-constant elasticity result of the Quadratic Lag Model. The Polynomial Lag Model remains the same. However, the Spline Lag Model becomes more strongly consistent with a non-constant elasticity as the effect of the tenth decile increases. The results are strongest when quadratic time trends are included in the models. All three models contain statistically significant higher order SPP terms; all three clearly imply an elasticity that varies with the scale of imprisonment. The evidence is compelling because the results occur in the presence of the quadratic time trends. Even after filtering out the overall state-specific quadratic trend of crime rates, there is evidence of the non-constant elasticity.

COINTEGRATION ANALYSES

Prior research has found that crime rates and imprisonment are cointegrated (Levitt, 1996; Marvell and Moody, 1994) . If cointegrated, both series—crime rates and SPP—contain unit roots [are I(1)], but a linear combination of the two series is stationary [is I(0)]. Cointegrated series require a specialized modeling approach. As discussed, evidence was found that the series do not contain unit roots and are not I(1). However, an additional model specification appropriate for such situations is estimated, for completeness, and because the model estimates contemporaneous effects of imprisonment on crime. This model can be written as

$$\ln(crime\ rate_{it}) = b_0 + b_1(\ln SPP_{it}) + b_2(\ln SPP_{i(t-1)}) + \\ \gamma(\ln(crime\ rate_{i(t-1)})) + \sum b_k X_{kit} + \delta_i + \lambda_t + \varepsilon_{it}.$$

Note that this model is an error-correction, or equilibrium-correction, model (ECM) incorporating both short-run (contemporaneous) effects and a long-run equilibrium correction effect. The short-run elasticity is identified with the coefficient b_1, whereas the long-run equilibrium elasticity is determined as $(b_1 + b_2)/(1 - \gamma)$. This specification of the ECM, although not visibly identical to the Engle–Granger model employed by Marvell and Moody (1994), is indeed the same model (a detailed comparison is presented in an appendix available from the authors). When quadratic or polynomial terms of SPP are added, a quadratic or polynomial

TABLE 4. ML REGRESSIONS OF Ln(CRIME RATES/ 100,000): ROBUSTNESS SPECIFICATIONS

	Model 1 Quadratic Lag Model w/Linear Time Trend	Model 2 Polynomial Lag Model w/Linear Time Trend	Model 3 Spline Lag Model w/ Linear Time Trend	Model 4 Quadratic Lag Model w/Quadratic Time Trends	Model 5 Polynomial Lag Model w/Quadratic Time Trends	Model 6 Spline Lag Model w/ Quadratic Time Trends
Intercept	7.994***	7.928***	8.021***	8.027***	7.810***	8.087***
	(0.180)	(0.151)	(0.193)	(0.309)	(0.207)	(0.307)
lag [Ln (SPP/1000)]	–0.121**	–0.120**	–0.104**	–0.105*	–0.103**	–0.111**
	(0.047)	(0.045)	(0.040)	(0.047)	(0.034)	(0.038)
lag $[\text{Ln (SPP/1000)}]^2$	0.052	–0.006		0.042	–0.045	
	(0.039)	(0.031)		(0.034)	(0.024)	
lag $[\text{Ln (SPP/1000)}]^3$		0.012			0.005	
		(0.016)			(0.011)	
lag $[\text{Ln (SPP/1000)}]^4$		0.008			0.013***	
lag $[\text{Ln (SPP/1000)}]^4$		(0.005)			(0.003)	
Second Decile Increment			–0.011			0.023
of lag [Ln (SPP/1000)]			(0.042)			(0.041)
Third Decile Increment			0.072			0.100
of lag [Ln (SPP/1000)]			(0.063)			(0.063)
Fourth Decile Increment			0.041			0.042
of lag [Ln (SPP/1000)]			(0.046)			(0.043)
Fifth Decile Increment			–0.049			–0.052
of lag [Ln (SPP/1000)]			(0.052)			(0.054)
Sixth Decile Increment			–0.008			–0.020
of lag [Ln (SPP/1000)]			(0.080)			(0.088)
Seventh Decile Increment			0.080			0.091
of lag [Ln (SPP/1000)]			(0.075)			(0.077)
Eighth Decile Increment			0.003			0.033
of lag [Ln (SPP/1000)]			(0.035)			(0.035)
Ninth Decile Increment			0.057			0.047
of lag [Ln (SPP/1000)]			(0.070)			(0.070)
Tenth Decile Increment			0.368*			0.323**
of lag [Ln (SPP/1000)]			(0.157)			(0.116)
% Population 16–19	2.050	2.945	2.072	3.328	4.768	2.943
	(3.022)	(2.814)	(3.053)	(3.322)	(2.599)	(3.355)
% Population 20–24	0.288	0.916	0.498	–0.572	1.174	–0.371
	(1.125)	(1.403)	(1.277)	(1.553)	(1.668)	(1.472)
% Population 25–34	0.345	0.335	0.385	0.124	0.558	0.183
	(0.674)	(0.645)	(0.650)	(0.903)	(0.729)	(0.848)
Unemployment Rate	0.648*	0.643*	0.688*	0.870**	0.866**	0.871**
	(0.303)	(0.289)	(0.299)	(0.291)	(0.291)	(0.299)
% Black Population	1.443	1.251	1.119	0.479	0.488	0.435
	(1.295)	(1.120)	(1.105)	(0.703)	(0.692)	(0.708)
% Metro Population	–0.152	–0.111	–0.145	–0.306	–0.229	–0.260
	(0.241)	(0.232)	(0.238)	(0.276)	(0.247)	(0.254)
Mean Wage	0.069**	0.071**	0.064**	0.055*	0.050*	0.047
	(0.026)	(0.024)	(0.025)	(0.028)	(0.024)	(0.026)
–2 log likelihood	–3846.8	–3898.2	–3883.9	–4092.2	–4180.4	–4124.4
BIC	–3304.2	–3347.7	–3309.9	–3376.6	–3456.9	–3373.4
df (parameters estimated)	138	140	146	182	184	191
N	1308	1308	1308	1308	1308	1308

*p < 0.05; **p < 0.01; ***p < 0.001.

NOTES: For all models, fixed state and year effects are included, along with an AR(1) error structure.

ECM is then estimated.[18]

The results of estimating a (constant elasticity) standard ECM and (non-constant elasticity) quadratic ECM and polynomial ECM are presented in Table 5. The standard ECM is reported as Model 1. There is a statistically significant short-run SPP elasticity of –0.056, and a statistically significant long-run SPP elasticity of –0.132, which means that a 10% increase in SPP will reduce crime rates in the short- run by 0.56%. The long-run equilibrium is such that a 10% increase in SPP will produce a cumulative reduction in crime rates of 1.32%.

In Model 2, a quadratic ECM model is estimated. There is a statistically significant short-run linear and quadratic effect; the expression for the short-run SPP elasticity is –0.098 + 0.040(lnSPP), which means that at the 50th-percentile of SPP, a 10% increase in SPP will reduce crime rates by 0.05%. The inflection point at which short-run crime rates will rise is at 3.40 inmates per 1000 population. The long-run SPP elasticity can be expressed as –0.053 + 0.010(lnSPP); at the 50th-percentile of SPP, a 10% increase in SPP has a cumulative reduction of 2.45% on crime rates.

Finally, Model 3 reports the result of estimating a Polynomial ECM model. For the Polynomial ECM, only the linear short-run effect is significant; none of the higher order effects are significant. This result is in contrast to the parallel estimation of the Lag Quadratic and Lag Polynomial models discussed. However, it must be noted that the Polynomial ECM does not fit significantly better than the Quadratic ECM ($G^2 = 8.7$, $df = 4$, $p < 0.10$).

HOW IMPORTANT ARE THE VARIABLE SPP EFFECTS?

To aid interpretation, Table 6 provides the estimated percentage change in crime rates for a 10% increase in SPP at the 10th-, 25th-, 50th-, 75th-, 90th-, and 95th-percentiles of SPP for the various non-constant elasticity models. These models include the Quadratic, Polynomial, and Spline Lag models, with and without time-trends and the Quadratic ECM model. For comparison, it should be noted that the constant elasticity baseline Lag Model reduces crime by 0.72% for a 10% increase in SPP at all percentile levels, whereas the constant elasticity ECM Model reduces crime by 0.56% in the short run, and 1.32% in the long run, for a 10% increase in SPP at all percentile levels.

The Quadratic Lag and Polynomial Lag models (columns 1 and 2) both

18. An ECM that parallels the Spline Lag model estimated above cannot be readily estimated, because in the ECM model, both lagged and unlagged SPP are included in the model, but decile splits occur at different values for lagged SPP and unlagged SPP.

TABLE 5. ML REGRESSIONS OF Ln(CRIME RATES/ 100,000): ERROR-CORRECTION SPECIFICATIONS

	Model 1 Error-Correction Model	Model 2 Error-Correction Quadratic Model	Model 3 Error-Correction Polynomial Model
Intercept	0.997***	1.152***	1.154***
	(0.125)	(0.128)	(0.130)
Ln (SPP/1000)	−0.056*	−0.098***	−0.110**
	(0.022)	(0.026)	(0.034)
lag [Ln (SPP/1000)]	0.023	0.045	0.058
	(0.022)	(0.025)	(0.032)
Ln $(SPP/1000)^2$		0.040***	0.006
		(0.010)	(0.017)
lag $[Ln (SPP/1000)]^2$		−0.030**	0.001
		(0.010)	(0.017)
Ln $(SPP/1000)^3$			0.009
			(0.011)
lag $[Ln (SPP/1000)]^3$			−0.008
			(0.010)
Ln $(SPP/1000)^4$			0.002
			(0.003)
lag $[Ln (SPP/1000)]^4$			−0.002
			(0.003)
lag[Ln(Index crimes/100,000)]	0.850***	0.831***	0.829***
	(0.015)	(0.016)	(0.016)
% Population 16–19	2.163***	2.536***	2.726***
	(0.529)	(0.537)	(0.554)
% Population 20–24	−0.228	−0.301	−0.371
	(0.337)	(0.334)	(0.340)
% Population 25–34	0.712***	0.719	0.781***
	(0.214)	(0.212)	(0.213)
Unemployment Rate	−0.053	2.536***	0.009
	(0.127)	(0.537)	(0.127)
% Black Population	−0.143	−0.301	−0.250
	(0.174)	(0.334)	(0.235)
% Metro Population	0.080	0.719***	0.062
	(0.052)	(0.212)	(0.052
Mean Wage	0.005	0.016	0.019
	(0.025)	(0.025)	(0.025)
−2 log likelihood	−4043.8	−4068.6	−4077.3
BIC	−3405.1	−3415.6	−3395.5
df (parameters estimated)	89	91	95
N	1308	1308	1308

*$p < 0.05$; **$p < 0.01$; ***$p < 0.001$.

NOTES: For all models, fixed state and year effects are included, along with an AR(1) error structure.

show the impact on crime weakens over the range of SPP, even becoming positive (a crime-augmentation result) at the 90th-percentile for the Quadratic Lag model. The Spline Lag Model (column 3) also indicates crime-augmentation properties of striking size at the 95th-percentile of SPP. When time-trends are added to the Quadratic Lag Model (column 4), a

TABLE 6. ESTIMATED IMPACT OF 10% INCREASE IN SPP ON CRIME RATES

SPP Percentile	Quadratic Lag Model (Table 3, Model 1)	Polynomial Lag Model (Table 3, Model 2)	Spline Lag Model (Table 3, Model 3)	Quadratic Lag w/Quadratic Time Trends (Table 4, Model 4)	Polynomial Lag w/Quadratic Time Trends (Table 4, Model 5)	Spline Lag w/Quadratic Time Trends (Table 4, Model 6)	ECM Quadratic Model (Table 5, Model 2)	
							Short Run	Long Run
10th	–1.547%	–1.339%	–1.033%	–1.362%	–0.705%	–1.112%	–1.277%	–3.548%
25th	–1.123%	–1.352%	–0.621%	–1.004%	–1.080%	0.117%	–0.938%	–3.066%
50th	–0.579%	–1.014%	0.091%	–0.547%	–1.407%	–0.177%	–0.050%	–2.450%
75th	–0.083%	–0.359%	0.647%	–0.129%	–1.162%	1.058%	–0.109%	–1.887%
90th	0.298%	0.368%	0.812%	0.192%	–0.376%	1.533%	0.195%	–1.455%
95th	0.469%	0.759%	3.941%	0.336%	0.199%	4.758%	0.331%	–1.260%

NOTES: All value are positive unless indicated. For comparison, impact for Lag Model is –0.072% at all percentiles of SPP. For comparison, impact for ECM Model is –0.558% for the short run and –2.157% for the long run, at all percentiles of SPP.

declining impact of imprisonment is observed as the scale of imprisonment increases, with a crime-augmentation effect observed past the 90th-percentile of imprisonment. The Polynomial Lag model time-trends (column 5) also show a pattern of decreasing effectiveness of imprisonment, with the crime-augmentation effect also beginning when the 90th-percentile of SPP is reached. The Spline Lag Model indicates crime-augmentation properties at even moderately high levels of SPP (column 6). The Quadratic Error-Correction model (column 7 and 8) indicates declining effectiveness in both the short run and the long run, although crime-augmentation effects only the short run.

This set of results has several implications. First, the effect on crime of expanding the use of incarceration may be different in different jurisdictions depending on how extensively the jurisdictions are already using prison as punishment. For example, compare California in 1998 (with an incarceration rate of 4.8 per 1000) with Oregon in the same year (with an incarceration rate of 2.6 per 1000). Our estimates imply that expanding prison population by 10% in California would be associated with a 0.42% increase in crime, whereas a similar expansion in Oregon would be associated with a 0.22% decrease in crime, net other effects in the quadratic lag model with time-trends (employing estimates from Table 4, Model 1).

A second implication is that studies estimating a constant elasticity between SPP and crime are likely to find different results depending on the time period studied. One way to see this result is to note that the mean level of incarceration in the 1970s was 1.11 inmates per 1000 population, the mean level in the 1980s was 2.07, and the mean level in 1990s was 3.97. Studies from the 1970s would have had less than 1.5% of their observations above the estimated inflection point of the quadratic lag model (Table 4, Model 1) and less than 1% above the estimated short-run inflection of the quadratic ECM model. Studies from the 1980s would have had 7.5% of their observations above the estimated inflection point from the quadratic lag model and 5.5% of their observations above the estimated short-run inflection point from the quadratic ECM model. Studies from the 1990s would have had 48.8% of their observations above the estimated inflection point from the quadratic lag model and 42.9% of their observations above the estimated short-run inflection point from the quadratic ECM model. As a result, the constant elasticity model on U.S. data will yield estimates of the effect of imprisonment that become less negative as more recent years are added to the analysis. This result provides a caution against using estimates from one period of time to extrapolate to another period with far different conditions.

It is somewhat surprising that some models estimated imply crime augmentation effects at moderate or high levels of incarceration. We are cautious about interpretation because of concerns that it may in part reflect simultaneity bias. Nonetheless, it is provocative enough to be considered in future work, for it implies that additional prison growth may cause crime—the supposed remedy causing more of the disease.

However, we are fully confident of the more general point that the effect of prison on crime depends on the scale of incarceration. Across a variety of models, as the prison population increases, all else being equal, its proportional effect on crime falls. These estimates are closely in line with those reported in the earlier literature, except that the estimated constant elasticity is smaller than previously thought. Furthermore, these new findings of an elasticity that declines with the scale of imprisonment are robust to a wide range of alternative specifications of empirical models and various flexible controls for time. The essential pattern of the results is emphasized: The prison elasticity of crime declines with the scale of imprisonment.

CRIME TYPES

Although these analyses point to a particular pattern in elasticities over the range of the scale of incarceration, the models employed the overall UCR crime rate. This process may not be as helpful as presenting the results broken down by crime type. Thus, all of the various models discussed were estimated but for each crime type—murder, rape, robbery, aggravated assault, burglary, larceny-theft, and motor vehicle theft. Rather than replicate tables for each crime type as above, results are presented only for the spline model specification.[19]

These results are shown in Table 7. This table presents a summary of the spline estimates for each crime type, analogous to Table 3, Model 3. To simplify the table, the estimates of the intercept and control variables are suppressed.

The general pattern across crime type is similar to that found with the analysis of index crime rates. However, there are some crucial differences. All crime types have significant, positive effects for the tenth decile, which indicate an elasticity that turns positive. The major difference is the pattern of effects for rape, where the ninth and tenth decile effects are significant and negative, which means that for rape, the increase in imprisonment has led to a greater reduction in rates of rape.

For murder, the initial negative effect (–0.130) is swamped by significant, positive effects at the third, sixth, and tenth deciles. For robbery and aggravated assault, the only significant effect is the positive effect at the tenth decile. The estimates for burglary, larceny-theft, and motor vehicle

19. A total of 28 additional tables would be needed to reproduce Tables 3–6 for each of the seven crime types. This full set of tables is available from the authors upon request.

TABLE 7. ML REGRESSIONS OF Ln(CRIME RATES/100,000): SPLINE SPECIFICATIONS BY CRIME TYPE

	Murder	Rape	Robbery	Assault	Burglary	Theft	MV Theft
lag [Ln (SPP/1000)]	–0.130*	0.144	–0.108	0.016	–0.136*	–0.077*	–0.243**
	(0.064)	(0.082)	(0.085)	(0.088)	(0.060)	(0.037)	(0.079)
Second Decile Increment	0.088	0.003	0.021	–0.070	–0.062	–0.007	–0.039
of lag [Ln (SPP/1000)]	(0.172)	(0.110)	(0.104)	(0.122)	(0.046)	(0.050)	(0.069)
Third Decile Increment	0.543**	0.192	–0.202	0.031	0.077	0.065	0.041
of lag [Ln (SPP/1000)]	(0.197)	(0.139)	(0.196)	(0.129)	(0.093)	(0.059)	(0.114)
Fourth Decile Increment	0.317	0.196	–0.114	–0.138	0.044	0.124*	0.033
of lag [Ln (SPP/1000)]	(0.202)	(0.151)	(0.149)	(0.080)	(0.069)	(0.063)	(0.073)
Fifth Decile Increment	0.149	0.203	–0.204	–0.102	–0.048	–0.002	0.047
of lag [Ln (SPP/1000)]	(0.220)	(0.167)	(0.107)	(0.099)	(0.081)	(0.045)	(0.084)
Sixth Decile Increment	0.650**	0.098	–0.228	0.117	–0.010	–0.016	0.056
of lag [Ln (SPP/1000)]	(0.227)	(0.110)	(0.177)	(0.105)	(0.084)	(0.077)	(0.065)
Seventh Decile Increment	0.305	0.012	–0.205	–0.034	0.096	0.056	0.116
of lag [Ln (SPP/1000)]	(0.267)	(0.120)	(0.177)	(0.144)	(0.071)	(0.078)	(0.140)
Eighth Decile Increment	0.382	0.080	0.000	–0.116	0.063	–0.008	–0.072
of lag [Ln (SPP/1000)]	(0.219)	(0.104)	(0.115)	(0.112)	(0.053)	(0.042)	(0.086)
Ninth Decile Increment	–0.129	–0.351**	0.176	0.065	0.042	–0.029	0.149*
of lag [Ln (SPP/1000)]	(0.198)	(0.121)	(0.141)	(0.180)	(0.089)	(0.055)	(0.072)
Tenth Decile Increment	0.509**	–0.458***	0.437***	0.541***	0.299**	0.220***	0.774***
of lag [Ln (SPP/1000)]	(0.196)	(0.102)	(0.129)	(0.150)	(0.103)	(0.053)	(0.200)
–2 log likelihood	13.6	–1332.1	–1105.8	–1374.1	–2692.0	–3473.7	–1708.2

*p < 0.05; **p < 0.01; ***p < 0.001.

NOTES: For all models, fixed state and year effects are included, along with an AR(1) error structure. N = 1308.

theft most closely parallel the results for index crimes, a result that is not very surprising because these offenses are the most common and constitute about 85% of reported index crimes.

These basic results, reported with the index crime rates, hold up when they are disaggregated by crime type, save for the case of rape. The patterns found in examining aggregated crime rates seem to hold for specific types of crime.

CONCLUSION

The core point of this study is to consider the relevance of the point that the effect of imprisonment depends on the scale of incarceration. Increasing imprisonment rates from its low levels must reduce crime; otherwise, everyone would be prison abolitionists. And endless prison expansion must have diminishing returns beyond a certain threshold. The interesting question is whether the abstract observation of a non-constant elasticity applies to the prison buildup over the last 30 years. Specifically, first, did the U.S. prison buildup reduce the crime rate in its initial stages, and second, did the buildup reach the point of declining effectiveness? The central empirical finding of this study is that the answer to both questions is "yes."

This answer provides a broad reconciliation of the mainly econometric studies that have found negative prison/crime elasticities and the critics' observations that the prison buildup damages the fabric of society. The results presented here suggest that during the course of a dramatic increase in incarceration, both stories are likely to be true—in succession. Of course, the details of these experiences operate on the individual and community levels, not on the "state-year" observations analyzed here. But these aggregate results point the literature in a useful direction—that of synthesizing various theories and analyses of the prison–crime relationship.

The United States has experienced three decades of rapid prison growth, and the prison population continues to grow, although at a slower rate. The findings developed here go beyond the claim, made by previous researchers, that this continued prison expansion has reached a point of declining marginal returns. Instead, accelerating diminishing marginal returns were found. Prison expansion is expensive in the costs it imposes on both those who serve time behind bars and in absorbing tax dollars. Policy discussion should be informed by the limitation of the fact that prison expansion, beyond a certain point, will no longer serve any reasonable purpose. It seems that that point has been reached.

REFERENCES

Becker, Gary
1968 Crime and punishment: An economic approach. Journal of Political Economy 76:169–217.

Bound, John, David A. Jaeger, and Regina M. Baker
1995 Problems with instrumental variables estimation when the correlation between the instruments and the endogenous explanatory variable is weak. Journal of the American Statistical Association 90:443-450.

Chaiken, Jan M. and Marcia R. Chaiken
1982 Varieties of Criminal Behavior. Santa Monica, Calif.: Rand.

Chambliss, William
1999 Power, Politics, and Crime. Boulder, Colo.: Westview Press.

Donziger, Steven A.
1996 The Real War on Crime: The Report of the National Criminal Justice Commission. New York: Harper Perennial.

Feeley, Malcom M. and Edward L. Rubin
1998 Judicial Policy Making and the Modern State: How the Courts Reformed America's Prisons. New York: Cambridge University Press.

Finkelman, Paul
1985 Exploring Southern legal history. North Carolina Law Review 64:77–120.

Fisher, Ronald A.
1932 Statistical Methods for Research Workers. 5th ed. Edinburgh: Oliver and Boyd.

Garland, David
2001 The Culture of Control: Crime and Social Order in Contemporary Society. Chicago: University of Chicago Press.

Gould, Eric D., Bruce A. Weinberg, and David B. Mustard
2002 Crime rates and Local Labor market opportunities in the United States: 1979-1997. Review of Economics and Statistics 84:45–61.

Granger, C. W. J.
1969 Investing causal relations by econometric models and cross-spectral methods. Econometrica 37:424–438.

Grasmick, Harold G. and George J. Bryjak
1980 The deterrent effect of perceived severity of punishment. Social Forces 59: 471–491.

Greenberg, David F.
2001 Time series analysis of crime rates. Journal of Quantitative Criminology 17:291–327.

Greenwood, Peter W.
1982 Selective Incapacitation. Santa Monica, Calif.: Rand.

Hagan, John and Ronit Dinovitzer
1999 Collateral consequences of imprisonment for children, communities, and prisoners. In Michael Tonry (ed.), Crime and Justice: A Review of Research, Vol 26. Chicago: University of Chicago Press.

Katyal, Neal Kumar
1997 Deterrence's difficulty. Michigan Law Review 95: 2385–2476.

Levitt, Steven D.
1996 The effect of prison population size on crime rates: Evidence from prison overcrowding litigation. Quarterly Journal of Economics 111:319–352.

Lynch, James P. and William Sabol
2004 Assessing the effects of mass incarceration on informal social control in communities. Criminology & Public Policy 3:267–294.

Maddala, G. S. and Shaowen Wu
1999 A comparative study of unit root tests with panel data and a new simple test. Oxford Bulletin of Economics and Statistics 61:631–652.

Marvell, Thomas B. and Carlisle E. Moody
1994 Prison population and crime reduction. Journal of Quantitative Criminology 10:109–139.

Mauer, Marc
1999 Race to Incarcerate. New York: New Press.

McKelvey, Blake
1977 American Prisons: A History of Good Intentions. Montclair, N.J.: P. Smith.

Meyer, Peter B. and Shawna Adkins Hopkins
1991. Making economically sound confinement decisions: A response to the Zedlewski thesis. The American Journal of Criminal Justice 15:106–132.

Nagin, Daniel S.
1998 Deterrence and incapacitation, In Michael Tonry (ed.), The Handbook of Crime and Punishment. New York: Oxford University Press.

Piehl, Anne M. and John J. DiIulio, Jr.
1995 Does prison pay? Revisited. The Brookings Review (Winter):21–25.

Piehl, Anne M., Bert Useem, and John J. DiIulio, Jr.
1999 Right-Sizing Justice: A Cost-Benefit Analysis of Imprisonment in Three States. A Report of the Manhattan Institute for Policy Research Center for Civic Innovation. New York: Manhattan Institute.

Raftery, Adrian E.
1995 Bayesian model selection tor social research. Sociological Methodology 25:111–163.

Rose, Dina R. and Todd R. Clear
1998 Incarceration, social capital, and crime: Examining the unintended consequences of incarceration. Criminology 36:441–479.

Schlanger, Margo
2003 Inmate litigation. Harvard Law Review 116:1555–1705.

Skolnick, Jerome H.
1995 What not to do about crime—The American Society of Criminology Presidential Address. Criminology 33:1–15.

Spelman, William
1994 Criminal Incapacitation. New York: Plenum.

2000 The limited importance of prison expansion. In Alfred Blumstein and Joel Wallman (eds.), The Crime Drop in America. New York: Cambridge University Press.

Stinchcombe, Arthur L.
1997 On the virtues of the old institutionalism. Annual Review of Sociology 23:1–18.

Wilson, James Q.
1983 Thinking About Crime. 2ed. New York: Basic Books.

Witt, R. and Anne Witte
2000 Crime, prison, and female labor supply. Journal of Quantitative Criminology 16:69–85.

Zedlewski, Edwin
1987 Making Confinement Decisions. NIJ Research in Brief. Washington, D.C.: U.S. Department of Justice, Bureau of Justice Statistics, U.S. Government Printing Office.

Zimring, Franklin and Gordon Hawkins
1988 The new mathematics of imprisonment. Crime & Delinquency 34:425–443.

Raymond V. Liedka is an assistant professor at Oakland University. He is interested in the application of quantitative models to problems in crime and criminal justice.

Anne Morrison Piehl is an Associate Professor in the Economics Department at Rutgers University, Faculty Affiliate of the Rutgers Program in criminal justice, and Research Associate at the National Bureau of Economic Research. She conducts research on the economics of crime and criminal justice.

Bert Useem is Professor of Sociology at Purdue University. He is interested in the conditions that produce order and disorder in criminal justice institutions.

Part IV
Deterrence and Capital Punishment

[10]

SPEECH IN FAVOUR OF CAPITAL PUNISHMENT

JOHN STUART MILL

. . . It would be a great satisfaction to me if I were able to support this Motion. It is always a matter of regret to me to find myself, on a public question, opposed to those who are called—sometimes in the way of honour, and sometimes in what is intended for ridicule—the philanthropists. Of all persons who take part in public affairs, they are those for whom, on the whole, I feel the greatest amount of respect; for their characteristic is, that they devote their time, their labour, and much of their money to objects purely public, with a less admixture of either personal or class selfishness, than any other class of politicians whatever. On almost all the great questions, scarcely any politicians are so steadily and almost uniformly to be found on the side of right; and they seldom err, but by an exaggerated application of some just and highly important principle. On the very subject that is now occupying us we all know what signal service they have rendered. It is through their efforts that our criminal laws—which within my memory hanged people for stealing in a dwelling house to the value of 40s.—laws by virtue of which rows of human beings might be seen suspended in front of Newgate by those who ascended or descended Ludgate Hill—have so greatly relaxed their most revolting and most impolitic ferocity, that aggravated murder is now practically the only crime which is punished with death by any of our lawful tribunals; and we are even now deliberating whether the extreme penalty should be retained in that solitary case. This vast gain, not only to humanity, but to the ends of penal justice, we owe to the philanthropists; and if they are mistaken, as I cannot but think they are, in the present instance, it is

Reprinted from *Hansard's Parliamentary Debates*, 3rd Series, 21 Apr. 1868 (London, 1868).

only in not perceiving the right time and place for stopping in a career hitherto so eminently beneficial. Sir, there is a point at which, I conceive, that career ought to stop. When there has been brought home to any one, by conclusive evidence, the greatest crime known to the law; and when the attendant circumstances suggest no palliation of the guilt, no hope that the culprit may even yet not be unworthy to live among mankind, nothing to make it probable that the crime was an exception to his general character rather than a consequence of it, then I confess it appears to me that to deprive the criminal of the life of which he has proved himself to be unworthy—solemnly to blot him out from the fellowship of mankind and from the catalogue of the living—is the most appropriate, as it is certainly the most impressive, mode in which society can attach to so great a crime the penal consequences which for the security of life it is indispensable to annex to it. I defend this penalty, when confined to atrocious cases, on the very ground on which it is commonly attacked—on that of humanity to the criminal; as beyond comparison the least cruel mode in which it is possible adequately to deter from the crime. If, in our horror of inflicting death, we endeavour to devise some punishment for the living criminal which shall act on the human mind with a deterrent force at all comparable to that of death, we are driven to inflictions less severe indeed in appearance, and therefore less efficacious, but far more cruel in reality. Few, I think, would venture to propose, as a punishment for aggravated murder, less than imprisonment with hard labour for life; that is the fate to which a murderer would be consigned by the mercy which shrinks from putting him to death. But has it been sufficiently considered what sort of a mercy this is, and what kind of life it leaves to him? If, indeed, the punishment is not really inflicted—if it becomes the sham which a few years ago such punishments were rapidly becoming—then, indeed, its adoption would be almost tantamount to giving up the attempt to repress murder altogether. But if it really is what it professes to be, and if it is realized in all its rigour by the popular imagination, as it very probably would not be, but as it must be if it is to be efficacious, it will be so shocking that when the memory of the crime is no longer fresh, there will be almost insuperable difficulty in executing it. What comparison can there really be, in point of severity, between consigning a man to the short pang of a rapid death, and immuring him in a living tomb, there to linger out what may be a long life in the hardest and most monotonous toil, without any of its alleviations or rewards—debarred from all pleasant sights and sounds, and cut off from all earthly hope, except a slight mitigation of bodily restraint, or a small improvement of diet? Yet even such a lot as this, because there is no one moment at which the suffering is of terrifying intensity, and, above all, because it does not contain the element, so imposing to the imagination, of the unknown, is universally reputed a milder punishment than death—stands in all codes as a mitigation of the capital penalty, and is thankfully accepted as such. For it is characteristic of all punishments which depend on duration for their efficacy—all, therefore, which are not corporal or pecuniary—that they are more rigorous than they seem; while it is, on the contrary, one of the strongest recommendations a punishment can have, that it should seem more rigorous than it is; for its practical power depends far less on what it is than on what it seems. There is not, I should think, any human infliction which makes an impression on the imagination so entirely out of proportion to its real severity as the punishment of death. The punishment must be mild indeed which does not add more to the sum of human misery than is necessarily or directly added by the execution of a criminal. As my hon. Friend the Member for Northampton (Mr Gilpin) has himself remarked, the most that human laws can do to anyone in the matter of death is to hasten it; the man would have died at any rate; not so very much later, and on the average, I fear, with a considerably greater amount of bodily suffering. Society is asked, then, to denude itself of an instrument of punishment which, in the grave cases to which alone it is suitable, effects its purposes at a less cost of human suffering than any other; which, while it inspires more terror, is less cruel in actual fact than any punishment that we should think of substituting for it. My hon. Friend says that it does not inspire terror, and that experience proves it to be a failure. But the influence of a punishment is not to be estimated by its effect on hardened criminals. Those whose habitual way of life keeps them, so to speak, at all times within sight of the gallows, do grow to care less about it; as, to compare good things with bad, an old soldier is not much affected by the chance of dying in battle. I can afford to admit all that is often said about the indifference of professional criminals to the gallows. Though of that indifference one-third is probably bravado and another third confidence that they shall have the luck to escape, it is quite probable that the remaining third is real. But the efficacy of a punishment which acts principally through the imagination, is chiefly to be measured by the impression it makes on those who are still innocent; by the horror with which it surrounds the first promptings of guilt; the restraining influence it exercises over the beginning of the thought which, if indulged, would become a temptation; the check which it exerts over the graded declension towards the state—never suddenly attained—in which crime no longer revolts, and punishment no longer terrifies. As for what is called the failure of death punishment, who is able to judge of that? We partly know who those are whom it has not deterred; but who is there who knows whom it has deterred, or how many human beings it has saved who would have lived to be murderers if that awful association had not been thrown round the idea of murder from their earliest infancy? Let us not forget that the most imposing fact loses its power over the imagination if it is made too cheap. When a punishment fit only for the most atrocious crimes is lavished on small offences until human feeling recoils from it, then, indeed, it ceases to intimidate, because it ceases to be believed in. The failure of capital punishment in cases of theft is easily accounted for; the thief did not believe that it would be inflicted. He had learnt by experience that jurors would perjure themselves rather than find him guilty; that Judges would seize any excuse for not sentencing him to death, or for recommending him to mercy; and that if neither jurors nor Judges were merciful, there were still hopes from an authority above both. When things had come to this pass it was high time to give up the vain attempt. When it is impossible to inflict a punishment, or when its infliction becomes a public scandal, the idle threat cannot too soon disappear from the statute book. And in the case of the host of offences which were formerly capital, I heartily rejoice that it did become impracticable to execute the law. If the same state of public feeling comes to exist in the case of murder; if the time comes when jurors refuse to find a murderer guilty; when Judges will not sentence him to death, or will recommend him to mercy; or when, if juries and Judges do not flinch from their duty, Home Secretaries, under pressure of deputations and memorials, shrink from theirs, and the threat becomes, as it became in the other cases, a mere *brutum fulmen*; then, indeed, it may become necessary to do in this case what has been done in those—to abrogate the penalty. That time may come—my hon. Friend thinks that it has nearly come. I hardly know whether he lamented it or boasted of it; but he and his Friends are entitled to the boast; for if it comes it will be their doing, and they will have gained what I cannot but call a fatal victory, for they will have achieved it by bringing about, if they will forgive me for saying so, an enervation, an effeminancy, in the general mind of the country. For what else than effeminancy is it to be so much more shocked by taking a man's life than by depriving him of all that makes life desirable or valuable? Is death, then, the greatest of all earthly ills? *Usque adeone mori miserum est?* Is it, indeed, so dreadful a thing to die? Has it not been from of old one chief part of a manly education to make us despise death—teaching us to account it, if an evil at all, by no means high in the list of evils; at all events, as an inevitable one, and to hold, as it were, our lives in our hands, ready to be given or risked at any moment, for a sufficiently worthy object? I am sure that my hon. Friends know all this as well, and have as much of all these feelings as any of the rest of us; possibly more. But I cannot think that this is likely to be the effect of their teaching on the general mind. I cannot think that the cultivating of a peculiar sensitiveness of conscience on this one point, over and above what results from the general cultivation of the moral sentiments, is permanently consistent with assigning in our own minds to the fact of death no more than the degree of relative importance which belongs to it among the other incidents of our humanity. The men of old cared too little about death, and gave their own lives or took those of others with equal recklessness. Our danger is of the opposite kind, lest we should be so much shocked by death, in general and in the abstract, as to care too much about it in individual cases, both those of other people and our own, which call for its being risked. And I am not putting things at the worst, for it is proved by the experience of other countries that horror of the executioner by no means necessarily implies horror of the assassin. The stronghold, as we all know, of hired assassination in the 18th century was Italy; yet it is said that in some of the Italian populations the infliction of death by sentence of law was in the highest degree offensive and revolting to popular feeling. Much has been said of the sanctity of human life, and the absurdity of supposing that we can teach respect for life by ourselves destroying it. But I am surprised at the employment of this argument, for it is one which might be brought against any punishment whatever. It is not human life only, not human life as such, that ought to be sacred to us, but human feelings. The human capacity of suffering is what we should cause to be respected, not the mere capacity of existing. And we may imagine somebody asking how we can teach people not to inflict suffering by ourselves inflicting it? But to this I should answer—all of us would answer—that to deter by suffering from inflicting suffering is not only possible, but the very purpose of penal justice. Does fining a criminal show want of respect for property, or imprisoning him, for personal freedom? Just as unreasonable is it to think that to take the life of a man who has taken that of another is to show want of regard for human life. We show, on the contrary, most emphatically our regard for it, by the adoption of a rule that he who violates that right in another forfeits it for himself, and that while no other crime that he can commit deprives him of his right to live, this shall. There is one argument against capital punishment, even in extreme cases, which I cannot deny to have weight—on which my hon. Friend justly laid great stress, and which never can be entirely got rid of. It is this—that if by an error of justice an innocent person is put to death, the mistake can never be corrected; all compensation, all reparation for the wrong is impossible. This would be indeed a serious objection if these miserable mistakes—among the most tragical occurrences in the whole round of human affairs—could not be made extremely rare. The argument is invincible where the mode of criminal procedure is dangerous to the innocent, or where the Courts of Justice are not trusted. And this probably is the reason why the objection to an irreparable punishment began (as I believe it did) earlier, and is more intense and more widely diffused, in some parts of the Continent of Europe than it is here. There are on the Continent great and enlightened countries, in which the criminal procedure is not so favourable to innocence, does not afford the same security against erroneous conviction, as it does among us;

countries where the Courts of Justice seem to think they fail in their duty unless they find somebody guilty; and in their really laudable desire to hunt guilt from its hiding places, expose themselves to a serious danger of condemning the innocent. If our own procedure and Courts of Justice afforded ground for similar apprehension, I should be the first to join in withdrawing the power of inflicting irreparable punishment from such tribunals. But we all know that the defects of our procedure are the very opposite. Our rules of evidence are even too favourable to the prisoner; and juries and Judges carry out the maxim, 'It is better that ten guilty should escape than that one innocent person should suffer', not only to the letter, but beyond the letter. Judges are most anxious to point out, and juries to allow for, the barest possibility of the prisoner's innocence. No human judgement is infallible; such sad cases as my hon. Friend cited will sometimes occur; but in so grave a case as that of murder, the accused, in our system, has always the benefit of the merest shadow of a doubt. And this suggests another consideration very germane to the question. The very fact that death punishment is more shocking than any other to the imagination, necessarily renders the Courts of Justice more scrupulous in requiring the fullest evidence of guilt. Even that which is the greatest objection to capital punishment, the impossibility of correcting an error once committed, must make, and does make, juries and Judges more careful in forming their opinion, and more jealous in their scrutiny of the evidence. If the substitution of penal servitude for death in cases of murder should cause any declaration in this conscientious scrupulosity, there would be a great evil to set against the real, but I hope rare, advantage of being able to make reparation to a condemned person who was afterwards discovered to be innocent. In order that the possibility of correction may be kept open wherever the chance of this sad contingency is more than infinitesimal, it is quite right that the Judge should recommend to the Crown a commutation of the sentence, not solely when the proof of guilt is open to the smallest suspicion, but whenever there remains anything unexplained and mysterious in the case, raising a desire for more light, or making it likely that further information may at some future time be obtained. I would also suggest that whenever the sentence is commuted the grounds of the commutation should, in some authentic form, be made known to the public. Thus much I willingly concede to my hon. Friend; but on the question of total abolition I am inclined to hope that the feeling of the country is not with him, and that the limitation of death punishment to the cases referred to in the Bill of last year will be generally considered sufficient. The mania which existed a short time ago for paring down all our punishments seems to have reached its limits, and not before it was time. We were in danger of being left without any effectual punishment, except for small offences. What was formerly our chief secondary punishment—transportation—before it was abolished, had become almost a reward. Penal servitude, the substitute for it, was becoming, to the classes who were principally subject to it, almost nominal, so comfortable did we make our prisons, and so easy had it become to get quickly out of them. Flogging—a most objectionable punishment in ordinary cases, but a particularly appropriate ones for crimes of brutality, especially crimes against women—we would not hear of, except, to be sure, in the case of garrotters, for whose peculiar benefit we re-established it in a hurry, immediately after a Member of Parliament had been garrotted. With this exception, offences, even of an atrocious kind, against the person, as my hon. and learned Friend the Member for Oxford (Mr Neate) well remarked, not only were, but still are, visited with penalties so ludicrously inadequate, as to be almost an encouragement to the crime. I think, Sir, that in the case of most offences, except those against property, there is more need of strengthening our punishments than of weakening them; and that severer sentences, with an apportionment of them to the different kinds of offences which shall approve itself better than at present to the moral sentiments of the community, are the kind of reform of which our penal system now stands in need. I shall therefore vote against the Amendment.

[11]

Refuting Reiman and Nathanson

ERNEST VAN DEN HAAG

I shall consider Jeffrey Reiman's view of the punishment offenders deserve before turning to his moral scruples, alleged to justify lesser punishments, and to the discriminatory distribution of the death penalty which Stephen Nathanson stresses.

Reiman believes the death penalty is deserved by some murderers, but should never be imposed. Moral scruples should preclude it. If the punishment deserved according to the *lex talionis* is morally repugnant, we may impose less, provided the suffering imposed *in lieu* of what is deserved is proportional to the suffering inflicted on the crime victim. However, suffering exceeding that of his victim can never be deserved by the offender; to impose it would be "unjust for the same reasons that make punishment of the innocent unjust."[1]

Measurement

How do we know whether the punitive suffering to be imposed on the offender is less or "equal to that which he imposed on the victim" so as not to exceed what he deserves?[2] Cardinal and interpersonal measurement of suffering would be required to find out. Although ordinal measurement is possible in some cases, the cardinal and interpersonal meas-

1. See Jeffrey H. Reiman, "Justice, Civilization, and the Death Penalty: Answering van den Haag," *Philosophy & Public Affairs* 14, no. 2: 128. Unless otherwise noted, all my quotations are taken from Reiman's article.

2. This question arises only when the literal *lex talionis* is abandoned—as Reiman proposes to do, for good reason—in favor of the proportional retribution he suggests. How, by the way, would we punish a skyjacker? Summing up the suffering of all the skyjacked passengers? What about the damage to air traffic?

urement required by Reiman's scheme is not.[3] How many days must the kidnapper be confined, to suffer as much, but no more, than his victim? If he kept his victim three days, are three days of confinement correct? Or three hundred? Or one thousand? If he half-starved his victim, should we do as much to him, or, how do we commute starvation into additional time?

Punishment for kidnapping can be, within limits, of the same kind as the crime, although all we can actually do to conform to Reiman's prescription even here is to confine for a longer time the kidnapper who kept his victim for a longer time. We have no way of comparing the victim's suffering with the victimizer's, and to limit the latter accordingly. Execution too bears some similarity to the murderer's crime. But confinement? How do we make it commensurate with murder? What about the punishment for assault, burglary, or rape? How do we compare the pain suffered by the victims with the pain to be imposed on the offender by confinement, to make sure that the latter not exceed the former? There is no way of applying Reiman's criterion of desert. Fortunately, we don't need to.

Actual Desert

Even if, somehow, we knew that three days' confinement inflicts as much pain as his victim suffered on the kidnapper who kept his victim three days, we would feel that the kidnapper deserves much more punishment. That feeling would be appropriate. The offender imposed undeserved suffering on his victim. Why should society not impose undeserved (in Reiman's terminology) suffering on the offender? It would be undeserved only if one accepts Reiman's flawed view of retribution, for, in addition to whatever he deserves for what his victim suffered, the offender also deserves punishment for breaking the law, for imposing undeserved, unlawful suffering on someone. Retributionism of any kind cannot authorize less, despite Reiman's view that suffering imposed on the criminal is unjust when it exceeds the suffering of his victim.

Although occasionally he indicates awareness of the social harm caused by crime and even of the social function of punishment, Reiman treats crimes as though involving but a relationship between victim and offender

3. The order of punishments is notoriously hard to coordinate with the order of crimes: even when punishments are homogenous, crimes are not.

167 Refuting Reiman and Nathanson

implemented by judicial authorities.[4] From this faulty premise he infers that retribution should not exceed the harm done to the victim, an idea derived from the *lex talionis*. But that primitive rule was meant to limit the revenge private parties could exact for what was regarded as private harm. The function of the rule was to guard against social disruption by unlimited and indefinitely extended vengeance.

Crimes are no longer regarded merely as private harms. Retribution for the suffering of the individual victims, however much deserved, is not punishment any more than restitution is. Punishment must vindicate the disrupted public order, the violated law, must punish for the social harm done. If my neighbor is burglarized or robbed, he is harmed. But we all must take costly precautions, and we all feel and are threatened: crime harms society as it harms victims. Hence, punishment must, whenever possible, impose pain believed to exceed the pain suffered by the individual victim of crime. No less is deserved. Punishment must be determined by the total gravity of the crime, the social as well as the individual harm, and by the need to deter from the harmful crime. There are ordinal limits to deserved punishments, but cardinal upper limits are set only by harm, habit and sentiment—not by victim suffering.

Let me now turn to the moral scruples which should lead us to reduce punishment to less than what is deserved in some cases. I share some of Reiman's scruples: although he deserves it, I do not want to see the torturer tortured. Other scruples strike me as unjustified.

Poverty and Culpability

Reiman believes "that the vast majority of murders in America are a predictable response to the frustrations and disabilities of impoverished social circumstances" which could be, but are not remedied because "others in America benefit," wherefore we have "no right to exact the full cost . . . from our murderers until we have done everything possible to rectify the conditions that produce their crimes."[5] Murder here seems to become the punishment for the sins of the wealthy. According to

4. Perhaps Reiman's excessive reliance on the Hegelian justification of retribution (to vindicate the equality of victim and offender) or on the Kantian version (to vindicate the rationality of both) is to blame.

5. Reiman does not say here that murder deserves less than the death penalty, but only that "the vast majority of murderers" deserve less because impoverished. However, wealthy murderers can be fully culpable, so that we may "exact the full cost" from them.

Reiman, "the vast majority" of current murderers are not fully culpable, since part of the blame for their crimes must be placed on those who fail to "rectify the conditions that produce their crimes."

I grant that certain social conditions predictably produce crime more readily than others. Does it follow that those who commit crimes in criminogenic conditions are less responsible, or blameworthy, than they would be if they did not live in these conditions? Certainly not. Predictability does not reduce responsibility. Reiman remains responsible for his predictable argument. Culpability is reduced only when the criminal's ability to control his actions, or to realize that they are wrong, is abnormally impaired. If not, the social conditions in which the criminal lives have no bearing on his responsibility for his acts. Conditions, such as poverty, just or unjust, may increase the temptation to commit crimes. But poverty is neither a necessary nor a sufficient condition for crime, and thus certainly not a coercive one. If there is no compulsion, temptation is no excuse. The law is meant to restrain, and to hold responsible, those tempted to break it. It need not restrain those not tempted, and it cannot restrain those who are unable to control their actions.

Reiman's claim, that even "though criminals can control their actions, when crimes are predictable responses to unjust circumstances, then those who benefit from and do not remedy those conditions bear some responsibility for the crimes and thus the criminals cannot be held *wholly* responsible for them . . ." seems quite unjustified. Those responsible for unjust conditions must be blamed for them,[6] but not for crimes that are "predictable responses to unjust circumstances," if the respondents could have avoided these crimes, as most people living in unjust conditions do.

If crimes are political, that is, address not otherwise remediable "unjust circumstances," they may be held to be morally, if not legally, excusable, on some occasions.[7] But the criminal's moral, let alone legal, responsibility for a crime which he committed for personal gain and could have avoided, is not diminished merely because he lives in unjust circumstances, and his crime was a predictable response to them. Suppose the predictable

6. Who are they? They are not necessarily the beneficiaries, as Reiman appears to believe. I benefit from rent control, which I think unjust to my landlord, but I'm not responsible for it. I may benefit from low prices for services or goods, without being responsible for them, or for predictable criminal responses to them. Criminals benefit from the unjust exclusionary rules of our courts. Are they to blame for these rules?

7. See my *Political Violence & Civil Disobedience, passim* (New York: Harper & Row, 1972) for a more detailed argument.

169 *Refuting Reiman and Nathanson*

response to unjust wealth were drunken driving, or rape. Would his wealth excuse the driver or the rapist? Why should poverty, if wealth would not?[8]

Crime is produced by many circumstances, "just" and "unjust." The most just society may have no less crime than the least just (unless "just" is defined circularly as the absence of crime). Tracing crime to causal circumstances is useful and may help us to control it. Suggesting that they *eo ipso* are excuses confuses causality with nonresponsibility. *Tout comprendre ce n'est pas tout pardonner*, Mme. de Staël's followers to the contrary notwithstanding. Excuses require specific circumstances that diminish the actor's control over his actions.

Since "unjust circumstances" do not reduce the responsibility of criminals for their acts, I shall refrain from discussing whether Reiman's circumstances really are unjust, or merely unequal, and whether they do exist because someone benefits from them and could be eliminated if the alleged beneficiaries wished to eliminate them. I am not sure that unjust circumstances always can be remedied, without causing worse injustices. Nor do I share Reiman's confidence that we know what social justice is, or how to produce it.

Civilization

Reiman thinks that the death penalty is not civilized, because it involves the total subjugation of one person to others, as does slavery, or prostitution.[9]

Whereas slavery usually is not voluntary, the murderer runs the risk of execution voluntarily: he could avoid it by not murdering. I find nothing uncivilized in imposing the risk of subjugation and death on those who decide to murder.

Nota bene: Persons who act with diminished capacity, during moments of passion, are usually convicted of manslaughter rather than murder.

8. Suppose unjust wealth tends to corrupt, and unjust poverty does not. Would the wealthy be less to blame for their crimes?

9. Prostitution does not involve total subjugation and is voluntary. In an ambiguous footnote Reiman asserts that it is the perception of prostitution as subjugation that makes it offensive. But this perception, derived from pulp novels more than from reality, is not what makes the voluntary act offensive. Rather, it is the sale of sex as a fungible service, divorced from affection and depersonalized that is offensive. Anyway, when something is offensive because misperceived it is not the thing that is offensive.

Even if convicted of murder, they are not sentenced to death; only if the court believes that the murderer did have a choice, and intended to murder, can he receive the death sentence.

Reiman refers to research finding a brutalization effect, such that executions lead to more homicides. The data are unpersuasive. Some researchers find an increase, some a decrease, of homicides immediately after an execution.[10] Either effect seem ephemeral, involving bunching, rather than changes in the annual homicide rate.

To argue more generally, as Reiman also does, that capital punishment is inconsistent with the advancement of civilization, is to rely on arbitrary definitions of "advancement" and "civilization" for a circular argument. If civilization actually had "advanced" in the direction Reiman, quoting Durkheim, thinks it has, why is that a reason for not preferring "advancement" in some other, perhaps opposite, direction? I cannot find the *moral* (normative) argument in Reiman's description.

Deterrence

The death penalty should be retained if abolition would endanger us, Reiman believes. But he does not believe that abolition would. He may be right. However, some of his arguments seem doubtful.

He thinks that whatever marginal deterrent effect capital punishment has, if it has any, is not needed, since life imprisonment provides all the deterrence needed. How can it be ascertained that punishment x deters "everyone who can be deterred" so that punishment x-plus would not deter additional persons? I can see no way to determine this, short of experiments we are unlikely to undertake. Reiman may fear life imprisonment as much, or more, than death. Couldn't someone else fear death more and be insufficiently deterred by life imprisonment?

I cannot prove conclusively that the death penalty deters more than life imprisonment, or that the added deterrence is needed. Reiman cannot prove conclusively that the added deterrence is not needed, or produced. I value the life of innocents more than the life of murderers. Indeed, I value the life of murderers negatively. Wherefore I prefer over- to under-protection. I grant this is a preference.

10. David P. Phillips, "The Deterrent Effect of Capital Punishment: New Evidence on an Old Controversy," *The American Journal of Sociology* (July 1980). For further discussion see loc. cit., July 1982. See also Lester, *Executions as a Deterrent to Homicides* 44 *Psychological Rep.* 562 (1979).

171

Refuting Reiman and Nathanson

Self-Defense

Reiman also believes that murderers who are not deterred by the risk they run because their victims may defend themselves with guns will not be deterred by the risk of execution. This seems unrealistic. Murderers rarely run much risk from self-defense since they usually ambush unsuspecting victims.

Torture

On my reasoning, Reiman contends, torture should be used, since it may deter more than execution; or else, even if more deterrent than alternatives, the death penalty should be abolished as torture was: "either we must abolish the electric chair or reinstitute the rack," is his colorful phrase. But there is a difference. I do not oppose torture as undeserved or nondeterrent (although I doubt that the threat of the rack, or of anything adds deterrence to the threat of execution), but simply as repulsive. Death is not; nor is the death penalty. Perhaps repulsiveness is not enough to exclude the rack. If Reiman should convince me that the threat of the rack adds a great deal of deterrence to the threat of execution he might persuade me to overcome my revulsion and to favor the rack as well. It certainly can be deserved.

Moral Theory

In *The Death Penalty: A Debate*[11] I noted that only when punishments are based not on retribution alone, but also on deterrence, they rest on a theory, that is, on a correlation of recurrent facts to a prediction: punishment x will, *ceteris paribus*, reduce the rate of crime y by 10%, and x-plus will bring a reduction of 20%. Reiman censures me for using "theory" when I should have written "empirical theory." He is right. Further, deterrence does not morally justify any punishment, unless one has first accepted the moral desirability of reducing crime, and the tolerability of the costs. I should have pointed that out. Finally, I did not mean to deny that there are moral theories to justify retribution. They strike me as more dependent on feeling than empirical theories are. More to the point, unlike deterrence theory, justice theories are not meant to predict the effect of various punishments, and are not capable of deter-

11. Ernest van den Haag and John P. Conrad (New York: Plenum Press, 1983).

mining, except ordinally, what these punishments should be, although they can help to justify the distribution of punishments.[12]

Modes of Execution

As Reiman stresses, the spectacle of execution is not pretty. Nor is surgery. Wherefore both should be attended only by the necessary personnel.[13] I do not find Reiman's aesthetic or moral scruples sufficient to preclude execution or surgery. However, I share his view that lethal injections are particularly unpleasant, not so much because of the subjugation which disturbs him, but because of the veterinary air. (We put animals "to sleep" when sick or inconvenient.) In contrast, shooting strikes me as dignified; it is painless too and probably the best way of doing what is necessary.

Life Imprisonment

Reiman proposes life imprisonment without parole instead of execution. Although less feared, and therefore likely to be less deterrent, actual lifelong imprisonment strikes me as more cruel than execution even if perceived as less harsh. Its comparative cruelty was stressed already by Cesare Bonesana, Marchese di Beccaria, and by many others since.

Life imprisonment also becomes undeserved over time. A person who committed a murder when twenty years old and is executed within five years—far too long and cruel a delay in my opinion—is, when executed, still the person who committed the murder for which he is punished. His identity changes little in five years. However, a person who committed a murder when he was twenty years old and is kept in prison when sixty years old, is no longer the same person who committed the crime for which he is still being punished. The sexagenarian is unlikely to have much in common with the twenty-year-old for whose act he is being punished; his legal identity no longer reflects reality. Personality and actual identity are not that continuous. In effect, we punish an innocent

12. See my *Punishing Criminals* (New York: Basic Books, 1975) which is superseded to some extent by the views expressed in my "Criminal Law as a Threat System 73, *Journal of Criminal Law and Criminology* 2 (1982).

13. Both spectacles when graphically shown may also give rise to undesirable imitations or inspirations.

sexagenarian who does not deserve punishment, instead of a guilty twenty-year-old who did. This spectacle should offend our moral sensibilities more than the deserved execution of the twenty-year-old. Those who deserve the death penalty should be executed while they deserve it, not kept in prison when they no longer deserve any punishment.

Discrimination

Disagreeing with the Supreme Court, Stephen Nathanson believes that the death penalty still is distributed in an excessively capricious and discriminatory manner. He thinks capital punishment is "unjust" because poor blacks are more likely to be sentenced to death than wealthy whites. Further, blacks who murdered whites are more likely to be executed than those who murdered blacks.[14] This last discrimination has been thrown into relief recently by authors who seem to be under the impression that they have revealed a new form of discrimination against black murderers. They have not. The practice invidiously discriminates against black victims of murder, who are not as fully, or as often, vindicated as white victims are. However, discrimination against a class of victims, although invidious enough, does not amount to discrimination against their victimizers. The discrimination against black victims, the lesser punishment given their murderers, actually favors black murderers, since most black victims are killed by black murderers. Stephen Nathanson and Jeffrey Reiman appear to think that they have captured additional discrimination against black defendants. They are wrong.

Neither the argument from discrimination against black victims, nor the argument from discrimination against black murderers, has any bearing on the guilt of black murderers, or on the punishment they deserve

Invidious discrimination is never defensible. Yet I do not see wherein it, in Reiman's words, "would constitute a separate and powerful argument for abolition," or does make the death penalty "unjust" for those discriminatorily selected to suffer it, as Stephen Nathanson believes.[15] If we grant that some (even all) murderers of blacks, or, some (even all) white and rich murderers, escape the death penalty, how does that reduce

14. Despite some doubts, I am here granting the truth of both hypotheses.

15. Stephen Nathanson, "Does It Matter if the Death Penalty Is Arbitrarily Administered?" *Philosophy & Public Affairs* 14, no. 2 (this issue). Unless otherwise noted, all further quotations are taken from Nathanson's article.

the guilt of murderers of whites, or of black and poor murderers, so that they should be spared execution too? Guilt is personal. No murderer becomes less guilty, or less deserving of punishment, because another murderer was punished leniently, or escaped punishment altogether. We should try our best to bring every murderer to justice. But if one got away with murder wherein is that a reason to let anyone else get away? A group of murderers does not become less deserving of punishment because another equally guilty group is not punished, or punished less. We can punish only a very small proportion of all criminals. Unavoidably they are selected accidentally. We should reduce this accidentality as much as possible but we cannot eliminate it.[16]

Equal Injustice and Unequal Justice

Reiman and Nathanson appear to prefer equal injustice—letting all get away with murder if some do—to unequal justice: punishing some guilty offenders according to desert, even if others get away. Equal justice is best, but unattainable. Unequal justice is our lot in this world. It is the only justice we can ever have, for not all murderers can be apprehended or convicted, or sentenced equally in different courts. We should constantly try to bring every offender to justice. But meanwhile unequal justice is the only justice we have, and certainly better than equal injustice—giving no murderer the punishment his crime deserves.

More Discrimination

Nathanson insists that some arbitrary selections among those equally guilty are not "just." He thinks that selecting only bearded speeders for ticketing, allowing the cleanshaven to escape, is unjust. Yet the punishment of the bearded speeders is not unjust. The escape of the cleanshaven ones is. I never maintained that a discriminatory distribution is just—only that it is irrelevant to the guilt and deserved punishment of those actually guilty.

16. Discrimination or capriciousness is (when thought to be avoidable and excessive) sometimes allowed by the courts as a defense. Apparently this legal device is meant to reduce discrimination and capriciousness. But those spared because selected discriminatorily for punishment do not become any less deserving of it as both Reiman and Nathanson think, although not punishing them is used as a means to foster the desired equality in the distributions of punishments.

175 *Refuting Reiman and Nathanson*

Nathanson further suggests that it is not just to spare some student plagiarizers punishment for (I suppose) irrelevant reasons, while punishing others. Again the distribution is discriminatory, i.e., unjust. But the punishment of the plagiarizers selected is not. (The non-punishment of the others is.) Nathanson thinks that giving a prize only to one of three deserving children (his own) is unjust. Not to the deserving child. Only to the others, just as it was unjust not to punish the others who deserved it, but not unjust to punish the deserving plagiarizers who were irrelevantly selected.[17]

Nathanson taxes me with inconsistency because in a footnote I wrote that irrelevant discriminations are "not acceptable to our sense of justice." They are not. But I did not say that those who deserved the punishment received, or the reward, were unjustly treated, that is, did not deserve it and should not have received it. Rather those equally situated also should have received it, and the distribution was offensive because they did not. Whenever possible this inequality should be corrected, but certainly not by not distributing the punishment, or the reward at issue, or by not giving it to the deserving. Rather by giving it as well to those who because of discrimination did not get it. (I might have done better to write in my footnote that discriminatory distributions offend our sense of *equal* justice. But neither the Constitution nor I favor replacing justice with equality.)

Nathanson quotes the late Justice Douglas suggesting that a law which deliberately prescribes execution only for the guilty poor, or which has that effect, would be unconstitutional. Perhaps. But the vice would be in exempting the guilty rich; the guilty poor would remain guilty, and deserving of prescribed punishment even if the guilty rich escape legally or otherwise.[18]

Further on Nathanson points out that the inevitable capriciousness in the distribution of punishments (only a very small percentage of offenders are ever punished and the selection unavoidably is morally arbitrary) while no reason to abolish punishment in general, may still be an argument for abolishing capital punishment because of its unique severity, and because we could survive without. We can survive without many

17. There will be some difficulty in explaining to the children who did not get the reward, why they did not, but no difficulty in explaining why one deserving child got it—unless the children share Nathanson's difficulty in distinguishing between justice and equality.

18. See footnote 16.

things, which is not reason for doing without, if one thinks, as I do, that we survive *better* with. As for the unique severity of the death penalty it is, of course, the reason for imposing it for uniquely heinous crimes. The guilt of those who committed them is not diminished, if they are selected by a lottery from among all those guilty of the crime.

Following Charles Black, Nathanson notes that those executed are not necessarily the worst murderers, since there is no way of selecting these. He is right. It seems quite sufficient, however, that those executed, though not the worst, are bad enough to deserve execution. That others who deserved it even more got away, does not make those executed insufficiently deserving.

Nathanson goes on to insist that "not every person who kills another is guilty of the same crime." True. Wherefore the law makes many distinctions, leaving only a small group of those guilty of homicide eligible for the death penalty. Further, capital punishment is not mandated. The court must decide in each case whether or not to impose it. To impose capital punishment, courts must find that the aggravating circumstances attending the murder outweigh the mitigating ones, both of which must be listed in the law. Nathanson is right in pointing out that the criteria listed in the law are not easy to apply. If they were, we would not need the judgment of the court. That judgment is not easy to make. It may seem too severe, or not severe enough, in some cases, as would mandated penalties. So what else is new?

[12]

Is Capital Punishment Morally Required? Acts, Omissions, and Life-Life Tradeoffs

Cass R. Sunstein* and Adrian Vermeule**

Many people believe that the death penalty should be abolished even if, as recent evidence seems to suggest, it has a significant deterrent effect. But if such an effect can be established, capital punishment requires a life-life tradeoff, and a serious commitment to the sanctity of human life may well compel, rather than forbid, that form of punishment. The familiar problems with capital punishment—potential error, irreversibility, arbitrariness, and racial skew—do not require abolition because the realm of homicide suffers from those same problems in even more acute form. Moral objections to the death penalty frequently depend on a sharp distinction between acts and omissions, but that distinction is misleading in this context because government is a special kind of moral agent. The widespread failure to appreciate the life-life tradeoffs potentially involved in capital punishment may depend in part on cognitive processes that fail to treat "statistical lives" with the seriousness that they deserve. The objection to the act/omission distinction, as applied to government, has implications for many questions in civil and criminal law.

---

* Karl N. Llewellyn Distinguished Service Professor of Jurisprudence, the University of Chicago Law School, Department of Political Science, and the College.

** Bernard D. Meltzer Professor of Law, the University of Chicago. The authors thank Larry Alexander, Ron Allen, Richard Berk, Steven Calabresi, Jeffrey Fagan, Robert Hahn, Dan Kahan, Andy Koppelman, Richard Lempert, Steven Levitt, James Liebman, Daniel Markel, Frank Michelman, Tom Miles, Eric Posner, Richard Posner, Joanna Shepherd, William Stuntz, James Sullivan, and Eugene Volokh for helpful suggestions, and Blake Roberts for excellent research assistance and valuable comments. Thanks too to participants in a work-in-progress lunch at the University of Chicago Law School and a constitutional theory workshop at Northwestern University Law School.

INTRODUCTION

Many people believe that capital punishment is morally impermissible. In their view, executions are inherently cruel and barbaric.[1] Often they add that capital punishment is not, and cannot be, imposed in a way that adheres to the rule of law.[2] They contend that, as administered, capital punishment ensures the execution of (some) innocent people and also that it reflects arbitrariness, in the form of random or invidious infliction of the ultimate penalty.[3]

Defenders of capital punishment can be separated into two different camps. Some are retributivists.[4] Following Immanuel Kant,[5] they claim that for the most heinous forms of wrongdoing, the penalty of death is morally justified or perhaps even required. Other defenders of capital punishment are consequentialists and often also welfarists.[6] They contend that the deterrent

1. *See, e.g.*, Furman v. Georgia, 408 U.S. 238, 309, 371 (1972) (Marshall, J., concurring).

2. *See* Stephen B. Bright, *Why the United States Will Join the Rest of the World in Abandoning Capital Punishment*, *in* DEBATING THE DEATH PENALTY: SHOULD AMERICA HAVE CAPITAL PUNISHMENT? 152 (Hugo Adam Bedau & Paul G. Cassell eds., 2004) [hereinafter DEBATING THE DEATH PENALTY].

3. *See, e.g.*, James S. Liebman et al., *A Broken System: Error Rates in Capital Cases, 1973-1995* (Columbia Law Sch., Pub. Law Research Paper No. 15, 2000) (on file with authors).

4. *See, e.g.*, Luis P. Pojman, *Why the Death Penalty Is Morally Permissible*, *in* DEBATING THE DEATH PENALTY, *supra* note 2, at 51, 55-58.

5. *See* IMMANUEL KANT, THE PHILOSOPHY OF LAW: AN EXPOSITION OF THE FUNDAMENTAL PRINCIPLES OF JURISPRUDENCE AS THE SCIENCE OF RIGHT 198 (W. Hastrie trans., 1887) (1797).

6. Arguments along these lines can be found in Pojman, *supra* note 4, at 58-73.

effect of capital punishment is significant and that it justifies the infliction of the ultimate penalty. Consequentialist defenses of capital punishment, however, tend to assume that capital punishment is (merely) morally permissible, as opposed to being morally obligatory.

Our goal here is to suggest that the debate over capital punishment is rooted in an unquestioned assumption and that the failure to question that assumption is a serious moral error. The assumption is that for governments, acts are morally different from omissions. We want to raise the possibility that an indefensible form of the act/omission distinction is crucial to some of the most prominent objections to capital punishment—and that defenders of capital punishment, apparently making the same distinction, have failed to notice that according to the logic of their theory, capital punishment is morally obligatory, not just permissible. We suggest, in other words, that on certain empirical assumptions, capital punishment may be morally required, not for retributive reasons, but rather to prevent the taking of innocent lives.[7]

The suggestion bears not only on moral and political debates, but also on constitutional questions. In invalidating the death penalty for juveniles, for example, the Supreme Court did not seriously engage the possibility that capital punishment for juveniles may help to prevent the death of innocents, including juvenile innocents.[8] And if our suggestion is correct, it relates to many questions outside of the context of capital punishment. If omissions by the state are often indistinguishable, in principle, from actions by the state, then a wide range of apparent failures to act—in the context not only of criminal and civil law, but of regulatory law as well—should be taken to raise serious moral and legal problems. Those who accept our arguments in favor of the death penalty may or may not welcome the implications for government action in general. In many situations, ranging from environmental quality to appropriations to highway safety to relief of poverty, our arguments suggest that in light of

---

7. In so saying, we are suggesting the possibility that states are obliged to maintain the death penalty option, not that they must inflict that penalty in every individual case of a specified sort; hence we are not attempting to enter into the debate over mandatory death sentences, as invalidated in *Lockett v. Ohio*, 438 U.S. 586 (1978), and *Woodson v. North Carolina*, 428 U.S. 280 (1976). For relevant discussion, see Martha C. Nussbaum, *Equity and Mercy*, 22 PHIL. & PUB. AFF. 83 (1993).

8. Roper v. Simmons, 125 S. Ct. 1183 (2005). Here is the heart of the Court's discussion:

> As for deterrence, it is unclear whether the death penalty has a significant or even measurable deterrent effect on juveniles, as counsel for the petitioner acknowledged at oral argument. . . . [T]he absence of evidence of deterrent effect is of special concern because the same characteristics that render juveniles less culpable than adults suggest as well that juveniles will be less susceptible to deterrence. . . . To the extent the juvenile death penalty might have residual deterrent effect, it is worth noting that the punishment of life imprisonment without the possibility of parole is itself a severe sanction, in particular for a young person.

Id. at 1196. These are speculations at best, and they do not engage with the empirical literature; of course, that literature does not dispose of the question whether juveniles are deterred by the death penalty.

imaginable empirical findings, government is obliged to provide far more protection than it now does, and it should not be permitted to hide behind unhelpful distinctions between acts and omissions.

The foundation for our argument is a significant body of recent evidence that capital punishment may well have a deterrent effect, possibly a quite powerful one.[9] A leading national study suggests that each execution prevents some eighteen murders, on average.[10] If the current evidence is even roughly correct—a question to which we shall return—then a refusal to impose capital punishment will effectively condemn numerous innocent people to death. States that choose life imprisonment, when they might choose capital punishment, are ensuring the deaths of a large number of innocent people.[11] On moral grounds, a choice that effectively condemns large numbers of people to death seems objectionable to say the least. For those who are inclined to be skeptical of capital punishment for moral reasons—a group that includes one of the current authors—the task is to consider the possibility that the failure to impose capital punishment is, prima facie and all things considered, a serious moral wrong.

Judgments of this sort are often taken to require a controversial commitment to a consequentialist view about the foundations of moral evaluation. One of our principal points, however, is that the choice between consequentialist and deontological approaches to morality is not crucial here. We suggest that, on certain empirical assumptions, theorists of both stripes might converge on the idea that capital punishment is morally obligatory. On

9. *See, e.g.*, Hashem Dezhbakhsh et al., *Does Capital Punishment Have a Deterrent Effect? New Evidence from Postmoratorium Panel Data*, 5 AM. L. & ECON. REV. 344 (2003); H. Naci Mocan & R. Kaj Gittings, *Getting Off Death Row: Commuted Sentences and the Deterrent Effect of Capital Punishment*, 46 J.L. & ECON. 453, 453 (2003); Joanna M. Shepherd, *Deterrence Versus Brutalization: Capital Punishment's Differing Impacts Among States*, 104 MICH. L. REV. 203 (2005) [hereinafter Shepherd, *Deterrence Versus Brutalization*]; Joanna M. Shepherd, *Murders of Passion, Execution Delays, and the Deterrence of Capital Punishment*, 33 J. LEGAL STUD. 283, 308 (2004) [hereinafter Shepherd, *Murders of Passion*]; Paul R. Zimmerman, *Estimates of the Deterrent Effect of Alternative Execution Methods in the United States*, 65 AM. J. ECON. & SOC. (forthcoming 2006) [hereinafter Zimmerman, *Alternative Execution Methods*], *available at* http://papers.ssrn.com/sol3/papers.cfm?abstract_id=355783; Paul R. Zimmerman, *State Executions, Deterrence, and the Incidence of Murder*, 7 J. APPLIED ECON. 163, 163 (2004) [hereinafter Zimmerman, *State Executions*].

10. *See* Dezhbakhsh et al., *supra* note 9, at 344. In what follows, we will speak of each execution saving eighteen lives in the United States, on average. We are, of course, suppressing many issues in that formulation, simply for expository convenience. For one thing, that statistic is a national average, as we emphasize in Part IV. For another thing, future research might find that capital punishment has diminishing returns: even if the first 100 executions deter 1800 murders, it does not follow that another 1000 executions will deter another 18,000 murders. We will take these and like qualifications as understood in the discussion that follows.

11. In recent years, the number of murders in the United States has fluctuated between 15,000 and 24,000. FED. BUREAU OF INVESTIGATION, CRIME IN THE UNITED STATES tbl.1 (2003), *available at* http://www.fbi.gov/ucr/03cius.htm.

consequentialist grounds, the death penalty seems morally obligatory if it is the only or most effective means of preventing significant numbers of murders; much of our discussion will explore this point. For this reason, consequentialists should have little difficulty with our arguments. For deontologists, a killing is a wrong under most circumstances, and its wrongness does not depend on its consequences or its effects on overall welfare. Many deontologists (of course not all) believe that capital punishment counts as a moral wrong. But in the abstract, any deontological injunction against the wrongful infliction of death turns out to be indeterminate on the moral status of capital punishment *if* the death is necessary to prevent significant numbers of killings.

The unstated assumption animating much opposition to capital punishment among intuitive deontologists is that capital punishment counts as an "action" by the state, while the refusal to impose it counts as an "omission," and that the two are altogether different from the moral point of view. A related way to put this point is to suggest that capital punishment counts as a "killing," while the failure to impose capital punishment counts as no such thing and hence is far less problematic on moral grounds. We shall investigate these claims in some detail. But we doubt that the distinction between state actions and state omissions can bear the moral weight given to it by the critics of capital punishment. Whatever its value as a moral concept where individuals are concerned, the act/omission distinction misfires in the general setting of government regulation. If government policies fail to protect people against air pollution, occupational risks, terrorism, or racial discrimination, it is inadequate to put great moral weight on the idea that the failure to act is a mere "omission."

No one believes that government can avoid responsibility to protect people against serious dangers—for example, by refusing to enforce regulatory statutes—simply by contending that such refusals are unproblematic omissions.[12] If state governments impose light penalties on offenders or treat certain offenses (say, domestic violence) as unworthy of attention, they should not be able to escape public retribution by contending that they are simply refusing to act. Where government is concerned, failures of protection, through refusals to punish and deter private misconduct, cannot be justified by pointing to the distinction between acts and omissions.

It has even become common to speak of "risk-risk tradeoffs," understood to arise when regulation of one risk (say, a risk associated with the use of DDT) gives rise to another risk (say, the spread of malaria, against which DDT has been effective).[13] Or suppose that an air pollutant creates adverse health effects

12. Indeed, agency inaction is frequently subject to judicial review. *See* Ashutosh Bhagwat, *Three-Branch Monte*, 72 NOTRE DAME L. REV. 157 (1996).

13. *See generally* RISK VERSUS RISK: TRADEOFFS IN PROTECTING HEALTH AND THE ENVIRONMENT (John D. Graham & Jonathan Baert Wiener eds., 1995) (considering "risk-risk tradeoffs" on topics such as DDT, the use of estrogen for menopause, and clozapine theory

but also has health benefits, as appears to be the case for ground-level ozone.[14] It is implausible to say that, for moral reasons, social planners should refuse to take account of such tradeoffs; there is general agreement that whether a particular substance ought to be regulated depends on the overall effect of regulation on human well-being.

As an empirical matter, criminal law is pervaded by its own risk-risk tradeoffs. When the deterrent signal works, a failure to impose stringent penalties on certain crimes will increase the number of those crimes. A refusal to impose such penalties is, for that reason, problematic from the moral point of view. It should not be possible for an official—a governor, for example—to attempt to escape political retribution for failing to prevent domestic violence or environmental degradation by claiming that he is simply "failing to act." The very idea of "equal protection of the laws," in its oldest and most literal sense, attests to the importance of enforcing the criminal and civil law so as to safeguard the potential victims of private violence.[15] What we are suggesting is that to the extent that capital punishment saves more lives than it extinguishes, the death penalty produces a risk-risk tradeoff of its own—indeed, what we will call a *life-life tradeoff.*

Of course, the presence of a life-life tradeoff does not resolve the capital punishment debate. By itself, the act of execution may be a wrong, in a way that cannot be said of an act of imposing civil or criminal penalties for, say, environmental degradation. But the existence of life-life tradeoffs raises the possibility that for those who oppose killing, a rejection of capital punishment is not necessarily mandated. On the contrary, it may well be morally compelled. At the very least, those who object to capital punishment, and who do so in the name of protecting life, must come to terms with the possibility that the failure to inflict capital punishment will fail to protect life—and must, in our view, justify their position in ways that do not rely on question-begging claims about the distinction between state actions and state omissions, or between killing and letting die.

We begin, in Part I, with the facts. Raising doubts about widely held beliefs based on older studies or partial information, recent studies suggest that capital punishment may well save lives. One leading study finds that as a national average, each execution deters some eighteen murders. Our question whether capital punishment is morally obligatory is motivated by these findings; our central concern is that foregoing any given execution may be equivalent to condemning some unidentified people to a premature and violent death. Of course, social science can always be disputed in this contentious domain, and spirited attacks have been made on the recent studies;[16] hence, we mean to

for schizophrenia).

14. *See* Am. Trucking Ass'ns, Inc. v. EPA, 175 F.3d 1027, 1051-53 (D.C. Cir. 1999).

15. *See* RANDALL KENNEDY, RACE, CRIME, AND THE LAW (1997).

16. *See* Richard Berk, *New Claims About Executions and General Deterrence: Déjà*

outline, rather than to defend, the relevant evidence here. But we think that to make progress on the moral issues, it is productive and even necessary to take those findings as given and consider their significance. Those who would like to abolish capital punishment, and who find the social science unconvincing, might find it useful to ask whether they would maintain their commitment to abolition if they were firmly persuaded that capital punishment does have a strong deterrent effect. We ask such people to suspend their empirical doubts in order to investigate the moral issues that we mean to raise here.

In Part II, the centerpiece of the Article, we offer a few remarks on moral foundations and examine some standard objections to capital punishment that might seem plausible even in light of the current findings. We focus in particular on the view that capital punishment is objectionable because it requires affirmative and intentional state "action," not merely an "omission." The act/omission distinction, we suggest, systematically misfires when applied to government, which is a moral agent with distinctive features. The act/omission distinction may not even be intelligible in the context of government, which always faces a choice among policy regimes, and in that sense cannot help but "act." Even if the distinction between acts and omissions can be rendered intelligible in regulatory settings, its moral relevance is obscure. Some acts are morally obligatory, while some omissions are morally culpable. If capital punishment has significant deterrent effects, we suggest that for government to omit to impose it is morally blameworthy, even on a deontological account of morality. Deontological accounts typically recognize a consequentialist override to baseline prohibitions. If each execution saves an average of eighteen lives, then it is plausible to think that the override is triggered, in turn triggering an obligation to adopt capital punishment.

Once the act/omission distinction is rejected where government is concerned, it becomes clear that the most familiar, and plausible, objections to capital punishment deal with only one side of the ledger: the objections fail to take account of the exceedingly arbitrary deaths that capital punishment may deter. The realm of homicide, as we shall call it, is replete with its own arbitrariness. We consider rule-of-law concerns about the irreversibility of capital punishment and its possibly random or invidious administration, a strict scrutiny principle that capital punishment should not be permitted if other means for producing the same level of deterrence are available, and concerns about slippery slopes. We suggest that while some of these complaints have

Vu All over Again?, 2 J. EMPIRICAL LEGAL STUD. 303 (2005); *see also Deterrence and the Death Penalty: A Critical Review of New Evidence*: *Hearings on the Future of Capital Punishment in the State of New York Before the New York State Assemb. Standing Comm. on Codes, Assemb. Standing Comm. on Judiciary, and Assemb. Standing Comm. on Correction*, 2005 Leg., 228th Sess. 1-12 (N.Y. 2005) (statement of Jeffrey Fagan, Professor of Law and Pub. Health, Columbia Univ.), *available at* www.deathpenaltyinfo.org/FaganTestimony.pdf [hereinafter *Deterrence and the Death Penalty*]. For a response to Fagan's testimony, see generally Shepherd, *Deterrence Versus Brutalization*, *supra* note 9.

merit, they do not count as decisive objections to capital punishment, because they embody a flawed version of the act/omission distinction and generally overlook the fact that the moral objections to capital punishment apply even more strongly to the murders that capital punishment apparently deters.

In Part III, we conjecture that various cognitive and social mechanisms, lacking any claim to moral relevance, may cause many individuals and groups to subscribe to untenable versions of the distinction between acts and omissions or to discount the lifesaving potential of capital punishment while exaggerating the harms that it causes. An important concern here is a sort of misplaced concreteness, stemming from heuristics such as salience and availability. The single person executed is often more visible and more salient in public discourse than any abstract statistical persons whose murders might be deterred by a single execution. If those people, and their names and faces, were highly visible, we suspect that many of the objections to capital punishment would at least be shaken. As environmentalists have often argued, "statistical persons" should not be treated as irrelevant abstractions.[17] The point holds for criminal justice no less than for pollution controls.

Part IV expands upon the implications of our view and examines some unresolved puzzles. Here we emphasize that we hold no brief for capital punishment across all contexts or in the abstract. The crucial question is what the facts show in particular domains. We mean to include here a plea not only for continuing assessment of the disputed evidence, but also for a disaggregated approach. Future research and resulting policies would do well to take separate account of various regions and of various classes of offenders and offenses. We also emphasize that our argument is limited to the setting of life-life tradeoffs—in which the taking of a life by the state will reduce the number of lives taken overall. We express no view about cases in which that condition does not hold—for example, the possibility of capital punishment for serious offenses other than killing, with rape being the principal historical example, and with rape of children being a currently contested problem. Such cases involve distinctively difficult moral problems that we mean to bracket here. A brief conclusion follows.

I. EVIDENCE

For many years, the deterrent effect of capital punishment was sharply disputed.[18] In the 1970s, Isaac Ehrlich conducted the first multivariate

17. Lisa Heinzerling, *The Rights of Statistical People*, 24 HARV. ENVTL. L. REV. 189, 189 (2000).

18. *Compare, e.g.*, Isaac Ehrlich, *The Deterrent Effect of Capital Punishment: A Question of Life and Death*, 65 AM. ECON. REV. 397, 398 (1975) (estimating each execution deters eight murders), *with* William J. Bowers & Glenn L. Pierce, *The Illusion of Deterrence in Isaac Ehrlich's Research on Capital Punishment*, 85 YALE L.J. 187, 187 (1975) (finding Ehrlich's data and methods unreliable). A good overview is Robert Weisberg, *The Death*

regression analyses of the death penalty, based on time-series data from 1933 to 1967, and concluded that each execution deterred as many as eight murders.[19] But subsequent studies raised many questions about Ehrlich's conclusions—by showing, for example, that the deterrent effects of the death penalty would be eliminated if data from 1965 through 1969 were eliminated.[20] It would be fair to say that the deterrence hypothesis could not be confirmed by the studies that have been completed in the twenty years after Ehrlich first wrote.[21]

More recent evidence, however, has given new life to Ehrlich's hypothesis.[22] A wave of sophisticated multiple regression studies have exploited a newly available form of data, so-called "panel data," that uses all information from a set of units (states or counties) and follows that data over an extended period of time. A leading study used county-level panel data from 3054 U.S. counties between 1977 and 1996.[23] The authors found that the murder rate is significantly reduced by both death sentences and executions. The most striking finding was that *on average, each execution results in eighteen fewer murders*.[24]

Other econometric studies also find a substantial deterrent effect. In two papers, Paul Zimmerman uses state-level panel data from 1978 onwards to measure the deterrent effect of execution rates and execution methods. He estimates that each execution deters an average of fourteen murders.[25] Using state-level data from 1977 to 1997, H. Naci Mocan and R. Kaj Gittings find that each execution deters five murders on average.[26] They also find that increases in the murder rate result when people are removed from death row

---

Penalty Meets Social Science: Deterrence and Jury Behavior Under New Scrutiny, 1 ANN. REV. L. & SOC. SCI. 151 (2005).

19. *See* Ehrlich, *supra* note 18, at 398; Isaac Ehrlich, *Capital Punishment and Deterrence: Some Further Thoughts and Additional Evidence*, 85 J. POL. ECON. 741 (1977).

20. For this point and an overview of many other criticisms of Ehrlich's conclusions, see Richard O. Lempert, *Desert and Deterrence: An Assessment of the Moral Bases of the Case for Capital Punishment*, 79 MICH. L. REV. 1177 (1981).

21. *See id.*; Weisberg, *supra* note 18, at 155-57.

22. Even as this evidence was being developed, one of us predicted, perhaps rashly, that the debate would remain inconclusive for the foreseeable future. *See* Adrian Vermeule, *Interpretive Choice*, 75 N.Y.U. L. REV. 74, 100-01 (2000).

23. *See* Dezhbakhsh et al., *supra* note 9, at 359.

24. *Id.* at 373.

25. Zimmerman, *Alternative Execution Methods*, *supra* note 9; Zimmerman, *State Executions*, *supra* note 9, at 190.

26. Mocan & Gittings, *supra* note 9, at 453. Notably, no clear evidence of a deterrent effect from capital punishment emerges from Lawrence Katz et al., *Prison Conditions, Capital Punishment, and Deterrence*, 5 AM. L. & ECON. REV. 318, 330 (2003), which finds that the estimate of deterrence is extremely sensitive to the choice of specification, with the largest estimate paralleling that in Ehrlich, *supra* note 18. Note, however, that the principal finding in Katz et al., *supra*, is that prison deaths *do* have a strong deterrent effect and a stunningly large one—with each prison death producing a reduction of "30-100 violent crimes and a similar number of property crimes." *Id.* at 340.

and when death sentences are commuted.[27]

A study by Joanna Shepherd, based on data from all states from 1997 to 1999, finds that each death sentence deters 4.5 murders and that an execution deters 3 additional murders.[28] Her study also investigates the contested question whether executions deter crimes of passion and murders by intimates. Although intuition might suggest that such crimes cannot be deterred, her own finding is clear: all categories of murder are deterred by capital punishment.[29] The deterrent effect of the death penalty is also found to be a function of the length of waits on death row, with a murder deterred for every 2.75 years of reduction in the period before execution.[30] Importantly, this study finds that the deterrent effect of capital punishment protects African-American victims even more than whites.[31]

In the period between 1972 and 1976, the Supreme Court produced an effective moratorium on capital punishment, and an extensive unpublished study exploits that fact to estimate the deterrent effect. Using state-level data from 1977 to 1999, the authors make before-and-after comparisons, focusing on the murder rate in each state before and after the death penalty was suspended and reinstated.[32] The authors find a substantial deterrent effect: "[T]he data indicate that murder rates increased immediately after the moratorium was imposed and decreased directly after the moratorium was lifted, providing support for the deterrence hypothesis."[33]

A recent study offers more refined findings.[34] Disaggregating the data on a state-by-state basis, Joanna Shepherd finds that the nationwide deterrent effect of capital punishment is entirely driven by only six states—and that no deterrent effect can be found in the twenty-one other states that have restored capital punishment.[35] What distinguishes the six from the twenty-one? The answer, she contends, lies in the fact that states showing a deterrent effect are executing more people than states that are not. In fact the data show a

27. Mocan & Gittings, *supra* note 9, at 453, 456.

28. Shepherd, *Murders of Passion*, *supra* note 9, at 308.

29. *Id.* at 305. Shepherd notes:

> Many researchers have argued that some types of murders cannot be deterred: they assert that murders committed during arguments or other crime-of-passion moments are not premeditated and therefore undeterrable. My results indicate that this assertion is wrong: the rates of crime-of-passion and murders by intimates—crimes previously believed to be undeterrable—all decrease in execution months.

Id.

30. *Id.* at 283.

31. *Id.* at 308.

32. Hashem Dezhbakhsh & Joanna M. Shepherd, *The Deterrent Effect of Capital Punishment: Evidence from a "Judicial Experiment,"* at tbls.3-4 (Am. Law & Economics Ass'n Working Paper No. 18, 2004), *available at* http://law.bepress.com/cgi/viewcontent.cgi?article=1017&context=alea (last visited Dec. 1, 2005).

33. *Id.* at 3-4.

34. Shepherd, *Deterrence Versus Brutalization*, *supra* note 9.

35. *Id.* at 207.

"threshold effect": deterrence is found in states that had at least nine total executions between 1977 and 1996. In states below that threshold, no deterrence effect can be found.[36] This finding is intuitively plausible. Unless executions reach a certain level, murderers may act as if the death penalty is so improbable as not to be worthy of concern.[37] Shepherd's main lesson is that once the level of executions reaches a certain level, the deterrent effect of capital punishment is substantial.

All in all, the recent evidence of a deterrent effect from capital punishment seems impressive, especially in light of its "apparent power and unanimity."[38] But in studies of this kind, it is hard to control for confounding variables, and reasonable doubts inevitably remain. Most broadly, skeptics are likely to question the mechanisms by which capital punishment is said to have a deterrent effect. In the skeptical view, many murderers lack a clear sense of the likelihood and perhaps even the existence of executions in their states; further problems for the deterrence claim are introduced by the fact that capital punishment is imposed infrequently and after long delays. Emphasizing the weakness of the deterrent signal, Steven Levitt has suggested that "it is hard to believe that fear of execution would be a driving force in a rational criminal's calculus in modern America."[39] And, of course, some criminals do not act rationally: many murders are committed in a passionate state that does not lend itself to an all-things-considered analysis on the part of perpetrators.

More narrowly, it remains possible that the recent findings will be exposed as statistical artifacts or found to rest on flawed econometric methods. Work by Richard Berk, based on his independent review of the state-level panel data from Mocan and Gittings, offers multiple objections to those authors' finding of deterrence.[40] For example, Texas executes more people than any other state, and when Texas is removed from the data, the evidence of deterrence is severely weakened.[41] Removal of the apparent "outlier state[s]" that execute the largest numbers of people seems to eliminate the finding of deterrence

36. *Id.* at 239-41.

37. Less intuitively, Shepherd finds that in thirteen of the states that had capital punishment but executed few people, capital punishment actually *increased* the murder rate. She attributes this puzzling result to what she calls the "brutalization effect," by which capital punishment devalues human life and teaches people about the legitimacy of vengeance. *Id.* at 40-41.

38. *See* Weisberg, *supra* note 18, at 159.

39. *See* Steven D. Levitt, *Understanding Why Crime Fell in the 1990s: Four Factors that Explain the Decline and Six that Do Not*, 18 J. ECON. PERSP. 163, 175 (2004).

40. *See* Berk, *supra* note 16; *Deterrence and the Death Penalty*, *supra* note 16, at 6-12.

41. Berk, *supra* note 16, at 320. It has also been objected that the studies do not take account of the availability of sentences that involve life without the possibility of parole; such sentences might have a deterrent effect equal to or beyond that of capital punishment. *See Deterrence and the Death Penalty*, *supra* note 16. A response to Berk can found in Shepherd, *Deterrence Versus Brutalization*, *supra* note 9.

altogether.[42] Berk concludes that the findings of Mocan and Gittings are driven by six states with more than five executions each year. Berk, however, proceeds by presenting data in graphic form; he offers no regression analyses in support of his criticism.

These concerns about the evidence should be taken as useful cautions. At the level of theory, it is plausible that if criminals are fully rational, they should not be deterred by infrequent and much-delayed executions; the deterrent signal may well be too weak to affect their behavior. But suppose that like most people, criminals are boundedly rational, assessing probabilities with the aid of heuristics.[43] If executions are highly salient and cognitively available, some prospective murderers will overestimate their likelihood, and will be deterred as a result. Other prospective murderers will not pay much attention to the fact that execution is unlikely, focusing instead on the badness of the outcome (execution) rather than its low probability.[44] Few murderers are likely to assess the deterrent signal by multiplying the harm of execution against its likelihood. If this is so, then the deterrent signal will be larger than might be suggested by the product of that multiplication. Levitt's theoretical claim assumes that prospective murderers are largely rational in their reaction to the death penalty and its probability—standing by itself, a plausible conjecture but no more.

As for the recent data, it is true that evidence of deterrence is reduced or eliminated through the removal of Texas and other states in which executions are most common and in which evidence of deterrence is strongest.[45] But removal of those states seems to be an odd way to resolve the contested questions. States having the largest numbers of executions are most likely to deter, and it does not seem to make sense to exclude those states as "outliers."[46] By way of comparison, imagine a study attempting to determine what characteristics of baseball teams most increase the chance of winning the World Series. Imagine also a criticism of the study, parallel to Berk's, which complained that data about the New York Yankees should be thrown out, on the ground that the Yankees have won so many times as to be "outliers." This would be an odd idea, because empiricists must go where the evidence is; in the case of capital punishment, the outliers provide much of the relevant evidence. Recall here Shepherd's finding, compatible with the analysis of some skeptics, that the deterrent effect occurs only in states in which there is some threshold

---

42. Berk, *supra* note 16, at 320-24; Shepherd, *Deterrence Versus Brutalization*, *supra* note 9.

43. On bounded rationality in general, see RICHARD H. THALER, QUASI-RATIONAL ECONOMICS (1991).

44. *See* Yuval Rottenstreich & Christopher K. Hsee, *Money, Kisses, and Electric Shocks: On the Affective Psychology of Risk*, 12 PSYCHOL. SCI. 185, 188 (2001); Cass R. Sunstein, *Probability Neglect: Emotions, Worst Cases, and Law*, 112 YALE L.J. 61 (2002).

45. *See* Shepherd, *Deterrence Versus Brutalization*, *supra* note 9.

46. *Id.*

number of executions.[47]

But let us suppose, plausibly, that the evidence of deterrence remains inconclusive. Even so, it would not follow that the death penalty as such fails to deter. As Shepherd also finds in her most recent study,[48] more frequent executions, carried out in closer proximity to convictions, are predicted to amplify the deterrent signal for both rational and boundedly rational criminals. We can go further. A degree of doubt, with respect to the current system, need not be taken to suggest that existing evidence is irrelevant for purposes of policy and law. In regulation as a whole, it is common to embrace some version of the precautionary principle[49]—the idea that steps should be taken to prevent significant harm even if cause-and-effect relationships remain unclear and even if the risk is not likely to come to fruition. Even if we reject strong versions of the precautionary principle,[50] it hardly seems sensible that governments should ignore evidence demonstrating a significant possibility that a certain step will save large numbers of innocent lives.

For capital punishment, critics often seem to assume that evidence on deterrent effects should be ignored if reasonable questions can be raised about the evidence's reliability. But as a general rule, this is implausible. In most contexts, the existence of legitimate questions is hardly an adequate reason to ignore evidence of severe harm. If it were, many environmental controls would be in serious jeopardy.[51] We do not mean to suggest that government should commit what many people consider to be, prima facie, a serious moral wrong simply on the basis of speculation that this action will do some good. But a degree of reasonable doubt need not be taken as sufficient to doom a form of punishment if there is a significant possibility that it will save large numbers of lives.

It is possible that capital punishment saves lives on net, even if it has *zero* deterrent effect. A life-life tradeoff may arise in several ways. One possibility, the one we focus on here, is that capital punishment deters homicides. Another possibility is that capital punishment has no deterrent effect, but saves lives just

47. *See id.*

48. *Id.*

49. For overviews of the precautionary principle and related issues, see INTERPRETING THE PRECAUTIONARY PRINCIPLE (Tim O'Riordan & James Cameron eds., 1994); ARIE TROUWBORST, EVOLUTION AND STATUS OF THE PRECAUTIONARY PRINCIPLE IN INTERNATIONAL LAW (2002).

50. *See, e.g.*, Julian Morris, *Defining the Precautionary Principle*, *in* RETHINKING RISK AND THE PRECAUTIONARY PRINCIPLE (Julian Morris ed., 2000).

51. Indeed, those skeptical of capital punishment invoke evidence to the effect that capital punishment did not deter, and argue, plausibly, that it would be a mistake to wait for definitive evidence before ceasing with a punishment that could not be shown to reduce homicide. *See* Lempert, *supra* note 20, at 1222-24. This is a kind of precautionary principle, arguing against the most aggressive forms of punishment if the evidence suggested that they did not deter. We are suggesting the possibility of a mirror-image precautionary principle when the evidence goes the other way.

by incapacitating those who would otherwise kill again in the future.[52] Consider those jurisdictions that eschew capital punishment altogether. What sanction can such jurisdictions really apply to those who have already been sentenced to life in prison without parole? Sentences of this sort may take more lives overall by increasing the number of essentially unpunishable within-prison homicides of guards and fellow inmates.[53] Many murderers are killed in prison even in states that lack the death penalty.[54] And if murderers are eventually paroled into the general population, some of them will kill again. Overall, it is quite possible that the permanent incapacitation of murderers through execution might save lives on net. A finding that capital punishment deters—and deterrence is our focus here—is sufficient but not necessary to find a life-life tradeoff.

In any event, our goal here is not to reach a final judgment about the evidence. It is to assess capital punishment given the assumption of a substantial deterrent effect. In what follows, therefore, we will stipulate to the validity of the evidence and consider its implications for morality and law. Those who doubt the evidence might ask themselves how they would assess the moral questions if they were ultimately convinced that life-life tradeoffs were actually involved—as, for example, in hostage situations in which officials are authorized to use deadly force to protect the lives of innocent people.

II. Capital Punishment: Moral Foundations and Four Objections

Assume, then, that capital punishment does save a significant number of innocent lives. On what assumptions should that form of punishment be deemed morally unacceptable, rather than morally obligatory? Why should the deaths of those convicted of capital murder, an overwhelmingly large fraction of whom are guilty in fact, be considered a more serious moral wrong than the deaths of a more numerous group who are certainly innocents?

We consider, and ultimately reject, several responses. Our first general contention is that opposition to capital punishment trades on a form of the distinction between acts and omissions. Whatever the general force of that distinction, its application to government systematically fails, because government is a distinctive kind of moral agent. Our second general contention is that, apart from direct state involvement, the features that make capital punishment morally objectionable to its critics are also features of the very murders that capital punishment deters. The principal difference, on the empirical assumptions we are making, is that in a legal regime without capital punishment far more people die, and those people are innocent of any

52. *See* Ronald J. Allen & Amy Shavell, *Further Reflections on the Guillotine*, 95 J. Crim. L. & Criminology 625, 630-31 (2005).

53. *See id.* at 630 n.9.

54. *See* Katz et al., *supra* note 26, at 340.

wrongdoing. No one denies that arbitrariness in the system of capital punishment is a serious problem. But even if the existing system is viewed in its worst light, it involves far less arbitrariness than does the realm of homicide. Let us begin, however, with foundational issues.

A. *Morality and Death*

On a standard view, it is impossible to come to terms with the moral questions about capital punishment without saying something about the foundations of moral judgments. We will suggest, however, that sectarian commitments at the foundational level are for the most part irrelevant to the issues here. If it is stipulated that substantial deterrence exists, both consequentialist and deontological accounts of morality will or should converge upon the view that capital punishment is morally obligatory. Consequentialists will come to that conclusion because capital punishment minimizes killings overall. Deontologists will do so because an opposition to killing is, by itself, indeterminate in the face of life-life tradeoffs; because a legal regime with capital punishment has a strong claim to be more respectful of life's value than does a legal regime lacking capital punishment; and because modern deontologists typically subscribe to a consequentialist override or escape hatch, one that makes otherwise impermissible actions obligatory if necessary to prevent many deaths—precisely what we are assuming is true of capital punishment. Only those deontologists who both insist upon a strong distinction between state actions and state omissions *and* who reject a consequentialist override will believe the deterrent effect of capital punishment to be irrelevant in principle.

Suppose that we accept consequentialism and believe that government actions should be evaluated in terms of their effects on aggregate welfare. If we do so, the evidence of deterrence strongly supports a moral argument in favor of the death penalty—a form of punishment that, by hypothesis, seems to produce a net gain in overall welfare. Of course, there are many complications here; for example, the welfare of many people might increase as a result of knowing that capital punishment exists, and the welfare of many other people might decrease for the same reason. A full consequentialist calculus would require a more elaborate assessment than we aim to provide here. The only point is that if capital punishment produces significantly fewer deaths on balance, there should be a strong consequentialist presumption on its behalf; any argument against capital punishment, on consequentialist grounds, will face a steep uphill struggle.

To be sure, it is also possible to imagine forms of consequentialism that reject welfarism as implausibly reductionist and see violations of rights as part of the set of consequences that must be taken into account in deciding what to do.[55] For some such consequentialists, killings are, under ordinary circumstances, a violation of rights, and this point is highly relevant to any judgment about killings. But even if the point is accepted, capital punishment may be required, not prohibited, on consequentialist grounds, simply because and to the extent that it minimizes rights violations. Private murders also violate rights, and the rights-respecting consequentialist must take those actions into account.

But imagine that we are deontologists, believing that actions by government and others should not be evaluated in consequentialist terms; how can capital punishment be morally permissible, let alone obligatory? For some deontologists, capital punishment is obligatory for moral reasons alone.[56] But suppose, as other deontologists believe, that under ordinary circumstances, the state's killing of a human being is a wrong and that its wrongness does not depend on an inquiry into whether the action produces a net increase in welfare. For many critics of capital punishment, a deontological intuition is central; evidence of deterrence is irrelevant because moral wrongdoing by the state is not justified even if it can be defended on utilitarian grounds. Compare a situation in which a state seeks to kill an innocent person, knowing that the execution will prevent a number of private killings; deontologists believe that the unjustified execution cannot be supported even if the state is secure in its knowledge of the execution's beneficial effects. Of course, it is contentious to claim that capital punishment is a moral wrong. But if it is, then significant deterrence might be entirely beside the point. It is simply true that many intuitive objections to capital punishment rely on a belief of this kind: just as execution of an innocent person is a moral wrong, one that cannot be justified on consequentialist grounds, so too the execution of a guilty person is a moral wrong, whatever the evidence shows.

Despite all this, our claims here do not depend on accepting consequentialism or rejecting the deontological objection to evaluating unjustified killings in consequentialist terms. The argument is instead that by itself and in the abstract, this objection is indeterminate on the moral status of capital punishment. To the extent possible, we intend to bracket the most fundamental questions and to suggest that whatever one's view of the foundations of morality, the objection to the death penalty is difficult to sustain under the empirical assumptions that we have traced. Taken in its most sympathetic light, a deontological objection to capital punishment is unconvincing *if* states that refuse to impose the death penalty produce, by that

55. Amartya Sen, *Rights and Agency*, 11 PHIL. & PUB. AFF. 3, 15-19 (1982).

56. *See* Pojman, *supra* note 4, at 58-59. As noted below, the case of Israel is a good test for such deontologists; Israel does not impose the death penalty, in part on the ground that executions of terrorists would likely increase terrorism. Do deontologists committed to capital punishment believe that Israel is acting immorally? In our view, they ought not to do so, at least if the empirical assumption is right and if the protection of lives is what morality requires.

very refusal, significant numbers of additional deaths. Recall the realm of homicide: for deontologists who emphasize life's value and object to the death penalty, the problem is acute if the refusal to impose that penalty predictably leads to a significant number of additional murders. In a hostage situation, police officers are permitted to kill (execute) those who have taken hostages if this step is reasonably deemed necessary to save those who have been taken hostage. If the evidence of deterrence is convincing, why is capital punishment so different in principle?

Of course, these points might be unresponsive to those who believe that execution of a guilty person is morally equivalent to execution of an innocent person and not properly subject to a recognition of life-life tradeoffs. We will explore this position in more detail below. And we could envision a form of deontology that refuses any exercise in aggregation—one that would refuse to authorize, or compel, a violation of rights even if the violation is necessary to prevent a significantly larger number of rights violations. But most modern deontologists reject this position, instead admitting a consequentialist override to baseline deontological prohibitions.[57] Although the threshold at which the consequentialist override is triggered varies with different accounts, we suggest below that if each execution deters some eighteen murders, the override is plausibly triggered.

To distill these points, the only deontological accounts that are inconsistent with our argument are those that *both* (1) embrace a distinction between state actions and state omissions *and* (2) reject a consequentialist override. To those who subscribe to this complex of views, and who consider capital punishment a violation of rights, our argument will not be convincing. In the end, however, we believe that it is difficult to sustain the set of moral assumptions that would bar capital punishment *if* it is the best means of preventing significant numbers of innocent deaths. Indeed, we believe that many of those who think that they hold those assumptions are motivated by other considerations—especially a failure to give full weight to statistical lives—on which we focus in Part III.

B. *Acts and Omissions*

A natural response to our basic concern would invoke the widespread intuition that capital punishment involves intentional state "action," while the failure to deter private murders is merely an "omission" by the state. In our view, this appealing and intuitive line of argument goes rather badly wrong. The critics of capital punishment have been led astray by uncritically applying the act/omission distinction to a regulatory setting. Their position condemns the "active" infliction of death by governments but does not condemn the "inactive" production of death that comes from the refusal to maintain a system

57. For an overview, see Larry Alexander, *Deontology at the Threshold*, 37 SAN DIEGO L. REV. 893, 898-901 (2000).

of capital punishment. The basic problem is that even if this selective condemnation can be justified at the level of individual behavior, it is difficult to defend for governments.[58] A great deal of work has to be done to explain why "inactive," but causal, government decisions should not be part of the moral calculus. Suppose that we endorse the deontological position that it is wrong to take human lives, even if overall welfare is promoted by taking them. Why does the system of capital punishment violate that position, if the failure to impose capital punishment also takes lives?

Perhaps our argument about unjustified selectivity is blind to morally relevant factors that condemn capital punishment and that buttress the act/omission distinction in this context. There are two possible points here, one involving intention and the other involving causation. First, a government (acting through agents) that engages in capital punishment intends to take lives; it seeks to kill. A government that does not engage in capital punishment, and therefore provides less deterrence, does not intend to kill. The deaths that result are the unintended and unsought byproduct of an effort to respect life. Surely—it might be said—this is a morally relevant difference. Second, a government that inflicts capital punishment ensures a simple and direct causal chain between its own behavior and the taking of human lives. When a government rejects capital punishment, the causal chain is much more complex; the taking of human lives is an indirect consequence of the government's decision, one that is mediated by the actions of a murderer. The government authorizes its agents to inflict capital punishment, but it does not authorize private parties to murder; indeed, it forbids murder. Surely that is a morally relevant difference, too.

We will begin, in Part II.B.1, with questions about whether the act/omission distinction is conceptually intelligible in regulatory settings. Here the suggestion is that there just is no way to speak or think coherently about government "actions" as opposed to government "omissions," because government cannot help but act, in some way or another, when choosing how individuals are to be regulated. In Part II.B.2, we suggest that the distinction between government acts and omissions, even if conceptually coherent, is not morally relevant to the question of capital punishment. Some governmental actions are morally obligatory, and some governmental omissions are blameworthy. In this setting, we suggest, government is morally obligated to adopt capital punishment and morally at fault if it declines to do so.

1. *Is the act/omission distinction coherent with respect to government?*

In our view, any effort to distinguish between acts and omissions goes

---

58. Compare debates over going to war: Some pacifists insist, correctly, that acts of war will result in the loss of life, including civilian life. But a refusal to go to war will often result in the loss of life, including civilian life.

wrong by overlooking the distinctive features of government as a moral agent. If correct, this point has broad implications for criminal and civil law. Whatever the general status of the act/omission distinction as a matter of moral philosophy,[59] the distinction is least impressive when applied to government, because the most plausible underlying considerations do not apply to official actors.[60] The most fundamental point is that, unlike individuals, governments always and necessarily face a choice between or among possible policies for regulating third parties. The distinction between acts and omissions may not be intelligible in this context, and even if it is, the distinction does not make a morally relevant difference.

Most generally, government is in the business of creating permissions and prohibitions. When it explicitly or implicitly authorizes private action, it is not omitting to do anything or refusing to act.[61] Moreover, the distinction between authorized and unauthorized private action—for example, private killing—becomes obscure when the government formally forbids private action but chooses a set of policy instruments that do not adequately or fully discourage it.

To be sure, a system of punishments that only weakly deters homicide, relative to other feasible punishments, does not quite authorize homicide, but that system is not properly characterized as an omission, and little turns on whether it can be so characterized. Suppose, for example, that government fails to characterize certain actions—say, sexual harassment—as tortious or violative of civil rights law and that it therefore permits employers to harass employees as they choose or to discharge employees for failing to submit to sexual harassment. It would be unhelpful to characterize the result as a product of governmental "inaction." If employers are permitted to discharge employees for refusing to submit to sexual harassment, it is because the law is allocating certain entitlements to employers rather than employees. Or consider the context of ordinary torts. When Homeowner *B* sues Factory *A* over air pollution, a decision not to rule for Homeowner *B* is not a form of inaction: it is the allocation to Factory *A* of a property right to pollute. In such cases, an apparent government omission is an action simply because it is an allocation of legal rights. Any decision that allocates such rights, by creating entitlements

59. For discussion of the philosophical controversy over acts and omissions, see generally RONALD DWORKIN, LIFE'S DOMINION: AN ARGUMENT ABOUT ABORTION, EUTHANASIA, AND INDIVIDUAL FREEDOM (1993); Frances M. Kamm, *Abortion and the Value of Life: A Discussion of* Life's Dominion, 95 COLUM. L. REV. 160 (1995) (reviewing DWORKIN, *supra*); Tom Stacy, *Acts, Omissions, and the Necessity of Killing Innocents*, 29 AM. J. CRIM. L. 481 (2002).

60. Here we proceed in the spirit of Robert Goodin by treating government as a distinctive sort of moral agent with respect to whom many quotidian moral distinctions have little purchase. *See* ROBERT E. GOODIN, UTILITARIANISM AS A PUBLIC PHILOSOPHY (1995). Goodin, we should note, does not address the act/omission distinction at any length, although he seems to reject it. *See id.* at 89.

61. *See* STEPHEN HOLMES & CASS R. SUNSTEIN, THE COST OF RIGHTS: WHY LIBERTY DEPENDS ON TAXES (1999).

and prohibitions, is not inaction at all.

Suppose that government officials face a choice between two (and only two) packages of policies for reducing the murder rate. Suppose that Package *A* contains a range of legal instruments, such as ordinary imprisonment, imprisonment without parole (perhaps for life), postincarceration programs to prevent recidivism, and so on. Package *B* contains all the same instruments *plus* capital punishment.

Stipulating to the validity of the evidence discussed in Part I, the crux of the issue is this: to opt for Package *A* over Package *B* will inevitably ensure a significant increase in the number of deaths. In this setting, it is hard to make sense of the claim that capital punishment involves intentional government "action" in some morally distinctive way. It is tautologically true that a package lacking capital punishment does not include the particular "action" of imposing that form of punishment. But for government to opt for Package *A*—even in the sense of simply leaving in place previously enacted laws that adopted Package *A*—is no less an intentional "action" than it is to opt for Package *B*. Some criminal justice policy or other will necessarily be in place. The only interesting or even meaningful question government ever faces is not whether to act, but what action should be taken—what mix of criminal justice policies government ought to pursue. The policy mix that does not include capital punishment is not an "omission" or a "failure to act" in any meaningful sense. If a government chooses that mix, it is allocating a certain set of rights to both murderers and their victims; the latter are certainly given a right to be free from murder, but the right is limited by the terms of the anticipated punishment. In the extreme case, suppose that a state failed to punish certain classes of murders (say, those who kill African-Americans), that it punished such murders only infrequently, or that it punished such murders with just a slap on the wrist. Under any of these approaches, the distinction between authorizing murder and failing to prevent it would become thin.

To be sure, officials and citizens who opt for a system that lacks capital punishment do not "intend" to kill anyone in particular. But consider a situation in which regulators refuse to adopt motor vehicle or drug-safety regulations that would prevent significant numbers of statistical deaths. Is the refusal acceptable because it leads to deaths that are not, strictly speaking, intended? The very concept of "intentional" action, and the moral relevance of intention, are both obscure when government is the pertinent moral agent. The executioner who administers the injection acts intentionally, but so does the private murderer. Those who emphasize intention presumably do not mean to focus narrowly on the actual individual who carries out the final action on the state's behalf. (Does it matter so much that the executioner is on the government's payroll? What if the executioner is a volunteer?) The real point is that in a regime of capital punishment the executioner acts pursuant to an explicit government policy, whereas (the idea runs) there is never a government policy to murder the particular citizens whose deaths would have been deterred by capital punishment.

It is true that there is no such policy, and intuition seems to suggest that its absence is important, but the moral relevance of its absence is obscure. If the point appears intuitively important, it is only because of the abstract or statistical character of the eighteen persons whose murders are deterred by each execution (a theme to which we return in Part III). People generally pay little attention to statistical deaths, but this lack of attention seems to be a cognitive failure, not a proper basis for morality or policy.[62] The legal regime whose package of crime-control instruments happens not to include capital punishment does indeed embody an explicit government policy: a policy that inevitably and predictably opts for more murders over fewer. That the victims of those murders cannot be personally identified in advance does not seem to be a morally impressive basis for favoring the regime that makes their murders inevitable. If we put aside the intentional actions of low-level officials, the relevant policies in either regime will be set by a complex process of democratic and regulatory interaction among voters, legislators, administrators, and judges. In this large-scale process of collective decisionmaking, the concept of intention might be coherent, but it becomes too attenuated to bear the moral weight often put upon it.[63] The regime with capital punishment does not seem importantly different, on the score of intentions, than the regime without it.

In this light, the idea that the government "authorizes" capital punishment but "forbids" private murder is too simple. Two points are important. First, of course, it is true that the government does not authorize private killings in a retail sense, barring cases of self-defense or defense of others. At the wholesale level, however, to adopt a package of criminal justice policies that does not include capital punishment is to ensure the murders of a large number of (as yet unidentified) victims. The government's inability to identify the victims before the fact must be morally irrelevant. Second, there is a sense in which the regime without capital punishment comes perilously close to licensing private killings, because in that regime policymakers know or should know that the prohibition on murder is supported by a weaker deterrent signal.

To be sure, government creates property rights, and it does not create lives in the same sense; however, the cash value of a prohibition lies in the scheme

62. *See* George Loewenstein et al., *Statistical, Identifiable and Iconic Victims and Perpetrators* (Stanford Law Sch., John M. Olin Law & Econ. Working Paper No. 301, Mar. 2005), *available at* http://ssrn.com/abstract=678281.

63. There is a large philosophical literature that considers whether the concept of culpability for intentional wrongdoing applies meaningfully to governments. *See, e.g.*, CHRISTOPHER KUTZ, COMPLICITY: ETHICS AND LAW FOR A COLLECTIVE AGE (2000). There are also large literatures in jurisprudence and literary theory that consider whether the concept of intention can meaningfully be transposed from individual to collective decisionmakers. *See, e.g.*, JEREMY WALDRON, LAW AND DISAGREEMENT (1999); Steven Knapp & Walter Benn Michaels, *Against Theory*, 8 CRITICAL INQUIRY 723 (1982); Max Radin, *Statutory Interpretation*, 43 HARV. L. REV. 863 (1930).

of punishments that enforce it. Where the enforcement scheme is feeble, the prohibition is as well. On the empirical assumptions we are making, a government that eschews capital punishment rejects an effective mechanism for enforcing the baseline prohibition of murder. In the extreme case, ineffective enforcement mechanisms make the prohibition of murder begin to look like something of a sham. (Recall that 15,000 to 25,000 people are killed in the United States each year.)

It is no objection, to any of the foregoing points, that "government" is merely a convenient shorthand for a way of organizing individuals. Of course, government is staffed by natural persons and can only act through individual agents. But where those agents are invested with regulatory authority over third parties—when natural persons are acting as officials rather than as the subjects of regulation—there is no escaping the duty to choose policies in some fashion or other. To see this, imagine an absolute monarch who defines homicide, defines the limits of self-defense, sets the terms of imprisonment for homicide, and so forth. Now imagine that, when subjects kill each other, the monarch invokes her liberty as a natural person to decline to "intervene," or to "act." Accordingly, the monarch chooses not to adopt capital punishment. Here the invocation of the natural liberty of the monarch-as-person is farcical, even unintelligible. The monarch-as-monarch has already set all the ground rules that help to determine the frequency and incidence of homicide; as monarch, she has already structured the terrain. It is irresponsible, indeed incoherent, for her then to disavow her regulatory role by invoking the natural person's liberty not to "act." She might decide not to execute anyone, of course. But that decision would have to be justified on other grounds than the distinction between governmental acts and governmental omissions.

2. *Is the act/omission distinction morally relevant to capital punishment?*

So far we have argued that the act/omission distinction is conceptually obscure when applied to government, whatever its merits when applied to individuals. The arguments that most plausibly support the distinction do not make much sense in the context of public officials, and in any case the category of government inaction is hard to understand, except by tautology, in the context of criminal punishment. Even if that argument fails, however, capital punishment may still be morally obligatory for governments. The relevant acts may be morally required or the relevant omissions morally blameworthy. We begin by reviewing the considerations that underpin the act/omission distinction as applied to individuals; these considerations lose their force where government is the moral agent at issue. We then turn to the ideas that declining to adopt capital punishment is a culpable omission and that adopting capital punishment is a morally obligatory act.

Suppose that there is some clear and nontautologous sense in which a system of capital punishment counts as "action" and that this is not the case for a refusal to impose capital punishment, which therefore counts as a kind of omission or failure to act. What is the moral importance of this distinction? Individuals, let us suppose, are prima facie obligated not to harm others, but they have no obligation to assist them. Of course, this view raises many puzzles, not least in the definition of the relevant categories, but let us accept it for present purposes and ask how it applies where government is the moral agent.

With respect to individuals, the act/omission distinction is sharply contested, but consider some grounds on which it might be defended. First, those who injure others, and who commit harms, are far more vicious than those who fail to take steps to prevent harm to others. By their deeds, actors display a far worse character than omitters, and this difference is properly taken into account by both morality and law. Second, human beings have a presumptive right to go about their private lives without official interference; if omissions were sanctioned, through morality or law, liberty would be badly compromised. It is no infringement on liberty, or rights, to tell people that they must not harm others. But it is a significant infringement to tell people that they must assist others. On this view, the act/omission distinction is defensible, for individuals, because it respects liberty. Third, it is fully plausible to think that an all-things-considered assessment of consequences justifies the act/omission distinction, at least in most domains. Of course, it is possible to find cases in which an omission causes a serious welfare loss on balance, as, for example, when a bystander refuses to take relatively simple steps to prevent a homicide. But for a legal system, an assessment of the consequences of omissions, in individual cases, would be quite overwhelming, and many of those who are omitting to help some are, at the same time, helping others (for example, their children or others who need assistance). An insistence on an act/omission distinction might well have good consequences at the systemic level. We are not contending that for individuals this distinction makes sense in specific cases or in general; we are attempting more modestly to isolate the reasons that best justify it.

Those reasons, however, lose their force in the regulatory setting. It is possible that government officials are more "vicious" when they engage in, say, unlawful and environmentally destructive behavior than when they fail to take steps against such behavior by private parties; it is hard to see the moral relevance of that difference in the evaluation of government policy. Government officials cannot plausibly claim that their liberty is abridged when citizens ask them to take steps against, say, domestic violence, occupational deaths, or rape. At first glance, it is difficult to see how consequentialist considerations could justify an approach that would draw a sharp distinction between problematic actions (e.g., in the form of unjustified enforcement proceedings against alleged violators of the Clean Air Act) and problematic omissions (e.g., in the form of unjustified refusal to enforce the Clean Air

Act).[64]

The government cannot easily claim that it is under no duty to assist people, at least when those people are at risk of criminal violence. In administrative law, it is greatly contested whether agency inaction is subject to some special immunity from judicial review, and any such immunity turns largely on pragmatic considerations involving the limits of oversight by federal judges.[65] Likewise, governmental failure to protect people against private violence generally does not give rise to constitutional liability,[66] but this too is largely because judges have a limited capacity to enforce liability in such cases. Apart from law, there is no reason to think that omissions of this kind are properly insulated from moral criticism if significant numbers of deaths are a predictable consequence. Consider the question of famines. Amartya Sen has famously shown that in governments with a free press and democratic elections, no nation in the history of the world has ever experienced a famine.[67] It would be implausible to say that a government's failure to prevent a famine is morally unproblematic, and, indeed, anticipated public outrage at the prospect of mass starvation lies at the heart of Sen's finding.

Alternatively, and equivalently, we can put these points within the usual language of the act/omission distinction. It is standard that an omission can count as an action when there is a "duty" to act, especially where the party subject to the duty has himself created the conditions that threaten harm. Where government is concerned, these requirements will often be fulfilled far more often than for typical private parties. Where citizens are murdering each other, government is not a bystander, innocent or otherwise, because the decision whether to murder is made, at least in part, in light of the government's criminal justice policies. The background rules against which citizens act to threaten the lives of others or to protect their own lives, including rules about and limitations on self-defense, are themselves products of government action—including the action of the special bureaucracies that lawyers call "criminal courts."

The previous points suggest that even if inflicting capital punishment is an "act" while declining to inflict it is an "omission," the omission may nonetheless be morally culpable. Conversely, the act may be morally obligatory if large numbers of lives are saved. Even strict deontological accounts of the impermissibility of killing typically build in a threshold exception: when the

64. The proper role of judicial review is, of course, contested, mostly for pragmatic reasons, but even here the distinction is not so sharp. *See* Bhagwat, *supra* note 12; Cass R. Sunstein, *Reviewing Agency Inaction After* Heckler v. Chaney, 52 U. CHI. L. REV. 653 (1985).

65. *See* Heckler v. Chaney, 470 U.S. 821 (1985).

66. *See* DeShaney v. Winnebago County Dep't of Soc. Servs., 489 U.S. 189 (1989).

67. *See* AMARTYA SEN, POVERTY AND FAMINES: AN ESSAY ON ENTITLEMENT AND DEPRIVATION (1981). We are grateful to William Stuntz for the example.

threshold is crossed, the moral agent is obliged[68] to commit otherwise impermissible acts in order to save third-party lives.[69] Moral theorists are typically vague as to where the threshold lies, but if each execution saves eighteen lives, then we are right in the neighborhood at which most theorists blanch at the collateral costs of deontological prohibitions.[70] We offer more general remarks on deontology and its relation to the act/omission distinction below. The point here is that capital punishment may be morally obligatory even if capital punishment counts as an act while failing to impose capital punishment counts as an omission.

We have questioned both the coherence and the moral relevance of the act/omission distinction as applied to capital punishment. We want to be clear, however, that in this setting, as elsewhere, rejecting the act/omission distinction only begins the analysis. For government to opt for a large highway-building project, for example, inevitably and predictably results in the deaths of a statistical set of workers who are no less real for being unidentifiable in advance. The reason the highway project is acceptable (if it is) might be either that more deaths would occur on net absent the project or, more broadly, that the social benefits are higher than the costs. Likewise, capital punishment might or might not be shown to save lives, on net; might or might not turn out to be welfare-enhancing, all things considered; and might or might not turn out to be just, depending on whether we hold a welfarist conception of justice. Our point here is limited: the crucial questions that determine whether capital punishment is life-saving, welfare-enhancing, or otherwise just are not questions about the difference between actions and omissions.

Consider, in this regard, the "reasonable doubt" standard of criminal law, under which it is better that some number of guilty defendants go free than an innocent person be convicted. It is possible to imagine a defense of the reasonable doubt standard on act/omission grounds: perhaps the government "acts" when it convicts and "fails to act" when it does not convict; perhaps government errors through action are much worse than government errors through inaction. Yet this seems an unlikely description. To acquit, or to decline to convict, is government "action" whether performed by a judge or by

---

68. A more precise formulation would be "permitted or obliged," because it is unclear which moral modality holds, according to threshold deontology, once the baseline deontological prohibition is waived. Without digressing too far into moral theory, we suggest that, conditional on accepting threshold deontology, the agent is obliged (not merely permitted) to promote the best overall consequences once the threshold has been crossed. In our view, it would be distinctly odd to say that a moral agent is permitted to infringe deontological constraints to save a large number of lives, but is not obliged to do so. For the related question whether general consequentialism entails an obligation to promote best consequences overall, or instead recognizes a class of supererogatory acts, see SHELLY KAGAN, NORMATIVE ETHICS 153-70 (1998).

69. For an overview, see Alexander, *supra* note 57, at 898-900.

70. *See* KAGAN, *supra* note 68, at 81 (stating that a "low threshold might permit killing one to save ten").

a jury acting as the state's agents[71] under rules and procedures set by the state. Yet the reasonable doubt standard can still be straightforwardly defended on a claim that the overall social consequences of false convictions are much worse than the overall social consequences of false acquittals. If so defended, the standard is perfectly sensible and need not be justified by reference to an obscure distinction between acts and omissions. So, too, in our setting: apart from the distinction between acts and omissions, there is a reasonable question about whether capital punishment really does provide net social benefits. The relevant material for answering that question, however, is the empirical evidence discussed in Part I, rather than conceptual arguments that struggle to adapt the act/omission distinction to the state.

Those who object to capital punishment typically favor life imprisonment, or even life imprisonment without parole, as a morally acceptable alternative. But once an empirical lens is introduced, this preference becomes quite puzzling. A significant number of those who have committed egregious murders, and might otherwise be subject to capital punishment, are killed in prison. State officials must be aware of this fact. Indeed, one study finds an extremely large deterrent effect from prison deaths, with a reduction of 30 to 100 violent crimes and an equivalent reduction in property offenses per death.[72] Is it so clear that an official execution is much worse than a statistical risk of murder? Is it so much worse for the state to authorize its officials to execute people than for the state to imprison people with the knowledge that many of those imprisoned will be killed by private or public actors—not expressly authorized to be killed, to be sure, but with little likelihood of official punishment? We think that those who oppose capital punishment ought not to see life imprisonment as substantially better if many convicted murderers are going to be killed, directly by state actors or with the acquiescence of state actors, in prison.

C. *The Arbitrary and Discriminatory Realm of Homicide*

Of course, there are important objections to capital punishment that do not trade on (some version of) the distinction between acts and omissions. Some of the most powerful of these objections invoke values associated with the rule of law. There are several concerns here.

Some innocent people are executed, and their deaths are obviously irreversible.[73] No legal system can ensure complete accuracy in criminal convictions. Even under the "no reasonable doubt" standard, errors are made.

---

71. *See* Gary J. Simson & Stephen P. Garvey, *Knockin' on Heaven's Door: Rethinking the Role of Religion in Death Penalty Cases*, 86 CORNELL L. REV. 1090, 1108 (2001).

72. *See* Katz et al., *supra* note 26, at 340.

73. *See* Liebman et al., *supra* note 3; Lawrence Marshall, *The Innocence Revolution and the Death Penalty*, 1 OHIO ST. J. CRIM. L. 573 (2004).

But errors are sometimes said to be intolerable when the state is depriving people of their lives, precisely because mistaken deprivations cannot be reversed.

The death penalty inevitably contains a degree of arbitrariness. Justice Stewart famously made the point when he wrote that receiving the death penalty is "cruel and unusual in the same way that being struck by lightning is cruel and unusual."[74] Justice Stewart's point is undoubtedly overstated for current capital punishment systems. But if any such system operates as a kind of death lottery, in which similarly situated people are not treated similarly, perhaps it is unacceptable for that reason alone.

Even within the set of guilty defendants, the death penalty may be administered in a way that reflects objectionable or invidious discrimination. In 2003, forty-two percent of the death row population was African-American and fifty-six percent was white.[75] In some times and places, African-American defendants have been more likely to receive capital punishment than whites. More recently, those who kill white people appear to be more likely to receive capital punishment than those who kill African-Americans.[76] The system of capital punishment might reflect a form of institutional racism; even if not, the system might simply operate against the background of racial injustice, ensuring intolerable inequalities in the imposition of death. In any event, capital defendants who are poor, or otherwise unlikely to have good lawyers, are far more likely to face the death penalty.

Some people believe that even if capital punishment could be morally acceptable if it were fairly administered, the inevitability of unfair administration means that we must eliminate it. These arguments point to strong reasons for reforming the existing system to increase accuracy and decrease arbitrariness. But the arguments do not succeed as objections to capital punishment as such. Once the act/omission distinction is no longer central, it becomes clear that *the standard moral objections to capital punishment apply even more powerfully to the murders prevented by capital punishment*. Those murders also cause irreversible deaths: those of the victims. Private murders are also often highly arbitrary, involving selectivity on any number of morally irrelevant or objectionable grounds. African-Americans, for example, are far more likely than other groups to be the victims of murder. In

74. Furman v. Georgia, 408 U.S. 238, 309 (1972) (Stewart, J., concurring).

75. THOMAS P. BONCZAR & TRACY L. SNELL, BUREAU OF JUSTICE STATISTICS, CAPITAL PUNISHMENT, 2003 (2004), *available at* http://www.ojp.usdoj.gov/bjs/pub/pdf/cp03.pdf.

76. For a well-known discussion, see Randall Kennedy, McCleskey v. Kemp*: Race, Capital Punishment, and the Supreme Court*, 101 HARV. L. REV. 1388, 1401 (1988). For recent evidence, see John Blume et al., *Explaining Death Row's Population and Racial Composition*, 1 J. EMPIRICAL LEGAL STUD. 165 (2004). On the basis of data analyzed by Blume et al., it is possible to estimate the rate at which death sentences are issued (per 1000 murders): for cases involving black offenders and black victims, the rate is 6.7%; black offenders and white victims, 62.2%; white offenders and white victims, 28.4%; and white offenders and black victims, 18.6%.

2003, forty-eight percent of murder victims were white and forty-eight percent were African-American—meaning that the racial disparity in the probability of becoming a murder victim is even greater than the racial disparity in the probability of ending up on death row.[77] An important corollary is that the benefits of capital punishment, to the extent that it operates as a powerful deterrent of murder, are likely to flow disproportionately to African-Americans.[78]

To be sure, this effect will be attenuated if death sentences are imposed less frequently on those who murder African-Americans. In the most pessimistic projection, capital punishment is likely to be disproportionately inflicted on African-Americans, and because that punishment is most likely to be imposed when whites have been killed, the resulting savings are likely to go largely to whites. On this view, the "life-life tradeoffs" may turn out, all too often, to be "African-American-life to white-life tradeoffs." In the abstract, it may be unclear how to make that tradeoff—even if it involves larger numbers, and innocence, on one side of the ledger. The simplest response is that on the current numbers, this projection is unrealistic. Because interracial murders are only a small fraction of all murders, and because death sentences for interracial murders are only a small fraction of all death sentences, capital punishment does not, in fact, make it necessary to trade off African-American lives against white ones.

To spell the claim out in more detail: most murder is intraracial, not interracial.[79] African-Americans are disproportionately victims of homicide, and their murderers are disproportionately African-American. For this reason, they have a great deal to gain from capital punishment if it does have a deterrent effect—very plausibly more, on balance, than white people do.[80] In

77. *See* FED. BUREAU OF INVESTIGATION, *supra* note 11, at tbl.2.3.

78. *See* Kennedy, *supra* note 76, at 1401.

79. *See* FED. BUREAU OF INVESTIGATION, *supra* note 11, at tbl.2.7 (tabulating murders as follows: white murdering white: 3017; African-American murdering African-American: 2864; white murdering African-American: 226; African-American murdering white: 501).

80. This judgment is supported by Blume et al., who provide figures relevant to the demographics of murder:

National Estimate of Death Row Composition Using Seven States' Data, 1976-1978

	Black Offender-Black Victim	Black Offender-White Victim	White Offender-White Victim	White Offender-Black Victim
National Known Murderers	113,649	19,987	118,488	7048
Estimated Number of Death Sentences	767	1243	3368	131
Estimated Percent of Death Row	14.6%	23.8%	55.0%	2.5%

Note: Using seven states with known race of offender-race of victim data, the table estimates the percentage of death row consisting of the indicated racial combinations for the thirty-one states in this study. The percentages in the third row do not total 100% because we limit our

any event, the more natural response to existing racial disparities is to lower them, rather than to eliminate the penalty altogether.

For the rule-of-law questions, as for all others, the core problem of capital punishment is that it presents a risk-risk tradeoff, or a life-life tradeoff. To say the least, it is extremely desirable to prevent arbitrary or irreversible deaths, but this consideration is on both sides of the ledger. The relevant analogy is not, say, to a policy that uses racial classifications to increase security or national wealth. The closer analogy would be one that uses racial classifications in order to minimize the overall use of racial classifications, or to hasten the day when racial classifications are no longer useful.[81] A still closer analogy would be a policy that increases certain risks but that in the process decreases other risks of greater magnitude. Whatever the merits of such tradeoffs across different settings, a one-sided complaint about a harm or loss that is on both sides of the ledger is not a sufficient objection to a policy of this sort.

On this view, the crucial point is that on the empirical assumptions we are making, a legal regime with capital punishment predictably produces far *fewer* arbitrary and irreversible deaths than a regime without capital punishment. In a sensible regime of capital punishment, legal rules, enforced by administrative, judicial, and citizen oversight, attempt to reduce arbitrariness and error up to the point where further reductions would inflict unacceptable harms.[82] Where killing is carried out by private parties, however, there are no such institutions for keeping arbitrariness in check. Most striking is the potential size of the opportunity cost of foregone capital punishment. Stipulate that for every foregone execution (conducted under procedural safeguards), the cost is, on average, some eighteen arbitrary and irreversible murders—as some of the evidence in Part I suggests. Suppose, for example, that five hundred additional death row inmates were executed in the next year.[83] Unless the marginal deterrent benefit of each additional execution diminishes very rapidly, the result would be to save thousands of innocent people—in all probability, far

national murder sample to those cases with whites and blacks as offenders and victims. *See* Blume et al., *supra* note 76, at 26. Because cases of white victims and African-American offenders are such a small percentage of the total number of murders, the pessimistic scenario discussed in the text is not a plausible reading of the numbers.

81. *See, e.g.*, Grutter v. Bollinger, 539 U.S. 306, 341-43 (2003) ("We expect that 25 years from now, the use of racial preferences will no longer be necessary to further the interest approved today."); United Steelworkers of Am., AFL-CIO v. Weber, 443 U.S. 193, 208 (1979) (upholding voluntary private affirmative action plans "designed to break down old patterns of racial segregation and hierarchy"); Regents of Univ. of Cal. v. Bakke, 438 U.S. 265, 407 (1978) (Blackmun, J., concurring in part and dissenting in part) ("In order to get beyond racism, we must first take account of race.").

82. This formulation is meant as a placeholder for the appropriate degree of reduction. We bracket the relevant questions here, beyond noting that the courts typically use a calculus of decision costs and error costs to assess the marginal value of additional procedures. *See* Matthews v. Eldridge, 424 U.S. 319 (1976).

83. The death row population is now over 3000. *See* BONCZAR & SNELL, *supra* note 75, at 1.

more people than were killed in the terrorist attacks of September 11, 2001. The people whose lives are lost, and whose deaths could be averted, are killed arbitrarily and without fair process. In short, rule-of-law criticisms of capital punishment either smuggle in the distinction between acts and omissions or else overlook the fact that the same objections apply even more powerfully to the utterly arbitrary killings that capital punishment prevents.

D. *Preferable Alternatives and the Principle of Strict Scrutiny*

Some critics of the death penalty believe that there are other, better ways of deterring murder, and states ought to use those methods instead.[84] Deterrence might occur through superior law enforcement efforts. Or it might occur through taking steps to reduce people's incentives to engage in violent crime, such as education, job training, and other steps toward poverty reduction. On this view, capital punishment reduces the pressure to take better and less barbaric steps to control homicide.

Here there is an analogy, though an imperfect one, to the principle of "strict scrutiny" found in many areas of constitutional law. Although constitutional law often permits government to act in ways that burden important rights, government must typically show that no alternative policy would promote the same goals with less burden on the affected right.[85] The analogy is imperfect because strict scrutiny in the courts is often "strict in theory but fatal in fact,"[86] with courts often barring government from satisfying strict scrutiny by reference to arguments that are routinely acceptable in the process of policy evaluation. Here we use "strict scrutiny" as a shorthand for the argument that capital punishment is justified only if, and when, a rational policy evaluation would show that no alternative policies could do as much to reduce murder rates. The Supreme Court has not accepted this idea as a matter of constitutional law.[87] But perhaps it should be accepted as a normative matter.

Here is the simplest response: on the basis of the evidence that we are assuming to be true, a plausible inference is that whatever steps states take to reduce homicide, capital punishment will provide further deterrence. Whatever states do, some level of homicide is inevitable; so long as liberty is respected, a significant number of murders will continue to occur in every state. If states undertook the steps that are recommended as less restrictive alternatives—and they surely should undertake some of them—then capital punishment would

84. *See* Hugo Bedau, *An Abolitionist's Survey of the Death Penalty in America Today*, *in* DEBATING THE DEATH PENALTY, *supra* note 2, at 15.

85. *See, e.g.*, *Grutter*, 539 U.S. at 326-27.

86. Gerald Gunther, *The Supreme Court, 1971 Term—Foreword: In Search of Evolving Doctrine on a Changing Court: A Model for a Newer Equal Protection*, 86 HARV. L. REV. 1, 8 (1972).

87. *See, e.g.*, Gregg v. Georgia, 428 U.S. 153, 175 (1976).

still reduce that level from what it would otherwise be. In other words, a key assumption of the strict scrutiny view is that the alternative policies are substitutes for capital punishment. Yet they would likely turn out to be complements instead. Many steps can be taken simultaneously to reduce violent crime, and reform of the criminal justice system is only one of those steps.

Moreover, the strict scrutiny position rests upon an excessively simple view of legal policymaking. The first question is always what policies lie in the feasible set. Political constraints will rule out some policies that might be even better, from the standpoint of deterring murders, than capital punishment. Switching to a Swedish-style welfare state might (or might not) reduce crime dramatically, but we will never know because we will never try it. So too, increasing job-training funds by several orders of magnitude might result in many fewer murders, but such policies are simply not in the cards anytime soon. Capital punishment, by contrast, is very much a live policy option, even in many states that do not currently use it.[88]

Perhaps the apparent political constraints are partially endogenous; perhaps capital punishment reduces the political incentive to adopt other strategies, and if this were so, the argument for capital punishment would surely be weakened. But there is little reason to believe that if capital punishment were abolished, there would be significantly larger efforts to reduce violent crime through education and training programs. We cannot rule out the possibility that abolition would result in a better mix of measures, all things considered. But if the death penalty has the deterrent effect suggested by the recent literature, then this would be a surprising conclusion.

In general, there is no reason to say that capital punishment must be prohibited unless and until all available alternatives have been tried and proven inferior. No sensible principle of policymaking bars regulators from adopting a clearly desirable practice, unless and until they show that all other potential projects are inferior. Such a view overlooks the opportunity cost of searching through the policy space and exhausting the available alternatives. In the setting of capital punishment, the alternatives might be tried and fail; even if they succeed, approaches based on education and social-welfare provision will often have a longer lag time before they bear fruit. In either case, while the policy experiments are ongoing, a large number of murders will go undeterred. The hard question is what the *interim* policies should be while regulators search for optimal arrangements, and it begs the question to say that the interim policy must be a regime without capital punishment. Why should that be so, if there is powerful evidence that instituting capital punishment today will save many lives starting tomorrow?

88. *See, e.g.*, Rick Klein, *Science Key in Building Case for Death Law*, BOSTON GLOBE, Sept. 30, 2003, at B1 (reporting that a majority of Massachusetts residents support the death penalty and that the state's governor is developing a capital punishment proposal).

As the last point shows, the strict scrutiny idea goes wrong in the same sort of way that the earlier arguments go wrong: by overlooking the possibility that the regime without capital punishment itself inflicts even larger net harms—harms to the very same values that animate opposition to capital punishment. This is a version of the act/omission mistake. Stipulating that capital punishment saves many more innocent lives than it takes, the strict scrutiny argument has the default position backwards. Criminal justice policy would do well to adopt capital punishment while the search for regulatory alternatives proceeds; it is the alternatives that should be strictly scrutinized, to be rejected unless and until they prove themselves superior.

E. *Slippery Slopes*

Our argument might seem to have serious slippery-slope problems. Suppose, for example, that the best way to deter heinous crimes is to torture perpetrators. Suppose that if torture were undertaken, there would be a significant reduction in the number of such crimes. The logic of our hypothesis is that torture would be morally obligatory on certain factual assumptions.

We accept this claim about what our hypothesis entails. To make the case as simple as possible, suppose that some criminals torture their victims and that if such criminals were themselves tortured, the incidence of torture would decrease substantially. Suppose, that is, a ban on (state) torture ensures that (private) torture will occur far more often than it otherwise would. In our view, the ban on state torture reflects a use of the act/omission distinction in a context in which the distinction is not easy to defend. If, for example, state torture of a torturer would prevent eighteen acts of torture—of, say, children—the argument for banning state torture would be greatly weakened.

None of this means that a ban on state torture is indefensible.[89] Here, as always, rejecting the act/omission distinction says nothing, by itself, about what policies are best from any point of view. State practices of torture might actually increase torture, rather than diminish it, perhaps by weakening the social prohibition on torture. This is an empirical issue, and no evidence, so far as we are aware, either undermines or confirms it. Hence, state torture might be self-defeating if its goal is to reduce private torture. In any case, a ban on torture might, or might not, have a rule-consequentialist defense. Suppose, not implausibly, that the benefits of state torture are low; suppose that its costs, prominently including the risks of abuse, are high; and suppose that front-line decisionmakers cannot be trusted to sort good instances from bad instances. Everything depends on what the facts turn out to be.

The last point is crucial. Because arguments about policies such as capital

89. For relevant considerations, see Eric A. Posner & Adrian Vermeule, *Should Coercive Interrogation Be Legal?*, 104 MICH. L. REV. (forthcoming 2005) (on file with authors).

punishment and torture are hostage to what the facts turn out to show in particular domains, slippery-slope arguments are disabled; instead of a slope, there is just a series of discrete policy problems. Support for capital punishment need not, by analogical reasoning or otherwise, commit policymakers to support for public floggings or punitive mutilation or other horrors. Nor is there any obvious mechanism that would push policymakers or citizens to adopt those other practices once they have adopted capital punishment.[90] Not only is there no slope, there is no a priori reason to believe the ground slippery.

Perhaps the torture example fails to get to the heart of what is most objectionable in our argument. Return to a problem raised above and focus on the following situation: suppose that holding a show trial to frame and convict one innocent person of murder would deter eighteen real murders. Wouldn't you be obliged to defend that, crazy as it is? Or consider an analogous situation: suppose that the state could withhold exonerating information and ensure the execution of several innocent people. Is it legitimate, or even mandatory, for the state to withhold that information? On one view, these questions are fair. It is possible to imagine a finding that conviction of innocent people would deter murders, so that the failure to hold show trials or to withhold exonerating information is, in effect, condemning large numbers of people to unjustified deaths. On utilitarian grounds, the show trials might be permissible or even mandatory. On deontological grounds, the answer is at first clear: the state cannot take the lives of innocent people. But if our argument is correct, the deontological argument might not be so clear after all: might not the failure to conduct show trials or to exonerate innocent people be a way of taking the lives of innocent people, too?

An initial problem with slippery-slope questions of this kind is that they often obscure more than they clarify.[91] First, as John Rawls pointed out long ago, the systemic effects of a government policy that allowed sham convictions of the innocent, including debilitating uncertainty for other innocents, would

90. For criticism of slippery-slope arguments that lack a specific mechanism, see Frederick Schauer, *Slippery Slopes*, 99 HARV. L. REV. 361 (1985); Eugene Volokh, *The Mechanisms of the Slippery Slope*, 116 HARV. L. REV. 1026 (2003).

91. It is tempting to think that there is a kind of moral floor for the infliction of severe punishment. On this view, such punishment cannot be inflicted unless the defendant has done something very grave—and considerations of deterrence cannot justify severely punishing, for example, parking tickets or minor traffic offenses. For those who endorse this view, it is possible to believe that government cannot punish innocent people or impose sentences that are grossly excessive in comparison to the crime. But it is also possible to believe that government can impose the death penalty after people have, under stringent standards, been convicted of committing especially egregious murders. Of course any moral "floor" will be controversial, and the most adamant opponents of capital punishment might believe that it is below the floor by its very nature. We do not mean to untangle the moral complexities here. Our only suggestion is that even for those who insist on a moral floor, the death penalty may be acceptable if it is imposed on those who have committed especially egregious murders.

themselves have to be folded into the overall assessment.[92] From a consequentialist standpoint, executing the innocent would be a very poor strategy for government to follow. For one thing, there will always be plenty of convicts in the pipeline whose guilt is certain. why take the extra risk and trouble of executing the innocent? More important still is the following: each execution of someone known to be innocent, or whose guilt is doubted, would dilute the deterrent signal that the government would (by hypothesis) be attempting to strengthen. In the limiting case, if capital punishment were entirely random, falling with utter arbitrariness upon innocent and guilty alike, there would be no deterrence at all; there would be no reason for any prospective criminal to take the threat of capital punishment into account. To the extent that deterrence occurs, Justice Potter Stewart's comparison of capital punishment to being struck by lightning does not hold.

Note that, if the findings discussed in Part I are valid, it must be the case that the present system of capital punishment is *not* a wholly capricious system of punishment, pervaded by false positives. At the very least, some or many prospective murderers must believe that the system has a high degree of accuracy. We do not mean to overstate this point. Of course, it remains undeniable that capital punishment is sometimes imposed erroneously[93] and undeniable too that it is sometimes imposed arbitrarily or on invidious grounds *within* the set of guilty defendants. Nothing we say here is meant to suggest that states should be content with erroneous or arbitrary death sentences. But the evidence plausibly suggests that there is substantial accuracy, in the sense of avoiding false positives, in the infliction of capital punishment.

A corollary to Rawls's point about the systemic costs of executing the innocent is that a government policy of executing the innocent could be implemented only if the policy were itself a secret; only a conspiracy to keep the policy secret would prevent it from unraveling. No such conspiracy is likely to succeed. Put in less consequentialist terms, such a policy would violate the publicity principle emphasized by Rawls and others. It could not be defended publicly and still accomplish its central goal.[94] The publicity principle is a principle of political morality that can be given both deontological and consequentialist justifications,[95] so moral theorists of many stripes could reject this sort of hypothetical.

---

92. *See* John Rawls, *Two Concepts of Rules*, 64 PHIL. REV. 3, 32 & n.27 (1955).

93. Independent estimates of the number of innocent people who have been executed since the reinstatement of capital punishment in the mid-1970s are "remarkably low." Allen & Shavell, *supra* note 52, at 629 n.7. One estimate puts the number at five people in the last three decades. *See* FRANKLIN E. ZIMRING, THE CONTRADICTIONS OF AMERICAN CAPITAL PUNISHMENT 170 (2003). A slightly earlier study, by opponents of capital punishment, identified no more than three. *See* MICHAEL L. RADELET ET AL., IN SPITE OF INNOCENCE: ERRONEOUS CONVICTIONS IN CAPITAL CASES 279 (1992).

94. On the publicity condition, see JOHN RAWLS, A THEORY OF JUSTICE 177 (1971).

95. For an overview of issues, see David Luban, *The Publicity Principle*, *in* THE THEORY OF INSTITUTIONAL DESIGN 154 (Robert E. Goodin ed., 1996).

Second, it is not clear how policymakers could have reliable evidence about the deterrent effects of conviction of the innocent, torture, or other disturbing practices without first experimenting on hapless victims—and the necessary experimentation might well be impermissible on moral grounds ex ante, even if the policies themselves would be permissible given certain experimental findings ex post. Capital punishment, however, is already the status quo in most states, and policymakers already have many decades' worth of data about its deterrent effects.

Finally, and most fundamentally, we doubt that the intuitions which drive extreme hypotheticals of this sort have moral significance in any event. Of course, it is prima facie objectionable, worse than outrageous, if the state proposes to kill people whom it knows to be innocent. The widely held moral and legal norm against executions of innocent people is certainly an individual and social good, whatever one's views about the foundations of morality. But suppose that a situation arises in which execution of an innocent person really is the only way to save eighteen, or eighty, or eighteen hundred innocent people. We are not sure how to handle such situations. There is no reason to think that intuitions about the extreme cases are reliable trackers of moral truth, or to assume that such intuitions have any privileged connection to what a considered moral theory would permit or require. Consider the fact that innocent people die in war and even in attacks that are well short of war; consider also the obvious tension between some apparently pro-life intuitions and the accepted practice of killing (executing) hostage-takers. (Do opponents of capital punishment reject this practice?) We offer more remarks on the moral status of particular intuitions below and in Part III.

Overall, the possibility of a deliberate decision to execute the innocent seems to us too lurid to have a place in serious discussions of the death penalty. Of course, real-world systems of capital punishment tolerate some risk that unidentified persons will be erroneously executed; in that aggregate sense, real-world systems of capital punishment cannot absolutely ensure that only the guilty are executed.[96] As we have emphasized, however, the world of homicide also ensures the deaths of a number of statistical, unidentified victims—indeed a much larger number. From the standpoint of a government attempting to deter homicide, moreover, executing the innocent is costly and indeed counterproductive from the deterrence point of view—a practice to be minimized on the very same deterrence grounds that animate capital punishment in the first place.

F. *Deontology and Consequentialism Again*

What is the relationship between the foregoing argument, particularly our

96. Note, however, that on existing estimates, the number of executions of innocent people appears to be very small. *See supra* note 93.

rejection of the act/omission distinction as applied to government's policy choices, and standard debates about deontological and consequentialist approaches in moral theory? We do not think this is a crucial analytic lens for the questions we address.[97] We are aware that some deontologists will disagree. But as we have emphasized, our argument does not challenge deontological claims as such, except insofar as they apply the act/omission distinction to government and reject any consequentialist override of deontological injunctions. The simple injunction "thou shalt not kill" is too general to cut between the relevant options at the lower level of policy choice. If capital punishment strongly deters killings, and if the government that eschews capital punishment can fairly be charged with those killings, then the government's only choices are to kill more or to kill fewer; the deontological injunction might then be interpreted to require rather than to forbid capital punishment.

To be sure, some opponents of capital punishment tend to build the act/omission distinction directly into the deontological injunction itself. "Thou shalt not kill" might be interpreted just to mean that the state and its agents shall not themselves kill. Moreover, opponents sometimes assume away the problem of consequentialist overrides. But as we have seen, both the act/omission distinction and the idea that deontological injunctions are absolute are highly contentious assumptions, above all for government actors. They assume, implausibly, that the moral distinctions and considerations that apply to individuals apply without qualification to government officials and that they require independent arguments on their behalf. In many cases, no such argument is offered; all that is typically offered is an intuition that the state must not kill, period.

We do not believe that, upon reflection, the intuition can be defended, nor do we think that case-specific intuitions should be morally dispositive. In part this is because of familiar arguments in moral theory that commitments to generalizable moral principles should trump intuitions in particular cases.[98] In part it is because the reliability of such intuitions is highly suspect. Recent research in cognitive psychology, which we discuss in Part III, suggests that the intuitions underpinning the act/omission distinction may represent cognitive errors, without any moral relevance or larger importance. The only point we emphasize here is that, stipulating that capital punishment powerfully deters killings, an opposition to killing is most naturally understood to support capital punishment rather than to undercut it. Opponents of capital punishment who build the act/omission distinction directly into an absolutist deontological

97. For a recent argument that most or all substantive moral positions can be formulated at will in either deontological or consequentialist terms, see Campbell Brown, Consequentialise This (unpublished manuscript), *available at* http://personal.bgsu.edu/~browncf/papers/ConsequentialiseThis.pdf (last revised Sept. 10, 2004).

98. *See generally* R.M. HARE, MORAL THINKING: ITS LEVELS, METHODS, AND POINT (1981).

injunction, by stating a position against *state* killing with no consequentialist override, face the prospect that their position will ultimately come to rest upon little more than an inarticulate intuition, a conclusion masquerading as an argument.

Overall, the crucial question is what the facts show, a point to which we return in Part IV. Perhaps capital punishment might best be restricted to certain classes of offenders or offenses, or even to certain geographic regions; different polities might, in their different factual circumstances, each do well by adopting or rejecting capital punishment as appropriate. It might even turn out that the system of capital punishment is so riddled with errors and arbitrariness that it would be unwise and unjust to adopt it, simply because it is a hopelessly defective tool of criminal justice. Although we doubt that this is so, for the reasons given in Part I, it *could* be so, and a belief that it is true would supply a very respectable reason for opposing capital punishment. What does not supply such a reason is an indeterminate and unprocessed intuition that the state should not "kill."

None of this is to suggest that intuitionism is the only possible basis for opposing capital punishment; of course it is not. Perhaps the death penalty is opposed (as it is sometimes endorsed) on expressivist grounds; perhaps the social meanings of capital punishment are what drive opponents as well as advocates.[99] But if the evidence outlined here is correct, expressivist opposition is not so easy to sustain. A failure to protect women against domestic violence or workers against severe occupational risks is objectionable on expressive grounds because it reflects contempt for the safety of women and workers.[100] A failure to take steps that would prevent significant numbers of murders is itself expressively objectionable, on parallel grounds.

There is a final point involving democracy itself. On one view, government's central obligation is to follow the public will, assuming that it has been properly focused and channeled through processes of public deliberation.[101] If the public opposes capital punishment, and insists on an act/omission distinction, then officials should oppose it too, unless, perhaps, opposition can be shown to be ill informed or to have failed the minimal requirements of political deliberation. And on this view, public support for capital punishment would be presumptively binding as well. We do not mean to say anything contentious about democratic legitimacy here. Both citizens and representatives must ask themselves what morality requires. If a life-life tradeoff is involved, the moral question is inevitably affected. And if capital punishment saves large numbers of innocent lives, then participants in democracies are obliged to take note of that fact.

99. *See* Dan M. Kahan, *The Secret Ambition of Deterrence*, 113 HARV. L. REV. 413 (1999).

100. *See* ELIZABETH ANDERSON, VALUE IN ETHICS AND ECONOMICS (1993).

101. *See* WILLIAM BESSETTE, THE MILD VOICE OF REASON (1994).

III. COGNITION AND CAPITAL PUNISHMENT

Those who object to capital punishment, and who believe that evidence of deterrence is irrelevant, think that they are operating in accordance with a freestanding moral principle. They will not be enthusiastic about the suggestion that their moral judgments are instead a product of some kind of cognitive error. But in the regulatory domain as a whole, it has become standard to say that cognitive processes contribute to large mistakes, at least on questions of fact.[102] For risk regulation, people do seem to focus on a subset of the harms at stake in a way that produces both excessive and insufficient reactions to environmental problems.[103] More generally, a form of "tradeoff neglect" pervades regulatory policy,[104] and it is easy to imagine that the moral domain has its own kinds of tradeoff neglect. For example, it is common, in the environmental domain, to focus on the risks associated with some kind of environmental degradation but to neglect the risks associated with environmental regulation; those who focus on the costs of regulation often neglect the risks of inaction.[105]

In a related vein, a great deal of recent work has emphasized the possibility that heuristics and biases can be found in the moral arena, making it possible that deeply felt moral intuitions are a result of errors and confusions.[106] This is a possibility and no more. Certainly we cannot demonstrate that moral opposition to capital punishment is sometimes rooted in selective attention or an identifiable heuristic. But, return to the hostage situation to which we have referred: police officers are permitted to kill those who have taken hostages, at least if the killing is reasonably believed to be necessary to save human lives. If capital punishment is deemed different, it might be because the lives to be saved are merely statistical, as compared with the lives of hostages, which are entirely vivid. Statistical lives and harms are pervasively neglected in policy, in part for cognitive reasons.[107] More generally, consider two points, the first involving salience and the second involving the foundations of the act/omission distinction.

---

102. Roger G. Noll & James E. Krier, *Some Implications of Cognitive Psychology for Risk Regulation*, 19 J. LEGAL STUD. 747, 777 (1990).

103. This is the theme of HOWARD MARGOLIS, DEALING WITH RISK: WHY THE PUBLIC AND THE EXPERTS DISAGREE ON ENVIRONMENTAL ISSUES (1996).

104. *Id.*

105. *Id.*

106. *See, e.g.*, Jonathan Baron, *Heuristics and Biases in Equity Judgments: A Utilitarian Approach*, *in* PSYCHOLOGICAL PERSPECTIVES ON JUSTICE: THEORY AND APPLICATIONS 109 (Barbara A. Mellers & Jonathan Baron eds., 1993); Jonathan Haidt, *The Emotional Dog and Its Rational Tail: A Social Intuitionist Approach to Moral Judgment*, 108 PSYCHOL. REV. 814 (2001); Cass R. Sunstein, *Moral Heuristics*, 28 BEHAV. & BRAIN SCI. 531 (2005).

107. *See* Loewenstein et al., *supra* note 62.

A. *Salience*

It is obvious that people's reactions to factual and moral questions are greatly affected by vividness or *salience*.[108] If an event, such as a terrorist attack, seems salient, people will think it is more likely to occur. And if an event is salient, people may not pay much attention to less salient possibilities, such as the risk that a response to a terrorist attack will cause a significant number of deaths of its own. When people neglect tradeoffs, it is often because one aspect of the situation is highly visible, or "on screen," while other aspects are less visible or perhaps invisible.

Consider in this regard the life-life tradeoffs potentially involved with capital punishment. Those subject to capital punishment are real human beings, with their own backgrounds and narratives. Some of them have been subject to multiple forms of unfairness, in the legal process and elsewhere. At least some were wrongly convicted. By contrast, those whose lives are or might be saved by virtue of capital punishment are mere "statistical people."[109] They are both nameless and faceless, and their deaths are far less likely to be considered in moral deliberations. It is for this reason, perhaps, that the advocates of capital punishment often focus on the heinousness of the (salient) offender, while the abolitionists focus on his or her humanity. We suspect that the discussion would take a different form if the victims of a regime lacking capital punishment were salient too,[110] and the example of police behavior in hostage situations supports the suspicion. None of this argument establishes the claim that the death penalty is morally required if it saves far more lives than it ends. But it does raise the possibility that moral intuitions, for many people, are a product of the salience of one set of deaths and the invisibility or speculative nature of another.

B. *Acts, Omissions, and Brains*

Outside of the domain of government, we have not questioned the act/omission distinction. But in some settings, it may be worth considering the possibility that the act/omission distinction operates as a heuristic for a more complex and difficult assessment of the moral issues at stake.[111] Consider in

108. *See* SCOTT PLOUS, THE PSYCHOLOGY OF JUDGMENT AND DECISION MAKING 125-26, 178-80 (1993) (discussing the salience heuristic and the closely related heuristics of vividness and availability); *cf.* Robert M. Reyes et al., *Judgmental Biases Resulting from Differing Availabilities of Arguments*, 39 J. PERSONALITY & SOC. PSYCHOL. 2, 5-12 (1980) (demonstrating that vivid, concrete information exerts greater influence on mock jury deliberations than abstract, pallid information).

109. *See* Heinzerling, *supra* note 17, at 189.

110. *Cf.* PHILIP K. DICK, THE MINORITY REPORT (2002).

111. The argument is ventured in JONATHAN BARON, JUDGMENT MISGUIDED: INTUITION AND ERROR IN PUBLIC DECISION MAKING (1998).

this regard the dispute over two well-known problems in moral philosophy.[112] These problems do not involve the act/omission distinction, but they implicate closely related concerns. We suggest that people's asymmetrical reactions to the two problems say a great deal about the operation of the act/omission distinction.

The first, called the trolley problem, asks people to suppose that a runaway trolley is headed for five people, who will be killed if the trolley continues on its current course. The question is whether you would throw a switch that would move the trolley onto another set of tracks, killing one person rather than five. Most people would throw the switch. The second, called the footbridge problem, is the same as that just given, but with one difference: the only way to save the five is to throw a stranger, now on a footbridge that spans the tracks, into the path of the trolley, killing that stranger but preventing the trolley from reaching the others. Most people will not kill the stranger. What is the difference between the two cases, if any? A great deal of philosophical work has been done on this question, much of it trying to suggest that our firm intuitions can indeed be defended in principle.[113]

Without engaging these arguments, consider a suggestive experiment designed to see how the human brain responds to the two problems.[114] The experiment's authors do not attempt to answer the moral questions in principle, but they find "that there are systematic variations in the engagement of emotion in moral judgment"[115] and that brain areas associated with emotion are far more active in contemplating the footbridge problem than in contemplating the trolley problem. An implication of the authors' finding is that human brains are hardwired to distinguish between bringing about a death "up close and personal" and doing so at a distance.[116]

Of course, this experiment is far from decisive; emotions and cognition are not easily separable,[117] and there may be good moral reasons why certain brain areas are activated by one problem and not by the other. Perhaps the brain is closely attuned to morally relevant differences. But consider the case of fear, where an identifiable physical region of the brain makes helpfully immediate but not entirely reliable judgments[118]—something analogous, very plausibly, is

---

112. *See* JUDITH JARVIS THOMSON, RIGHTS, RESTITUTION, AND RISK: ESSAYS IN MORAL THEORY 94-116 (1986).

113. *Id.*

114. Joshua D. Greene et al., *An fMRI Investigation of Emotional Engagement in Moral Judgment*, 293 SCI. 2105 (2001).

115. *Id.* at 2107.

116. *Id.* at 2106-07.

117. *See* MARTHA C. NUSSBAUM, UPHEAVALS OF THOUGHT: THE INTELLIGENCE OF EMOTIONS (2001).

118. *See* Joseph E. LeDoux & Jeff Muller, *Emotional Memory and Psychopathology*, 352 PHIL. TRANSACTIONS: BIOLOGICAL SCI. 1719, 1719 (1997).

true in the context of morality.[119]

For capital punishment, the implication is straightforward. For many people, the prospect of lethal executions is akin to the prospect of throwing the stranger into the path of a train in the footbridge problem. We expect that the relevant part of the brain would light up for most people who sincerely imagine themselves in the position of executioner. But for almost everyone, no such lights would be found after learning that the consequence of abolishing capital punishment was to ensure somewhere between eight and twenty-eight statistical deaths for each foregone execution. No unambiguous moral lesson follows from an understanding of the operation of the human brain. But, it is perhaps illuminating if moral judgments are caused by rapid intuitions that do not involve a great deal of cognitive work and that have no obvious connection to the morally relevant features of the situation.

C. *A Famous Argument that Might Be Taken as a Counterargument*

Our general claims might be thought to run up against Bernard Williams's well-known critique of utilitarianism, rooted largely in a story about an unfortunate tourist named Jim.[120] In Williams's tale, Jim is a tourist in a small town in South America. He notices that twenty Indians are about to be shot. The leader of the shooters gives Jim a chance to save all but one of the Indians, but for a price: Jim has to shoot one of them. Williams believes that for utilitarians, the moral answer is clear: Jim should shoot. But in his view, it is not clear that this is what morality requires. In Williams's words, utilitarianism

> cuts out a kind of consideration which for some others makes a difference to what they feel about such cases: a consideration involving the idea, as we might first and very simply put it, that each of us is specially responsible for what he does, rather than for what other people do.[121]

Williams asks:

> [H]ow can a man, as a utilitarian agent, come to regard as one satisfaction among others, and a dispensable one, a project or attitude round which he has built his life, just because someone else's projects have so structured the causal scene that that is how the utilitarian sum comes out?[122]

We believe that an intuition akin to Williams's helps to explain opposition to capital punishment even in the face of evidence of the sort that we have outlined. But there are three responses:

Most modestly: Capital punishment, on the evidence given here, more closely resembles a hostage situation than Jim's case. Recall that police officers

---

119. Joshua Greene & Jonathan Haidt, *How (and Where) Does Moral Judgment Work?*, 6 TRENDS COGNITIVE SCI. 517, 522-23 (2002).

120. *See* J. J. C. SMART & BERNARD WILLIAMS, UTILITARIANISM: FOR AND AGAINST 98-99 (1973).

121. *Id.* at 99.

122. *Id.* at 116.

are permitted, even expected, to use deadly force against those who have taken hostages if that is the only way to save innocent people. Those who are subject to capital punishment are (almost always) egregious wrongdoers, not innocents.

Somewhat less modestly: An understanding of the attitudes around which people have built their lives might constrain people, but such an understanding does not constrain states, at least not in the same way. If Jim is a police officer, asked to save twenty hostages, he might well be morally obliged to shoot one of them if that is the only way to save the other nineteen. If Jim is the head of state, asked to engage in military intervention to prevent a mass slaughter (say, in Rwanda), it is not so clear that he should refuse even if he knows that military intervention will also result in innocent deaths at the hands of his own military. At the very least, the moral question cannot be answered, at the level of the state, by insisting "that each of us is especially responsible for what he does, rather than for what other people do."[123]

Less modestly still: Williams's own arguments seem to us to rely on question-begging claims about causation and about what counts as intentional action. He is right to say that we are particularly responsible for what we do, but in Jim's case, how does that precept cash out, exactly? Granted, Jim faces bad choices through no fault of his own, but can Jim disclaim responsibility for the unnecessary deaths of nineteen people?

It is more than plausible to say that for rule-utilitarian reasons, societies benefit from strong moral prohibitions on the taking of innocent life. Perhaps we do better if most people share Jim's reluctance to shoot the innocent. In the real world, relevant Jims, engaged in on-the-spot consequentialist analyses, may well engage in killings that are unjustified even on consequentialist grounds. Here, as elsewhere, a moral norm may operate as a kind of heuristic, one from which individuals and societies gain a great deal.[124] But for the reasons that we have given, no moral heuristic can provide an adequate moral objection to capital punishment, at least if the empirical evidence can show strong evidence of deterrence.

IV. IMPLICATIONS AND FUTURE PROBLEMS

In this Part, we expand upon the implications of our approach and highlight some remaining puzzles, not with the goal of resolving all issues, but with a view to indicating the contours of existing puzzles and some possible directions for future research. We also emphasize that our argument is limited to the setting of life-life tradeoffs: cases in which capital punishment is used to deter killing, rather than other offenses.

123. *Id.* at 99 (emphasis omitted).

124. *See* Sunstein, *supra* note 106, at 531.

A. *Threshold Effects (?) and Regional Variation*

The statistic that each execution saves eighteen lives, on average, is an aggregated statistic based on national-level data—something like a national average. Averages can be misleading, of course, and a look at regional variation suggests a potentially complicated picture. The most recent work suggests the possibility that states fall into three sets: a set of states in which capital punishment deters very strongly, a set in which it has no deterrent effect at all, and even a set in which capital punishment has perverse effects, slightly raising murder rates. The pronounced deterrent effect at the level of the national average occurs because, where capital punishment does deter, it deters powerfully. As we mentioned in Part I, Joanna Shepherd suggests there is a "threshold effect" at work here: in states that execute very few people, capital punishment either has no effect or even backfires, perhaps because (Shepherd conjectures) a "brutalization effect" operates, while in states that execute a larger number, there are large deterrent effects.[125] Whatever the validity of the particular mechanisms Shepherd proposes, it seems plausible that capital punishment deters strongly in one set of states and has little effect in others. If this is correct, does it undermine our thesis?

The simple answer is no, not at all, because we hold no brief to promote capital punishment everywhere, at all times and places. Where capital punishment is a powerful deterrent, we have suggested that states may well be morally obligated to adopt it. Where capital punishment does not powerfully deter, the empirical predicate for that obligation disappears. Retributivists might continue to argue for capital punishment on other grounds, but we are not retributivists and see no inherent moral necessity for capital punishment if it produces little in the way of benefits in the protection of human life. If future work were to overturn the recent evidence that capital punishment deters, that work would also, in our view, overturn the case for capital punishment altogether.

B. *International Variation*

What holds for variation across states within the United States holds a fortiori for variation across liberal democratic polities. The European Union and its member states firmly reject capital punishment as violative of human dignity; more broadly, the United States is one of only a small number of nations that permit capital punishment. How does this international variation bear upon our thesis?

The short answer is that we have nothing to say about such polities, because the relevant facts are not yet known. It might turn out that, due to variation in some relevant factor, capital punishment is appropriate for our

125. *See supra* Part I and corresponding references.

circumstances but not for the circumstances of (some set of) other polities; nothing in our view excludes this stance. If capital punishment turns out to deter strongly in some populations, or given some background legal and economic systems, but not otherwise, then the scope of the moral obligation to adopt capital punishment would vary accordingly. Israel does not execute terrorists, in part because of a belief that executions of terrorists would breed more terrorism; if the belief is correct, as seems plausible, then the failure to use capital punishment is correct, too. Those who favor capital punishment might well ask whether they reject Israel's policy on retributive grounds. For pro-capital punishment deontologists, no less than for anti-capital punishment deontologists, serious life-life tradeoffs might be involved. Is it possible to sustain a deontological argument for executing terrorists if the consequence is to produce many more terrorists? We think that retributivists should hesitate before giving an affirmative answer.

C. *Offenders and Offenses*

Other dimensions of variation include differences in classes of offenses (e.g., murders for profit versus murders animated by passion) and classes of offenders (e.g., juvenile murderers, mentally disabled murderers, and so on). As we noted in discussing the slippery-slopes argument in Part II.E, no a priori argument either precludes or mandates extending capital punishment to all such cases, because a priori arguments are not helpful here.

Let us consider the example of juvenile offenders. In a recent decision, the Supreme Court held that capital punishment may not be inflicted upon offenders who were under eighteen years old at the time of the offense.[126] Acknowledging the paucity of evidence either way, the Court speculated that such offenders are less deterrable than adults.[127] Below, we will review findings suggesting, by analogy to crimes of passion, that this speculation is mistaken. What if the facts turn out to be otherwise than the Court guessed? Suppose that there turns out to be a significant class of fifteen-year-old murderers, perhaps predominantly murdering other fifteen-year-old innocents, and suppose that relevant data suggested that allowing capital punishment for fifteen-year-old murderers would significantly deter those murders.

In our view, there is a strong argument that states would then be morally obligated to extend capital punishment to such cases (bracketing whether such a course would be legally permitted). If the obligation would attach, it is precisely because killing fifteen-year-old innocents is morally unacceptable and because capital punishment would be the best system for reducing the overall number of such killings. Only an implausible version of the act/omission distinction would suggest otherwise. On the other hand, suppose that the

126. Roper v. Simmons, 125 S. Ct. 1183, 1196 (2005).

127. *Id.*

Court's speculation is correct and that murders by juveniles turn out to be genuinely undeterrable, perhaps because juveniles are not yet capable of reasoning clearly about the expected costs and benefits of crime or frequently act out of uncontrollable passion. Then the factual predicate for our view would simply fail to apply.

The same holds true for classes of offenses. Recent work has suggested, contrary to the intuitions of many, that capital punishment may well deter types of murders previously thought undeterrable.[128] In particular, the frequent conjecture that murders animated by passion are undeterrable may turn out to be erroneous. Should future work identify such a category of undeterrable murders, however, our view would straightforwardly entail that capital punishment ought not extend to such cases.

D. *Life-Life Tradeoffs and Beyond*

Every case we have discussed so far involves what we have called life-life tradeoffs: cases in which state execution deters many private executions. A very different set of moral and institutional problems arises when the issue is whether capital punishment should be used to deter serious offenses other than killing. Consider the sentence of capital punishment for particularly serious forms of rape, which the Supreme Court invalidated as cruel and unusual punishment.[129] Apart from constitutional constraints, would states be morally obligated to employ capital punishment if it could be shown, empirically, that each such execution would deter many future rapes?

We have given simple answers to the foregoing questions about variation in regional and international circumstances, and in classes of offenders and offenses, but no simple answers are possible here. The reason is that, unlike the other cases, the harms on the two sides of the ledger are not the same. Where capital punishment of murderers is at issue, the taking of life is the only morally relevant action in the picture, and the state's taking of life is entirely commensurable with the crimes it deters.[130] When other offenses are at issue, additional moral questions of commensurability and aggregation arise. May the state inflict a permanent deprivation of all personhood (death) upon a few to deter serious, but temporary, deprivations of autonomy (rape) that would otherwise be inflicted upon many? What if the many are children? The moral analysis here will necessarily be more complicated. If a utilitarian or consequentialist framework is used, the effects must be "translated" in some

128. Shepherd, *Murders of Passion*, *supra* note 9, at 305.

129. *See* Coker v. Georgia, 433 U.S. 584, 598 (1977).

130. This assumes that one rejects, as we did in *supra* Part II, the attempt to build the act/omission distinction right into the definition of the relevant action. We have rejected, in other words, the idea that the state's taking of life is itself a morally different act from the "private" taking of life that is made possible by the state's choice of a criminal justice policy that does not include capital punishment.

way so as to permit tradeoffs to occur. Suppose that an execution of a rapist would deter thirty rapes. How should capital punishment be evaluated in that event? It is most unclear how to think about these and similar cases; here we mean to bracket such questions entirely.

Likewise, nothing we say here entails a view, one way or another, on the question (for example) whether drunk drivers who kill recklessly or negligently should be subject to capital punishment. A relevant question is, of course, what the facts would show. Perhaps executing drunk drivers would not, in fact, save any lives, because drunk driving is not sensitive to criminal sanctions. More importantly, however, the question is different in principle from the ones we have addressed above. As with rape, capital punishment for nonpremeditated homicide is no longer an apples-to-apples comparison. We have argued that, once the act/omission distinction is rejected as to government action, the moral objections to capital punishment apply even more strongly to the murders that capital punishment apparently deters. This is not clearly true with respect to homicides caused by drunk driving. In such cases, the homicides deterred by capital punishment might stand on a different moral footing.

In short, nothing in our argument is inconsistent with the view that there are deontological constraints, or constraints of proportionality, that forbid the use of capital punishment for unintentional or merely reckless wrongdoing. As we have noted, some opponents of capital punishment believe that deontological constraints forbid the use of capital punishment even in cases of egregious intentional killing. We make no attempt to argue, from within deontology, that they are wrong. But if life-life tradeoffs are involved, we believe that the deontological objection, shorn of act/omission confusion, is much harder to defend than a similar objection to the death penalty for drunk drivers.

CONCLUSION

We conjecture that something like the following set of views about capital punishment has been, and probably still is, widespread in the legal academy: capital punishment does not deter, or at least no one has set out even plausible evidence that it does so;[131] some categories of murders, especially crimes of passion, are undeterrable (at least by capital punishment);[132] even if capital punishment has a deterrent effect, the effect is trivial, perhaps because of the relatively small number of capital sentences and the long time lags between sentencing and execution;[133] and the system of capital punishment is rife with error and arbitrariness.[134]

131. *See* Lempert, *supra* note 20, at 1222.

132. *See id.* at 1193-94.

133. *See id.* at 1192-93.

134. *See id.* at 1224.

The recent evidence raises legitimate doubts about all of these views: capital punishment may well have deterrent effects; there is evidence that few categories of murders are inherently undeterrable, even so-called crimes of passion; some studies find extremely large deterrent effects; and error and arbitrariness undoubtedly occur, but the evidence of deterrence suggests the possibility that some or even many prospective murderers may be receiving a clear signal.

The moral and legal commentary on capital punishment ought to be sensitive to any significant revision in what we know. The realm of homicide is replete with problems of discrimination, injustice, and arbitrariness, and these problems are far more severe than they are in the world of capital punishment as presently administered. If deterrence occurs, life-life tradeoffs are inescapably involved. And if deterrence occurs, a government that settles upon a package of crime-control policies that does *not* include capital punishment might well seem, at least prima facie, to be both violating the rights and reducing the welfare of its citizens—just as would a state that failed to enact simple environmental measures promising to save a great many lives.

The most common basis for resisting this conclusion, and our principal target here, is some version of the distinction between acts and omissions. With respect to government, at least, we mean to raise objections to that distinction in general, and the objections extend well beyond the domain of capital punishment. Death penalty opponents frequently appeal to an intuition that intentional killing by the government and its agents is morally objectionable in a way that simply allowing private killings is not. Whatever the moral relevance of the distinction between acts and omissions for individual conduct, we think it gets little purchase on questions of governmental policy. Government cannot help but act in ways that affect the actions of citizens; where citizens decide whether or not to kill each other in light of government policies, it is not clear even as a conceptual matter what it would mean for government not to act. For government to adopt a mix of criminal justice policies that happens not to include capital punishment is not an "omission" or a "failure to act" in any meaningful sense.

Likewise, deontological injunctions against unjustified killing, which we have not questioned here, are of little help in these settings. Unjustified killing is exactly what capital punishment prevents. In any case, the strongest arguments in favor of the act/omission distinction, involving individual liberty and overall consequences, do not apply in the context of public officials.

If this argument is correct, it has broad implications, some of which may not be welcomed by advocates of capital punishment. Government engages in countless omissions, many of which threaten people's health and safety. Consider the failure to reduce highway fatalities, to regulate greenhouse gas emissions, to prevent domestic violence, to impose further controls on private uses of guns, or even to redistribute wealth to those who most need it. Suppose that it is not sensible, in these and other contexts, to characterize government omissions as such. Or suppose that even if the characterization is sensible, it lacks moral relevance. If so, then government might well be compelled, on one or another ground, to take steps to protect people against statistical risks, even if those steps impose costs and harms; everything will depend on what the facts show and on the costs and benefits of alternative policies.[135]

Any objection to capital punishment, we believe, must rely on something other than abstract injunctions against the taking of life. If the recent evidence of deterrence is ultimately shown to be correct, then opponents of capital punishment will face an uphill struggle on moral grounds. If each execution saves many innocent lives, the harms of capital punishment would have to be very great to justify its abolition, far greater than most critics have heretofore alleged. There is always residual uncertainty in social science and legal policy, and in this domain the empirical controversy continues; we have attempted to describe, rather than to defend, the recent findings. But if those findings are right, capital punishment has a strong claim to being not merely morally permissible, but morally obligatory—above all from the standpoint of those who wish to protect life.

135. For a general attack on the act/omission distinction from a utilitarian perspective, see BARON, *supra* note 111. If our argument is correct, some of Baron's arguments should be appealing to deontologists as well, and his controversial commitment to utilitarianism is not a necessary foundation for his conclusions.

Part V
Deterrence and Corporate Crime

[13]

Corporate Crime and Deterrence

Assaf Hamdani* & Alon Klement**

This Article sheds new light on the controversial doctrine of corporate criminal liability and other forms of collective sanctions. Critics contend that the use of criminal law to target business entities is undesirable given the disastrous consequences for firms convicted of misconduct, as graphically illustrated by the unraveling of the accounting firm Arthur Andersen. At the same time, the threat of going out of business is commonly perceived as providing firms with powerful incentives to contain misconduct. In this Article, we challenge the conventional view concerning the deterrence value of corporate criminal liability. Specifically, we show that harsh entity-level penalties might discourage monitoring for misconduct and undermine compliance incentives within professional firms. We also identify the conditions under which civil fines might enhance deterrence. Our analysis has implications for entity criminal liability and collective sanctions more generally. We call for greater reliance on purely financial corporate penalties and provide a deterrence-based justification for modifying the existing doctrine for holding firms criminally liable. We also explain why prohibiting law and accounting firms from organizing as limited-liability entities might be unwise.

---

* Associate Professor, Faculty of Law, Hebrew University.

** Associate Professor, Radzyner School of Law, Interdisciplinary Center, Israel. This Article greatly benefited from comments and criticism by Lucian Bebchuk, Avi Bell, Tsilly Dagan, Alon Harel, Barak Orbach, Gideon Parchamovsky, Mitch Polinsky, Ariel Porat, Ed Rock, Eric Talley, and participants in workshops at the Hebrew University, Tel Aviv University, and the University of Pennsylvania Law School. We also thank Efrat Nachalon for excellent research assistance and the Handler Foundation for financial support.

INDEX OF FIGURES AND TABLES

INTRODUCTION

The doctrine of corporate criminal liability is notoriously controversial. For decades, scholars have argued that imposing criminal liability on business entities is both ineffective and inconsistent with the fundamental principles of individual culpability and moral condemnation underlying criminal law.[1] It is therefore not surprising that the federal government's post-Enron campaign against corporate crime has reignited debate over the proper use of criminal law to target business entities.[2]

Critics of corporate criminal liability often invoke the disastrous impact of a criminal conviction on firms, employees, suppliers, and other innocent third parties.[3] Consider the case of Arthur Andersen LLP. Formerly one of the "Big Five" accounting firms, Arthur Andersen was convicted in 2002 of obstruction of justice for its destruction of Enron-related documents.[4] The conviction forced the firm to go out of business, thereby making 28,000 employees in the United States lose their jobs.[5] Not surprisingly, Arthur Andersen's tragic fate has sparked calls for sharply limiting the prosecution of business entities.[6]

But while the dramatic consequences of corporate liability occupy a prominent role in the ongoing policy debate, the deterrence effect of these harsh consequences remains largely unexplored by legal academics.[7] This omission is troubling, as the predominant justification for corporate criminal liability is its effectiveness as a necessary tool for combating organizational misconduct.

Commentators typically assume that harsh corporate penalties, including the threat of going out of business, provide firms with powerful incentives to contain wrongdoing.[8] Some find these incentives to be excessive,[9] while others

---

1. *See, e.g.*, Brent Fisse, *Reconstructing Corporate Criminal Law: Deterrence, Retribution, Fault, and Sanctions*, 56 S. CAL. L. REV. 1141, 1183 (1983) (referring to corporate criminal liability jurisprudence as "the blackest hole in the theory of corporate criminal law").

2. *See, e.g.*, Symposium, *Corporate Criminality: Legal, Ethical, and Managerial Implications*, 44 AM. CRIM. L. REV. 1269 (2007); *see also* Brandon L. Garrett, *Structural Reform Prosecution*, 93 VA. L. REV. 853, 854 (2007) ("In the past few years, federal prosecutions of organizations have sharply accelerated . . . .").

3. *See, e.g.*, Sara Sun Beale, *Is Corporate Criminal Liability Unique?*, 44 AM. CRIM. L. REV. 1503, 1522 (2007).

4. This conviction was overturned by the Supreme Court in 2005. Arthur Andersen LLP v. United States, 544 U.S. 696 (2005).

5. *See* Elizabeth K. Ainslie, *Indicting Corporations Revisited: Lessons of the Arthur Andersen Prosecution*, 43 AM. CRIM. L. REV. 107, 107 (2006).

6. *See* COMM. ON CAPITAL MKTS. REGULATION, INTERIM REPORT, at xii (2006) ("[C]riminal enforcement against companies, in light of the experience of Arthur Andersen, should truly be a last resort . . . ."); Ainslie, *supra* note 5, at 110 ("[C]riminal prosecution of business entities should be considered only when it is clear that no civil sanction . . . will suffice to deter the corporate misconduct.").

7. *But see* V.S. Khanna, *Corporate Criminal Liability: What Purpose Does It Serve?*, 109 HARV. L. REV. 1477, 1499-1512 (1996) (considering the extent to which reputational penalties could deter corporate crime).

8. *See, e.g.*, Christopher A. Wray & Robert K. Hur, *Corporate Criminal Prosecution in a Post-Enron World: The Thompson Memo in Theory and Practice*, 43 AM. CRIM. L. REV. 1095, 1097 (2006) (referring to such penalties as providing "deterrence on a massive scale" (quoting Memorandum from Larry D. Thompson, Deputy Attorney Gen., to Heads of Dep't

posit that only the threat of going out of business can effectively deter organizational misconduct. Yet, the prevailing view is that prosecutors should balance the need to deter corporate crime against a conviction's dire consequences for employees and other innocent stakeholders.[10]

In this Article, we show that subjecting business entities to criminal liability carrying severe collateral consequences might, in fact, undermine deterrence. Indeed, purely financial penalties could contain misconduct more effectively than the threat of going out of business. To be sure, severe corporate penalties might produce powerful compliance incentives in some cases. As we shall explain, however, such penalties are likely to fail precisely when entity liability is vital from a deterrence standpoint, i.e., in decentralized organizations where individual wrongdoers are difficult to identify.

Part I begins our analysis by providing necessary background concerning both the doctrine of corporate criminal liability and its collateral consequences. The prevailing respondeat superior doctrine holds entities criminally liable for every offense committed by an agent within the scope of employment.[11] At the same time, a conviction can deal corporate defendants a fatal blow even when courts impose relatively modest penalties. Firms may thus unravel due to a variety of non-criminal sanctions triggered by a conviction, such as delicensing, exclusion from government contracts, and irreparable damage to reputation. Indeed, the most telling evidence of the fatal consequences associated with a conviction is the growing success of prosecutors in compelling companies under investigation to assist them in bringing charges against their own employees and officers.[12]

Components, U.S. Attorneys (Jan. 20, 2003), *available at* http://www.usdoj.gov/dag/cftf/corporate_guidelines.htm)).

9. It is difficult to find an economic justification for corporate sanctions that aim at putting firms out of business, as optimal deterrence requires that penalties equal social harm (discounted by the probability of detection). *See* Gary S. Becker, *Crime and Punishment: An Economic Approach*, 76 J. POL. ECON. 169, 192 (1968). To be sure, an offense may be strictly undesirable from a social perspective, thereby justifying an attempt to secure full deterrence. Yet, legal economists believe that this objective should not dictate the magnitude of firm-level sanctions. *See* Daniel R. Fischel & Alan O. Sykes, *Corporate Crime*, 25 J. LEGAL STUD. 319, 322-27 (1996).

10. *See* Garrett, *supra* note 2, at 859 ("The DOJ could seek to impose optimally deterrent fines, but the dire collateral consequences of such an approach make it highly undesirable.").

11. *See* Kathleen F. Brickey, *Andersen's Fall from Grace*, 81 WASH. U. L.Q. 917, 929 (2003) ("Under the respondeat superior rule applicable to federal criminal trials, the acts and intent of agents at any level of an entity's hierarchy—including those at the lower end of the organizational ladder—are imputable to the firm."). For suggestions that imposing liability for misconduct committed by employees against corporate policy or without management's involvement is unfair, see William S. Laufer & Alan Strudler, *Corporate Intentionality, Desert, and Variants of Vicarious Liability*, 37 AM. CRIM. L. REV. 1285, 1297 (2000).

12. *See* Lisa Kern Griffin, *Compelled Cooperation and the New Corporate Criminal Procedure*, 82 N.Y.U. L. REV. 311, 331 (2007) (noting that the threat of indictment induces companies to hand over internal documents and rat out individual employees as targets for

Our analysis then focuses on two distinct channels through which entity liability affects compliance. Part II considers *professional firms*. As the Arthur Andersen case demonstrates, holding a professional firm criminally liable would most likely trigger its demise.[13] Unlike shareholders of a corporation, members of professional firms are both part-owners and potential wrongdoers. This overlap is commonly believed to strengthen compliance incentives. Penalties imposed on professional firms, the argument goes, would not only encourage hierarchical monitoring,[14] but also directly penalize members to the extent of their equity investment,[15] thereby discouraging them from committing misconduct.

We demonstrate, however, that holding professional firms criminally liable might undermine this unique deterrence effect. When a conviction triggers the firm's demise, members decide whether to commit misconduct in a strategic setting: there are many potential wrongdoers within the firm, but liability can be imposed only once before the firm unravels. When other members of the firm are likely to commit misconduct, each member expects to bear her share of the loss associated with the firm's demise regardless of her own actions. The risk of going out of business due to others' wrongdoing thus undercuts the deterrence power of the firm's liability.

Part III considers the second channel—monitoring against misconduct—which applies to all types of business organizations. The threat of going out of business appears to provide firms with powerful monitoring incentives. Most modern firms, however, cannot realistically expect to eliminate wrongdoing even when they implement adequate compliance measures.[16] Under the prevailing entity-liability regime, a firm might unravel even for an isolated violation that took place notwithstanding the firm's compliance effort.

---

prosecution).

13. *See also* Julie Creswell, *U.S. Indictment for Big Law Firm in Class Actions*, N.Y. TIMES, May 19, 2006, at A1 (reporting the federal indictment of Milberg Weiss Bershad & Schulman, a leading U.S. class-action law firm, for making illegal payments to clients); Nathan Koppel, *Fatal Vision: How a Bid to Boost Profits Led to a Law Firm's Demise*, WALL ST. J., May 17, 2007, at A1 (describing the demise of a prominent Dallas law firm as a result of an investigation concerning its role in marketing illegal tax shelters).

14. The profit-sharing quality of professional firms might also improve the monitoring incentives among partners. *See, e.g.*, Armen A. Alchian & Harold Demsetz, *Production, Information Costs, and Economic Organization*, 62 AM. ECON. REV. 777, 786 (1972) (suggesting that profit-sharing induces monitoring of each employee by every other employee). *But see* Eugene Kandel & Edward P. Lazear, *Peer Pressure and Partnerships*, 100 J. POL. ECON. 801, 813 (1992) (indicating that "there is little incentive to engage in mutual monitoring, even with profit sharing").

15. Henry Hansmann labels this effect of profit sharing "self monitoring." *See* Henry Hansmann, *When Does Worker Ownership Work? ESOPs, Law Firms, Codetermination, and Economic Democracy*, 99 YALE L.J. 1749, 1762 (1990).

16. *See* Poonam Puri, *Judgment Proofing the Profession*, 15 GEO. J. LEGAL ETHICS 1, 9-10 (2001) (listing rapid growth, globalization, and increased specialization as factors that explain the inability of law firms to monitor their members).

When they cannot eliminate misconduct, firms might respond to the threat of harsh sanctions by *reducing* their monitoring effort. After all, if the firm is about to unravel regardless of its investment in compliance, then why bother? More precisely, the marginal reduction in expected liability might be too low to justify additional monitoring efforts. Entity-level criminal liability can therefore undermine incentives to implement costly compliance measures when such measures merely reduce—but do not eliminate—misconduct.

Our analysis gives rise to several insights concerning corporate liability and collective sanctions.[17] First, as a matter of theory, we demonstrate that harsh penalties could undermine deterrence in group settings. Law and economics scholars recognize that subjecting offenders to severe penalties might fail to produce optimal deterrence.[18] Yet, this Article offers a novel framework to analyze the deterrence effect of harsh penalties imposed on business entities or other groups.

Second, as a matter of enforcement policy, we caution against subjecting firms to harsh sanctions—whether criminal, administrative, or other—that can be imposed only once.

Third, as a matter of criminal law doctrine, we offer a deterrence-based justification for targeting firms only for *pervasive* wrongdoing. While legal economists generally believe that the respondeat superior doctrine provides firms with optimal incentives,[19] our analysis shows that this regime might fail when the defendant entity is unlikely to survive a conviction. A pervasiveness standard, however, can provide both firms and their members with adequate compliance incentives. Interestingly, the federal guidelines for prosecuting business organizations require that prosecutors consider the extent to which wrongdoing is pervasive within the organization.[20] Our analysis thus lends support to this element of the guidelines.

Fourth, our analysis sheds a new light on the debate about unlimited liability for professional firms. Professional firms were traditionally prohibited from incorporating as limited liability entities. In recent years, however, lawmakers have allowed such firms to enjoy the shield of limited liability, by organizing as an LLP, for example.

---

17. For a comprehensive analysis of collective sanctions, see Daryl J. Levinson, *Collective Sanctions*, 56 STAN. L. REV. 345 (2003). *See also* Thomas J. Miceli & Kathleen Segerson, *Punishing the Innocent Along with the Guilty: The Economics of Individual Versus Group Punishment*, 36 J. LEGAL STUD. 81 (2007).

18. Economists have shown that, under certain conditions, it may be desirable to lower the sanctions on relatively light offenses in order to enhance the deterrence of more severe ones. *See generally* Dilip Mookherjee & I.P.L. Png, *Marginal Deterrence in Enforcement of Law*, 102 J. POL. ECON. 1039 (1994); Steven Shavell, *A Note on Marginal Deterrence*, 12 INT'L REV. L. & ECON. 345 (1992).

19. *See* sources cited *infra* note 99.

20. *See* Memorandum from Larry D. Thompson, Deputy Attorney Gen., to Heads of Dep't Components, U.S. Attorneys, *supra* note 8.

While critics argue that reinstituting unlimited liability for professional firms is vital for enhancing deterrence,[21] our analysis questions the deterrence value of unlimited liability. Under a regime of unlimited liability, each partner could suffer a severe financial penalty even for wrongdoing by a single, rogue member of the firm. In modern, large professional firms—where members cannot fully eliminate wrongdoing—subjecting members to such potential liability might dilute their incentives to refrain from wrongdoing.

I. Respondeat Superior and Collateral Consequences

Before turning to analyze the deterrence effect of corporate criminal liability, we would like to set the background by describing the collateral effect of a conviction and the existing regime of corporate criminal liability.

The notion that criminal liability can dramatically affect business entities is widespread among scholars, policymakers, and prosecutors.[22] Subpart A considers the channels through which criminal liability can produce disastrous effects for firms and their employees. We identify three sources for such collateral consequences: criminal law, non-criminal rules and regulations, and market reaction. Subpart B presents the expansive standard governing entity criminal liability. As the remainder of this Article will show, the combination of the existing liability regime with a conviction's collateral consequences can undermine the deterrence effect of corporate criminal liability.

A. *Collateral Consequences*

1. *The "corporate death penalty"*

Courts that convict a corporation for committing misconduct can impose

21. *See, e.g.*, Jonathan Macey & Hillary A. Sale, *Observations on the Role of Commodification, Independence, and Governance in the Accounting Industry*, 48 VILL. L. REV. 1167, 1181 (2003) (arguing that the shift to the LLP organization form deprived members of accounting firms of incentives to monitor their peers); Deborah L. Rhode & Paul D. Paton, *Lawyers, Ethics, and Enron*, 8 STAN. J.L. BUS. & FIN. 9, 30-31 (2002) ("Reducing this insulation from accountability could give lawyers greater incentives to address collegial misconduct and to establish the internal oversight structures that can check abuses.").

22. *See, e.g.*, Pamela H. Bucy, *Trends in Corporate Criminal Prosecutions*, 44 AM. CRIM. L. REV. 1287, 1288 (2007) ("[T]here is no question that criminal prosecution of a corporation has a tremendous impact on the corporation and its community, employees, customers and lenders."); Kern Griffin, *supra* note 12, at 330 (noting that prosecutors may decide against prosecuting business organizations because they are "justifiably reluctant to cause such extensive economic harm"); Eric Holder, Op-Ed., *Don't Indict WorldCom*, WALL ST. J., July 30, 2002, at A14 ("[T]o ensure that even more innocent Americans are not harmed, prosecutors must not give in to the pressures of the day and feel compelled to indict more corporations simply because they can.").

sanctions that aim at putting the defendant out of business. The Federal Organizational Sentencing Guidelines require courts to impose a fine that would be sufficiently large to divest a corporation of all of its assets "[i]f . . . the court determines that the organization operated primarily for a criminal purpose or primarily by criminal means . . . ."[23] Courts typically impose this so-called corporate death penalty on firms with no legitimate business operations.[24]

Commentators occasionally call for expanding the scope of the corporate death penalty by, for example, revoking the charters of corporations convicted of environmental crimes.[25] Financial penalties, the argument goes, are simply no different than any other cost of doing business. The threat of a firm's demise, in contrast, would compel firms to implement effective measures for containing misconduct.[26]

Finally, firms convicted of crimes could unravel simply because they lack the assets necessary to pay the fines. To be sure, the Organizational Sentencing Guidelines allow courts to depart from the recommended fine range if it would jeopardize the continuing viability of the corporation.[27] Courts, however, are not required to adjust the fines down whenever the fine amount would trigger the firm's demise.[28]

2. *Delicensing, exclusion, and debarment*

A conviction could have fatal consequences for business entities even when the criminal trial ends with a modest penalty for the defendant firm. Indeed, a variety of laws and regulations can effectively put out of business firms convicted of a crime.

Firms in regulated industries could lose their license as a result of a criminal conviction. Consider the Arthur Andersen case. The courts imposed relatively modest penalties on the firm—a $500,000 fine and five years of

23. U.S. SENTENCING GUIDELINES MANUAL § 8C1.1 (2008).

24. *See* Christopher A. Wray, Note, *Corporate Probation Under the New Organizational Sentencing Guidelines*, 101 YALE L.J. 2017, 2027 (1992).

25. *See, e.g.*, Mitchell F. Crusto, *Green Business: Should We Revoke Corporate Charters for Environmental Violations?*, 63 LA. L. REV. 175, 189-92 (2003) (analyzing recent proposals to revoke the charter of corporations that committed crimes against the environment).

26. *See, e.g.*, Thomas Linzey, *Awakening a Sleeping Giant: Creating a Quasi-Private Cause of Action for Revoking Corporate Charters in Response to Environmental Violations*, 13 PACE ENVTL. L. REV. 219, 221 (1995) ("The power . . . to revoke corporate charters, and thereby end the corporate life, may be the only effective deterrent for corporate polluters.").

27. *See* U.S. SENTENCING GUIDELINES MANUAL § 8C3.3.

28. *See* United States v. Eureka Labs., Inc., 103 F.3d 908, 910, 912 (9th Cir. 1996) (holding that the Sentencing Guidelines do not preclude courts from imposing a fine jeopardizing the firm's continued viability).

probation.[29] Nevertheless, the firm unraveled because SEC rules prohibit any accounting firm convicted of a felony from serving as the auditor of publicly traded corporations.[30] KPMG, another global accounting firm, barely escaped a similar fate when prosecutors decided against bringing charges against the firm for marketing tax shelters.[31]

Likewise, the federal government is authorized to forfeit the franchise of national banks convicted of certain money laundering offenses.[32] Firms in other regulated industries also can lose their licenses as a result of a conviction.[33]

Furthermore, firms convicted for certain offenses—health care fraud, for example—might be excluded from further contracting with the government.[34] A conviction also can cause government agencies to suspend or debar firms from conducting business with the government.[35] Several federal statutes impose *mandatory* debarment or suspension on business entities convicted for violating the statute.[36] These provisions might deal a fatal blow to firms for which government contracts are a key sources of revenue.

3. *Market reaction*

Firms' ability to survive in the marketplace depends on their reputation for honesty and quality of service.[37] Given the market value of reputation, legal scholars have claimed that business entities cannot survive a conviction—not even an indictment.[38] Some further posit that the devastating effect of a

---

29. *See* Ainslie, *supra* note 5, at 107.

30. The SEC prohibits any accounting firm convicted of a felony from serving as the auditor of a publicly traded corporation. *See* 17 C.F.R. § 201.102(e)(2) (2008); Stephan Landsman, *Death of an Accountant: The Jury Convicts Arthur Andersen of Obstruction of Justice*, 78 CHI.-KENT L. REV. 1203, 1223-24 (2003).

31. *See* discussion *infra* Part IV.B.

32. *See* 12 U.S.C. § 93(d) (2000).

33. *See* Commodity Exchange Act, 7 U.S.C. § 12a (2000); Federal Deposit Insurance Act, 12 U.S.C. § 1818(a)(2) (2000); Securities Act of 1933, 15 U.S.C. § 77t(b) (2000); Securities Exchange Act of 1934, 15 U.S.C. §§ 78o(b)(4)–(6), 78u(d)–(e) (2000); Investment Advisers Act of 1940, 15 U.S.C. § 80b-3(e)–(f) (2000); Social Security Act, 42 U.S.C. § 1320a-7 (2000).

34. *See* Pamela H. Bucy, *Civil Prosecution of Health Care Fraud*, 30 WAKE FOREST L. REV. 693, 720-37 (1995) (discussing the exclusion remedy for health care fraud under which providers might become ineligible to receive any payment under Medicare or any state health care program).

35. *See* 48 C.F.R. § 9.406-2 (2008) (listing causes for debarment).

36. *See* Andrew T. Schutz, Comment, *Too Little Too Late: An Analysis of the General Service Administration's Proposed Debarment of WorldCom*, 56 ADMIN. L. REV. 1263, 1273 (2004) (discussing mandatory debarment).

37. Khanna, *supra* note 7, at 1499 ("The most powerful sanction that society can impose on a corporation is lost reputation or stigma.").

38. *See, e.g.*, Preet Bharara, *Corporations Cry Uncle and Their Employees Cry Foul: Rethinking Prosecutorial Pressure on Corporate Defendants*, 44 AM. CRIM. L. REV. 53, 73

criminal conviction on corporate reputation is the principal feature that distinguishes criminal from civil liability.[39]

Recent high-profile cases demonstrate the potentially destructive impact of an indictment on firms' reputations. Consider the indictment of Milberg Weiss for bribery and fraud charges.[40] Once a leading class action law firm, the firm has been crippled by its indictment and agreed to pay a $75 million fine to avoid trial.[41] Another prominent law firm has recently unraveled as a result of a government investigation concerning its role in marketing abusive tax shelters.[42]

Unfortunately, there are no empirical studies to support the claim that criminal liability has a distinctively harsh impact on firms' reputations. But the most telling evidence in this context is the behavior of top management.[43] The perception that the reputational consequences of a conviction could exceed even the substantial monetary penalties in any parallel civil litigation can explain why firms under investigation for criminal violations are willing to do almost whatever it takes—including waiving attorney-client privilege, assisting the government's prosecution of their senior officers, and paying millions of dollars in civil fines—to avoid an indictment.[44]

4. *The existing regime*

The previous Subpart reviewed the harsh consequences associated with a firm's criminal conviction. In this Subpart, we outline the conditions under which entities can be held liable. As we will explain, firms can go out of

(2007) ("[C]orporate defendants, subject as they are to market pressures, may not be able to survive indictment, much less conviction and sentencing."); Pamela H. Bucy, *Organizational Sentencing Guidelines: The Cart Before the Horse*, 71 WASH. U. L.Q. 329, 352 (1993) ("In some instances adverse publicity alone can cause corporate devastation . . . .").

39. *See* Khanna, *supra* note 37, at 1508-09.

40. For a thorough analysis of the indictment and its aftermath, see Bruce H. Kobayashi & Larry E. Ribstein, *The Hypocrisy of the Milberg Indictment: The Need for a Coherent Framework on Paying for Cooperation in Litigation*, 2 J. BUS. & TECH. L. 369, 372-75 (2007).

41. The firm agreed to pay $75 million to settle the criminal charges against it. *See* Jonathan D. Glater, *Big Penalty Set for Law Firm, but Not a Trial*, N.Y. TIMES, June 17, 2008, at A1.

42. *See* Nathan Koppel, *Fatal Vision: How a Bid to Boost Profits Led to a Law Firm's Demise*, WALL ST. J., May 17, 2007, at A1 (describing the demise of Jenkens & Gilchrist).

43. *See* Samuel W. Buell, *The Blaming Function of Entity Criminal Liability*, 81 IND. L.J. 473, 504 (2006) ("Managers and their counsel apparently do not see civil and criminal sanctions as substitutes . . . .").

44. *Id.* at 505-07 (assessing the practice of firms waiving their procedural safeguards to avert an indictment); Kern Griffin, *supra* note 12, at 327 ("Because virtually no company will risk indictment, prosecutors have come to expect compliance with every government demand.").

business for a single violation that took place notwithstanding their compliance effort.

The prevailing respondeat superior doctrine holds an organization criminally liable for every offense committed by an employee within the scope of employment.[45] In other words, an entity can be convicted regardless of the rank of the person committing the offense or her authority within the organization.[46] Firms cannot escape liability by establishing that they have made an extensive effort to monitor against employee misconduct or that the offense was in clear violation of company policy.[47]

The existing regime does not require that the crime benefit the corporation.[48] Moreover, under the so-called collective knowledge doctrine, business organizations can be convicted for a crime although no single individual within the organization was aware of all the information required for the crime to materialize.

To summarize, under the existing regime of enterprise liability, a business entity can unravel even for the misdeeds of a single, low-level rogue employee. As the remainder of this Article explains, the prevailing regime might undermine organizational incentives to prevent misconduct.

II. PROFESSIONAL FIRMS

We begin by assessing the impact of criminal liability on professional firms. In the next Part, we expand our analysis to consider a broader range of business entities.

Wrongdoers in professional firms often are part owners.[49] This profit-sharing quality is commonly viewed as bolstering compliance incentives within professional firms. This Part, however, shows that the severe consequences of entity-level criminal liability might undermine the deterrence effect associated with member ownership. We also demonstrate that the legal system can enhance deterrence by using civil fines or, alternatively, by holding firms criminally liable only for sufficiently pervasive wrongdoing.

45. *See* Brickey, *supra* note 11, at 929 ("Under the respondeat superior rule applicable to federal criminal trials, the acts and intent of agents at any level of an entity's hierarchy—including those at the lower end of the organizational ladder—are imputable to the firm.").

46. Samuel W. Buell, *Criminal Procedure Within the Firm*, 59 STAN. L. REV. 1613, 1662 (2007) ("Under current law, a firm faces criminal liability for virtually any criminal act by an agent.").

47. For suggestions that imposing liability for misconduct committed by employees against corporate policy or without management's involvement is unfair, see Laufer & Strudler, *supra* note 11, at 1297.

48. *See infra* text accompanying notes 85-86.

49. *But see* Note, *Collective Sanctions and Large Law Firm Discipline*, 118 HARV. L. REV. 2336, 2337 (2005) (arguing that the law should provide law firms with incentives to prevent wrongdoing by nonpartners).

We do not argue that criminal liability carrying harsh collateral consequences will always undermine deterrence within professional firms. Rather, our objective in this Part is to demonstrate that there are cases in which purely financial penalties or the pervasiveness standard for criminal liability can bolster compliance among professional firms' members.

Before we proceed, we would like to comment on our terminology. To simplify the discussion, we will refer to the threat of going out of business as representative of the collateral consequences of criminal liability.

A. *Organizational Liability and Member Incentives*

Legal entities do not commit crimes; individuals do. Ideally, the legal system would target only culpable individuals within organizations. But a system of pure personal liability would likely fail to produce adequate deterrence.[50] In the criminal context,[51] the principal challenge confronting prosecutors is to identify individual offenders within large, decentralized organizations,[52] and to gather sufficient evidence to establish their culpability—including the requisite mental state—beyond reasonable doubt.[53]

The conventional justification for entity liability is that holding firms liable would be a cost-effective way to overcome the shortcomings of personal liability.[54] Specifically, holding firms criminally liable would induce them to police their employees and prevent them from committing misconduct.[55]

Like other business entities, professional firms would attempt to minimize their liability exposure by policing their agents. In professional firms, however,

50. *See, e.g.*, Lewis A. Kornhauser, *An Economic Analysis of the Choice Between Enterprise and Personal Liability for Accidents*, 70 CAL. L. REV. 1345 (1982); Reinier Kraakman, *Corporate Liability Strategies and the Costs of Legal Controls*, 93 YALE L.J. 857 (1984); Alan O. Sykes, *The Economics of Vicarious Liability*, 93 YALE L.J. 1231 (1984).

51. Another common justification for entity-level liability is that wrongdoers might lack the financial resources to pay fines. *See* V.S. Khanna, *Corporate Liability Standards: When Should Corporations Be Held Criminally Liable?*, 37 AM. CRIM. L. REV. 1239, 1243-44 (2000). While it can justify the prevalence of vicarious liability in torts, the assumption that wrongdoers are judgment-proof cannot satisfactorily explain the decision to hold firms *criminally* liable. The government can overcome offenders' limited wealth by subjecting them to imprisonment. Indeed, the government's ability to impose jail sentences explains why personal liability is essential even under a regime of corporate criminal liability. *See* A. Mitchell Polinsky & Steven Shavell, *Should Employees Be Subject to Fines and Imprisonment Given the Existence of Corporate Liability?*, 13 INT'L REV. L. & ECON. 239 (1993).

52. *See* Jennifer Arlen & Reinier Kraakman, *Controlling Corporate Misconduct: An Analysis of Corporate Liability Regimes*, 72 N.Y.U. L. REV. 687, 695-96 (1997).

53. *See, e.g.*, Stacey Neumann Vu, *Corporate Criminal Liability: Patchwork Verdicts and the Problem of Locating a Guilty Agent*, 104 COLUM. L. REV. 459 (2004).

54. Subjecting firms to liability also might induce them to adopt an optimal scale of production. *See* Khanna, *supra* note 7, at 1496.

55. While commentators normally agree on the justification for firms' vicarious liability, there is disagreement whether this liability should be criminal or civil. *See, e.g.*, *id.*

wrongdoers are often part owners. This overlap translates into a unique self-enforcing deterrence advantage: imposing a sanction on the firm immediately translates into a personal cost for each member-wrongdoer even when the prosecution cannot establish the wrongdoer's culpability in court.

At first sight, the threat of a firm's demise should supply members with powerful incentives to refrain from wrongdoing. After all, so the argument goes, the firm's collapse will render worthless each member's ownership stake. This Part, however, shows that such a threat might undermine the effect of firms' profit-sharing arrangements on member-compliance incentives.

In order to study the impact of organizational liability on member incentives, we make two simplifying assumptions in this Part. First, we assume that members face no meaningful threat of personal liability for their misconduct.[56] Second, we assume that firms cannot adopt effective measures to police members and prevent them from engaging in misconduct.[57]

Consider a decision by a professional firm's member as to whether to commit misconduct. Under our assumptions, each member would weigh her share of the firm-level expected penalty against her benefit from misconduct. Yet, since a firm can unravel only once, the effective magnitude of the firm-level liability depends on other members' conduct. Simply put, the expected cost of another violation is zero when the firm is going to unravel anyway.

The firm's dissolution turns each member's decision whether to commit misconduct into a *strategic* one—each member's cost-benefit calculus is shaped not only by her own actions, but also by the conduct of her colleagues. The interaction of legal rules and organizational attributes can deepen the strategic nature of members' decisions. Recall that a firm can be held liable even for a single violation by any of its agents. Moreover, members of large professional firms often lack information concerning their peers' behavior. The upshot is that even a small probability that someone within the organization would commit misconduct can undermine the deterrence effect of the firm's liability.

To illustrate, let us use the following example. A law firm has two equal members (attorneys), John and Elizabeth. Each attorney can commit misconduct, say issue legal opinions to facilitate the marketing of illegal tax shelters.[58] At the time of committing misconduct, each attorney does not know

56. When members are held liable for their misconduct, the effect that we identify in this Part is less likely to take place, as each member will bear the cost of committing misconduct regardless of other members' conduct. As explained earlier, however, the difficulty of identifying culpable agents within the firm provides the principal justification for subjecting firms to liability.

57. This assumption is made for simplicity only. In a more realistic setting, this Part's analysis applies to the extent that monitoring is imperfect. We return to this issue when we consider the negligence standard. *See infra* Part IV.B. We also assume that firms cannot turn in wrongdoers after the offense has been committed in order to induce prosecutors to waive a criminal indictment.

58. We discuss such an example below. *See infra* Part IV.B.

whether the other has committed misconduct as well. While committing misconduct would provide the wrongdoer with some personal benefit,[59] it may also lead to the firm's indictment and trigger its demise. The probability of conviction following misconduct is 0.9.[60] The firm total value is 160. Each attorney would thus suffer a loss of 80 upon the firm's demise.

Assume that John's benefit from issuing the questionable tax opinion is 30. At first sight, one could expect the threat of the firm's criminal liability to discourage John from issuing the opinion. After all, John's benefit from committing misconduct is clearly outweighed by his expected loss (i.e., his loss upon the firm's demise discounted by the probability of conviction) of 72.[61]

This conclusion, however, overlooks the strategic environment in which John makes his decision. Specifically, John's action in this example will depend on his beliefs concerning Elizabeth's likelihood of committing misconduct. This likelihood depends on Elizabeth's benefit from committing misconduct, which John, by hypothesis, does not know. Denote this benefit by B_E. The following matrix describes John's situation.

Table 1. The Strategic Decision Under Criminal Liability

		Elizabeth	
		Don't Commit	Commit
John	Don't Commit	0, 0	-72, B_E-72
	Commit	30-72, -72	30-79.2, B_E-79.2

The left expression in each cell represents John's payoff; the right expression represents Elizabeth's. In the upper left cell, neither attorney commits misconduct. In both the lower left cell and the upper right cell, only one attorney commits an offense. This offender benefits from misconduct, but the law firm is held liable with a probability of 0.9, thereby subjecting each attorney to a loss of 80 (or an expected loss of 72). In the lower right cell, both attorneys commit misconduct, and the probability that the firm will be

59. The analysis assumes that the firm as such does not benefit from wrongdoing. In other words, we assume that corporate crime is to a large extent the byproduct of the so-called agency problem. *See, e.g.*, Jonathan R. Macey, *Agency Theory and the Criminal Liability of Organizations*, 71 B.U. L. REV. 315, 319 (1991) ("The real aim of criminal behavior by organizations is to advance the careers of the responsible corporate actors."). For a critique of this perception of corporate crime, see generally Kimberly D. Krawiec, *Organizational Misconduct: Beyond the Principal-Agent Model*, 32 FLA. ST. U. L. REV. 571 (2005).

60. We assume for simplicity that the probabilities of conviction for each violation are statistically independent. Relaxing this assumption would not change our qualitative results.

61. John's loss when the firm unravels is 80. The probability that the firm will unravel due to John's misconduct is 0.9. John's expected loss thus equals $0.9 \times 80 = 72$.

convicted is 0.99.[62] Under these circumstances, the expected liability cost for each attorney is therefore 0.99 × 80 = 79.2.

The matrix shows that John's optimal strategy depends on Elizabeth's actions, and vice versa. When Elizabeth acts lawfully, John expects to lose 72 if he issues the illegal tax opinion. Since his benefit from doing so is only 30, he would not engage in wrongdoing.

But if Elizabeth is likely to commit misconduct, the difference between John's expected loss if he commits the offense, 79.2, and his expected loss if he does not commit it, 72, is only 7.2. In this case, John would clearly prefer to issue the opinion, gain 30 with certainty, and increase his expected liability cost by only 7.2. Thus, if he expects Elizabeth to commit misconduct, John will issue the illegal tax opinion notwithstanding the firm's likely demise.

The analysis thus far has focused on John's decision. Elizabeth, however, also has to decide whether to commit misconduct given her uncertainty concerning John's actions. A full model, which we develop in the Appendix, would therefore incorporate both attorneys' incomplete information. As neither attorney knows the other's benefit from wrongdoing, each attorney would act based on her estimate of the other's probability of committing misconduct.

This setup of the game allows us to predict members' actions by finding their threshold benefit, i.e., the benefit from wrongdoing above which each member is expected to commit misconduct given her belief concerning the other's likely actions. An equilibrium of this game is a threshold benefit such that, given the implied probability of offense by one member,[63] the other member's best response is to commit the offense if her benefit is higher than the *same* threshold, and not to commit it if her threshold is lower.[64]

This threshold benefit, which we denote as B^*, is a useful proxy for the impact of organizational liability on deterrence at the individual member level. An increase in B^* implies that members will commit misconduct only if their benefit from wrongdoing is higher. In other words, an increase in B^* represents an increase in the level of deterrence.

The Appendix develops a model that formally studies the impact of various liability regimes on the threshold benefit under the assumption that members' benefits are uniformly distributed between 0 and 100.[65] The Appendix shows that, when the probability of conviction is 0.9, this threshold equals 20.45. Based on the Appendix's model, the following figure describes the threshold B^* as a function of the probability of convicting the firm, p.

62. This probability equals 0.9 + (1 - 0.9) × 0.9.

63. By implied probability we mean the probability that a member will commit misconduct given that she will do so if and only if her benefit is higher than the threshold.

64. We thus restrict attention to symmetric equilibria only.

65. The same analysis can be applied for any other probability distribution of benefits. Note, however, that if the benefit could never exceed 80 (discounting for the probability of detection), the threat of putting the firm out of business would likely deter all members from committing misconduct.

Figure 1. The Effect of Probability of Conviction on Deterrence

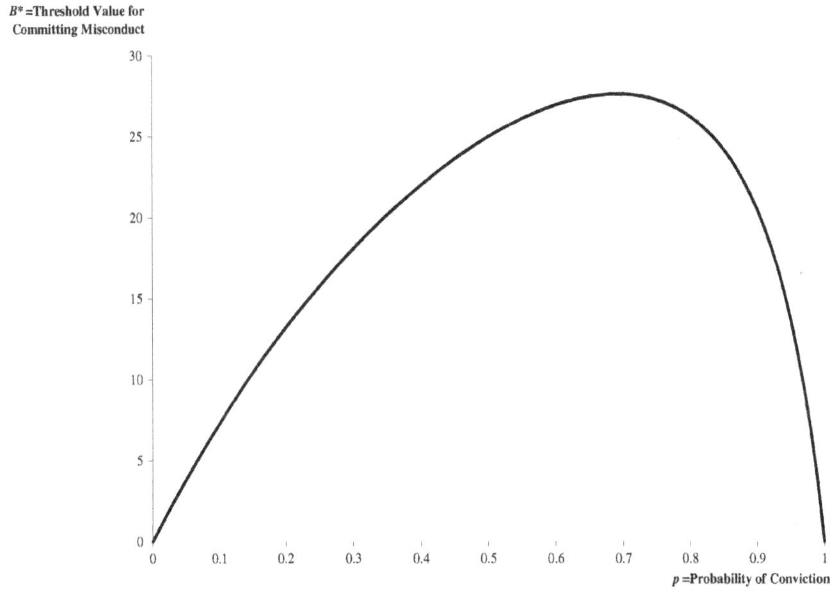

Figure 1 illustrates two somewhat surprising results. First, the maximal level of deterrence that combining criminal liability with the threat of the firm's dissolution can produce in this example is fairly low. Since each attorney would lose 80 upon the firm's unraveling, one could expect members to commit misconduct only when their illicit gain exceeded this amount. Our model, however, shows otherwise. When deterrence is highest, attorneys will commit misconduct whenever their benefit from doing so exceeds 28.[66]

Second, there is a range of probabilities within which *increasing* the probability of detection *reduces* the level of deterrence. Optimal deterrence theory suggests that increasing the probability of detection increases the expected sanction, thereby enhancing deterrence.[67] Our analysis, however, shows that the level of deterrence under the threat of going out of business dramatically decreases as the probability of detection approaches 1.

The intuition underlying this observation follows the logic of marginal deterrence.[68] John's expected sanction equals his share of loss upon the firm's dissolution discounted by the probability of convicting the firm. John's expected loss from committing misconduct thus increases as the firm's

66. It can be verified that at the maximum p=0.69, and that B^*=27.64. The explanation for this result is that the strategic environment significantly reduces the magnitude of the effective penalty facing each member.

67. *See* Becker, *supra* note 9, at 176; A. Mitchell Polinsky & Steven Shavell, *The Optimal Tradeoff Between the Probability and the Magnitude of Fines*, 69 AM. ECON. REV. 880 (1979).

68. *See supra* note 18.

probability of conviction rises. This explains the upward sloping left-hand side of the graph.

Yet, John's misconduct will not affect his expected costs if Elizabeth also commits an offense for which the firm is convicted. Under the assumption that Elizabeth is likely to commit an offense, John's misconduct cannot further increase the magnitude of the sanction imposed on the firm. Rather, it can increase the firm's overall probability of conviction. When Elizabeth is likely to commit misconduct, therefore, committing misconduct increases John's expected costs only in those cases in which Elizabeth is not detected. As the probability of detection increases, John expects his commission of the offense to matter less, as the firm would unravel with higher probability if Elizabeth committed an offense. This explains the downward sloping right-hand side of the graph.

B. *Can Lenient Regimes Enhance Deterrence?*

This Subpart identifies two liability schemes that can discourage members from committing misconduct more effectively than the existing criminal liability regime. We first consider a regime that would impose only a civil fine for each violation. For the purposes of our analysis, a civil fine means a purely financial penalty with no collateral consequences. We then consider a regime that preserves criminal liability, but conditions it on the pervasiveness of wrongdoing within the firm.

1. *Civil fines*

Returning to our example, assume that the fine for each offense is 80 (recall that the probability of detection and conviction is 0.9). The following table describes John's options under the assumption that his benefit from wrongdoing is 30:

Table 2. The Strategic Decision Under Civil Fines of 80

		Elizabeth	
		Don't Commit	Commit
John	Don't Commit	0, 0	-36, B_E-36
	Commit	*30*-36, -36	*30*-72, B_E-72

Reducing the entity-level fine to 80 clearly enhances deterrence in this example: regardless of Elizabeth's likely course of action, John will not commit misconduct. This is because with a fine of 80, the expected liability cost for each attorney contemplating misconduct is 36 even when the other attorney is likely to commit an offense as well.[69] An attorney will thus commit misconduct if and only if her benefit is higher than 36. This threshold is higher than the threshold under the death-penalty regime, i.e., 20.45.

Reducing the fine in this example can enhance marginal deterrence by making each member's expected loss from misconduct independent of the other member's actions. As the previous Subpart showed, criminal liability might lose its deterrent effect when members expect their peers' conduct to trigger the firm's demise. With a civil fine of $80, each member knows that, regardless of others' actions, her own conduct will further increase the firm's liability costs, as it increases both the probability of the firm's conviction and the total value of the sanction. Relatively modest civil penalties can therefore effectively enhance the expected sanction when members lack information concerning their peers' conduct.

2. *The pervasiveness standard*

Consider next a criminal liability regime under which firms are held criminally liable only for sufficiently pervasive wrongdoing. In our example, we take the pervasiveness standard to require that both members commit the offense for the firm to be convicted. As discussed earlier, a criminal conviction leads to the firm's dissolution. John's game matrix under this standard is the following:

Table 3. The Strategic Decision Under the Pervasiveness Standard

		Elizabeth	
		Don't Commit	Commit
John	Don't Commit	0, 0	0, B_E
	Commit	*30*, 0	*30*-72, B_E-72

Under the pervasiveness standard, each attorney knows that the firm cannot be liable unless she commits the offense. In other words, this standard turns each member into a pivotal figure in determining the sanction to be imposed on the firm. The pervasiveness standard thus enhances deterrence when there is a high likelihood that at least one member will commit misconduct. It is not subject to the risk that an isolated case of wrongdoing would trigger the firm's

69. The entity-level fine is 80. Each member's share of the entity-level fine is 40. Since the probability of detection is 0.9, the expected liability cost for each member is 0.9 × 40 = 36.

demise, thereby undermining the deterrence effect of criminal liability on all the remaining members.[70]

Indeed, the Appendix shows that the threshold B^* under this regime is 39.3, which exceeds the threshold under the existing criminal liability regime, 20.45.

3. *Taking stock*

We do not purport to argue that civil penalties or the pervasiveness standard will *always* outperform the existing regime of criminal liability carrying severe collateral consequences. Nor do we argue that these regimes will optimally deter organizational wrongdoing. Rather, our goal here is to demonstrate that civil penalties or the pervasiveness standard could discourage wrongdoing more effectively than the threat of going out of business under the existing regime of entity liability.

Figure 2 compares the level of deterrence in our example for three regimes: the existing entity-liability regime, a pervasiveness standard of entity liability, and civil penalties. This figure presents the level of deterrence, measured by B^*, as a function of the firm's probability of conviction.

Figure 2. Comparing Deterrence Under Alternative Regimes

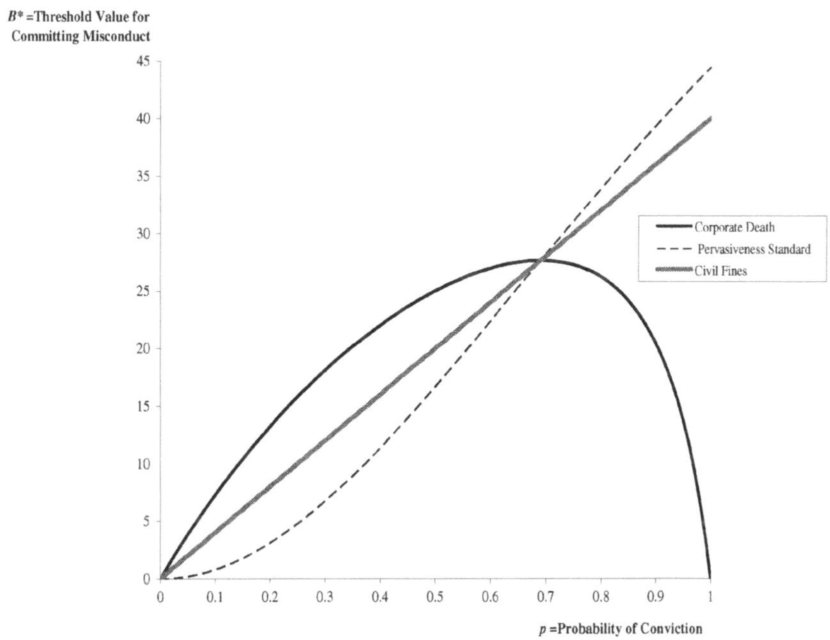

70. For similar reasons, the pervasiveness standard may under certain conditions encourage wrongdoing. A member who believes that other members will always refrain from wrongdoing will expect her misconduct to go unpunished under this standard.

This figure shows that the threat of going out of business tends to be powerful when the probability of the firm's conviction following misconduct is relatively small. Once the probability of conviction exceeds a certain threshold, however, the pervasiveness standard or civil fines would contain misconduct more effectively.

For simplicity of exposition, our analysis has thus far focused on a firm with two members. Our framework, however, can be extended to firms with a large number of members. In fact, as an organization increases in size, the threat of going out of business is more likely to reduce criminal liability's deterrence power. In a firm with numerous members, each member is less likely to view her actions as having a pivotal effect on the firm's fate. In other words, as the number of members (and other agents) increases, it becomes more likely that at least one case of wrongdoing will take place. Expecting other members to commit misconduct, members become more likely to commit offenses.

III. Monitoring Against Misconduct

The previous Part focused on the compliance incentives of individual members within professional firms. One might argue, however, that the threat of going out of business can provide the firm itself with powerful incentives to monitor against misconduct by its agents.

Indeed, as we explained earlier, entity liability primarily aims at inducing organizations to monitor against misconduct. In this Part we show that the threat of going out of business might frustrate this goal as well. Again, we do not argue that threatening firms with harsh penalties will *always* distort monitoring incentives. In some cases, the threat of going out of business can compel firms to make an effort—perhaps even an excessive one—to prevent their agents from breaking the law.[71] We do show, however, that corporate liability carrying severe collateral consequences might be inferior from a deterrence perspective to alternative liability regimes. Moreover, while our findings in the previous case were limited to professional firms, our findings in this Part apply to all forms of business organizations.

A. *Firms' Monitoring Incentives*

Firms can adopt a variety of measures to prevent their agents from committing misconduct. They can respond to wrongdoing ex post—by disciplining wrongdoers or reporting them to the authorities. They can also implement internal controls and other ex ante policing measures to detect

71. Deterrence theory predicts that entity liability will produce overdeterrence when the expected sanction exceeds the expected social harm.

agents contemplating wrongdoing or otherwise thwart misconduct.[72] Our analysis focuses on the ex ante measures that firms may take to prevent wrongdoing.[73]

1. *Criminal liability: the existing regime*

Assume that criminal liability will cause the defendant entity to unravel. At first glance, the threat of going out of business appears to be a powerful deterrent. To the extent that the loss associated with a firm's unraveling outweighs monitoring cost, this threat would encourage firms to monitor their agents to prevent them from committing misconduct.

This initial impression, however, may be misleading. The principal drawback of criminal corporate liability in this example is that it imposes the harshest sanction even on firms that made an adequate effort to police their agents. The existing regime holds firms—regardless of their monitoring effort—vicariously liable whenever an employee commits an offense within the scope of employment.[74] Firms, however, often cannot eliminate wrongdoing altogether. A firm may therefore go out of business even for a single violation that took place despite its monitoring effort.

From the firm's perspective, investment in compliance is valuable only to the extent that it reduces expected liability costs. When criminal liability triggers dissolution, however, a decrease in the level of wrongdoing will not necessarily translate into an equal decrease in the firm's expected liability costs.

This Part will use the following stylistic example to compare the deterrence effect of enterprise criminal liability to that of more lenient regimes. A firm has two employees. Without monitoring, each employee will surely commit an offense. Each case of fraud is ultimately detected and leads to the firm's conviction.[75] The firm has only 100 in assets, and a criminal conviction leads it to dissolve.

Assume that the firm can choose between two measures to monitor its employees—*Extensive* and *Moderate*. Extensive monitoring has a 50% success

---

72. *See* Arlen & Kraakman, *supra* note 52, at 696 & n.22.

73. The corporate death sanction might also adversely affect ex post measures. For example, a firm that is surely going out of business has no reason to impose private sanctions on culpable individuals.

74. Under the Federal Sentencing Guidelines for Business Organizations, firms' monitoring policies can affect the magnitude of the sanction imposed on the firm. *See* Krawiec, *supra* note 59, at 584 (noting that fines can be "reduc[ed] to as little as one-twentieth or increase[ed] by as much as four hundred percent" based on the presence of an internal compliance program). This mitigation, however, is unavailable when criminal liability triggers the firm's unraveling.

75. To focus on the impact of criminal liability on the incentives of *firms*, we assume in this Part that employees face no meaningful threat of personal liability for their misconduct.

rate in preventing fraud. With Moderate monitoring, the likelihood of preventing each offense is only 20%. The following table describes the probability that the firm's employees commit one, two, or no offenses under each monitoring level:

Table 4. Employee Misconduct and Monitoring

Number of Offenses	Probability with Moderate Monitoring	Probability with Extensive Monitoring
0	0.04	0.25
1	0.32	0.5
2	0.64	0.25

Now consider the firm's expected liability costs under the assumption that the government ultimately detects each offense. With no monitoring, the firm would surely go out of business, i.e., its expected liability cost would be 100 (that is, the total value of its assets). The firm's expected liability cost is 96 with Moderate monitoring,[76] and 75 with Extensive monitoring.[77] The firm's marginal benefit from Extensive monitoring—i.e., the amount it expects to save by moving from Moderate to Extensive monitoring—is therefore 21.

The remainder of this Part shows that the liability schemes that we considered in the previous Part—civil fines and criminal liability under the pervasiveness standard—might contain misconduct more effectively than the current criminal liability regime. For each liability scheme, we demonstrate that the firm's incentive to implement Extensive monitoring may be stronger than under the threat of going out of business.

2. *Civil fines*

Limiting the sanction to civil fines (assuming such fines do not exceed the firm's assets of course) can enhance deterrence because it ensures that firms' liability costs will rise with the number of violations committed by their agents. In other words, a regime of purely financial penalties allows enforcement officials to create a gradual penalty schedule, thus preserving marginal incentives to monitor. Each violation increases the total amount of fines that the

76. With a probability of 0.32, only one offense will take place and the firm will pay a fine of $100. With a probability of 0.64, two offenses will take place. Even if two offenses take place, the effective fine remains $100. The total expected cost under Moderate monitoring is thus $0.32 \times 100 + 0.64 \times 100$.

77. With a probability of 0.5, only one offense will take place and the firm will pay a fine of $100. With a probability of 0.25, two offenses will take place. Again, even if two offenses take place, the effective fine remains $100. The total expected cost under Extensive monitoring is thus $0.5 \times 100 + 0.25 \times 100$.

firm would ultimately have to pay, and, accordingly, each offense that the firm prevents reduces its expected liability costs.

In our example, assume that the fine for each violation is 50. The firm thus faces a fine of 50 if one employee commits fraud, and a fine of 100 if two employees commit fraud. The firm's expected sanction is 80 with Moderate monitoring,[78] and 50 with Extensive monitoring.[79] The firm's benefit from shifting from Moderate to Extensive monitoring is therefore 30. This benefit exceeds the marginal benefit from Extensive monitoring under a fine of 100 for each violation, which was 21.

3. *Criminal liability: pervasiveness*

Consider next a regime under which firms are held criminally liable only when wrongdoing is sufficiently pervasive. In our example, we take the pervasiveness standard to hold firms liable only when at least two employees commit an offense.

Although it allows firms to escape liability for certain offenses (when only one employee commits misconduct), the pervasiveness standard will bolster the firm's monitoring incentives in this example. The firm's expected sanction is 64 with Moderate monitoring,[80] and 25 with Extensive monitoring.[81] The firm's benefit from shifting from Moderate to Extensive monitoring is 39. Therefore, firms for which the cost of increasing monitoring from Moderate to Extensive is between 21 and 39 would not adopt Extensive monitoring under the existing criminal liability regime, but would do so under the pervasiveness standard.

The intuition is as follows. In our example, a firm that increases its monitoring effort will reduce the expected number of offenses below two, but adopting Extensive monitoring cannot reduce the expected number of offenses below one. Under the existing vicarious liability regime for entity liability, however, an investment in monitoring is economically worthwhile for the firm only to the extent that it reduces the expected number of offenses to zero (or below one). In contrast, under the pervasiveness standard, monitoring is valuable if it reduces the expected number of offenses below two.

78. With a probability of 0.32, only one employee commits fraud, thereby subjecting the firm to a fine of 50. With a probability of 0.64, two employees will commit fraud, thereby subjecting the firm to a total fine of 100.

79. With a probability of 0.5, only one employee commits fraud, thereby subjecting the firm to a sanction of 50. With a probability of 0.25, two employees will commit fraud, thereby subjecting the firm to a total fine of 100.

80. Recall that the probability that two employees will commit fraud under Moderate monitoring is 0.64.

81. The probability that two employees will commit fraud under Extensive monitoring is 0.25.

Another way to understand the deterrence value of the pervasiveness standard is to consider the following perspective: the government's task is to encourage monitoring while using a sanction that can be deployed only once given the collateral consequences of the firm's criminal liability. To achieve this goal, the government needs to target only firms that failed to monitor.[82] The government therefore should impose liability only when the outcome—the number of offenses in this case—is more likely to indicate the firm's failure to monitor rather than a failure of the monitoring measures that the firm did adopt. Because even optimal monitoring may fail to eliminate misconduct, a small number of offenses would often be a poor signal for the firm's monitoring effort. In contrast, a relatively large number of violations credibly signals that the firm did fail to monitor for wrongdoing.[83]

B. *When Will Corporate Criminal Liability Fail?*

We have thus far shown that the collateral consequences that normally follow a business entity's conviction might adversely affect firms' incentives to police their agents, and undermine the deterrence effect of professional firms' profit-sharing arrangements. We have also explained, however, that harsh penalties might sometime be quite effective. Before we turn to explore the policy implications of our analysis, we would like to address an important question. Can one predict the cases in which the threat of going out of business would likely fail to deter organizational misconduct?

This Subpart identifies the conditions under which the existing regime of corporate criminal liability is likely to fail. These conditions vary by offense type, organizational structure, enforcement policy, and the availability of effective compliance measures. For our present purposes, however, it is important to stress that the existing regime undermines the deterrence of exactly those firms for which the need to provide compliance incentives is strongest.

For simplicity, assume that criminal liability would force firms to go out of business. The threat of going out of business can distort monitoring incentives when firms are likely to be convicted notwithstanding their effort to prevent wrongdoing. Likewise, it will undermine deterrence of professional firms' members when each member expects the firm to unravel regardless of her own conduct. Other things equal, therefore, the dissolution threat becomes less effective when: (i) firms are unlikely to eliminate wrongdoing by monitoring; (ii) employees (or members) are prone to commit misconduct; (iii) the probability that the government will detect misconduct is high. We discuss each

82. A negligence standard also is likely to achieve this goal. *See infra* Part IV.B.

83. For some offenses, even a single offense can indicate that the firm did not monitor. We discuss this point below. *See infra* Part III.B.2.

of these conditions below with respect to both professional firms and business organizations more generally.

1. *Monitoring technology*

Firms rely on a variety of internal control mechanisms to prevent their agents from committing misconduct. When the available monitoring devices are relatively ineffective at averting violations, it is likely that at least one violation will take place notwithstanding the firm's compliance measures. This in turn would undermine marginal incentives to monitor, as firms could unravel notwithstanding their investment in policing measures. An ineffective monitoring technology thus increases the likelihood that criminal liability carrying harsh collateral consequences would undermine monitoring incentives.

The effectiveness of the firm's monitoring measures can also affect member incentives in professional firms. When the firm has an effective monitoring scheme in place, members expect the firm to detect and prevent violations. Effective monitoring thus makes members less likely to act under the assumption that the firm will unravel anyway for others' actions. Each member then becomes more pivotal, as her actions are likely to increase substantially the firm's exposure to the risk of dissolution. In other words, a relatively effective system of internal controls reduces the likelihood that members will make decisions in a strategic setting.

2. *Personal gain from wrongdoing*

Firms' success rate in preventing agent misconduct is determined not only by the degree to which monitoring is effective, but also by the extent to which agents are prone to commit offenses to begin with. Individuals, in turn, are more likely to commit misconduct when they derive a *personal* benefit from doing so.[84]

Accordingly, criminal liability carrying severe collateral consequences is more likely to undermine firms' monitoring incentives when agents derive substantial personal benefits from wrongdoing. Likewise, when the personal gains from misconduct are relatively significant, members of professional firms are more likely to expect other members to commit violations that would trigger the firm's demise.

To be sure, the existing federal regime holds organizations criminally liable only for actions that were taken with the intent to benefit the organization.[85] Courts, however, often convict corporations even for offenses that were committed primarily for the benefit of the individual offender.[86]

84. *See supra* note 59.

85. *See* Alan C. Michaels, *Fastow and Arthur Andersen: Some Reflections on Corporate Criminality, Victim Status, and Retribution*, 1 OHIO ST. J. CRIM. L. 551, 554

3. *Firm size and structure*

An organization's size and structure undoubtedly affect its ability to eliminate agent misconduct. When a firm has numerous agents, it becomes likely that some agents will commit misconduct notwithstanding the firm's policing effort. This description also applies to business organizations with a decentralized structure under which decision making and responsibility are diffuse. This in turn increases the risk that an organization that has adopted adequate policing measures would nevertheless go out of business as a result of a single violation of one of its agents. Thus, a regime under which even a single violation can trigger a firm's demise may turn out to undermine deterrence especially in large organizations.

Firm size also matters for professional firms. A member of a professional firm with a relatively large number of members (perhaps even working at different locations) is unlikely to possess information concerning his colleagues' conduct. In other words, such a member would decide whether to commit misconduct under conditions of uncertainty. Moreover, the increase in the number of members and other employees also increases the probability that at least one of the firm's agents will commit an offense, thereby causing the firm to unravel anyway. Members' expectations that one of the firm's agents would commit misconduct significantly undermine their compliance incentives under the threat of going out of business.

4. *Enforcement policy*

The threat of going out of business is more likely to undermine deterrence when the probability of the firm's conviction following misconduct is high. The previous Part explained the connection between such probability and deterrence in professional firms.[87] In this Part, we explore the link between the probability of conviction and organizations' monitoring incentives.

Other things equal, when the government's probability of detecting each offense is relatively small, detecting even a small number of violations is more likely to indicate the firm's failure to monitor. Conversely, if the probability of government's detection is high, detecting a small number of offenses is less likely to indicate the firm's failure to invest in monitoring.[88] Holding the firm criminally liable would then operate to dilute deterrence instead of enhancing it.

(2004).

86. *See* Buell, *supra* note 46, at 1662 ("[C]ourts have all but read the 'intent to benefit' element out of the law."); *see also* United States v. Potter, 463 F.3d 9, 25 (1st Cir. 2006).

87. *See supra* Part II.B.3.

88. Likewise, when the probability of detection is small, firms can benefit from imperfect monitoring by reducing the probability of a conviction.

Note that the probability of conviction is affected by the legal regime in place. The probability of going out of business as a result of criminal liability is determined by the probability of detection and the probability of the firm's conviction. The intensity of the government's enforcement efforts affects the probability of detecting violations. The likelihood of conviction, in contrast, is largely determined by the applicable liability regime. Under the existing regime—which subjects firms to liability for virtually all offenses committed within the scope of employment—prosecutors have a relatively light burden when trying to convict an organization for its agents' crimes. This makes the probability of conviction roughly equal to the probability that the government would detect a violation.[89]

To summarize, the precise conditions under which the firm's possible dissolution might undermine deterrence vary by offense type, firm attributes, and governmental policy. The analysis in this Part, however, suggests that the threat of going out of business may be an inferior deterrent in those firms for which entity-level criminal liability is important from a deterrence perspective.

One of the primary goals of entity criminal liability is to overcome the difficulty of identifying culpable individuals within firms.[90] The government's task of identifying individual offenders and establishing their culpability in court becomes more challenging when the violation took place within a large organization with diffused decision-making structures.[91] Even professional firms are now large, geographically dispersed organizations with many members and other employees. Arthur Andersen, for example, had 85,000 employees in approximately 390 offices in 85 countries prior to its conviction.[92]

Entity criminal liability is thus vital for combating misconduct within large, decentralized firms. In many cases, however, such firms are virtually incapable of eliminating wrongdoing even when they properly invest in monitoring, policing, or other compliance measures.[93] In these firms, therefore,

89. *See* Garrett, *supra* note 2, at 879 ("[T]he DOJ can readily obtain convictions given broad respondeat superior liability and substantive criminal law."); Gerard E. Lynch, *The Role of Criminal Law in Policing Corporate Misconduct*, 60 LAW & CONTEMP. PROBS. 23, 24 (1997) ("[T]here is often no distinction between what the prosecutor would have to prove to establish a crime and what the relevant administrative agency or a private plaintiff would have to prove to show civil liability.").

90. *See supra* text accompanying notes 51-53.

91. *See, e.g.*, Note, *supra* note 49.

92. *See* Ainslie, *supra* note 5, at 109.

93. *See* United States *ex rel.* Porter v. Kroger Grocery & Baking Co., 163 F.2d 168, 177 (7th Cir. 1947) ("As the magnitude of a business increased, with its personal supervision further removed, we apprehend that the difficulties were correspondingly enhanced. Certainly 100% compliance could not be expected in any event; in fact, it would be impossible."). This is also evidenced by the blooming industry of compliance programs that apparently fail to eliminate misconduct. *See generally* Kimberly D. Krawiec, *Cosmetic Compliance and the Failure of Negotiated Governance*, 81 WASH. U. L.Q. 487 (2003) (noting that internal compliance mechanisms fail to deter misconduct and merely reduce

trying to bolster deterrence by subjecting the entity to criminal liability carrying severe collateral consequences can ultimately backfire.

IV. IMPLICATIONS: CRIMINAL LAW AND BEYOND

This Part explores the policy implications of our findings. We first put forward several prescriptions concerning the criminal liability of business organizations. In Subpart A, we argue that legal systems should generally abandon entity-level penalties carrying severe collateral consequences. In Subpart B, we explore the conditions under which a firm should be held liable when a conviction is likely to trigger its dissolution. We then explore the implications of our analysis outside criminal law. Subpart C explains why prohibiting professional firms from incorporating as entities with limited liability might undermine deterrence.

A. *The Case for Purely Monetary Penalties*

Finding a business entity criminally liable can trigger a variety of sanctions that aim at—or have the collateral effect of—putting firms out of business. Not surprisingly, these sanctions raise a host of fairness-based objections.[94] After all, a firm's demise can impose undue hardship on innocent parties, such as the firm's employees, suppliers, and even entire communities. This Article, however, offers a novel deterrence rationale for abandoning such penalties—or any other severe penalties that can be deployed only once.[95]

We have shown that purely financial sanctions would contain organizational misconduct more effectively than harsher entity-level sanctions. To be sure, the threat of going out of business might provide firms with powerful compliance incentives in some cases. As we explained in the previous Part, however, harsh entity-level penalties are especially prone to undermine the deterrence of those firms for which the need for corporate liability is strongest.

Given the uncertain impact of sanctions with severe collateral consequences, we believe that lawmakers should generally limit penalties—whether imposed directly in the criminal trial or as a collateral consequence of conviction—to monetary fines that would not trigger firms' demise.[96]

---

legal liability and improve market legitimacy).

94. For a comprehensive analysis, see generally Darryl K. Brown, *Third Party Interests in Criminal Law*, 80 TEX. L. REV. 1383 (2002) (assessing the implications of considering the collateral consequences of prosecution and punishment).

95. *See* Ted Schneyer, *Professional Discipline for Law Firms?*, 77 CORNELL L. REV. 1, 20-21 (1991) (arguing that dissolving law firms or temporarily shutting their doors for attorney misconduct would be inappropriate and ineffective).

96. *See* Ainslie, *supra* note 5, at 110 ("[M]andatory, automatic and drastic civil sanctions in the wake of criminal convictions are unnecessarily harsh and rigid.").

This prescription has several doctrinal implications. First, lawmakers could significantly cut back on the collateral consequences following a conviction. Second, lawmakers could make sure that debarment, delicensing, and other similar sanctions would apply only when consistent with deterrence, as explained in the next Subpart.[97] Finally, as we explained earlier, there is a widespread belief that the devastating effect of a criminal conviction on corporate reputation is the principal feature that distinguishes criminal from civil liability. To the best of our knowledge, there is no empirical study that proves this belief to be accurate across industries, that is, that shows that the sheer act of convicting an entity for a crime—regardless of any collateral legal consequences—will cause a firm to unravel. Yet, to the extent that the disastrous effects of entity criminal liability are indeed beyond the government's control, lawmakers should narrow down the conditions under which entities could be held criminally liable.

B. *Reforming Entity Criminal Liability*

The goal of eliminating all forms of severe collateral consequences is likely unattainable. For example, the SEC rule disqualifying an accounting firm convicted of a felony from auditing public companies is unlikely to be repealed, and it is equally unlikely that accounting firms will get blanket immunity from criminal liability. In this Subpart, we consider what liability standard should apply when a conviction will trigger the firm's demise.

The respondeat superior doctrine, which governs corporate criminal liability under federal law, holds firms liable whenever their agent commits an offense within the scope of employment. Legal economists, who have been skeptical of any attempt to incorporate notions of individual fault into the entity-liability context,[98] generally believe that this doctrine provides business entities with optimal incentives to prevent misconduct.[99]

97. The debarment provisions, for example, permit excusing debarment if "the contractor had effective standards of conduct and internal control systems in place at the time of the activity which constitutes cause for debarment or had adopted such procedures prior to any Government investigation of the activity cited as a cause for debarment." 48 C.F.R. § 9.406-1(a)(1) (2008).

98. *See generally* Fischel & Sykes, *supra* note 9 (arguing against criminal prosecution for corporate crimes); V.S. Khanna, *Is the Notion of Corporate Fault a Faulty Notion?: The Case of Corporate Mens Rea*, 79 B.U. L. REV. 355 (1999) (considering when corporate mens rea is appropriate in prosecution and punishment).

99. *See, e.g.*, Fischel & Sykes, *supra* note 9. Jennifer Arlen has shown that strict corporate liability might produce perverse incentives for firms to adopt measures that could increase the likelihood of detecting offenses. *See* Jennifer Arlen, *The Potentially Perverse Effects of Corporate Criminal Liability*, 23 J. LEGAL STUD. 833 (1994). For a comprehensive analysis of modifications that may rectify these distortions, see Arlen & Kraakman, *supra* note 52.

The previous Parts, however, demonstrated that combining the death penalty with respondeat superior might undermine deterrence. So what liability standard should apply when a firm's criminal conviction is likely to trigger its demise?

1. *Top management involvement*

The principal alternative to respondeat superior focuses on the extent to which senior management was involved in wrongdoing.[100] Under the Model Penal Code, for example, entity criminal liability for "mens rea" offenses requires the involvement of an agent with sufficient seniority.[101]

At first blush, top management's involvement appears to alleviate the concern that the threat of going out of business will undermine deterrence. After all, one could argue that senior management's participation is the best evidence for a firm's failure to make a genuine effort to prevent misconduct. Relatedly, such participation is less likely to reflect some coordination failure afflicting members within professional firms.

This liability standard, however, has two principal flaws. First, the involvement of senior officers does not eliminate the concern that the threat of going out of business will undercut deterrence. Even senior officers are agents who need to be monitored by the entity's ultimate owners—shareholders (or members of professional firms). And even senior officers might commit crimes with neither the cooperation nor the knowledge of other members of management. In fact, monitoring senior management by shareholders (or members) might be far more costly than monitoring rank-and-file employees.[102]

Second, this standard distorts organizational incentives for gathering and sharing information.[103] Regardless of the penalty accompanying liability,

100. Another group of standards focuses on organizational measures of culpability, which can be loosely defined as corporate ethos or corporate culture. These standards of organizational culpability tend to be somewhat indeterminate. *See, e.g.*, Pamela H. Bucy, *Corporate Ethos: A Standard for Imposing Corporate Criminal Liability*, 75 MINN. L. REV. 1095 (1991).

101. *See* MODEL PENAL CODE § 2.07(1)(c) (1985); *see also* Commonwealth v. L.A.L. Corp., 511 N.E.2d 599, 602 (Mass. 1987) ("The Commonwealth must prove that the individual for whose conduct it seeks to charge the corporation criminally was placed in a position by the corporation where he had enough power, duty, responsibility and authority to act for and in behalf of the corporation to handle the particular business or operation or project . . . ." (emphasis omitted)). For a survey of states that adopted various formulations of the MPC standard, see RICHARD S. GRUNER, CORPORATE CRIME AND SENTENCING §§ 7.025-.036 (2d ed. 1997). Management's involvement also can dramatically affect the magnitude of sanctions under the federal sentencing guidelines. *See* William S. Laufer, *Corporate Liability, Risk Shifting, and the Paradox of Compliance*, 52 VAND. L. REV. 1343, 1384-86 (1999).

102. *See* Fischel & Sykes, *supra* note 9, at 324-25.

103. *See, e.g.*, Assaf Hamdani, *Mens Rea and the Cost of Ignorance*, 93 VA. L. REV.

holding firms liable only when senior executives are involved would discourage firms from monitoring for violations by rank-and-file employees, and encourage senior officers to distance themselves from any knowledge concerning misconduct.[104]

2. *Negligence*

A well functioning negligence regime could provide firms with optimal incentives to monitor their agents. Under a negligence standard, firms would be liable only when they failed to make an adequate investment in monitoring their employees. Firms that implemented proper monitoring measures would be insulated from liability even when some offenses were committed notwithstanding their compliance effort. Combining harsh entity-level penalties with negligence is therefore unlikely to distort monitoring incentives even when monitoring is not foolproof.[105]

A negligence regime, however, might perform even worse than respondeat superior with respect to professional firms' members. Consider a professional firm that implements an optimal monitoring scheme that leaves some misconduct undetected. Given the limited success of the firm's policing measures, one could expect the firm's profit-sharing arrangements to kick in and discourage members from committing misconduct. Yet, under a negligence standard, the firm will be exempt from liability given its investment in monitoring. Accordingly, members would have no self-enforcing incentive to refrain from wrongdoing.

We should also note the inherent weakness of all negligence regimes: they require courts to possess both the expertise necessary to set the optimal level of monitoring for each firm and sufficient information to determine whether firms did make an adequate investment in monitoring.[106] Courts, however, may find these tasks to be relatively complex in the corporate setting.

3. *Pervasiveness*

Federal guidelines for prosecuting business organizations direct prosecutors to take into account the extent to which wrongdoing is pervasive

415, 446-47 (2007) (explaining how the "responsible corporate officer" doctrine might discourage monitoring by officers).

104. For the general case against making the involvement of top management a factor in setting corporate sanctions, see Vikramaditya S. Khanna, *Should the Behavior of Top Management Matter?*, 91 GEO. L.J. 1215 (2003).

105. Steve Shavell has shown that negligence standards can be more effective than strict liability in inducing judgment-proof injurers to take care. *See* S. Shavell, *The Judgment Proof Problem*, 6 INT'L REV. L. & ECON. 45, 47-48 (1986).

106. Firms' efforts to create the impression that they take the necessary steps to prevent misconduct have been referred to as the problem of cosmetic compliance. *See* Krawiec, *supra* note 93.

within the firm.[107] The guidelines provide that pressing criminal charges against organizations is generally inappropriate in the case of the prototypical rogue employee.[108] The guidelines explain, however, that charging a corporation may be appropriate where the wrongdoing was pervasive and was undertaken by a large number of employees or by all the employees.

Commentators often criticize the guidelines' departure from the strictures of respondeat superior.[109] Our analysis, in contrast, provides a deterrence-based justification for adopting the pervasiveness standard when the collateral consequences of a conviction are likely severe.

The previous Parts used a stylized example of a firm with only two employees. But how many offenses would qualify as sufficiently pervasive in larger firms? Ideally, lawmakers would devise a bright-line rule to determine when wrongdoing is sufficiently pervasive to justify an indictment notwithstanding a conviction's harsh collateral consequences. As it turns out, however, there is no single prescription to determine how many offenses render misconduct sufficiently pervasive.

In order to induce firms to invest optimally in monitoring, the number of violations that qualifies as "pervasive" is one that signals the organization's failure to police its agents. As we showed above,[110] this number is a function of the firm's size, its monitoring capabilities, the government's enforcement policy, and agents' private benefit from wrongdoing.

The pervasiveness standard may also prove elusive with respect to professional firms. In this context, the number of violations that qualifies as "pervasive" is one that prevents each member from expecting the firm to unravel irrespective of his decision whether to commit the offense.

The precise meaning of "pervasiveness" thus varies across firms and offense types. However, the factors that predict whether the threat of going out of business would fail also affect the threshold number of offenses under the pervasiveness standard.[111] The threshold number of offenses is thus likely to increase with the probability of the firm's conviction, the difficulty of uprooting misconduct, organizational structure, and agents' gain from

107. *See* Memorandum from Paul J. McNulty, Deputy Attorney Gen., to Heads of Dep't Components, U.S. Attorneys 4 (Dec. 2006) [hereinafter McNulty Memorandum], *available at* http://www.usdoj.gov/dag/ speeches/2006/mcnulty_memo.pdf.

108. *See id.* at 6 ("[I]t may not be appropriate to impose liability upon a corporation, particularly one with a compliance program in place, under a strict respondeat superior theory for the single isolated act of a rogue employee.").

109. *See, e.g.*, Laufer, *supra* note 101; Wray & Hur, *supra* note 8, at 1187 (stressing the need for consistency in federal corporate crime enforcement). On the difference between the federal regime of criminal liability and prosecution policy, see Darryl K. Brown, *The Problematic and Faintly Promising Dynamics of Corporate Crime Enforcement*, 1 OHIO ST. J. CRIM. L. 521, 542 (2004) (noting other ways in which prosecution policy and strict respondeat superior differ).

110. *See supra* Part III.B.

111. *See supra* Part III.B.

wrongdoing. In some cases, even a single violation would satisfy the pervasiveness standard.[112] In others, a larger number of detected offenses would be required to justify an indictment.

Given the context-specific nature of the pervasiveness standard, the best practical approach might be to entrust prosecutors and courts with the task of applying it on a case-by-case basis. To be sure, leaving the application of this standard to prosecutorial discretion has the obvious drawbacks associated with any measure that grants the prosecution considerable authority.[113] We take no position here on the proper limits on prosecutorial power. Rather, we highlight one advantage of leaving this standard somewhat open-ended.

The guidelines further require prosecutors to consider the collateral consequences of a criminal conviction, including the possibility of "suspension or debarment from eligibility for government contracts or federal[ly] funded programs such as health care."[114] We believe, however, that the link between collateral consequences and pervasiveness should become more explicit. When the consequences of a criminal conviction are limited to financial penalties, there is little reason to rely on the pervasiveness standard. Prosecutors should be instructed to take pervasiveness into account only when the collateral consequences of a criminal conviction are sufficiently severe.

The difference between the law on the books—under which firms can be held liable for any offense committed within the scope of employment—and the law in action—under which firms are normally indicted only for pervasive wrongdoing—might provide an answer to the following objection. One might argue that our thesis—that is, criminal liability carrying several collateral consequences might undermine deterrence—seems at odds with the common perception that the existing regime of entity liability does provide firms with strong incentives to prevent misconduct. The response to this objection is that one's perception of the existing regime is largely shaped by the law in action, i.e., the federal guidelines for prosecuting business organizations. To the extent that they actually take into account the pervasiveness of wrongdoing within organizations, prosecutors make it significantly unlikely that entity criminal liability would undermine firms' compliance incentives.

---

112. As we explained above, the corporate death penalty would not always undermine deterrence. When even a single offense is sufficiently indicative of the firm's failure to monitor, or when the probability of the government's detection is sufficiently low, there is little risk that the putting firms out of business for a single offense would undermine deterrence.

113. *See generally* William S. Laufer, *Corporate Prosecution, Cooperation, and the Trading of Favors*, 87 IOWA L. REV. 643, 647, 650-57 (2002) (questioning "the fairness of trading corporate cooperation for government-granted favors" and discussing "the dark side of guideline incentives"); Geraldine Szott Moohr, *Prosecutorial Power in an Adversarial System: Lessons from Current White Collar Cases and the Inquisitorial Model*, 8 BUFF. CRIM. L. REV. 165 (2004).

114. *See* McNulty Memorandum, *supra* note 107, at 16.

4. *Personal liability*

The apportionment of liability among the firm and its officers is one of the toughest challenges for policymakers and legal scholars alike.[115] We have no intention of resolving this issue here. Rather, we argue that when a criminal conviction would produce severe collateral consequences, prosecutors should make an extra effort to subject culpable individuals within the firm to liability.

As we explained earlier,[116] the goal of entity liability is to rectify the likely failure of personal liability to deter misconduct. But when the collateral consequences of criminal liability are too severe, targeting the entity might undermine rather than enhance deterrence. Personal liability, in contrast, ensures that each actor bears the consequences of her misdeeds.

At first glance, our prescription in this Subpart appears inconsistent with one premise underlying this Article, namely, that subjecting the firm to liability is necessary to overcome the difficulty of establishing individual culpability beyond a reasonable doubt.[117] Indeed, our recommendation would be of little value if it were impossible for the prosecution to identify the culpable individual within the organization.

But identifying such an individual is often a matter of cost, i.e., the extent to which the government is willing to undertake the costly effort to acquire evidence. For example, the prosecutors in charge of the Enron investigation spent considerable resources on gathering sufficient evidence to indict Enron's top management. Their effort included two years of attempts to overcome legal stonewalling by Ken Lay, the company's former chairman, to allow investigators to acquire relevant documents,[118] and a complex "building-block" approach of entering into plea bargains with Enron's executives, where these executives agreed to cooperate with investigators' efforts.[119] More generally, the President's Corporate Fraud Task Force has since 2002 secured the convictions of hundreds of senior officers.[120] Our claim is that, other things

115. *See, e.g.*, Jennifer H. Arlen & William J. Carney, *Vicarious Liability for Fraud on Securities Markets: Theory and Evidence*, 1992 U. ILL. L. REV. 691 (arguing that management—and not issuers—should be held liable for certain types of securities fraud); Laufer, *supra* note 101, at 1346 ("[T]he evolution of corporate criminal law in the United States . . . is understood best by examining the shifting risks of liability and loss between corporations and their agents . . . ."). For an insightful analysis of the considerations affecting the choice between entity and personal liability, see Kraakman, *supra* note 50.

116. *See supra* Part II.A.

117. *See supra* Part II.A.

118. *See* Kathleen F. Brickey, *Enron's Legacy*, 8 BUFF. CRIM. L. REV. 221, 273-74 (2004).

119. *Id.* at 272.

120. *See* Press Release, Dep't of Justice, Fact Sheet: President's Corporate Fraud Task Force Marks Five Years of Ensuring Corporate Integrity (July 17, 2007), *available at* http://www.usdoj.gov/opa/pr/2007/July/07_odag_507.html (reporting the fraud-related convictions of 214 CEOs and presidents, 53 chief financial officers, and 129 vice presidents).

equal, the investment in gathering evidence against individual wrongdoers becomes more justified when indicting the entity might trigger its dissolution.

5. *The KPMG affair*

We conclude this Subpart by considering the recent investigation against the accounting firm KPMG in light of our analysis. Although it seriously considered pressing charges against the firm for marketing tax shelters, the Department of Justice eventually decided against taking such a step, presumably in light of concerns that the demise of yet another big accounting firm would increase the concentration in the market for auditing services. However, after admitting wrongdoing, the firm had to pay a fine and enter into a deferred prosecution agreement in order to avoid a criminal indictment. In other words, the firm barely escaped criminal liability that would have led to its demise.[121]

Interestingly, KPMG was not the only professional firm allegedly involved in this tax shelter affair. It turns out that Raymond J. Ruble, a partner at the law firm Sidley Austin Brown & Wood LLP, issued numerous legal opinions supporting the legality of the transactions at stake. The government indeed indicted Ruble for his role in marketing these tax shelters.[122]

Under the existing regime of respondeat superior, the government could have indicted not only the partner involved, but also the law firm itself. Indeed, Sidley Austin settled a lawsuit filed by investors in those tax shelters and agreed to pay to the IRS a *civil* penalty of $39.4 million for its role in the tax shelter affair.[123] Unlike in the case of KPMG, however, federal prosecutors did not press charges against (or enter into a deferred prosecution agreement with) the law firm, citing the fact that its tax shelter work had been primarily carried out by one person.[124]

Our analysis sheds a new light on the government's distinction between KPMG and Sidley Austin. The reported evidence shows that a relatively large number of senior KPMG officials participated in the scheme to market the allegedly abusive tax shelter.[125] In other words, wrongdoing was pervasive and not the result of an isolated decision taken by members of the firm in a strategic

121. David Reilly, *Narrow Escape: How a Chastened KPMG Got By Tax-Shelter Crisis*, WALL ST. J., Feb. 15, 2007, at A1.

122. *See* Carrie Johnson, *9 Charged over Tax Shelters in KPMG Case*, WASH. POST, Aug. 30, 2005, at A1.

123. *See* Ben Hallman, *Damage Control: Sidley Agrees to Pay $40 Million for a Rogue Partner's Tax Shelter Schemes. But the Tab Is Still Running*, AM. LAW., Nov. 2005, at 18.

124. *See* Lynnley Browning, *Court Ruling Jeopardizes U.S. Tax Case*, N.Y. TIMES, May 24, 2007, at C1.

125. *See* Buell, *supra* note 43, at 488-89 (reporting KPMG's admission that the conduct involved "dozens of KPMG partners and other personnel").

setting. There was thus little risk that subjecting the firm to criminal liability for its tax-shelter activities would undermine deterrence in future similarly situated firms.

On the other hand, the publicly available evidence indicates that Ruble acted alone, with neither cooperation nor endorsement by his partners. In fact, Ruble was subsequently forced to resign after it turned out that he did not accurately report to his own firm the amount of the fees he received for providing legal opinions to tax shelter clients.[126] Under these circumstances, holding the law firm criminally liable (with the probable outcome of putting it out of business) would have been unwise from a deterrence perspective.

We should stress that we do not argue that firms should face no liability whatsoever for the acts of rogue employees. Rather, we believe that when liability is likely to trigger an entity's demise, convicting the firm for a single employee's misconduct might undermine compliance incentives.

C. *Unlimited Liability of Professional Firms*

The implications of our analysis are not limited to criminal law. Our core insight—that harsh penalties might undermine deterrence in group settings—applies to other cases of collective sanctions, whether civil or criminal. In this Subpart, we use our analysis to shed a new light on the controversy over unlimited liability for professional firms.

For many years, the law required professional firms to organize as general partnerships. Under partnership law, general partners are jointly and severally liable for wrongful acts committed by partners. In recent years, however, there has been a widespread trend among states to allow professional firms to enjoy the benefits of limited liability.[127] This move has always been controversial,[128] and it became even more so in the aftermath of the recent spate of corporate scandals.[129]

Like in the case of the harsh corporate penalties, critics of limited liability for professional firms posit that unlimited liability would bolster deterrence, increase incentives to monitor,[130] and further discourage members from

126. *See* Lynnley Browning, *Top Tax Shelter Lawyer No Longer at a Big Firm*, N.Y. TIMES, June 30, 2004, at C1.

127. Partners are still liable for their own wrongful acts under all limited liability statutes for professional firms. Some states also hold partners liable for the acts of those whom they supervise and control. *See* Jennifer J. Johnson, *Limited Liability for Lawyers: General Partners Need Not Apply*, 51 BUS. LAW. 85, 94-95 (1995).

128. *See generally* Martin C. McWilliams, Jr., *Who Bears the Costs of Lawyers' Mistakes?—Against Limited Liability*, 36 ARIZ. ST. L.J. 885 (2004); Puri, *supra* note 16.

129. *See* sources cited *supra* note 21.

130. *See, e.g.*, Larry E. Ribstein, *Ethical Rules, Agency Costs, and Law Firm Structure*, 84 VA. L. REV. 1707, 1727 (1998) ("A public interest rationale for some form of mandatory vicarious liability is that it increases monitoring beyond what lawyers otherwise would do in the absence of a mandatory rule.").

committing misconduct.[131] Supporters of limited liability contend that it would reduce internal agency costs and allow firms to grow larger.[132] Our analysis, however, shows that holding individual partners liable for the misconduct of their peers might prove counterproductive by diluting deterrence.

Under a regime of unlimited liability, individual partners might lose all their wealth for a single act of misconduct, producing a catastrophic loss.[133] On the one hand, this increase in liability exposure might strengthen partners' incentives to monitor against misconduct.[134] With their personal wealth at risk, partners—whether individually or as a group—would likely increase the investment in monitoring and policing employees and other partners. On the other hand, subjecting individual partners to harsh financial consequences as a result of others' misconduct might undermine deterrence.

Consider first the paradigmatic small professional firms. When partners can cheaply monitor their colleagues, holding them liable for wrongdoing committed by their partners will likely motivate them to effectively police their peers. In this case, therefore, unlimited liability will likely bolster deterrence.

But the effect of unlimited liability might differ with respect to the modern professional firm, with a large number of partners working at different locations. Members of such firms are incapable of monitoring their colleagues to eliminate wrongdoing. Moreover, the liability exposure of members of large firms is greater—both in terms of the likely magnitude of damages and the higher probability of misconduct given the large number of members. A partner might thus face a decision whether to engage in wrongdoing in a strategic setting—when a partner's wealth depends not only on her own decision but also on the acts of others. Under conditions of uncertainty, a partner might estimate that her entire wealth is at a serious risk anyway. In this case, a regime of unlimited liability would undermine deterrence at the level of the individual partner.[135] Indeed, there is evidence that a limited liability organizational form is more likely to be adopted by larger law firms.[136]

131. For a review of the arguments for unlimited liability of professional firms, see Larry E. Ribstein, *Limited Liability of Professional Firms After Enron*, 29 J. CORP. L. 427, 429 (2004).

132. *See, e.g.*, Ribstein, *supra* note 130, at 1707-08 (asserting that limited liability allows law firms to grow larger).

133. *See, e.g.*, Floyd Norris, *Will Big Four Audit Firms Survive in a World of Unlimited Liability?*, N.Y. TIMES, Sept. 10, 2004, at C1 (reporting a concern that auditor liability would cause audit firms to become insolvent). In theory, partners who are required to bear the cost associated with liability could recover from other partners. However, this is unlikely to provide a meaningful relief. *See* Ribstein, *supra* note 131, at 435.

134. The literature typically depicts unlimited liability as inducing partners to intensify their own monitoring effort rather than increasing the amount that the *firm* expends on monitoring. *See, e.g.*, Scott Baker & Kimberly D. Krawiec, *The Economics of Limited Liability: An Empirical Study of New York Law Firms*, 2005 U. ILL. L. REV. 107, 115 ("[U]nlimited liability encourages monitoring of each partner by every other partner.").

135. The problem might be mitigated, but not eliminated, to the extent that the regime of unlimited liability requires each partner to bear only her share of the damages. *See* Henry

V. CONCLUSION

Since Enron imploded in late 2001, the government has increasingly relied on criminal law to combat organizational misconduct. Targeting business organizations, however, can lead them to unravel, thereby subjecting employees, communities, and other innocent parties to harsh collateral consequences.

The dire consequences of entity criminal liability occupy center stage in the decades-old debate concerning corporate criminal liability. Critics contend that these consequences render entity criminal liability unjust. Others, however, believe that the uniquely severe impact of criminal liability turns it into the most effective tool for combating organizational misconduct.

This Article, however, demonstrated that using the threat of going out of business as a deterrent may be unwise. Harsh corporate penalties might distort firms' incentives to monitor for misconduct, and undermine deterrence of professional firms' members. Moreover, more lenient regimes—such as holding firms liable only for pervasive wrongdoing—might bolster compliance incentives within organizations.

Given the uncertainty concerning their ultimate effect, policymakers should generally ensure that entities are not subject to penalties carrying severe collateral consequences. Alternatively, we explored what liability standard should apply when a conviction would inevitably lead a firm to unravel.

The implications of our analysis are not limited to entity criminal liability. Our core insight—that harsh penalties might undermine deterrence in group settings—illuminates other instances of collective sanctions as well. For example, our analysis suggests that prohibiting law and accounting firms from organizing as limited liability entities might undermine rather than enhance the incentives of their members to refrain from wrongdoing.

Hansmann & Reinier Kraakman, *Toward Unlimited Shareholder Liability for Corporate Torts*, 100 YALE L.J. 1879 (1991). Also, the problem could be solved if professional firms could purchase satisfactory liability insurance.

136. *See* John Romley & Eric Talley, *Uncorporated Professionals* (U.S.C. CLEO Res. Paper No. C04-18, U.S.C. Law & Econ. Res. Paper No. 04-22), *available at* http://ssrn.com/abstract=587982.

APPENDIX: MEMBER INCENTIVES IN PROFESSIONAL FIRMS

This Appendix generalizes the example that we discuss in Part I.B.[137]

A. *The Threshold B* Under the Existing Criminal Liability Regime*

Let p be the probability that an offense is detected and triggers a conviction. An attorney's gain from misconduct is his private information, whereas the other only knows that it is drawn from a uniform distribution on [0,100]. Denote this benefit by B_E for Elizabeth and B_J for John.

Table 5. The Professional Firm Misconduct Game: Criminal Liability

		Elizabeth	
		Don't Commit	Commit
John	Don't Commit	0, 0	$-80p$, B_E-80p
	Commit	B_J-80p, $-80p$	$B_J-80(1-(1-p)^2)$, $B_E-80(1-(1-p)^{2)}$

We look for a symmetric Bayesian Nash Equilibrium.[138] Denote by B^* the threshold benefit in such equilibrium, so that all attorneys whose benefit exceeds B^* commit misconduct, and all attorneys whose benefit is lower than B^* do not commit it. By hypothesis, an attorney whose benefit is B^* must be indifferent between committing and not committing an offense. Using simple algebra it can be shown that the indifference condition is:

$$B^* - 80p - 80p(1-p)\left(1-\frac{B^*}{100}\right) = -80p\left(1-\frac{B^*}{100}\right)$$

Rearranging this condition we get:

$$B^* = \frac{80p(1-p)}{1-0.8p^2}$$

Substituting 0.9 for p, as we do in the example in Part I.A, we get B^*=20.45. The graph in Figure 1 is obtained by finding the threshold B^* for each probability of conviction, p, between 0 and 1.

---

137. For a description of the game's setup, see *supra* Part II.A.

138. For a definition of a Bayesian Nash Equilibrium, see DREW FUDENBERG & JEAN TIROLE, GAME THEORY 215 (1991).

B. *The Threshold B* Under Civil Fines*

When the fine for each offense is 80, the game matrix is:

Table 6. The Professional Firm Misconduct Game: Civil Fines

		Elizabeth	
		Don't Commit	Commit
John	Don't Commit	0, 0	$-40p$, B_E-$40p$
	Commit	B_J-$40p$, $-40p$	B_J-$80p$, B_E-$80p$

Now an attorney would commit the offense if and only if $B>40p$. The threshold is, therefore, $B^*=40p$. If $p=0.9$ then $B^*=36$.

C. *The Threshold B* Under the Pervasiveness Standard*

Under the pervasiveness standard the matrix is the following:

Table 7. The Professional Firm Misconduct Game: Pervasiveness Standard

		Elizabeth	
		Don't Commit	Commit
John	Don't Commit	0, 0	0, B_E
	Commit	B_J, 0	B_J-$80p^2$, B_E-$80p$

The indifference condition for each player is then:

$$B^* - 80p^2\left(1 - \frac{B^*}{100}\right) = 0$$

Rearranging, we get:

$$B^* = \frac{80p^2}{1 + 0.8p^2}$$

Substituting 0.9 for p, as we do in our example in Part I.B, we get $B^*=39.3$.

Part VI
Critics

[14]

THE SECRET AMBITION OF DETERRENCE

Dan M. Kahan

TABLE OF CONTENTS

THE SECRET AMBITION OF DETERRENCE

*Dan M. Kahan**

In this Article, Professor Kahan identifies the political and moral economies of deterrence theory in legal discourse. Drawing on an extensive social science literature, he shows that deterrence arguments in fact have little impact on citizens' views on controversial policies such as capital punishment, gun control, and hate crime laws. Citizens conventionally defend their positions in deterrence terms only because the alternative is a highly contentious expressive idiom, which social norms, strategic calculation, and liberal morality all condemn. But not all citizens respond to these forces. Expressive zealots have an incentive to frame controversial issues in culturally partisan terms, thereby forcing moderate citizens to defect from the deterrence détente and declare their cultural allegiances as well. Accordingly, deliberations permanently cycle between the disengaged, face-saving idiom of deterrence and the partisan, face-breaking idiom of expressive condemnation. These dynamics, Professor Kahan argues, complicate the normative assessment of deterrence. By abstracting from contentious expressive judgments, deterrence arguments serve the ends of liberal public reason, which enjoins citizens to advance arguments accessible to individuals of diverse moral persuasions. But precisely because deterrence arguments denude the law of social meaning, the prominence of the deterrence idiom impedes progressives from harnessing the expressive power of the law to challenge unjust social norms. There is no stable discourse equilibrium between the deterrence and expressive idioms, either as a positive matter or a normative one.

I don't say all I think in the opinion. — Oliver Wendell Holmes, Jr.[1]

IN his provocative essay, "The Secret History of Self-Interest," political philosopher Stephen Holmes suggests that classical liberal thought harbors more ambitions than meet the eye.[2] The impetus for Holmes's inquiry is the view that derides the liberal ideal of self-interest as demeaning to our higher ends and corrosive of friendship, public-spiritedness, and other self-effacing virtues. This antiliberal critique, according to Holmes, is naïvely ahistorical. Classical liberals,

---

* Professor, Yale Law School. I am grateful to Yale Law School and to the Russell J. Parsons Faculty Research Fund at the University of Chicago for generous financial support; to Darwin Roberts and Jeremy Bates for research assistance; to Kenworthey Bilz, James Boyle, Jules Coleman, Alon Harel, Elena Kagan, Brian Leiter, Lawrence Lessig, Jerry Mashaw, Bernie Meltzer, Eric Posner, Robert Post, Judith Resnik, Daria Roithmayer, Tanina Rostain, Peter Schuck, and Cass Sunstein for comments on an earlier draft; to participants in workshops at Cardozo Law School, the University of Chicago Law School, Harvard Law School, St. John's University School of Law, and Yale Law School for discussion; and to Bruce Ackerman and Stephen Holmes for inspiration.

[1] Letter from Oliver Wendell Holmes, Jr. to Harold J. Laski (May 12, 1921), *in* 1 HOLMES-LASKI LETTERS: THE CORRESPONDENCE OF MR. JUSTICE HOLMES AND HAROLD J. LASKI 1916–1935, at 262 (Mark DeWolfe Howe ed., Alger Hiss abr. ed. 1963).

[2] *See* Stephen Holmes, *The Secret History of Self-Interest*, *in* STEPHEN HOLMES, PASSIONS AND CONSTRAINT: ON THE THEORY OF LIBERAL DEMOCRACY 42–68 (1995) [hereinafter HOLMES, PASSIONS AND CONSTRAINT].

including Hume and Smith, celebrated self-interest not because they believed it to be a complete moral virtue, but because they saw it as displacing an alternative moral idiom that prized glory and hierarchy and that had produced centuries of violent contention. Exhorted to overcome love of self, individuals are more likely to display heroic *male*volence than heroic *bene*volence. The self-interested pursuit of material wealth, the classical liberals hoped, would calm the violent passions of honor, revenge, and pride. By waging an assault on self-interest, contemporary antiliberals, Holmes suggests, risk inflaming the selflessly *cruel* passions that the classical liberals endeavored to extinguish.[3]

My goal in this Article is to offer a parallel account of *deterrence theory* in American criminal law. I will suggest that the real value of deterrence — its secret ambition — is to quiet illiberal conflict between contending cultural styles and moral outlooks. To attack deterrence theorizing is to invite such conflict.

By "deterrence" I intend to refer broadly to the consequentialist theory, propounded by Bentham and refined by his economist successors, that depicts punishment as a policy aimed at creating efficient behavioral incentives.[4] Deterrence arguments of this sort figure prominently in public debates over capital punishment, gun control, domestic violence, "hate crimes," drugs, and many other criminal law issues.[5]

---

[3] *See id.* at 42–59; *see also* ALBERT O. HIRSCHMAN, THE PASSIONS AND THE INTERESTS: POLITICAL ARGUMENTS FOR CAPITALISM BEFORE ITS TRIUMPH 32 (1977) (providing an account, on which Holmes draws, of the rise of self-interest as a relatively peaceful alternative to the violent passion for glory); James Boyle, *Anachronism of the Moral Sentiments? Integrity, Postmodernism, and Justice*, 51 STAN. L. REV. 493, 510–14 (1999) (proving that one need not be a classical liberal to see the error of equating self-interest with immorality).

[4] The classic exposition is Jeremy Bentham's *The Principles of Morals and Legislation* (Hafner Press 1948) (1823). *See also* Gary S. Becker, *Crime and Punishment: An Economic Approach*, 76 J. POL. ECON. 169 (1968); Richard A. Posner, *An Economic Theory of the Criminal Law*, 85 COLUM. L. REV. 1193 (1985) (providing contemporary accounts).

[5] *See, e.g.*, JOHN R. LOTT, JR., MORE GUNS, LESS CRIME: UNDERSTANDING CRIME AND GUN-CONTROL LAWS 5–18 (1998) (describing the centrality of deterrence claims to the gun control debate); Phoebe C. Ellsworth & Lee Ross, *Public Opinion and Capital Punishment: A Close Examination of the Views of Abolitionists and Retentionists*, 29 CRIME & DELINQ. 116, 145 (1983) ("[B]elief in the deterrent efficacy of the death penalty has generally been the rationale most frequently offered by Retentionists."); Ed Hayward, *Sex-Based Hate Crime Proposal Angers Dads*, BOSTON HERALD, Mar. 7, 1997, at 21 (quoting a supporter of legislation that would allow domestic battering to be prosecuted as a "hate crime": "The only real deterrent for batterers is the threat of serious jail time."); Robert L. Jackson, *Study Assails Mandatory Drug Crime Sentences*, L.A. TIMES, May 13, 1997, at A14, *available in* LEXIS, News Library, News Group File, All (reporting the remarks of Rep. Bill McCollum: "The principal value of mandatory minimum sentences is the certainty of punishment and the deterrent message that that sends.").

Deterrence arguments also draw incessant fire from academic theorists. Empirically, deterrence claims are speculative.[6] Conceptually, they are question-begging, because they ignore (or resolve peremptorily) the issue of what state of affairs the law should be trying to maximize.[7] Evaluatively, they are impoverished: we assess actions and laws for their meanings, individuals for their characters, emotions for the values they embody — all features of our moral experience for which the deterrence theory seems to make no allowance.[8]

Each of these criticisms, I believe, is correct; yet it also seems to me that they all completely miss the point. Consistent with Stephen Holmes's defense of classical liberalism, I want to suggest that the real significance of deterrence theory lies not in what it says but in what it stops us from saying. Just as the moral idiom of "self-interest" displaces an illiberal idiom that focuses on glory, so the rhetoric of deterrence displaces an alternative expressive idiom that produces incessant illiberal conflict over status.

Eruptions of controversy are a familiar, if somewhat puzzling, feature of American criminal law. Pivotal elections are decided on the basis of candidates' positions on capital punishment,[9] millions of dollars are spent by lobbying organizations to influence legislation on gun control,[10] state governors reverse ideological field to accommodate the angry demand that they grant clemency to women convicted of mur-

---

[6] *See generally* NATIONAL RESEARCH COUNCIL, DETERRENCE AND INCAPACITATION: ESTIMATING THE EFFECTS OF CRIMINAL SANCTIONS ON CRIME RATES 4–7 (Alfred Blumstein, Jacqueline Cohen & Daniel Nagin eds., 1978) (describing the inconclusive nature of data on deterrent effects); Franklin M. Fisher, *Multiple Regression in Legal Proceedings*, 80 COLUM. L. REV. 702, 730–35 (1980) (discussing practical constraints on econometric analysis of deterrence effects).

[7] *See* Alvin K. Klevorick, *On the Economic Theory of Crime*, *in* CRIMINAL JUSTICE: NOMOS XXVII 289, 292–94, 301–04 (J. Roland Pennock & John W. Chapman eds., 1985) (maintaining that the economic theory of deterrence fails to account for societal norms that define licit utility); *see also* Paul H. Robinson & John M. Darley, *The Utility of Desert*, 91 NW. U. L. REV. 453, 471–88 (1997) (arguing that the conventional utilitarian conception of deterrence is defective because it neglects to consider how the departure from moral norms diminishes the willingness of citizens to obey the law).

[8] *See* Dan M. Kahan & Martha C. Nussbaum, *Two Conceptions of Emotion in Criminal Law*, 96 COLUM. L. REV. 269, 350–57 (1996).

[9] *See, e.g.*, E.J. Dionne Jr., *Bush Is Elected by a 6–5 Margin with Solid G.O.P. Base in South; Democrats Hold Both Houses*, N.Y. TIMES, Nov. 9, 1988, at A1 (crediting George Bush's presidential victory in large part "to the power of the Vice President's advertising, which attacked . . . Governor[] [Michael Dukakis's] opposition to the death penalty"); Kevin Sack, *New York Voters End a Democratic Era*, N.Y. TIMES, Nov. 9, 1994, at A1 ("George Elmer Pataki, a lanky lawyer-legislator from the Hudson Valley who has promised to slash income taxes and restore the death penalty, was elected the 53d Governor of New York yesterday . . . .").

[10] *See* ROBERT J. SPITZER, THE POLITICS OF GUN CONTROL 105 (1995).

dering abusive mates,[11] and national politics becomes convulsed over flag-burning laws.[12] The intensity of the debate that these policies excite cannot convincingly be explained in terms of their behavioral consequences, which are patently negligible in most cases and exceedingly ambiguous in the rest.

Rather, these disputes are best understood, I will argue, as battles to control the *expressive capital* of the criminal law. They break out when positions on a criminal law issue are associated with the moral understandings of competing subcommunities — whether regional or racial, cultural or economic. Their resolution is often understood to signal whose stock is up and whose is down in the market for social status. Their permanence reflects the abiding illiberal ambition to see one's own distinctive conception of virtue authoritatively confirmed and one's cultural adversaries' officially repudiated.

Deterrence theory helps to cool these expressive disputes. Its disembodied idiom of costs and benefits elides the points of moral contention that motivate public positions on these disputed issues. Citizens of diverse commitments converge on the deterrence idiom to satisfy social norms against contentious public moralizing; public officials likewise converge on it to minimize opposition to their preferred policy outcomes. Ultimately, the deterrence idiom takes the political charge out of contentious issues and deflects expressive contention away from the criminal law. This condition of suppressed expressive contention persists until citizens are impertinently pushed to signal their motivating commitments on these issues by expressive zealots.

I have two objectives. One is to deepen our understanding of how legal discourse contributes to the maintenance of a liberal political order. It is a common theme of contemporary legal and political theory that liberalism depends on forms of "public reason" that mute moral contention.[13] Deterrence theory, I will show, performs exactly this

---

[11] *See, e.g.*, Ray Long & Fran Spielman, *Some See Politics in Clemency Order*, CHI. SUN-TIMES, May 15, 1994, at 5 (reporting on controversial commutations granted by a Republican governor facing a female Democratic candidate in his reelection bid).

[12] *See, e.g.*, ROBERT JUSTIN GOLDSTEIN, BURNING THE FLAG: THE GREAT 1989–1990 AMERICAN FLAG DESECRATION CONTROVERSY (1996).

[13] JOHN RAWLS, *The Idea of Public Reason*, *in* POLITICAL LIBERALISM 212, 212 (1993); *see also* BRUCE A. ACKERMAN, SOCIAL JUSTICE IN THE LIBERAL STATE 8–12 (1980) (arguing for constraints on "power talk" that are grounded in the idea that nobody can claim a privileged insight into the moral universe); AMY GUTMANN & DENNIS THOMPSON, DEMOCRACY AND DISAGREEMENT 52–53 (1996) (concluding that deliberative democracy requires participants to seek "fair terms of cooperation for their own sake"); CASS R. SUNSTEIN, LEGAL REASONING AND POLITICAL CONFLICT 35–48 (1996) (arguing that agreements that are "incompletely theorized" promote liberal goals); David A. Strauss, Legal Argument and the Overlapping Consensus 4–5 (July 12, 1998) (unpublished manuscript, on file with the Harvard Law School Library) (proposing that legal institutions that command widespread allegiance enable liberal societies to function in the face of deep moral divisions).

function in a critical domain of American law. The contribution that deterrence makes to taming public discourse, moreover, complicates the prevailing accounts of what liberal "public reason" should be expected to look like.

My second objective is to expose the unappreciated complexity of the normative status of deterrence. The role that deterrence theory plays in staunching expressive conflict acquits it of the standard arguments against it, all of which ignore its contribution to sustaining liberal politics. Indeed, the conceptual and evaluative poverty of deterrence, along with its false empirical confidence, is exactly what gives this theory its liberal bracketing power. The impertinent debunking of deterrence always risks unleashing divisive public moralizing, a lesson that liberal critics of deterrence theory have largely failed to perceive.

At the same time, the role of deterrence in muting expressive conflict should feed a distinctive *antiliberal* anxiety. The aspirations of liberal public reason notwithstanding, contestable social meanings pervade our politics and law.[14] Not talking about these meanings in a public way doesn't render them inert; if anything, norms that discourage divisive public discourse extend the life of these meanings by making it harder for their critics to expose them and easier for their beneficiaries to disclaim their significance in the law. Deterrence is vulnerable to exactly that objection: by leaching the meaning out of criminal law, deterrence rhetoric extinguishes a powerful resource for reshaping the social norms that construct unjust systems of status and privilege.

My argument unfolds in three parts. In Part I, I discuss the dual function of theories of punishment as normative guides for action and as strategies for managing public discourse. Deterrence theory, I argue, is demonstrably inferior to expressive condemnation along the former dimension but a serious competitor of it along the latter.

Part II examines the influence of deterrence rhetoric on public debate over three important issues: capital punishment, gun control, and hate crimes. Although prominent on both sides of these disputes, deterrence arguments don't genuinely explain why most citizens hold the positions they do on any of them. What does are citizens' understandings of how these issues cohere with the more general moral commitments of the social groups that they favor and despise, and what particular resolutions of such issues would express about the status of these groups in American society. Citizens resort to deterrence rhetoric in response to norms, principles, and strategic interests that enjoin them to minimize conflict and expressions of disrespect in

---

[14] *See generally* Lawrence Lessig, *The Regulation of Social Meaning*, 62 U. CHI. L. REV. 943 (1995) (describing the role of social meaning in reinforcing existing social arrangements).

their face-to-face interactions with those who harbor cultural commitments that differ from their own. None of these forces is especially stable, however, which is why deterrence détentes are prone to break down.

Finally, in Part III, I evaluate the secret ambition of deterrence. The power of deterrence to mute expressive conflict, I will try to show, supplies both the strongest argument *for* and the strongest argument *against* deterrence theorizing. There simply is no right answer — at least in the abstract — to the question whether deterrence theory furnishes a morally appropriate idiom for public discussion of criminal law.

I. THEORIES OF PUNISHMENT AND POLITICAL CONFLICT

Normative legal theories do more than justify particular legal doctrines. They also furnish vocabularies and concepts that determine *how* we talk to each other about what the law should be. The manner in which citizens routinely talk about contentious matters — whether they speak softly or raise their voices, use terms that connote respect or express contempt — influences how likely they are to reach agreement, and how easily they'll be able to get along with each other if they don't. Indeed, the vocabulary the law uses to frame an issue can determine whether citizens of diverse commitments even see anything to disagree about.[15]

We can thus evaluate theories of punishment both as normative guides for action and as strategies for managing the tone of public discourse. In this Part, I assess two prominent theories of punishment — expressive condemnation and deterrence — along both of these dimensions.

A. Expressive Condemnation

1. As Normative Theory. — The expressive theory of punishment is part of a more general expressive account of rationality.[16] According

[15] *See* SUNSTEIN, *supra* note 13, at 35–44 (identifying and praising people's tendency to agree on the basic contours of principles while refusing to fill in the details); Strauss, *supra* note 13, at 21–22 (arguing that the legal culture's emphasis on technical forms of argumentation helps to shift the focus away from underlying moral disagreements, thereby promoting tolerance).

[16] For general accounts of expressive rationality, see ELIZABETH ANDERSON, VALUE IN ETHICS AND ECONOMICS 17–43 (1993) and Lessig, cited in note 14 above. *See also* Richard H. Pildes & Elizabeth S. Anderson, *Slinging Arrows at Democracy: Social Choice Theory, Value Pluralism, and Democratic Politics*, 90 COLUM. L. REV. 2121 (1990) (arguing that rational choice theory must take greater account of the inseparability of rationality and social practices, institutions, and norms); Richard H. Pildes, *The Unintended Cultural Consequences of Public Policy: A Comment on the Symposium*, 89 MICH. L. REV. 936 (1991) (criticizing modern public law thinking for focusing exclusively on the instrumental outcomes of policies while ignoring cultural consequences). For expressive theories of punishment, see JOEL FEINBERG, DOING & DESERVING:

to this account, we can't make sense of individual and group behavior without considering its social meaning. Social norms define how persons (or communities) who value particular goods — whether the welfare of other persons, their own honor or dignity, or the beauty of the natural environment — should behave. Against the background of these norms, actions and laws express attitudes toward these goods. Individuals take these social meanings into account when deciding what actions to take, as do communities when deciding what laws to enact.

The expressive theory of punishment says we can't identify criminal wrongdoing and punishment independently of *their* social meanings. Economic competition may impoverish a merchant every bit as much as theft. The reason that theft but not competition is viewed as *wrongful*, on this account,[17] is that against the background of social norms theft expresses disrespect for the injured party's moral worth whereas competition (at least ordinarily) does not. Military service and imprisonment may be equally destructive of a person's liberty; the reason that imprisonment but not conscription is regarded as *punishment* is that against the background of norms only imprisonment expresses society's moral condemnation.[18] The meanings of wrongdoing and punishment, moreover, are related: the condemning retort of punishment signals society's commitment to the values that the wrongdoer's act denies.

This account supplies a powerful tool for making sense of common intuitions about criminal law. The belief that wrongs are distinguished by their meanings, for example, helps to show why rape, which evinces profound contempt for a woman's agency, is seen as more reprehensible than an assault that imposes equivalent or greater physical injury.[19] The expectation that punishments should condemn, and not just regulate, explains why non-evocative sanctions such as fines are

---

ESSAYS IN THE THEORY OF RESPONSIBILITY 95–118 (1970); JEFFRIE G. MURPHY & JEAN HAMPTON, FORGIVENESS AND MERCY (1988); ROBERT NOZICK, PHILOSOPHICAL EXPLANATIONS 370–76 (1981); Henry M. Hart, Jr., *The Aims of the Criminal Law*, 23 LAW & CONTEMP. PROBS. 401 (1958); and Dan M. Kahan, *What Do Alternative Sanctions Mean?*, 63 U. CHI. L. REV. 591 (1996).

17 There are, of course, other accounts. *See, e.g.*, Posner, *supra* note 4, at 1195–96 (claiming that the law criminalizes behavior that bypasses an available market to effect a pure coercive transfer of wealth).

18 *See* Hart, *supra* note 16, at 404–05 (identifying moral condemnation by the community as the sine qua non of criminal punishment).

19 *Cf.* People v. Liberta, 474 N.E.2d 567, 574–75 (N.Y. 1984) (holding that the "marital rape exception" violates the Equal Protection Clause and rejecting the argument that ordinary assault prosecution is sufficient when a husband forces sex on his wife: "The fact that rape statutes exist ... is a recognition that the harm caused by a forcible rape is different, and more severe, than the harm caused by an ordinary assault .... 'Short of homicide, [rape] is the "ultimate violation of self."'" (quoting Coker v. Georgia, 433 U.S. 584, 597 (1977))).

regarded as inappropriate substitutes for more evocative ones such as imprisonment.[20] The idea that punishment evidences societal values accounts for the complaint that the lenient treatment of certain offenses — such as domestic violence or hate crimes — reveals that certain persons just "don't count" in the eyes of the law.[21]

Moreover, the expressive theory gives us the power not only to explain but also to appraise criminal law. Voluntary manslaughter doctrine distinguishes among angry killers, mitigating the punishment of the cuckold, for example, but not that of the spurned suitor.[22] Such distinctions are intelligible insofar as we see a person's emotions as expressing valuations; they are normatively justified to the extent that we think that the law is accurately apportioning punishment based on the moral truth or falsity of the valuations that offenders' emotions express.[23] Sodomy laws, even when unenforced, express contempt for certain classes of citizens.[24] The injustice of this message supplies a much more urgent reason to oppose the persistence of these rarely enforced laws than does their supposed impingement on anyone's liberty to engage in particular sexual practices.

2. As Discourse Strategy. — So far, I've been assessing expressive condemnation as a normative theory of punishment; it's also possible to assess it as a strategy for managing public discourse. In this respect, the expressive theory is a recipe for contention. Punishment, the expressive theory tells us, conveys an authoritative schedule of moral values. Society, however, is marked by profound moral dissensus. Accordingly, to the extent that citizens see the positions that the law takes as adjudicating the claims of diverse moral views, we can expect the criminal law to be a site of conflict.

Indeed, we can expect such conflict to be intense by virtue of the connection between the expressive function of law and *status*. Individuals value status — in the form of approval, respect, and deference

---

[20] *See* Kahan, *supra* note 16, at 617–24.

[21] *See, e.g.*, *Judge Draws Protests After Cutting Sentence of Gay Man's Killer*, N.Y. TIMES, Aug. 17, 1994, at A15 (quoting a gay activist's reaction to a sentence reduction for a man convicted of manslaughter for the intentional killing of a homosexual: it says "that it's O.K. to kill faggots"); Sheridan Lyons & Robert Guy Matthews, *Oust Judge Cahill, Protesters Urge*, BALTIMORE SUN, Oct. 22, 1994, at 1B (reporting the reaction of a female protester that an 18-month work-release sentence for a man who killed his wife after discovering her infidelity sends the message that "murder is no big deal — in fact, is a fitting punishment" for unfaithful wives).

[22] *See* Kahan & Nussbaum, *supra* note 8, at 308.

[23] *See id.* at 308–09.

[24] *See* Terry S. Kogan, *Legislative Violence Against Lesbians and Gay Men*, 1994 UTAH L. REV. 209, 233 (concluding that the rare enforcement of sodomy laws demonstrates that "our society exhibits little interest in implementing direct control over sexual activity in private bedrooms. . . . Rather, the purpose of sodomy statutes is to proclaim the message that society hates homosexuals, whoever that category happens to encompass and whatever those people happen to do in bed.").

— both as a means to an end and as an end itself. As a result, they are motivated to master the norms that signify that they merit such esteem. These norms, however, are always specific to particular subcommunities — whether religious sects, ethnic groups, geographic regions, or more loosely defined cultural styles — and are contested in society at large. Inevitably, then, the pursuit of status impels individuals to defend *their* subcommunities' norms, as well as the claims to esteem that these norms construct, against rival subcommunities' norms and claims.[25]

The expressive function of law is an important resource in this struggle. Because criminal law is widely understood to signify a society's authoritative moral values, culturally embattled groups can use it to demonstrate — to themselves and to others — that *their* norms are worthy and ascendant and their cultural adversaries' bankrupt and deviant.[26] "The courtroom decision or the legislative act often glorifies the values of one group and demeans those of another."[27] "The public support of one conception of morality at the expense of another enhances the prestige and self-esteem of the victors and degrades the culture of the losers."[28]

Expressive conflict of this sort becomes especially pronounced when traditional norms are contested. For it is in that circumstance that traditionally ascendant groups are most likely to value official confirmation of their status and traditionally dominated ones are most likely to see opportunities for establishing their claims to respect.[29] Law is thus an instrument for the redistribution of status as well as material wealth. "The struggle to control the symbolic actions of government is often as bitter and fateful as the struggle to control its tangible effects."[30]

Many of America's most fiercely contested criminal law issues have involved battles to control the law's expressive capital. Well into the middle of the nineteenth century, the nation was consumed by disputes over corporal punishment, which was perceived by its opponents and

---

25 *See* JOSEPH R. GUSFIELD, SYMBOLIC CRUSADE: STATUS POLITICS AND THE AMERICAN TEMPERANCE MOVEMENT 13–24, 62–65, 172–75 (2d ed. 1986); J.M. Balkin, *The Constitution of Status*, 106 YALE L.J. 2313, 2326–31 (1997).

26 *See generally* Balkin, *supra* note 25, at 2326 (discussing groups' struggle for prestige through minor, symbolic changes to statutes).

27 Joseph R. Gusfield, *On Legislating Morals: The Symbolic Process of Designating Deviance*, 56 CAL. L. REV. 54, 57 (1968).

28 GUSFIELD, *supra* note 25, at 5.

29 *See id.* at 17–18, 20, 177, 205–06; Balkin, *supra* note 25, at 2334–35. *See generally* Richard H. McAdams, *The Origin, Development, and Regulation of Norms*, 96 MICH. L. REV. 338, 402–03 (1997) (depicting legislation as a way of signaling consensus in the formation of norms).

30 GUSFIELD, *supra* note 25, at 167; *see also* MURRAY EDELMAN, THE SYMBOLIC USES OF POLITICS 5 (1964) (declaring that "[p]olitics is for most of us a passing parade of abstract symbols," a "series of pictures in the mind" that we "fear or cheer").

proponents alike as emblematic of contested forms of social hierarchy, including slavery.[31] Contentious votes in Congress on the use of corporal punishment in the navy were thus regarded as tests of the status and power of these competing sectional factions.[32]

No sooner had the corporal punishment controversy abated than the nation was fractured by the temperance debate, which was similarly expressive in nature. Temperance supporters tended to be nativist, rural, and overwhelmingly Protestant; for them, abstinence from drink connoted the virtues of self-reliance and discipline.[33] Temperance opponents were largely immigrant, urban, and Catholic; they celebrated commerce and leisure and chafed at the perceived regimentation and asceticism of agrarian norms.[34] Prohibition marked an attempt to shore up the norms that had underwritten the cultural preeminence of America's traditional rural elite.[35] Repeal marked a decisive defeat for the norms of that subcommunity,[36] although only on that particular battlefront.[37]

Expressive disagreements continue to be central to many contemporary criminal law disputes. The centuries-old rule affording mitigation to cuckolds who kill their unfaithful wives is now an object of intense controversy. The reason is not that the number of such killings is on the rise, but rather that the patriarchal norms that such rules express are on the decline.[38] Overthrowing the old rule is a way for those committed to contemporary feminist norms to display their strength.

Flag desecration is another example. Few individuals burn flags.[39] Legislation to punish such behavior generates intense controversy nonetheless because votes on such legislation are understood to be tests

---

[31] *See generally* MYRA C. GLENN, CAMPAIGNS AGAINST CORPORAL PUNISHMENT: PRISONERS, SAILORS, WOMEN, AND CHILDREN IN ANTEBELLUM AMERICA 55–57 (1984) (observing that condemnation of corporal punishment reflected shifting attitudes toward a variety of hierarchical relationships); HERBERT ARNOLD FALK, CORPORAL PUNISHMENT: A SOCIAL INTERPRETATION OF ITS THEORY AND PRACTICE IN THE SCHOOLS OF THE UNITED STATES 15, 108–09 (1941) (recognizing corporal punishment as distinctive of hierarchical societies).

[32] *See* GLENN, *supra* note 31, at 129–31 (detailing the political disagreements between northern and southern congressmen on naval flogging).

[33] *See* GUSFIELD, *supra* note 25, at 4.

[34] *See id.* at 4, 6–8.

[35] *See id.* at 8.

[36] *See id.*

[37] *See id.* at 11 (identifying success on issues including fluoridation, domestic communism, and school curricula in the struggle between the traditional rural cultural style and the modern urban style).

[38] *See* Kahan & Nussbaum, *supra* note 8, at 346–50.

[39] *See* GOLDSTEIN, *supra* note 12, at 381 (noting the "paucity of recent flag burnings").

of the national commitment to patriotism and of the status of those for whom patriotism is an unproblematic virtue.[40]

Of course, criminal law does not monopolize expressive conflict. According to Kristin Luker, abortion laws (both civil and criminal) spark controversy because they confer esteem on women who occupy traditional domestic roles and express contempt for those who inhabit modern professional ones.[41] Robert Ellickson traces the dispute over range-closure laws to the desire of western ranchers to erect a symbolic barrier to the erosion of their status.[42] Disputes over public monuments, Sanford Levinson has shown, reflect the rivalries spawned by multiculturalism.[43] Jack Balkin demonstrates how such rivalries affect interpretation of the Constitution.[44] But because criminal law is viewed as distinctively charged with vindication of moral norms, it is not surprising that it draws a disproportionate share of expressive controversy.

This relationship between the expressive theory and political conflict is not immutable, at least in theory. In a society unmarked by fundamental moral dissensus, the expressive function of criminal law might simply reinforce solidarity.[45] Moreover, even in a morally pluralistic society, it is possible to imagine the law expressing only those values on which there is "overlapping consensus,"[46] and thereby reinforcing liberal accommodation.

There's little reason to suppose, however, that such expressive harmony is realistically attainable in our society. Whether we choose to celebrate or lament it, pluralism is a permanent social fact.[47] Nor should we expect groups that hold discordant moral and cultural visions to renounce their aspirations to see their distinctive values confirmed by law. Indeed, if even a small minority of cultural zealots remain committed to using the law to project the ascendancy of their

---

40 *See id.* at 190–91, 369–70, 381–84, 407–10 (documenting the influence of veterans groups in flag desecration debates and the importance of flag-burning laws as a symbolic affirmation of patriotic values).

41 *See* KRISTIN LUKER, ABORTION AND THE POLITICS OF MOTHERHOOD 193–94 (1984).

42 *See* ROBERT C. ELLICKSON, ORDER WITHOUT LAW: HOW NEIGHBORS SETTLE DISPUTES 116–18 (1991).

43 *See, e.g.*, SANFORD LEVINSON, WRITTEN IN STONE: PUBLIC MONUMENTS IN CHANGING SOCIETIES 23–25 (1998) (surveying some modern disputes over the names of public places).

44 *See* Balkin, *supra* note 25, at 2316–20.

45 This apparently was Durkheim's view, for example. *See* EMILE DURKHEIM, DIVISION OF LABOR IN SOCIETY 87–89, 103–06 (George Simpson trans., The MacMillan Co. 1933).

46 RAWLS, *supra* note 13, at 133.

47 *See id.* at 37 (describing moral pluralism as the "inevitable outcome of free human reason"); *see also* GUTMANN & THOMPSON, *supra* note 13, at 18–26 (canvassing sources of persistent moral disagreement, including interest, scarcity of resources, and incomplete understanding, as well as ultimate plurality of values).

norms, the less culturally ambitious majority will be goaded into expressive competition by way of self-defense. Thus, criminal law will furnish an irresistible target for public moralizing so long as citizens see criminal law issues in expressive terms.

B. Deterrence

1. As Normative Theory. — Whereas expressive theory focuses on meanings, deterrence theory focuses on consequences. According to deterrence theory, society should punish if, and to the extent that, doing so maximizes social welfare.[48] This directive generates a series of practical axioms: that the expected penalty must exceed the expected gain from the offense in order to deter it; that society should invest in punishment up to the point where the marginal cost of additional punishment equals the marginal benefit in averted crimes; that society should allocate punishment across crimes so as to discourage the substitution of more serious for less serious ones — and so forth.[49] Deterrence theorists typically assess the efficiency of a punishment for its contribution both to "general deterrence," which refers to the effect that punishing a particular offender has on the behavior of the population generally, and to "specific deterrence," which refers to the impact of a punishment on the offender's own behavior, a usage that brings the aim of incapacitation within the ambit of deterrence broadly understood.[50] The optimal punishment so derived might correspond to our perception of the form and degree of punishment necessary to counter the message expressed by a wrongful act and the emotional motivations that inspired it. But if it doesn't, then it is our naïve expressive sensibilities, not the prescription generated by deterrence theory, that must yield.[51]

The aspiration to be normative for expressive sensibilities, however, is one that deterrence theory can never genuinely realize. The reason is that deterrence theory presupposes an external theory of value, which we are always free to derive from our expressive sensibilities.[52]

---

[48] *See* BENTHAM, *supra* note 4, at 170.

[49] *See generally id.*, at 170–73, 179–84 (presenting Bentham's principles for shaping the criminal law); RICHARD POSNER, ECONOMIC ANALYSIS OF LAW 223–231 (4th ed. 1992) (using an economic model to evaluate criminal punishment); Becker, *supra* note 4, at 183–84 (same).

[50] *See* Johannes Andenaes, *The General Preventive Effects of Punishment*, 114 U. PA. L. REV. 949, 949–54 (1966).

[51] *See, e.g.*, BENTHAM, *supra* note 4, at 126–35 (asserting that whether good or bad, the moral quality of an individual's motivations or character dispositions should not affect punishment independently of the individual's propensity to frustrate the maximization of social welfare).

[52] *See generally* ANDERSON, *supra* note 16, at 29–30 (making this point about consequentialist theories generally).

Imagine two intentional killers: a woman who, in anger, kills the sexual abuser of her young child;[53] and a man who, out of humiliation, kills his wife for seeking a divorce.[54] One thing that deterrence theory tells us is that to deter a crime of a particular sort the expected penalty — that is, the severity of the punishment discounted by the probability that it will be imposed — must exceed the gain to the offender.[55] Assume that the angry mother (and others in her situation) and the dishonored husband (and others in his) get roughly the same psychic returns from their killings, and that they are equally likely to be convicted when society commits comparable resources to detecting and prosecuting their offenses. Does deterrence theory imply under those circumstances that the two killers should receive the same punishment?

The answer is, "Not necessarily." To identify the optimal punishments, we must also determine what value society gets from deterring these types of killings.[56] Society might attach relatively little value to the lives of child molesters: private acts of retaliation against them might make members of society happy and help to deter further child molestation. If so, then the social benefit of deterring deadly violence against child molesters might be small or even negative. The social benefit of deterring deadly attacks on women who want divorces, in contrast, might be great: members of society might attach a relatively high value to the innocent victims of such killings and experience intense indignation in response to the killers' patriarchal motivations; they might worry, too, that such killings will intimidate women seeking to escape abusive marriages. If so, then it might make sense, from a consequentialist or economic standpoint, for society to devote more of its limited punishment resources to punishing the dishonored husband, because the social benefit of deterring his type of killing would be greater than the benefit of deterring the angry mother's type.

Of course, matters could be otherwise. Maybe members of society are even less disturbed by the killing of disobedient wives than they are by the killing of child molesters, in which case the deterrence theory might justify punishing the angry mother more severely. Or

---

[53] *See, e.g.*, People v. Shields, 575 N.E.2d 538, 546 (Ill. 1991) (finding victim's admission that he had raped defendant's daughter and statement that he would do so again to be one of several factors that constituted sufficient provocation to mitigate murder to manslaughter).

[54] *See, e.g.*, State v. Klimas, 288 N.W.2d 157, 165–67 (Wis. Ct. App. 1979) (holding that the defendant's mental state during a period of marital breakdown in which his wife had an affair and sought a divorce was not grounds for mitigating intentional homicide from murder to manslaughter).

[55] *See* BENTHAM, *supra* note 4, at 179, 184; Becker, *supra* note 4, at 183–84.

[56] *See generally* BENTHAM, *supra* note 4, at 172 (Punishment is unjustified "[w]here it is *unprofitable*, or too *expensive*: where the mischief it would produce would be greater than what it prevented.").

maybe they disvalue these killings equally, in which case the punishments should in fact be equal.

The point, however, is that from a deterrence point of view, the optimal level of punishment for these, and for all other offenses, depends critically on how bad we perceive them to be. Unless we know whether and how much we disvalue a particular species of conduct, we can't determine whether the cost of deterring any particular amount of it is worth paying. Nor can we make a rational judgment about how to allocate punishment resources between crimes that impose different levels of harm.[57]

Deterrence, in short, presupposes a consequentialist theory of value. Yet nothing intrinsic to the deterrence theory supplies one.

Our expressive sensibilities, in contrast, do. We can judge the relative culpability of the dishonored husband and the angry mother by considering our perception of whether the valuations their actions and motivations express (the importance of one's sovereignty in the household in the one case; the importance of the well-being of one's child in the other) are morally reasonable or not. If we decide to construct our consequentialist theory of value in this way, deterrence theory, at least, is powerless to object.[58]

This conclusion by itself, however, doesn't establish that deterrence theory lacks critical force relative to the expressive theory. A "pure" expressive approach would have us set punishments based solely and directly on our perceptions of what different species of wrongdoing mean. The deterrence theory, even if informed by an expressive theory of value, suggests that we should be prepared to qualify our expressive appraisals in light of factual considerations relating to the cost-effectiveness of punishment. Suppose we discover that it is in fact substantially harder to obtain convictions of angry mothers than dishonored husbands; or that angry mothers on average derive substantially more psychic pleasure from killing; or that the "demand" for deadly retaliation against independent wives is inelastic relative to the expected punishment for — or the "price" of — such killings. These considerations could imply that it would be cost-effective to punish the angry mother more severely than the dishonored husband even if we conclude, based on expressive considerations, that revenge killings of child molesters are less harmful to society than are honor-inspired killings of independent women.

But this is the point at which the empirically speculative nature of deterrence becomes unbearable. We will rarely have reliable informa-

[57] *See generally id.* at 181 ("The greater the mischief of the offence, the greater is the expense, which it may be worth while to be at, in the way of punishment.").

[58] *See* Kahan & Nussbaum, *supra* note 8, at 354–55.

tion on the probability of conviction, average psychic gains, elasticity of demand, and like variables, the measurement of which depends on seemingly intractable empirical problems. Our confidence in the information we do have on these facts will nearly always be less than the confidence we have in the relative expressive reprehensibility of diverse wrongs, a matter that each of us is in a position to determine through personal introspection.[59] Cognitive psychology tells us that individuals tend to resolve uncertainty about disputed empirical matters — from the safety of nuclear power to the deterrent efficacy of the death penalty — consistently with their prior evaluative judgments.[60] Consequently, even if we commit ourselves to a deterrence framework, the raw expressive judgments that inform our consequentialist theory of value are much more likely to dominate the cost-benefit axioms of deterrence than vice versa.

Indeed, even if we could attain perfect confidence in the relevant empirical variables, deterrence theory wouldn't dictate that we put cost-effectiveness ahead of our raw expressive judgments. The reason is that, consequentially or economically speaking, the satisfaction of those judgments creates a species of social wealth. Within a consequentialist or economic framework, we are entitled to trade off this species of wealth against the species of wealth created by efficient behavioral incentives. If society decided for expressive reasons to devote a greater share of its limited punishment resources to dishonored husbands notwithstanding evidence that angry mothers are more responsive to threatened punishments, that decision would reflect the judgment that the utility of indulging its members' expressive sensibilities more than offsets the disutility associated with creating suboptimal behavioral incentives. To say that such a trade-off offends *deterrence theory* would reveal an arbitrary (or at least undefended) exclusion of expressive utility from the social welfare function.[61]

2. As Discourse Strategy. — I have been arguing that deterrence is inferior to expressive condemnation as a normative theory of punishment. But how does it rate as a strategy for managing public discourse? Through a particular example, I will demonstrate that the de-

---

59 This isn't to say that each of us will agree with everyone else on these issues, but only that each of us is likely to have better access to our own values than to reliable information on the empirical variables upon which the deterrence theory depends.

60 *See* JULIAN V. ROBERTS & LORETTA J. STALANS, PUBLIC OPINION, CRIME, AND CRIMINAL JUSTICE 239, 242–43 (1997) (death penalty); Paul Slovic, Baruch Fischhoff & Sarah Lichstenstein, *Facts Versus Fears: Understanding Perceived Risk*, *in* JUDGMENT UNDER UNCERTAINTY: HEURISTICS AND BIASES 463, 485 (Daniel Kahneman, Paul Slovic & Amos Tversky eds., 1982) (nuclear power).

61 *See* Dan M. Kahan, *Social Meaning and the Economic Analysis of Crime*, 27 J. LEGAL STUD. 609, 615–16 (1998); Kenworthey Bilz, Populist Wealth in Legal Economic Analysis (Oct. 12, 1998) (unpublished manuscript, on file with the Harvard Law School Library).

fects of deterrence as a normative theory don't detract at all from its function in guiding public discussion of criminal law issues, and may in fact *enhance* its power to discharge the potential for conflict associated with expressive theory.

Most American jurisdictions follow the rule that a person confronted with a deadly attack in public may repel it with deadly force even if she could have safely fled.[62] Consider two justifications for this doctrine, the first articulated by the Missouri Supreme Court in 1902,[63] and the second by Justice Oliver Wendell Holmes, writing for the U.S. Supreme Court, in the 1921 decision of *Brown v. United States*:[64]

> [1] It is true, human life is sacred, but so is human liberty. One is as dear in the eye of the law as the other, and neither is to give way and surrender its legal status in order that the other may exclusively exist, supposing for a moment that such an anomaly to be possible. In other words, the wrongful and violent act of one man shall not abolish or even temporarily suspend the lawful and constitutional right of his neighbor. And this idea of the nonnecessity of retreating from any locality where one has the right to be is growing in favor, as all doctrines based upon sound reason inevitably will .... [No] man, because he is the physical inferior of another, from whatever cause such inferiority may arise, is, because of such inferiority, bound to submit to a public horsewhipping. We hold it a necessary self-defense to resist, resent, and prevent such humiliating indignity, — such a violation of the sacredness of one's person, — and that, if nature has not provided the means for such resistance, art may; in short, a weapon may be used to effect the unavoidable necessity.[65]
>
> [2] The law has grown, and even if historical mistakes have contributed to its growth, it has tended in the direction of rules consistent with human nature .... Detached reflection cannot be demanded in the presence of an uplifted knife. Therefore, in this court, at least, it is not a condition of immunity that one in that situation should pause to consider whether a reasonable man might not think it possible to fly with safety, or to disable his assailant rather than to kill him.[66]

Although they get to the same place, these two justifications for the "no retreat" rule travel along strikingly different normative paths. The position of the Missouri Supreme Court is unapologetically expressive. The man who stands his ground and fights has done nothing wrong because his "resent[ment]" reveals that he appropriately attaches more value to his "rights," "liberty," and "sacredness of . . . person" than he does to the life of a "wrongful" aggressor. Indeed, other courts of the day defended the same result on the ground that "a true man" — one

---

[62] *See* WAYNE R. LAFAVE & AUSTIN W. SCOTT, JR., CRIMINAL LAW § 5.7(f), at 460–61 (2d ed. 1986).

[63] *See* State v. Bartlett, 71 S.W. 148, 151–52 (Mo. 1902).

[64] 256 U.S. 335 (1921).

[65] *Bartlett*, 71 S.W. at 151–52.

[66] *Brown*, 256 U.S. at 343.

whose character and values are straight rather than warped — cannot be expected "to fly from an assailant, who, by violence or surprise, maliciously seeks to take his life or do him enormous bodily harm."[67] Extending the privilege to use deadly force to repel such an attack is the appropriate way for the law to acknowledge the courage of the defender's decision to stand firm; indeed, punishing him for killing the aggressor would send the "anomal[ous]" message that the law values the sanctity of "human life" but not the goods — from "liberty" to "rights" to "dignity" to honor — that make life sacred.

Justice Holmes's argument, in contrast, is a concession to futility. A deadly attack triggers an unthinking impulse to fight; it disregards "human nature" to believe that the threat of subsequent criminal punishment will induce "detached reflection" on the prospects for safe retreat. Although there is certainly more than one way to interpret Holmes's argument, Holmes, who saw "[p]revention" as the "only universal purpose of punishment,"[68] can plausibly be read (and has plausibly been read) as making a deterrence argument. Because punishment cannot be expected to influence behavior in such circumstances, it would be a waste to punish a man for not taking flight in the face of deadly aggression.[69]

As an exercise in normative justification, Holmes's account is manifestly less satisfying than the Missouri Supreme Court's. For one thing, Holmes's defense of the "no retreat" doctrine displays the characteristic empirical speculativeness of deterrence arguments. Why so quickly assume that "human nature" makes it impossible for a person confronted with aggression to hear a legal directive to retreat? Physically threatened people run in fear all the time; adding the prospect of being killed down the road by the state to the prospect of being killed instantly by the attacker should only make running in fear all the more likely.

---

67 Erwin v. State, 29 Ohio St. 186, 199–200 (1876).

68 OLIVER WENDELL HOLMES, JR., THE COMMON LAW 46 (Dover 1991) (1881).

69 *See* Richard Singer, *The Resurgence of Mens Rea: II — Honest but Unreasonable Mistake of Fact in Self Defense*, 28 B.C. L. REV. 459, 501 (1987); *see also* Mitchell Keiter, *Just Say No Excuse: The Rise and Fall of the Intoxication Defense*, 87 J. CRIM. L. & CRIMINOLOGY 482, 498 n.98 (1997) (reading Holmes as arguing that punishing a reasonable defender will overdeter legitimate self-defense because of a defender's inability to assess the probability of a safe retreat). Another reading of the argument would be that because the threatened individual is incapable of detached reflection, he cannot be said to be acting "freely" when he chooses to kill rather than run and thus cannot be blamed. This voluntarist reading, however, would be inconsistent with Holmes's philosophical skepticism about "free will" and his related opposition to treating subjective blameworthiness as relevant to liability in criminal law and elsewhere. *See* HOLMES, *supra* note 68, at 49–51; G. EDWARD WHITE, JUSTICE OLIVER WENDELL HOLMES: LAW AND THE INNER SELF 143–44, 161–62, 165 (1993).

Even assuming that certain people won't run no matter what, it still might make sense to punish *all* non-retreaters for the sake of general deterrence. The prospect of a defense for the person who stands his ground and fights might induce some premeditating killers to stage deadly attacks or to provoke them; steadfastly denying a defense would discourage this form of strategic behavior and in fact encourage individuals to steer clear of situations in which they might be confronted with a deadly attack that triggers their supposedly unreasoning fighting impulses. Of course, denying a defense to the person who stands his ground might encourage aggressors to initiate more deadly confrontations. But if our goal is to maximize lives, it's just not clear which of these empirical effects we should expect to dominate.[70]

These empirical issues are much less of a problem for the Missouri Supreme Court, because it doesn't see maximizing lives per se as the goal. Life has sacred value only because liberty, dignity, and honor do; legally obliging a person either to "retreat[] from [a] locality where [he] has the right to be"[71] or "to submit to a public horsewhipping"[72] when he could effectively repel the attack would express contempt for these values. If we accept this account, then it doesn't much matter whether the "true man" doctrine leads to the unnecessary taking of aggressors' lives, for the virtue of the "true men" would be worth much more than the lives of wrongful aggressors.

We needn't, of course, accept the Missouri Supreme Court's account of what's valuable. Less than a year after the Missouri Supreme Court issued its decision, Joseph Beale argued that the norms that the "true man" doctrine expresses ought to be condemned, not endorsed:

> The ideal of [the] courts [that have propounded the "true man" doctrine] is found in the ethics of the duelist, the German officer, and the buccaneer. . . . The feeling at the bottom of the [rule] is one beyond all law; it is the feeling which is responsible for the duel, for war, for lynching; the feeling which leads a jury to acquit the slayer of his wife's paramour; the feeling which would compel a true man to kill the ravisher of his daughter. We have outlived dueling, and we deprecate war and lynching; but it is only because the advance of civilization and culture has led us to control our feelings by our will.[73]

For Beale, it is the man who endures the embarrassment of retreat to avoid the shedding of blood whose values are true:

> A *really* honorable man, a man of *truly* refined and elevated feeling, would perhaps always regret the apparent cowardice of a retreat, but he

[70] *See* Alon Harel, *Efficiency and Fairness in Criminal Law: The Case for a Criminal Law Principle of Comparative Fault*, 82 CAL. L. REV. 1181, 1217–19 (1994).

[71] State v. Bartlett, 71 S.W. 148, 151 (Mo. 1902).

[72] *Id.* at 154.

[73] Joseph H. Beale, Jr., *Retreat from a Murderous Assault*, 16 HARV. L. REV. 567, 577, 581 (1903).

would regret ten times more, after the excitement of the contest was past, the thought that he had the blood of a fellow-being on his hands. It is undoubtedly distasteful to retreat; but it is ten times more distasteful to kill.[74]

If we accept Beale's account, then the duty to retreat is appropriate because it tells us what good persons really care about. If we attach as much value to having the law get that message across as Beale does, then we have a reason to impose a duty to retreat even if Holmes is right in his wobbly empirical guess that doing so won't change the behavior of individuals who are attacked in the public square.

Beale and the Missouri Supreme Court have thus clearly joined issue on the question of what state of affairs the law should be trying to promote, whereas Holmes, displaying another characteristic vice of deterrence theorists, has begged that question. It also won't do to assert that, from an optimal deterrence perspective, the proper rule on retreat just *is* the one that maximizes lives saved regardless of what that rule expresses about norms and character.[75] For that would amount to an indefensible exclusion of something people value — social meaning — from the social welfare calculus.

In sum, Holmes's defense of the "no retreat" rule fails in all the ways typical of deterrence arguments relative to their expressive alternatives. Nevertheless, this assessment of Holmes's position is incomplete. Just as the antiliberal critique of "self-interest" misunderstands the ambition of the classic liberals to displace the contentious moral idiom of glory, so the expressive critique of Holmes overlooks how his use of the deterrence idiom predictably calmed illiberal jockeying over the content of America's public morality.

From the end of the Civil War well into the early part of this century, the duty to retreat was an unsettled and fiercely contested issue in American criminal law. Like the disputes over corporal punishment and temperance, the battle over the "true man" doctrine was one for the control of the law's expressive capital. The judicial proponents of the "true man" doctrine — which constituted a sharp break with English common law — were located in the South and West.[76] By virtue of the slave culture in the former and the frontier culture in the latter, both of these regions had inherited rich systems of honor that put a premium on physical displays of courage and on violent reactions to

[74] *Id.* at 581 (emphasis added).

[75] Indeed, it is unrealistic to assess a legal doctrine's behavioral incentives apart from its expressive content, because the norms that the law expresses are likely to be internalized by members of society generally and thus to affect their behavior. *See* Kahan & Nussbaum, *supra* note 8, at 355–57.

[76] *See, e.g.*, La Rue v. State, 41 S.W. 53, 54 (Ark. 1897); People v. Lewis, 48 P. 1088, 1089–90 (Cal. 1897); Ragland v. State, 36 S.E. 682, 684–85 (Ga. 1900); McCall v. State, 29 So. 1003 (Miss. 1901).

slights.[77] Opponents of the "true man" doctrine, such as Beale, tended to come from the East, which viewed traditional honor norms with alarm and contempt in part because of their historical association with slavery.[78] Western judges derided the English common law requirement that a man "retreat to the wall" before using deadly force as contrary to "the tendency of the American mind";[79] in fact, the dispute over the "true man" doctrine was about *whose* minds — those of the aristocratic South and the ruggedly individualistic West, on the one hand, or those of the more egalitarian and cosmopolitan East, on the other — would be proclaimed *genuinely* "American" by the law.

Against this background, Holmes's use of the deterrence idiom can be understood as a gesture of expressive neutrality. Reformulated in Holmes's language, the "no retreat" rule is transformed from a story about the righteous "resent[ment]" of the "true man" into one about the paralyzing fear of the terrified man. Its adoption marks not the "inevitable" triumph of "sound reason" in the law, but a mature concession to the unreasoning necessity of "human nature." Without expressly mentioning the southern and western decisions that had initiated the rift with the English common law, Holmes implies that *their* morally aggressive defenses of honor and freedom can be seen as "historical mistakes" that happily "contributed to [the law's] growth" nevertheless.[80] Having gotten what they wanted, the southern and western proponents of the "no retreat" rule were in no position to complain. But having been spared an official endorsement of the honor norms they abhorred, the eastern opponents had little to complain about either.

If Holmes's goal was to short-circuit the no-retreat conflict, then the empirically speculative and morally question-begging nature of deterrence made that theory singularly appropriate. Stated at a high level of abstraction, the idea that the law should promote security but avoid futility is unlikely to offend any group's deeply held values. To be sure, the empirical premise of Holmes's futility argument is open to dispute — but if that narrow empirical issue is *all* the "no retreat" dispute is really about, why become agitated about it? Precisely because deterrence fails to address the most important value-laden issues that surround the "no retreat" rule, Holmes's authoritative reconceptualiza-

---

77 *See generally* RICHARD E. NISBETT & DOV COHEN, CULTURE OF HONOR: THE PSYCHOLOGY OF VIOLENCE IN THE SOUTH (1996) (discussing systems of honor in the South).

78 *See, e.g.*, State v. Brown, 53 A. 354, 356 (Del. 1902); People v. Constantino, 47 N.E. 37, 39 (N.Y. 1897); Commonwealth v. Drum, 58 Pa. 9, 20–22 (1868); State v. Roberts, 21 A. 424, 425 (Vt. 1891); RICHARD MAXWELL BROWN, NO DUTY TO RETREAT 24–28 (1991).

79 Runyan v. State, 57 Ind. 80, 84 (1877).

80 Brown v. United States, 256 U.S. 335, 343 (1921).

tion of the rule strips it of the evocative vitality that it needs to underwrite expressive conflict.

This account of Holmes's objectives can be supported by extrinsic evidence. In a letter to his long-time confidant Harold Laski, Holmes disclosed more candidly his motives for upholding the "no retreat" rule. Invoking a conception of "human nature" more cognizant of socialization and less steeped in mechanistic necessity than the one in his *Brown* opinion, Holmes wrote: "[L]aw must consider human nature and make some allowances for the fighting instinct at critical moments. In Texas where this thing happened, . . . it is well settled, as you can imagine, that a man is not born to run away . . . ."[81]

This approving nod in the direction of southern and western honor norms resonated with Holmes's own pride in having been part of a Civil War regiment that "never ran."[82] In his famous 1884 Memorial Day Address, Holmes spoke not of the thoughtless impulses of those who survived hand-to-hand combat, but rather of the "swift and cunning thinking on which once hung life or freedom."[83] Acknowledging how much less passionately he defended the "no retreat" rule in *Brown*, Holmes tells Laski, "I don't say all I think in the opinion."[84]

Holmes's decision *not* to say all that he thought about the "true man" doctrine stemmed from his more basic jurisprudential commitments. Holmes entertained a hard-edged belief in the permanence of social and moral conflict.[85] Nevertheless, he viewed the judicial system as a decidedly less desirable location for such conflict than the legislative arena, where unrestrained and cacophonous interaction of competing interests was far more likely to yield stable compromise. Holmes's aspiration to channel conflict away from the judicial process accounts for his famous project to demoralize the language of common law tort standards.[86] Deterrence theory, which is more important for

---

81 Holmes, *supra* note 1, at 262.

82 MARK DEWOLFE HOWE, JUSTICE OLIVER WENDELL HOLMES: THE SHAPING YEARS, 1841–70, at 126 (1957) (quoting Holmes); *see* WHITE, *supra* note 69, at 477 ("Holmes emerged from the Civil War with what became, in the course of his life, an anachronistic, tribalist perspective, glorifying war and its codes, such as duty, honor, chivalry, self-abnegation."); *see also* Albert W. Alschuler, *The Descending Trail: Holmes'* Path of the Law *One Hundred Years Later*, 49 FLA. L. REV. 353, 358 (1997) (describing Holmes as a "Nietzschean" who "venerated power, conflict, violence, death, and survival" (emphasis omitted)).

83 Oliver Wendell Holmes, Memorial Day, Address Before John Sedgwick Post No. 4, Grand Army of the Republic (May 30, 1884), *in* THE MIND AND FAITH OF JUSTICE HOLMES: HIS SPEECHES, ESSAYS, LETTERS AND JUDICIAL OPINIONS 11 (Max Lerner ed., 1946).

84 Holmes, *supra* note 1, at 262.

85 *See generally* Grant Gilmore, *Some Reflections on Oliver Wendell Holmes, Jr.*, 2 GREEN BAG 2d 379, 385 (1999) ("Holmes had arrived at a tragic view of the human condition. In the life of an individual as in the life of a society there is nothing but force, violence, and a never-ending struggle for bare survival.").

86 *See* Richard A. Posner, *Introduction* to THE ESSENTIAL HOLMES, at xi (Richard A. Posner ed., 1992) (identifying the "severance of law from morals" as a "basic element" of Holmes's

what it does *not* say than for what it does, carries this philosophy forward into the world of criminal law.

Since Holmes recast the "true man" doctrine, public controversy over the duty to retreat has largely disappeared. It's difficult to say, of course, whether and to what extent the abatement of the "true man" controversy is due to Holmes's reconceptualization of the rule. Nevertheless, it should be clear that this is one of the questions that we ought to ask if we are trying to evaluate Holmes's argument.

Because deterrence theory can be seen as a strategy for managing public discourse, it misses the point to evaluate arguments such as Holmes's solely as normative justifications. We should consider, in addition, what function such arguments play in moderating expressive conflict, how effective they are in performing this function, and whether their aspiration to denude criminal law of its social meaning is itself a worthy objective. These are the issues that guide the remainder of this Article.

II. THE SECRET AMBITION REVEALED

Just as deterrence theory enabled Justice Holmes not to say all that he thought about the "true man" doctrine, so deterrence enables the rest of us not to say all we think about a host of controversial issues in criminal law. Deterrence arguments play a large role in public debate. The prominence deterrence enjoys, however, is misleading. Even if they honestly believe the deterrence arguments they are making, the vast majority of citizens and officials don't believe such arguments are essential to their positions on highly charged issues. They emphasize deterrence arguments nevertheless only to satisfy a social norm against the open expression of contentious moral judgments or to avoid exciting expressively motivated opposition to their own policy positions. This rhetorical self-restraint can and often does break down, but so long as it persists it functions to dissipate expressive conflict. I will support this argument by analyzing public opinion on three disputed issues: capital punishment, gun control, and hate crimes.[87]

---

jurisprudence). *See generally* WHITE, *supra* note 69, at 290–91, 324, 328, 391–92 (discussing Holmes's views and his use of political economy principles rather than rights in his opinions).

[87] As should be clear, I do *not* mean to claim that deterrence arguments never influence *anyone* on *any* issue. There may be some forms of behavior — perhaps speeding or tax evasion — on which moral and cultural disagreement is minimal (if not nonexistent) and on which instrumental issues loom much larger. Even with respect to some culturally charged issues, some individuals may honestly believe that the deterrent impact of a particular law or policy is all that matters — although even when they honestly believe that, it is likely that their perceptions of what is instrumentally effective are being decisively if imperceptibly shaped by their expressive values. *See*

A. Capital Punishment

Following two decades of intense political contention, New York in 1995 became the latest state to restore the death penalty in the (receding) wake of *Furman v. Georgia*.[88] Only days before the legislature passed the death penalty bill, a *New York Times* poll had shown that New Yorkers believed, by a margin of fifty-seven percent to forty percent, that capital punishment would deter murders.[89] In signing the new law, Governor George Pataki, who had emerged from obscurity to dethrone prominent incumbent Mario Cuomo by attacking Cuomo's opposition to capital punishment, stated:

> The citizens of New York State have spoken loudly and clearly in their call for justice for those who commit the most serious of crimes by depriving other citizens of their very lives. *The citizens of New York State are convinced the death penalty will deter these vicious crimes and I, as their Governor, agree.* The legislation I approve today will be the most effective of its kind in the nation. It is balanced to safeguard defendants' rights while ensuring that our state has a fully credible and enforceable death penalty statute. *This law significantly buttresses the twin pillars of an effective criminal justice system — deterrence and true justice for those convicted of violent crimes.*[90]

New Yorkers and their Governor are not the only ones who purport to give primary consideration to deterrence when evaluating the death penalty. Polls have consistently shown that most Americans are likely to put deterrent efficacy or inefficacy first when asked to rank their motives for supporting or opposing the death penalty.[91]

To anyone who has reflected on the death penalty debate, however, this feature of public opinion ought to seem puzzling. No issue of criminal justice has been subjected to greater empirical study than whether the death penalty is an effective deterrent, and on none is the evidence more ambiguous and conflicting.[92] It is genuinely astonish-

---

supra p. 425. But as I will try to show, there is ample evidence that deterrence has little impact on what most individuals believe about highly charged issues.

[88] 408 U.S. 238 (1972). The state legislature had enacted a death penalty bill every year for 18 years, but every bill had been vetoed by Democratic Governors Hugh Carey and Mario Cuomo. *See What's News — World-Wide*, WALL ST. J., Mar. 8, 1995, at A1.

[89] *See* Tom Kuntz, *Killings, Legal and Otherwise, Around the U.S.*, N.Y. TIMES, Dec. 4, 1994, § 4, at 3.

[90] William C. Donnino, Practice Commentary, N.Y. PENAL LAW § 125.27 (McKinney 1998) (quoting memorandum of New York Governor George Pataki on the death penalty) (emphasis added).

[91] *See, e.g.*, Dov Cohen, *Law, Social Policy, and Violence: The Impact of Regional Cultures*, 70 J. PERSONALITY & SOC. PSYCHOL. 961, 970 (1996); Ellsworth & Ross, *supra* note 5, at 145–49; *see also* Tom R. Tyler & Renee Weber, *Support for the Death Penalty: Instrumental Response to Crime, or Symbolic Attitude?*, 17 LAW & SOC'Y REV. 21, 24–25 (1982).

[92] *See generally* DAVID LESTER, THE DEATH PENALTY: ISSUES AND ANSWERS 83–109 (2d ed. 1998); Ruth D. Peterson & William C. Bailey, *Is Capital Punishment an Effective Deterrent for*

ing, then, that *only three percent* of the respondents in a poll such as the one conducted in New York claim to be uncertain when asked whether the death penalty deters.

What's more, only someone who is morally obtuse could fail to perceive how charged the issue of capital punishment is with fundamental questions of value. Is there any satisfactory public gesture *other than* the death penalty for reaffirming the sanctity of the life of a murder victim? But doesn't taking the life of the murderer itself demean the sanctity of life? Even if the death penalty is just in the abstract, doesn't the racially disparate administration of it in practice — an empirical issue on which there is relatively little doubt[93] — make capital punishment unacceptable? Depending on one's view on these and many other issues, one could easily come out for or against the death penalty irrespective of its deterrent impact, which is bound to be small relative to life imprisonment without parole. So *why* do citizens put deterrence first when they are deciding whether they are for or against the death penalty?

The answer is, *they don't*. The story of what citizens believe about the death penalty and why is much more complicated than their simple profession of deterrence claims suggests.

1. Deterrence Doesn't Matter. — There is ample evidence that deterrence doesn't really have the decisive significance that individuals say that it has in shaping their opinions on the death penalty. For example, pollsters often ask whether respondents would change their view if they were shown conclusive evidence that the death penalty either does or does not deter. The vast majority of respondents, both for and against the death penalty, indicate that they would not.[94] In other words, even when individuals say that deterrence is the most important consideration, it turns out that what they believe about deterrence is neither necessary nor sufficient to explain their opinion about the appropriateness of the death penalty.

Less direct but equally compelling sources of evidence point in the same direction. The value that individuals attach to deterring crime presumably reflects how serious they take crime to be. There is no significant correlation, however, between support for the death penalty

Murder? An Examination of Social Science Research, *in* AMERICA'S EXPERIMENT WITH CAPITAL PUNISHMENT (James R. Acker, Robert M. Bohm & Charles S. Lanier eds., 1998).

[93] *See, e.g.*, DAVID C. BALDUS, GEORGE WOODWORTH & CHARLES A. PULASKI, JR., EQUAL JUSTICE AND THE DEATH PENALTY (1990) (discussing the racially disparate impact of the death penalty).

[94] *See* Phoebe C. Ellsworth & Samuel R. Gross, *Hardening of the Attitudes: Americans' Views on the Death Penalty*, 50 J. SOC. ISSUES 19, 27, 32 (1994); Tyler & Weber, *supra* note 91, at 26.

and fear of crime.[95] To be sure, national support for the death penalty began to climb in the late 1960s — from a low of forty-two percent in 1966 to some seventy-five percent by the late 1980s — at the same time that homicide rates began to rise significantly.[96] But these high levels of support have persisted as homicide rates have declined.[97] Moreover, professed belief in the deterrent efficacy of the death penalty (while well over fifty percent) did not rise as steadily as support for the death penalty itself did throughout the 1970s.[98] In the main, individuals' assessments of the death penalty clearly do not derive from their beliefs about deterrence.

Indeed, it seems more likely that individuals' beliefs in deterrence derive from their independent evaluative assessments of the death penalty. To avoid dissonance, individuals tend to resolve factual uncertainty consistently with their existing convictions.[99] Experimental work shows that this is exactly what happens when individuals assess the deterrent effect of the death penalty. When asked to evaluate conflicting empirical studies, subjects credit those that confirm their prior beliefs and dismiss those that conflict with them.[100]

Finally, the reluctance of death penalty supporters to make one species of deterrence argument casts doubt on the strength of their commitment to the rest. In its conventional economic or utilitarian form, deterrence theory favors not the most effective punishment per se, but the most *cost*-effective one. It costs a lot less to pass a fatal surge of electricity through a person's body or to inject a lethal dose of poison into his veins than it does to house him for decades in a prison. Thus, even if death penalty abolitionists are correct that life imprisonment without parole is an equally severe disincentive to murder, deterrence theory could be used to justify capital punishment as the most *cost-effective* disincentive. Yet most proponents of deterrence refuse to make this cost-effectiveness argument.[101]

In truth, once the multiple layers of judicial review for death sentences are taken into account, it costs more to execute an offender than to imprison him for life.[102] But most members of the public don't re-

---

95 *See* Dennis R. Longmire, *Americans' Attitudes About the Ultimate Weapon: Capital Punishment*, *in* AMERICANS VIEW CRIME AND JUSTICE: A NATIONAL PUBLIC OPINION SURVEY 93, 95–96 (Timothy J. Flanagan & Dennis R. Longmire eds., 1996).

96 *See* Ellsworth & Gross, *supra* note 94, at 40, 41 fig.4.

97 *See id.* at 42; Samuel R. Gross, *Update: American Public Opinion on the Death Penalty — It's Getting Personal*, 83 CORNELL L. REV. 1448, 1449 (1998).

98 *See* Ellsworth & Gross, *supra* note 94, at 27.

99 *See* LEON FESTINGER, A THEORY OF COGNITIVE DISSONANCE 271 (1957).

100 *See* ROBERTS & STALANS, *supra* note 60, at 239, 242.

101 *See* Ellsworth & Gross, *supra* note 94, at 29–30.

102 *See, e.g.*, PHILIP COOK & DONNA SLAWSON, THE COSTS OF PROCESSING MURDER CASES IN NORTH CAROLINA 98 (1993) (finding that the extra cost per execution of prosecuting a case capitally is over $2.16 million).

alize this.[103] Moreover, Congress has now drastically streamlined (that is, truncated) federal habeas corpus procedures.[104] In the years of contentious debate that led up to these reforms, supporters criticized the existing procedures as visiting unjustified burdens on the states, but *didn't* argue that reducing these costs would make execution a more "efficient" penalty.[105] Not only does public support of the death penalty depend on some value other than deterrence, but that value, it seems, would be demeaned were the death penalty to be defended in the naked cost-effectiveness terms that are distinctive of deterrence theory.[106]

2. *Expressive Judgments Do Matter.* — Deterrence judgments don't explain the death penalty debate; expressive ones do. The death penalty debate has all the trappings of a battle for the law's expressive capital. Individuals hold the positions that they do on the death penalty because of what those positions signify about the norms of competing subcommunities. Adopting one position or another is a way for individuals to sharpen their own senses of group allegiance and to signal those allegiances to others; thus, individuals "do not so much form opinions [on the death penalty] as choose sides."[107] The death penalty issue enjoys the prominence that it does in contemporary politics because its resolution signifies the relative social status of the groups whose norms are at stake. Whether or not they affect the behavior of criminals, death penalty laws "confer[] prestige on the law-abiding" population,[108] or at least on that segment of it that sees its status as bound up with the messages that the death penalty projects.

(a) Expressive Attitudes. — Individual opinions on the death penalty correlate with membership in various groups. All else equal, support for the death penalty is more prevalent among whites than blacks;[109] among men than women;[110] among rich than poor;[111] among

---

[103] *See* ROBERTS & STALANS, *supra* note 60, at 238.

[104] *See* Antiterrorism and Effective Death Penalty Act of 1996, Pub. L. No. 104-132, 110 Stat. 1214, 1217–26 (1996).

[105] *See, e.g.*, H.R. REP. NO. 104-23, at 9–11 (1995); 32 WEEKLY COMP. PRES. DOC. 719 (April 24, 1996).

[106] *See* LOUIS MICHAEL SEIDMAN & MARK V. TUSHNET, REMNANTS OF BELIEF: CONTEMPORARY CONSTITUTIONAL ISSUES 149 (1996) (stating that "cost-benefit" rhetoric "gut[s] the moral core of" the retentionist position).

[107] Ellsworth & Gross, *supra* note 94, at 23; *see* Gross, *supra* note 97, at 1452 ("For most Americans, a position on capital punishment is an aspect of self-identification. We say, 'I'm for the death penalty,' the same way we say, 'I'm a Republican,' or 'I'm a Red Sox fan.'").

[108] Barbara Ann Stolz, *Congress and Capital Punishment: An Exercise in Symbolic Politics*, 5 LAW & POL'Y Q. 157, 167 (1983).

[109] *See* ROBERTS & STALANS, *supra* note 60, at 228; Longmire, *supra* note 95, at 98.

[110] *See* Longmire, *supra* note 95, at 98.

[111] *See id.* at 100.

country dwellers than city dwellers;[112] and among adherents of fundamentalist and evangelical religious denominations than adherents of other sects.[113] Generally speaking, individuals tend to adopt the views of the persons with whom they associate or identify as a means of earning approval and signaling solidarity and belonging.[114] The demographic patterns that characterize death penalty views suggest that the same expressive dynamics help to determine those attitudes.[115]

Even stronger evidence of the expressive underpinnings of death penalty attitudes comes from the clustering of positions on the death penalty with positions on other issues. Death penalty proponents are more likely to oppose abortion, for example, and to take relatively conservative stances on civil rights and civil liberties.[116] There is no necessary *philosophical* link between the death penalty and these latter positions; one could (and some persons do) oppose both the death penalty *and* abortion on the ground that the state should never condone the taking of life,[117] or favor the death penalty for civil rights violations. The relative infrequency of these pairings, however, suggests again that death penalty positions are largely symbolic or expressive: in order to understand themselves and to be understood by others as the sorts of persons who belong to particular ideological communities, individuals adopt the position on the death penalty that is *conventionally* associated with those allegiances.[118]

Finally and most compellingly, positions on the death penalty correlate with a range of other more abstract evaluative dispositions. Death penalty proponents are more likely to value obedience to authority, to believe more fervently in the power of individual will, and to accept the permanence of warfare.[119] They are more likely to see morality as absolute, whereas death penalty opponents are more likely to see it as contextual and relative to persons or communities.[120]

---

[112] *See id.* at 99.

[113] *See id.* at 94.

[114] *See generally* ELLIOT ARONSON, THE SOCIAL ANIMAL (7th ed. 1994).

[115] *See* SEIDMAN & TUSHNET, *supra* note 106, at 162–63 ("[E]xpression of opinion about capital punishment is a way of defining oneself and signaling to others which side one is on.").

[116] *See* Tyler & Weber, *supra* note 91, at 29, 37.

[117] This, of course, is the position of the Catholic Church. Most American Catholics, however, disagree with the Church's stance on capital punishment. *See* Michele Dillon, *Rome and American Catholics*, 558 ANNALS AM. ACAD. POL. & SOC. SCI. 122, 123 (1998).

[118] *See* Ellsworth & Gross, *supra* note 94, at 23–24 (interpreting data as suggesting that positions on the death penalty are part of an individual's "self-identification"); Aaron Wildavsky, *Choosing Preferences by Constructing Institutions: A Cultural Theory of Preference Formation*, 81 AM. POL. SCI. REV. 4, 17 (1987) (suggesting that social relationships help form political opinions).

[119] *See* Tyler & Weber, *supra* note 91, at 29–30, 37.

[120] *See* O.J. Harvey, *Belief Systems and Attitudes Toward the Death Penalty and Other Punishments*, 54 J. PERSONALITY 659, 661–62, 668–69 (1986).

Death penalty proponents are less tolerant of social deviance.[121] They trust their fellow citizens less.[122] Death penalty opponents are more likely to care about racial equality.[123] These attitudinal variables furnish the most powerful predictors of death penalty opinion.[124]

Again, there is no intrinsic connection between these abstract evaluative dispositions and the death penalty. In the abstract, there is nothing incongruous in saying that one opposes the death penalty because one is a moral absolutist, or that one is for it because, morality being contextual, one cannot identify any compelling moral reason to oppose the majority who want it. There is nothing conceptually inconsistent about being against the death penalty because one is so universally distrustful of others that one doesn't believe that anyone should be afforded the power to impose it, or about favoring it because one is so universally trusting that one thinks that the state would invariably impose the death penalty only in appropriate circumstances. It's idiosyncratic, but not senseless, to say that one favors the death penalty to promote equality for African Americans because they are victimized more often by homicide than are whites.[125]

If these positions *do* seem discordant or even unreal, that's only because the death penalty bears connotations that make it fit better with certain evaluative stances than others. By virtue of its history, the death penalty is imbued with social meanings. Those meanings make it signify something attractive for those who understand themselves, and who want to be understood by others, as strong believers in moral truth and as respecters of authority; they make it signify something repulsive for those who see themselves, and want others to perceive them, as nonjudgmental and egalitarian.

Based on the social science data that I've been reviewing, it's possible to sketch out rough expressive profiles of the proponents and opponents of the death penalty. The proponent believes that there is a single moral truth that others in his society should adopt and should be judged by. He thinks that individuals are responsible for their circumstances, resents being obliged to contribute to the well-being of unrelated others, and is himself wary of relying on others overmuch. He is likely to be politically conservative on a range of issues and most

---

121 *See id.*; Paul M. Valliant & Carrie L. Oliver, ***Attitudes Toward Capital Punishment: A Function of Leadership Style, Gender, and Personality***, 25 SOC. BEHAV. & PERSONALITY 161, 165 (1997).

122 *See* Longmire, *supra* note 95, at 95.

123 *See* ROBERTS & STALANS, *supra* note 60, at 228–29.

124 Tyler and Weber, for example, found that social and political attitudes explain 11 times more of the variance in death penalty opinions than does individuals' fear of crime. *See* Tyler & Weber, *supra* note 91, at 37.

125 *Cf.* Randall L. Kennedy, McCleskey v. Kemp: ***Race, Capital Punishment, and the Supreme Court***, 101 HARV. L. REV. 1388, 1391 (1988).

likely believes that individuals are duty-bound to respect society's rules and institutions. He may well belong to a social group — ethnic, regional, or religious — many of whose members share these outlooks. To him, the death penalty embodies and expresses these values and commitments.

The opponent is different from the proponent along all of these dimensions. She may hold strong moral beliefs herself, but recognizes that others, who were raised in different circumstances, have different views that are worthy of her respect. She believes that individuals' circumstances are often determined by forces outside their control and that as a result society is responsible for the well-being of all citizens, whom she generally views as good and worthy of trust. She is likely to be a political liberal, and in any event is skeptical of official authority. She, too, is likely to belong to a social group — ethnic, regional, or religious — many of whose members share these outlooks. To her, being against the death penalty embodies and expresses these values and commitments.

The communities made up of persons of these sorts are more diffuse and loosely defined than are religious, ethnic, or professional allegiances. It makes more sense to think of them as "cultural styles" than as cultural groups.

These collective orientations, however, can still furnish a ready ground for status conflict. They correspond to what Gusfield calls "status collectivities," groups that "have no church, no political unit, and no associational units," but that nonetheless furnish coherent norms for granting and withholding esteem. "Examples of these are cultural generations, such as the traditional and the modern; characterological types, such as 'inner-directed and other-directed'; and reference orientations, such as 'cosmopolitans and locals.'"[126]

Many of the most charged social and political issues of the past century can be understood as conflicts between individuals who identify with competing cultural styles and who see their status as bound up with the currency of those styles in society at large.[127] The death penalty is one of these issues.

(b) Expressive Politics. — If the death penalty is assessed apart from its social meaning, its political significance seems mysterious. The federal government, for example, has jurisdiction over an exceedingly tiny fraction of the homicides that can result in a sentence of death. Yet the issue of the death penalty looms large in national elec-

---

[126] GUSFIELD, *supra* note 25, at 21.

[127] *See id.* at 21–23, 140–47 (linking a variety of issues to these polarities, including civil rights, temperance, and populist economic regulation).

tions and consumes a large number of lawmaking hours in Congress.[128]

Even the significance of the issue in state politics seems odd from a consequentialist perspective. Pataki defeated Cuomo in an election that centered on the death penalty, yet the Pataki-supported law that the New York legislature enacted is so narrow that it may never be applied.[129] California rarely executes offenders.[130] Nevertheless, the issue embroils state politics and in fact resulted in the nonretention of Chief Justice Bird in 1986.[131]

Considered expressively, however, the pivotal nature of the death penalty debate is perfectly understandable. Positions on the death penalty reflect deeper, community-defining commitments on a range of contentious values. What's at stake, then, when Congress or a state legislature considers death penalty legislation is whose basic commitments will be affirmed and whose repudiated by the law. Moreover, to the extent that positions on the death penalty do cluster with positions on other ideologically charged issues, citizens can use a political candidate's positions on the death penalty to gauge whether that candidate is likely to vote consistently with their desires (expressive and otherwise) on various other matters, many of which might not even be foreseeable at the time of the election.[132] None of these expressive consequences depends necessarily on the death penalty being imposed in any significant number of cases. Thus, "[c]apital punishment is an issue of largely symbolic importance, but symbols count."[133]

The one study of federal legislators' attitudes toward the death penalty confirms this interpretation. Political scientist Barbara Ann Stolz extensively surveyed and interviewed the members of Congress

---

128 *See, e.g.*, HERBERT H. HAINES, AGAINST CAPITAL PUNISHMENT: THE ANTI-DEATH PENALTY MOVEMENT IN AMERICA, 1972–1994, at 112 (1996).

129 *See* Andrea E. Girolamo, Note, ***Punishment or Politics? New York State's Death Penalty***, 7 B.U. PUB. INT. L.J. 117, 117 (1998) (observing that safeguards meant to insulate law "from constitutional challenge . . . may realistically and ironically prevent an execution from ever taking place in New York").

130 California has imposed only seven of the 584 executions carried out by American states since 1977. *See U.S.A. Executions by Year and State* (visited Nov. 12, 1999) <http://www.smu.edu/~deathpen/execyrst1.html>.

131 *See* Mark I. Pinsky, *Times Poll: Law and Order, Spending, Bird Top the Issues*, L.A. TIMES, Nov. 5, 1986, at 2-I ("[One of the] dominant issues in the minds of Orange County voters Tuesday" was "Chief Justice Rose Elizabeth Bird's death penalty rulings. . . . [In an exit poll] more than 80% of voters . . . said they support the death penalty. Not surprisingly, they voted against confirming Bird . . . .").

132 *See generally* SAMUEL L. POPKIN, THE REASONING VOTER: COMMUNICATION AND PERSUASION IN PRESIDENTIAL CAMPAIGNS 51–52, 213 (2d ed. 1994) (describing "information shortcut[s]" that voters use "to estimate [a candidate's] future positions," including "past political positions" and ideological stances).

133 FRANKLIN E. ZIMRING & GORDON HAWKINS, CAPITAL PUNISHMENT AND THE AMERICAN AGENDA, at xiv (1986).

who were most active on the capital punishment issue between 1972 and 1982, a period during which Congress dealt repeatedly with the question of what federal offenses should be subject to the death penalty.[134] Deterrence arguments, she found, figured prominently both in congressional debates and in the self-reported motivations of both proponents and opponents of federal death penalty legislation. Nevertheless, in personal interviews members indicated that "their answers were not rooted in the academic literature," which many characterized as "just a statistical game."[135]

The survey and interview data suggested that members had a much more vivid sense, in contrast, of the symbolism of the death penalty. Proponents, Stolz found, depicted the "enactment of federal capital punishment legislation [as] a means of communicating society's moral indignation toward a type of behavior"; "capital punishment," they stressed, "more clearly emphasizes the outrage at these crimes than other sanctions would."[136] Sometimes proponents depicted this expressive upshot as itself reinforcing deterrence by instilling aversions to killing in potential wrongdoers.[137]

But even more significant, according to Stolz, were the messages that the death penalty conveyed to, and about, committed law-abiders. Proponents expected the enactment of a federal death penalty, even if infrequently imposed, to reassure law-abiders that their representatives are resolutely opposed to crime.[138] They also saw it as a means of affirming the virtue of the "upright" — those citizens who stake their claim to respect on their successful adherence to society's norms.[139] "Such legislation indicates that government has taken sides" in a battle for social esteem.[140] "[S]upport for capital punishment *and criticism of opponents*," Stolz writes, "may be interpreted as a desire to grant status" to those who see their standing as expressively linked to emphatic moral condemnation of law-breakers.[141]

Congressional opponents of the death penalty, according to Stolz, see the issue in equally expressive terms. They worry that the death penalty will "brutal[ize]" society.[142] It sends the message that society bears no responsibility for the wrongdoer's situation and hence no obligation to improve it.[143] Just as proponents see the death penalty as a

---

134 *See* Stolz, *supra* note 108.

135 *Id.* at 172.

136 *Id.* at 166.

137 *See id.*

138 *See id.* at 161, 165.

139 *See id.* at 166–67.

140 *Id.* at 167.

141 *Id.* (emphasis added).

142 *See id.* at 168–69.

143 *See id.*

means of siding with the upright, so opponents see repeal as a means of siding with those who are emotionally invested in equality and collective attention to social welfare and whose status is threatened by the harsh repudiation of the worth of offenders.[144]

Thus, expressive considerations energize both sides in the political debate over capital punishment. For opponents and proponents alike, the issue is whose defining commitments and allegiances will be symbolically credited, and whose repudiated, by the law.

3. Deterrence Talk and Public Discourse Norms. — But if the capital punishment debate is really expressive, why don't people say so? Why does deterrence rhetoric dominate public discourse?

The answer does not seem to be that opponents and proponents are themselves deluded about the moral foundations of their positions. Although they may be likely to cite deterrence or lack thereof *first*, they never cite it as the *only* reason that they support or oppose the death penalty. Rather, those on both sides of the issue cite a variety of moral and emotional bases for their positions: that executing a convicted murderer is just/is itself murder; that the death penalty comports with/defies religious teachings; that the death penalty affirms/demeans the sanctity of life.[145] Indeed, opinion polls show that citizens invariably signify their agreement with *all* the conventional rationales that point in the direction of their preferred position on the death penalty.[146] Deterrence occupies a central place in public debate only because those on both sides consciously choose to emphasize it to the near exclusion of other arguments.

The most convincing account of why they make this choice is that talking openly of the expressive foundations of their positions would violate a social norm against public moralizing. Liberal political culture stigmatizes public appeals to contested moral values.[147] This taboo applies most forcefully to religious convictions,[148] but extends as well to secular evaluative judgments, which are also likely to be dismissed as "mere opinions" that cannot legitimately support imposing obligations on those who disagree. Politics (or at least "comprehensive

---

[144] *See id.*

[145] *See* Ellsworth & Ross, *supra* note 5, at 150.

[146] *See* Ellsworth & Gross, *supra* note 94, at 26.

[147] *See generally* Stephen Holmes, *Gag Rules or the Politics of Omission*, *in* HOLMES, PASSIONS AND CONSTRAINT, *supra* note 2, at 203 (describing the "range and variety of self-censorship common in liberal democratic societies"); Strauss, *supra* note 13, at 39 ("It is not true that in politics, anything goes. There is general agreement on an elaborate set of both procedural and substantive limits on the acceptable ways of resolving political disputes. . . . [W]e underestimate the extent to which political decisionmaking is the product of constrained disputation.").

[148] *See generally* STEPHEN CARTER, THE CULTURE OF DISBELIEF: HOW AMERICAN LAW AND POLITICS TRIVIALIZE RELIGIOUS DEVOTION 1–6 (1993).

views" of politics) and religion are unfit topics of conversation — not only at the dinner table, but also in the public square.[149]

The idiom of deterrence avoids triggering the injunction against contentious public moralizing. As open as they are to dispute, arguments about the empirical consequences of deterrence have an "objective" or "scientific" veneer; those who rely on such arguments need not be seen as relying solely on their "subjective opinions."

But even better, deterrence rhetoric elides the major points of expressive contention that separate proponents and opponents of the death penalty. The conventional expressive arguments on the death penalty are pregnant with accusation: if *I favor* the death penalty because it's essential to vindicating the worth of the victim, then *you* must be *against* it because you don't sufficiently appreciate her worth and overvalue the worth of the wrongdoer; if *I oppose* the death penalty because it is administered in a way that devalues the lives of African Americans, then *you* must be *for* it because you are a racist. In contrast, if I claim to be for/against the death penalty because it is/is not the penalty most likely to protect lives — a claim that is abstract enough to fit within essentially all recognizable cultural and ideological commitments — then I can be seen as saying only that you are factually misinformed, rather than morally obtuse, for feeling otherwise. In much the way that Justice Holmes resorted to deterrence rhetoric because he resented being implicated in fundamental moral conflict as a judge, we resort to it because we resent being implicated in such conflict as citizens.

The social science evidence, although relatively thin in this respect, again supports this interpretation. Those who have analyzed survey responses, for example, posit that "the belief in deterrence is seen as more 'scientific' or more socially desirable than other reasons; people mention it first because its importance is obvious, not because its importance is real."[150] Stolz, too, finds that the emphasis on deterrence by members of Congress reflects their belief that "'statistical/scientific' explanation is perceived as more 'rational,' hence more 'legitimate,'" than unadorned appeals to values.[151] Given the ideologically charged nature of the debate, moreover, proponents perceive that it is more "acceptable" to cite the deterrent benefits of executing a killer than it

---

149 *See generally* MURRAY EDELMAN, THE SYMBOLIC USES OF POLITICS 8 (1964) ("[Individuals] are likely to talk politics with those who agree with them, avoid the subject with those who do not, and sometimes shade or change their opinions to create agreement."); JON ELSTER, ALCHEMICS OF THE MIND: RATIONALITY AND THE EMOTIONS 157 (1999) (discussing the role of social norms in suppressing expression of condemnatory emotions); Holmes, *supra* note 147, at 234 ("[S]trategic self-censorship seems to be an almost universally employed technique of self-management and self-rule.").

150 Ellsworth & Ross, *supra* note 5, at 149.

151 Stolz, *supra* note 108, at 174.

"would be to say 'the bastard deserved it.'"[152] Private citizens are similarly loath to be perceived as vindictive; proponents of the death penalty will thus much more readily acknowledge experiencing "outrage" when a murderer escapes the death penalty than taking "satisfaction" when one is executed, although the two emotional sensibilities are obviously conjoined.[153]

Of course, participants in the death penalty debate might also be making deterrence arguments because they think that those are the ones most likely to change their opponents' minds. Indeed, that would be an understandable conclusion, given how adamantly their adversaries purport to be relying on deterrence. In this way, arguments that disclaim judgmental valuations invite counterarguments that do the same, creating a feedback effect that likely reinforces the norm against public moralizing.

But if they choose to employ deterrence claims in order to persuade, then participants in the public debate *are* deluding themselves. Again, experiments suggest that empirical studies carry little weight with those on either side of the death penalty issue. Proponents and opponents alike conform their assessments of the quality of such studies to their preexisting expressive evaluations.[154]

What does make people change their minds are shocking spectacles that create evaluative dissonance. Thus, a state is most likely to repeal the death penalty in the aftermath of a "botched" execution, particularly one in which a sympathetic person who is perceived to be innocent gets put to death.[155] This is not surprising: proponents of the death penalty see it as a singularly apt gesture for remarking viciousness and depravity; such miscarriages cloud the death penalty's symbolic import. There is also evidence that death penalty abolitionists can change their minds when they confront gruesome, racially inspired murders: the fitness of the death penalty for remarking an emphatic

[152] *Id.* at 176.

[153] *See* Ellsworth & Ross, *supra* note 5, at 155.

[154] *See supra* p. 438.

[155] *See* Herb Haines, *Flawed Executions, the Anti-Death Penalty Movement, and the Politics of Capital Punishment*, 39 SOC. PROBS. 125, 131–35 (1992). The prospect of innocent individuals being sentenced to death was instrumental in the recent defeat of a death penalty bill in Massachusetts. *See* Gross, *supra* note 97, at 1475. The release of an innocent offender from death row in Illinois moved the Illinois House of Representatives to enact a nonbinding resolution in favor of a moratorium on executions in the state and led the Nebraska state legislature to enact a binding one. *See* Robynn Tysver, *Pause in Deaths to Get Debate this Week*, OMAHA (NEB.) WORLD-HERALD, April 11, 1999, at 1B (discussing the influence of Illinois developments on the Nebraska debate). Had the Nebraska measure not been vetoed by the state's Governor, *see* Robynn Tysver, *Moratorium Vetoed*, OMAHA (NEB.) WORLD-HERALD, May 26, 1999, at 1, *available in* 1999 WL 4501362, then Nebraska would have become the first state since *Furman v. Georgia*, 408 U.S. 238 (1972) (per curiam), to suspend the death penalty after reinstituting it.

opposition to racism starts to erode in opponents' minds the penalty's conventional signification of racial domination.[156]

This evidence suggests that deterrence arguments not only fail to persuade. By masking the effective expressive motivations behind death penalty positions, they also obscure from participants on both sides of the debate their best rhetorical opportunities to change their opponents' minds.

4. The Cooling Effect of Deterrence. — I suggested earlier that Justice Holmes invoked the idiom of deterrence not only to avoid saying all he thought about honor and deadly violence, but also to defuse a contentious expressive controversy in the law. It might seem doubtful that the deterrence idiom similarly dissipates controversy on the death penalty issue. The death penalty is one of the most divisive issues in criminal law even though it is dominated by deterrence rhetoric.

But the relevant question, of course, is not how divisive the death penalty debate *is* when it focuses on deterrence, but how divisive it *would be* if it did not. We have been treated to glimpses of this in American history. The last time that it happened was in 1988, when the simmering death penalty debate boiled over with George Bush's victory over Michael Dukakis in the race for President. What raised the temperature was the social meaning of Willie Horton.

Willie Horton was a Massachusetts inmate serving a life term for murdering a teenage gas station attendant. Under a program strongly supported by Governor Dukakis, Horton received regular weekend furloughs to visit his young daughter. During one furlough, Horton fled to Maryland, where he terrorized an innocent couple, torturing the man and repeatedly raping the woman while holding them hostage in their home for hours. The Bush campaign seized on this episode to depict Dukakis as soft on crime. It occupied pride of place in campaign manager Lee Atwater's plan to focus voter attention on "social fabric" issues such as crime and patriotism, a strategy that is credited with erasing Dukakis's seemingly insurmountable lead in the polls as he emerged from the Democratic National Convention.[157]

The Bush campaign invariably coupled Willie Horton with the death penalty. Thus, campaign ads introduced the furlough issue by underscoring that Bush was for the death penalty and Dukakis against

---

[156] *Cf.* Greg Hernandez, *O.C. Jury Votes Death for Hate Crime Murder*, L.A. TIMES (ORANGE COUNTY EDITION), Oct. 10, 1997, at A1, *available in* 1997 WL 13988485 ("[Human Relations] Commission Chairman Rusty Kennedy said that although he is personally opposed to the death penalty, 'the fact that this man was convicted of this heinous crime and given the maximum penalty is good. I do think it's going to send a message to other purveyors of hate in our community and across the nation that we take this very seriously.'").

[157] *See* DAVID C. ANDERSON, CRIME AND THE POLITICS OF HYSTERIA: HOW THE WILLIE HORTON STORY CHANGED AMERICAN JUSTICE 214 (1995).

it.[158] The unmistakable implication was that Dukakis deserved censure not only for letting Horton out on weekends but also for having opposed a regime in which Horton would have been executed for his commission of the earlier murder. Indeed, Willie Horton and the death penalty became so closely identified that when Bush criticized Dukakis's position on the death penalty in the first debate, Dukakis — to the horror of his campaign handlers — answered by defending his support for the Massachusetts furlough program. Bush's answer affirmed the Horton/death penalty link: "When a narcotics wrapped-up guy goes in and murders a police officer, I think they ought to pay with their life . . . . So I am not going to furlough men like Willie Horton . . . ."[159]

The Bush operatives also invariably coupled the Horton issue with all the excruciatingly judgmental expressive themes that motivate death penalty support. Televised advertisements featured the enraged husband and the humiliated wife and trumpeted Dukakis's refusal to reexamine his position on prison furloughs and the death penalty;[160] the message was that death-penalty opponent Dukakis did not care about the worth of innocent crime victims and the indignity that they suffer at the hands of brutal criminals. Bush operatives televised Horton's sullen and hostile-looking mug shot, which they viewed as making Horton "look[] like an animal";[161] Bush depicted Horton as drug-crazed and implied (falsely) that he had killed a cop.[162] The implication was that Dukakis, like other death penalty opponents, could not be counted on to employ the brute force necessary to repel the threat posed by the dangerous, unreasoning, and beastly foes of lawful authority. A Republican party fundraising letter juxtaposed photos of Dukakis and Horton, asking, "Is this your pro-family team for 1988?"[163] Death-penalty opponent Dukakis, we were being told, did not care about family values and other timeless and absolute elements of morality. Even the continual reminder that Horton had escaped from Massachusetts, a New England state that does not have the death penalty, to Maryland, a southern state that does, was calculated to enflame the regional schisms that lurk in the background of the death penalty controversy.

Predictably, Democrats answered expressive arguments with expressive arguments. For them, the Horton/death-penalty issue reflected pure and simple racism. Horton was a *black man*; he raped a

158 *See id.* at 215, 228, 231.

159 *Id.* at 241–42 (quoting George Bush).

160 *See id.* at 228–29.

161 *Id.* at 233.

162 *See id.* at 242.

163 *Id.* at 236–37.

white woman. There can be no more potent historical symbol of white America's racial anxieties, resentments, and fears, Dukakis campaign officials pointed out.[164] Bush campaign officials later expressed indignation at the charge that they framed the Horton/death-penalty issue to appeal to racial animosity.[165] But even assuming that they were telling the truth, their *inability to see* how the Horton/death-penalty issue would be interpreted by African Americans and by citizens who cared passionately about civil rights only confirmed to death penalty opponents the deficiency of their adversaries' commitment to equality.

The social meaning of Willie Horton and the death penalty constructed a conflict between two fundamentally opposed cultural styles. Authoritarianism clashed with egalitarianism, righteousness with tolerance, southernness and westernness with easternness, compassion for victims of crime with compassion for victims of social deprivation. As divisive as the death penalty debate can be when it focuses on deterrence, it rarely achieves this level of polarization.

At the same time, the dynamics that generated the Willie Horton dispute suggest that the heat of the death penalty debate is bound to reach this temperature periodically, notwithstanding the cooling potential of deterrence. *Most* of us don't want to talk in the way that Americans talked to each other during the 1988 presidential campaign. But *some* of us do want to talk this way, at least when there's some obvious political gain to be had in doing so. Once these expressive zealots succeed in framing the death penalty issue in their terms, even those who prefer the milder idiom of deterrence must fight expressive fire with expressive fire or else face the risk of rhetorical immolation.

This, too, is one of the lessons of the 1988 campaign. Michael Dukakis's prospects for winning the election died with his answer to the first question of the final presidential debate. "Governor," asked CNN anchorman Bernard Shaw, "if [your wife] were raped and murdered, would you favor an irrevocable death penalty for the killer?"[166] As distasteful as the question was, it offered Dukakis a chance to dig himself out of the expressive hole that the Willie Horton issue had put him in. Obviously, Dukakis couldn't have changed his position on the death penalty at that point. But he could have shown how enraged and anguished contemplating such a crime could make him, and how severely he thought that the perpetrators of such an abomination should be punished short of execution. An answer like that could have

---

164 *See, e.g.*, Stephen Chapman, *Would It Matter If Willie Horton Were White?*, CHI. TRIB., Oct. 27, 1988, at C23 ("Susan Estrich, Dukakis'[s] campaign manager, sees nothing accidental about these facts: 'There is no stronger metaphor for racial hatred in our country than the black man raping the white woman.'").

165 *See* ANDERSON, *supra* note 157, at 216–17.

166 *Id.* at 243.

gone a long way toward dispelling the negative meanings associated with his opposition to the death penalty — that he lacked compassion for victims, was ambivalent toward government authority, was only weakly committed to traditional moral values, and the like. Instead he said: "No, I don't, Bernard. And I think you know that I've opposed the death penalty during all of my life. *I don't see any evidence that it's a deterrent* . . . ."[167]

It was understandable, and maybe even honorable, that Dukakis would seek to discharge the moral tension by drawing attention to the instrumental effect of the death penalty. But by that point in the debate, deterrence talk was clearly not up to the task of returning the expressive genie to its bottle.

B. Gun Control

The gun control debate has a profile similar to that of the death penalty debate. Again, both sides tend to frame their arguments in deterrence terms: supporters of gun control say that banning firearms, particularly handguns, will discourage violent criminals from arming themselves and preying on innocent victims;[168] opponents say that permitting potential *victims* to arm *themselves* will deter violent criminals from preying on them.[169]

But again, citizens generally don't say all they think when they are justifying their positions on gun control. Deterrence considerations don't genuinely explain opinions on either side. Expressive considerations matter much more: for proponents and opponents alike, guns and gun control bear social meanings that go to the heart of their fundamental moral commitments and cultural identities. The protagonists in the gun control debate, like those in the death penalty debate, are fighting to control the expressive capital of the law. Deterrence rhetoric conceals, but barely contains, each side's illiberal ambition to proclaim its cultural and moral ascendancy through the law.

1. Deterrence and Public Opinion. — The perceived effect of gun control on crime does not have nearly as significant an impact on attitudes towards gun control as the rhetoric of proponents and opponents

---

167 *Id.* at 243–44 (emphasis added).

168 *See, e.g.*, *83rd Congressional District: Election '94*, HARTFORD COURANT, Nov. 3, 1994, at G23 (quoting Democratic congressional candidate James Abrams) ("I support retention of the ban on assault weapons and other gun-control measures as a cost-effective method of fighting violent crime.").

169 *See, e.g.*, Nelson Lund, *Gunning Down Crime*, WKLY. STANDARD, June 1, 1998, at 35 ("Even taking account of evidence that some criminals substitute crimes of stealth (like burglary) for crimes of violence (like robbery) and that some criminals migrate to jurisdictions that forbid their citizens to carry guns, concealed-carry permits remain the most cost effective crime-control measure ever studied. Such laws are cheaper than increased law enforcement or incarceration, and they do not rely on tax dollars.").

might suggest. The majority of persons who say that they favor gun control to reduce crime nevertheless answer "no" when asked if they believe that crime would in fact go down if the government enacted stricter gun control laws.[170] Similarly, most Americans favor stricter gun control, yet only a small fraction list it when asked to specify the policies that they think the government should enact in order to reduce crime.[171] And although crime is perennially put at or near the top of citizens' biggest concerns, the vast majority of Americans rank gun control as less important to them than a host of non-crime policies and issues that bear on public welfare.[172]

Opponents argue that gun control interferes with the use of firearms for lawful self-defense. But whether one accepts or rejects this argument turns out not to predict one's position on gun control.[173]

If individuals did base their gun control positions on their beliefs about its effect on crime, then one would expect variation in the perceived pervasiveness of crime to influence individuals' opinions on gun control. But it doesn't. Survey data show no significant correlation between prior victimization or fear of victimization and positions on gun control. Nor can variation in opinions about gun control be fully explained by variations in violent crime rates across space or time or by variations in the perception of such crime rates.[174] Whatever they say in public, those involved in the gun control debate are not really motivated by beliefs about guns and crime.

2. *The Social Meanings of Guns.* — What *does* motivate them, a wealth of sociological and historical literature suggests, is their attachment to competing cultural styles that assign social meanings to guns. Indeed, the gun control debate is, in many important respects,

---

170 *See* GARY KLECK, POINT BLANK: GUNS AND VIOLENCE IN AMERICA 370 (1991); SPITZER, *supra* note 10, at 121; Don B. Kates, Jr., *Public Opinion: The Effects of Extremist Discourse on the Gun Debate*, *in* THE GREAT AMERICAN GUN DEBATE 93, 95 (Don B. Kates, Jr. & Gary Kleck eds., 1997); *see also* JAMES D. WRIGHT, PETER H. ROSSI & KATHLEEN DALY, UNDER THE GUN: WEAPONS, CRIME, AND VIOLENCE IN AMERICA 236 (1983) (noting that the number of persons who believe gun control would be effective in reducing crime is smaller than the number of persons who support gun control).

171 *See* ROBERTS & STALANS, *supra* note 60, at 281.

172 *See* WILBUR EDEL, GUN CONTROL: THREAT TO LIBERTY OR DEFENSE AGAINST ANARCHY? 72 (1995); ROBERTS & STALANS, *supra* note 60, at 281; Kates, *supra* note 170, at 94.

173 *See* Tom W. Smith, 1996 National Gun Policy Survey of the National Opinion Research Center: Research Findings 8, 33 tbl.6 (Mar. 1998) (unpublished report, on file with the Harvard Law School Library).

174 *See* ARTHUR L. STINCHCOMBE, REBECCA ADAMS, CAROL A. HEIMER, KIM LANE SCHEPPELE, TOM W. SMITH & D. GARTH TAYLOR, CRIME AND PUNISHMENT — CHANGING ATTITUDES IN AMERICA 103–04, 121 (1980); Kenneth Adams, *Guns and Gun Control*, *in* AMERICANS VIEW CRIME AND JUSTICE: A NATIONAL PUBLIC OPINION SURVEY 109, 123 (Timothy J. Flanagan & Dennis R. Longmire eds., 1996); Gary Kleck, *Crime, Culture Conflict, and the Sources of Support for Gun Control: A Multilevel Application of the General Social Surveys*, 39 AM. BEHAV. SCI. 387, 394–99 (1996).

the successor of the "true man"[175] and temperance[176] debates. As in those controversies, one side is disproportionately rural, southern or western, and Protestant, as well as male and white; the other is disproportionately urban, eastern, Catholic or Jewish, as well as female and black.[177] The two sides also subscribe to competing cultural ethics reminiscent of those at stake in the earlier controversies. For the former, the "model is that of the independent frontiersman who takes care of himself and his family with no interference from the state."[178] To them, "the . . . gun symbolizes much that is right in [American] culture," including "manliness, self-sufficiency, and independence."[179] The latter "take bourgeois Europe as a model of a civilized society [—] . . . just, equitable, and democratic[,] but well ordered, with the lines of responsibility and authority clearly drawn, and with decisions made rationally and correctly by intelligent men for the entire nation."[180] To them, "the gun is symbolic of much that is wrong in American culture," including "violence, aggression, . . . male dominance,"[181] individualism, and racism.

Obviously, it would be a mistake to speak as if there were only two cultural styles in America that attach social meaning to guns. The inner-city gang member who carries a gun to signify defiance of authority and indifference to deadly risk,[182] for example, has little in common with either the western NRA member who prizes his gun as an emblem of his frontier heritage or the liberal Urban Leaguer who despises the gun as a badge of anachronistic honor norms and individualism. No doubt there are still other coherent styles and systems of meanings that differ from all three of these.

At the same time, I don't think it's a mistake to speak of two *dominant* cultural styles in this setting. These are the ones that belong to the middle and upper classes in American society, whose members exercise disproportionate influence in the political conflict over gun control, particularly at the federal level. Because that is the conflict that I am trying to explain, I will focus on what guns mean to them and why.

---

175 *See supra* pp. 432–35.

176 *See supra* p. 423.

177 *See* Kleck, *supra* note 174, at 390, 398; Smith, *supra* note 173, at 6.

178 B. Bruce-Briggs, *The Great American Gun War*, PUB. INTEREST, Fall 1976, at 37, 61.

179 James D. Wright, *Ten Essential Observations on Guns in America*, SOC'Y, Mar.–Apr. 1995, at 63, 68.

180 Bruce-Briggs, *supra* note 178, at 61.

181 Wright, *supra* note 179, at 68.

182 *See* Deanna L. Wilkinson & Jeffrey Fagan, *The Role of Firearms in Violence "Scripts": The Dynamics of Gun Events Among Adolescent Males*, 59 LAW & CONTEMP. PROBS. 55, 81–84 (1996); Mary E. Pattillo & Reuben A.B. May, Gun Talk: Culture & Social Control in an African-American Community 19–21 (1996) (unpublished manuscript, on file with the Harvard Law School Library).

The positive meanings that fuel opposition to gun control derive from two historical sources. The first is America's militia heritage.[183] Through their use in revolutionary-era militias, guns came to symbolize the "civic virtue and military prowess of the yeoman" as well as the "degeneration of England and . . . the sharp decline of the 'liberties of Englishmen' on their original home soil."[184] These connotations became institutionalized in the Second Amendment.[185]

The second historical source is the frontier heritage of the American West.[186] Frontiersmen depended on guns for many practical purposes, including hunting and security. But in the course of performing these missions, guns became suffused with meaning. "[C]arried openly on the person, firearms serve[d] as badges that enable[d] those individuals displaying them to mark themselves off as being worthy of special attention without even firing a shot."[187] One could draw inferences about another's social competence, economic class, profession, and even desirability as a suitor from whether he carried a "Kentucky rifle," an "English shotgun," or a dueling pistol.[188] To prevent the appropriation of status — and to repel subversive threats to authority — norms and laws regulated who could possess such weapons.[189] Thus, "[w]ell into the nineteenth century the gun was a more widely held badge of membership in the body politic than the ballot."[190]

Through "cultural momentum," remnants of these meanings have outlived the utilitarian role that guns played in arming militias and settling the frontier.[191] A number of institutions and practices contribute to this dynamic. One is the use of guns for recreation, including target shooting and hunting. In the South and West, proficiency in

---

183 *See* Richard Hofstadter, *America as a Gun Culture*, 21 AM. HERITAGE, Oct. 1970, at 4, 82 (connecting the persistence of gun culture to "the anti-militaristic traditions of radical English Whiggery").

184 *Id.*

185 *See id.* at 83; Don B. Kates Jr., *The Second Amendment and the Ideology of Self-Protection: Essays on Firearms & Violence*, *in* THE GREAT AMERICAN GUN DEBATE, *supra* note 170, at 271, 278–82.

186 *See* SPITZER, *supra* note 10, at 8–12; Hofstadter, *supra* note 183, at 7.

187 WILLIAM R. TONSO, GUN AND SOCIETY: THE SOCIAL AND EXISTENTIAL ROOTS OF THE AMERICAN ATTACHMENT TO FIREARMS 318 (1982).

188 *Id.* at 247–50, 281–82, 317–19.

189 *See* Hofstadter, *supra* note 183, at 84 ("[I]n the historic system of the South, having a gun was a white prerogative."); *see also* LEE KENNETT & JAMES LA VERNE ANDERSON, THE GUN IN AMERICA: THE ORIGINS OF A NATIONAL DILEMMA 167 (1975) (noting that early regulation was inspired by concerns about aliens and political radicals); TONSO, *supra* note 187, at 256–57 (noting that the earliest regulations against the possession of firearms were aimed at disarming immigrants, labor agitators, poor whites, and blacks).

190 KENNETT & ANDERSON, *supra* note 189, at 250.

191 Pauline Gasdow Brennan, Alan J. Lizotte & David McDowall, *Guns, Southernness, and Gun Control*, 9 J. QUANTITATIVE CRIMINOLOGY 289, 292, 305 (1993); *see* TONSO, *supra* note 187, at 30–35, 39.

these activities continues to signal a man's social competence, whereas the refusal to participate in them risks making him into a social outcast.[192] Collecting likewise sustains the positive connotations of guns: "Just to hold [a Colt Model 'P'] in your hand produces a feeling of kinship with our western heritage — an appreciation of things like courage and honor and chivalry and the sanctity of a man's word."[193]

Finally and most importantly, the positive social meaning of guns is sustained by the market, which simultaneously exploits and creates the appetite to share in the culture of martial virtue and frontier independence that the gun connotes. Since the 1950s, the entertainment industry has ceaselessly glamorized the frontier gunslinger.[194] So has the firearms industry:

> An advertisement for the old Colt, for example, shows a photograph of one of these revolvers with a 7 1/2-inch cavalry-length barrel under a color drawing of the lower extremities of galloping horses and the legs of their uniformed riders flashing past a feathered Indian spear imbedded in the ground. Printed on the drawing is: "A COLT says: distant drums, hoof beats, pursuit, confidence."[195]

These connotations are reflected in a host of regional attitudes and practices. The firearm's signification of responsibility, masculinity, and (male) status is reflected in the custom of awarding an adolescent boy his "first gun" — "the *bar mitzvah* of the rural WASP."[196] Its connotation of suspicion of government is reflected in the positive correlation between opposition to gun control and distrust of the police (a correlation that cannot be explained by greater fear of crime).[197] Its affiliation with individualism is reflected in the correlation of opposition to gun control with opposition to social welfare policies and support of punitive measures such as capital punishment.[198] Its resonance with martial virtues is reflected in the greater propensity of gun own-

---

192 *See* TONSO, *supra* note 187, at 329–30.

193 *Id.* at 287–88 (quoting a gun collector) (internal quotation marks omitted).

194 *See* KENNETT & ANDERSON, *supra* note 189, at 218; *cf.* SPITZER, *supra* note 10, at 12, 22 n.46 (noting the power of frontier mythology about the gun and concluding that "the admittedly ambivalent relationship between movies and guns has nevertheless helped cultivate America's gun tradition"). Indeed, as early as 1870, live entertainment and novels were trading on the evocative connections between guns and the frontier. *See* TONSO, *supra* note 187, at 248.

195 TONSO, *supra* note 187, at 293.

196 Bruce-Briggs, *supra* note 178, at 41; *see* Hofstadter, *supra* note 183, at 82 (describing first guns as "milestones of life, veritable rites of passage" that signify "arrival at manhood"); *see also* TONSO, *supra* note 187, at 285 (noting that in some communities the gift of a gun marks the coming of age for males).

197 *See* Adams, *supra* note 174, at 122–24.

198 *See* WRIGHT, ROSSI & DALY, *supra* note 170, at 104, 112.

ers to join the military.[199] In all these ways, commitment to the gun remains deeply enmeshed in a coherent cultural style.

Hostility toward guns is enmeshed in a coherent cultural style as well. Indeed, gun control supporters attach many of the same meanings to guns that opponents do, but invert the relevant valuations of these meanings.

Thus, gun control proponents resent guns because they find frontier ethics abhorrent. Residents of the urban North and East have historically been, and continue to be, leery of rural honor norms.[200] Whereas the typically southern or western collector celebrates the gun as redolent of "chivalry" and "courage,"[201] the northern control proponent derides it as "uncivilized" and "atavistic," and exhorts America to follow the lead of other "modern nations" in banning private weapons possession.[202] Gun owners are not men of honor; they are "rednecks."[203] Their belief that guns are symbols of "manliness" (it is said) displays their subconscious anxiety about sexual potency.[204]

The relationship between gun control and the repudiation of traditional honor norms has two important components. One is aversion to violence. Whereas gun-related journals promote guns as a way to introduce young boys to the tradition of the West, more mainstream journals such as *Parents' Magazine* warn readers not to buy toy guns for their children lest they develop an appetite for aggression and war.[205] Gun control supporters are also ambivalent about the use of weapons even in self-defense.[206]

Another component of the anti-gun/anti-honor style is resistance to gender hierarchy, or at least certain conventional forms of it. The vir-

---

199 *See id.* at 118. According to Wright, Rossi, and Daly, military service does not predict opposition to gun control when other demographic and attitudinal variables are controlled for; in other words, the same cluster of attributes that incline individuals to be pro-gun also incline them to military service. *See id.*

200 *Cf.* NISBETT & COHEN, *supra* note 77, at 25–38, 62–63, 72–78 (describing the differences between the South and other regions of the country in attitudes towards the use of violence in various circumstances).

201 TONSO, *supra* note 187, at 287.

202 Bruce-Briggs, *supra* note 178, at 61 ("To [gun control proponents], hunting is atavistic, personal violence is shameful, and uncontrolled gun ownership is a blot upon civilization."); Hofstadter, *supra* note 183, at 4 (asserting that America is the "only nation so attached to the supposed 'right' to bear arms that its laws abet assassins, professional criminals, berserk murderers, and political terrorists at the expense of the orderly population" and that "[in other countries in which] rights are rather better protected than in ours . . . our arms control policies would be considered laughable").

203 *See* Raymond G. Kessler, *Ideology and Gun Control*, 12 Q.J. IDEOLOGY, No. 2, at 1, 4–5 (1988).

204 *See* EDEL, *supra* note 172, at 97–98; Kates, *supra* note 170, at 97–98.

205 *See* KENNETT & ANDERSON, *supra* note 189, at 215.

206 *See* Kates, *supra* note 170, at 106–10; *see also* Smith, *supra* note 173, at 8, 33 tbl.6 (finding belief that gun control impedes self-defense does not predict position on gun control).

tues that honor norms construct — "courage," "self-reliance," "chivalry" — are traditionally *male* virtues; guns function as symbols of these virtues in rural communities for *men*; the practices that forge this symbolic link — from hunting, to target shooting, to the custom of presenting guns to adolescent boys — are predominantly *male* practices. Indeed, women who possess guns are likely to be perceived (unflatteringly) as possessing male traits.[207]

It is not surprising, then, that guns became an issue early on for women's groups, whose advocacy of gun control in between the First and Second World Wars reflected their distinctive ambition to infuse politics with "maternal" values.[208] Gun control opponents of that time depicted control as inspired by women, who, they said, "instinctively fear and mistrust guns."[209] These resonances persist: women continue disproportionately to favor gun control,[210] which is therefore seen as a position geared to appeal to female voters.[211]

Men who resent the gender-specific expectations and dispositions constructed by honor norms are also more likely to favor gun control. Thus, one study found that support for gun control correlated with tolerance for homosexuality, disdain for "macho" behavior, opposition to pornography, and other attitudes opposed to traditional, hierarchical gender roles.[212] The proponents of gun control are also repulsed by the individualism that guns connote. Proponents believe that society is responsible for the well-being of individuals: they tend to support social welfare policies and to oppose punitive measures, including capital punishment, that signify a belief that individuals are solely to blame when they transgress society's rules.[213]

Thus, for the same reasons that control proponents see guns as proclaiming "individual self-reliance," control supporters see them as denying civic solidarity. "Every handgun owned in America is an implicit declaration of war against one's neighbor."[214] The gun owner is an "anti-citizen[]," an "enem[y] of [his] own *patriae*."[215]

---

207 *See* H. Taylor Buckner, Sex and Guns: Is Gun Control Male Control? 3 (Aug. 5, 1994) (unpublished manuscript, on file with the Harvard Law School Library).

208 *See* KENNETT & ANDERSON, *supra* note 189, at 214.

209 *Id.* at 215 (quoting a pro-gun magazine) (internal quotation marks omitted).

210 *See, e.g.*, Smith, *supra* note 173, at 18, 36 tbl.14.

211 *See, e.g.*, Alison Mitchell & Frank Bruni, *Suburban Districts Seen as a Key In the Debate Over Gun Control*, N.Y. TIMES, June 16, 1999, at A1 ("In a pointed appeal to suburban women, Mr. Clinton cast gun control as a women's issue, saying, 'Women who belong to both parties in America, all over this country, have been in the forefront of this fight.'").

212 *See* Buckner, *supra* note 207, at 22–24.

213 *See* STINCHCOMBE, ADAMS, HEIMER, SCHEPPELE, SMITH & TAYLOR, *supra* note 174, at 104, 111–13.

214 Kates, *supra* note 170, at 109 (quoting Gary Wills) (internal quotation marks omitted).

215 *Id.* at 97 (quoting Gary Wills) (internal quotation marks omitted).

> Give up your gun the gun nut says, and you give up your freedom. . . . *Trust no one but yourself to vindicate your cause. Not the law. Not your representatives. Not your fellow citizens.* . . . When the chips are down, [the gun] owner says, he will not trust any other arbiter but force personally wielded.[216]

The idea that arming private citizens is the way to deter crime "ought to disgust rather than cheer the civilized observer."[217] To accept it is "to embrace a society based on an internal . . . balance of terror,"[218] "a jungle where each relies on himself for survival."[219] There is "[n]o reason . . . why anyone in a *democracy* should own a weapon."[220]

Finally, for control proponents the gun means racism. Historically, at least, the status conferred by gun ownership was not only an important symbol of *male* status, but also "an important symbol of *white* male status": the earliest forms of gun control were aimed at keeping weapons out of the hands of African Americans.[221] The gun's connotations of white supremacy were no doubt renewed and intensified by the assassinations of Martin Luther King, Jr. and Medgar Evers and by the generally violent reaction to the civil rights movement in the South,[222] which experienced soaring weapons purchases during that period.[223] These meanings persist: African Americans continue disproportionately to favor gun control, as do whites who favor civil rights policies.[224] Commitment to racial equality, moreover, reinforces the social meaning of the gun as a denial of solidarity: because poverty and criminality are both racially concentrated, the expressive equation of guns with opposition to assisting strangers and with punitiveness makes every handgun a declaration of war against one's *black* neighbors in particular.[225]

---

216 *Id.* at 109 (quoting various articles by Gary Wills) (internal quotation marks omitted).

217 H. Laurence Ross, Book Review, 98 AM. J. SOC. 661, 662 (1992).

218 *Id.*

219 RAMSEY CLARK, CRIME IN AMERICA 107 (1970).

220 William R. Tonso, *Social Science and Sagecraft in the Debate over Gun Control*, 5 LAW & POL'Y. Q. 325, 333 (1983) (emphasis added) (quoting sociologist Morris Janowitz) (internal quotation marks omitted).

221 Hofstadter, *supra* note 183, at 84 (emphasis added); *see* TONSO, *supra* note 187, at 256–57; Don B. Kates, Jr., *Gun Control: Separating Reality from Symbolism*, 20 J. CONTEMP. L. 353, 370 (1994).

222 *See* TONSO, *supra* note 187, at 236.

223 *See* KENNETT & ANDERSON, *supra* note 189, at 224–25.

224 *See* Smith, *supra* note 173, at 5; *cf.* STINCHCOMBE, ADAMS, HEIMER, SCHEPPELE, SMITH & TAYLOR, *supra* note 174, at 106, 110–113 (finding that African Americans, as well as whites who supported busing, were less likely than others to own guns, and finding that gun ownership is correlated with decreased support for gun control).

225 Gun control opponents fuel this association when they attribute the demand for gun control to inner-city crime problems that do not affect rural areas, an argument that could be taken to imply that the right of virtuous white citizens to own guns should not be compromised by the vi-

Thus, much more is at stake in the gun control debate than crime control. At bottom, the disagreement embodies "two alternative views of what America is and ought to be."[226]

3. Illiberalism and Expressive Zealotry. — As in the death penalty debate, overtly expressive arguments figure in the gun control debate only intermittently. They emerged, for example, in the late 1960s: primed by a decade of political assassinations, gun control proponents aggressively flooded the market with expressive currency, unapologetically invoking the themes of race, solidarity, and civilized nonaggression.[227] They emerged again in the 1980s: using the issue to frame politics as a conflict between the virtuous and the vicious, NRA member Ronald Reagan heralded his opposition to gun control to show that "our side" supports "law-abiding people who want to protect their home and family," and his adversaries' pro-control stance to show that "the liberals" are "indifferent to the safety and welfare of the average American."[228] And they are surfacing once more in the wake of a series of school ground massacres, which have provoked waves of contempt for "hicksville cowboy[s]" with "oversized belt buckles"[229] who need guns to overcome their "macho, Freudian hang-ups."[230] Most of the time, however, politicians and ordinary citizens alike blunt the sharp edges of their expressive commitments with the softer idiom of deterrence, the logic of which doesn't assault either sides' fundamental commitments, at least not frontally.

---

cious behavior of African-American citizens. *See, e.g.*, 145 CONG. REC. H4371 (daily ed. June 16, 1999) (statement of Rep. Cunningham of San Diego) ("I went to Mr. Schumer's district, and I understand why he hates guns. They have all the projects, and they shoot each other, and they do drugs, and they kill each other, and that is bad. But the answer is not just to be negative, but to look and see what is reasonable.").

226 Bruce-Briggs, *supra* note 178, at 61.

227 *See* KENNETT & ANDERSON, *supra* note 189, at 234–36.

228 EDEL, *supra* note 172, at 112, 121 (quoting Ronald Reagan) (internal quotation marks omitted).

229 Margery Eagan, *Rally Proves Gun Lovers are Still Out There*, BOSTON HERALD, May 18, 1999, at 4, *available in* 1999 WL 3398695; *see also* Richard Cohen, *The Tame West*, WASH. POST, July 15, 1999, at A25 ("[Republican gun control opponents] all pretend to be upholding American tradition and rights, citing in some cases an old West of their fervid imagination and suggesting remedies that can only be considered inane."); Ted Flickinger, Letter to the Editor, *Dodge City, USA*, PITTSBURGH POST-GAZETTE, June 1, 1999, at A10 ("The widespread availability of guns in a society in which many so-called adult males still embrace the frontier mentality makes it a certainty these periodic adolescent outbursts will be tragically repeated. It's still Dodge City out there, boys. Wahoo."); Perry Young, *We Are All to Blame*, CHAPEL HILL HERALD, April 24, 1999, at 4, *available in* LEXIS, News Group File ("[W]e seem crippled by a mythological 'tradition' (a frontier gun world that ceased to exist 100 years ago and was wrong even then) and bullied into submission by a ridiculous minority of airheads like B-movie actor Charlton Heston and the National Rifle Association.").

230 Norman W. Nielsen, Letter to the Editor, L.A. TIMES, Apr. 30, 1999, at B6; *see also In Shadow of Littleton, NRA Refuses Scapegoat Role*, MILWAUKEE J. SENTINEL, May 2, 1999, at 1 (describing a sign displayed at a gun control rally that read: "Gun owners have penis envy").

What deterrence rhetoric helps each side to avoid disclosing, moreover, are their culturally imperialistic ambitions. Neither side can point to conclusive empirical evidence on whether handguns increase or decrease crime,[231] and in the end neither side is decisively motivated by beliefs about guns and crime control anyway. The dispositive point is what the enactment or defeat of gun control legislation *says*, not what it *does*. Both sides see the law as an instrument for affirming the moral commitments associated with the cultural style they admire and condemning those of the style they despise.

This is as true for the politically liberal proponents of gun control as it is for the conservative opponents of it. Liberals normally think that law should be confined to the regulation of other-regarding conduct and should not be used to promote a moral orthodoxy.[232] The commitments that gun control signifies to its supporters — including opposition to violence, support for gender and race equality, and concern with common welfare — are all proper objects of coercive law under the liberal standard (or at least under plausible conceptions of it). But gun control advocates don't support that policy because they believe that it will *itself* stop violent crime (most think it won't),[233] block racism and sexism, or remedy social deprivation; they support it because they think that it *expresses* the value of these objectives. Even more to the point, they support gun control because they see it as officially condemning a cultural style that prizes aggression, traditionally white male forms of status, and uncompassionate and punitive individualism. By taking private citizens' guns away, the law visits a decisive *symbolic* defeat on "macho men," "anti-citizens," and "uncivilized rednecks" who are obsessed with their sexual inadequacies. In effect, gun control is to the party of equality and solidarity what flag-desecration laws are to the party of patriotism.

Ironically, gun owners and their allies have repelled all but the most trivial forms of federal gun control in large measure because the ambitions of the gun controllers are perceived as expressive in nature. National polls have shown for decades that Americans prefer stricter gun control.[234] Why does Congress consistently side with the anti-

---

231 *Compare* LOTT, *supra* note 5, at 94 (presenting empirical evidence that states with permissive concealed handgun possession laws enjoy lower rates of violent crime), *with* Jens Ludwig, *Concealed-Gun-Carrying Laws and Violent Crime: Evidence from State Panel Data*, 18 INT'L REV. L. & ECON. 239, 241–43 (1998) (finding flaws in the Lott study).

232 *See, e.g.*, West Va. State Bd. of Educ. v. Barnette, 319 U.S. 624, 642 (1943) ("If there is any fixed star in our constitutional constellation, it is that no official, high or petty, can prescribe what shall be orthodox in politics, nationalism, religion, or other matters of opinion . . . ."); ACKERMAN, *supra* note 13, at 8–11; John Rawls, *The Idea of Public Reason Revisited*, 64 U. CHI. L. REV. 765–66, 773 (1997).

233 *See supra* p. 452 & note 170.

234 *Cf.* EDEL, *supra* note 172, at 70–73 (chronicling public support for gun registration).

control minority? The answer is that gun control opponents care much more intensely about the issue than do proponents and are much more willing to participate in gun control politics, either by voting against candidates who support control, by voicing their opinions to their representatives, or (most importantly) by giving money to anti-gun control interest groups such as the NRA.[235] And the reason that members of the anti-control minority care so intensely is that they know the aim of gun legislation is to disparage their cultural identities. Gun registration might be no more onerous than auto registration, but the social meaning of the former makes it impossible for gun owners to bear: "car regulation is not premised on the basis that cars are evils from which any decent person would recoil in horror — that anyone wanting to possess such an excrescence is atavistic and warped sexually, intellectually, educationally, and ethically."[236]

Expressive zealotry is inevitably answered in kind. Thus, the NRA became the force that it is today thanks to a huge influx of members and cash in the late 1960s when gun control rhetoric had reached its feverish expressive peak.[237] The organization continues to thrive on, and hence to fuel, its members' perception that control proponents are motivated by animus toward frontier and militia values.[238] Indeed, when gun control proponents tried to leverage national anguish over recent school yard shootings into stricter gun control laws, control opponents in the House of Representatives countered with a *Kulturkampf Blitzkrieg*, linking gun control to abortion, promiscuity, irreligiosity, and myriad other practices and policies perceived to be threatening to their constituents' cultural identities.[239] This tactic not only succeeded in stalling serious gun legislation but also secured the passage of measures condemning the low ethical standards of the entertainment indus-

235 *See* KENNETT & ANDERSON, *supra* note 189, at 238; Adams, *supra* note 174, at 119–20; *cf.* SPITZER, *supra* note 10, at 14 (detailing the success of the NRA).

236 Kates, *supra* note 170, at 96. This is a familiar dynamic in expressive politics. *Cf.* Joseph R. Gusfield, *On Legislating Morals: The Symbolic Process of Designating Deviance*, 56 CAL. L. REV. 54, 73 (1968) (noting that "redefining moral crusades tend to generate strong counter movements [sic]": "The threat to the legitimacy of the norm is a spur to the need for symbolic restatement in legal terms. . . . [I]t is when consensus is least attainable that the need for legal expression appears to be greatest.").

237 *See* KENNETT & ANDERSON, *supra* note 189, at 240–42.

238 *See* Kates, *supra* note 170, at 100 ("Indispensable to gun lobby success is an anti-gun discourse that convinces gun owners that 'gun control' is not a criminological imperative but a matter of culturally or ethically based hatred of them."); *cf.* SPITZER, *supra* note 10, at 9–12 (discussing the militia and frontier ethos of gun culture).

239 *See* Francis X. Clines, *In a Bitter Cultural War, An Ardent Call to Arms*, N.Y. TIMES, June 17, 1999, at A26.

try and recognizing the authority of state officials to post the Ten Commandments in public schools.[240]

This "action-reaction" dynamic makes expressive arguments for gun control inexpedient as well as illiberal. To dampen the intensity of opposition, it is essential to assure gun owners that control is *not* motivated by disgust for their cultural identities. Indeed, moderate advocates of control implore their allies to disavow strident, ideologically charged rhetoric.[241] This strategic motivation, along with the norm against public moralizing, helps to explain the prevalence of deterrence arguments in the gun control debate.[242]

But such expressive détentes are inherently unstable. Like anti-control interest groups, pro-control interest groups have a stake in fomenting expressive controversy in order to generate financial support from their membership. Even more fundamentally, to the extent that the gun control controversy aims to capture the expressive capital of the law, the battle can't be decisively won unless the social meaning of gun control is made express; control premised on deterrence grounds won't authoritatively repudiate martial and frontier virtues. Ultimately, then, the gun control movement is constrained by a social meaning paradox: the proponents of control can win only if they give up expressive talk, but if they give up expressive talk they can't win anything they really value.

C. Hate Crimes

What to do about "hate crimes" — violent offenses motivated by animus toward victims' group identities — is now a matter of intense national debate. At this point, the majority of states have hate crime laws, which typically impose enhanced penalties (including death, in

---

240 *See* Alison Mitchell & Frank Bruni, *House Vote Deals a Stinging Defeat to Gun Controls*, N.Y. TIMES, June 18, 1999, at A1.

241 *See, e.g.*, SPITZER, *supra* note 10, at 97 (arguing that the "white-hot rhetoric" of debate makes rational discussion impossible and urging proponents to stop screaming obscenities at the other side); Bruce-Briggs, *supra* note 178, at 61–62 (noting that the perception of cultural siege makes gun owners "a dangerous group to cross," and suggesting that "some of the mindless passion, on both sides, could be drained out of the gun-control issue"); Kates, *supra* note 170, at 100–02 (attributing the resistance to gun control to extremist pro-control rhetoric); Susan Tyrey-Jefferson, *Gun Control: Understanding the Policy Battle*, 20 CRIM. JUST. REV. 191, 198 (1995) (book review) ("Perhaps the most confounding question raised by the gun control debate, however, is that of why there is even a debate going on. . . . Until we stop fighting simply for the sake of a fight, no meaningful legislation can be enacted or implemented.").

242 Borrowing from successful campaigns to regulate smoking, control advocates have recently begun to frame gun control as an element of public health policy. *See* William J. Vizzard, *The Impact of Agenda Conflict on Policy Formulation and Implementation: The Case of Gun Control*, *in* GUNS IN AMERICA 131, 139 (Jan E. Dizard, Robert Merrill Muth & Stephen P. Andrews, Jr. eds., 1999). Like the use of deterrence language, this tactic "avoids the need for demonization by moving to . . . cost-benefit language." *Id.*

the case of homicide, in some jurisdictions) for offenses based on race, religion, or national origin.[243] But many citizens criticize such laws as creating "special rights," and oppose extending them to additional categories, including offenses based on animus toward gays, a motivation specified in less than half of the existing statutes.[244] Indeed, in some jurisdictions, intense disgust or loathing toward homosexuality is treated as a ground for *mitigating* the punishment for homicide under either the voluntary manslaughter, self-defense, or "diminished capacity" doctrines.[245]

Like the debates over capital punishment and gun control, the political fight over hate crimes is aimed at capturing the expressive capital of the law. Those who support hate crime laws see enhanced punishments as countering the message of group inferiority that such crimes convey, as symbolically affirming the political community's dedication to a particular conception of equality, and as recognizing the status of citizens whose social standing is insecure. Those who oppose hate crime laws intensely see those laws as condemning the conceptions of virtue that underwrite their own claim to status and recognition.[246]

The hate crimes debate, however, is a much younger expressive controversy than is either the capital punishment or gun control debate. Consequently, the rhetorical structure of the debate has not fully matured. Both sides continue to speak in an unselfconscious expressive idiom that makes their true motivations transparent. But deterrence arguments are also familiar and show up often in the pronouncements of judges and legislators. These arguments, which invariably lack cogency, *conceal* their proponents' true motivations. Nevertheless, deterrence arguments can be expected to become increasingly common as participants in the hate crime debate recoil from the cultural tension that expressive claims reveal.

1. Expressive Claims. — The expressive theory holds that both wrongdoing and punishment are defined in significant part by their social meanings.[247] The participants in the hate crime debate disagree about what bias-motivated crimes mean and what the law should say in response.

---

[243] *See* JAMES B. JACOBS & KIMBERLY POTTER, HATE CRIMES: CRIMINAL LAW & IDENTITY POLITICS 29 (1998).

[244] *See id.* at 30.

[245] *See* Gary David Comstock, *Dismantling the Homosexual Panic Defense*, 2 L. & SEXUALITY 81, 81–82 (1992).

[246] *See* Dan M. Kahan, The Anatomy of Disgust *in Criminal Law*, 96 MICH. L. REV. 1621, 1635–39 (1998) (book review).

[247] *See supra* Part I.A.1.

Proponents of hate crime laws argue that crimes motivated by homophobia, racism, religious bigotry, and like emotions have a distinctive social meaning.[248] Such crimes, the proponents argue, "send a message" that the victim and those who share his identity are not full members of society. Hate crimes say, in effect, "Fags" — or Blacks or Jews — "are not wanted here."[249] Indeed, hate crime offenders often select — or just as significantly are understood to select — modes of killing that convey that message in express terms: by tying African-American James Byrd to the bumper of their car and dragging his body for miles, his white supremacist killers traded on the evocative connotations of lynching;[250] by leaving the severely beaten and unconscious body of gay man Matthew Shepard dangling from a fence post, his killers were said to be patterning their behavior on "the Old West practice of nailing a dead coyote to a ranch fence as a warning to future intruders."[251]

These meanings, hate crime proponents argue, make such offenses worthy of special condemnation.[252] In American society, many individuals see their group commitments — from their ethnicity to their religious affiliation to their sexual orientation — as essential compo-

---

248 *See* Kahan & Nussbaum, *supra* note 8, at 350–53 (dealing with the role of emotion in criminal law).

249 Sam Fulwood III, *Dissent Blocks Tougher Hate Crime Laws*, L.A. TIMES, Oct. 14, 1998, at A14 (quoting the executive director of the National Coalition of Anti-Violence Programs) (internal quotation marks omitted); *see* Richard Lacayo, *The New Gay Struggle*, TIME, Oct. 26, 1998, at 32 ("What people mean when they say Matthew Shepard's murder was a lynching is that he was killed to make a point. When he was 21 years old, the world's arguments reached him with deadly force and printed their worst conclusions across him. So he was stretched along a Wyoming fence not just as a dying young man but as a signpost. 'When push comes to shove,' it says, 'this is what we have in mind for gays.'").

250 *See* Les Payne, *Exploitation and Dismissal of a Victim*, NEWSDAY (New York), June 21, 1998, at B6 ("It was a lynching so heinous that the Ku Klux Klan was moved to deny any involvement. . . . Byrd was chained to a pickup truck and dragged so roughly that his head, neck and arms were torn off along a mile of bad Texas road in Jasper. The three men charged with raising their white hands against Byrd bore a gallery of tattoos, some reportedly suggesting links to the Klan and the prison-bred Aryan Brotherhood."); *see also* Editorial, *Race, Memory and Justice*, N.Y. TIMES, June 14, 1998, § 4, at 14 ("In Jasper, [Texas,] the community has rallied around a sheriff bent on color-blind prosecution of this lynching by pickup truck.").

251 James Brooke, *Gay Man Dies from Attack, Fanning Outrage and Debate*, N.Y. TIMES, Oct. 13, 1998, at A1.

252 *See, e.g.*, 144 CONG. REC. E2291 (Oct. 15, 1998) (statement of Rep. Kucinich) ("The message that Mr. Shepard's attackers intended to send is clear. Their message was that lesbian and gay people should not feel welcome anywhere, a message that lesbian and gay Americans everywhere should fear for their safety. This message is the wrong message in a democratic society."); Gary Norman, *Time Texas Has a Gay-Inclusive Hate-Crime Law*, HOUSTON CHRON., Oct. 20, 1998, at A19 ("Hate-crime laws increase punishment and send a message that crimes motivated by hate are different from other crimes and will not be tolerated."); Ed Vogel, *Nevada Gays Protected by '95 Hate Crime Law*, LAS VEGAS REV.-J., Oct. 18, 1998, at 2B ("We are not tolerant of [hate crimes] and we are willing to extract more punishment.") (quoting Nevada assemblywoman Jan Evans, author of hate crimes legislation) (internal quotation marks omitted).

nents of their identities.[253] Accordingly, as much as rape conveys a more profound denial of a woman's worth than does an ordinary assault, so a hate crime connotes a more profound denial of worth than does another type of crime. This indignity, moreover, is visited not just upon the individual victim, but upon all those who share his defining commitments.[254]

Proponents defend enhanced punishment for such crimes in expressive terms as well. Hate crime laws "send the message" that the offender was *wrong* to see the victim as lower in worth by virtue of his group commitments.[255] In this way, they assure the victim and those who share his commitments that they *are* full members of society.[256]

Hate crime laws also affirm the larger community's commitment to the value of equality. They make it clear that "[t]here is nothing more important to the future of this country than our standing together against intolerance, prejudice, and violent bigotry."[257] Indeed, by denouncing the values of the hate criminals, such laws convey that those who refuse to stand *with* us in support of equality so conceived are not

---

253 *See, e.g.*, Note, *A Communitarian Defense of Group Libel Laws*, 101 HARV. L. REV. 682, 690 (1988).

254 *See, e.g.*, 144 CONG. REC. H4535 (June 11, 1998) (statement of Rep. Northup) ("I think it is important that we remember that when one black man is brutalized, every other person of race feels a greater sense of unease, and rightfully so. The effects of what happened in Texas will live long beyond one person. It would be impossible to measure the sense of dis-ease, dis-ease, that black Americans all across this country feel as a result of this act. Because of that, it is important that we register our outrage and our agony."); Norman, *supra* note 252, at A19 ("Unlike other crimes, hate crimes terrorize entire communities and instill fear into our society's already marginalized populations of people."); Janet Saidi, *Why Hate-Crime Laws Make Sense*, SAN DIEGO UNION-TRIB., Oct. 21, 1998, at B11 ("The difference between hitting someone to take their money and hitting someone because of their sexual orientation is that the latter affects not just an individual, but sends a message to an entire group of people.").

255 *See, e.g.*, George R. Nock, *Attack on Hate-Crimes Legislation Lacks Reason*, NEWS TRIB. (Tacoma, Wash.), Oct. 22, 1998, at A8 ("Hate-crime laws send a message: It is terribly wrong to act against people who are members of groups for no other reason than their membership."); *Reno Urges Expansion of Hate-Crime Laws*, N.Y. TIMES, Oct. 19, 1998, at A12 ("[Attorney General Janet Reno] said a bill introduced nearly a year ago — but not passed by the current Congress — would send 'a clear message from the Federal Government, if we can get it passed, that hate crimes will not be tolerated.'").

256 *See, e.g.*, John Anthony Melson, Letter to the Editor, *Hate-Crime Myths*, CHI. TRIB., Oct. 19, 1998, at 18 ("Hate-crime laws send back an important message of hope and support to the victim, and a strong message to potential perpetrators that hate-mongering will not be tolerated.").

257 President William J. Clinton, Statement on the Attack of Matthew Shepard (Oct. 10, 1998), *in* 34 WKLY. COMPILATION OF PRESIDENTIAL DOCUMENTS, 1998, at 2029; *see also* 144 CONG. REC. S12729 (Oct. 20, 1998) (statement of Sen. Kerry) ("The Declaration of Independence [gives us] certain inalienable rights; life, liberty, and the pursuit of happiness. Mr. President, those two young high school dropouts threaten [sic] each and every one of us when they stole Matthew's rights and life itself. That kind of hate is the real enemy of our civilization — and we come here to call on all people of good conscience to pass the laws that help us protect every citizen and we ask all Americans to make the personal commitment to live their lives each day in a way that brings us together.").

genuinely *of* us; *they* are the ones who "are not wanted here," who are "not part of [our] culture," "not part of [our] vision."[258] Projecting this meaning might be defended in instrumental terms as contributing to the inculcation of values such as toleration and respect. But the authoritative affirmation of equality also has inherent value as "a message about how the people of the state feel."[259]

Hate crime opponents respond in similarly expressive terms. They say that punishing bias-motivated crimes more severely "sends the message" that victims of other, non-hate-related crimes matter less in the eyes of the law than do hate crime victims.[260] This interpretation necessarily assumes that the proponents are wrong — perhaps descriptively, but more likely normatively — to see a person's group commitments as more central to her identity and worth than other facts about her.

Indeed, many critics of hate crime laws don't just assume but expressly argue that the law *shouldn't* convey respect for those who hold certain group commitments. Enhanced punishment for crimes motivated by animus toward homosexuality "would criminalize pro-family beliefs," argues an official of a prominent Christian advocacy group; such a law "basically sends a message that you can't disagree with the political message of homosexual activists."[261] "The reason they bring the Feds into this debate," adds another, "is that it's a way of legitimizing homosexual activity. They can't force the culture to accept their life but they are trying to do it legislatively."[262]

Expressive claims of this nature can even be used to justify *mitigating* the punishment of homophobic killers. Various doctrines of substantive criminal law, including voluntary manslaughter, reduce the punishment of impassioned offenders whose emotions express morally

258 James Brooke, *Crowd in Denver Rallies Against Skinhead Violence*, N.Y. TIMES, Nov. 26, 1997, at A20 (reporting speech of Denver mayor); *cf. ABC This Week* (ABC television broadcast, June 14, 1998) ("[The killing of James Byrd was] a contemptuous act — a heinous, subhuman crime.") (quoting Reverend Jesse Jackson) (internal quotation marks omitted).

259 Vogel, *supra* note 252, at 2B (reporting the opinion of a state legislator who authored a hate crime law).

260 *See, e.g.*, Steve Chapman, *A Dubious Case for Hate-Crimes Laws*, LAS VEGAS REV.-J., Oct. 21, 1998, at 11B ("It is a mistake, though, for the president to suggest that certain types of violence and intimidation are more tolerable than others."); Fulwood, *supra* note 249, at A14 ("'All crime is hate crime,' said Andrea Sheldon, executive director of the Traditional Values Coalition, an umbrella group of conservative religious organizations. 'Is that poor boy any more dead because he was homosexual? We shouldn't label some crimes more hateful than other crimes to advance a political agenda.'"); Debra Saunders, *Let Debate Begin on Hate Crimes*, IDAHO STATESMAN, Oct. 20, 1998, at 7B (stating that non-hate-crime victims "believe that disparate laws send a message that some lives are worth more than others").

261 Brooke, *supra* note 251, at A1 (quoting Steven A. Schwalm of the Family Research Council) (internal quotation marks omitted).

262 Fulwood, *supra* note 249, at A14 (quoting Andrea Sheldon, executive director of the Traditional Values Coalition) (internal quotation marks omitted).

reasonable valuations.[263] Thus, if the homophobic killer is right to attach a low value to his victim, if his anger or disgust reflects appropriate "pro-family beliefs," then he is entitled, so the argument goes, to the benefit of one of these doctrines.

This is exactly what one judge in Texas concluded. Justifying a lenient sentence for a defendant convicted of killing two homosexuals for allegedly propositioning him, the judge reasoned, "I put prostitutes and gays at about the same level, . . . and I'd be hard put to give somebody life for killing a prostitute."[264] "I don't care much for queers cruising the streets," the judge continued, "I've got a teen-age boy."[265] A reduced sentence was thus the appropriate way to affirm the low valuation of homosexuals expressed by the defendant's disgust. Gay rights activists predictably attacked the sentence as "send[ing] messages to the community that it's still open season on gay and lesbian citizens."[266]

2. *Deterrence as Normative Theory.* — Neither side in the hate crimes debate, however, limits itself to expressive arguments. Both also make deterrence arguments, which are no more cogent in this setting than they are in others in which deterrence claims compete with expressive ones.

Proponents of hate crime legislation typically make two types of deterrence arguments. First, they argue that larger penalties are necessary to counteract the unusually strong impulses of criminals motivated by group animus, which is thought to emanate from historically rooted social norms.[267] Second, they argue that penalty enhancements are necessary because hate crimes harm society more than other types of crimes. "[B]ias-motivated crimes," the defenders of hate crime laws argued to the Supreme Court in *Wisconsin v. Mitchell*,[268] "are more likely to provoke retaliatory crimes, inflict distinct emotional harms on

---

263 *See* Kahan & Nussbaum, *supra* note 8, at 306–21.

264 Lisa Belkin, *Texas Judge Eases Sentence for Killer of 2 Homosexuals*, N.Y. TIMES, Dec. 17, 1988, at 8.

265 *Id.*

266 *Id.*

267 *See, e.g.*, Robert T. Altman, Letter to the Editor, *Hate Crime Legislation*, L.A. TIMES, Oct. 21, 1998, at B6 (quoting a state court judge: "We punish wrongdoers in order to protect innocent people and to deter potential criminals. It is rather obvious that members of certain groups, for example, gays and African Americans, have long been abused simply because they are members of a group, and it seems similarly obvious that they should receive the additional protection that longer sentences hopefully afford."). *See generally* Gregory M. Herek, *Psychological Heterosexism and Anti-Gay Violence: The Social Psychology of Bigotry and Bashing*, *in* HATE CRIMES: CONFRONTING VIOLENCE AGAINST LESBIANS AND GAY MEN 149 (Gregory M. Herek & Kevin T. Berrill eds., 1992) [hereinafter Herek, *Psychological Heterosexism*] (discussing common motivations behind hate crimes).

268 508 U.S. 476 (1993).

their victims, and incite community unrest."[269] Given limited punishment resources, society should (all else equal) invest more in deterring more harmful crimes.[270] So assuming that hate crimes do in fact cause more harm than other types of crimes, society is justified in investing more to deter them even if hate criminals' violent propensities are no greater than those of other criminals. Turning aside the First Amendment challenge in *Mitchell*, the Supreme Court agreed that this "greater harm" argument "provides an adequate explanation for . . . penalty-enhancement provision[s] over and above mere disagreement with offenders' beliefs or biases."[271]

Opponents of hate crime legislation typically offer two sets of counterarguments. First, they challenge the empirical foundation of the claim that hate crimes cause greater harm.[272] Second, they suggest that enhanced penalties are wasteful. Offenders who lash out in racist or homophobic rage tend to act on impulse; consequently, they are unlikely to respond rationally to the threat of higher penalties.[273] After all, "[t]he conduct which hate crime laws aim at is already criminal."[274] If those who engage in such conduct are willing to "ignore existing criminal laws and punishment threats" — including, potentially, the death penalty in the case of homicide — there is no reason to think that "the additional threat promised by hate crime laws [will] add[] much, if any, marginal deterrence."[275]

In fact, the wasted-punishment argument can be used to justify punishing some hate criminals *less severely* rather than more. According to deterrence theory, the level of punishment should match the dangerousness of the offender. The mitigating consequence of the voluntary manslaughter doctrine can be justified on the ground that individuals who experience homicidal passion only in response to strong and unusual provocations are less dangerous than people who kill without provocation or when only mildly provoked.[276] Homosexual propositions seem fairly uncommon. Accordingly, a decisionmaker might well conclude that the impassioned killing of someone who makes such a proposition is a "one-time tragedy" committed by a per-

269 *Id.* at 488 (internal quotation marks omitted).

270 *See, e.g.*, BENTHAM, *supra* note 4, at 181.

271 *Mitchell*, 508 U.S. at 488; *see* Saidi, *supra* note 254, at B11.

272 *See* JACOBS & POTTER, *supra* note 243, at 81–87.

273 *See* Richard A. Posner, *Emotion Versus Emotionalism in Law*, *in* THE PASSIONS OF LAW 309 (Susan A. Bandes ed., forthcoming 2000).

274 JACOBS & POTTER, *supra* note 243, at 130.

275 *Id.*; *see, e.g.*, Editorial, *The Hate Debate*, NEW REPUBLIC, Nov. 2, 1998, at 7 ("It's hard to see how Matthew Shepard's killers would have been deterred by the prospect of federally assisted prosecution and a tough federal penalty. Under Wyoming law, and that of most states, murder is already punishable by the ultimate penalty: death.").

276 *See, e.g.*, Jerome Michael & Herbert Wechsler, *A Rationale of the Law of Homicide II*, 37 COLUM. L. REV. 1261, 1280–82 (1937).

son who the decisionmaker can be "confident ... [will] not kill again."[277]

The deterrence arguments both for and against hate crimes display all the shortcomings characteristic of this species of justification. To begin with, they are empirically speculative. The "impulsive" nature of hate crimes can cut either way. Perhaps additional punishment will have no effect and thus be wasted, as critics of hate crime laws (such as Richard Posner) suggest.[278] Or perhaps as deterrence theorists (including Richard Posner) have emphasized in other contexts, the prospect of extra punishment might be just what it takes to counteract the strength of these killers' impulses.[279] Alternatively, if these offenders are so consumed with unreasoning hate that no punishment of any size will *deter* them, then (as Richard Posner has stressed outside the hate crimes context) incarcerating them for longer periods of time or even executing them might be cost-justified for purposes of incapacitative *specific deterrence* because offenders of that sort clearly *are* very dangerous.[280] Or maybe not, because hate criminals are generally youthful (Richard Posner reminds us)[281] and can be expected to mellow with age.

Perhaps some homophobic killers are so unlikely to kill again that there is essentially no value in *incapacitating* them. But then again, perhaps mitigating punishment on that ground, as some jurisdictions do, will unacceptably detract from the *general deterrence* of individuals who find themselves faced with a homosexual proposition for the

277 *Judge Draws Protests After Cutting Sentence of Gay Man's Killer*, N.Y. TIMES, Aug. 17, 1994, at A15 (reporting a judge's explanation for the lenient sentence that he gave for a man who hunted down and killed a gay man who had fondled him); *see also* Posner, *supra* note 273 (arguing that a killing by a "'homophobe,' who, deeply concerned about his own sexual identity, kills a homosexual who propositions him" is a "category of hate crime [that] overlaps with the crime of passion and [thus] raises the issue whether provocation should not result in a lighter punishment for many hate crimes").

278 *See, e.g.*, Posner, *supra* note 273 (speculating that "impulsive juveniles, who are in fact responsible for the majority of hate crimes," might be "less deterrable because of the emotionality of youth").

279 *See generally* Posner, *supra* note 4, at 1223 ("There might seem to be another reason for punishing the impulsive crime less severely than the deliberated one: the impulsive crime is less deterrable; punishment is less efficacious, less worthwhile, and therefore society should buy less of it. But this analysis is incomplete. To begin with, the fact that a given increment of punishment will deter the impulsive criminal less than the deliberate one could actually point to heavier punishment for the former.").

280 *See id.* ("And we must not forget the incapacitative effect of imprisonment. The fact that certain criminals may not be deterrable argues for greater emphasis on their incapacitation, which implies long prison terms.").

281 *See* Posner, *supra* note 273 (emphasizing the youthfulness of most hate offenders).

first time. Furthermore, some premeditating killers might invite or stage homosexual propositions in order to escape severe punishment.[282]

Perhaps, as proponents of hate crime laws suggest, higher penalties are necessary to counteract the emotional and reputational pressure created by bigoted social norms. But it is also possible that higher penalties will *accentuate* rather than counteract those pressures. If skinheads and white supremacists already pride themselves on deviating from the norms of society at large, then penalty enhancements might actually magnify the status that homophobic and racist violence confers within those groups.

All of these effects are plausible. It is impossible to say, without the benefit of more solid empirical evidence than anyone in the hate crimes debate has marshaled so far, which of them predominates and under what circumstances.

The ineffectiveness of existing punishments is similarly inconclusive. Contrary to what critics of hate crime laws argue, the willingness of offenders to brave existing punishments does not imply that special hate crime penalties would be ineffective. For noncapital offenses, hate crime legislation supplies a penalty enhancement; for capital offenses, it supplies an additional aggravating factor for the death penalty, which isn't (and indeed can't be) mandatory under existing law.[283] Federal hate crime legislation permits *federal* prosecution, which might compensate for the reluctance of state officials to prosecute hate crimes aggressively.[284] By forcefully condemning bigotry, hate crime legislation could make factfinders more likely to convict and sentencers more likely to exercise their discretion to punish severely. Even if hate crime laws have no actual effect on the expected penalty, the information that they convey about society's attitudes might cause offenders to revise upward their *assessment* of the expected penalty, or induce them to revise downward the *value* that they attach to committing such crimes. Of course, similar arguments have been advanced in favor of severe punishments, including the death

282 Many cases in which a homosexual "provocation" is asserted seem to fit this pattern. *See* Comstock, *supra* note 245, at 96–97; Robert B. Mison, Comment, *Homophobia in Manslaughter: The Homosexual Advance as Insufficient Provocation*, 80 CAL. L. REV. 133, 167–70 (1992).

283 *See, e.g.*, Woodson v. North Carolina, 428 U.S. 280, 305 (1976).

284 *See Reno Urges Expansion of Hate-Crime Laws*, *supra* note 255, at A12 ("[Attorney General] Reno . . . said such nationwide legislation was needed to address 'situations where the state cannot or will not take action.'").

penalty, in other settings[285] and have been empirically documented in none of them.[286]

The "greater harm" argument is also unsatisfying. As mentioned, critics of hate crime laws challenge the "greater harm" claim on empirical grounds. The real problem, however, is conceptual. The Supreme Court's conclusion in *Mitchell* notwithstanding, the "greater harm" argument *doesn't* genuinely avoid crediting societal aversions to the "offenders' beliefs or biases."[287] For if such crimes really do "inflict distinct emotional harms . . . and incite community unrest,"[288] what is traumatizing victims and enraging onlookers is what they understand these crimes to *mean*, which does in fact depend on their perception of the perpetrators' motivations. As is characteristic of deterrence claims, the "greater harm" argument obscures a contentious decision about what kinds of public sensibilities can be legitimately included in the social welfare function.

But so do the deterrence arguments *against* penalty enhancements for hate crimes. The justification for punishing, from a deterrence standpoint, is to maximize social welfare.[289] The satisfaction that citizens take in denouncing the motivations of hate criminals, in repairing the social status of historically despised groups, or in celebrating societal commitment to a particular conception of equality can be regarded as a species of social welfare. Securing it furnishes a justification for hate crime laws even if enhanced penalties fail to produce efficient behavioral incentives or are unnecessary for incapacitation. Those critics of hate crime laws who argue that the *only* pertinent consideration is the relative "dangerousness" of hate crime offenders[290] are using deterrence arguments to conceal the undefended *exclusion* of certain values from the social welfare function.

The only parties who are not concealing their motivations are the ones who criticize or defend hate crime laws in overtly expressive terms. However reprehensible his remarks, the Texas judge who miti-

---

285 *See, e.g.*, Jack P. Gibbs, *Preventive Effects of Capital Punishment Other than Deterrence*, 14 CRIM. L. BULL. 34, 40–41 (1978) (referring to the argument that legal punishments serve the purpose of "normative validation" by helping maintain "the condemnation of a particular kind of act").

286 Empirical studies consistently find that increasing the certainty of punishment has a much more significant deterrent effect on all manner of crime than does increasing the severity of it. *See, e.g.*, JAMES Q. WILSON & RICHARD J. HERRNSTEIN, CRIME AND HUMAN NATURE 398 (1985) (drunk driving); Alfred Blumstein & Daniel Nagin, *The Deterrent Effect of Legal Sanctions on Draft Evasion*, 29 STAN. L. REV. 241, 269 (1977) (draft evasion); Isaac Ehrlich, *Participation in Illegitimate Activities: A Theoretical and Empirical Investigation*, 81 J. POL. ECON. 521, 544–47 (1973) (robbery).

287 Wisconsin v. Mitchell, 508 U.S. 476, 488 (1993).

288 *Id.*

289 *See generally* BENTHAM, *supra* note 4; Posner, *supra* note 4.

290 *See, e.g.*, Posner, *supra* note 273.

gated the punishment of the homophobic killer presented an argument that was cogent. *If* prostitutes and gays aren't worth as much as other citizens, *then* punishing those who kill them less severely than those who kill others *does* express exactly that valuation. Maybe that sentence will "send [a] message[] . . . that it's still open season on gay and lesbian citizens,"[291] and thus invite even more violence against them, but that's not a problem for someone who, like the Texas judge, doesn't "care much for queers cruising the streets."[292]

Similarly, those who *support* hate crime laws on expressive grounds can be seen as saying that they value the messages of respect for minorities and condemnation of homophobes and other bigots that such laws convey, *regardless* of the behavioral consequences such laws produce. "I don't think an enhancement statute provides a deterrent effect," acknowledges the legislator who sponsored Nevada's hate crimes statute.[293] But even if the "law may not stop hate crimes," she explains, "it sends a message about how the people of the state feel."[294] "The criminal law is an expression of the nation's basic moral standards," observes a representative of the American Jewish Congress.[295] Consequently, "enactment of a [federal hate crimes] statute . . . serves a valuable purpose *even if no one is ever sentenced to an enhanced penalty* as a result of its enactment."[296] "[W]ill this stop violence against women . . . ?" asks the sponsor of the federal Violence Against Women Act. "The answer is no, [but] that is not my intention. My intention in making this a civil rights violation is to change the Nation's attitude."[297]

At this point, no rigorous public opinion testing has been done to determine whether deterrence arguments genuinely explain why those who make such arguments feel the way that they do about hate crime legislation. But given how absurdly weak those arguments are relative to the expressive claims made for and against such laws, it seems unlikely that deterrence is doing any more work in the hate crimes debate than it is in the gun control and death penalty debates.

3. Deterrence as Discourse Strategy. — The work that deterrence arguments *do* do in the gun control and death penalty debates, however, is substantial. Notwithstanding their empirically speculative and evaluatively question-begging nature — indeed, partly by virtue of

---

291 Belkin, *supra* note 264, at 8 (internal quotation marks omitted).

292 *Id.*

293 Vogel, *supra* note 252, at 2B (internal quotation marks omitted).

294 *Id.*

295 JACOBS & POTTER, *supra* note 243, at 76.

296 *Id.* (emphasis added).

297 *Legislation to Reduce the Growing Problem of Violent Crime Against Women: Hearing Before the Senate Comm. on the Judiciary*, 101st Cong. 2 (1990) (statement of Senator Joseph R. Biden) (internal quotation marks omitted).

that — deterrence arguments play a critical role in muting expressive controversy over those issues. This same discourse management function explains the emergence of deterrence arguments in the hate crimes debate.

The hate crimes debate is a struggle between opposing communities that pits competing cultural styles against each other. Work in social psychology, for example, suggests that individuals who hold homophobic views tend to belong to communities that assign status according to traditional hierarchical gender norms. These individuals express loathing toward homosexuality (sometimes violently) both to gain esteem within their subcommunities and to vindicate their communities' norms within society at large.[298] Individuals who belong to communities that prize egalitarian norms, in contrast, tend to have positive attitudes toward homosexuality and are likewise motivated to express those views publicly as a way to affirm their membership in those communities and to earn approval within them.[299]

The members of these groups care deeply about hate crime laws because they see those laws as adjudicating their competing claims to status and recognition.[300] Thus, gay advocacy groups lobbied intensely for the inclusion of homophobic crimes in the federal Hate Crime Statistics Act of 1990[301] and later celebrated it as "the first time in history that sexual orientation will be included in a federal civil rights law."[302] Right wing Christian groups opposed it just as passionately. To them, the law equated disapproval of homosexuality with racism and religious bigotry, a message that they found deeply insulting.[303] The legislation ultimately overcame the opposition of powerful conservative Senator Jesse Helms only after its sponsors consented to a preamble that proclaimed, "Nothing in this Act shall be construed . . . to promote or encourage homosexuality."[304] The same factions are

[298] *See* Karl M. Hamner, *Gay-Bashing: A Social Identity Analysis of Violence Against Lesbians and Gay Men*, *in* HATE CRIMES: CONFRONTING VIOLENCE AGAINST LESBIANS AND GAY MEN, *supra* note 267, at 179, 182–83; Gregory M. Herek, *Beyond "Homophobia": A Social Psychological Perspective on Attitudes Toward Lesbians and Gay Men*, *in* BASHERS, BAITERS & BIGOTS: HOMOPHOBIA IN AMERICAN SOCIETY 1, 12 (John P. De Cecco ed., 1985) [hereinafter Herek, *Beyond "Homophobia"*]; Herek, *Psychological Heterosexism*, *supra* note 267, at 153–54; *see also* Richard A. Berk, Elizabeth A. Boyd & Karl M. Hamner, *Thinking More Clearly About Hate-Motivated Crimes*, *in* HATE CRIMES: CONFRONTING VIOLENCE AGAINST LESBIANS AND GAY MEN, *supra* note 267, at 123, 127 (characterizing "hate-motivated violence" as "symbolic crimes" among competing groups).

[299] *See* Herek, *Psychological Heterosexism*, *supra* note 267, at 153–54.

[300] *See generally* JACOBS & POTTER, *supra* note 243, at 65 (arguing that the passage of hate crime laws can be "explained by the growing influence of identity politics").

[301] Pub. L. No. 101-275, 104 Stat. 140 (codified as amended at 28 U.S.C. § 534 note (1994)).

[302] JACOBS & POTTER, *supra* note 243, at 71 (quoting Tim McFeeley, executive director of the Human Rights Campaign Fund) (internal quotation marks omitted).

[303] *See id.* at 70.

[304] 104 Stat. at 141.

girding for expressive battle over federal and state legislation in the aftermath of the grisly slaying of Matthew Shepard.[305]

Competition over the law's expressive capital can pit not only the Christian right against civil rights groups, but also civil rights groups against one another. For example, the groups that supported the Hate Crime Statistics Act successfully opposed feminist efforts to add rape to the Act out of concern that doing so would detract from their efforts to call attention to homophobic and racist assaults. Angered feminists thereafter turned their attention to securing their own hate crimes law, an effort that led to the Violence Against Women Act of 1994.[306] Feminists also squared off against African-American civil rights advocates over the *O.J. Simpson* case: whereas some feminists lobbied the prosecutor to seek the death penalty to "get[] society to take domestic violence and female victims seriously," African-American leaders lobbied against it on the ground that it could reinforce social disapproval of interracial marriages.[307] African-American and Jewish groups in New York City have clashed repeatedly over whether the "hate crime" label should be afforded to assaults committed by blacks against Jews and vice versa.[308]

Even if deterrence theory lacks the power to resolve these expressive conflicts as a matter of normative theory, it might still be rhetorically potent enough (that is, rhetorically inert enough) to discharge those conflicts in practice. On its face, at least, the cost-benefit logic of deterrence abstracts from the contentious social meanings that motivate the warring cultural factions in the hate crimes battle. Accordingly, those who speak in a deterrence idiom need not be seen (at least from a distance) as picking sides.

More specifically, we should expect deterrence arguments to appeal to three important constituencies. First are ordinary citizens who have a position on hate crime laws but do not hold it passionately. For them, the value of revealing their expressive allegiances in public is

305 *See, e.g.*, Brooke, *supra* note 251, at A1 ("Gay leaders hope that Mr. Shepard's death will galvanize Congress and state legislatures to pass hate-crime legislation or broaden existing laws. Conservatives, particularly Christian conservatives, generally oppose such laws, saying they extend to minorities 'special rights.'").

306 *See* JACOBS & POTTER, *supra* note 243, at 72–76.

307 Scott Armstrong, *Case Against Simpson Intensifies Death-Penalty Debate in U.S.*, CHRISTIAN SCI. MONITOR, Sept. 6, 1994, at 2; *see also* Haya El Nasser & Richard Price, *"Race Factor Begins to Emerge"/L.A. Fear: Reopening Old Wounds*, USA TODAY, July 20, 1994, at 3A (noting concern of African-American civil rights activists that the Simpson case would "reinforce negative opinions about interracial marriages").

308 *See* JACOBS & POTTER, *supra* note 243, at 138. For a comic example of the conflict that hate crime legislation can provoke among civil rights advocacy groups, see Hayward, cited above in note 5, quoting a so-called "fathers' rights" activist opposed to domestic abuse legislation: "At every opportunity, this administration seeks to demonize fathers and destroy the institution of fatherhood."

smaller than the gains of complying with the liberal social norm against contentious public moralizing. So just as citizens do when forced to declare their position on the death penalty, these individuals will opt for the morally unambitious and culturally unaggressive idiom of deterrence.

Second, deterrence arguments should appeal to officials and opinion leaders who are committed to cleansing public debate of moralizing as a matter of principle. They will frame the hate crime issue in deterrence terms as a means of steering expressive controversy away from the hate crimes issue ex ante and blunting the expressive import of hate crime laws ex post. Motivations of this sort plausibly explain the Supreme Court's acceptance of the fallacious argument in *Mitchell* that penalty enhancements are warranted by the "greater harms" associated with hate crimes rather than by societal aversions to the messages that such crimes express.[309] They explain, too, why an economist as smart as Richard Posner would focus only on the "dangerousness" of criminal offenders in evaluating hate crime laws: Posner excludes expressive sensibilities from the social welfare calculus not because he is obtuse but because, like Justice Holmes, he sees the infusion of expressive sensibilities into the criminal law as productive of incessant illiberal conflict.[310]

Third, deterrence arguments will recommend themselves to strategically sophisticated (and emotionally disciplined) proponents of hate crime legislation. Like opposition to gun control, opposition to hate crime laws draws much of its force from the perceived cultural ambitions of those who support such laws; the Christian right sees hate crime legislation as equating disapproval of homosexuality with racist bigotry and therefore as "criminaliz[ing]" supposedly "pro-family beliefs."[311] Muting the expressive overtones of such laws should thus reduce the intensity of the opposition to them. A moderate legislator

---

309 *See supra* pp. 467–68.

310 Posner writes:

> [My] objection [to hate crime laws], in short, is not to varying the punishment for crime according to the harm suffered by the victim or the deterrability of the criminal but to varying it in order to make a political or ideological statement, or (what is often the same thing) to accommodate the pressures of politically influential groups. Ideology and interest-group politics have no proper place in a criminal justice system. In rejecting this precept, the supporters of hate-crime laws, some of whom are deficient in historical memory, are playing with fire. It was not long ago that a political or ideological conception of the role of criminal law would have justified less, rather than more, protection of that law for blacks, homosexuals, and other minorities. Proponents of hate-crime law may respond that in those bad old days the enforcement of the criminal law on behalf of these groups was often unenthusiastic, and this is true. But there is a difference between failing to protect people adequately against private hostility and making that hostility a basis for punishment. The first practice is wrong; the second is wrong and dangerous.

Posner, *supra* note 273.

311 *See supra* p. 466.

who acquiesces in the enactment of a hate crime statute will get in less trouble with her most conservative constituents if the sponsors of hate crime legislation *say* their goal is only to "deter" violence than she will if the stated aim of the legislation is to "send the message" that gays deserve as much respect as heterosexuals, Jews as much as Christians, blacks as much as whites, etc. Of course, once such laws are on the books, their sponsors are free to celebrate them as symbolic acknowledgements of the status of the protected groups — just as gay rights advocates did after enactment of the Hate Crime Statistics Act, its absurd preamble notwithstanding.[312] These dynamics can explain why public officials who support hate crime laws gravitate toward the deterrence idiom.[313]

For all of these reasons, we should expect deterrence arguments, already prominent in the debate over hate crime laws, to become even more so as the debate progresses. Those who are content merely to debunk such arguments as normatively facile are, at a minimum, overlooking the role that these arguments play in discourse management.

Worse yet, the deterrence critics might also be making a grievous moral blunder. By loudly discrediting deterrence arguments — by demonstrating, in particular, that such arguments cannot really compel a position on hate crimes independent of contentious judgments of value — normative theorists risk impairing the cooling effect of deterrence as a strategy for discourse management. *If* the secret ambition of deterrence is a morally honorable one, then it is morally wrong to be (or at least to talk like) anything other than a Benthamite. ***Whether*** the secret ambition of deterrence is morally honorable is the question to which I now turn.

III. THE SECRET AMBITION APPRAISED

So far I have concerned myself with the positive question of why deterrence theory figures so prominently in public debate over criminal law. The answer, I have argued, is ***not*** that deterrence speaks authoritatively to the moral issues posed by capital punishment, gun control, hate crimes, and the like; on the contrary, the attraction of deterrence

---

312 *See supra* pp. 473–74.

313 *See, e.g.*, Nock, *supra* note 255, at A8 ("When the Tacoma City Council voted, 8–1, to include sexual orientation as a protected category, one of the council members, an opponent of gay rights, noted he was voting for the provision because it was a safety issue."); *see also* Altman, *supra* note 267, at B6 (quoting a state court judge: "We punish wrongdoers in order to protect innocent people and to deter potential criminals. It is rather obvious that members of certain groups, for example, gays and African Americans, have long been abused simply because they are members of a group, and it seems similarly obvious that they should receive the additional protection that longer sentences hopefully afford.").

is precisely that it *doesn't* speak to the contested expressive values that make these matters so contentious. We resort to the culturally ecumenical idiom of deterrence to avoid a style of public moralizing that principle, interest, and etiquette all condemn. In this way, deterrence cools — with intermittent success — an engine of debate that is predisposed to run at a white hot temperature.

I now want to take up the normative question of whether the discourse management function of deterrence is itself good or bad. Does it cleanse public debate of expressive zealotry? Or contaminate it with hypocrisy? Does it facilitate convergence by citizens of diverse cultural identities? Or conceal the influence of dominant subcommunities? Does it promote the ultimate triumph of enlightened policies? Or prolong the influence of morally bankrupt social norms?

The unhappy truth is that there just are no final answers to questions such as these. The contribution that deterrence makes to discourse management is both the strongest argument for and the strongest argument against this theory of punishment. The best we can do is pragmatically adapt our style of talk to the nature of the issue at hand, although even this strategy tends to defeat itself when self-consciously pursued.

My argument in this Part proceeds dialectically. I begin with a liberal defense of deterrence theory as a form of discourse management. I then counter that position with an antiliberal critique. Finally, I attempt a pragmatic reconciliation of these positions, one that I regard as only partially successful.

A. Liberal Thesis

Expressive condemnation and optimal deterrence are not so much competing ways to *identify* morally justified laws (the latter never contradicts the former) as they are competing ways to *describe* what makes such laws morally justified. The expressive theory is excruciatingly judgmental. It endorses the behavior of the individual who opts to kill rather than to run because he is a "true man," whose "resent[ment]" of the "humiliating indignity" of flight appropriately values "liberty" and "rights" more than the life of a wrongful aggressor;[314] it withholds severe punishment for homophobic killers because it "do[es]n't care much for queers," whom it puts "at about the same level" as "prostitutes";[315] it supports gun control to condemn the "anticitizen," whose vision of individual self-sufficiency "ought to disgust . . . the civilized observer."[316] Deterrence, by contrast at least, is

[314] *See supra* pp. 429–430.
[315] *See supra* p. 467.
[316] *See supra* pp. 457–58.

soothingly detached: it talks of persons who can't behave rationally "in the presence of . . . uplifted kni[ves],"[317] of the disutility of incapacitating offenders who we can be "confident . . . [will] not kill again,"[318] and of the effect that banning handguns will have in reducing violent crime.[319]

To choose between expressive condemnation and optimal deterrence, then, we must consider which form of public discourse — judgmental or detached, face-breaking or face-saving[320] — is better. In particular, since we know that citizens by and large are motivated by expressive considerations even when they profess to be relying on instrumental ones, the deterrence theory can be defended only if we think that it is appropriate for citizens to hide their true moral feelings — to refrain from "saying all [they] think," in Justice Holmes's words — when they deliberate about criminal law. Is there any theory of public discourse that would justify rhetorical indirection of this sort?

There is: modern liberalism. Liberalism is famously opposed to public moralizing, or at least to certain robust forms of it. Rawls calls this the liberal principle of "public reason," which enjoins public officials and private citizens alike "not to appeal to comprehensive religious and philosophical doctrines — to what [they] as individuals or members of associations see as the whole truth —"[321] when engaging in political deliberation, but rather "to explain the basis of their actions to one another in terms each could reasonably expect that others might endorse as consistent with their freedom and equality."[322] Rawls confines the directive of public reason to certain fundamental issues relating to the structure of government and the content of basic rights.[323] Other liberal theorists, however, see the obligation of citizens to disclaim reliance on "privileged insight into the moral universe,"[324] and instead to confine themselves "to reasons or principles that can be shared by fellow citizens" of diverse moral persuasions,[325] as coextensive with the domain of coercive state authority.

Liberal legal theorists put the same constraints on judicial discourse. Formalism, "minimalism," and related techniques of judicial

---

317 *See supra* pp. 429–430.

318 *See supra* pp. 468–69.

319 *See supra* notes 168–169.

320 *Cf.* GUSFIELD, *supra* note 25, at 185 ("Since status conflicts involve opposition between styles of life, it is necessary to break the 'face' of the opponent by degrading his cultural content.").

321 RAWLS, *supra* note 13, at 224–25.

322 *Id.* at 218.

323 *See id.* at 214. He does allow, however, that "it is usually highly desirable" that even less fundamental political issues be resolved "by invoking the values of public reason." *Id.* at 215.

324 ACKERMAN, *supra* note 13, at 10.

325 GUTMANN & THOMPSON, *supra* note 13, at 55.

restraint, they argue, can be seen as strategies for grounding legal decisions in reasons acceptable to persons of diverse moral outlooks and commitments.[326]

The liberal commitment to public reason rests on two motivations. The first is a practical one. The avoidance of contentious public moralizing is thought to promote popular acceptance of law. Because fundamental moral dissensus is a permanent feature of the modern condition,[327] we can expect citizens to submit to a regime in which democratic majorities continually get their way only if citizens are "assured that 'ultimate values' — the things they care about most — will not be dragged through the mud of contestation."[328] Once "emotionally charged solidarities and commitments are displaced from the political realm," moreover, democratic politics become more cooperative.[329] Citizens of diverse persuasions are more likely to converge on solutions to their common problems if they agree not to treat politics as a site for adjudicating the fundamental issues of value that divide them and if accommodation and compromise are not taxed with connotations of moral collaboration or surrender.[330]

The second motivation behind the principle of public reason is liberalism's foundational commitment to individual autonomy. Abiding moral dissensus is the "inevitable outcome of free human reason."[331] Consequently, in order to respect each individual's capacity to choose her own ends, citizens and legislators must refrain from grounding their support for coercive policies in reasons that are compatible with only some comprehensive views and not with others.[332] By rooting legal conclusions in formally authoritative sources such as precedent or textualism, rather than in raw invocations of morality, participants in the legal culture likewise "convey mutual respect and a desire to maintain connections."[333] Because such decisions disclaim any grounding in contentious moral presuppositions, dissenting citizens can acquiesce in them without feeling that they are being forced to renounce their defining outlooks and commitments.[334]

---

326 *See* SUNSTEIN, *supra* note 13, at 46–47 (comparing "incompletely theorized agreements" to "overlapping consensus"); Cass R. Sunstein, *The Supreme Court, 1995 Term — Foreword: Leaving Things Undecided*, 110 HARV. L. REV. 4, 37–38 (1996) (defending "minimalism" as morally unambitious in the liberal sense); Strauss, *supra* note 13, at 17–20 (connecting "techniques of legal argument" to the Rawlsian notion of "overlapping consensus").

327 *See* GUTMANN & THOMPSON, *supra* note 13, at 18–26.

328 Holmes, *supra* note 147, at 217.

329 *Id.* at 207.

330 *See* SUNSTEIN, *supra* note 13, at 37–39; Strauss, *supra* note 13, at 20–21.

331 RAWLS, *supra* note 13, at 37.

332 *See id.* at 216–17.

333 Strauss, *supra* note 13, at 21; *see also* SUNSTEIN, *supra* note 13, at 39 (arguing that "incompletely theorized agreements" help citizens show each other mutual respect).

334 *See* SUNSTEIN, *supra* note 13, at 41.

The strongest defense of deterrence theory is that using it to justify contentious criminal law policies satisfies the basic demands of liberal public reason. Expressive arguments overtly appeal to values — from hierarchical conceptions of honor to contested conceptions of equality, from individualism to civic solidarity — that belong only to particular moral visions and cultural styles; indeed, when they take the form of battles over the law's expressive capital, disputes over the death penalty, gun control, hate crimes, and like issues all aim at the exaltation of one subcommunity's moral view and the disparagement of another's. But when citizens and officials frame their positions on these same issues in deterrence terms, they avoid directly challenging each other's fundamental commitments. None of the cultural styles in conflict denies, in the abstract, that the law should "reduce crime"; *all* of them can agree that the law should be used to promote desirable states of affairs — so long as they don't have to say anything about what those states of affairs are. It's true that deterrence arguments have a certain caginess about them, insofar as they invariably reflect unstated expressive theories of value. But this evaluative modesty (how thoughtless to deride it as "emptiness"!) is exactly what makes deterrence theory congenial to liberal public reason, which counsels us "*not* [to] appeal to the *whole* truth as we see it, even when it might be readily available."[335]

To the extent that it succeeds in displacing its contentious expressive rival, deterrence theorizing secures both of the general goals of liberal public reason. First, it makes the criminal law more acceptable to persons of diverse moral persuasions. Once the law gets out of the business of "sending messages" about whose values and commitments count and whose don't, it no longer serves as a lightning rod for expressive zealotry. Citizens can determine their positions on issues like the death penalty, gun control, and hate crimes based solely on whether they believe such policies contribute to their security as opposed to their relative social standing. Indeed, shielded from the distorting influences of symbolic politics, legislators and judges are more likely to resolve disputed issues in a rational fashion that genuinely *does* furnish cost-effective security to *all* citizens.

Deterrence arguments are also open to dispute, of course, but the empirical issues that they involve excite much less contention than do the moral ones posed by the expressive arguments. Consider how little emotional blood is spilled over the duty to retreat from a deadly encounter once dispensing with it is seen to reflect, not the virtue of the "true man," but the perceived imperviousness of a terrified person to

---

[335] RAWLS, *supra* note 13, at 218 (emphasis added).

legal incentives.[336] By leaching the meaning out of issues like the death penalty and gun control, deterrence similarly lowers the expressive stakes of these debates, whether or not it makes the proper resolution of them any clearer.

Second, as a substitute for overtly expressive arguments, deterrence claims show respect for individual autonomy. When citizens publicly defend or oppose a law based *not* on its perceived behavioral consequences but on their desire to see the law repudiate values that they abhor, they show contempt for the persons who see such values as central to their identities. This is clearly so, for example, when legislators voice their support for unenforced sodomy laws to express condemnation of homosexuality;[337] but it's just as true when citizens say that they support gun control to show that they are "disgusted" with the frontier ethic of individual self-sufficiency. Like the decision of a judge to invoke formal grounds rather than moral ones, the decision of a citizen to rely on deterrence rather than on expressive arguments shows respect for her cultural adversaries. When citizens and public officials debate controversial policies in deterrence terms, moreover, they spare the losers in those debates from having to see their cultural and moral identities as incompatible with their civic ones.

Although some might object that Rawls's conception of liberal public reason taints deliberation with an objectionable lack of candor, the liberal defense of deterrence does not imagine that citizens will engage in deceit. Because individuals tend to resolve empirical uncertainty consistently with their values,[338] most citizens will sincerely believe that deterrence is best promoted by the policies that they actually support for expressive reasons. Even if they perceive (as is likely) that deterrence is not the *only* reason that they support those policies, citizens who choose to use deterrence arguments to avoid "saying all they think" are not lying, but are merely restraining their advocacy in the interest of civility and respect.[339]

Similarly, the liberal defense doesn't necessarily imagine that deterrence exercises its cooling effect by "tricking" or "duping" anyone. We are perfectly aware that those who make deterrence arguments on behalf of policies such as the death penalty, hate crimes, and gun control likely hold culturally partisan expressive beliefs that point in the same direction. But for exactly that reason, the decision of an individual to frame her position in the bland idiom of deterrence, rather than in the

---

[336] *See supra* pp. 432–435.

[337] *See* Kogan, *supra* note 24, at 233.

[338] *See supra* p. 428, 438.

[339] *Cf.* Bruce Ackerman, *Why Dialogue?*, 86 J. PHIL. 5, 19 (1989) (arguing that the liberal principle of "conversational restraint" does not "require people to say things they believe are false" but only "to repress their desire to say many things which they believe are true").

caustic and assaultive one of expressive condemnation, effectively conveys her desire to avoid moral confrontation. Resort to deterrence is the rhetorical equivalent of extending the hand — a ceremonial gesture of goodwill and accommodation that signals that one is not about to let another's competing cultural commitments stand in the way of mutually advantageous undertakings.

I have been using liberal theory to justify the role of deterrence theory in public deliberations over criminal law; the role of deterrence theory, however, can also be used to deepen our understanding of liberal theory. The function of deterrence as a strategy for managing public discourse furnishes an example of what something approaching liberal public reason looks like in practice. It looks different, moreover, from what either liberal political theorists or liberal legal theorists imagine.

Rawls understands liberal public reason to preclude arguments rooted in a "comprehensive view," which he defines as any "precisely articulated scheme of thought" — religious or philosophical — that "includes conceptions of what is of value in human life, as well as ideals of personal virtue and character, that are to inform much of our nonpolitical conduct (in the limit our life as a whole)."[340] For Rawls, "[u]tilitarianism is a familiar example" of a comprehensive view.[341] Other liberal theorists likewise assume that utilitarianism and related consequentialist systems of justification are too ambitious in defining the good to be an acceptable basis for policymaking in a liberal regime.[342]

The function of deterrence theory as a strategy for managing political conflict calls this suspicion of utilitarianism into question. Deterrence theory is utilitarian or consequentialist in nature, yet it succeeds in muting illiberal conflict in criminal law. That it is able to do so notwithstanding its "comprehensive" underpinnings is likely a consequence, in part, of a rhetorical framing effect: because deterrence arguments are so much *less* contentious than their familiar expressive counterparts, one's choice to speak in a deterrence idiom is an unambiguous gesture of ideological compromise and self-restraint. Deterrence is also able to mute expressive conflict because of the relative *looseness* of utilitarian or consequentialist arguments as they actually

340 RAWLS, *supra* note 13, at 175.

341 *Id.* at 13.

342 *See, e.g.*, ACKERMAN, *supra* note 13, at 49 ("[T]he problem with utilitarianism is its teleological character, its effort to evaluate distribution rules by how much 'good' they produce. *Any* such effort requires a specification of the good that will be contested by *some* citizens who insist on measuring their good by a different yardstick . . . ."); GUTMANN & THOMPSON, *supra* note 13, at 184–96 (arguing that consequentialist forms of policymaking supply neither a theoretically cogent nor a practically feasible approach for aggregating the preferences of citizens of diverse moral persuasions).

appear in political debate. Consequentialist arguments are likely to strike citizens as imperialistic about conceptions of the good only when those arguments clearly specify the account of the good that they are trying to maximize; deterrence arguments in American criminal law nearly always elide that question, and thus appeal widely across groups that subscribe to antagonistic conceptions of what makes for a valuable life.

The lesson for liberal political theory is that those who want to implement public reason need fairly fine-grained and contextual understandings of how citizens perceive different styles of argument. What sounds comprehensive to the ear of a philosopher might not to the ear of the ordinary citizen.

The function of deterrence as a strategy for managing public discourse also challenges certain conclusions of liberal legal theory, which unlike liberal political theory does pay close attention to actual practice. Sunstein, for example, sees American judicial discourse as contributing to liberal political ends through the device of "incompletely theorized agreements," by which he means (primarily) consensus on "concrete outcomes"[343] in the absence of any commonly stated agreement on the "general theory that accounts for" them.[344] Sunstein points out that it's often easier for citizens, lawmakers, or judges to agree about *what* the law should do — protect endangered species, recognize labor unions, respect the right to abortion — than about *why* the law should do it, in which case deliberation over "abstractions" such as utilitarianism or Kantianism will produce needless illiberal conflict.[345]

Deterrence, however, is an example of one "abstraction" that *lessens* conflict over the content of the law. Indeed, it is precisely because deterrence arguments *abstract from* contentious social meanings that they are able to cool debates over issues like the duty to retreat, gun control, and the death penalty, the concrete outcomes of which polarize the body politic.

Although it is hazardous to generalize about the respective functions of "generality" and "concreteness" in managing political conflict

---

[343] SUNSTEIN, *supra* note 13, at 4.

[344] *Id.* at 5.

[345] *See id.* at 4–8, 36–37. Sunstein states that "incompletely theorized agreements" characterize the decisionmaking culture of the judiciary and not that of the political branches. *Id.* at 45, 60. Many of his examples of the salutary role of such agreements in discharging conflict, however, deal with policies made by legislatures or administrative agencies. The benefits of "incompletely theorized agreements" in the courts would surely be minimal were politics treated as a moral free-fire zone. *See, e.g.*, Strauss, *supra* note 13, at 39 ("There is general agreement on an elaborate set of both procedural and substantive limits on the acceptable ways of resolving political disputes. . . . [W]e underestimate the extent to which political decisionmaking is the product of constrained disputation like that found much more obviously in legal discourse.").

in legal discourse, the lesson to be learned from deterrence theory seems to be that the relative clarity of an argument's *social meaning* matters more than its theoretical abstractness. Legal and political issues become the site of illiberal conflict when citizens perceive that the resolution of them will signify whose side the government is taking in disputes between contending social groups and related cultural and moral styles. At least outside of law school and political philosophy seminar rooms, citizens usually *don't* get agitated about abstractions such as utilitarianism and Kantianism. Accordingly, one way to defuse moral contestation in law, especially when we can anticipate that citizens are *not* disposed to agree on the outcome of a legal question, is to envelop that issue in the anesthetizing (indeed, downright narcotizing) idiom of abstract theory.

Of course, the theorists who are positioned to learn the most from the function of deterrence as a strategy for managing public discourse are the ones who favor liberal values in criminal law. The lesson for them, plainly enough, is that they ought to speak in the idiom of deterrence.

This directive is far from obvious. Commentators of a liberal bent are not invariably deterrence theorists. Indeed, the two most sophisticated contemporary accounts of the *expressive* theory were developed by liberal moral philosophers: Jean Hampton, who saw it as an appropriate vehicle for infusing the criminal law with a Kantian theory of individual dignity;[346] and Joel Feinberg, who is famous for his project to conform the criminal law to liberal principles.[347]

Indeed, liberal criminal law theorists are much more likely to reject deterrence than to embrace it.[348] Bentham's fanatic commitment to the "greatest good for the greatest number" makes no allowance for the contemporary liberal commitment to individual rights. The bureaucratic fascism of Justice Holmes, who not only conceived of "[p]revention" as the "only universal purpose of punishment" but who imputed to the criminal law the precept that "the individual [i]s a means to an end, . . . a tool to increase the general welfare,"[349] seems a singularly inapt vehicle for advancing liberalism's humanist project. Yet given the latent illiberality that deterrence rhetoric holds in check, the best course for criminal law liberals is to throw their lot in with the modern-day Benthamites and Holmesians.

---

346 *See* Jean Hampton, *The Retributive Idea*, *in* MURPHY & HAMPTON, *supra* note 16, at 135.

347 *See* FEINBERG, *supra* note 16, at 95–251.

348 *See, e.g.*, H.L.A. HART, PUNISHMENT AND RESPONSIBILITY 40–49 (1968) (describing the concept of excuse in criminal law as evidence that law ranks respect for individual autonomy over societal utility).

349 HOLMES, *supra* note 68, at 46–47.

Certainly, one can imagine many other ways of talking about criminal law that would also be consistent with liberal ideals. The question, however, is whether these *theoretically* available liberal idioms are also *practically* available. No merely imagined liberal alternative to deterrence has its track record in staunching expressive zealotry.[350]

Under these circumstances, liberals who disparage deterrence are guilty of indefensible recklessness. Whatever its shortcomings as a normative theory, the power of deterrence as a strategy for managing public discourse makes it liberalism's best hope for containing divisive public moralizing.

B. Antiliberal Antithesis

Deterrence theorizing might be liberals' best hope for insulating criminal law from divisive public moralizing, but that only puts the question whether we should *be* criminal law liberals. The argument I want to advance now is addressed to those who are committed, as I am, to the progressive values of egalitarianism and civic solidarity, and who believe that the existing regime of criminal law systematically disserves those values. Those who hold these views ought to see the liberal defense of deterrence, precisely because it seeks to suppress moral controversy, as a strategy for entrenching the status quo and as an invitation to the critics of the existing regime unilaterally to disarm.

As the liberal defense of deterrence theory recognizes, deterrence theorizing never genuinely resolves contested issues of policy. Its operational axioms demand better empirics than policymakers could ever have. Even more fundamentally, reasoning within those axioms presupposes a contestable theory of value that tells us what states of affairs the law should be trying to maximize; without such a theory, we can't rationally decide what forms of conduct the law should be deterring, how much it should spend to deter them, and what the most efficient allocation of resources is across different forms of wrongdoing.

---

[350] One readily imagined liberal alternative — voluntarism — has never been able to contain it. Voluntarism holds punishment to be deserved if and to the extent that an individual self-consciously chooses to break the law. For the classic exposition, see H.L.A. HART, PUNISHMENT AND RESPONSIBILITY 140–45 (1968). But whether or not voluntarism successfully brackets contentious moral visions as a matter of theory, in practice it is deeply pervaded by them. Told that they can excuse a crime only if an offender suffered "impaired volition," for example, legal decisionmakers predictably perceive this invisible condition only in the offenders whose behavior expresses the decisionmakers' preferred social norms — whether the cuckold who executes his unfaithful wife, or the battered woman who assassinates her tyrannical husband. When defenses are conceived of in voluntarist terms, expressive warfare continues unabated, with cultural factions trading rival charges of "abuse excuse." *See, e.g.*, Victoria Nourse, *The New Normativity: The Abuse Excuse and the Resurgence of Judgment in the Criminal Law*, 50 STAN. L. REV. 1435, 1441–51 (1998) (exposing political presuppositions underlying the "abuse excuse" critique).

These issues always get resolved by recourse to unstated expressive valuations that citizens and their representatives use to construct a usable theory of value and to help them screen conflicting empirical data.[351]

Accordingly, the liberal defense of deterrence as a strategy for managing public discourse gives us a program not for *extricating* contentious expressive valuations from the law but only for *concealing* their influence. Justice Holmes indeed didn't *say* all that he thought — namely, that "in Texas . . . a man is not born to run away" and that the law should recognize the glory of the "swift and cunning" combatant — but that's the unstated expressive evaluation that *motivated* him to reject the duty to retreat.[352] The judge who mitigates the sentence of the homophobic killer on the ground that the event was a "one-time tragedy" committed by a person who the judge is "confident . . . [will] not kill again" doesn't tell us all he thinks either, but his decision to emphasize specific deterrence to the exclusion of general deterrence reveals that he harbors (consciously or otherwise) the same expressive valuations as the judge who candidly tells us that he doesn't "care much for queers cruising the streets."[353]

The implicit expressive valuations that underlie decisions such as these are not self-generating; they are constructed, as all expressive judgments are, by social norms. Thus, deterrence as a strategy for managing public discourse amounts to a plan for concealing the patterning of the law on the contestable social norms of the dominant social groups from whose ranks most judges, legislators, and politically influential citizens come.

If one believes that those norms are likely to be *bad*, then one should see nothing *good* in deterrence as a form of liberal "public reason." For by obscuring the influence of these norms, deterrence theorizing insulates them from the forces in both politics and law that have the best prospect for dislodging them.

Social norms are not static. Indeed, the transformation of norms is a familiar phenomenon in contemporary political and social life. The once pervasive and unquestioned norms that underwrote white supremacy have now been disavowed, if not extinguished, by the cultural mainstream. The same is true in the domains of gender and sexuality, where traditional, hierarchical norms are today highly contested and in some cases completely discredited.

These norm shifts can be intentionally triggered and, at least to an extent, accelerated. Individuals tend to conform to the behavior and

---

351 *See supra* Part I.B.1.

352 *See supra* p. 434.

353 *See supra* pp. 467, 469.

expectations of those around them.[354] What others do and say reveals information from which individuals infer the social acceptance of different courses of action; they furnish cues about how individuals should conduct themselves to gain approval and to avoid the stigma of deviance; and they supply examples of appropriate conduct that individuals are likely to internalize.[355] Advertisers, fund raisers, political campaign managers, and other "influence professionals" exploit these dynamics by bombarding us with images of persons engaging in the behavior or expressing the opinions that the professionals wish to promote.[356] Political and social reformers frequently use this same strategy. By staging or publicizing dramatic events — from mass demonstrations to campaigns of civil disobedience to examples of individual heroism — they seek to create the self-reinforcing impression of a groundswell of opinion in favor of their causes.[357]

Law is an important source of the information that determines the vitality of a nascent norm. Because it is commonly understood to express community values, criminal law in particular is an important cue about what others believe.[358] This is one of the reasons that contending social groups battle so fiercely to control the law's expressive capital: if the law conveys that *others believe* that gays warrant respect, or that the ideal of individual self-sufficiency expressed by handguns warrants disgust, then individuals — reformers and their adversaries both believe — are more likely to adopt that assessment. Indeed, the value of law as a signal of common attitudes is greatest for those who are trying to establish (or defend) contested norms, for in that case private behavior is least likely to convey a self-reinforcing signal in favor of the norm spontaneously.[359] Thus, by seeking to drain the law of its expressive vitality, deterrence as liberal public reason threatens to strip progressives of a potent weapon in their project to overthrow hierarchical and individualistic social norms.

---

[354] *See, e.g.*, ELLIOT ARONSON, THE SOCIAL ANIMAL 13–56 (7th ed. 1994); ROBERT B. CIALDINI, INFLUENCE: THE PSYCHOLOGY OF PERSUASION 1–16 (2d ed. 1993).

[355] *See, e.g.*, Dan M. Kahan, *Social Influence, Social Meaning, and Deterrence*, 83 VA. L. REV. 349, 352–61 (1997) (discussing social influence on individual behavior).

[356] *See generally* CIALDINI, *supra* note 354, at 95–133 (discussing how society influences personal behavior).

[357] *See* Gusfield, *supra* note 27, at 56 (describing "[m]oral entrepreneurs" who trigger crusades to change the norms of deviancy); Timur Kuran, *Ethnic Norms and Their Transformation Through Reputational Cascades*, 27 J. LEGAL STUD. 623, 654–55 (1998) (stating same for "ethnification entrepreneurs"); Cass R. Sunstein, *Social Norms and Social Roles*, 96 COLUM. L. REV. 903, 912 (1996) (stating same for "norm entrepreneurs"); *cf.* MICHAEL WALZER, INTERPRETATION AND SOCIAL CRITICISM 38–39, 50 (1987) (discussing strategies of the "connected critic").

[358] *See* Kahan, *supra* note 355, at 362–65.

[359] *See* GUSFIELD, *supra* note 25, at 17–18, 20, 177, 205–06; McAdams, *supra* note 29, at 400–03.

Of course, two (or more) can play the norm-manipulation game. Political reactionaries can exploit the expressive function of law to reinforce bad norms just as political progressives can use it to promote good ones. Indeed, some of the most dramatic examples of expressive politics, including Prohibition, have been aimed at shoring up norms essential to the status of embattled dominant groups.[360] There is no reason, a liberal might argue, for the progressives to assume that they are going to win the expressive game. Out of prudence, progressives too should advocate that criminal law speak in the idiom of deterrence lest expressive condemnation add self-reinforcing insult to material injury when judges mitigate the punishment for homophobes when citizens elect pro-death-penalty Presidents and Governors, and when legislatures refuse to enact gun control.

There are three basic flaws in this liberal defense of expressive détente. First, it embodies an unjustifiable bias in favor of the status quo. The law as it stands — from the widespread adoption of the death penalty to the absence of effective gun control on a national level to the persistence of mitigation for homophobic killers under the voluntary manslaughter doctrine — already reflects hierarchical and individualistic norms. The progressives who oppose these norms would thus be giving up much more than the reactionaries who support them were both sides to agree to a moratorium on expressive criminal law politics.

Indeed, because contested expressive valuations determine how citizens and officials feel about the law even when they *say* their positions reflect deterrence considerations, the defenders of the status quo don't need to engage in expressive politics to construct a legal regime that reflects their values. Sodomy laws just *do* demean gays even when those law are universally applicable on their face. The death penalty just *does* express authoritarianism and devaluation of African Americans, whether or not politicians make those meanings express. Consequently, a prohibition on expressive rhetoric imposes costs *only* on progressive critics of the status quo, because they are the only ones who need the norm-shifting power of overt social meanings.

Second, the expressive détente defended by liberals lacks credible mechanisms of enforcement. "Public reason" is a classic "public good": the benefits of public reason — stability, legitimacy, respect for dignity, and the like — are enjoyed by all members of society and not only by the individual who renounces public moralizing, except insofar as she is benefited by the like restraint of others. Like all other public goods,

360 *See* GUSFIELD, *supra* note 25, at 7–8 (Prohibition); Gusfield, *supra* note 27, at 62 (describing anti-gambling laws in Boston in 1930 as symbolically protecting "Yankee social and political superiority").

then, public reason is vexed by a collective action problem. Individuals are being expected to confer benefits on others who aren't obliged to reciprocate. Why should a self-interested individual restrain herself from engaging in divisive public moralizing when she can get the benefit of her principled adversaries' restraint for nothing? Why should a *prudent* individual agree to restrain *herself* if she can anticipate that her self-interested rival will free-ride?

Absent formal sanctions for public moralizing — a system that we don't have and couldn't have under the First Amendment — this collective action problem can be solved only by social norms backed up by the informal sanctions of personal guilt and public scorn. There are in fact such norms in our political culture.[361] But they are weak. Expressive zealots — including the leaders of interest groups that thrive on ideological conflict and ambitious politicians who see opportunities for immediate electoral gains — invariably breach the expressive peace and force more moderate citizens to take up arms as well.[362]

Common experience, moreover, suggests that defections from the norm against public moralizing are not uniform across moral commitments and cultural styles. Citizens who support egalitarianism and civic solidarity are more likely to see appeal in liberal public reason, whether out of principle or pragmatic calculation; citizens who support hierarchy and individualism tend to put little value on liberal public reason and are in fact likely to be horrified by the suggestion that moralizing be banished from political discourse. If *we* give up on enhanced penalties for gay bashing, *they* will still insist on the Defense of Marriage Act.[363] In these circumstances, progressives who voluntarily assent to the constraints of public reason are fools. They've failed to learn from the experience of Michael Dukakis, whose attempt to use deterrence talk to extinguish the flames of expressivism ignited by the Willie Horton issue left his campaign a smoldering heap of ashes.[364]

Third and finally, the liberal defense of expressive détente grossly overstates the costs of public moralizing by reactionaries. Persuading reactionaries to justify bad laws in deterrence terms achieves little, since those arguments will continue to persuade so long as decisionmakers remain responsive to unjust social norms. Things aren't necessarily worse, however, when reactionaries justify their positions ex-

361 *See supra* pp. 445–46.

362 *See supra* Parts II.A.4, II.B.3.

363 Pub. L. No. 104-199 § 2, 110 Stat. 2419 (1996) ("No State, territory, or possession of the United States, or Indian tribe, shall be required to give effect to any public act, record, or judicial proceeding of any other State, territory, possession, or tribe respecting a relationship between persons of the same sex that is treated as a marriage under the laws of such other State, territory, possession, or tribe, or a right or claim arising from such relationship.").

364 *See supra* pp. 450–51.

pressively. For once their underlying normative commitments are exposed, their defenders can no longer disclaim their influence, and their critics can more readily organize public opposition to them.

To illustrate, consider the story of Maryland Judge Robert Cahill. Cahill gave an eighteen-month work-release sentence to a truck driver who had shot and killed his wife (execution style, as she slept) after discovering that she had committed adultery. So far there is nothing remarkable about this story; the vengeful cuckold has been the beneficiary of the mitigating effect of the voluntary manslaughter doctrine for centuries. What *is* remarkable about this case was how Cahill justified the lenient sentence. Rather than resorting to bland deterrence rationales — the futility, say, of trying to influence the behavior of someone in the grip of unreasoning passion, or the relative lack of dangerousness of a man who kills only when seriously provoked — Cahill opted for an overtly expressive one. He expressed sympathy for the defendant, stating that he could imagine nothing that would enrage "a happily married man" more than "to be betrayed in your personal life, when you're out working to support the spouse."[365] "I seriously wonder how many men married five, four years," the Judge continued, "would have had the strength to walk away without inflicting some corporal punishment."[366] This language bore the unmistakable signature of hierarchical gender norms, against the background of which the defendant's anger expressed an appropriate valuation of male domestic sovereignty, and the victim's "betrayal" of her husband a wrongful disvaluation of the same.

Just as remarkably, Cahill's statement provoked an immense political reaction. Newspapers across the country ran critical editorials.[367] Protesters picketed the courthouse, calling for Cahill's removal. Members of the Maryland General Assembly introduced a resolution condemning him.[368] And the Maryland judiciary agreed to withhold new sentencing guidelines so that provisions relating to domestic vio-

---

365 Sheridan Lyons, *Court Panel to Probe Judge in Sentencing*, BALTIMORE SUN, Oct. 20, 1994, at 1B (quoting Judge Cahill).

366 *She Strays, He Shoots, Judge Winks*, N.Y. TIMES, Oct. 22, 1994, at A22 (quoting Judge Cahill).

367 *See, e.g.*, *A Judge Who Dishonors the Bench*, HARTFORD COURANT, Oct. 21, 1994, at A16; *Justice Mocked in Maryland*, BOSTON HERALD, Oct. 24, 1994, at 26; *"Passion Killing" Sentence Absurd*, SUN-SENTINEL (Fort Lauderdale, Fla.), Oct. 22, 1994, at 18A; *She Strays, He Shoots, Judge Winks*, *supra* note 366, at A22; Ann G. Sjoerdsma, *Justice: 18 Months for a Wife's Life*, CHI. TRIB., Nov. 14, 1994, at 21; *Unequal Justice*, ST. LOUIS POST-DISPATCH, Nov. 1, 1994, at 12B.

368 *See* John W. Frece, *Ouster of Judge Sought*, BALTIMORE SUN, Dec. 8, 1994, at 1B; Sheridan Lyons & Robert G. Matthews, *Oust Judge Cahill, Protesters Urge*, BALTIMORE SUN, Oct. 22, 1994, at 1B.

lence could be reviewed and possibly strengthened.[369] Cahill's remarks, in short, became the focal point for exactly the kind of orchestrated publicity that signals widespread opposition to an unjust norm in the law.

Had Cahill spoken in the deterrence idiom, things would likely have turned out differently. The *result* in the case would have been the same; relying implicitly on expressive valuations, Cahill would still have seen leniency as justified in cost-benefit terms. But precisely because deterrence arguments hide the speaker's theory of value, it would have been much more difficult to make citizens *see* what really motivated Cahill's decision and to make them outraged about it. Indeed, notwithstanding the contested status of hierarchical gender norms in contemporary society, judges who talk deterrence continue to mitigate the punishment of vengeful cuckolds all the time without provoking controversy.[370] At the end of the day, then, Cahill's use of expressive rhetoric, far from making things worse than they otherwise would have been, at least arguably made them *better* by showing citizens the influence of bad norms in their law and by showing legislators, judges, and juries that many citizens do in fact view those norms as *bad*.

This conclusion generalizes. Expressive rhetoric makes the reliance on contestable valuations salient and thus enables effective organizing against bad norms. The Texas judge who told us that he "do[es]n't much care for queers," for example, was defeated in an election in which gays and women furnished critical support for his opponent;[371] in the aftermath of this and similar cases, Texas (home of the "true man"!) enacted a hate crimes law that expressly enhances the penalty for crimes motivated by bias against any group, including gays.[372] Deterrence rhetoric, in contrast, lowers the profile of potentially contentious laws. By transforming the evocative "true man" doctrine into the expressively inert "paralyzed man" doctrine, Justice Holmes discharged the controversy surrounding the rule excusing individuals from an obligation to retreat before using deadly violence.[373] It is tempting to

---

369 *See* Janet Naylor, *Maryland Judges Delay Relaxation of Sentence Guidelines*, WASH. TIMES, Jan. 26, 1995, at A1.

370 *See, e.g.*, JEREMY HORDER, PROVOCATION AND RESPONSIBILITY 72–127 (1992); Donna K. Coker, *Heat of Passion and Wife Killing: Men Who Batter/Men Who Kill*, 2 S. CAL. REV. L. & WOMEN'S STUD. 71, 76–99 (1992) (discussing the historical and continuing use of the voluntary manslaughter doctrine for wife killers).

371 *See Gay Rights Groups Hail Defeat of Judge in Texas*, N.Y. TIMES, Dec. 4, 1992, at B20.

372 *See* TEX. PENAL CODE ANN. § 12.47 (West Supp. 1999); TEX. CODE CRIM. P. ANN. art. 42.014 (West Supp. 1999); *see also* Clay Robison, *Richards Signs Hate Crimes Bill into Law*, HOUSTON CHRON., June 20, 1993, at 3D (noting that the purpose of the legislation is to punish "criminal offenses motivated by the victims' race, religion, ethnicity, sexual orientation or national origin").

373 *See supra* pp. 432–35.

believe that that doctrine continues as the majority rule in the United States only because Holmes's formulation broke courts of the habit of talking about the rule in a way that would alert citizens today to the doctrine's grounding in contested honor norms. Thus, accepting the expressive détente urged by liberalism would make progressives complicit in extending the life of hierarchical and individualistic norms that are in fact ripe for annihilation.

However well-meaning, the liberal aversion to moral conflict is in reality a powerful instrument for entrenching the reactionary status quo. Precisely because deterrence theory seeks to exclude contentious public moralizing from criminal law, progressives should without qualification oppose deterrence theorizing.

C. Pragmatic Synthesis?

Yet in truth, unqualified opposition to deterrence is just as indefensible as unqualified support of it. The best stance is one that seeks to negotiate the extremes of the liberal and antiliberal positions, employing deterrence theory selectively in the manner best calculated to express respect for individual dignity *and* to promote progressive values. The problem, sadly, is that this strategy tends to defeat itself.

The antiliberal critique effectively dispatches the practical liberal defense of deterrence but does not give sufficient credit to the principled liberal defense of it as a means of respecting individual dignity. Respect for the freedom of individuals to pursue their own conception of the good in a manner that does not impose harm on others — the core ideal of liberalism[374] — is as much a progressive value as are egalitarianism and civic solidarity. Conventional liberalism tends to define harm to third parties too narrowly, overlooking how norms and laws can construct social meanings that coerce individuals or undermine their status.[375] But when the pursuit of particular moral visions and cultural styles does not cause this or any other form of harm, the law should not be used as an instrument for expressing contempt for these styles of life, no matter how noxious they might seem. The antiliberal critique overlooks the potential utility of deterrence as a form of public "soft-spokenness" that allows the law to avoid imposing "counterproductive humiliation."[376]

Equally important, the antiliberal critique reflects undue optimism about the dynamics of norm reform. Substitute "reactionary" for "pro-

374 *See, e.g.*, JOHN STUART MILL, ON LIBERTY 13 (Stefan Collini ed., Cambridge Univ. Press 1989) ("[T]he only purpose for which power can be rightfully exercised over any member of a civilised community, against his will, is to prevent harm to others.").

375 *See generally* Lessig, *supra* note 14 (exploring the construction and regulation of social meaning).

376 Holmes, *supra* note 147, at 206.

gressive," "hierarchy" for "equality," "individualism" for "civic solidarity," and vice versa, and the argument in the last section becomes a defense of expressive zealotry on behalf of those who seek to conserve or restore the influence of morally bankrupt norms. Informational and reputational cascades have no politics. Contrast the successful orchestration of the cues of public sentiment by the Civil Rights Movement with the similarly successful orchestration of cues by contemporary conservatives, who have nurtured the campaign against "political correctness" into a bandwagon of political defeats for affirmative action.[377] If they enfeeble norms against public moralizing in criminal law, then expressive appeals by progressives could inadvertently enable counterappeals that strengthen reactionary norms.

These concerns do *not* rehabilitate deterrence as liberal public reason, a position that invites passivity in the face of expressive aggression. They merely highlight the necessity of formulating a more moderate strategy that uses deterrence with pragmatic discretion.

Such a strategy should distinguish between three categories of policy positions. The first includes positions motivated by commitment to good norms that already enjoy the backing of overwhelming consensus or by opposition to bad norms that are already so far outside the cultural mainstream as to be largely inert. Supporters of these positions should avail themselves of the deterrence idiom to avoid inflicting gratuitous humiliation on those who subscribe to the deviant but harmless norms. The second category includes policy positions motivated by opposition to hierarchical or individualistic norms that continue unjustly to constrain the flourishing of some group of citizens *and* that can be effectively renounced by adoption of the policies in question. In that case, proponents should overtly avail themselves of the expressive idiom to maximize the prospects for successful norm reform. The third category includes policy positions that express opposition to vital hierarchical or individualistic norms but that have only a remote likelihood of prevailing. Here, proponents should express their views in deterrence terms to obscure the meaning of defeat and should wait for a more opportune moment to strike expressively.

An example of a policy in the first category is the prohibition on "extreme fighting."[378] This is a spectator sport in which two contestants fight, bare-fisted and unconstrained by rules against head-butting, kicking, elbowing, and the like, until one surrenders in disgrace or is knocked unconscious.[379] By now the vast majority of states ban this

[377] *See* TIMUR KURAN, PRIVATE TRUTHS, PUBLIC LIES 137–54 (1996).

[378] This example is inspired by an exchange between Gerald Dworkin and Martha Nussbaum at a recent Quinnipiac Law School symposium on Nussbaum's works.

[379] *See* David Ferrell, *A Brutal Sport Fights for Its Life*, L.A. TIMES, Nov. 1, 1997, at A1.

practice.[380] Extreme fighting obviously appeals to a minority of citizens who take pleasure in watching human beings inflict physical injury on each other. That taste is recognizable but clearly deviant in society at large, which is why there is overwhelming majority support for banning such contests. It would be far-fetched if not downright silly to defend the "right" to watch extreme fighting: the majority that is disgusted by this practice is no less entitled to have its sensibilities respected than is the minority that relishes this spectacle. Nevertheless, there is already a vital norm against the enjoyment of actual bloodshed, and the ban needn't be defended as expressing that norm in order to protect the norm from erosion. Consequently, to avoid expressing gratuitous disrespect for the deviant minority, the majority that supports the ban should premise its position on deterrence grounds — that, say, extreme fighting could lead to violent behavior in society generally — even though such arguments are completely speculative and don't really explain the motivation behind the law.[381]

Enhanced penalties for homophobic crimes are an example of a policy that falls into the second category. Homophobic norms retain vitality in many segments of society and underwrite an array of practices that harm gay and lesbian citizens. At the same time, it's clear that these norms are now contested: as they encounter more individuals in private and public life who identify themselves as gay or lesbian, some members of the public shed their biases; in response, other citizens, whose status is tied to conventional gender roles, feel impelled to resist this growing acceptance through dramatic expressive gestures, including homophobic violence and homophobic legislation such as the Defense of Marriage Act.

Because individuals tend to conform their attitudes to those of persons around them, it is essential that the opponents of homophobic norms forcefully engage their cultural adversaries in the battle to control the law's expressive capital. Hate crime laws, which legislatures are most likely to enact in the aftermath of gruesome instances of homophobic violence, do just that. Because the value of such laws depends on the clarity with which they express condemnation of homophobia, and because those who support traditional gender roles will oppose such laws intensely no matter how they are defended, the pro-

---

380 *See id.*

381 In fact, opponents of extreme fighting do nothing to hide their revulsion. *See* James Dao, *Senate Chief in Albany, Reversing Himself, Says He Backs a Ban on Ultimate Fighting*, N.Y. TIMES, Feb. 11, 1997, at B7 (quoting the legislative sponsor of the ban, State Senator Roy M. Goodman: "This is the culmination of a yearlong campaign to end what I call human cockfighting, a disgraceful, animalistic and disgusting contest which can result in severe injuries to contestants and sets an abominable example for our youth.").

ponents of enhanced penalties for homophobic hate crimes should defend those laws in unambiguously expressive terms.

Federal gun control and the abolition of the death penalty, in contrast, are examples of policies that fit into the third category. These positions also take aim at norms that construct a host of objectionable policies and practices. Nevertheless, the immediate prospects for significant federal gun control or for death penalty abolition are bleak. Because it is clear that those who favor these policies can't win the expressive game (at least for now), their best strategy is *not to play it*.

Participants in public debate tend to address the specific arguments advanced by their adversaries. Accordingly, if death penalty abolitionists and proponents of federal gun control religiously confine themselves to deterrence talk, then their opponents are likely to answer them in the same idiom. Deterrence arguments are unlikely to change the mind of those who favor the death penalty or oppose gun control, because those positions are in fact grounded in expressive considerations. But to the extent that they succeed in framing the debate in deterrence rather than expressive terms, gun control supporters and death penalty abolitionists can obscure the social meaning of their own defeat. In a climate in which everyone is talking deterrence, less committed members of the public are less likely to infer from the retention of the death penalty or from defeat of gun control legislation that those around them subscribe to the contested norms that in truth motivate the more ardent and politically influential advocates of these outcomes.

Of course, the expressive restraint of federal gun control proponents and of death penalty abolitionists shouldn't be permanent. At the moment that they think that they *can* win the game, they should resume the expressive defense of their positions in order to realize the norm-shaping benefits of policies so defended. Such moments are most likely to arise in the aftermath of dramatic events — such as horrific acts of gun violence, or botched executions — that expose the latent tension between the norms that block gun control and entrench the death penalty and other norms that many members of the public accept.[382]

Indeed, the opportunity for decisive expressive strikes will arise sooner if the supporters of such positions strategically restrain themselves in the near term. The intensity of the opposition to gun control, for example, is largely an artifact of the perceived expressive ambitions of those who support this policy.[383] Thus, by muting their expressive

382 *See, e.g.*, Haines, *supra* note 155, at 131–35 (describing the backlash against the death penalty in the wake of flawed executions as an example of a "suddenly realized grievance").

383 *See supra* pp. 460–62.

aims, gun control proponents deprive the organized leadership of the pro-gun lobby of a resource for maintaining the zeal of their own constituency. Patience in the short- to medium-term, then, will diminish the readiness of the defenders of frontier and militia virtues to repel an opportune expressive attack on behalf of gun control.

Or at least that is the theory. The reality of the pragmatic position is more complicated, for at least three reasons. First, the pragmatic strategy assumes an unrealistically sophisticated and complete understanding of the norm-shaping consequences of different styles of discourse. It is exceedingly difficult to know whether one's policy position falls into the third pragmatic category, in which the expressive idiom will accentuate the undesirable meaning of political defeat, or the second category, in which a resort to the expressive idiom will transmit desirable meanings to the public. Michael Dukakis, for example, played a category-three strategy when in hindsight it surely would have been better for him to have used a category-two strategy.

Likewise, it is difficult to know whether one's policy position really falls into the first category, in which the contribution of expressive arguments to good norms is too negligible to justify imposing a humiliating defeat on a cultural subcommunity. For example, I might be wrong to view the norms that inform the pleasure that some take in extreme fighting as clearly deviant. Indeed, they might be closely related to the norms that construct homophobia or the social meaning of guns. If that's the case, then highlighting the disgust that motivates the extreme-fighting ban might create an expressive surplus that could be profitably reinvested in the campaigns for hate crime laws and gun control.

Because it depends on contentious empirical premises, the pragmatic strategy will inevitably result in errors. Maybe the cost of these errors will be smaller than the costs of uniformly following either the liberal or antiliberal discourse strategies. But that's an empirically speculative conclusion. Anyone who purports to be confident that one strategy or another minimizes error costs is likely conforming her assessment of the evidence to unstated expressive valuations of her own.

Second, the pragmatic strategy assumes an unrealistic degree of coordination and control. The progressives have their own zealots, who either out of self-interest, extreme preferences, or simple lack of discipline advance expressive claims with reckless indifference to how such appeals affect the prospects of the causes that they believe in. Thus, even if they could acquire the empirical knowledge that the pragmatic strategy contemplates, the progressives would be unable to force their own zealots to hold their tongues. And their zealotry would predictably invite expressive retorts from the reactionaries, whose zeal would in turn force the hand of even more moderate progressives. The pragmatic strategy is no more stable than is the liberal defense of expressive détente.

Third and most importantly, the pragmatic strategy is likely to unravel in the face of a public-discourse effect equivalent to the economic axiom of rational expectations. Whereas the liberal defense of deterrence as public reason assumes that individuals believe what they say,[384] the pragmatic strategy contemplates that progressives will employ deterrence arguments only when they wish to hide their true expressive motivations. But if the progressives' best strategic move is to constrain their discourse in this way, then their adversaries will infer that that is exactly what the progressives are doing when they talk deterrence. As a result, deterrence arguments are likely in short order to acquire the very social meanings that they are meant to suppress.[385] (Indeed, many citizens no doubt think of deterrence arguments as "rationalizations" of this sort.)

The pragmatic strategy refuses to treat the secret ambition of deterrence as a *secret*. And once the secret is out, the ambition cannot be realized.

CONCLUSION

In this article, I have tried to answer two questions: *why* do citizens use deterrence rationales to justify their positions on controversial issues of criminal law, and *should* they?

The answer to the first question — why deterrence talk? — isn't that citizens are actually persuaded by deterrence claims. They probably are, but only because they are relying on unstated theories of value to identify what's worth deterring at what cost and to resolve disputed empirical issues. These theories of value supply sufficient grounds for the positions that individuals say they subscribe to based on deterrence. Sometimes, as in the hate crimes debate, individuals will readily admit that this is so. But even when they do not readily admit that deterrence is superfluous, deterrence-related considerations play little role in determining the positions citizens hold on contentious issues like capital punishment and gun control.

The real reason that deterrence is so prominent in public debate over criminal law is that citizens generally don't want to say all they think about such contentious issues. Their positions on gun control, the death penalty, hate crimes, and the like reflect their allegiances in the ceaseless battle for status between contending social groups or between looser cultural styles. The natural idiom for signaling such allegiances is expressive condemnation, which is bristling with indignation and disgust. The consequentialist idiom of deterrence is much less

---

384 *See supra* p. 482.

385 *Cf.* ELSTER, *supra* note 149, at 328 (noting that disingenuous attempts to manipulate ideology "tend to fail for reasons well understood by social psychologists").

passionate and confrontational. Avoiding illiberal status conflict is the secret ambition of deterrence.

A series of interlocking incentives motivates citizens to favor the face-saving idiom of deterrence over the face-breaking one of expressive condemnation. Social norms discourage overt moralizing in our dealings with those who we know harbor cultural commitments that differ from our own. Moral partisans pay a steep reputational price, at least within the social mainstream. This dynamic seems especially prominent in debate over the death penalty.

Such restraint is often reinforced by strategic calculation. By strengthening the resistance of those with opposing commitments, the open profession of expressive motivations can sometimes make it harder to garner legislative support for contested symbolic legislation. This explains the appeal of deterrence rhetoric on issues like gun control and hate crimes.

Finally, some citizens are moved by principle to disavow the confrontational stance of expressivism. These citizens talk deterrence because they view the injection of overt moralizing into public discourse as imprudent and disrespectful. Such individuals engage in an heroic form of rhetorical self-sacrifice, speaking in mechanistic or economistic terms that make them appear morally obtuse when in fact they know full well that that way of talking is empty.

None of these incentives, however, is particularly robust. Expressive zealots, who are unmoved by the norm against moralizing, conspire with professional ideologues, who know that they can mobilize their constituencies by invoking the specter of cultural aggression. Their lack of restraint forces the hand of more moderate citizens, who are drawn into the fray either to protect the norms on which their status depends or to remove ambiguity as to their allegiances at a time when those around them seem to be demanding conspicuous displays of loyalty. Political actors, too, are moved to release the divisive energy of expressivism when they perceive the opportunity for immediate electoral gain. When these dynamics bring simmering expressive controversy to a boil, political actors who try to defuse the controversy with deterrence will look more like fools than heroes.

There is thus no stable discourse equilibrium as a positive matter. We are constrained to cycle back and forth between deterrence détentes and bursts of expressive zeal.

Should citizens talk deterrence in these circumstances? Unsurprisingly, there is no stable discourse equilibrium as a moral matter either.

The cooling effect of deterrence can be seen as the strongest argument in favor of this style of justification. By muting expressive controversy, deterrence arguments make it easier for citizens of diverse moral and cultural commitments to agree on policy outcomes. Just as important, by leaching the social meaning out of such outcomes, deterrence theory spares those who *disagree* with a policy from the indignity of having their most fundamental commitments authoritatively repudiated by the law. In this way, deterrence theory secures the goals of liberal public reason, which enjoins us to disclaim privileged moral insight when we engage in public deliberations.

This benefit of deterrence, moreover, does not depend on the cogency of deterrence as a normative theory. Indeed, deterrence is able to mute expressive controversy precisely *because* it has nothing to say about the contentious issues of expressive value that are really at stake in debates about the death penalty, gun control, and hate crimes. Those who criticize deterrence for being evaluatively empty are missing the point of deterrence as a strategy for managing public discourse.

That doesn't mean, however, that the role deterrence plays in managing public discourse is beyond criticism. In fact, its cooling effect can also be seen as the strongest argument *against* deterrence theorizing.

Many of the social meanings that motivate citizens to support particular criminal law policies are *bad*. They are constructed by hierarchical and individualistic social norms that unjustly deny status to certain groups of citizens and constrain their material well-being in numerous ways. Deterrence theorizing doesn't make those norms go away; it merely obscures them beneath narcotizing layers of abstraction. Such obscurity is itself bad, because it makes the influence of such norms less salient and thus deprives norm reformers of opportunities to expose and critique them.

Even worse, deterrence theory risks lulling the critics of bad norms into a posture of decided rhetorical disadvantage. As a species of liberal public reason, deterrence contemplates a condition of mutual rhetorical self-restraint. But such a condition is unstable; expressive zealots have incentives to defect. Indeed, we should anticipate that supporters of unjust norms will defect the most readily since they are, by hypothesis, the citizens least inclined to show respect to their fellow citizens. Consequently, if the critics of bad norms assent voluntarily to the public discourse constraints of deterrence, they will more often than not be restraining themselves unilaterally, thereby allowing their adversaries exclusive access to the expressive capital of the law.

Since the secret ambition of deterrence is both the strongest argument for and the strongest argument against deterrence theorizing, a mixed rhetorical strategy might seem like the most promising one. Such a strategy would use the idiom that's best for the circumstances, shifting back and forth between optimal deterrence and expressive condemnation based on the prospects for effective norm reform, the risk of reactionary backlash, the need to repel expressive aggression, and the imperative to respect harmless moral deviance.

But this pragmatic stance also collapses. For one thing, it presupposes an unrealizable degree of both foresight and central control.

There are lots of teams and players but no effective coaches in the expressive politics game. Even more fundamentally, it is too nakedly instrumental. If deployed in a self-consciously strategic fashion, deterrence arguments become too transparent as rationalizations and thus lose their power to signal a spirit of moral and cultural accommodation.

The secret ambition of deterrence is thus only a slice of an insoluble discourse dilemma. The liberal defense of deterrence as public reason respects individual dignity and mutes counterproductive political conflict, but also subsidizes bad social norms by shielding them from critical appraisal. The antiliberal critique of deterrence liberates the norm-reforming potential of expressive condemnation, but gratuitously stigmatizes harmless deviancy and risks provoking reactionary backlashes. A pragmatic strategy, which shifts between deterrence and expressive condemnation, promises to combine the best elements of both approaches and to avoid the worst, but is impossible to execute as a practical matter.

So what theory is the best for managing public discourse? There simply is no answer, at least when the question is posed this globally. All we can do is try to understand all that is at stake and make the best decisions we can about how to speak in particular contexts. What strikes us as best, moreover, will be as much a matter of personal style as a matter of high principle or prudent calculation. Those who criticize others for the way they choose to speak either are misguided about the consequences of any individual's choice about how to talk, or are themselves drawn to a style of discourse imperialism that insists everyone talk one way even though nothing of real consequence is at stake.

[15]

The Deterrence Hypothesis and Picking Pockets at the Pickpocket's Hanging

David A. Anderson, *Centre College*

The tenet that harsher penalties could substantially reduce crime rates rests on the assumption that currently active criminals weigh the costs and benefits of their contemplated acts. Existing and proposed crime strategies exhibit this belief, as does a large and growing segment of the crime literature. This study examines the premise that criminals make informed and calculated decisions. The findings suggest that 76% of active criminals and 89% of the most violent criminals either perceive no risk of apprehension or are incognizant of the likely punishments for their crimes.

In the late eighteenth and early nineteenth centuries, picking pockets was among 220 capital crimes in England. Thousands were executed before the attending masses. Undeterred by the fate of their colleagues, pickpockets routinely worked the crowds at public hangings (Gatrell, 1994, p. 62).[1] The irony of this practice begs several questions of importance to modern policy making: In what ways do punishments matter? To what extent can we address current crime problems with increased

---

The 3M Foundation and the Northpoint Training Center provided assistance with the prison research component of this project. I thank Mark A. Cohen, Thomas D. Rowe, Jr., Edward P. Schwartz, Alex Tabarrok, and W. Kip Viscusi for helpful comments. Kathy Carr, Sarah M. Harvieux, Charles Hokayem, and Stephanie Holbrook provided excellent research assistance. All errors are mine.

Send correspondence to: David A. Anderson, Department of Economics, Centre College, 600 West Walnut Street, Danville, KY 40422; Fax: (859) 236-7925; E-mail: David@Centre.edu.

1. The effectiveness of formal policing in Regency England is questionable. Nonetheless, vigilante justice and a (literal) lynch mob mentality can make for a larger expected punishment than more formal justice systems. Viscusi (1991, p. 65) and others point out that individuals place relatively high subjective probabilities on visible, compelling events like public hangings.

punishments? And what stake can we place on the assumptions that criminals are rational and informed?[2] The purpose of this article is to present new evidence of myopia and self-perceived invincibility among criminals that speaks to each of these questions and helps to explain a thing or two about Regency England.

Life in a crime-laden society is restricted and costly. Considering all facets of the crime burden, including victim expenses, deterrence, and health losses, the cost of crime exceeds $1.7 trillion annually in the United States (Anderson, 1999). Crime prevention is a priority at every level of government, yet a persistent nemesis. Despite a long history of experimentation with the penal code, between 1960 and 1997 the number of violent crimes known to police increased from 288,460 to 1,634,770, and the number of inmates in state and federal prisons increased from 212,953 to 1,176,807 (U.S. Bureau of Justice Statistics, 1998c, pp. 260, 479).[3] This study tests the basic premise behind most recent anticrime legislation, that stricter sanctions turn would-be offenders away from crime, and finds it to hold for only a minority of criminals.

One form of stricter sanctions, the extension of prison terms, achieves more than an increase in the stakes for crime. Lengthened imprisonment serves victims' desires for greater retribution. It also incapacitates the criminal, preventing that individual from committing additional offenses (outside of prison) for the duration of his or her sentence. Levitt (1998), Greenwood (1983), and others suggest that incapacitation is not a strong deterrent, perhaps because violent criminals generally do not commit crimes routinely enough for their incarceration to engender a significant reduction in crime, and because profitable property crimes seem to face no shortage of labor supply. These observations are consistent with

2. For punishments to matter it is not necessary for potential criminals to have full information on the true effectiveness of the criminal justice system, provided that perceptions vary systematically with law enforcement policies. Deterrence effects require potential criminals to perceive a positive probability of detection and some type of punishment. For *changes* in the penal code to have a beneficial effect on crime, potential criminals must further be aware that punishments have escalated.

3. Property crimes also increased dramatically over the 1960–1997 period, from 3,095,200 to 11,540,300. These increases do not simply track population growth. The rates of incidents per 100,000 inhabitants increased over the same period from 160.9 to 610.8 for violent crimes and from 1,726 to 4,312 for property crimes (U.S. Bureau of Justice Statistics, 1998a, pp. 261, 479).

the concurrent 386% increase in the incarceration rate, 380% increase in the violent crime rate, and 250% increase in the property crime rate over the past four decades (U.S. Bureau of Justice Statistics, 1998a, pp. 260, 490).

The existing theory and empirical evidence is entirely too controversial to settle the critical deterrence issue. Avio (1998, p. 204) asserts that "theorizing about the causes of criminal activity is not at this time, nor ever will be, sufficiently well developed to reconcile conflicting viewpoints independent of empirical evidence." At the same time, as outlined in the literature review to follow, most empirical studies suffer from the aggregate level of available crime and enforcement data and the sensitivity of regression model specifications, among other obstacles. Rather than reformulating models or regressing crime on punishment with yet another data set, the present study takes a step back and addresses two questions fundamental to the deterrence hypothesis: Are potential criminals sufficiently aware of the likely punishments to respond to them? And do criminals act on the basis of a contemporaneous notion of apprehension and conviction? If most do not, the deterrence hypothesis and associated policy are amiss.

The prospect of increasing the stakes for crime up to and including a routinely enforced death penalty provides a perennial controversy among crime scholars. "Three strikes" and similar mandatory sentencing legislation caters to calls for harsher penalties, often with disappointing results.[4] Without completely dismissing the criminal deterrence hypothesis, the current research suggests that punishment is not the key to a substantial reduction in crime. The results include evidence that most criminals are impervious to harsher punishments, either because they perceive no risk of apprehension and conviction, or because they have no knowledge of the likely punishments for their contemplated crimes. Note that this is not an argument for *decreased* punishments. Existing punishments deter an unknown quantity of potential criminals. Of those crimes that remain, however, the findings indicate that few could be eliminated by increased punishments.

4. For a thorough discussion, see Tonry (1996, pp. 134–64).

1. Previous Research

In his seminal work on the economics of crime, Gary Becker (1968) suggests that crimes are a rational response to situations in which the benefits of breaking the law outweigh the costs. According to the ensuing economic model, criminals commit crimes until the marginal cost exceeds the marginal benefit. The past three decades have produced a large literature reliant on the assumptions of informed and rational criminal behavior.[5] One of the intuitive results of rationality-based crime models is that harsher penalties or increased apprehension rates will result in fewer crimes. That is, after raising the expected cost of committing crimes, fewer crime opportunities will provide a marginal benefit in excess of the marginal cost.[6]

Becker's model of criminal behavior makes a number of assumptions about the criminal's information and mindset. In order to respond properly to the costs of a particular crime, the criminal must have some understanding of the likelihood of being apprehended and convicted, and have an idea of the likely punishment if convicted. Further, the criminal must have the proper mindset to process this information while contemplating the crime. That is, being adequately informed is a necessary but not sufficient condition for an appropriate response to expected penalties. A criminal who knows the punishment for murder but kills in the heat of the moment with no thought of the punishment is not a rational decision maker.

---

5. Examples include Block and Heineke (1975), Becker and Murphy (1988), and Polinsky and Shavell (1999).

6. From Becker (1968, p. 177), if EU is a representative criminal's expected utility from committing a crime, p is the probability of being punished, Y is the criminal's monetary and psychic income, and f is the fine or monetary value of the punishment, then

$$\text{EU} = pU(Y - f) + (1 - p)U(Y). \tag{1}$$

The theorized decrease in expected utility from crime resulting from increased punishment or detection rates is seen by

$$\frac{\partial \text{EU}}{\partial p} = U(Y - f) - U(Y) < 0 \tag{2}$$

and

$$\frac{\partial \text{EU}}{\partial f} = -pU'(Y - f) < 0. \tag{3}$$

The important policy implications of the deterrence hypothesis have inspired a large literature discussing its validity. Surveys include Avio (1998), Cameron (1994, 1988), and Nagin (1998). Capital punishment has been central to debates over the influence of punishment on crime rates. Ehrlich (1975, 1977) suggests that each execution of a death row criminal might reduce the number of subsequent murders by between seven and twenty-four.[7] In contrast, Bowers and Pierce (1980) estimate that, by devaluing life, each execution results in two or three additional murders. Leamer (1983) and McManus (1985) argue that prior beliefs taint empirical evidence in support of the deterrence hypothesis, whereas Ehrlich and Liu (1999) defend the methods employed.[8] Others finding a notable deterrent effect include, Kessler and Levitt (1999), Layson (1985), and Rubin, Dezhbakhsh, and Shephard (2001); those finding otherwise include Avio (1988), Cameron (1989), Grogger (1990), and McAleer and Veall (1989).

The lack of consensus on the value of harsher penalties among outcome-based studies is the result of a series of data and modeling issues.[9] The available data tend to be aggregated, and lack several potentially important variables.[10] Many crimes go unreported by victims, and others are missed when only the most severe crime in a multicrime incident is recorded.[11] Increased enforcement leads to the detection of more existing crimes, resulting in spurious correlation between crime and

7. Note that Ehrlich's larger estimate of the number of avoided murders is formed on the basis of a log-log function and analysis at the low existing number of executions. If the number of executions were to increase along such a function, the number of prevented murders would fall and become negligible for a high level of executions.

8. Leamer (1983) and McManus (1985) advocate Extreme Bound Analysis to deal with uncertainty about the proper specification of regression models and use EBA to demonstrate the fragility of past findings on criminal deterrence. Ehrlich and Lui (1998) show that the application of Extreme Bound Analysis would permit investigators to dismiss popular economic concepts such as the law of demand and reassert the validity of the deterrence hypothesis based on traditional regression methods.

9. A past review of deterrence studies performed by the National Academy of Sciences (Blumstein, Cohen, and Nagin, 1978) concluded that available data prove neither the existence nor the magnitude of deterrence effects. As discussed above, conflicting findings continue to confound this line of inquiry.

10. Typical examples include alternative sanctions for the studied crimes, sanctions for alternative crimes, opportunity costs of time, exposure to violence, and measures of drug use.

11. In 1997 there were 1,634,770 violent crimes and 11,540,300 property crimes known to police. In the same year, based on the National Crime Victimization Survey

enforcement variables. The simultaneity of law enforcement levels and crime rates leads to an identification problem with little conceptual basis for excluding predetermined variables. Law enforcement policies can alter the mix and location of crimes, reducing the rates of particular crimes (typically murder) in particular areas by more than the net decrease in all crimes in all locations.[12] The bottom line is that time-series equations in crime rate studies have not proven to be stable, nor have regression results proven to be robust.[13]

The present study considers the deterrence dilemma from an alternative perspective. Rather than trying to sort out the influence of punishments on crimes based on aggregated and imprecise counts, it creates an individual-level data set that explicitly measures the capacity of criminals to respond to punishment schemes. In order to carry out cost-benefit analysis, criminals must possess a minimal knowledge of the penalties for their crimes and the likelihood of conviction. The findings support those previous studies which suggest that adjusted penalties are not the answer to our crime epidemic. Further, the crimes found here to be the most impervious to punishment—deadly and sex crimes—are the same crimes determined by previous studies to inflict the greatest costs on victims and society.[14]

2. The Sample

The data came from 278 interviews of male inmates at two medium-security state prisons and one county jail.[15] A random subset of 159

of 80,000 residents in 43,000 housing units, there were an estimated 8,614,000 crimes of violence and 25,817,000 property crimes (U.S. Bureau of Justice Statistics, 1998a, pp. 172, 260).

12. For example, Forst, Filatov, and Klein (1978) and McKee and Sesnowitz (1978) find a substitution effect in the supply for murder that eliminates the deterrence effect when the rates of other types of crimes are added to the murder supply function.

13. For example, Fox and Radelet (1989) demonstrate the near instability of the conditional risk of execution variable in one of Layson's (1985) equations, and Passell and Taylor (1977) reject the stability of the underlying structure over Ehrlich's (1975) sample. For further discussion of regression results and related problems, see Avio (1998), Viscusi (1986), Cook (1980), and Taylor (1978).

14. Miller, Cohen, and Wiersema (1996) found rape to result in $141 billion in victim costs per year, and Anderson (1999) found deadly crimes to result in $463 billion worth of lost life (both figures are adjusted to 2000 dollars, using the CPI).

15. Interviews were conducted at the Northpoint Training Center and the Frankfort County Jail in Kentucky, and the Piedmont Correctional Institute in North Carolina.

inmates was asked supplemental questions about possible causes and influences behind their behavior. Participation by the inmates was anonymous, voluntary, and uncompensated. Participants were generally representative of the prison population at large in terms of age, race, drug use, and crimes committed. The data were collected between 1997 and 1999.

The fact that everyone in the sample was apprehended may mean that the sample is biased towards those who are more likely to be apprehended. If so, the results are conservative in their estimation of the percentage of criminals that would be impervious to harsher penalties, assuming that those who are more likely to be apprehended are accordingly more likely to consider the possibility of being apprehended. There is also the possibility that those who are apprehended are less intelligent and therefore less likely to think about the punishment and the likelihood of being apprehended. This would act as a countervailing bias; the extent to which either is present is uncertain. In any case, the results speak directly to the behavior of convicted criminals, whose incarceration costs $35.8 billion annually in the U.S.[16]

It is also the case that everyone in the sample carried out a crime. There are undoubtedly individuals who consider committing a crime and do not for fear of punishment. This unmeasured group of deterred criminals may be overrepresented by those most cognizant of apprehension and conviction risks, and those whose estimates of the likelihood and severity of punishment are on the accurate-to-excessive side. The deterrence of such would-be offenders is a sound reason to maintain a penal code. The purpose of this research is to determine to what extent *current* offenders could be dissuaded by more severe sentencing. If most of the potential criminals that *are* responsive to punishment are currently inactive, alternative strategies will be necessary to subvert the existing crime burden.

Survey research is subject to the honesty of the participants. This is true for data sources that serve as the basis for large portions of the law and economics literature, including Census Bureau data, the Current Population Survey, and the Panel Study of Income Dynamics. The current study asked participants how aware they were of the likelihood of punishment

16. Another possibility inherent in survey data is that some responses were not truthful. If, as one might expect, any resulting bias is towards understated ignorance of apprehension risks and punishments, then these results are conservative in their estimation of the percentage of criminals impervious to punishment.

and apprehension, and most indicated low levels of awareness. If anything, one might expect dishonesty to bias responses in the direction of greater awareness. That is, participants would cover up some of their foolishness. To the extent that this is the case, criminals are even less aware than the results suggest, and these findings are conservative. The survey instrument appears in the Appendix.[17]

3. Results

The mere existence of crime cannot be construed to discount the deterrence hypothesis. If criminals were informed, the rationality of their behavior would hinge upon a comparison of expected costs and benefits. Even if respondents knew that apprehension was likely and that the punishment was steep, it would be perfectly rational to commit a crime if the potential payoff were large enough. There are several results that could indicate problems with the deterrence hypothesis. The hypothesis assumes that criminals are both informed and rational. If they are uninformed about punishments, they cannot respond to them. If they are irrational, they might not respond to them in the desired way.

Table 1 indicates the reported degree of certainty about apprehension and punishment held by participants at the times of their offenses.

17. There is an instruction on the survey instrument saying that those who claim not to have committed the crime should be asked to respond as if they did. This note was inserted in anticipation of inmates who might claim to be innocent. Many claim innocence at trial; pleasingly, only about three to five inmates made this claim to us, perhaps because we held no control over their fates. Some of those inmates may indeed have been innocent, and some in that subset may never have committed similar crimes or had other experiences that would provide them with insight. They have, however, been screened by a legal system that demands a high standard of proof. It appears unlikely that there were enough truly innocent participants to have had a significant influence on the results of this study. The statement in the survey, "I did not think that I would be caught," could be open to interpretation in another context. During the survey, however, participants were asked to choose among a range of likelihood levels in decreasing order of likelihood: "very likely," "somewhat likely," "possible, but not likely," and then the statement in question. In this context, is should be clear that the last choice reflects thoughts of apprehension that are less than "possible, but not likely." Further, most of those who did not think that they would be caught also did not know or did not think about the punishment. Thus, they would have been impervious to punishment anyway.

Table 1. Cognizance of Apprehension-Risk and Punishment

	All	Deadly	Sex	Robbery	Assault	Burglary	Drugs	DUI	Other*
When you committed this crime, how likely did you think it was that you would be caught?									
Very likely	0.17	0.11	0.09	0.05	0.40	0.14	0.19	0.20	0.42
Somewhat likely	0.07	0.05	0.00	0.04	0.04	0.06	0.15	0.18	0.05
Possible, but not likely	0.13	0.11	0.09	0.12	0.00	0.17	0.19	0.09	0.16
I did not think I would be caught.	0.21	0.18	0.18	0.32	0.08	0.19	0.23	0.18	0.05
I did not think about it.	0.42	0.55	0.64	0.47	0.48	0.43	0.25	0.36	0.32
When you committed the crime, did you know what the likely punishment would be if you were caught?									
I knew exactly what the punishment would be.	0.22	0.16	0.09	0.26	0.04	0.21	0.25	0.36	0.47
I had a good idea.	0.13	0.08	0.00	0.14	0.16	0.08	0.25	0.09	0.16
I had some idea.	0.11	0.08	0.18	0.09	0.16	0.14	0.11	0.09	0.05
I had no idea, or thought I knew but was wrong.	0.18	0.13	0.45	0.19	0.28	0.19	0.13	0.00	0.21
I didn't think about it.	0.35	0.55	0.27	0.32	0.36	0.38	0.26	0.45	0.11
Totally incognizant of one or both factors	0.76	0.89	0.91	0.88	0.72	0.76	0.64	0.64	0.53
Observations	278	38	11	57	25	63	53	12	19

*Includes nonpayment of child support, forgery, escape, and parole violations.

Sixty-three percent of the criminals either did not think they would be apprehended or did not think about the possibility. Fifty-three percent either did not know what the punishment would be if they were convicted or did not think about it. The union of these four categories, 76% of the sample, represents those lacking at least one of the necessary conditions for making a rational response to punishments. This group would be unable to make informed, systematic decisions about their crimes. Some of those who had "some idea" of the likely punishment would also have been unable to apply appropriate cost-benefit analysis to their decisions, making the reported figures conservative. Still others would be impervious to harsher punishments, despite their cognizance of the risks, because drugs, rage, psychosis, or heat-of-the-moment impulses would circumvent rational responses to traditional deterrence methods.[18]

The result that 83% of the criminals thought it was not very likely that they would be caught echoes earlier findings from the National Bureau of Economic Research (NBER) Survey of Inner City Black Employment. In the NBER study of 2,358 inner-city youths as reported in Viscusi (1986), 87% of the respondents considered there to be only a "low" risk of arrest, conviction if arrested, or imprisonment if convicted. In reality, clearance rates (the percent of known offenses resulting in an arrest or associated resolution) are 66.9% for murder and nonnegligent manslaughter, 58.0% for aggravated assault, 51.9% for forcible rape, 47.4% for all violent crime, and 18.1% for all property crime. Felony conviction rates are 73% for drug trafficking; 67% for murder, burglary, and weapons offenses; and in no case lower than the 41% rate for assault (U.S. Bureau of Justice Statistics, 1998a). Of course, if some of those acquitted are innocent, the conviction rates among true offenders are even higher. Seventy-one percent of all convicted felons are sentenced to a period of confinement, and 41% are ordered to pay a fine or victim restitution, receive treatment, perform community service, or comply with some other additional penalty (U.S. Bureau of Justice Statistics, 1998b).

18. Among the irrational responses would be a hypersensitivity to threatened punishments, but individuals with this proclivity are unlikely to partake in crime to begin with. The purpose of this study is to examine the role of punishments in deterring active criminals.

This study is able to isolate differing potentials for responses to punishment among crime categories. Regardless of whether punishments are known well enough for enhancements to be noted, some crimes lend themselves more readily to cost-benefit trade-offs based on expectations. Parking illegally or speeding to the hospital when time is of the essence are common examples of potentially rational crimes.[19] In contrast to those involved in such minor offenses, the data suggest that 89% of deadly criminals, 91% of sex offenders, and 88% of robbers may lack the requirements necessary to make informed, rational judgments and to respond as intended to harsher punishments.[20] Although the remaining 9%–12% have at least some thought of apprehension and some concept of likely punishments, this does not imply a knowledge of or response to *changes* in punishments, or that these criminals are close to the margin between committing and not committing an offense. From the perspective of the criminals themselves, *of those with the information and mindset to respond to harsher punishments*, 72% of violent offenders and 66% of all offenders reported that no punishment or detection method would have prevented them from committing their crimes.

Those who had committed nonviolent crimes (burglary, drugs, driving under the influence, nonpayment of child support, escape, parole violations, and forgery) appeared more aware of the risks associated with their crimes than violent criminals. For crimes that are more likely to be repeated (robbery, burglary, drugs, DUI, and forgery), between 21% and 43% of the criminals knew exactly what the punishment would be. In contrast, for the violent crimes that are more likely to be spontaneous, only 4%–16% of the criminals knew what the punishment would be. Beyond the 21% of criminals that did not think they would be caught and the 18% that were completely ignorant of the likely punishment if caught, another 42% and 35% gave no thought to apprehension or possible punishments, respectively.

19. For example, in his Nobel lecture, Becker (1993) noted that he was inspired to study rational crime after deciding to park illegally in order to make it to a student's dissertation defense on time.

20. With 11 observations in the sex offender category and 12 in the DUI category, crime-specific generalizations on the basis of these small samples might not be reliable.

4. Discussion

It is appealing to think that with harsher punishments would come increased awareness, simply because raised stakes become more notable. Unfortunately, this is unlikely to make punishments more potent for several reasons. First, for every type of crime except assault, the more prominent reason why punishments fail to deter is that criminals do not perceive a positive probability of being caught, regardless of their awareness of punishments. Second, it would take more than a minor adjustment in the severity of a punishment to seize criminals' attention. The restrictions on excessive fines and cruel and unusual punishments imposed by the Eighth and Fourteenth Amendments to the U.S. Constitution are open to interpretation but would likely prohibit the more memorable punishments of lore and afar.[21] Of course, the ethical considerations that spurred these amendments can also be limiting. Finally, while the punishments for some lesser crimes have room for sizeable growth, many punishments have grown considerably in the past, and even so, this study indicates that few are common knowledge, even among criminals.

According to King (1999), "[C]riminologists agree that about-to-be lawbreakers don't look up penalties in the law books; they plan, if at all, on how to avoid being caught." The prospect of incomplete information or perceived invincibility does not undermine the law of demand. Criminals acting in the heat of the moment may disregard price and exhibit vertical demand curves, while others have downward sloping demand curves associated with inaccurate perceptions of the marginal cost of their behavior. Since criminals respond to perceived and not actual expected marginal costs for crimes, legislation changing the actual marginal costs may incite little or no behavioral change if perceived marginal costs are zero or invariant.[22]

21. In *A Tale of Two Cities*, Charles Dickens (1980, p. 69) describes a most memorable punishment: "He'll be drawn on a hurdle to be half hanged, and then he'll be taken down and sliced before his own face, and then his inside will be taken out and burnt while he looks on, and then his head will be chopped off, and he'll be cut into quarters. That's the sentence."

22. For this author, the most compelling reality check for the finding that criminals tend not to know the punishments for their crimes is to consider what anyone knows about the specific punishments for acts of malfeasance that tempt and occupy the average citizen. Many exceed the speed limit routinely while driving, but only five

Alongside perceived invincibility and unstudied punishments, rebellion and thrill-seeking effects counteract the intent of sanctions. Forty percent of the criminals reported boredom at the time of their criminal acts. While many of those with the option spend a collective $150 billion annually on various forms of legal entertainment (U.S. Bureau of the Census, 1998, p. 260), others gain stimulation from mischief. Reasons for committing crimes, as stated by the criminals in this sample, included "glamour," "excitement," "boredom," "enjoyed the attention," and "liked the fast life." Just as individuals who derive utility from driving fast relish faster cars, criminals who seek thrills from dodging punishment may see the avoidance of harsher punishment in the same light as an opportunity to drive a faster car. The effect of alcohol prohibition sent this message clearly in the 1920s; teenage drinking and smoking may result from a similar desire for rebellion.[23] In regard to illicit drug use, Friedman and Szasz (1992) go so far as to advocate legalization, which Friedman has suggested would remove the "forbidden fruit" aspect of drugs which "serves to make them attractive to young people" (Frost, 1998, p. 1).

It must also be recognized that formal punishment is simply a fraction of the full cost of committing a crime. Just as the associated increases in insurance costs are likely to eclipse fines for traffic offenses, weightier crimes and subsequent imprisonment may involve the associated costs of career loss, embarrassment, and severed relationships. The direct labor and capital costs of committing the crimes are further considerations. If the expected formal punishment constitutes, say, half of the expected cost of committing a crime, then a 10% increase in the associated fine or prison term results in only a 5% increase in the full-expected cost of the crime.

---

out of the approximately 350 students, economists, and law professors I have unscientifically surveyed have had a good guess of the punishment for this violation of the law. Does the reader know typical punishments for pirating software, copying copyrighted materials, or jaywalking? Have sanctions become more or less severe than five years ago? Indeed, if the reader does not know, the truth does not matter.

23. For example, Johnston, O'Malley, and Bachman (1981) studied the decriminalization of marijuana in seven states in the mid-1970s. They report that among their sample group of high school seniors there was a small net decline in monthly, annual, and lifetime marijuana use after decriminalization. Venkatesh (1994) reports that for certain groups, serving time in prison is positively regarded as a rite of passage.

The watered-down relative impact of formal punishments helps to explain the limited attention they receive.

It should be clear that the results of this study do not refute the idea that harsher punishments would deter some crimes. As previous studies have suggested (e.g., Ehrlich, 1973; Viscusi, 1986), there are some criminals on the margin that respond to the risks of crime. The 24% of survey respondents that had some sense of the expected cost of their behavior are candidates for such a response. However, the finding that a large majority of active criminals, including over nine out of ten of the most violent offenders, would not be responsive to a more severe penal code forces consideration of alternative means to a sizeable reduction in crime.

5. Conclusion

This research suggests that the popular strategy of addressing crime with adjustments in the penal code is unlikely to provide substantial reductions in crime rates and that solutions to the trillion-dollar crime burden must involve a new emphasis on alternative deterrents. The findings speak against more severe sentencing, not for emotional reasons, but because most current criminals do not have the information or mindset required to respond to these incentives for compliance. At the times of their offenses, 76% of the criminals in the sample and 89% of the most violent offenders were incognizant of either the possibility of apprehension or the likely punishments associated with their crimes. Still more active criminals are impervious to harsher punishments because no feasible detection rate or punishment scheme would arrest the impelling forces behind their behaviors, which might include drugs, fight-or-flight responses, or irrational thought.

Although the usual caveats apply regarding survey data, these results are not subject to the same aggregation, endogeneity, and specification problems inherent in regression-based studies of the deterrence hypothesis. The findings suggest that common models of criminal behavior may be misleading and viable crime-prevention efforts must include alternative strategies. The effectiveness of new approaches based, for example, on improved educational offerings, drug rehabilitation, youth programs, or the elimination of profit incentives for drug pushers through selective legalization, is left for further investigation.

Appendix

Survey Instrument

1) What type of crime were you arrested for? (Note: If you did not commit the crime that you were arrested for, please reply to each question based on your knowledge of those who do commit such crimes.)

2) How much time did you spend planning and carrying out this incident?

3) If you had a legal job when the crime was committed, how much were you earning?

_____ per _____ (hour/year/etc.) In what year? ________

4) How much do you think you could be earning now if you weren't involved in crime?

_____ per _____ (hour/year/etc.)

5) What was the last grade in school that you completed?

6) When you committed this crime, how likely did you think it was that you would be caught?

a) very likely
b) somewhat likely
c) possible, but not likely
d) I did not think I would be caught.
e) I did not think about it.

7) When you committed the crime, did you know what the likely punishment would be if you were caught?

a) I knew exactly what the punishment would be.
b) I had a good idea.
c) I had some idea.
d) I had no idea, or I thought I knew but I was wrong.
e) I didn't think about it.

8) Were the following items available, and if not, would they have prevented the crime?

	Available?		Prevented?		
	Yes	No	Yes	No	Maybe
drug rehabilitation	☐	☐	☐	☐	☐
father living with you	☐	☐	☐	☐	☐
evening/weekend sports programs	☐	☐	☐	☐	☐
awareness of punishment if caught	☐	☐	☐	☐	☐
awareness of likelihood of being caught	☐	☐	☐	☐	☐
legal employment	☐	☐	☐	☐	☐
death penalty for this crime	☐	☐	☐	☐	☐

Is there any other type of program, punishment, or detection method that would have prevented you from committing this crime?

9) If the following items existed, would the crime have occurred without them?

	Existed?		Caused?		
	Yes	No	Yes	No	Maybe
drug use	☐	☐	☐	☐	☐
friends who were a bad influence	☐	☐	☐	☐	☐
financial needs	☐	☐	☐	☐	☐
boredom	☐	☐	☐	☐	☐
violence in TV/movies you watched	☐	☐	☐	☐	☐

Is there anything else that might have caused this crime?

References

Anderson, David A. 1999. "The Aggregate Burden of Crime," 42(2) *Journal of Law and Economics* 611–42.

Avio, Kenneth L. 1988. "Capital Punishment is Canada: Statistical Evidence and Constitutional Issues," 30 *Canadian Journal of Criminology* 331–49.

———. 1998. "Capital Punishment," in Peter Newman, ed., *The New Palgrave Dictionary of Economics and the Law*. London: Macmillan.

Becker, Gary S. 1968. "Crime and Punishment: An Economic Approach," 76(2) *Journal of Political Economy* 169–217.

———. 1993. "Nobel Lecture: The Economic Way of Looking at Behavior," 101(3) *Journal of Political Economy* 385–409.

Becker, Gary S., and Kevin M. Murphy. 1988. "A Theory of Rational Addiction," 96(4) *Journal of Political Economy* 675–700.

Block, M. K., and J. M. Heineke. 1975. "A Labor Theoretic Analysis of the Criminal Choice," 65(3) *American Economic Review* 314–25.

Blumstein, Alfred, Jacquelin Cohen, and Daniel Nagin, eds. 1978. *Deterrence and Incapacitation: Estimating the Effects of Criminal Sanctions on Crime Rates*. Washington, DC: National Academy of the Sciences.

Bowers, William J., and Glenn L. Pierce. 1980. "Deterrence or Brutalization: What Is the Effect of Executions?" 26(4) *Crime and Delinquency* 453–84.

Cameron, Samuel. 1988. "The Economics of Crime Deterrence: A Survey of Theory and Evidence," 41 *KYKLOS* 301–23.

———. 1989. "Victim Compensation Does Not Increase the Supply of Crime," 16(4) *Journal of Economic Studies* 53–60.

———. 1994. "A Review of the Econometric Evidence on the Effects of Capital Punishment," 23 *Journal of Socio-Economics* 197–214.

Cook, Philip J. 1980. "Research in Criminal Deterrence: Laying the Groundwork for the Second Decade," in N. Morris and M. Tonry, eds., *Crime and Justice: An Annual Review of Research, Vol. 2*. Chicago: University of Chicago Press.

Dickens, Charles. 1980. *A Tale of Two Cities*. New York: Signet.

Ehrlich, Isaac. 1973. "Participation in Illegitimate Activities: A Theoretical and Empirical Investigation," 81(3) *Journal of Political Economy* 521–65.

———. 1975. "The Deterrent Effect of Capital Punishment: A Question of Life and Death," 65(3) *American Economic Review* 397–417.

———. 1977. "Capital Punishment and Deterrence: Some Further Thoughts and Additional Evidence," 85(4) *Journal of Political Economy* 741–88.

Ehrlich, Isaac, and Zhiqiang Lui. 1999. "Sensitivity Analyses of the Deterrence Hypothesis: Let's Keep the Econ in Econometrics," 42(1, part 2) *Journal of Law and Economics* 455–88.

Forst, B., V. Filatov, and L. R. Klein. 1978. "The Deterrent Effect of Capital Punishment: An Assessment of the Estimates," in Alfred Blumstein, Jacquelin Cohen, and Daniel Nagin, eds., *Deterrence and Incapacitation: Estimating the Effects of Criminal Sanctions on Crime Rates*. Washington DC: National Academy of the Sciences.

Fox, J. A., and M. L. Radelet. 1989. "Persistent Flaws in Econometric Studies of the Deterrent Effect of the Death Penalty," 23 *Loyola of Los Angeles Law Review* 29–44.

Friedman, Milton, and Thomas Szasz. 1992. *On Liberty and Drugs*. Washington, DC: Drug Policy Foundation.

312 American Law and Economics Review V4 N2 2002 (295–313)

Frost, Bob. 1998. "Leading Question: Milton Friedman," *San Jose Mercury News*, May 17.

Gatrell, V. A. C. 1994. *The Hanging Tree*. New York: Oxford University Press.

Greenwood, Peter W. 1983. "Controlling the Crime Rate through Imprisonment," in James Q. Wilson, ed., *Crime and Public Policy*. San Francisco: Institute for Contemporary Studies.

Grogger, Jeffrey. 1990. "The Deterrent Effect of Capital Punishment: An Analysis of Daily Homicide Counts," 85(410) *Journal of the American Statistical Association* 295–303.

Johnston, Lloyd D., Patrick M. O'Malley, and Jerald Bachman. 1981. "Marijuana Decriminalization: The Impact on Youth, 1975–1980," Monitoring the Future Occasional Paper 13. Ann Arbor: University of Michigan Institute of Social Research.

Kessler, Daniel, and Steven D. Levitt. 1999. "Using Sentence Enhancements to Distinguish Between Deterrence and Incapacitation," 42 *Journal of Law and Economics* 343–63.

King, Rufus. 1999. "It's Time to Open the Doors of Our Prisons," *Newsweek*, 10 April 19.

Layson, S. 1985. "Homicide and Deterrence: A Reexamination of the United States Time-Series Evidence," 52 *Southern Economic Journal* 68–89.

Leamer, Edward E. 1983. "Let's Take the Con out of Econometrics," 73 *American Economic Review* 31–43.

Levitt, Steven D. 1998. "Why Do Increased Arrest Rates Appear to Reduce Crime: Deterrence, Incapacitation, or Measurement Error?" 36(1) *Economic Inquiry* 353–72.

McAleer, Michael, and Michael R. Veall. 1989. "How Fragile Are Fragile Inferences? A Reevaluation of the Deterrent Effect of Capital Punishment," 71(1) *Review of Economics and Statistics* 99–106.

McKee, D. L., and M. L. Sesnowitz. 1977. "On the Deterrent Effect of Capital Punishment," 6 *Journal of Behavioral Economics* 217–24.

McManus, Walter S. 1985. "Estimates of the Deterrent Effect of Capital Punishment: The Importance of the Researcher's Prior Beliefs," 93(2) *Journal of Political Economy* 417–25.

Miller, Ted R., Mark A. Cohen, and Brian Wiersema. 1996. "Victim Costs and Consequences: A New Look," National Institute of Justice Research Report (Feb.) NCJ-155282.

Nagin, Daniel S. 1998. "Criminal Deterrence Research: A Review of the Evidence and a Research Agenda for the Outset of the 21st Century," in M. Tonry, ed., *Crime and Justice: An Annual Review of Research, Vol. 23*. Chicago: University of Chicago Press.

Passell, P., and J. B. Taylor. 1977. "The Deterrent Effect of Capital Punishment: Another View," 67 *American Economic Review* 445–51.

Polinsky, A. Mitchell, and Steven Shavell. 1999. "On the Disutility and Discounting of Imprisonment and the Theory of Deterrence," 28(1) *Journal of Legal Studies* 1–16.

Rubin, Paul H., Hashem Dezhbakhsh, and Joanna Mehlop Shepherd. 2001. "Does Capital Punishment Have a Deterrent Effect? New Evidence from Post Moratorium Panel Data," Emory University Working Paper.

Taylor, J. B. 1978. "Econometric Models of Criminal Behavior: A Review," in J. M. Heineke, ed., *Economic Models of Criminal Behavior.* Amsterdam: North-Holland.

Tonry, Michael. 1996. *Sentencing Matters*. New York: Oxford University Press.

U.S. Bureau of the Census. 1998. *Statistical Abstract of the Unites States: 1998*, (118th ed.), Washington, DC: U.S. Government Printing Office.

U.S. Bureau of Justice Statistics. 1998a. *Criminal Case Processing Statistics*, ⟨http://www.ojp.usdoj.gov/bjs/cases.htm⟩, accessed December 1998.

———. 1998b. *Criminal Sentencing Statistics*, ⟨http://www.ojp.usdoj.gov/bjs/cases.htm⟩, accessed December 1998.

———. 1998c. *Sourcebook of Criminal Justice Statistics*. Washington, DC: U.S. Government Printing Office.

Venkatesh, Sudhir. 1994. "Learnin' the Trade: Conversations with a Gangsta'," Winter 1994 *Public Culture* 319–41.

Viscusi, W. Kip. 1986. "The Risks and Rewards of Criminal Behavior: A Comprehensive Test of Criminal Deterrence," 4(3) *Journal of Labor Economics* 317–40.

———. 1991. *Reforming Products Liability*. Cambridge: Harvard University Press.

Name Index